endorsed by edexcel

BTEC Level 3 National in IT

Second Edition

Mark Fishpool and
Bernadette Fishpool

HODDER EDUCATION

Orders: please contact Bookpoint Ltd, 130 Milton Park, Abingdon, Oxon OX14 4SB. Telephone: (44) 01235 827720. Fax: (44) 01235 400454. Lines are open from 9.00 to 5.00, Monday to Saturday, with a 24 hour message answering service. You can also order through our website www.hoddereducation.co.uk

If you have any comments to make about this, or any of our other titles, please send them to educationenquiries@hodder.co.uk

British Library Cataloguing in Publication Data
A catalogue record for this title is available from the British Library

ISBN: 978 1 444 110517

First Edition Published 2007
This Edition Published 2011
Impression number 10 9 8 7 6 5 4 3 2 1
Year 2016, 2015, 2014, 2013, 2012, 2011

Cover photo © Yury Kosourov/iStockphoto.com
Typeset by Pantek Arts Ltd, Maidstone, Kent
Printed in Italy for Hodder Education, an Hachette UK Company,
338 Euston Road, London NW1 3BH.

Contents

The Introduction, Unit 5 Managing networks, and Unit 14 Event Driven Programming are covered on the supporting website www.hodderplus.co.uk/BtecIT You will need the username, ITstudent and password hodderIT. Answers for activities and Braincheck activities can also be found on this site.

Acknowledgements

Mark – for Ken Blackwell, with love.
Bernie – For Mum, Gloria and Didda – my safe harbours in a storm.

Every effort has been made to trace and acknowledge ownership of copyright. The publishers will be glad to make suitable arrangements with any copyright holders whom it has not been possible to contact.

The authors and publishers would like to thank the following for the use of images in this volume. Screenshots of Microsoft products used with permission from Microsoft.

1.24 E-mail from Tesco.com; **2.54**, **2.56** used with permission from Linux; **2.57**, **2.74**, **13.11** AVG Technologies CZ, s.r.o.; **2.59**, **8.20** Firefox®; **3.15** NHS Direct; **4.14**, **8.03**, **8.07**, **8.08**, **8.09**, **8.10**, **8.11**, **8.12**, **8.18**, **8.19**, **8.33** Google.Inc; **4.16** W3Counter, StatOwl; **6.04** VisSim © 2007 Visual Solutions Inc.; **7.02** Ebay.co.uk; **8.04** **www.everyclick.com**; **8.15** © 2007 HMV; **8.21**, **8.34** **www.pcworld.co.uk**; **8.23** **www.rnib.org.uk**; **8.24** **www.goodsearch.com**; **8.25** **www.charitycafe.com**; **8.31** **www.pricerunner.co.uk**; **8.32** Royal Mail website; **8.35** Email from Olympus-europa.com; **8.36** Paypal ©; **8.38** **www.virginmedia.com**; **8.39** © 2010 Amazon.com Inc. and its affiliates. All rights reserved; **8.40** Connexions **www.connexionsdirect.com**; **8.41** **www.saga.co.uk**; **8.42** **www.howstuffworks.com**; **8.44** Email from Egg.com; **9.12** Usenet; **10.53** Lloyds TSB; **10.55** Live Journal; **10.57** Wikipedia – **www.wikipedia.org**; **10.58** AOL Instant Messenger; **11.09**, **11.10**, **11.11** **www.sage.co.uk**; **12.10** Flexibility.co.uk, the online journal of flexible work; **12.15** Instruction manual for **www.dlink.com/products/?pid=227**; **13.19** © copyright 2001–2007 The Sims Zone; **13.20**, **13.21** Brother MFC-660CN Printer manual; **13.24** **www.hse.gov.uk/electricity**; **13.25** Electrical Safety Council; **13.29** **http://firekills.direct.gov.uk/index.html**; **13.30** **www.itschoolsafrica.org**; **13.31** www.tecc.org.uk; **13.32** **www.hse.gov.uk/firstaid/index.htm**

Photo credits
1.04 © Stockbyte/Getty Images; **1.05** © Andrey Skat – Fotolia; **1.12** © iStockphoto.com/Steve Luker; **1.13** Shannon Mendes/Masterfile; **2.1** © iStockphoto.com/Dino Ablakovic; **2.17** © Artyom Rudenko – Fotolia; **2.18** © Alexandr Makarov – Fotolia; **2.19** © Johnny Lye – Fotolia; **2.21** © echolalia – Fotolia; **2.51** lewing@isc.tamu.edu/ The GIMP; **2.65** © iStockphoto.com/Andrew Howe; **3.14** Mower Magic Ltd; **4.01** © Roger Ressmeyer/CORBIS; **4.02** © Chad Ehlers / Alamy; **4.03** © deanm1974 – Fotolia.com; **4.04** Tim Robberts/The Image Bank/Getty Images; **4.07** © Dino Ablakovic/iStockphoto.com; **4.10** © Bulent Ince/istockphoto.com; **4.17** © Charlotte Moss / Alamy; **7.04** © iStockphoto.com/ pmphoto; **8.37** © Steven May / Alamy; **10.16** Aleksandr Ugorenkov – Fotolia; **10.59** © iStockphoto.com/Shaun Lowe; **13.6** © rlat – Fotolia; **13.7** © Dainis Derics/iStockphoto.com

Unit 1: Communication and employability skills for IT

By the end of this unit you should be able to:

1. Understand the personal attributes valued by employers
2. Understand the principles of effective communication
3. Be able to use IT to communicate effectively
4. Be able to address personal development needs

Whether you are in school or college, passing this unit will involve being assessed. As with most BTEC schemes, the successful completion of various assessment criteria demonstrates your evidence of learning and the skills you have developed.

This unit has a mixture of pass, merit and distinction criteria. Generally you will find that merit and distinction criteria require a little more thought and evaluation before they can be completed.

The colour-coded grid below shows you the pass, merit and distinction criteria for this unit.

To achieve a pass grade you need to:	To achieve a merit grade you also need to:	To achieve a distinction you also need to:
P1 Explain the personal attributes valued by employers		
P2 Explain the principles of effective communication		
P3 Discuss potential barriers to effective communication	**M1** Explain mechanisms that can reduce the impact of communication barriers	
P4 Demonstrate a range of effective interpersonal skills		
P5 Use IT to aid communications		
P6 Communicate technical information to a specified audience	**M2** Review draft documents to produce final versions	**D1** Evaluate interpersonal and written communications techniques
P7 Produce a personal development plan	**M3** Explain how an awareness of learning style can aid personal development	
P8 Follow a personal development plan		**D2** Review progress on a personal development plan, identifying areas for improvement

Introduction

Communication and employability skills for IT is a 10-credit unit that is designed to introduce you to the world of work. Being successful in business requires you to develop both technical and non-technical skills. The technical skills will be achieved in part through this Level 3 BTEC course.

The non-technical skills, such as inter-personal skills, communications skills and self-development skills will be explored in this unit. Although you may doubt it at first, these skills are absolutely vital for all IT professionals whether you'll be a Software Developer getting the correct requirements from clients or a Technical Support Analyst helping users with their hardware problems.

In addition, you will need to be prepared to undergo continual self-development in order to remain effective and competitive in this fast-changing world. The final outcome for this unit will help you to focus on your personal development needs.

How to read this chapter

This chapter is organised to match the content of the BTEC unit it represents. The following diagram shows the grading criteria that relate to each learning outcome.

1.1 Understand the personal attributes of employees valued by employers

This section will cover the following grading criterion:

Make the Grade P1

This criterion requires you to **explain the personal attributes valued by employers**. There are essentially three different categories (specific attributes, general attributes and attitudes), so you will need to explain at least one topic from each of the categories. It is not necessary to describe the attribute, you can simply say **what it is** and **why it is valued**.

You could be asked to create a poster or some other type of information product (for example, a leaflet) as evidence.

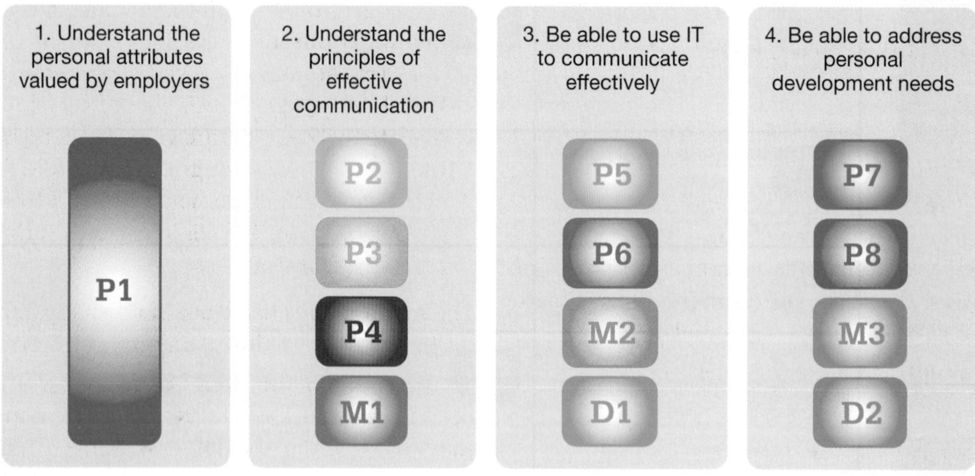

Figure 1.00

You'll find colour-matching notes in each chapter about completing each grading criterion.

Key terms

Attitudes These refer to your own personal behaviours in a work context. Examples would include that you show an interest in your work, that you show a willingness to put in effort, that you have a pride in your personal appearance, that you are polite and respectful.

Attributes and abilities These are the personal characteristics that employers expect you to have. Examples would be that you can solve problems, that you can be creative, that you have leadership qualities, that you can work as part of a team, that you can work with a minimum of supervision.

Skills These are relatively easy to measure. For example, do you have IT skills at a particular level? They will be shown by your qualifications or, in some cases, employers will give you a job-related test to measure particular skills that they expect you to have (although in many cases employers will be prepared to offer additional training, if needed).

1.1.1 Specific job-related attributes

Job description

In most situations, employers will be looking for particular skills when engaging a new employee. The exact requirements will be listed in a **job description** that lists and explains the tasks the employee will be expected to undertake.

A job description typically consists of:

- core information about the post (title, start date, salary range/grade etc.);
- job purpose (a broad overview of the post);
- job responsibilities and duties (what the person is expected to do in the role);
- information about the department and organisation;
- a person specification.

Fundamental to this process of employment is the development of a **person specification**. This is used to define the ***essential*** ('must haves') and ***desirable*** ('would be nice') skills and attributes required by a person applying for the post. Careful use of sensible descriptors will enable an experienced manager and personnel team (or Human Resources) to cut down a large number of applications to a manageable ***short list*** of four to six candidates for formal interview.

As a guide, a person specification usually sets out the requirements of the employee as follows:

- **Experience**: Usually this is a short profile detailing the type of previous experience that the candidate is required to have to take on the type of role. The required experience may be a result of previous, related employment or practice (**precursory role**) or it may be a result of changing from an **identical role**: both with a stated number of years service. Emphasis should also be placed on the vocational/industrial background that is being sought. Experience may even be very specific (for example, '...has developed database systems in Microsoft Visual Basic.NET® for the retail sector for at least two years').
- **Qualifications and training**: An outline of the educational requirements and professional qualifications that are necessary in order to perform the job. Most industries have a vocational body to guide this sort of decision.
- **Abilities**: These define the characteristics of the person being sought for the role. Typical abilities may include 'must be able to work in a team' or 'must be able to use own initiative to complete tasks'.

The requirements listed are often vitally important to the smooth running of an organisation.

The job description would usually have a section on **job circumstances**, describing the conditions that would make the job less/more difficult for some people. Common examples would include: mobile working, working in the evenings, working abroad, flexible hours, multi-site working, and so on.

Table 1.01 gives a completed person specification for a systems programmer.

Table 1.01

Attributes	Essential	Desirable
Experience	Three years' experience in a commercial environment using C++ and Visual Basic.NET®.	Java™ and C# experience would also be useful.
Qualifications and training	Educated to Level 3 Diploma Standard.	Evidence of professional updating in the last two years.
Abilities	Good team player, able to work unsupervised.	Has experience of leading a small project team.
Job circumstances (e.g. mobility/ late/early working)	Fully mobile because some visits to clients may be required.	Able to work to tight deadlines and prepared to work overtime.

When given a person specification, you should understand that an employer will expect you to show that you have the essential attributes as defined on it, and as many of the desirable attributes as possible. The more desirable attributes you can show you have, the more likely you are to get an interview.

Working procedures and systems

When you start your first job, you will realise that there is a lot more to employment than physically doing your job. You will need to familiarise yourself with organisational **working procedures** that affect the way that you work.

An example of a working procedure might be where an employer operates a flexible working system or process (this is called **flexi-time**). This is where you can choose your own start and finish times. In addition, quite often you will be able to accrue time worked for additional hours you are required to work when the organisation is busy, and that you will be allowed to take back when things are quieter. Most organisations that operate flexible working hours require employees to observe certain boundaries (for example, you have to work certain core hours and a minimum number of hours in a week or month).

It is usual with a flexible working patterns for you to keep a record (often referred to as a **timesheet**), which you will need to produce when required.

Figure 1.01 shows a sample of a completed timesheet.

Some employers allow you to work slightly less than your contracted hours in a week, providing you give the time back at busy periods. In many cases, timesheets are checked once a month by the payroll department to ensure that no one is taking advantage of the system.

Lee Office Supplies

TIMESHEET

Employee: *Anjum Smith* Department: *Delivery* Week commencing: *8th November 2010*

Day	Time in	Time out	Lunch	Hours worked
Monday	—	—	—	—
Tuesday	*7.00*	*15.30*	*30 mins*	*7hrs 30 mins*
Wednesday	*8.00*	*14.00*	*60 mins*	*5hrs*
Thursday	*7.30*	*16.30*	*60 mins*	*8hrs*
Friday	*7.00*	*17.00*	*60 mins*	*9hrs*
Saturday	*8.00*	*16.45*	*45 mins*	*8hrs*
Sunday	—	—	—	—

Total hours worked: *37.5* Total hours contracted: *37.5* Signed: *Anjum Smith*

Figure 1.01 Sample time sheet

There will be other procedures and systems that you will need to learn to ensure that you maximise your efficiency and work within the boundaries and expectations required by the organisation. It is likely that you will receive training early in your working life with the company to introduce and explain many of these. However, some information might have been omitted for some reason or you don't understand it, so you should ask for clarification if you are not sure about something. Watch others working with and around you and, again, ask if you think there's something you should know.

Health and safety

You will have been introduced to the concepts of Health and Safety at school or college. When you were younger, others would take the responsibility for ensuring that you were in a safe environment. As you get older, however, you will increasingly be expected to take responsibility for your own health and safety. By the time you start work, you will be expected to have an understanding of the ***Health & Safety at Work Act 1974*** and ***The Management of Health and Safety at Work Regulations 1999***.

These Acts set out the legal responsibilities of both employees and employers within the workplace. In terms of your responsibilities as a new employee, you will be expected to know the basic health and safety issues around the job for which you are engaged (for example, isolating high-voltage power supplies when working inside a computer case) before you start. In addition, there are more generic aspects of your responsibilities.

The most obvious and basic requirements for employees are:

- be observant in your own and others' working environments, and identify any obvious hazards or dangers;
- report any hazards or dangers you have identified to relevant individuals or groups of individuals to ensure the safety of yourself and others;
- anticipate any possible hazards and be proactive in helping the organisation overcome these.

Employers also have fundamental and legal responsibilities to ensure you have a safe working environment. These include giving you the correct tools and any Health and Safety equipment as required by your job.

Security

All organisations have sensitive and confidential data and information. Employees have a duty to keep this safe.

Some organisations ask employees to sign **non-disclosure agreements**, which mean that the employee is not allowed to discuss sensitive and confidential information with individuals or groups who are outside the organisation, either while employed by the organisation or after they leave.

In addition, organisations can implement a series of **physical** and **logical** security techniques to ensure that data and information are secure.

- Physical security techniques include locks on doors and alarm systems to prevent unauthorised access to computers and/or paper files. Many organisations also prohibit staff from using USB flash drives in their systems or from making CD or DVD copies of data. Some companies even remove these devices to reduce the temptation of copying files.
- Logical security techniques include encryption protocols (designed to scramble the data and make it useless to anyone who does not have the decryption software) and password protection.

1.1.2 General job-related attributes

There are a number of job-related skills that employers might look for in potential employees depending on the nature of the job. Your ability to show that you have these skills will be influential on whether or not you ultimately get the job.

Many of these are **transferable skills** that you take with you from employer to employer and which can be applied regardless of your job. You need to acquire these key skills (sometimes also called core skills or essential skills). Here are some examples:

Planning and organisational skills

These skills can be shown in several ways. They form part of the wider key skills syllabus for *Improving Own Learning and Performance and Problem Solving*. In addition, they are the types of skill that are discussed if your school or an employer is asked to provide a reference for you.

Future employers want to be reassured that you are able to plan your time effectively and organise your work, carefully prioritising it to meet organisational and departmental objectives (that is, deciding how important each task is and placing it in your plan accordingly).

Being well organised is fundamental, not only from an employment perspective, but also from a personal one.

Time management

Time management skills, like planning and organisational skills, are developed through *Improving Own Learning and Performance and Problem Solving* activities. Using flow charts, Gantt charts and other time management techniques, you will need to show that you can identify and allocate relevant times and durations as appropriate to meet deadlines when there can often be conflicting demands on your time.

One of the key issues with good time management is to be sensible about what you can achieve. Do not set yourself unrealistic deadlines that you do not have any hope of meeting. Sometimes it is easier if you create a visual representation of a series of tasks and how you might plan their completion. The Gantt chart in Figure 1.02 shows how a series of tasks will be handled over a given timeframe. This chart represents the order of tasks for a simple fictitious assignment that comprises five tasks.

This Gantt chart implies that Tasks 1, 2 and 3 must be completed in sequence and each must be finished before the next task begins. The same is true of Tasks 4 and 5 (that is Task 4 must be finished before Task 5 can begin). However, in this example, it is clear that Task 4 does not require Tasks 1, 2 and 3 to have been completed, implying that Task 4 can run in parallel to Task 1 (that is while the latter is being completed) and parallel to the beginning of Task 2.

Figure 1.03 shows an alternative Gantt chart. Here the chart suggests that all tasks can be started at the same time, implying that no task needs to be completed before another can begin. In addition, it shows that Task 3 is expected to take the longest and can be carried out throughout the week.

The Gantt chart is particularly useful when planning engineering projects (where some processes must run in sequence, and others may run in parallel).

Team working

Team working is part of the wider key skill *Working with others* that you may have been asked to do at your school or college. Being able to work effectively as part of a team is a skill that can be learned, although some people are natural team players anyway.

Employers consider that being able to work effectively as part of a team is as important as your being able to work independently.

When working as part of a team, it is important to remember that the role you play is only a part of an overall process. You will be expected to contribute to the project or task in hand, share ideas with other team members and compromise on a possible solution or a range of solutions. You will

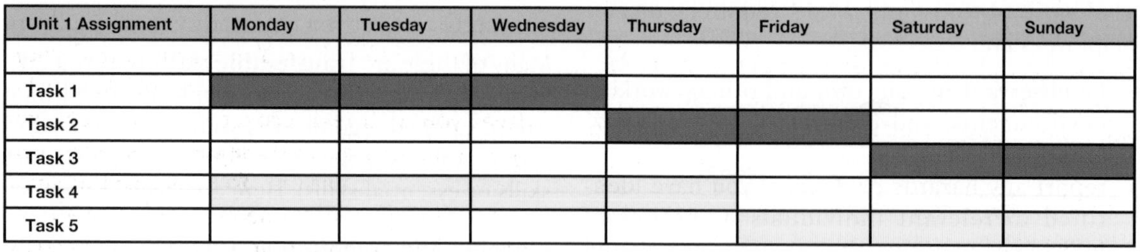

Unit 1 Assignment	Monday	Tuesday	Wednesday	Thursday	Friday	Saturday	Sunday
Task 1							
Task 2							
Task 3							
Task 4							
Task 5							

Figure 1.02 Gantt chart, example 1

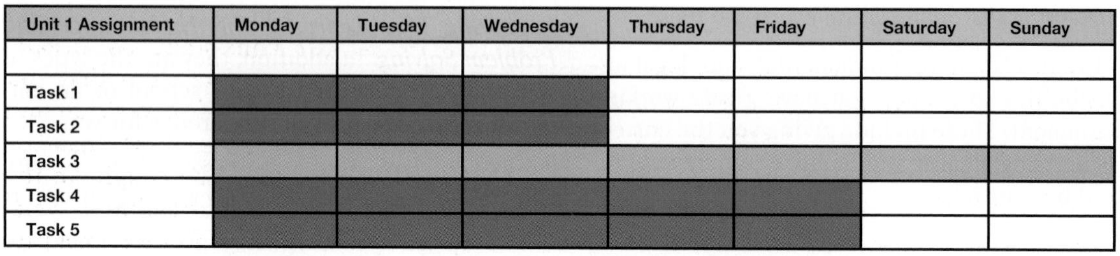

Unit 1 Assignment	Monday	Tuesday	Wednesday	Thursday	Friday	Saturday	Sunday
Task 1							
Task 2							
Task 3							
Task 4							
Task 5							

Figure 1.03 Gantt chart, example 2

need to be able to treat the ideas of others with respect, be able to collaborate and be prepared to share the responsibility for the overall outcome with other team members. It is possible, however, that when you are completing your allocated task you may be working individually.

An example of collaborative teamwork is with computer programming. It is very unlikely that if you develop your skills and are employed as a programmer that you will ever write a program from scratch in isolation. In fact, it is more likely that you (and other team members) will be asked to individually code sections of a larger program that will ultimately be put together once all the parts have been completed.

Verbal and written communication skills

Most employers use GCSE English as an indicator of your achievement in this subject, although the new *Functional Skills English* qualification completed at Level 2 is likely to be an accepted equivalent.

Numeracy skills

GCSE Mathematics is used as a national benchmark for achievement in this area, although as with English, the new *Functional Skills Maths* programme is also set to become a recognised equivalent.

An employer will want to be reassured that you are relatively numerate: that you can add numbers together, do simple multiplication, division and subtraction, and that you can work confidently with percentages (for example, calculating VAT).

Sometimes, if more technical number ability is required by a post or job, then the employer will seek to test this skill prior to (or during) the interview.

If you have any doubts about your maths skills, you should take any opportunities you are offered for basic support, to ensure that when you leave your Certificate or Diploma course, your number skills will be as strong as your IT skills. (The third Functional Skill to have been developed as a new qualification is *Functional IT*.)

Creativity

ICT creativity is a much harder transferable skill to demonstrate. It is common for students of art subjects (for example, fine art or photography) to create a portfolio of their work, which they will offer as evidence to a university or to an employer.

During this course (and dependent on the unit choices made by your centre), you will have an opportunity to create websites, to write computer programs and to work with digital graphics. Screenshots or printouts of these can be included in a personal portfolio that you can use during the applications process.

1.1.3 General attitudes

In terms of personal attributes, employers are looking for you to show that you possess a variety of positive traits. Work **attitudes** are a series of preferred behaviours that are thought to be desirable in employees. Here are a few examples:

- **Determination:** This is your strength of mind to achieve or succeed in a particular environment or with a project. For example, you should, at this stage, be determined to complete your BTEC National Diploma, Certificate or Award.
- **Independence:** Employers need to be reassured that their employees can work without much supervision. Although you will obviously have a supervisor or line manager, it is likely that this person will also have a number of other employees to look after. As such, being able to get on and do what you have been asked to do will be a valuable ability.
- **Integrity:** In simple terms, integrity is a measure of your honesty and your sense of duty and respect. Employers will want to trust you, for example, to arrive at work on time, even if there is no one there, to not steal (on any level) from the organisation, to always strive to do your best, to be respectful to your colleagues and others within the organisation.
- **Tolerance:** Working with other people is likely to have its difficulties. You may well find yourself working with people you do not like or who treat you with less respect than you feel you would treat them. In these circumstances, you will need to be tolerant. You will need to show that you respect other people's views, practices and opinions, even if you do not necessarily agree with them. A lack of tolerance is often what causes conflict between colleagues.
- **Dependability:** This means that you should be trustworthy and consistent. As already mentioned, you will need to show that you can work with a minimum of supervision and not knowingly take advantage of the organisation. You will be reliable, for example, in the quality of your work, your timeliness, your willingness to help the organisation, meet its objectives, etc.

- **A good problem-solving ability:** Your skill in finding alternative solutions to problems will need to be shown. This means that you can creatively find ways around issues or you can find new and innovative ways of doing something that is already taking place.

Other attributes include, for example, leadership qualities, confidence, self-motivation, and so on.

Whether or not you are a good leader is often difficult to assess. Many people think that if you can take charge of a group of people (for example, as part of a project), you must be a good leader. In fact, quite the opposite may be true – you might be an awful leader, particularly if you are bossy and controlling. Good leaders know how to support the people below them and get the best out of them, without having to boss them about!

Some people believe that aggression is a characteristic of confidence. In fact, confidence is about being self-assured, believing in yourself and having faith in your own abilities.

Self-motivation is an important attribute because if you are self-motivated it means that you do not constantly need to be kept on track by others (for example, a line manager or supervisor). You will be happy to be in control of your own work, you will move confidently between tasks, work to a high quality and meet deadlines, simply because you want to.

B Braincheck

1. Define **attribute** and give an example.
2. Define **skill** and give an example.
3. What is **flexi-time**?
4. Name **two** of your responsibilities in terms of Health and Safety in the workplace.
5. Define **one** logical and **one** physical security technique.
6. What is **collaboration**?
7. What does **tolerance** mean?
8. What is **integrity**?
9. What are the **three** new areas of Functional Skill?
10. What is an **attitude**?

How well did you do? See supporting website for answers.

1.2 Understand the principles of effective communication

This section will cover the following grading criteria:

1.2.1 Principles

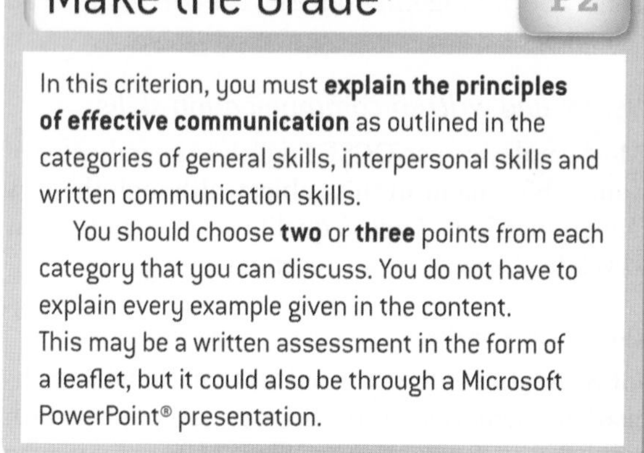

Communicating effectively relies on developing skills in three key areas:

- **General communication skills**, such as understanding cultural difference, finding ways to engage an audience and being able to adapt to a situation.
- **Interpersonal skills**, such as the use of language, and overcoming barriers to effective communication.
- **Written communication skills**, including adhering to organisational guidelines and taking care with spelling and grammar.

1.2.2 General communication skills

Cultural differences

You may already know that cultural differences exist between people from different nationalities. A serious misunderstanding can occur when a physical gesture, which in one country means 'wonderful', 'excellent' or 'first class', is interpreted as something exceedingly rude or derogatory in another country.

Simple English words or phrases can mean different things in different countries. For example, a 'cot'. In the UK, a cot is a small bed with high sides used for a baby (see Figure 1.04). In the USA, however, a cot is the term often used for a camp bed or other type of temporary bed (see Figure 1.05).

Figure 1.04 A cot (UK)

You also need to be aware that there are regional variations within the UK that can lead to misunderstandings. A simplistic example is that in parts of Scotland 'sausages' are known as 'links'. The latter word is usually used to means something completely different (for example, links in a chain, links between websites). It is unlikely that a Scottish person would not know the more usual meaning, but the example demonstrates that the context in which a word is used is important to avoid mistakes. It is no wonder that at times communication can be misunderstood, particularly if the two individuals communicating have a different understanding of some of the words used.

Adapting

Effective communication has a number of common elements. When communicating, remember the following:

- **Modulate your voice.** Vary the rate and pitch of your words as you speak. It isn't very interesting listening to someone who is talking like a robot.
- Ensure that communication is **unambiguous**. Speak as clearly and as accurately as possible. This is essential so that others understand what you are saying and do not misinterpret it.
- Use **terminology** that will be understood by all those involved in the communication. Most work disciplines have their own jargon, which will be understood by those working in the subject. However an outsider will probably not understand these special words. IT is especially subject to use of jargon.
- Choose a suitable **format**. Should the interaction be formal or can it be more relaxed and informal? Is a slide show really needed or could simple handouts and discussion be used instead?

Being able to adapt in style and approach makes effective communication more likely.

Provide accurate information

The information that you give should be completely accurate. It is easy to make mistakes in communicating information because you might make assumptions about what someone does or does not know.

Figure 1.05 A cot (USA)

Consider the example shown in Figure 1.06.

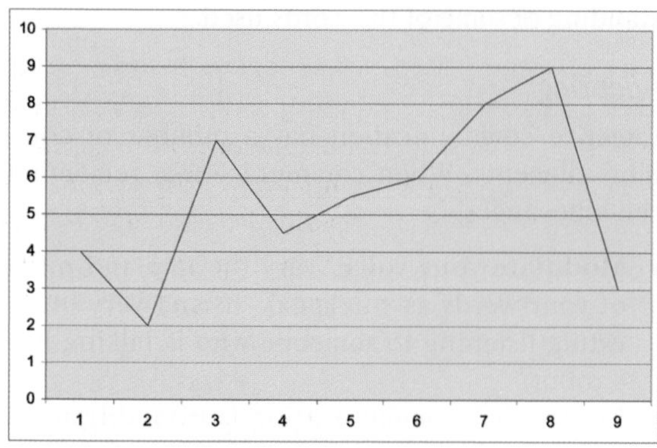

Figure 1.06 A chart with no meaning

What is the purpose of this line graph? It is clear that the y-valves values joined by the line are 4, 2, 7, 4.5, 5.5, 6, 8, 9 and 3, but there is no indication about what the graph is trying to convey. There is no title. The *x*-axis and *y*-axis both show numbers, but what do they mean?

Is the chart in Figure 1.07 better?

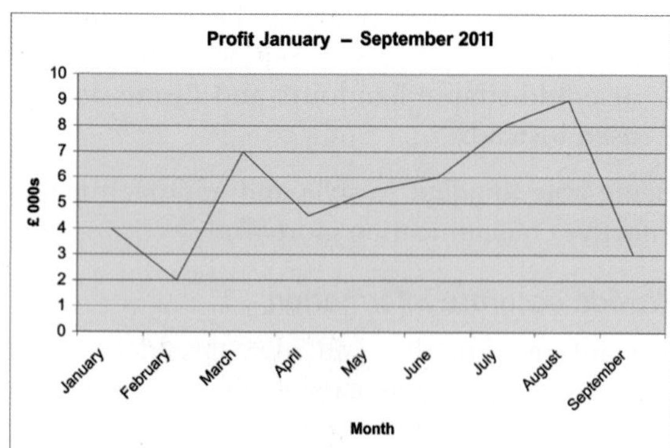

Figure 1.07 A chart with a title and axes labels

Even this chart could be further improved (for example, by a better use of colours, by possibly using a bar or column chart instead, by including the name of the organisation).

Techniques for engaging audience interest

If you are giving a presentation, think about what you like about lessons you attend. Do you like sitting and listening as someone goes through a series of PowerPoint® slides? Or do you prefer to be working practically, asking questions, using multimedia and the internet? Most learners would say the latter. If you like your classes to be interesting, with a mix of techniques, animated presentations and lots of interaction, then surely you should expect your audience to want the same from you. Here are some suggestions:

- **Change intonation:** This means changing the pitch of your voice when speaking.
- **Use technology:** This means using different types of technology to maintain the interest of your audience. Modern computers reliably play DVDs and CDs. Consider incorporating moving images, animation or sound into your presentations. Your school or college may well have interactive whiteboards and LCD projectors that are used as part of your lessons. You should endeavour to become familiar with this technology. Overhead projectors (OHPs) are common both in the classroom and in the workplace.
- **Question and answer sessions:** Give your audience an opportunity to interact with you. Allow them to ask questions. Asking them questions to liven up a presentation.

The best way to ensure that you keep an audience engaged is to use a variety of techniques to ensure that they stay interested and alert.

1.2.3 Interpersonal skills

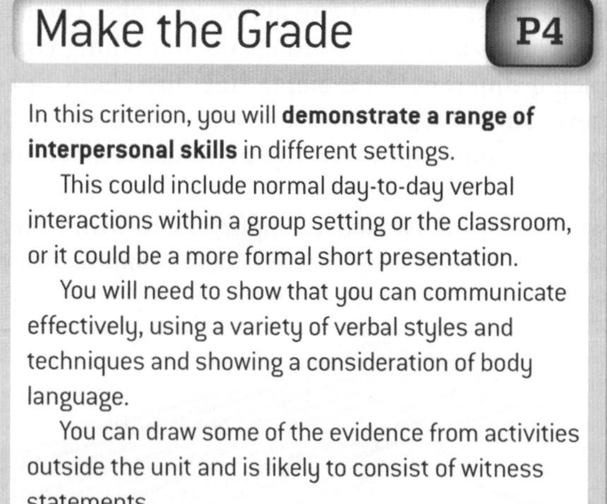

Make the Grade P4

In this criterion, you will **demonstrate a range of interpersonal skills** in different settings.

This could include normal day-to-day verbal interactions within a group setting or the classroom, or it could be a more formal short presentation.

You will need to show that you can communicate effectively, using a variety of verbal styles and techniques and showing a consideration of body language.

You can draw some of the evidence from activities outside the unit and is likely to consist of witness statements.

Interpersonal skills are how you interact with others. It's about your ability to relate to others. This section explains some ways that this can be done successfully.

Methods for communicating

There are a number of ways in which we physically communicate. The most common way is to enter into verbal exchanges (that is, we talk to each other). This is all very well for those individuals who have good hearing ability, but for those who do not there are two alternatives.

Signing is a common method of communicating with those who have hearing difficulties. There are, however, several standards for this method of communicating. The examples in Figures 1.08 and 1.09 each mean the letter A. The obvious difference is that the American system has been developed for one hand only, while the British system clearly uses two hands. That would tend to suggest that as a 'reader' you would know automatically which system you were looking at.

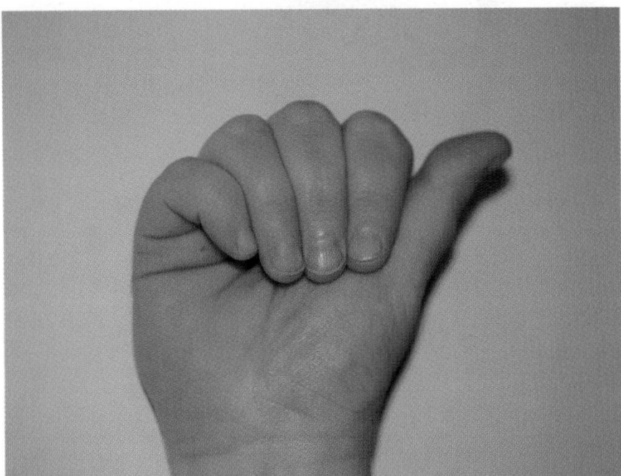

Figure 1.08 American Sign Language 'A' (American one-handed alphabet)

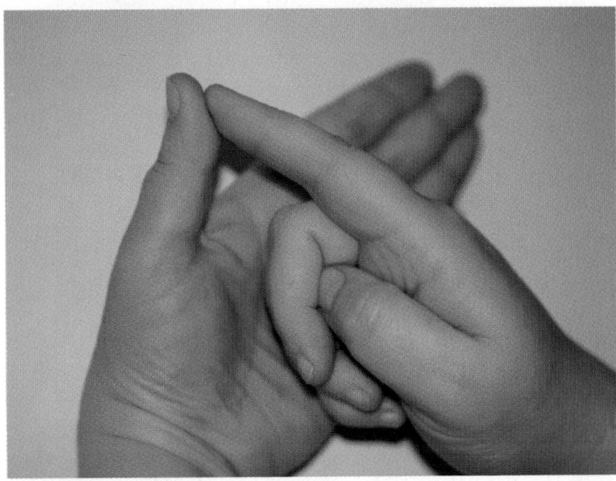

Figure 1.09 British Sign Language 'A' (British two-handed alphabet)

A third sign language, the Chinese sign language is based on ASL (American Sign Language), but it also has differences.

Lip reading is another common technique for those with hearing difficulty. Here, the recipient watches the mouth of the communicator. Often, it is something people are not aware they can do until they try it. With lip reading you are able to recognise letters by the way that they are formed with the mouth and lips. See the examples in Figures 1.10 and 1.11.

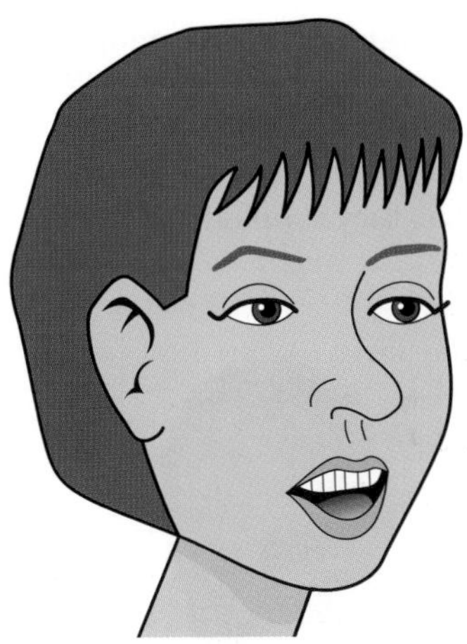

Figure 1.10 The 'th' sound

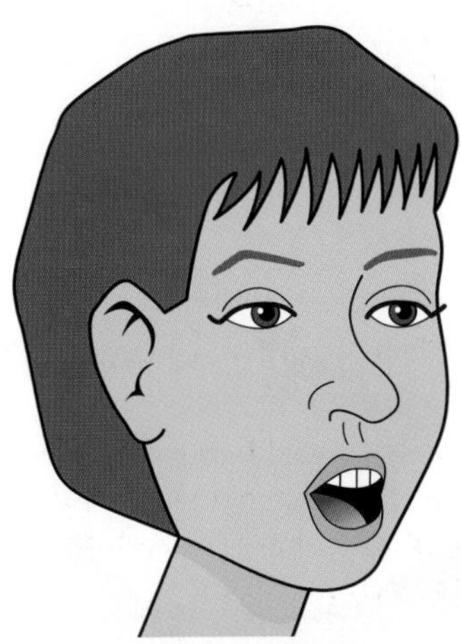

Figure 1.11 The 'o' sound

Some letters are easy to identify by lip reading, but for others you might need to see the rest of the word to make sense of a missing letter. For example, jar and char would look the same, but in a sentence you would assume that the person would not be asking for a char of honey! Thus, you would need to contextualise the word in order for it to make sense.

Lip reading can be a very useful technique if you are trying to hear what someone is saying when you are not close enough to hear the sounds.

Techniques and cues

In addition to communication by words, signs and sight, there are a number of other signals that a recipient can read that come from the communicator. Here are some examples:

- **Body language**: Most people would agree that the person in Figure 1.12 looks unhappy. Folded arms, a down-turned mouth and a frown are pretty obvious indicators that things are not as they should be.

Figure 1.12 Body language

- **Intonation**: Your vocal intonation (as suggested earlier in this chapter) can give the recipient clues about the way you are feeling. Changes in intonation are actually quite difficult to describe in writing, but here are a few examples:
  - Speaking slowly and deliberately often shows frustration on the part of the communicator.
  - Shouting is a clear indicator that the communicator is angry.
  - Raising your voice in pitch on the last syllable of a sentence indicates that you are asking a question.

Activity 1

What emotion do you think is being experienced by the people in Figures 1.22 and 1.23?

Figure 1.13 Facial Expression 1

Figure 1.14 Facial Expression 2

Activity answers are included on the supporting website.

Positive and negative language

There are many ways to say negative things without them sounding quite critical or rude. Here are some examples:

'*John, that painting is awful – you should have used better colour combinations.*'

Replaced with…

'*John, that's an interesting painting that might have been even better if you had considered your colour combinations.*'

Both of the above statements are critical of John, but the second one is not as aggressive or as negative as the first. In fact the second statement could be mistaken for guidance! Here's another example:

'*You don't appear to be particularly committed to your job.*'

'*At present, Sam, you are possibly not as dedicated to your job as I know you can be.*'

Again, the first statement is very direct. The second statement is actually saying the same thing, but leaves the recipient on a positive note.

Active engagement

There are times when it is useful if you can actually show that you are engaged in a particular discussion. **Nodding** is a useful tool to show that you are actively participating. It lets the speaker know that you are listening. **Summarising** (where you repeat the main points of an exchange), or **paraphrasing** (where you use other words to relay the same information to aid understanding and clarification) are also useful when used to show active participation, although these should be used carefully. Imagine you are talking to someone else and every time you stop, the other person immediately repeats everything you said back to you – you would obviously wonder what was going on! Equally, if the person you are talking to is constantly nodding or shaking their head, it can be equally disconcerting. Each technique should be used when appropriate and not excessively.

Types of questions

The type of question you ask will also have a bearing on how responsive the other party is in a communication. You will tend to mix the type of questions you use, depending on the situation. For this reason, you should understand different questioning techniques and the responses you are likely to receive.

- **Open question**: An open question is one where the question is structured in such a way as to allow the responder some control over how much they say in their response. For example, 'How are you today?' The responder might say, 'Very well, thank you', or could begin by saying, 'You know, I've had an awful day. I overslept this morning, got into work late and it meant that I spent hours trying to catch up with my work…'.
- **Closed question**: A closed question is one where the question is structured in such a way as to limit the possible responses. For example, 'Are you over 18 or under 18?' Here it would be likely that the response would be 'I'm over 18' or 'I'm under 18'. In some circumstances the responder might add, for example, 'I'm 17' or 'I'm 23' to further clarify their answer, but what else is there to say? Closed questions often result in a 'yes' or 'no' response.
- **Probing questions**: A probing question is one that is likely to encourage the responder to say more than they might have intended to. Quite often this is done intentionally, to make the responder believe that they are giving the information voluntarily, whereas the questioner was actually clever in the construction of the question in that a fuller response was always the intention. For example,

'Is that everything or is there anything else that you can think of?'

or

'Is there anything else you can tell me about the accident?'

Carefully selecting your questions prior to a meeting or discussion can be useful to a) ensure that the meeting moves at the pace you want it to and b) to ensure that you ask everything you need to, and receive the right level of detail.

Appropriate speeds of response

There is debate about the appropriateness of response speeds to questions or requests and what that says about the recipient.

A quick response could be interpreted in several ways:

- The responder is needy and over-eager.
- The responder is enthusiastic and interested.
- The responder has not fully considered their reply.

A slow response could also be interpreted in several ways:

- The responder doesn't care or couldn't be bothered to respond more quickly.
- The responder has taken a great deal of care and considered their response.
- The responder has misinterpreted the question and is taking longer to respond than you would have expected.

In most cases, a measured response is the most appropriate. In other words, don't respond too quickly or too slowly. Try to aim for somewhere in the middle.

Potential barriers to effective communication

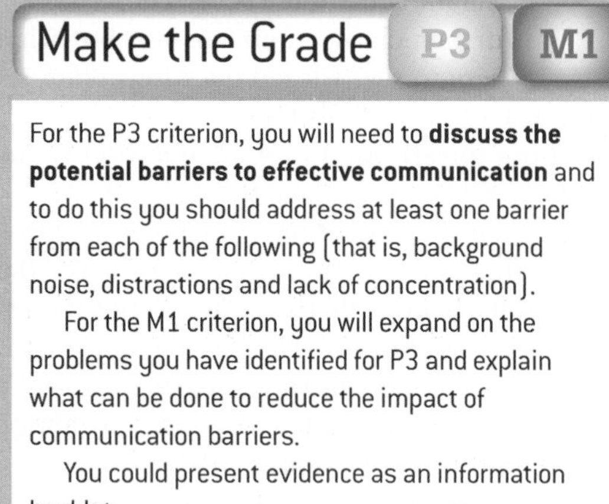

Make the Grade P3 M1

For the P3 criterion, you will need to **discuss the potential barriers to effective communication** and to do this you should address at least one barrier from each of the following (that is, background noise, distractions and lack of concentration).

For the M1 criterion, you will expand on the problems you have identified for P3 and explain what can be done to reduce the impact of communication barriers.

You could present evidence as an information booklet.

One of the key factors to improve interpersonal communication is to begin by removing any barriers to the communication. Examples of this could be:

- Moving away from an area where there is significant background noise, which can be very irritating, particularly if it also means that you have to shout to be heard.
- Move away from distractions, which could include a television that is on or another person. You can sometimes have a more meaningful discussion with someone if there is no one else present.

Both excessive background noises and distractions will ensure that you and/or the recipient will not be able to fully concentrate.

Consider also whether the person you wish to communicate with might be pre-occupied with other tasks. A lack of concentration on the part of either participant can make communication difficult and it can also be interpreted that one of the participants actually doesn't care very much about the conversation.

Poor diet and lack of exercise can be a cause of poor concentration, so it is the responsibility of anyone who finds concentration difficult to improve these things.

In general, to make discussions and communications more likely to be successful, you should ensure that you consider as many potential barriers as possible, and try to eradicate them.

Barriers can also prevent the content of written information from being communicated effectively. Distractions (such as noise, tiredness, overload of work, etc.) can all mean that you don't read something properly. It is very easy to scan text and think you know what it says, but in fact you might miss something entirely or misinterpret it. The reader of a message should try to avoid distraction, but the communicator can help by structuring a document or message carefully, by keeping the content unambiguous and by avoiding embellishments such as fancy fonts.

1.2.4 Communicate in writing

Organisational guidelines and procedures

Most organisations have written procedures and guidelines that they define and that they expect all employees to observe to portray the company's professionalism. These rules are usually known as a **house style**. The style will include guidelines on layout and fonts to be used, for example:

Left margin	3 cm
Right margin	2.5 cm
Top margin	4 cm (this is often to accommodate the organisation's own headed paper)
Bottom margin	2.5 cm
Justification	Full
Indentation	Blocked style
Line spacing	1.5 (except in an address)

Some organisations also define the line spacing of documents. For example, if you go on to university, it is likely that you will be asked to submit all your assignments in **double line** spacing. This is so that your tutor or lecturer can write comments between lines of your text. (see Figure 1.15).

Key terms

Justification This defines whether the edges of the page are consistent and in a straight line or not.

This paragraph is **left justified**. This means that the left edge of the text is aligned and the lines will be of different lengths making the right edge look ragged. **Ragged right** is another term for left justified!

This paragraph is **right justified**. This means that the right edge of the text is aligned and the left side will probably look ragged and have lines of different length. This is also known as **ragged left**. This style might be used for aligning a sender's address at the top of a letter.

This paragraph is **justified** (sometimes called **fully justified**). This means that each side of the text is aligned. This means that the word-processing software adjusts the gaps between words so they are of equal width within a line. If you look at a newspaper, you are likely to see all the columns printed in full justification.

This paragraph is centred. This means that the text is aligned centrally on the page. As you type a new line, the words start in the centre. Neither the left nor right edges of lines are aligned. If you like, this is effectively **ragged both**!

Indentation This is the amount of space from a margin before a line or paragraph. The indentation can be at the left- or right-hand side of a page. It identifies whether a paragraph starts at the edge of a page, or whether it begins a number of spaces in. For example:

This paragraph begins at the edge of the page. There is no indentation at the start of the paragraph. The writer immediately keys in text without pressing the space bar or tab key to show where the paragraph begins.

In this case, when a subsequent paragraph begins, a clear line is often left between paragraphs to make it clear where one paragraph ends and another starts. This is known as blocked style.

Alternatively, you could use what is called indentation.

Here, the first line of the paragraph is indented (moved in), with all subsequent text aligned to the left-hand margin. An easy way to set the space or gap is to press the tab key.

If you use this style, you need to make sure that you start each subsequent paragraph with its first line indented by the same distance.

Whichever style you use, you should ensure that the entire document is consistent!

Whole paragraphs can be indented, sometimes from both edges. This style is often used to display text for emphasis.

Good IT practice is to set a style within the word-processing application you use so that all new paragraphs start with the same indentation space. It is **not** considered good IT practice to use the space bar repeatedly to add a series of single spaces because you might forget how many to add and so end up with inconsistency in the style of your document.

According to Demszcinsky, et al (1994), the main reason for submitting this kind of

why many?

evidence is to ensure that the process has quality. Without quality the whole point of the

you have not said how!

exercise will be lost and there is a risk of misinterpretation.

Figure 1.15 Double line spacing

The text in this book is generally in **single line** spacing (that is, each line follows the line written above with no gap). In addition to single or double line spacing, most word processors let you set the spacing to be 1.5 or allow you to define a particular spacing.

Some envelopes have a transparent panel on their front (see Figure 1.16). This means that carefully positioned name and address details on a letter can be seen when the letter is folded and put into the envelope. It would probably be unwise to type the name and address on a letter in anything other than single line spacing because it would be unlikely that you would be able to see all of the details in the envelope window if you did otherwise.

Figure 1.16 Windowed envelopes

Professionalism

Communication using the internet (for example, by email or instant messaging) and the use of mobile phones for voice calls and texting has become commonplace. Texting, in particular, because of the restricted message length and keying methods, has caused a whole new language to develop. Poor use of words and the inability to see the person communicating the message, means that a sentence (for example, a jokey remark) might be misinterpreted. For example, if you received the comment

You looked really silly today

as a text or email you might be offended. If, however, you received the text like this:

You looked really silly today ☺

you would probably see that the sender was actually teasing you, and laughing with you.

The symbol is called an **emoticon** (from the words 'emotion' and 'icon') or a '**smiley**'.

There are many emoticons to depict different emotions, some of them are even animated. For more information, search the internet using the key word 'emoticon'.

However, it is very important to be professional. What you write to a friend, and how you write it, is often unsuitable in messages to colleagues. The use of abbreviated text messages and emoticons is bad practice in the workplace, where your messages have to be clear and concise, and must not cause offence.

Identifying and conveying key messages in writing

In our fast-paced world, where everyone is always busy, it is essential that when you are communicating you convey your message as quickly, efficiently and as simply as possible. Long and drawn out sentences and paragraphs are difficult to read and are time-consuming for the reader. It is best to plan a message in advance to ensure that your letters, faxes and emails are efficient.

1. Identify the key issues without which the communication will be deemed to have failed.
2. Identify what it is you want to say about these issues.
3. Decide how you want to say it (that is, its tone, etc.).

In these days of word processing, rather than in the days where letters had to be typed and changing a word would potentially require the whole letter to be retyped, there is no excuse for sending out poorly worded or incorrect correspondence. This is because the written word is now very easy to check, correct and reprint if necessary.

It is usually up to you what you put in a letter, fax or email (unless you have been asked to write it on somebody's behalf), but your employer will also have ideas about what should and should not be included.

Using correct grammar and spelling

When you consider that most word-processing software now has both spellchecking, grammar checking and thesaurus capabilities, there is really no reason why correspondence should be sent out unchecked and uncorrected.

Research suggests that the human brain does have the ability to interpret badly written English (see http://www.languagehat.com/archives/000840.php for further information).

However, there is no substitute for proofreading, as can be seen in Figure 1.17. The incorrectly written paragraph doesn't exactly look very professional does it? Poor spelling and grammar usually suggest that the writer did not take particular care in the presentation of his or her work. The recipient might then wonder if care has been taken with the work itself. This is paramount, particularly if you are writing to individuals outside an organisation as through the communication you are considered to be representing the organisation.

Some Peploe say "it dnso'et mtetar how txet is wittren as lnog as the frsit and lsat ltteres are in the rhgit oerdr and rghit psoitnios bacusee the hmaun bairn can srot out the maennig aynawy".

Can you read the above? Most people can. It should say:

Some people say "it doesn't matter how text is written as long as the first and last letters are in the right order and right positions, because the human brain can sort out the meaning anyway".

Figure 1.17 Proofreading

Key terms

Spellchecking Spellchecking facilities are often included in software packages to help the user to ensure that documents are correct. The software usually highlights words that it has assessed as being incorrectly spelled. The incorrectly spelled words in Figure 1.18 have been highlighted with a red wavy line.

Some Peploe say "it dnso'et mtetar how txet is wittren as lnog as the frsit and lsat ltteres are in the rhgit oerdr and rghit psoitnios, bacusee the hmaun bairn can srot out the maennig aynawy".

Figure 1.18 Spellchecking

Unfortunately, the system cannot identify correctly spelled words that are used in an incorrect context. For example, which is correct?

A I will not go their.

or

B I will not go there.

In this case, **B** is correct because the word 'their' means 'belonging to them'. There are a number of common words that are often incorrectly interchanged. Table 1.02 gives some examples to watch out for:

Table 1.02

Word	Meaning	Word	Meaning
There	In that place.	Their	Belonging to them.
Where	A place or scene of something.	Wear	To be dressed in
Pair	Two items as a set.	Pear	A fruit.
Whether	Often used to introduce a number of alternatives, for example, 'whether good or bad, we will proceed with the sale'.	Weather	Sunshine, rain, etc.
Fair	A place you go with dodgems and rides.	Fare	The cost of getting from A to B.

In each case, the word in the table would not throw up a spelling error. Only proofreading and an understanding of the word in its correct context will ensure that these errors are not made in written text.

Grammar check A grammar checker is built in to many software packages to check whether the sentences have been constructed correctly. Unfortunately, like the spellchecker, the grammar checker does not identify whether words have been used in an incorrect context. In the event that the grammar checker finds a sentence containing an error, the software will underline the incorrect words with a wavy green line.

Thesaurus The thesaurus is an extremely useful tool because when activated, it offers the user a selection of alternative words which more or less have the same meaning. Here's an example:

Actually, he was wrong when it came to his description of the actual man he had seen.

In this example, the word 'actual' has been used twice (once as 'actual' and the second time as the basis of the word 'actually'). It is good writing practice to vary the use of words, even if the words chosen say what you actually want them to say. In the example, the word 'actual' has been used to stress the point being made. Using the thesaurus, we can change both (or just one) of the occurrences of the word.

Here are some alternative words and phrases that a thesaurus might suggest for the word 'actually'.

in fact   really   in point of fact   in reality   truly   essentially

The following words are possible suggestions for alternatives to the word 'actual'.

real   definite   genuine   authentic   concrete   tangible

Using some of the alternative words, the sentence can be written.

In fact, he was wrong when it came to his description of the actual man he had seen.

In this example, we decided to keep the word 'actual' and only replace the word 'actually', because the words offered by the thesaurus to replace the word 'actual' didn't seem to fit the sentence. As such, the thesaurus is an extremely useful tool, but the you still need to make the final decision as to whether or not a suggested alternative word is suitable in a sentence. Knowing when it is appropriate to make changes and when it might be more suitable to leave words as they are, is part of your skill as a communicator.

Structuring writing into a logical framework

It is important to use a formal structure or framework for a written communication. Most letters have a format, for example, like that shown in Figure 1.19. A letter that uses this template is shown in Figure 1.20.

Name of organisation sending the letter
Address of organisation
Post Code
Telephone Number (if appropriate)

Date of letter
Reference (some organisations include information that they ask you to quote when responding)

Name of person/organisation the letter is going to
Address of person
Post Code of person

Dear Sir or Dear Mr Smith (known as the salutation)

Subject of the letter is often written here

This will be where the main content of the letter is typed. A sample of a completed letter from Lee Office Supplies follows this example.

Yours faithfully (if you wrote Dear Sir), or Yours sincerely (If you wrote Dear Mr Smith)

Room is left here to ensure that the person sending the letter has space to sign it.

Name of sender
Job in organisation

Figure 1.19 A sample letter template

Lee Office Supplies
21 Golden Road
Mytown
MY10 1BF
01166 878216

15 November 2011

Reference: BF/ja

Mr S Smith
Greenacres
Mytown
MY11 1MF

Dear Mr Smith

Order Number: 126552

We are delighted to inform you that the special envelopes and photographic paper you ordered are now in stock, a week earlier than anticipated. Furthermore, we were able to secure an additional discount and we will be reducing the cost of your order by a further 5 per cent.

Please call in at our offices at your earliest convenience to collect your order.

Yours sincerely

Bernie Fishpool
Sales Manager

Figure 1.20 A letter that uses the template shown in Figure 1.19

Firstly, note that the example letter closes with 'Yours sincerely' because the letter began with 'Dear Mr Smith'. If it had started with 'Dear Sir' or 'Dear Madam', it would have closed with 'Yours faithfully'.

The advantage of using a structure, such as the one shown in the examples, is a little bit like using a recipe to make a cake – if you follow the recipe you will have a usable product! In addition, if all organisations use a similar basic structure for their business documents (with organisational variations of course), then you will always know what information should be available in a document because you understand what the document is, how it works, and what is usually included. For example, any business documentation associated with money (sales invoices, purchase invoices, etc.) will have a VAT number on it if the company is registered for VAT. A company is not allowed to charge VAT on an invoice unless it a) is registered and b) has displayed its number on the documentation. Clearly, a letter isn't the same as a purchase or sales invoice, so it doesn't need to have the VAT number shown on it.

Particular documentation standards, which have been used by businesses for many years, have now provided the structure for many of the templates you will see within the software you use. Letters, memos, business cards, invoices, orders, delivery notes, greetings cards and many more have a similar format, with artistic variations to suit an organisation or individual.

Identifying relevant information in written communications

In order to explain this concept of relevancy in written communication, it is probably better to give an example. You have received the correspondence shown in Figure 1.21.

Dear Mrs Fishpool

We regret to inform you that your dental appointment has been postponed and will now be on Monday 2 April at 2.45 pm.

This is because the dentist has been asked to speak at a charity function and while this is actually a lunchtime appointment, we were concerned that he might be late and thus would keep you waiting. So we thought it better to change the time.

If this new date or time is inconvenient, please call and let us know as soon as possible.

Yours sincerely

Dental Practice

Figure 1.21 What information is truly necessary?

Review this letter and decide information it gives is relevant (and thus important). The answer is as follows:

> Your dental appointment is now on Monday 2 April at 2.45 pm.
>
> Please let us know if the new date or time is inconvenient.

You don't need to know why the appointment has been postponed? Does the knowledge of this fact have any influence on what you think about it? Probably not!

As such, the version of the letter in Figure 1.22 would have been wholly appropriate.

Identifying relevance

Being able to extract relevant information from writing is a skill. You have to decide which parts of the communication contain information you might want to use again or refer to at a later date. Here is an overview on how to do this:

1. Read the document through so that you understand in general what it is about.
2. Read again, and make notes about the important aspects of the text. Highlight the key points.
3. Write the relevant information in your own words.

Dear Mrs Fishpool

We regret to inform you that your dental appointment has been postponed and will now be on Monday 2 April at 2.45 pm.

If this new date or time is inconvenient, please call and let us know as soon as possible.

Yours sincerely

Dental Practice

Figure 1.22 The letter in Figure 1.21 amended to show only relevant information

If we use the dental appointment as an example, it would be likely that the patient would find her diary, cross through the original entry for the dental appointment, and write the new details on the appropriate date (as shown in Figure 1.23).

Figure 1.23 A diary extract

With experience you will soon be able to tell what information is likely to be important, and which information can be ignored. Similarly, you will learn to write letters that are to the point without waffling about things that have no relevance.

Reviewing and proofreading your own written work

It is absolutely essential that you learn to review and proofread your own written work. The more important a document is, the more carefully the document should have been reviewed and proofread.

Activity 2

You have been given the following typed record of a telephone message.

Mrs Jones rang about the missing items from the last order. She says that she really isn't very happy about the way that our organisation has dealt with this issue. She says that when she dealt with Smethurst Office Supplies she never had these kinds of problems. If something was missing from an order they would courier it to her immediately. She also said that she was always given goods on account and 30 days credit, and they didn't even chase her for an additional 15 days after the account was due. Her number is 01234 567891. She will be on this number from 3–4.30 pm today.

Extract the important information from this message.

Answers to the activity are given on the supporting website.

Key terms

Reviewing When you review text, you look at the factual content and check it is correct. Using the dental appointment example, the letter writer should check that the appointment details are correct for the patient in question. (Of course, it goes without saying that the writer should check that they have correctly entered the new times in their appointments' book, but this isn't really reviewing the content of the letter.)

Proofreading These are checks of the spelling and grammar of the text. If you are concerned about your proofreading skills, ask someone else to proofread for you or with you. You should, however, try to learn to do this yourself in the long term. As suggested earlier in this chapter, if you are using software to create your documents, you will be able to make use of the tools available. However, you should never rely on these tools, and you should always read the document through again yourself to be absolutely sure that it is correct.

Conveying alternative viewpoints

Often, one of the most important aspects of writing is that the writer should be able to convey alternative viewpoints – viewpoints with which he or she might not actually agree – when proposing that something should be adopted. This shows clear thinking. Emphasis will be given to the conclusion the writer is promoting, but the text should also show that other options have been considered and dismissed (with reasons).

Impartial reporting is an aspect of the above, but where an argument or case is not being put forward. Consider the following:

The Event – an election to select a local councillor

Martha Hargreaves is the Conservative candidate. Elena Malowski is the Labour candidate and Justin Newman is standing for the Independent Party. They were each asked to speak about the state of the county's roads. This is how the event was written up in two local papers.

Paper A	Paper B
Martha Hargreaves highlighted the dreadful state of the roads, particularly since the last election when the Independent Party took control of the council. 'There are increasing numbers of potholes in the streets, causing a trip hazard to the elderly and small children, and causing unnecessary stress on the suspension of local drivers' cars'. She said, 'Something needs to be done.' Elena Malowski and Justin Newman agreed.	After a debate the councillors agreed that something should be done about local roads in the county as potholes are increasingly a hazard for all road users.

It is clear that Paper A has focused on Martha Hargreaves and has only mentioned the other candidates at the end, almost dismissively. In addition, it makes Martha appear proactive and strong, and the other candidates weak because they simply agreed with her and didn't appear to have had any original thoughts of their own.

In Paper B's account no one councillor is quoted, just the summary of what was said. This does not emphasise a contribution from any one councillor and thus is more balanced. Obviously, if Paper A was a Conservative newspaper, it would be in its interest to get as much coverage for its own candidates as possible.

Note taking

The ability to take effective notes is a very useful skill, particularly if you need to make a paper record of a meeting. Taking notes in longhand is time-consuming. For this reason many people use some form of shorthand. Shorthand methods are written languages that use symbols that are quick to write as abbreviations for common words or sounds. A common shorthand technique is Speedwriting. With this technique, the words written down are abbreviations of the original words, symbols to denote a particular common word, and phonetic spellings (when a word is written as it actually sounds). For example:

Few	would be	fu	phonetic spelling
The	would be	.	symbol
Could	would be	cld	abbreviation

One very important aspect about taking notes is that you should always write up the notes in full as soon as possible after taking them, otherwise you might no longer be able to remember what you meant, particularly if you made errors.

Emphasis of text

CAPITALISATION is often used as a way to stress information in writing. Similar alternatives include underlining, **emboldening**, or *putting words in italics*, or even ***ALL FOUR SIMULTANEOUSLY***.

USING CAPITALISATION AS PART OF YOUR TEXT is considered to be bad etiquette, because it can be interpreted as shouting at the recipient.

Emphasis of words and phrases should be used sparingly. Care should be taken to consider what you really want to convey as being important. Over use of formatting to emphasise text can make a document look messy with the overall effect of distracting the reader, who then has to filter out irrelevant emphasis, thereby effectively negating the intention of highlighting what is important for quick recognition.

B Braincheck

Match the following terms with their correct explanation.

Term		Explanation	
A	Spellchecking	1	Where text is written in capital letters to stress a word or phrase.
B	Yours faithfully	2	Closes a letter that began with Dear Sir or Dear Madam.
C	Indented paragraph	3	Where each side of the text is aligned (straight).
D	A closed question	4	Where the first line is set in from the subsequent lines in a paragraph.
E	Proofreading	5	Offers a selection of alternative words that have an identical or similar meaning to the one selected.
F	Shouting when communicating in writing	6	Closes a letter that began with e.g. Dear Mr Smith.
G	Full justification	7	Using software to check the spelling accuracy of a piece of text.
H	Thesaurus	8	Checking the correctness of spelling and grammar in written text.
I	Yours sincerely	9	Where the answer can only be one of a limited number of options.

Answer to the Braincheck can be found on the supporting website.

1.3 Be able to use IT to communicate effectively

This section will cover the following grading criteria:

1.3.1 Communications channels

There are a number of common ways in which we communicate information today – some of which will be examined here.

Word-processed documents

Word processing has revolutionised the way in which organisations communicate. It has seen many organisations produce more professional and complex documents than they might have done in the days of typewriters.

It has become easier and cheaper to create mail-merge letters, leaflets, flyers, posters, etc. Most software also has a range of templates that can be used, and the facility for organisations and individuals to create their own templates. In addition, more and more design styles can be downloaded and incorporated within existing software as and when they are created by the manufacturers.

As suggested earlier in the unit, grammar and spellchecking facilities have ensured that written documentation looks more professional.

Presentations

Businesses frequently use presentations to pass a significant amount of information to a number of individuals simultaneously. You may well be asked to present some of your coursework in this format.

A presentation requires that the presenter speaks formally to the audience, using visual aids to help him or her get the message across. Slide shows, DVDs, leaflets and handouts may all be created for use during the presentation.

Email

Emails are increasingly being used in preference to letters. They have become the main method of communication, where less formal communication is required, particularly within organisations. They have all but replaced the concept of the office memorandum (which was laid out similarly to an email and was usually sent via an internal mail system).

The main advantages of email are that it is an extremely quick and cheap method of communication. In addition, if you ask for a 'receipt' reply, you can be advised when the recipient (person receiving your email) has opened it (although it doesn't actually confirm that they have read the content, and they can choose not to send the receipt if they don't want to!). This can be very useful in helping to get things done quickly, as someone could always say 'I didn't receive your memo', but would be less likely to claim that they had not received an email.

Web-based channels

- **Blog** is an abbreviation for weblog. This is a newsletter or information website (sometimes in diary form). It tends to be updated on a regular basis and is intended to be looked at by anyone who wishes to see it. A **vlog** (video blogging) is essentially the same as a blog, but uses video as part of its format.
- The term **podcast** is derived from the name of an Apple® product, the iPod® and the concept of the broadcast. Essentially a podcast is a media file that can be downloaded to an individual's own computer or mobile device to be played back. Depending on the originator, these files might be free or the receiver may have to pay a subscription.
- A **web page** is a document that can be created and uploaded to the World Wide Web (using the internet) or it can be included on an organisation's own internal website and accessed using the company's intranet. A web page is usually written in a **mark-up language**, such as HTML or XML and a web browser is needed to access and render the coding. A web page is usually only part of a larger website.

  One distinct advantage of web pages is that they can include **hyperlinks** to other web pages, thereby reducing the amount of information that an organisation might have to include on a page because the information can be accessed on another website.

  Some web pages are interactive (for example, a supermarket home-delivery service, where you can order and pay for goods or services). Other pages act as online brochures (for example, a tourist information website might have lists of attractions or accommodation that a visitor might like to know about before coming to your town or village).

Activity 3

Use a search engine such as Google®, Bing® or Yahoo®, to look at a tourist information website for your own town or area.

Try searching using the key words: Your town name + Tourist Information

- Video conferencing has significantly modernised the way in which businesses can communicate over distances. Where, in earlier years, executives would have had to travel to another office or a client's premises for a meeting, video conferencing has ensured that many people in different locations can come together for a meeting without actually having to travel anywhere. Using simple webcams or even fully integrated systems, users can see each other during the discussion. They can also see demonstrations of products, drawings, and so on.

Benefits and disadvantages

Table 1.03 gives an overview of the communication channels discussed.

1.3.2 Software

Make the Grade P5 P6

For the P5 criterion, you will need to demonstrate that you can use a variety of **IT techniques to help you communicate** (that is, word-processing, presentation, email and other specialist software). Evidence may come from this or other units as long as it is clear that it is your own work.

The P6 criterion requires you to **communicate technical information to a specific audience**. This might be creating some form of 'dummies' guide (for example, to explain the use of a word processor's proofing tools or how to create a master slide in presentation software such as Microsoft PowerPoint®. Any technical subject can be used, but you need to define your audience.

Table 1.03

Channel	Benefit	Disadvantage
Word-processed documents	Permanent record that can also be easily edited.	Users need reasonable word-processing skills, otherwise creating the documents can be laborious and time consuming.
Presentations	Information can be presented to a large number of individuals simultaneously.	Can be nerve-racking for those who are shy or who are not used to giving presentations.
Web pages	Can be interesting and interactive, and can reach many people across multiple time zones.	Need to be updated regularly and checked for accuracy, particularly taking into account any legal issues between countries.
Email	Quick and efficient.	They can be intrusive, and extensive **spam** (unsolicited emails from companies trying to sell things) can be irritating.
Blogs/vlogs/podcasts	These tools have ensured that there is now information on more or less anything on the Web.	Some might not be suitable for some age groups and they are difficult to police. Some might cause offence.
Video conferencing	Being able to communicate visually with others without having to travel.	Might involve expensive equipment and communication links.

Word-processing software

Using word processor applications, such as Microsoft Word® or Corel WordPerfect®, has transformed business communication. Open-source word processors, such as that in OpenOffice, are also rapidly becoming popular. All these products contain additional tools and templates that can help the less able user to create professional documentation with little effort.

Presentation software

As with word-processing software, there is a range of presentation software that can be purchased for a variety of operating systems.

Presentation software allows users to create slide shows. Each slide will usually contain text, images, graphs and charts (or a combination of these), with the advantage that the slideshow can be printed in the form of a handout to be taken away by delegates as a permanent record of the presentation.

Using presentation techniques ensures that if you give the same presentation on a number of occasions (possibly over a number of weeks or days), the content of each presentation is likely to be more or less the same.

Other specialist software

There is a variety of software available for many purposes (for example email, project management, graphic drawing, etc.). Some types have become more accepted and used than others.

A popular software application that interfaces to an Internet Service Provider (ISP) for sending and receiving emails is Microsoft Outlook® Express (which comes with Microsoft Office). Many (ISPs) have their own software interface for email. Microsoft Outlook® (which is similar to Outlook® Express, but has more functionality) is often used within companies. Some organisations have messaging software built in to their intranet to cut down on the number of internal phone calls made between people in different departments.

There are a number of Braille software products available for the visually impaired, such as Braille 'n Speak® and Braille Lite®.

Activity 4

Identify the following in a typical computer room at your school, college or institution.

- Types of common software installed (excluding the operating system).
- Types of specialist software installed.

Using this information, complete the following grid.

Software name (e.g. Microsoft® Word)	Function (e.g. word-processing)

You should keep this list to help you remember what software is available and what it is used for.

1.3.3 Review documents

Make the Grade M2

The evidence to meet the M2 criterion (**review draft documents to produce final versions**) can be taken from anywhere and will require you to review at least two documents where you will suggest corrections and amendments.

You don't need to learn any standard proofing symbols, but you will be expected to make notes or marks on the original document that indicate what has to be done.

Evidence will require the initial documents and the final documents, and some indication that it is your work.

Proofing tools

Certain types of application software help users to communicate more effectively by providing tools that carry out proofreading functions, such as spellchecking and grammar checking. In addition, they usually provide a thesaurus.

A **spellchecker**, as the name suggests, checks the spelling of individual words. Spellcheckers are able to identify whether letters in a word are missing or whether they have been transposed (switched around). However, this tool is unable to understand the sense of a word, so it is no substitute for reading the document through yourself. It can not differentiate between words that sound the same but have different spellings. In addition, the spellchecker must be compatible with the language in which you are writing. While this may sound silly, it would not be very helpful to use a spellchecker that is set for American spelling if you are writing documents in the UK for UK recipients. This is because some common words are spelled differently in the USA. For example:

colour (UK)	is	color (US)
centre (UK)	is	center (US)

A **thesaurus** is a very useful tool if you are unable to think of an alternative word. By selecting a typed word and activating the thesaurus, you will be offered a number of alternatives from which you can choose. Most have the same or very similar meaning (they are synonyms) to the word you highlighted. You should be cautious however that your choice of a substitute word doesn't change the sense of what you are trying to say.

As suggested earlier in this unit, proofreading documents you produce is essential to ensure that they are sensible, consistent and error free. Don't forget that in a working environment professionalism is largely demonstrated through communication skills.

Proofing tools

Make the Grade D1

For the D1 criterion, you will be required to **evaluate the interpersonal and written communication techniques** that you have used in this or other units.

Essentially, this is an evaluation of all the unit's Pass and Merit criteria, and you should be able to use it to provide strong insights into the ideas it covers.

The ideal evidence here is a brief report.

You should be able to name and evaluate a range of methods to demonstrate an understanding of interpersonal and written communications techniques. You should be able to contextualise each technique by giving a scenario of how and where a particular technique should be used.

1.4 Be able to address personal development needs

This section will cover the following grading criteria:

Make the Grade P7 P8 D2

The P7 and P8 criteria require you to put together a personal development plan.

For P7 you will need to create a learning plan, which you can present in any appropriate format. You can choose the timescale for your plan, but whatever you choose there should be sufficient time for you to have an opportunity to monitor progress.

Evidence for P8 can come from review points in the plan when you and your tutor discuss and evaluate your progress.

For D2 you will review your personal development plan and identify areas for improvement.

In order to be an effective individual (not just an effective employee) you will constantly need to review your own situation as you move through your personal and working life. Others will help you to identify your own training and developmental needs along the way, but primarily, you should be prepared to self-evaluate from time to time, to ensure that you are getting the best out of your life and your situation. Here are some examples of how needs are identified.

1.4.1 Identification of need

Formal reports

When you are in employment you will have regular **appraisals** with your line manager or supervisor. These usually take the form of a meeting. You will be asked to self-assess and you will discuss your positive and negative attributes and attitudes.

However, it is likely that your manager or supervisor will also have his or her own ideas about your good and bad traits! The appraisal is usually written up as a formal document and an action plan is established to help you to develop.

This plan could list a number of courses that might be useful to you. Alternatively, it might contain a personal attitude target, for example 'think before you speak' or 'arrive at work on time'. Targets that are set should be SMART (**S**pecific, **M**easurable, **A**ppropriate, **R**ealistic, **T**imed).

Self-assessment

Being introspective and thinking about your personal skills and abilities is known as self-assessment. You need to highlight what you feel you are good at and what you think you are bad at. In most cases, the things you think you are bad at are used to identify training and development needs. However, the list of what you feel you are good at also needs to be explored because human nature will dictate that we will sometimes think we are better at things than we really are.

Other assessment methods

Some organisations also use other information to help identify your developmental needs. It is common for organisations to ask customers for feedback. This can be through a phone call, where a series of questions are asked to rate the service, or more often via email, where the customer is invited to fill in an online survey (Figure 1.24).

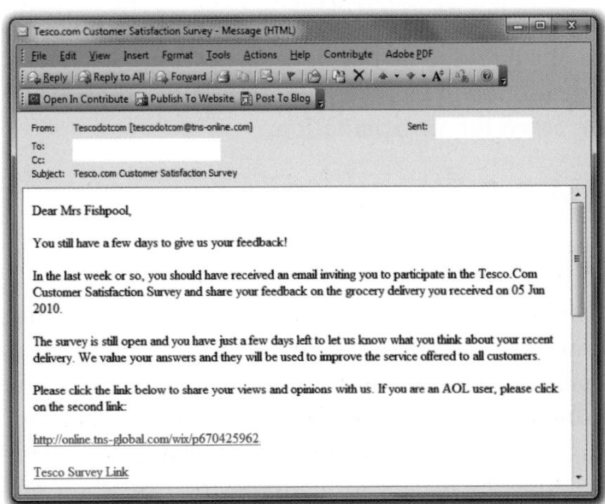

Figure 1.24 An example of a customer feedback request

The information or feedback from customers is often used as part of an employee's appraisal, particularly if the employee is identifiable. This information is then used to establish development needs.

Activity 5

You have been asked to undertake a skills audit in preparation for a job application. Using the following grid (similar to that which often records a person specification), you have been asked to consider your own strengths and weaknesses. Complete the grid and discuss what you have written with your personal tutor or learning mentor.

Attributes	Strengths	Weaknesses
Experience		
Qualifications and training		
Abilities		
Job circumstances (e.g. mobility/ late/early working)		

Based on this audit, create a short **Personal Development Plan** (PDP) that selects **two** weaknesses and plans activities to overcome them over the next three months. The plan should include timescales and monitoring points over the period.

In some environments there is what is called performance data which can help managers to assess the needs of their employees. For example, the sales records for a given area can be used to establish whether a sales representative is performing adequately. If he or she is over the target sales he or she might get a bonus. If under the sales target, questions will be asked and the representative will be asked for an explanation.

1.4.2 Records

Setting targets

As suggested in the previous section, an action plan is often created as part of the appraisal process. This is formalised so that it can be used in a subsequent review (where your work towards meeting these targets is discussed). Targets that have been set are usually formalised with a 'by when' notation, so that your development is not left open-ended, but is tied to specific dates in the calendar.

Other records

Most institutions will have their own version of an appraisal record. Figure 1.25 shows an example.

This form is usually filled in by the employee prior to the appraisal. It is given to the manager so that he or she is aware of the issues that the employee has identified.

During the subsequent appraisal meeting (sometimes also known as an interview), the second part of the appraisal record is filled in. In this section, the manager and the employee discuss the answers given by the employee, and the main points of the discussion are noted.

At the end of the session, an **action plan** will be completed, something like that shown in Table 1.04.

The action plan will be signed by both the employee and the line manager, both of whom will then receive a copy.

1.4.3 Methods of addressing needs

The ways that personal development for the employee will take place are dependent on a number factors, but particularly on the following:

- how much money the organisation has for staff development;
- the time needed for training.

Clearly an organisation will realise that making sure that its employees are adequately trained is good for its business, but it will want to ensure that it gets good value for the money it spends on training. Here are some methods of training that organisations use.

Appraisal Form

Name of Employee:	Department:
Position:	Name of Manager:

Please define your job role:

How has the period since the last appraisal been? Good/ satisfactory/bad (Please delete as appropriate and state why:

What have you achieved in the last year?

What do you find difficult about your job?

What do you like most about your job?

What can be done to help you improve?

What would you like to be doing in 3 years' time?

Figure 1.25 An example of an appraisal form

Table 1.04

Action point	How/by whom?	By when?
Improve time-keeping	Employee	1 month
Further Excel® training required	External training course/Training coordinator	July 2011
First aid training	External training course/Training coordinator	December 2010

Job shadowing

Let us suppose that an employee is asked to do some work in Reception. It might be possible for the employee to **shadow** (observe and help) the receptionist over a given period. The advantage to the employee of this activity would be that he or she would get first-hand experience of the job. The advantage to the employer would be that there would be another member of staff trained to cover this important business function. The main disadvantage for both the employer is that while the employee is shadowing the receptionist his or her usual job might not be getting done. The receptionist might also not work efficiently because he or she is spending time helping the learner.

Team meetings and events

In addition to formal training or job shadowing, you could be asked to attend team meetings. These might be for your own team or for teams from other areas, for example if you work in sales, you might be asked to attend a production meeting so that you can understand what that area does.

Alternatively, you might be offered an opportunity to attend a trade show (a computer fair or another exhibition relevant to your job). Here you would be able to gather information about products and services or even just about ways of doing things that will impact on how you do your own job.

Formal courses or training

If an organisation has the money, there is no substitute for formal training courses. Many organisations, to save money, pay for one employee to do a particular course and then use that employee to **cascade** the training to others who might need it.

External training courses are organised by schools, colleges and other training providers. An organisation might have some input into what is covered in the course. An external training provider might run the course at their own premises or, if there are enough attendees, at your company's site.

Internal training courses are run by the company itself. However, the time spent devising a course may mean that it is more cost-effective to use a ready-made externally provided course (for example, it would be cheaper to send employees on an external course on Microsoft Word® than to develop a new course in-house). Internal training is, however, the only option if specialised training for your job is required that only your company knows about.

There is a possibility that if you are doing a course on site (where you would normally work), you might be called out of the training course to deal with a problem, and as such you might miss important parts of the training.

1.4.4 Learning styles

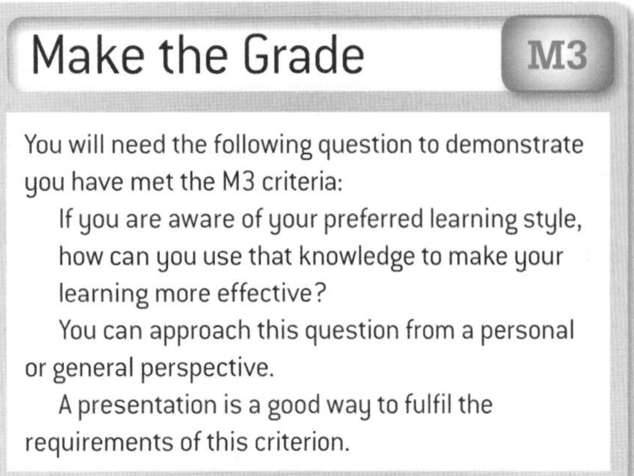

When your teachers and lecturers learned their profession, one of the most important things they had to learn was about the concept of individual learners having different learning styles. Some of us will be able to learn something merely because we read it in a book. This doesn't work for others who will only learn something if they do it practically. You may not be aware that someone at your own institution has probably carried out a learning style test on you, and your teachers generally know how you learn best.

Examples of systems

There are many examples of educational theories or systems that can be used to help you and your teachers identify how you like to learn. A simplified model is that we all learn by one or more of the styles shown in Table 1.05 on page 30, for example you might learn best through reasoning on your own (logical/solitary).

Identification of preferred style

A free online test to help you identify your own learning style can be downloaded from www.learning-styles-online.com/inventory/

By answering a series of questions the system will calculate your own learning-style profile. This will not give you a single learning style (e.g. kinaesthetic), but it will tell you how much of each of the

Table 1.05

Learning style	Learning activities
Aural	You learn best through music and sound.
Visual	You like to see images, pictures, demonstrations (for example, you particularly like the use of interactive whiteboards).
Physical (kinaesthetic)	Practical activities such as model making, using a computer, making finished products.
Logical	Mathematical reasoning, following steps like in a recipe.
Verbal	You learn through hearing or reading words.
Solitary	You prefer to learn on your own.
Social	You prefer to learn with others.

learning styles you have. For example, you might find you are a logical, kinaesthetic, social learner, which will mean that you like practical activities where you can apply mathematical reasoning and you like to do this with a group of people.

Once you have done a test like this (and there are many others online), you should not assume that your learning style is now set in stone – your learning style can change over time.

How to benefit from knowing your learning style

Two of the main benefits of knowing your own learning style is that you can make sure that you are on a suitable course or that you are using learning materials that you know in advance will ultimately teach you effectively. You will probably have noticed in your own classroom that the teacher or lecturer will be using a variety of different activities to help you learn a subject. You might watch a presentation, listen to the teacher talking, do some research using the internet and build a model. The teacher is teaching the subject in ways that will appeal to different learners in your group. That way, everyone has a better chance of learning.

Understanding how other people's learning styles impact on team working

We all have different preferred learning styles, so we need to take account other people's styles when we are working in a group or team. If you know that your colleague is a physical learner, it would not be very valuable to send him or her a video or DVD to watch.

Activity 6

Find out about your own preferred learning style using the website http://www.learning-styles-online.com/inventory/ or one of the many alternatives available.

Activity 7

Discuss your preferred learning style with your teacher or a tutor.

It is likely that they will already have formed their own ideas about how you learn best, and it might be interesting to compare what you think with what a professional sees in you.

Case Study

In this unit you have already been introduced to **Lee Office Supplies**, which is a small stationery and office equipment supplier trading with our other two organizations, **Frankoni T-shirts** and **KAM (Kris Arts & Media) Limited**.

Frankoni T-shirts Limited is a national company with outlets in larger towns. They specialize in producing personalized t-shirts on demand, using iron on designs that they buy in from other companies, but particularly from KAM Limited. The t-shirts themselves can be purchased from a range of alternative suppliers.

KAM (Kris Arts & Media) Limited is primarily a graphic design company. The company specialized in taking photographic images for use in advertising and other artistic pursuits, along with hand-drawn and computer-generated images, particularly used in t-shirt design. Trading only from one location, Kris' artistic reputation has seen a vast increase in his customer base.

The three companies seen here will be used throughout the text to underpin activities and to provide a contextual framework for some of the concepts you will meet.

Unit links

Unit 1 is a Mandatory unit for all qualifications and pathways of this Level 3 IT family.

Qualification (pathway)	Mandatory	Optional	Specialist optional
Edexcel BTEC Level 3 National Certificate in Information Technology	✓		
Edexcel BTEC Level 3 National Subsidiary Diploma in Information Technology	✓		
Edexcel BTEC Level 3 National Diploma in Information Technology	✓		
Edexcel BTEC Level 3 National Extended Diploma in Information Technology	✓		
Edexcel BTEC Level 3 National Diploma in IT (Business)	✓		
Edexcel BTEC Level 3 National Extended Diploma in IT (Business)	✓		
Edexcel BTEC Level 3 National Diploma in IT (Networking and System Support)	✓		
Edexcel BTEC Level 3 National Extended Diploma in IT (Networking and System Support)	✓		
Edexcel BTEC Level 3 National Diploma in IT (Software Development)	✓		
Edexcel BTEC Level 3 National Extended Diploma in IT (Software Development)	✓		

The specification makes no specific links to any units but, as noted, this unit complements many of the technical skills covered elsewhere in the programme.

Achieving success

In order to achieve success in each unit, you will complete a series of coursework activities. Each time you hand in work, your tutor will return this to you with a record of your achievement.

This particular unit has 13 criteria to meet: 8 Pass, 3 Merit and 2 Distinction.

For a Pass:	You must meet all 8 Pass criteria.
For a Merit:	You must meet all 8 Pass and all 3 Merit criteria.
For a Distinction:	You must meet all 8 Pass, all 3 Merit and both Distinction criteria.

Further reading

Barker, A. – *Improve Your Communication Skills, 2nd edition* (Kogan Page, 2006) ISBN-10 0749448229, ISBN-13 978-0749448226

Bolton, R. – *People Skills* (Simon & Schuster, 1986) ISBN-10 067162248X, ISBN-13 978-0671622480

Website

www.mindtools.com/page8.html

Unit 2: Computer systems

By the end of this unit you should be able to:

1. Understand the components of computer systems
2. Be able to recommend computer systems for a business purpose
3. Be able to set up and maintain computer systems

Whether you are in school or college, passing this unit will involve being assessed. As with most BTEC schemes, successful completion of various assessment criteria demonstrates your evidence of learning and the skills you have developed.

This unit has a mixture of pass, merit and distinction criteria. Generally you will find that merit and distinction criteria require a little more thought and evaluation before they can be completed.

The colour-coded grid below shows you the pass, merit and distinction criteria for this unit.

To achieve a pass grade you need to:	To achieve a merit grade you also need to:	To achieve a distinction grade you also need to:
P1 Explain the function of computer hardware components		
P2 Explain the purpose of operating systems	**M1** Compare the features and functions of different operating systems	
P3 Explain the purpose of different software utilities		**D1** Explain how software utilities can improve the performance of computer systems
P4 Recommend a computer system for a given business purpose	**M2** Justify choice of computer system to meet a given business purpose	
P5 Set up a standalone computer system, installing hardware and software components		
P6 Configure a computer system to meet user needs		
P7 Test a configured computer system for functionality	**M3** Evaluate the performance of a computer system	**D2** Explain and justify improvements that could be made to a computer system
P8 Undertake routine maintenance tasks on a standalone computer system		

Introduction

Computer systems is a 10-credit unit which is designed to introduce you to the hardware components that exist inside a typical computer. In addition, it also helps you to learn about important software such as the **operating system**, and crucial utilities such **antivirus** suites and **firewalls**.

Practical tasks are also covered. As part of your studies you will be required to build computer systems, tackle hardware and software maintenance, and configure and test a computer system to ensure that it meets user needs.

This unit provides a critical platform for your success in other units.

How to read this chapter

This chapter is organised to match the content of the BTEC unit it represents. The following diagram shows the grading criteria that relate to each learning outcome.

You'll find colour-matching notes in each chapter about completing each grading criterion.

2.1 Understanding the components of computer systems

This section will cover the following grading criterion:

Make the Grade P1

This criterion requires you to be able to explain the function of computer hardware components (that is, what they do). This will include all the internal components, the externally connected peripherals and backing storage devices. Typically, you may be asked to visually identify these or write about them during your assessment.

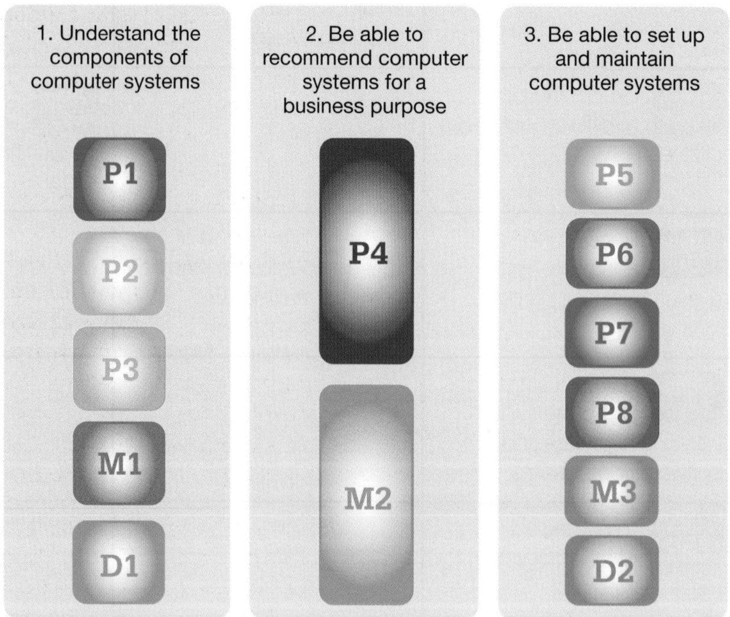

Figure 2.00

2.1.1 Internal system components

A typical computer system (Figure 2.01) consists of a base unit (or tower), monitor, keyboard and mouse.

Figure 2.01 A typical PC system (base unit, keyboard, mouse and monitor)

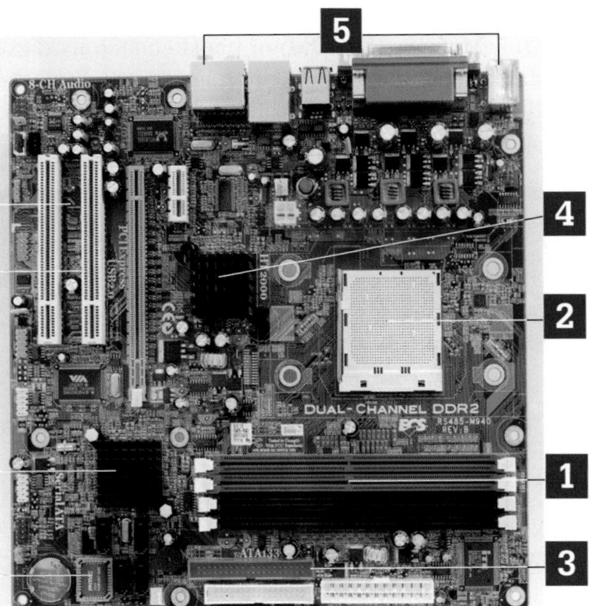

Figure 2.02 A typical ATX motherboard

Standardised components are used inside the base unit to create a number of different connected **subsystems**. Components and subsystems are built using industry-standard designs. This ensures that they are compatible and interoperable world-wide.

Motherboard

The **motherboard** is perhaps a computer's most important hardware component. It is located inside the computer system's case and other key components connect to it.

Most modern motherboards are based on a particular **form factor** (describing its dimensions and layout) called **A**dvanced **T**echnology E**x**tended (**ATX**). Standardised form factors ensure compatibility between different motherboards, cases and components.

A typical motherboard is shown in Figure 2.02 and the following explains the numbered components in the photograph.

1. **Random Access Memory (RAM) slots**, where memory modules are fitted. Usually two or four slots.
2. **Processor socket**, where the Central Processing Unit (CPU) chip is fitted. The socket has to have the same number of pin holes and pin configuration as the processor. Typically, a socket's name may reflect the number of pins (for example, Socket 754, Socket 939 or Socket 1366).
3. **Primary and secondary Enhanced Integrated Drive Electronics (EIDE) connector**. This connects to a hard disk, CD-ROM, DVD and so on. In addition this board supports Serial Advanced Technology Attachment (SATA) drives (SATA is the most recent standard for hard disk connectivity).
4. **Northbridge chip**, manages data traffic between the faster motherboard components (RAM, CPU and graphics subsystem).
5. **Motherboard backplane**, for external connectivity.
6. **Southbridge chip**, manages data traffic between slower components on the motherboard.
7. **Peripheral Component Interconnect (PCI) Express expansion slots** the most recent standard for specialised cards (for example, graphic cards).
8. **PCI expansion slots**.
9. **Basic Input Output System**, (BIOS) chip.

The motherboard chipset is the combination of the Northbridge and Southbridge processors. Some chipsets are more popular with system builders because they are more reliable or perform quicker in benchmarked tests. A Southbridge chip may not be present on all motherboards; some manufacturers prefer to delegate its role to separate subprocessors.

Basic Input Output System

The **B**asic **I**nput **O**utput **S**ystem (**BIOS**) is a small collection of programs that are stored in **R**ead-**O**nly **M**emory (**ROM**), **P**rogrammable **R**ead-**O**nly

Memory **(PROM)**, **E**rasable **P**rogrammable **R**ead-**O**nly **M**emory **(EPROM)** or (most commonly these days) **Flash** memory. Existing as a small chip, the BIOS is fitted onto the motherboard of a typical PC system (Figure 2.03).

Figure 2.03 A typical BIOS chip

Typically, the BIOS chip contains all the code required to control the keyboard, display, disk drives, serial communications and other critical functions. It can also monitor hardware (temperature, hard drive status etc.) and take action (that is, shut down the PC) to prevent any damage occurring to the hardware.

In addition, it has a BIOS set-up program (typically accessed by pressing a designated key on power-up, usually F2 or the Delete key), which lets the user configure the basic operation of the hardware.

Figure 2.04 A typical BIOS set-up screen

Another function of the BIOS is the **P**ower **O**n **S**elf **T**est **(POST)** procedure that checks to see that all connected peripherals (keyboard) and components (CMOS, BIOS, RAM and the Input/Output controller) are functioning correctly.

Malfunctioning devices are often reported via short on-screen messages (Figure 2.05) or, quite commonly, as a series of beep codes. Unfortunately, beep codes tend to be specific to different BIOS manufacturers.

An unsuccessful POST will usually cause the computer system to halt.

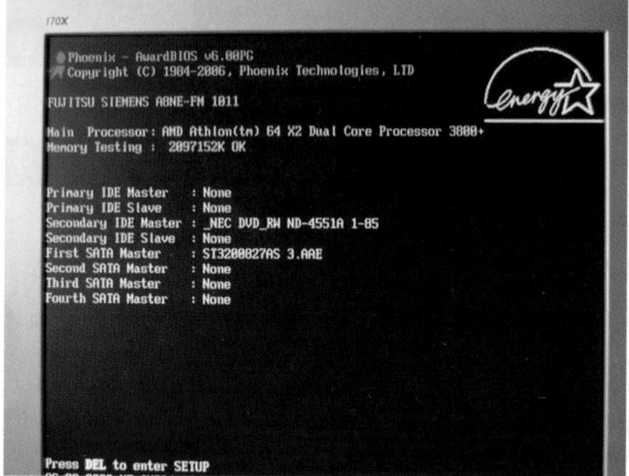

Figure 2.05 A typical BIOS POST screen

It is possible to update BIOS code by downloading new images over the internet. The process of updating the BIOS is called **flashing**. It is possible that flashing can go wrong and this can often kill the BIOS chip permanently, effectively rendering the motherboard useless.

BIOS updates are often used to add new functionality or fix existing bugs (problems) with the original BIOS firmware. Checking the motherboard manufacturer's website is usually the best way of finding out if new BIOS updates are available.

The final job of the BIOS is to seek an operating system on an available drive (floppy, hard disk or CD/DVD, USB pen drive) or via a network connection. Once found, the operating control is passed to the operating system as it is loaded into RAM. This is called the **boot process** (from the expression 'pulling oneself up by one's own bootstraps').

If the BIOS is unable to find an operating system, the boot process will halt.

> **Activity 1**
>
> *Accessing the BIOS*
>
> Using an available PC, switch it on and access its BIOS using the designated key (usually the F1, F2 or DEL key).
>
> Explore its menu system using the cursor keys and Enter.
>
> Make a list that details:
>
> - the name of the company that produced the BIOS;
> - the BIOS version number;
> - the 'top row' menu options;
> - the types of hardware monitoring the BIOS can perform.

CMOS

Complementary **M**etal **O**xide **S**emiconductor (**CMOS**) is a particular structure used in integrated circuit transistor manufacture. It is used to make memory chips that store the settings made by the BIOS set-up program. A 3 V lithium battery (Figure 2.06) is used to provide power to the memory circuit, ensuring that the information stored on it is retained when the mains power is switched off.

Figure 2.06 A CMOS memory back-up battery

If problems occur (usually when a PC refuses to boot after settings have been changed), these preferences may be reset to the manufacturer settings by either removing the battery or by using the 'clear CMOS' jumper that is usually located near to the battery or BIOS chip on the motherboard.

A motherboard may have a number of jumpers that change its performance or function. The CMOS jumper is often coloured differently (usually red, Figure 2.07) to emphasise its importance.

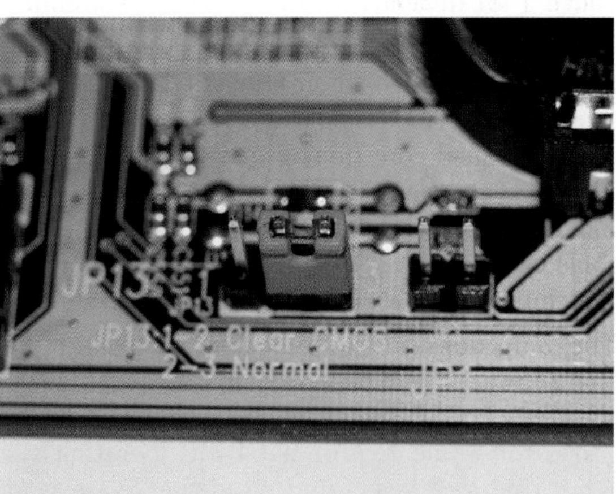

Figure 2.07 A 'clear CMOS' jumper

Central Processing Unit

In simple terms, the **C**entral **P**rocessing **U**nit (**CPU** or simply 'the processor') is the brain of the computer system. The CPU processes data and instructions. It is also responsible for coordinating system resources and performing arithmetic and logical operations.

The instructions are specific to the CPU in question and written in **machine code**. Machine code for one type of processor will not work on another unless they belong to the same family (in which case they are said to be **code compatible**).

For many years, Intel® have developed an x86 family of processors that included the 486, Pentium®, Pentium® 2, Pentium® 3, Pentium® 4 etc. Each later developed processor was **backwardly compatible** with earlier processors (which means that code written for an earlier processor would work on a later version, even if all the functionality of the later version could not be used). Other manufacturers, such as Advanced Micro Designs (AMD), created processors that were machine code compatible with Intel's. These processors included the K5™, K6™, Athlon™, Duron™, Sempron™ etc. Figure 2.08 on the next page shows an AMD Phenom™ processor.

Processor speed and architecture

Processor speed is measured in megahertz (**MHz**) or gigahertz (**GHz**).

The speed is actually the clock frequency of the processor and generally it is accepted that a faster processor will execute a program's instructions more rapidly (for example, a 3 GHz processor is faster at executing instructions than a 2.4 GHz processor), however, this isn't necessarily true because a lot depends on the processor's architecture (that is, its design).

Some processors have more efficient designs or have multiple cores, for example dual core (two processor units) or quad core (four processor units), within the same package. In addition, processors either handle 32-bit or 64-bit 'chunks' of data; at the same clock speed, a processor that can digest 64-bit 'chunks' of data would do so more efficiently.

The only downside to processor innovations is that software has to be written to take advantage of their efficient architecture. For example, a 64-bit processor would require a 64-bit operating system; Windows® Vista® and Windows® 7 are available in both 32-bit and 64-bit implementations.

Processor bus

The **processor bus** is also called the **F**ront **S**ide **B**us (**FSB**). It is the bidirectional link between the motherboard and the processor itself. Like the processor it operates at a certain clock speed, usually measured in megahertz.

Bus multiplier

A **bus multiplier** is a value used to calculate the maximum processor speed. The general equation for working this out is

maximum processor speed = processor bus speed × maximum multiplier

For example, 1992 MHz (2 GHz) = 166 MHz × 12

Overclocking and underclocking

Overclocking is the act of running a processor beyond its maximum rated performance.

In theory, if a processor can be kept cool (and other components, for example, RAM can run at the higher frequency), then it can be pushed beyond its rated speed limit by manipulation of the multiplier. Overclocking has the reputation of shortening the lifespan of a processor. Some processors are locked (they have their speeds fixed) by their manufacturers.

Underclocking is the opposite of overclocking in that the clock rate is reduced to keep a processor cool. This results in more reliable performance and it saves electrical power. Servers often have the ability to be underclocked when they are idle.

Power supply unit

A **P**ower **S**upply **U**nit (**PSU**) (Figure 2.09) converts the incoming mains alternating current (AC) voltage (240 V in the UK) into the different direct current (DC) voltages used by the computer's internal components (for example, 12 V to power a DVD-ROM drive.

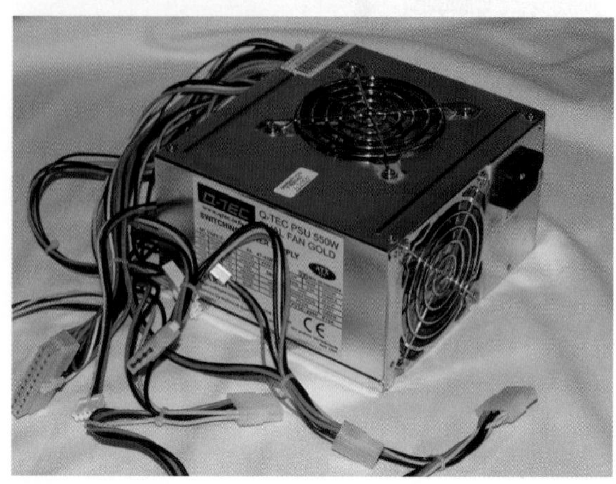

Figure 2.08 A typical ATX PSU

A power supply's power output is measured in watts (W). 450 W is a typical PSU power output in 2010.

Most PSUs come already fitted inside the computer system's case, but they may be purchased separately when a replacement is needed. They contain lethal voltages, so they should never, **under any circumstances**, be dismantled, **even after** the power has been removed.

> **Help**
>
> **Modern PC PSUs – what you need to know**
>
> The most common PSU types are:
>
> - AT – used in older PCs
> - ATX – most commonly used today
> - ATX-2 – a recently introduced standard.
>
> ATX PSUs introduced software-based power management (including standby mode) and the lower 3.3 V supply needed for newer processors.

A number of PSU connectors are commonly found:

- **Floppy Drive (FD) connector**: This is also known as a Four-pin Berg Connector (Figure 2.09).

Figure 2.09 Floppy drive connector

This is used to connect the PSU to small form factor devices, such as 3.5-inch floppy drives, or even supply supplementary power to a graphics card. They may also be used to power additional USB hubs.

They are often used on AT, ATX and ATX-2 PSUs.

- **Four-pin Molex connector** (Figure 2.10)

Figure 2.10 Four-pin Molex connector

This is used to power various components, including hard drives, optical drives and system fans. Molex is actually the name of the company that created this type of plastic in the 1930s.

They are often used on AT, ATX & ATX-2 PSUs.

- **20-pin ATX power connector** (Figure 2.11)

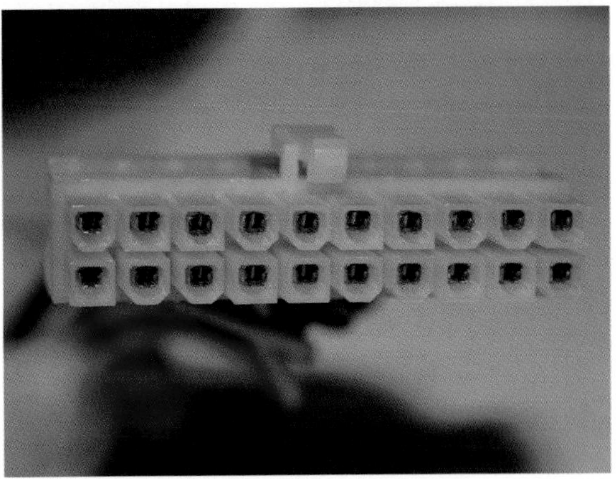

Figure 2.11 20-pin ATX power connector

This is used to provide the main power to the motherboard in ATX systems. ATX power supplies can be controlled by the BIOS and the operating system.

They are often used on the ATX PSU. (The ATX-2 PSU has 24 pins.)

- **4-pin auxiliary 12 V power connector** (Figure 2.12)

Figure 2.12 4-pin auxiliary 12 V power connector

These are very common on Pentium® 4 processor motherboards.

They are often used on ATX PSUs. (They are integrated into the power connector on ATX-2 PSUs, hence 24 pins.)

- 6-pin auxiliary connector (Figure 2.13)

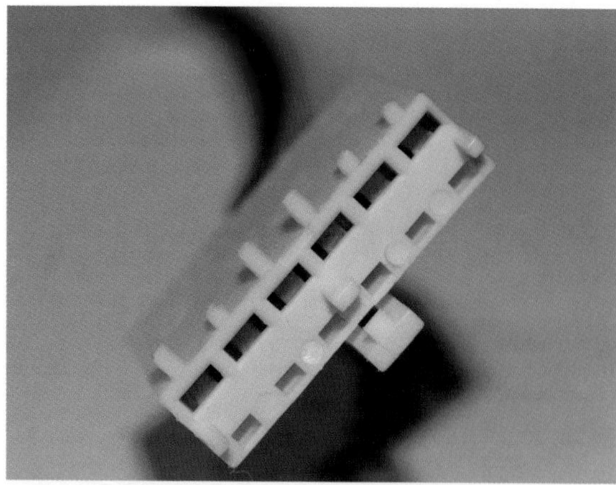

Figure 2.13 6-pin auxiliary connector

This provides +5 V DC and two connections of +3.3 V.

They are often used on ATX/ATX-2 PSUs.

Fan and heat sink

A CPU generates a lot of heat during operation. Although a CPU can operate at higher temperatures (well above 80°C), this is thought to shorten its lifespan. The simplest approach taken to keep the processor cool is to use a **heat sink** and **fan** combination (Figure 2.14).

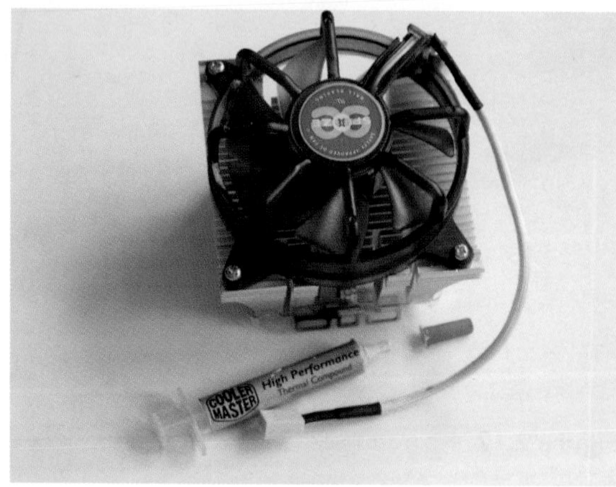

Figure 2.14 Heat sink, fan and thermal paste syringe

The heat sink, traditionally made from aluminium or copper (which is better), draws the radiated heat away from the top of the processor through a process called **conduction**. This process is made easier through the use of a thermal compound. This is a white paste, traditionally containing aluminium oxide or silver, which is spread thinly between the top of the CPU and the underneath of the heat sink.

A fan, usually revolving between 2000 and 4000 rpm (revolutions per minute) will draw the hot air away from the top of the heat sink through a process called **convection**.

The fan takes its 12 V power supply from a CPU three-pin fan header located near the processor socket on the motherboard (Figure 2.15). The red wire contains the 12 V supply, the black wire is ground and the yellow is used by the BIOS to monitor the CPU fan speed.

Figure 2.15 CPU fan header on the motherboard

It is through this monitoring that the BIOS health check program can switch off the system if the fan speed drops below a certain rotational speed. This is set in the BIOS set-up program (Figure 2.16). Similar settings may exist for 80 mm case ('system') fans present.

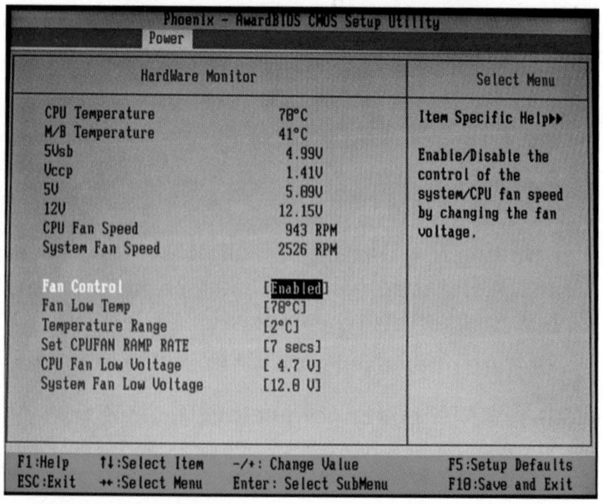

Figure 2.16 Health check settings for the CPU fan in the BIOS setup program

Liquid cooling

An alternative to traditional cooling is the use of liquids. Water is approximately 25 times more effective at conducting heat than air.

Help

Liquid cooling – what you need to know

Liquid cooling uses water or special coolant solution. Key components of the system are:

- a **reservoir** to store the coolant;
- a **pump** to circulate the coolant;
- **water blocks** to snap onto components needing cooling (for example, the CPU);
- a **radiator** to transfer heat from water to the air;
- **power input** (needs around 12 V power supply from typically a four-pin Molex connector from the PSU).

Scorecard – Liquid cooling

+ Quieter than traditional fans
+ More effective than traditional cooling techniques
– Can be difficult to install
– Can be dangerous if not installed properly

Hard drive–motherboard interface connectors

There are two connection standards in common use: **PATA** (or **ATA** or **EIDE**) and **SATA**. A motherboard may support either (or both) types, see table 2.01.

Ports

Modern computer systems use a number of different **ports** to enable a user to connect peripherals such as keyboards, mice, printers, scanners, cameras, graphic tablets and MP3 players etc. **USB** is by far the most common type of connector in use today.

Table 2.01

	PATA or ATA (or EIDE)	SATA
Stands for...	Parallel Advanced Technology Attachment Often referred to as ATA or EIDE (Enhanced Integrated Drive Electronics)	Serial Advanced Technology Attachment
Introduced	1986 (now being phased out)	2003 (now becoming the standard)
What the connector looks like...	**Figure 2.17** PATA or ATA connector	**Figure 2.18** SATA connector
Features	• PATA supports four devices: two devices on a primary channel and two devices on a secondary channel. • Each channel has a master and a slave drive. Typically, the master drive is the faster of the two. • Each channel's cable has two drive connections (master and slave). The master is connected to the end of the chain, the slave in the middle.	• SATA devices tend to connect one-to-one from the motherboard to the hard disk. This is called point-to-point architecture. • SATA uses fewer wires than PATA (seven instead of PATA's 40 or 80). • SATA is faster than PATA. • SATA supports hot-plugging (insertion and removal of the hard disk while the computer system is working).

Help

USB – what you need to know

USB stands for **U**niversal **S**erial **B**us.

The USB standard was devised in 1996. The most recent version is USB 2.0 (April 2000), which can transfer data at 480 Mbits/sec.

A single USB port can connect up to 127 devices through use of USB hubs. Multiple hubs can be **daisy-chained** to increase the number of connected devices further.

A USB cable can be up to 5 m long.

Operating systems can auto-detect USB devices and these devices are **hot-swappable** (that is, they can be inserted and removed while the computer system is powered. This process is called **hot-plugging**.

A USB port can supply power to a device (5 V at 500 mA). If a hub needs to supply electricity for a number of devices, it needs to be 'powered'.

USB cables have two ends with different connector types: an **'A' connector** and a **'B' connector**.

Table 2.02

Connector type	Looks like	Connects to...
A	**Figure 2.19** USB 'A' connector	...the computer system.
B	**Figure 2.20** USB 'B' connector	...the peripheral or device (for example, an MP3 player). Note that there are different types of 'B' connector – micro, mini and proprietary (that is, made by a company for a specific purpose, e.g. the Apple® iPod® connector). This type 'B' connector is often used to connect a printer to a computer system.

Figure 2.21 shows the common ports found on the backplane of a typical computer system's motherboard. Table 2.03 explains the numbered ports in the photograph.

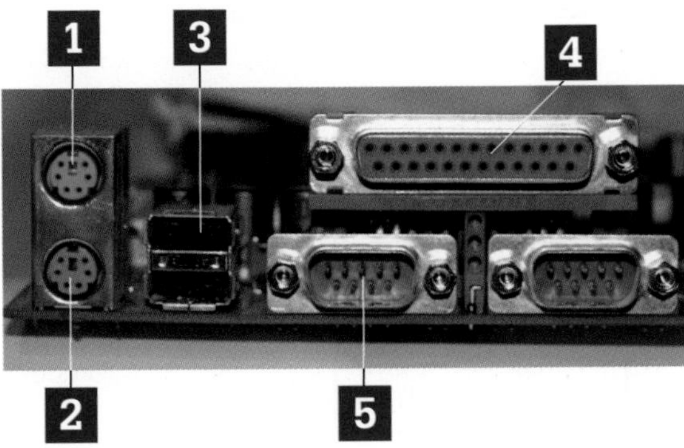

Figure 2.21 Motherboard backplane with common connectors

Table 2.03

Key to Figure 2.21	Type of connector and use	Data transfer speed
1	6-pin PS/2 (green) – Mouse	
2	6-pin PS/2 (purple) – Keyboard	
3	USB 1.1	1.5 Mbps (low) 12 Mbps (full)
	USB 2.0	480 Mbps (hi-speed)
4	25-pin parallel port (IEEE 1284)	2 Mbps (practically) 4 Mbps (theoretically)
5	9-pin serial port	115 000 bps (maximum)

Older connectors, such as serial, parallel and PS/2 ports, are called **legacy** ports. Some more recent motherboards do not have these types of connector, preferring to use USB and Firewire® instead. Other ports (Figure 2.22) may be present to connect a computer system's audio input/output through either a sound card or integrated sound chip.

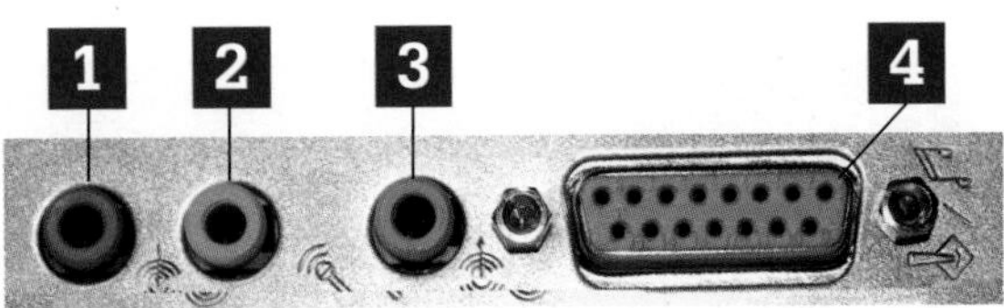

Figure 2.22 Audio ports

Table 2.04 explains the numbered ports in the photograph.

Table 2.04

Key to Figure 2.22	Type of connector and use
1	Blue **line-in** socket for a 3.5 mm jack plug. Used for connecting to a sound card from an external sound source.
2	Pink **microphone** socket for a 3.5 mm jack plug.
3	Green **headphones** socket for a 3.5 mm jack plug.
4	Yellow Musical Instrument Digital Interface (**MIDI**) or Gameport.

Internal memory

We have already mentioned ROM during the overview of the BIOS. Although ROM is important, **Random Access Memory (RAM)** is essential to the successful operation of the computer system.

RAM is the memory that stores the operating system, any programs (or part of a program) being run and, most importantly, the data being processed. It is also faster than ROM, which is why the BIOS is often **shadowed** (copied) to RAM and executed from there.

It is also important to remember that RAM is **volatile**. This means that the contents of RAM are completely lost when electrical power is removed.

Cache memory, typically high-speed RAM, is usually found on the motherboard (level 2) or inside the CPU (level 1). Cache memory is used to recall recently/frequently used instructions and data rather than making a slower request for them from main RAM. **Tertiary cache** is a new introduction to multi-core processors.

Help

Memory sizes – what you need to know

Table 2.05 lists common memory sizes so that you can reference them easily in the future.

Table 2.05

Unit	= bits	= bytes	= kilobytes
bit	1		
byte	8	1	
kilobyte	8,192	1024	1
megabyte	8,388,608	1,048,576	1024
gigabyte	8,589,934,592	1,073,741,824	1,048,576
terabyte	8,796,093,022,208	1,099,511,627,776	1,073,741,824

Larger data units of data exist, but they are not in everyday usage, for example, in ascending order: petabyte (PB), exabyte (EB), zettabyte (ZB) and yottabyte (YB)

It is useful to think about memory **size** when considering RAM. Data is grouped into collections of **bits** (binary digits) and **bytes** (8 bits make 1 byte), so memory storage capacity is measured similarly. You may have encountered larger multiples of these before (for example, kilobyte, megabyte etc.).

RAM exists in many different package formats. **D**ouble **D**ata **R**ate (**DDR**) and **DDR2** are currently the most popular formats. They offer enhanced data throughput by reading data on both the leading and failing edge of a clock 'tick'. Figures 2.23 and 2.24 show common memory packages. Figure 2.24 is a SDRAM DIMM (with 168 pins). Figure 2.23 is a DDR DIMM (with 184 pins).

Figure 2.23 PC3200 DDR DIMM

Figure 2.24 PC133 SDRAM DIMM

Modern motherboard design groups RAM slots by the CPU. Figure 2.25 shows four empty DDR slots on a motherboard. The white clips are used to secure each memory rail in place.

Figure 2.25 RAM slots on a typical motherboard

Help

Modern PC memory modules – what you need to know

Memory modules come in different forms. Table 2.06 gives you a basic comparison guide of the most popular modules.

Table 2.06

Module name	Module type and format	Clock frequency	Transfer rate
PC100	SDRAM DIMM	100 MHz	800 MBps
PC133	SDRAM DIMM	133 MHz	1,066 MBps
PC1600	DDR200 DIMM	100 MHz	1,600 MBps
PC2100	DDR266 DIMM	133 MHz	2,133 MBps per channel
PC2700	DDR333 DIMM	166 MHz	2,666 MBps per channel
PC3200	DDR400 DIMM	200 MHz	3,200 MBps per channel
PC2-3200	DDR2-400 DIMM	100 MHz × 2	3,200 MBps per channel
PC2-4200	DDR2-533 DIMM	133 MHz × 2	4,266 MBps per channel
PC2-5300	DDR2-667 DIMM	166 MHz × 2	5,333 MBps per channel
PC2-6400	DDR2-800 DIMM	200 MHz × 2	6,400 MBps per channel

As you can see, the early modules contain the frequency in their name, while later ones contain the transfer rate (or bandwidth).

Activity 2

1. Use the BIOS to identify the amount of RAM installed on an available PC. Write this down showing the correct units.
2. Use the operating system (for example, Microsoft® Windows®) to display the amount of RAM installed on an available PC. Does this agree with the figure reported in the BIOS?
3. With supervision as needed, safely disassemble the same PC to examine the RAM physically. What type and quantity of memory modules did you find?

Specialist cards

A key feature of a personal computer system is its **expandability**.

Motherboard slots, such as **PCI**, **AGP** and **PCI-Express**, offer both expansion and, in doing so, upgrade opportunities.

The correct type of card needs to be selected in order for an expansion or upgrade to be compatible. This is because any particular type of card (for example, a video or graphics card) could be available in PCI, AGP or PCI-Express formats. You must match the card to the available motherboard expansion slot.

Graphic card

Unless the motherboard has an **I**ntegrated **G**raphics **P**rocessor (**IGP** – also known as onboard graphics), the PC system will need a separate graphics card in order to translate data into video signals, which will be sent to a monitor.

IGPs are typically present if the motherboard's backplane has a blue VGA (or HD-15) female connector (Figure 2.26).

Figure 2.26 Blue VGA (or HD-15) female connector

Common terms associated with graphic cards include:

- **Refresh rate**: The refresh rate is how many times per second that an image is redrawn on a screen by the graphics card. The refresh rate is measured in **hertz** (Hz – a measurement of frequency). The refresh rate is sometimes called the **vertical refresh rate** or **vertical scan rate**. It is a particular feature of older **cathode ray tube (CRT)** displays. A standard definition television set usually uses 50 Hz or 100 Hz.

Figure 2.27 Changing the refresh rate in Windows Vista®

Refresh rates for computer displays less than 60 Hz tend to irritate the viewer because the viewer usually notices the flicker caused by the image being rescanned (updated). Viewers with 17″ or 19″ monitors often prefer refresh rates of 85 Hz or more for this reason.

Refresh rates are usually set in the operating system, effectively controlling the graphic card's output to the display device. Figure 2.27 shows the Microsoft Windows Vista® dialogue box where you can change the refresh rate.

If the refresh rate is set too high, and the display device cannot support it, the display device may go **out of synch(ronisation)** and the image may be temporarily lost. This is often signified by a flashing or red/orange light emitting diode (LED) on the monitor.

- **Resolution**: The display resolution is given in **pixels** (picture elements or cells). These are the miniscule dots that make up a display images. The resolution is expressed as number of pixels horizontally across the screen (X axis) by number of pixels vertically across the screen (Y axis), for example, 1024 × 768.

  Higher resolution images (which appear more realistic to the viewer) require more **Video RAM (VRAM)** to display and are often limited by the maximum resolution supported by the graphics card in use and the actual resolution of the display device.

  The resolution is controlled by the operating system. Figure 2.28 on page 47 shows the Windows® XP dialogue box where you can change the resolution.

  In this example the resolution has been set to 1280 × 1024 pixels. The amount of VRAM required to generate such a display cannot be calculated by resolution alone. In order to accurately calculate the VRAM requirement, it is also necessary to factor in the colour depth.

- **Colour depth**: Colour depth is the term used to describe the number of colours available in a particular graphics mode. Both the colour depth and resolution are needed in order to quantify the amount of VRAM required to generate a display image.

Other colour depths are far common, for example:

- 8-bit (256 colours);
- 16-bit (65,536 colours, often called **high colour** or **hi-color**);
- 24-bit (16,777,216 colours, often called **true colour**).

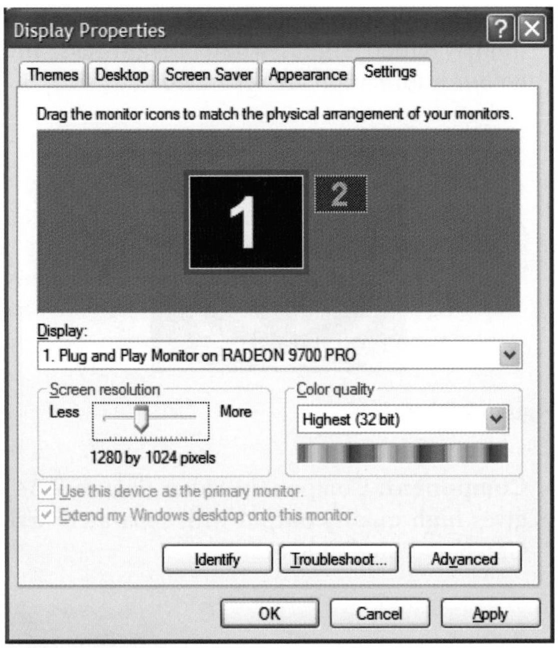

Figure 2.28 Changing the screen resolution in Windows XP®

True colour is a combination of 24-bits (eight bits for Red, eight bits for Green and eight bits for Blue) used to describe the **RGB** (**R**ed, **G**reen and **B**lue components) of any particular shade.

Scientists believe that the human eye is only actually capable of distinguishing between approximately 10 million different colour shades. In reality, this means that true colour displays are demonstrating ranges of colours which we can't actually fully tell apart.

Activity 3

How much VRAM is required to support a video mode with a resolution of 1024 × 768 pixels and 16-bit colour depth?

See supporting website for the answer.

In addition, a number of different types of video signal may be generated.

Help

Colour depth – What you need to know

Colour depth works on the **binary** (**base 2**) principle. For example, 4-bit colour would provide 16 different binary patterns that each represent a different colour. Any pixel's colour would be described by a 4-bit binary code (Figure 2.29).

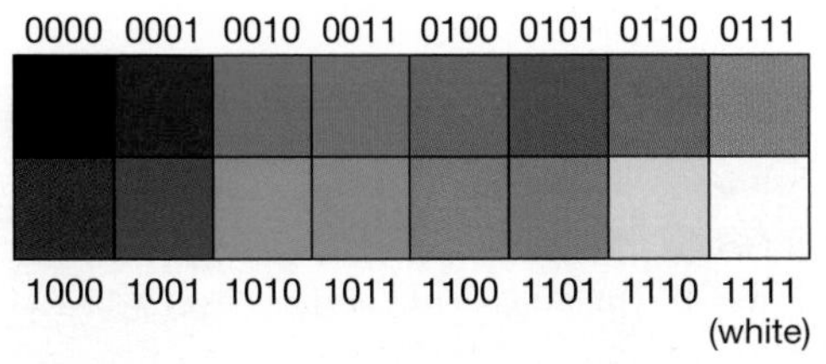

Figure 2.29 An example of colours using a 4-bit binary code

Given a resolution of 320 × 200 pixels with 4-bit colour requires 31.25 kB.

So how is this worked out?

320 × 200 pixels = 64,000 pixels

Each pixel = 4 bits

64,000 × 4 = 256,000 bits

256,000 bits / 8 (bits per byte) = 32,000 bytes

32,000 bytes / 1024 (bytes per kilobyte) = 31.25 kB

- **Digital Video Interface**: The Digital Video Interface (DVI – Figure 2.30) is replacing VGA connectors, especially for connecting to digital devices such as **L**iquid **C**rystal **D**isplay **(LCD)** panels.

Figure 2.30 Digital Visual Interface

- **High Definition Multimedia Interface**: The **H**igh **D**efinition **M**ultimedia **I**nterface **(HDMI** – Figure 2.31) is used to connect LCD flat panels, plasma televisions etc.

Figure 2.31 High Definition Multimedia Interface

- **Composite**: Composite video (Figure 2.31) gives a lower-quality image where brightness and colour information are compounded together to form the video signal..

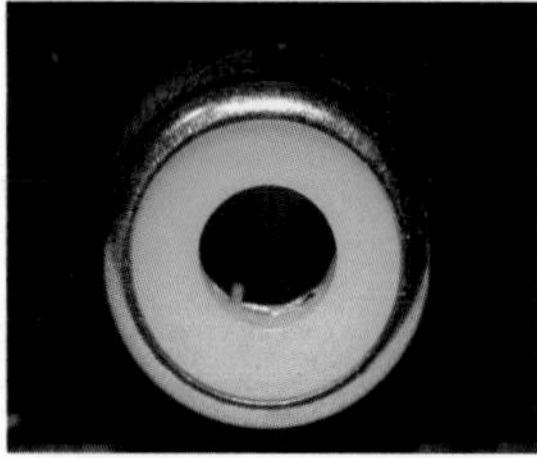

Figure 2.32 Composite video

- **S-Video**: S-Video (Figure 2.33) gives a better-quality video signal where brightness and colour information are separated.

Figure 2.33 S-Video

- **Component**: Component video (Figure 2.34) gives high-quality output with separated Red, Green and Blue signals.

Figure 2.34 Component video

Activity 4

Use your PC's operating system to find out the following about its graphics card.

- Whether of not the display is generated by an IGP or dedicated graphics card.
- The manufacturer of the graphics card.
- The model of the graphics card.
- The maximum display resolution.
- The maximum colour depth.
- The maximum refresh rate.
- The type of video signal being generated.

Write down your findings.

> Activity 5
>
> Kris Arts & Media (KAM) Ltd is investigating the purchase of a new graphics card to support the editing of video they have recorded. Research and recommend a suitable graphics card for this situation.

Scorecard – On-board graphics

- \+ Saves money
- \+ Drivers will come with motherboard
- \+ Upgrading is optional; usually will be acceptable for business use
- – average performance only
- – unlikely to support latest operating system features

Network cards

A **network card**, or more correctly, a **network interface card** (**NIC**) is a device that typically connects a computer system to a network. These cards may be wired (that is, they use cables) or be **wireless**. Again, it is common for network functionality to be built into modern motherboards.

Network cards can transmit and receive data at:

- 10 Mbps (megabits per second)
- 100 Mbps, or
- 1000 Mbps (often called **Gigabit Ethernet**)

Figure 2.35 shows a typical wired Ethernet NIC.

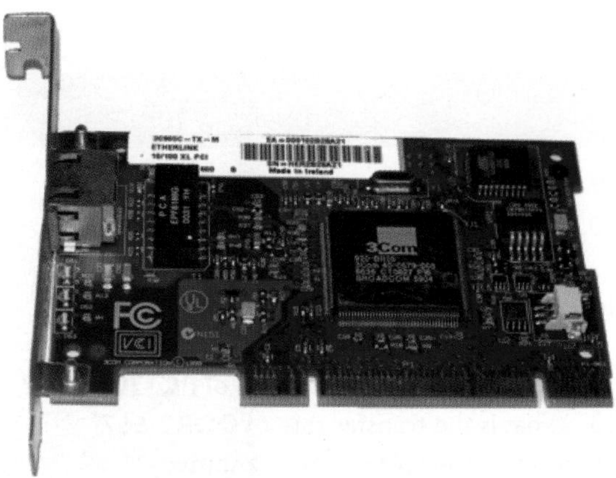

Figure 2.35 Wired network interface card (PCI adaptor)

Wireless NICs are less secure than wired NICs. The majority of notebooks and netbooks have this functionality built into the motherboard. Figure 2.36 shows a PCI WiFi card. Again, it uses a PCI bus edge connector to plug into the motherboard.

Figure 2.36 Wireless network card with aerial (PCI adaptor)

> **Help**
>
> **Network interface card technology – what you need to know**
>
> Popular network card manufacturers include 3Com, Belkin, Cisco, D-Link and Linksys.
>
> Every network device has its own unique physical address. This is called its **M**edia **A**ccess **C**ontrol (**MAC**) address. A typical MAC address is a string of six **hexadecimal** (**base 16**) paired digits, for example: **00-50-70-92-02-AB**

Network cards are very important in modern computer systems as users increasingly rely on internet online services and products. Network cards are used in conjunction with **routers** and **broadband modems** to supply broadband connections (whether via cable providers or ADSL).

> **Unit link**
>
> You can find out more about networking in Unit 10 – Communication Technologies.

Activity 6

Identify the manufacturer of your computer's network card.

In Windows® 7, click **Start**, then type **cmd** into search box and press the **Enter** key.

Type **ipconfig** and press the **Enter** key.

Find the **Physical Address** in the displayed information.

Use a web browser to visit the online resource: **www.curreedy.com/stu/nic/**

Type the physical address found on your PC and click the **Find Manufacturer** button.

The website should respond with the name of your network card's manufacturer.

2.1.2 Peripherals

A **peripheral** is often defined as any device that is connected externally to the CPU and main memory. In reality, this is revised to mean **connected outside the case**, that is, using one of the backplane connectors.

Peripherals are often categorised as **input** or **output** devices.

Figure 2.37 shows some common types of peripheral.

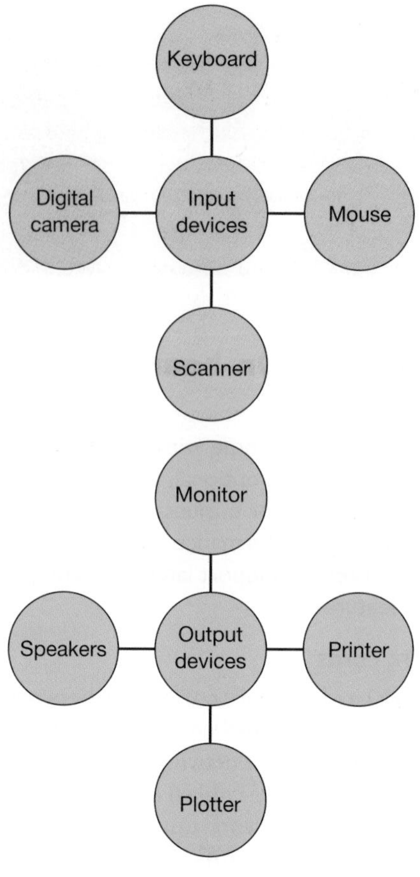

Figure 2.37 Common types of peripheral

Most modern peripherals use a USB connection and most users are now familiar with USB devices and their **plug and play** (**PnP**) approach to loading the correct drivers. (A **driver** is a small program that tells the operating system how to communicate with the hardware.)

B Braincheck

1. Which **four** basic components comprise a typically computer system?
2. What is the **BIOS**?
3. What is a motherboard's **form factor**?
4. What function does the **PSU** perform?
5. What is the purpose of the CPU **fan** and **heat sink**?
6. How do **parallel** and **serial** data transmission differ?
7. Each **IDE** channel has a __________ and __________ connection.
8. What is **USB**?
9. What does **IDE** mean?
10. What is the difference between **ROM** and **RAM**?
11. What is the difference between **DIMM** and **DDR RAM**?
12. What is the clock frequency of **PC3200** RAM?
13. What is the transfer rate of **DDR2-667**?
14. What is the role of **cache memory**?
15. Name **four** peripherals used for input.
16. Name **four** peripherals used for output.

How well did you do? See supporting website for answers.

2.1.3 Backing storage

As we have seen, a computer system's main memory (RAM) is typically **volatile**. This simply means that it **loses** its data once its electrical power is removed. In order to store data (and programs) more permanently, non-volatile storage must be used. This is called its **backing storage**.

There are a number of different types of backing storage, usually grouped by their storage mechanisms. The following are the three most common storage mechanisms.

Magnetic

Magnetic storage has been the primary backing storage technology since the mid-1970s and replaced older punched cards and paper tape. Magnetic media tends to be either fixed (a **hard disk**) or removable (a **floppy diskette**).

The 3.5-inch **floppy disk** that is still used today has been around since the mid-1980s, although larger format floppy disks (for example, 5.25-inch) were used before that time. Although they are a conveniently portable size, their storage capacity is only 1.44 MB, so their popularity has decreased in recent years because of the advent of large programs and data storage requirements. Many desktop and notebook PCs no longer have an internal floppy drive fitted as standard (although external floppy drives can be connected via USB).

There have been three hard-disk technology standards over the years (Figure 2.38). The oldest technology is Advanced Technology Attachment (ATA). This is now known as **Parallel ATA** (or just **PATA**). (P)ATA connects IDE hard drives to a motherboard via 40 or 80 wire cables. The most recent ATA standard is ATA133.

Figure 2.38 An external USB floppy drive

Another hard-disk technology is the Small Computer Systems Interface (**SCSI** – pronounced 'scuzzy') long favoured for server systems, which have a combination of large capacity storage, fast disk rotation speeds and superior transfer rates (when compared with ATA/IDE). Improvements in ATA/IDE technology have reduced the SCSI market somewhat in recent years.

A more recent development is **Serial ATA (SATA)**. This has quickly become popular with hardware manufacturers. **External SATA drives (eSATA)** are also available.

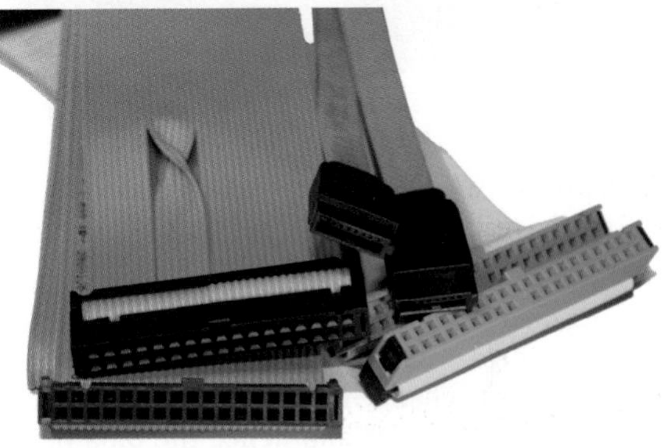

Figure 2.39 Floppy (with twist), SATA and PATA cables connect drives to the motherboard

> **Help**
>
> **SATA vs PATA – what you need to know**
>
> SATA has three primary advantages over the older PATA technology:
>
> - It's **hot-pluggable**. Drives can be connected/disconnected while the PC is still running.
> - **Thinner cables** reduce the footprint inside the case. They are easier to fit and help air flow and cooling.
> - It uses **T**agged **C**ommand **Q**ueuing (**TCQ**). This is a way of reordering a CPU's data access requests inside the drive so that data in neighbouring physical locations can be accessed sequentially, thereby saving time.
>
> The major disadvantage of SATA is that SATA drives are generally 10 per cent more expensive than their PATA equivalents.

Magnetic disks (Figure 2.40) have platters (glass or aluminium) evenly coated in a ferrous material that has magnetic properties. The disk drive's head can read the magnetic fields on the surface of the disk, converting them to electrical impulses (and then to data).

Figure 2.40 ATA/IDE hard drive exposed to show platters and read/write heads

Writing data to the disk requires creating a minute magnetic field from electrical impulses. The effect of this is to change the magnetic alignment of the surface of the disk and hence the data being stored there.

Optical

Optical backing storage devices use laser-generated light instead of magnetic fields to read and write data. In comparison, it is typically slower than magnetic mechanisms.

The most common optical storage devices are **Compact Disc (CD)** and **Digital Versatile Disc (DVD)**. They look physically similar and each has a similar diameter (120 mm) and thickness (1.2 mm). A typical DVD-ROM drive is shown in Figure 2.41.

Figure 2.41 A typical DVD-ROM drive

The majority of optical devices use removable media. You are certainly familiar with **CD-Digital Audio (CD-DA)** discs used for music and **DVD-Read Only Memory (DVD-ROM)** discs that hold popular films, television series and concerts.

CD-Read Only Memory (CD-ROM) discs are manufactured with data literally 'pressed' into them in the form of **pits** (small indentations) and **lands** (the flat area between the pits). These pits and lands exist in a long spiral starting at the centre of the disc and working to the outer edge (Figure 2.42). If the spiral was straightened, it would stretch approximately 6.5 km.

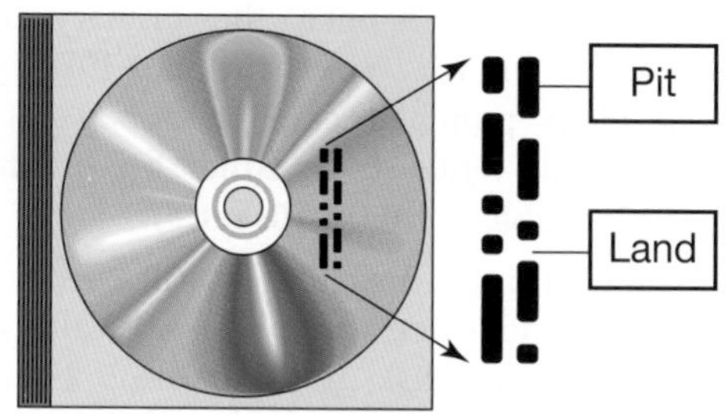

Figure 2.42 A magnified section of a CD showing its pits and lands

As you can see in the cross-section (Figure 2.43), when the CD-ROM's laser is fired at the surface of the disc, light hitting a land is mostly reflected back to the drive's lens.

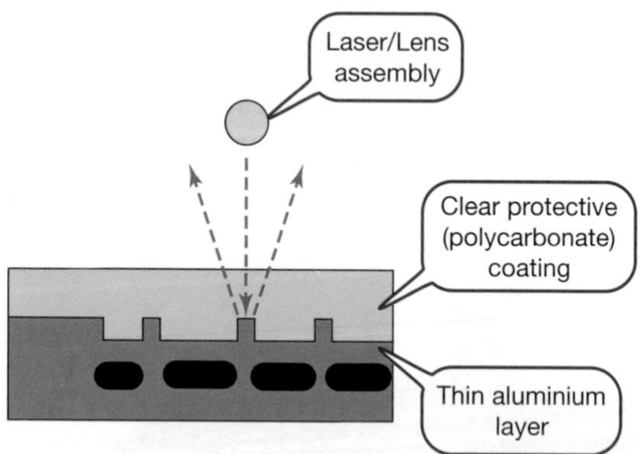

Figure 2.43 CD cross-section with laser light bouncing off a land

The light hitting a pit is scattered (Figure 2.44).

The amount of light received by the lens determines whether it is located over a pit or a land. The change from pit-to-land or land-to-pit represents a binary 1. Everything else is a binary 0 (for example, see Figure 2.45).

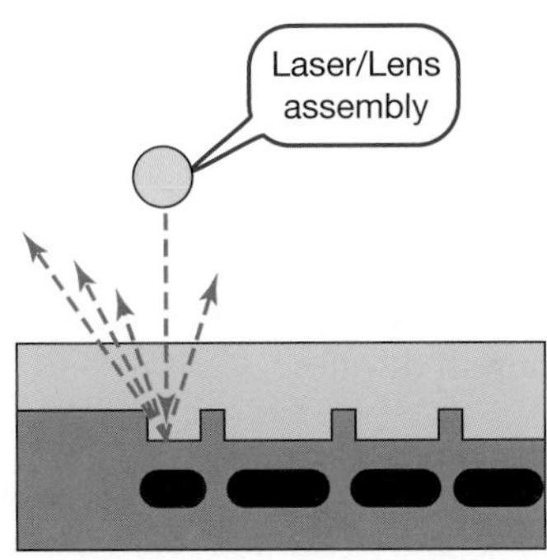

Figure 2.44 CD cross-section with laser light scattering off a pit

Figure 2.45 An example of binary CD data

These codes are then translated using a mechanism called **Eight to Fourteen Modulation (EFM)** into standard binary for the computer system to use as data.

A **CD-Recordable (CD-R)** disc uses a radiation-sensitive dye to record data sent by the CPU. The dye's colour can only be changed once. A **CD-Rewriteable (CD-RW)** uses a more chemically-complex dye to record and erase data. The dye is reusable. A more powerful recording laser is used to create the pit sequences using the changed dye colour.

A number of different recordable formats exist for both CD and DVD, and they are often not interchangeable. Care should be taken when building a computer system to ensure that the optical drive and media used are compatible. Many systems include **combo (combination)** drives, which include both CD-RW and DVD-ROM functionality for flexibility.

Flash (electronically-alterable)

Apart from in the BIOS chip inside the computer system itself, **flash memory** is commonly used in two types of device:

- **Pen drives** (also known as **USB Flash Drives** or **UFDs**)
- **Flash memory cards**

Pen drives were introduced in the late 1990s. They are an increasingly popular form of backing storage due to their portability, ease of use and value

Help

Optical drive speeds – what you need to know

Optical drives are often given using the following convention:

8× 16× 32× or **8/16/32**

In the case of a CD-Rewriter, this would mean:

8×	8 speed for burning CD-RW discs
16×	16 speed for burning CD-R discs
32×	32 speed for reading discs into the computer system's RAM

1× is approximately 150 Kbps.

for money. Based on NAND-flash architecture developed in the late 1980s, a pen drive consists of a male USB connector, a **printed circuit board (PCB)** containing the flash memory and a clock crystal (for synchronisation).

These components are typically housed in toughened plastic packaging (Figure 2.46) that includes a removable (or swivel) cap to protect the sensitive contents from **electrostatic discharge (ESD)**.

Figure 2.46 Inside a typical USB pen drive (left) and its casing (right)

Some pen drives might also have **light-emitting diodes (LEDs)** to indicate read/write status, a write-protect switch and a hoop for connecting a keychain or lanyard.

Pen drives are compatible with the majority of modern operating systems including Microsoft® Windows® (2000 onwards), Mac® OS (9.x onwards) and various Linux® distributions.

There are many different formats of flash memory card currently available and in use (Figure 2.47).

Figure 2.47 Various flash memory cards and flash card reader

Most use the same NAND-flash architecture as pen drives but come in a number of different form factors. Common varieties include:

- CompactFlash (CF) created by SanDisk in 1994.
- MultiMediaCard (MMC) created by SanDisk and Siemens AG in 1997.
- Memory Stick (MS) created by Sony in 1998. Varieties include Pro, Duo and micro.
- Secure Digital (SD) created by Panasonic, Toshiba and SanDisk in 1999.
- xD-Picture Card (xD) created by Olympus and Fujifilm in 2002.

It is becoming increasingly common for computer systems (especially PCs) to have front bezels that contain multi-format card-reading slots.

External card readers are also available and relatively inexpensive. These connect to the system via a standard USB port.

Although commonly used in **Personal Data Assistants (PDAs)**, **mobile cellular telephones** and **portable game consoles**, their most important application is undoubtedly in digital photography.

Backing store performance factors

There are three main performance factors for backing storage:

- **Capacity** – how much data it can store.
- **Data access time (DAT)** – how quickly specific data can be found.
- **Data transfer rate (DTR)** – how quickly data moves from the device into the computer.

Table 2.07 gives a comparison of performance factors for common devices.

Activity 7

Examine the backing storage options that exist in a selected computer system.

- Which mechanisms do they use?
- What capacities of data storage do they theoretically provide?
- Who manufactured the various backing storage devices in the selected computer systems?
- Does the system provide direct support for flash memory cards?

B Braincheck

1. Why is backing storage necessary for a computer system?
2. Name **three** different backing storage mechanisms.
3. What is a floppy disk's main disadvantage?
4. Name **three** different hard disk technologies.
5. A CD's surface contains…?
6. What is the storage capacity of a typical CD-ROM?
7. Name **three** components typically found inside a pen drive.
8. Name **three** different types of commercially available flash card.
9. What is DAT?
10. What is DTR?

How well did you do? See supporting website for the answers.

Table 2.07

Backing store name	Storage mechanism	Typical capacity	Typical DTR	Removable or fixed media
3.5-inch floppy diskette (FD)	Magnetic	1.44 MB	500 kBps	Removable
PATA IDE hard disk (HD)	Magnetic	60–500 GB	133 MBps (ATA133)	Fixed
SCSI hard disk (HD)	Magnetic	30–300 GB	320 MBps (Ultra320)	Fixed
SATA hard disk (HD)	Magnetic	60–500 GB	150 MBps (SATA150) 300 MBps (SATA300)	Fixed
CD-R	Optical	650–700 MB	150 kbps (x1)	Removable
CD-RW	Optical	650–700 MB	150 kbps (x1)	Removable
DVD-R	Optical	4.7–16 GB	1.3 MBps (x1)	Removable
DVD-RW	Optical	4.7–16 GB	1.3 MBps (x1)	Removable
USB pen drive	Flash	Up to 256 GB	1–25 MBps	Removable
Flash memory card (e.g. Magic Stick Pro)	Flash	Up to 128 GB (theoretically)	20 MBps	Removable

2.1.4 Operating system software

This section covers the following grading criteria:

Make the Grade P2 M1

The P2 criterion requires you **explain the purpose of operating systems**. You will need to explain what it is they do within a computer system. Reading carefully through this section should prepare you for this. Your understanding of operating system functions could be tested through a number of different activities (for example, a quiz, a written report, an electronic slideshow etc.).

The M1 criterion requires you to be able to **compare the features and functions of different operating systems**. Technically, 'compare' means seeking similarities and differences between two different things, so you will need to be able to identify these in **features** (for example, having file management) and **functions** (for example, being able to rename files, through the file management feature) between some selected operating systems. It would be very useful to have practical access to the selected systems before you attempt this task.

Again, it is likely that you will demonstrate your understanding of these comparisons by producing written evidence or presenting your findings.

An **operating system** (often abbreviated to **OS**) is classified as the system software that represents the essential layer between the BIOS and applications software, for example word processor, spreadsheet, graphics, database, web browsers etc. (Figure 2.48). This means that when a user opens a spreadsheet file the correct instruction needs to travel through the OS and BIOS levels before the appropriate electronic signals are generated to tell the disk drive's reading heads to find and transfer the required data into RAM.

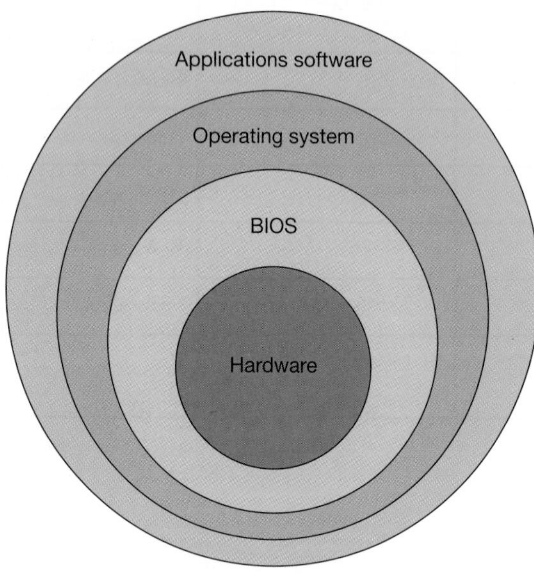

Figure 2.48 Computer system layers

The core interlocking components of an OS are:

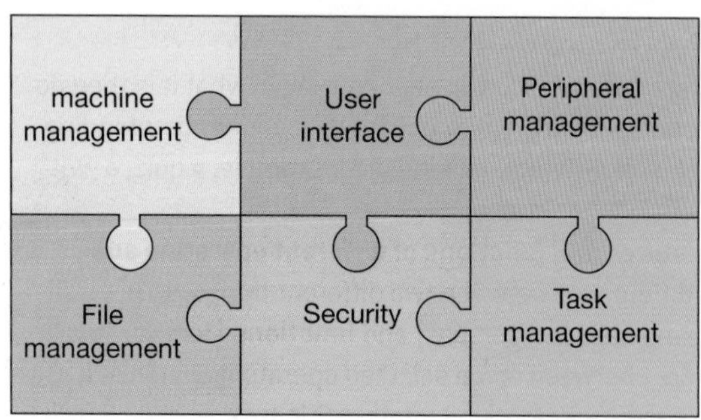

Figure 2.49 Interlocking components of an operating system

Let's examine these in a little more detail.

Machine management

Resources found on a modern computer system are:

- **physical memory** (RAM);
- **virtual memory** (disk space used as RAM);
- **disk cache** (RAM storing the most recently accessed data from the disk);
- **CPU** (the processor, particularly the balance between OS 'time' and application 'time');
- **bandwidth** (networking, video, bus etc.).

The operating system's job is to juggle these resources to keep the computer system running smoothly (avoiding too many peaks of activity where there is no free capacity).

User interface

An operating system has to have some form of user interface. The interface is responsible for:

- **accepting** user commands;
- **parsing** user commands (working out what the command actually is);
- **displaying** error or warning messages when processes or devices fail;
- **informing** a user of critical system events (for example, when the system is about to shut down);
- **confirming** that a command has been successfully completed.

As you will see later, there are two basic types of user interface: the **command line** and the **graphical user**. The trend towards **G**raphical **U**ser **I**nterfaces (**GUIs**) has made computer systems much more user friendly, especially for novice users.

Peripheral management

Modern operating systems are **Plug and Play (PnP)** compatible (that is, they recognise new devices when they are first connected). Through the use of a **driver**, the operating system can communicate with the hardware.

In addition, it is the operating system's job to control the amount of CPU attention that an input/output device receives. An operating system is also vital in scheduling input and output operations so that the CPU is not idly awaiting data.

File management

A modern operating system must be able to create and maintain a robust and reliable file management system (usually one that uses magnetic and optical disks).

Help

Drivers – what you need to know

A driver is a small program that tells an operating system how to communicate with a peripheral device.

Drivers are therefore specific to an operating system (that is, a Windows® 7 driver for a scanner won't work with Linux® – in fact it might not even work with Windows Vista® or Windows® XP!).

Usually, drivers can be:

- found on a CD/DVD that accompanies the device;
- downloaded from the manufacturer's website;
- already built into the operating system.

Drivers can be updated from time to time.

Devices don't work properly if a driver isn't installed.

The filing system's job is to store and organise data and program files on a backing storage device. It must also be able to retrieve the file when it is needed again.

In order to do this, the filing system must create some kind of logical index or table of contents, which maps parts of files to physical locations (for example, a disk's tracks and sectors) of the backing storage media.

File **A**llocation **T**able 32 (**FAT**32) and **N**ew **T**echnology **F**iling **S**ystem (**NTFS**) are popular filing systems used in Microsoft Windows® XP, Vista® and Microsoft Windows® 7.

Second extended file system (**ext2**) is a popular filing system used by Linux distributions. However, ext2 cannot be natively read by Windows® operating systems.

Modern Apple Mac® computer systems use **H**ierarchical **F**ile **S**ystem (**HFS+**).

Backing storage, such as hard disk drives, need to be **partitioned** (the act of splitting large physical drives into numerous, smaller logical volumes) and then formatted for the appropriate filing system before they can be used. It is typically the operating system's responsibility to perform these acts.

Security

Security is a critical component of modern operating systems, especially as increasing numbers of users are connected to other systems via the internet.

Security should encompass:

- user data;
- connectivity;
- access to applications software;
- access to system configuration;
- access to the filing system.

Task management

One of the principal jobs of an operating system is **task management**: the job of running other applications. There are many different ways that this can be achieved. Perhaps the most common method is **pre-emptive multitasking** as used by Windows® XP, Linux and MAC OS X®. Pre-emptive multitasking is the ability of an operating system to divide its resources between a number of processes. These resources include RAM, input/output and CPU processing time (Figure 2.50).

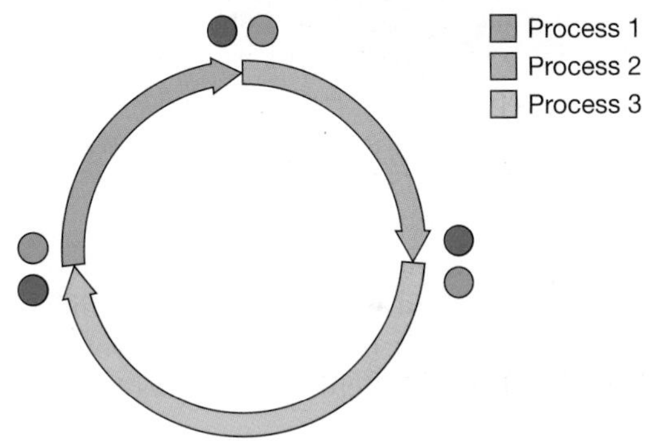

Figure 2.50 Pre-emptive multitasking

In pre-emptive multitasking, the operating system takes responsibility for starting and stopping different processes (each application that is running may consist of many different processes). In addition, it also allocates RAM and CPU time for each task. If a process is **more critical** the operating system may give it a **higher priority** (more CPU time) to accomplish its task. In Figure 2.50, Process 3 has been given a **higher priority** than Processes 1 and 2.

When a process is stopped, its state (where it was, what was happening inside the CPU) is frozen. This happens when each task is suspended. When each process is restarted, their states are unfrozen and the processes recommence as if they had never been paused. It appears that a single processor is running multiple tasks simultaneously because the process switching happens very quickly. The pre-emptive description reflects the fact that it is the operating system that decides when processes should halt, not the processes themselves. The allocated CPU period assigned to a process is sometimes called a **time slice**.

Examples of operating system

Although it is referred to as a 'piece of software', in reality an OS is not a single program. It is a collection of hundreds of smaller modules, with each module responsible for fulfilling a specific task.

Building an OS in a modular fashion ensures that it can be easily updated or patched (to fix any errors) in a more manageable way. An OS may receive many online patches via a live internet connection, typically to resolve security issues or mend bugs that have been reported.

Microsoft Windows®

There are many different commercial operating systems. Most home users are familiar with Microsoft® operating systems, particularly the older MS-DOS® line and the newer Windows® family. The most recent Microsoft® operating system is Windows® 7, released to retail shops in October 2009, and which will eventually replace the older Windows Vista® and XP® as support for these is gradually reduced. It is very likely that you regularly use a version of Microsoft Windows® at home, school or college.

Linux

Linux was initially created as a hobby project by a young student, Linus Torvalds, while studying at the University of Helsinki. Torvalds had a keen interest in a small Unix® system called Minix®; his goal quickly became to create an operating system that exceeded the Minix® functionality. Although he started work on this in 1991, the 1.0 version of the Linux® Kernel (the core part of the operating system) was not publicly released until 1994.

The Linux kernel is developed and released under the GNU General Public License and as such its source code is freely available to everyone.

These days other hands guide ongoing development of Linux, and there are literally hundreds of different Linux distributions ('distros') which are freely available for download. Each is geared for a particular purpose (for example, scientific research, education etc.). Some even fit on a floppy diskette!

Common distributions include:

- **Ubuntu** (www.ubuntu.com)
- **Fedora** (www.fedora.redhat.com)
- **OpenSuse** (en.opensuse.org).

Tux the Penguin (Figure 2.51) is the official mascot of the Linux® operating system, as created by Larry Ewing.

Figure 2.51 Tux the Penguin

> Activity 8
>
> Frankoni T-shirts are aiming to move to the Linux® operating system in order to reduce operating costs (costs of software licences, upgrades etc.). They are aware that Linux® is available in a number of different distributions but are uncertain which one best meets their needs. They would like to use Linux® as a desktop operating system for traditional administration tasks (that is, word-processing, spreadsheets and databases). No one in the company has a great deal of technical expertise, so they would like the graphical interface to be as user friendly as possible.
>
> Investigate popular Linux® distributions. Which one would you recommend for Frankoni? Hint: Try http://distrowatch.com/

Command line and GUIs

There are two different operating system user interfaces:

- **Command Line Interface (CLI)**
- **Graphical User Interface (GUI)**

The CLI is the oldest form of user interface, being present in early operating systems such as Unix®, Control Program for Microprocessors (CPM) and Microsoft® Disk Operating System (MS-DOS®). They typically feature:

- text-only output;
- keyboard-only input;
- basic command names;
- limited user help for commands;
- very basic error messages.

The most well known CLI is that represented by MS-DOS®. It still exists today as a **command prompt** in modern versions of Microsoft's Windows® OS.

In most versions of Windows®, the CLI is accessed clicking **Start** > **Run**, then typing **cmd** and clicking the **OK** button (Figure 2.52).

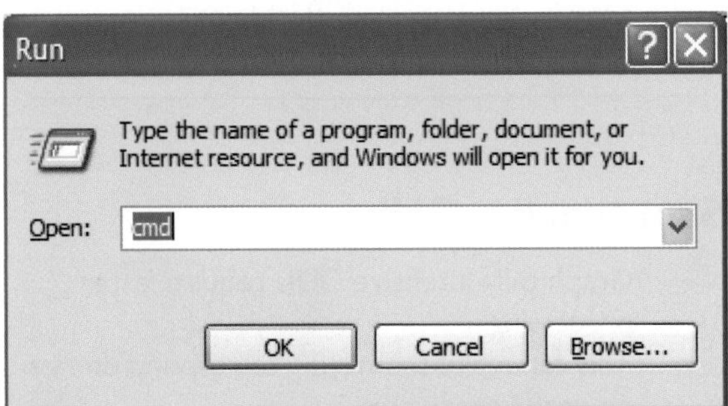

Figure 2.52 Windows® Run dialogue box

Figure 2.53 shows a typical view of a CLI in Windows®.

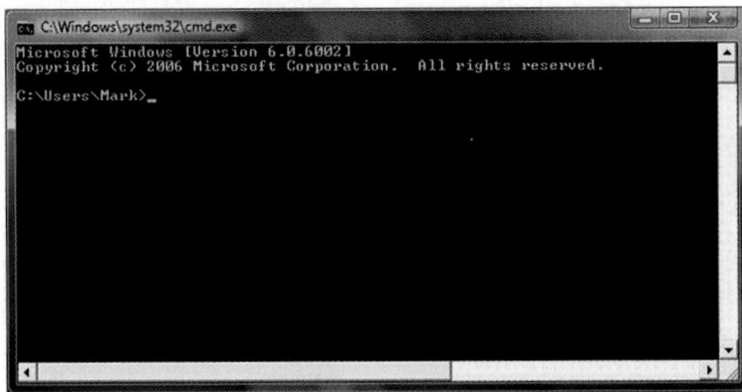

Figure 2.53 Windows® command prompt

The GUI is optional in Linux® distributions. In theory, all system functions can be controlled from the CLI. As such it is more powerful and has better user support in the form of online manuals (**MAN** files), which tell the user in detail how a command may be used.

The Linux command prompt is called the **Terminal** (Figure 2.54).

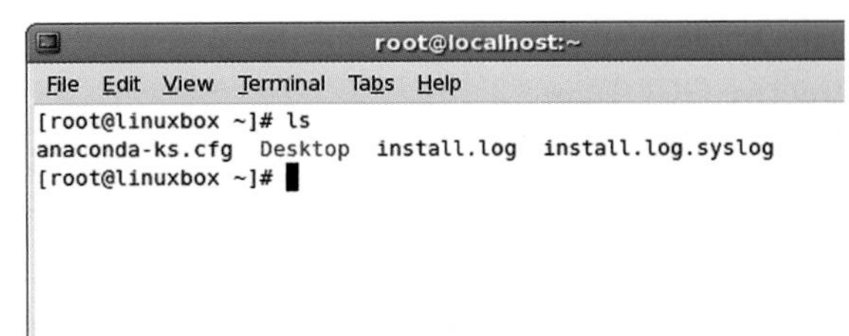

Figure 2.54 Linux command prompt

Help

Command Line Interfaces – what you need to know

A CLI is used to input basic OS commands, which the computer system typically executes when the **Enter** key is pressed.

Bad commands generate a brief error message, which the user must understand in order to try again.

The CLI is often seen as an unfriendly environment (compared with a GUI) because complex commands have to be remembered by the user.

Scorecard – CLI

– Not very user friendly
– Not very aesthetically pleasing
– Help may be limited
– Relies on good keyboard skills
– Error messages are generally not helpful
\+ Provides a quick response, even on slower equipment
\+ Proficient users can perform complex tasks very quickly
\+ Commands can be joined to form scripts to automate regular jobs

A **GUI** (pronounced 'goo-ey') is based on the **W**indows, **I**con, **M**enus and **P**ointer (**WIMP**) systems developed in the early 1970s.

A GUI creates a user-friendly, media-rich environment for users to explore, work and play within a combination of movable and resizable windows, representative icons and intuitive point-and-click mouse control.

Perhaps the most familiar GUI is the one presented by Microsoft Windows® (Figure 2.55).

The Apple Mac OS® also has an intuitive and attractive GUI (Figure 2.56).

Linux desktop managers are also becoming more intuitive, robust and aesthetically pleasing (Figure 2.57).

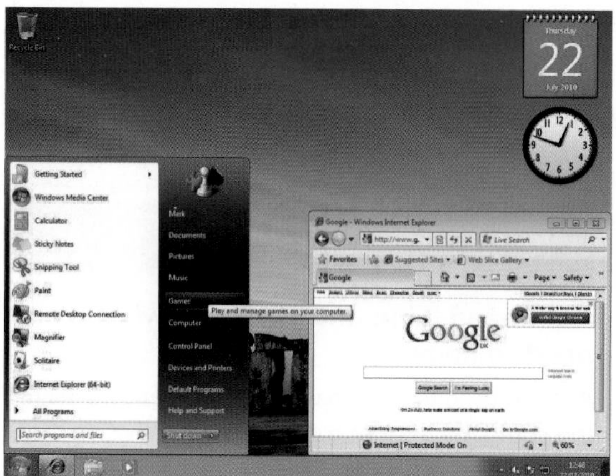

Figure 2.55 Microsoft Windows® 7 'Aero' desktop

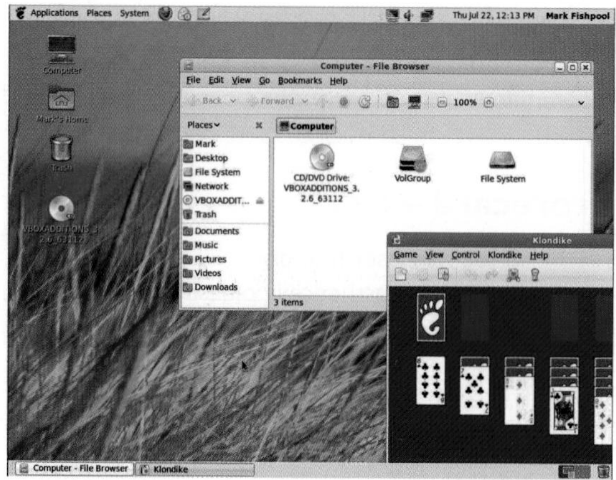

Figure 2.56 Linux Fedora Core 13 Gnome interface

GUIs are popular as they represent a good levelling tool: users of any age and IT experience can quickly feel at home, performing a combination of both simple and complex tasks with equal ease.

Help

Graphical User Interfaces – what you need to know

GUIs are now the standard interface for modern operating systems. Although they generally rely on a mouse and keyboard, some have voice recognition software that allows the operating system to respond to vocal commands. This is particularly useful to those with limited mobility. In addition, narrator software is also present to describe events and options on screen for those who are visually impaired. Both aim to improve equal opportunities amongst users.

Scorecard – GUIs

– Graphically intensive GUIs require faster processing
– This can make them slow to respond on less powerful hardware
– Newer operating systems require more hard disk space to install
– They need greater system resources (processor, memory etc.) to run
+ They are very user friendly
+ They are easy to configure to suit different user's preferences
+ They provide comprehensive input device support
+ There's no need to remember complex CLI instructions
+ Basic operations can take longer than using the CLI
+ More options are available to support users with disabilities

B Braincheck

1. Which **two** layers does the OS sit between?
2. Name any **four** core functions of the OS?
3. Where is an OS typically stored?
4. Which **two** types of OS user interface are available?
5. What is the process of updating part of an OS called?
6. What is multi-tasking?
7. What is virtual memory?
8. Complete the following CLI commands for Windows and Linux:

Objective	Windows®	Linux®
List files in a directory		
Create a new directory		
Delete a file		
Change to the 'root' directory		
Examine the computer's network adaptor information		

9. Describe **three** differences between Windows® 7 and a typical Linux distribution (e.g. Fedora, Ubuntu, Mint etc.).
10. Name **five** pieces of information that a file management system knows about a file.

How well did you do? See supporting website for answers.

2.1.5 Software utilities

This section will cover the following grading criteria:

Make the Grade

D1

The P3 criterion requires you to be able to explain the purpose of different software utilities, essentially explaining the roles they perform in a computer system.

In addition, criterion D1 asks you to explain **how software utilities can improve the performance** of computer systems.

These two criteria are clearly linked. For each utility you can think of, ensure that you know what it does and how it improves the system's performance.

Virus protection

A **virus** is a malicious program that infects a computer system. Viruses can spy on users and cause irreparable damage to personal or business data.

Initially, virus spread was limited by relying on physical transport through removable media such as floppy disks. However, growth in internet downloads and email attachments has made virus infection a very real threat to most users: An unprotected computer system could be infected with a virus within 1 minute of venturing online.

Virus authors typically target Microsoft Windows® operating systems (which count for the majority of users), but Linux and Mac OS® operating systems are starting to come under pressure.

Antivirus software (usually third party, that is not written by an operating system developer) is easily available. Regular updates are required to keep virus **definition files** or virus **signatures** up to date.

AVG Technologies offer examples of antivirus utilities.

Anti-spyware

Spyware is a type of malicious software **(malware)** that monitors the actions of a computer user. Sometimes the software has been legitimately installed, perhaps to keep an eye on an employee (for example, for security or workplace monitoring), but it may have been installed without the knowledge or permission of the user.

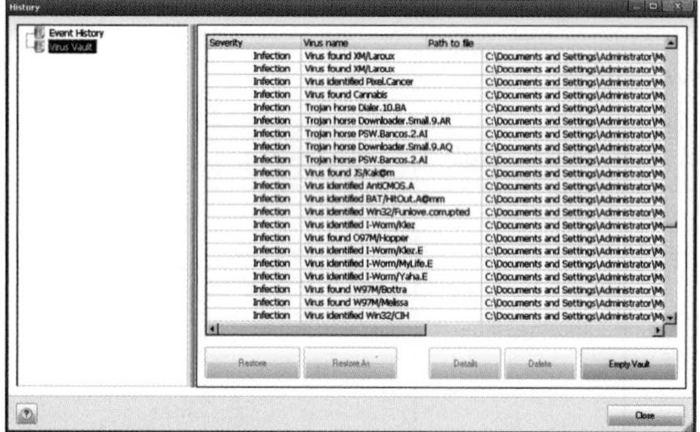

Figure 2.57 AVG Anti-virus shows its virus vault of quarantined files

The use of such monitoring tools is varied. A typical use is to collect marketing data, showing websites visited and goods purchased by a user. In most cases spyware is an annoyance rather than a threat (like a virus).

More intrusive spyware might report on user activities, permit a machine to be remotely controlled or create a security loophole that will allow a 'rogue user' to harvest personal information (for example, passwords, credit card information, account details etc.) in a bid to perform identity theft.

Anti-spyware is a piece of software that can identify, disable and remove such software Microsoft Defender® is a typical anti-spyware product (Figure 2.58).

Firewalls

A **firewall** is a program that runs on a computer system (client or dedicated) and filters network traffic coming in or out. In addition, it can also specify which programs are allowed to access the network.

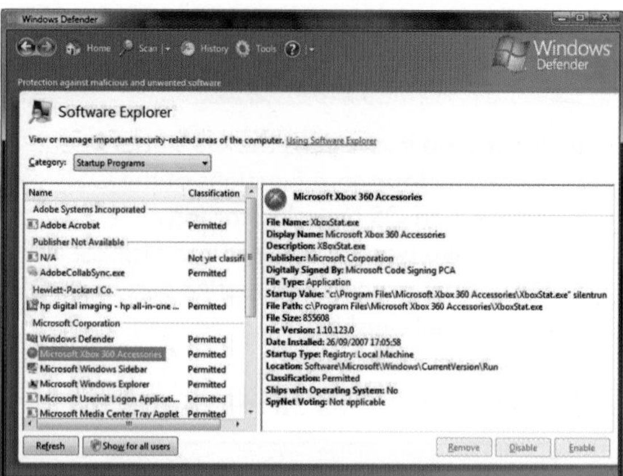

Figure 2.58 Microsoft Defender® explores programs loading at Start up

Typically, a firewall is placed between a trusted, private network and an unprotected public network (such as the internet), and is often built into a **router** or **gateway**.

Clean-up tools

Utilities are also available to protect the user's personal information from prying eyes, particularly when browsing the World Wide Web.

Defragmentation

Most operating systems have disk-filing systems that create **fragmentation** over a period of time. Fragmentation occurs when space reclaimed after a file is deleted is used to store parts of a larger file (Figure 2.60). The end result is that a file does not exist in **contiguous** (that is, adjacent) disk locations. (Windows® calls these **clusters**.)

Fragmented files are **slower to load into RAM**, simply because the hard disk drive has to work harder to physically locate and read all the physically separate clusters that form the file.

Most operating systems have utilities to defragment a file system (Figure 2.61). This utility may be run as an ad hoc (that is, unplanned, whenever

Help

Clean-up tools – what you need to know

Modern operating systems keep a detailed account of user activity (**footprint**). There are times when such accounts are now longer required. In order to manage the accounts, most operating systems and applications have options to clear personal data from the system.

In the internet age, the most common footprints to remove are:

- **internet history** (which web sites have been visited by whom and when);
- **cookies** (small text files stored on your machine containing personal data used by websites to recognise the user and their preferences);
- **temporary files** downloaded into a disk cache;
- **passwords**;
- **information entered** into **online forms**.

Options to specify what data is held and how to manage it may be located and set in the operating system or internet client software such as a web browser (for example, Figure 2.59).

Figure 2.59 Clean-up of personal data in Mozilla Firefox®

Of course, there may be situations where such user activity logs are important and should be kept intact, for example, students in a college and employees in the workplace may have to obey their organisation's communication policy. Third-party clean-up utilities are also available (for example, Piriform's CCleaner http://www.piriform.com/ccleaner)

needed) process or on a **regular schedule**. Doing so will speed up file access in the computer system. It is often recommended that a fragmentation of 10% or more should be fixed.

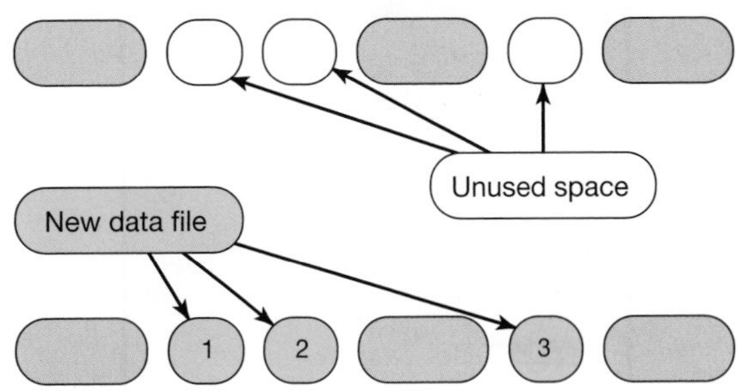

Figure 2.60 An example of disk fragmentation and reuse of space

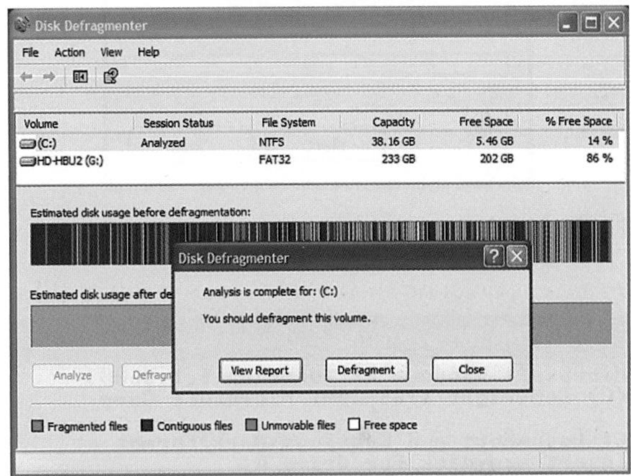

Figure 2.61 Windows® Defragmenter utility finds a problem

Drive formatting

Before a magnetic disk can be used, it must be prepared. This process is called **formatting**. Formatting theoretically erases all data previously stored on a disk. Formats are specific to the disk operating system in use, for example, a disk formatted for use on a Microsoft Windows® system cannot be read natively by an Apple Mac® and special drivers are required.

Operating systems such as Microsoft Windows® have GUI format utilities (Figure 2.62), but they can also perform the same process from the CLI (Figure 2.63).

A disk format:

- prepares the physical locations to be ready for recording;

- sets up a filing system (for example, **File Allocation Table (FAT)**) on the disk;
- checks the disk for physical or magnetic errors.

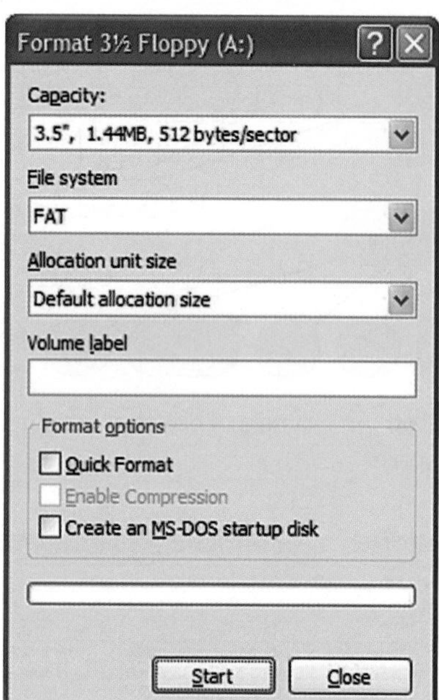

Figure 2.62 Windows® disk format (GUI)

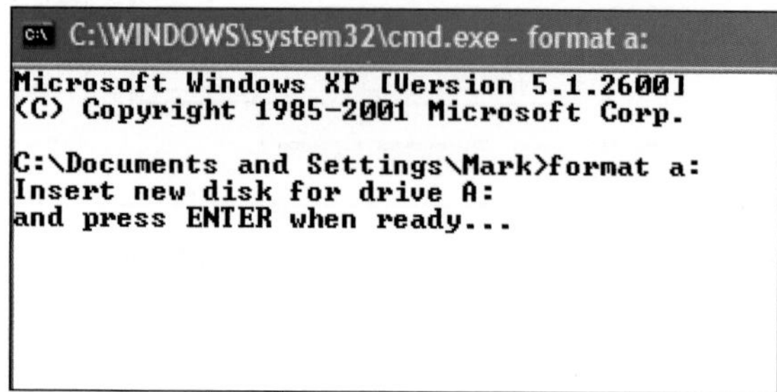

Figure 2.63 Windows® disk format (CLI)

In reality, formatting a disk clears the filing system's **table of contents**. The data is still present on the disk, but the operating system will have no idea where the various files are physically stored. This means that data may still be recoverable using specialist data recovery software. Sensitive data (personal or business) should be safely deleted using **data shredding software**. Of course, the surest way to erase data is to physically destroy the disk itself!

2.2 Be able to recommend computer systems for a business purpose

This section will cover the following grading criteria:

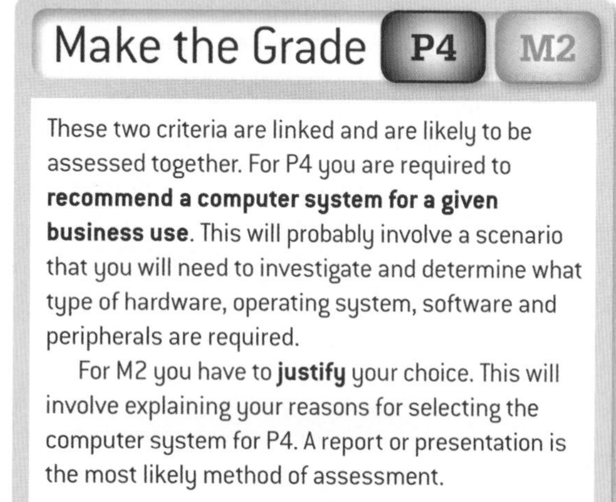

Make the Grade P4 M2

These two criteria are linked and are likely to be assessed together. For P4 you are required to **recommend a computer system for a given business use**. This will probably involve a scenario that you will need to investigate and determine what type of hardware, operating system, software and peripherals are required.

For M2 you have to **justify** your choice. This will involve explaining your reasons for selecting the computer system for P4. A report or presentation is the most likely method of assessment.

2.2.1 Considerations for selection

A number of factors have to be taken into consideration before recommending a new computer system. These should include:

- the cost of hardware, software and delivery;
- the user's requirements.

Of the two, the latter is the most difficult to determine because there are many different aspects that must be satisfied. Table 2.08 opposite lists some of these.

Table 2.08

User requirement	Details
Software to be used	Fact: Operating systems don't sell computer systems. Applications software does! The choice of operating system is less likely to be affected by budgetary concerns and more likely to be connected to what is needed to run a particular application. Therefore, the first user requirement to fulfil is to determine the kind of computer system needed to run the user's program (whatever it may be) successfully.
Need for maintenance	Fact: Computer systems go wrong from time to time. Although building a new computer system from scratch is possible, enjoyable and a worthwhile practical challenge, there is little backup when things go wrong (apart from manufacturer guarantees on individual components). A new 'ready-made' system will often give the user: • a period of RTB (return to base) if problems occur; • an extended warranty covering replacement parts and labour charges. Although this can significantly add to the cost of the computer system, it will give peace of mind. For businesses without a separate IT Support section, purchasing a separate maintenance contract for regular servicing of IT equipment is common practice.
Need for integration and connectivity	Modern computer systems are often bought as a part of a larger solution (for example, a home entertainment (media) system. Thought must be given to how a new system will integrate with existing systems. This could also include network connectivity.
Processing power	Modern programs are 'resource hungry'. Processing power is a vital tool in achieving good system performance. This usually means investment in a quality motherboard, processor, RAM and video card. Again, software will have minimum and recommended hardware requirements. Optimum performance always requires an excess of processing power, so always meet or exceed the recommended requirements for any software.
Storage capacity	User data requirements are increasing every year. As users move over to digital libraries (music, pictures and video), the need for larger hard-drive capacity increases too. In addition, any critical storage will need backup, effectively doubling the storage capacities required. Fortunately, costs of hard disks and flash memory continue to fall.
Ease of use and accessibility for disabled users	Modern users are concerned with functionality and ease of use. Any computer system has to be as intuitive as possible with a friendly GUI and informative feedback (which avoids technical jargon in its description). In addition, regular maintenance tasks should either be fully automated (and invisible) or be simple for a novice to operate safely. In addition, accessibility for less able users is also crucial. Modern computer systems should integrate voice commands (through speech recognition), support innovative Human Interface Devices, provide high-contrast displays for visually impaired and narration for on-screen events.
ICT competence of user and training requirements	When specifying a system, you must think about how IT literate the end user is. If the user is inexperienced, the system must be as user friendly as possible. If the tasks involve learning new software, then you may need to include training in your cost calculations.
Sustainability	Computer systems should last, or at least provide, the maximum amount of usage before components need replacing or upgrading. Options should also exist for ecologically friendly options (such as low emissions, refillable ink, safe disposal of toxic motherboard components, encouraging the use of electronic documents where possible etc.).

Activity 9

KAM Ltd is currently investigating the purchase of a new computer system for graphic design. The software they wish to use is:

- Adobe Photoshop® CS5

1 Investigate the minimum requirements for this package at www.adobe.com/products/photoshop/photoshop/systemreqs/

2 Give details of **two** possible computer systems that could be purchased by KAM to run this software successfully.

2.3 Set up and maintain computer systems

2.3.1 Connect and set up

The following sections will cover the following grading criterion:

P5

Make the Grade P5

This criterion requires you to be able to **set up a standalone computer system**, so there's no networking to worry about! This is a practical task so you will need to provide photographs, video, witness statements etc. If you have learnt about the different internal components, external peripherals and connectors you should be fine!

In addition, you'll need to be able **to install** and configure **different types of software**. Screen captures are acceptable evidence to demonstrate you have done this satisfactorily.

Most devices have distinctive connectors, so connecting the various components of a modern computer system is not difficult. In general, you are likely to have to make the connections in Figure 2.64 on page 67.

Help

Connection and set up – what you need to know

- RAM connects internally to the motherboard inside the base unit (see page 44).
- Speakers connect externally to the base unit backplane (see page 43).
- A hard drive connects internally to the motherboard inside the base unit (see page 35).
- A keyboard connects externally to the base unit backplane (see page 43).
- A mouse connects externally to the base unit backplane (see page 43).
- A monitor connects externally to the base unit backplane (see page 35).
- A printer connects externally to the base unit backplane (see page 43).

The base unit, monitor, printer and speakers will typically require their own power supply. As a safeguard, all devices should be switched off before connecting/disconnecting.

2.3.2 Install hardware

In addition to connecting external components of a computer system, it is sometimes necessary to install hardware which will mean opening the base unit to gain access to the motherboard. Typical hardware installations are:

- additional RAM;
- a new hard drive or optical drive (or change existing one);
- an upgrade CPU;
- a replacement CPU or case fan;
- a new PSU;
- an upgrade specialist card (for example, graphics card, sound card or NIC).

Never perform any of these operations while the base unit is still connected to an electrical supply.

Working with an open case provides extra challenges, for example components are often difficult to remove or replace due to cramped space inside the case. In addition, there are many sharp metal edges, which can cause cuts and abrasions.

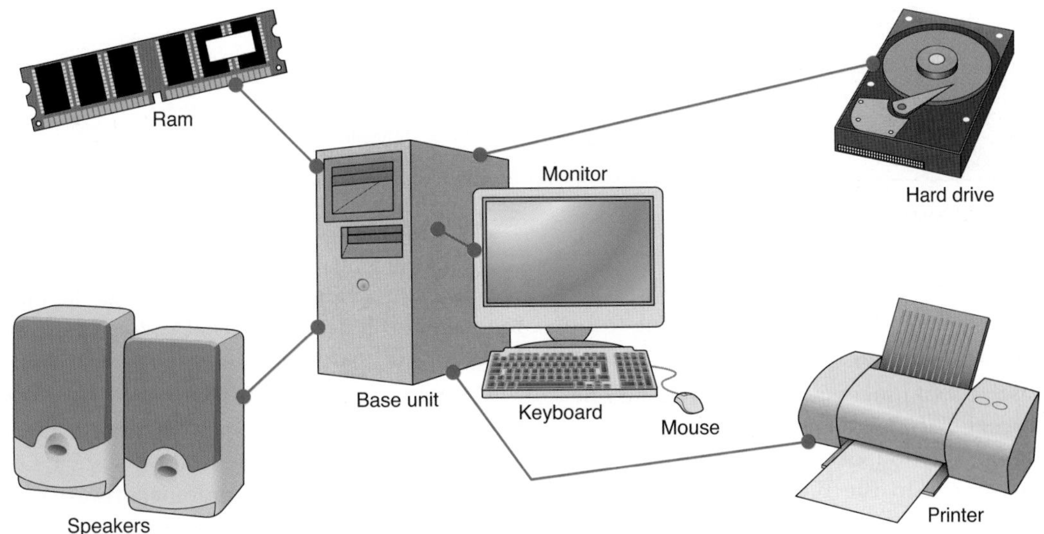

Figure 2.64 Connect and set up diagram

Protecting equipment

It is possible to damage electrical components through **electrostatic discharge (ESD)**. In order to prevent this from happening, both the technician and equipment should be electrically grounded: the former, by wearing an antistatic wrist strap, and the latter, by placing all of the components (including the case) on an antistatic workbench mat (Figure 2.65).

Figure 2.65 Safely installing more RAM into a notebook (note the use of an antistatic wrist strap)

2.3.3 Install software

The installation of new software has its own challenges and we will examine these for operating systems, applications software and security software.

> **Help**
>
> **Installing new hardware – what you need to know**
>
> You will be expected to install and configure new peripherals (for example, scanners, printers etc.).
>
> Modern peripherals are Plug and Play (PnP) and as long as the BIOS and operating system supports PnP, the correct device should be correctly identified and drivers loaded:
>
> - from the installation or drivers CD;
> - via the internet;
> - from default drivers stored in the operating system.
>
> Care should be taken to follow the installation instructions of any new piece of hardware. This is particularly important if the drivers are to be loaded **before** the device is connected.
>
> In addition, you should register peripherals with the manufacturers so that additional support (including free driver updates etc.) can be easily obtained.

Installing operating systems

Operating system software can be commercially purchased (for example, Microsoft® Windows®) or downloaded for free using the internet (for example, Linux®).

In general, when an operating system installation is performed on a hard drive, the drive's previous

What is the rationale for picking a particular operating system?	What hardware is required to run the operating system?	How is a copy of the operating system obtained?	How is the operating system installed?	Does the operating system need to be registered before use?

Figure 2.66 Installing an operating system

contents will be erased. As with any software, there is a logical order to follow when preparing for installation (Figure 2.66).

There are several processes for installing an operating system, but a common technique is to use a bootable installation CD or DVD (this usually requires a change to the BIOS so the CD/DVD is chosen before the hard disk in the boot order).

Modern operating system installations will lead the technician through the set-up process by asking simple questions that determine which features will be incorporated and what settings the operating system will default to (that is, for location settings for keyboard, clock and language, date and time etc.).

Some operating systems require **activation** through a telephone or online registration system before they can be used. This is to prevent **software piracy**.

> Activation 10
>
> Try using a Linux operating system.
>
> Many Linux distributions are available in **LiveCD** format.
>
> These special CDs let the user boot a version of Linux into the computer system's RAM without affecting the resident operating system that is installed on the hard drive. This lets the user 'test drive' a version of Linux without having to worry about installing it.
>
> Typically it works a little more slowly (due to CD access) than a fully installed version, but it gives a useful way of comparing and contrasting different operating systems.
>
> Useful links for some popular Linux® distributions are:
>
> - **Linux Mint** www.linuxmint.com/download.php
> - **Ubuntu** www.ubuntu.com/desktop/get-ubuntu/download
> - **Fedora** fedoraproject.org/en/get-fedora
>
> Note: Some Linux distributions can also be placed on USB pen drives.

Installing security software

The means of installing security software will vary greatly depending on the operating system being used. Modern versions of Microsoft Windows® have a **Security Centre**, which coordinates utilities such as firewalls, antivirus, anti-spyware, clean-up tools (cookies, history etc.) and parental controls.

Third-party security software (for example, antivirus suites from software manufacturers such as McAfee®, AVG, Symantec®) can be installed and these will integrate well with the operating system. Installation follows a similar technique to that of applications software (see *installing applications software*).

Installing device drivers

As explained device drivers ensure that the operating system and hardware correctly communicate with one another. Drivers are generally loaded when a device is first connected to a computer system. This is often achieved through a technique called Plug and Play (PnP). Most operating systems let a technician update a driver, especially for malfunctioning devices. Figure 2.67 shows the Windows® Device Manager as accessed through the Control Panel.

Installing applications software

Applications software needs an operating system in order to run. Although some applications software is called **cross-platform** (available for multiple operating systems), most are specifically designed to run on a particular operating system, and this may be a very specific version (for example, Microsoft Windows® 7 or Windows Vista® 64-bit only.)

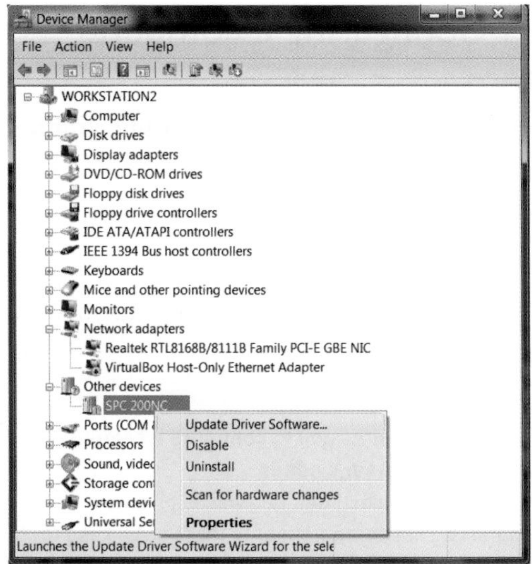

Figure 2.67 Windows® Device Manager showing a device which needs a driver update

An IT technician must be sure of the hardware and software requirements in order to install applications software. Table 2.09 lists requirements for Adobe's Photoshop® CS5 product, for both PCs and Apple® Macs.

As you can see in the table, software manufacturers will often refer to **minimum requirements** and **recommended requirements**. Minimum requirements are needed to get the software application to work. Recommended requirements will enable the application to work well.

Most software applications are installed via specially written **installation programs** (sometimes called a **set-up program** or **set-up wizard**). These lead the technician through the installation process in a step-by-step manner and require very little technical knowledge apart from selecting appropriate folders to store the application and its data (Figure 2.68).

Table 2.09 Requirements for Adobe® Photoshop® CS5

	PC	Apple® Mac®
CPU (processor)	Intel® Pentium® 4 or AMD Athlon® 64 processor	Multicore Intel® processor
Operating system	Microsoft Windows® XP with Service Pack 3; Windows Vista® Home Premium, Business, Ultimate, or Enterprise with Service Pack 1 (Service Pack 2 recommended); or Windows® 7	Mac OS® X v10.5.7 or v10.6
RAM	1 GB	1 GB
Hard drive space for installation	1 GB of available hard-disk space for installation; additional free space required during installation (cannot install on removable flash-based storage devices)	2 GB of available hard-disk space for installation; additional free space required during installation (cannot install on a volume that uses a case-sensitive file system or on removable flash-based storage devices)
Video display	1024 × 768 display (1280 × 800 recommended) with qualified hardware-accelerated OpenGL graphics card, 16-bit color, and 256 MB of VRAM	1024 × 768 display (1280 × 800 recommended) with qualified hardware-accelerated OpenGL graphics card, 16-bit color, and 256 MB of VRAM
Video card features	Some GPU-accelerated features require graphics support for Shader Model 3.0 and OpenGL 2.0	Some GPU-accelerated features require graphics support for Shader Model 3.0 and OpenGL 2.0
Optical drive	DVD-ROM drive	DVD-ROM drive
Other software	QuickTime® 7.6.2 software required for multimedia features	QuickTime® 7.6.2 software required for multimedia features
Connectivity	Broadband internet connection required for online services	Broadband internet connection required for online services

Source: http://www.adobe.com/products/photoshop/photoshop/systemreqs/

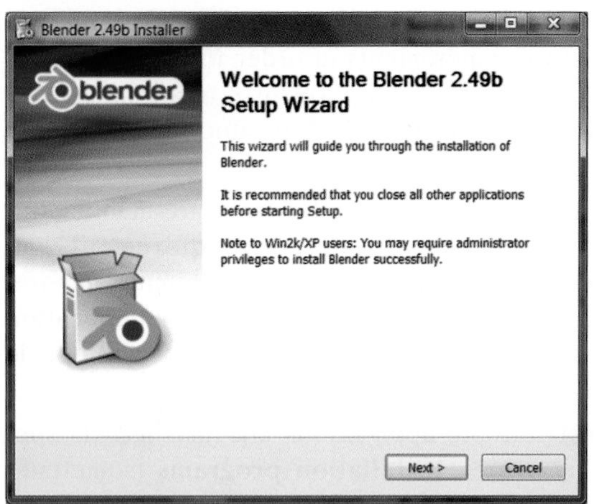

Figure 2.68 Blender Installer for Microsoft Windows®

Common installation program types are (for Microsoft Windows®): **.exe** (executable) and **.msi** (Microsoft® Installer) packages. Both make the appropriate changes to the operating system's settings in order for the application to function correctly.

An **uninstall program** is used to remove the software (when required) as fully and cleanly from the computer system as possible.

Most applications software will ask the technician to read and confirm their acceptance of a **E**nd **U**ser **L**icence **A**greement (**EULA**) before allowing the installation to continue. The EULA is a legal contract between the application's manufacturer/author and the user (Figure 2.69)

In most cases, a user must be an **administrator** (or have equivalent user rights) to install software onto a computer system.

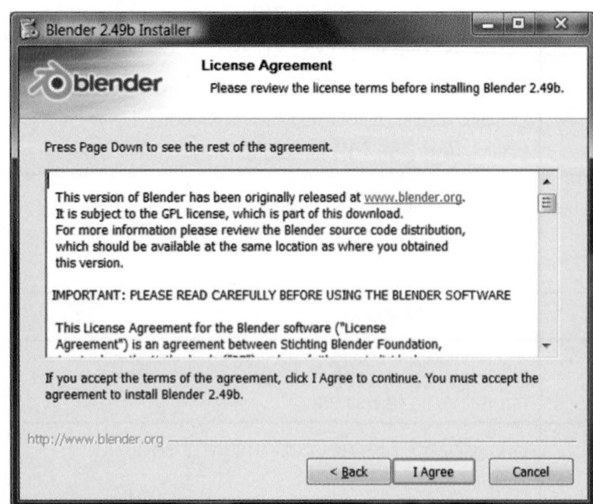

Figure 2.69 Blender's EULA

2.3.4 Configuring a computer system

This section will cover the following grading criterion:

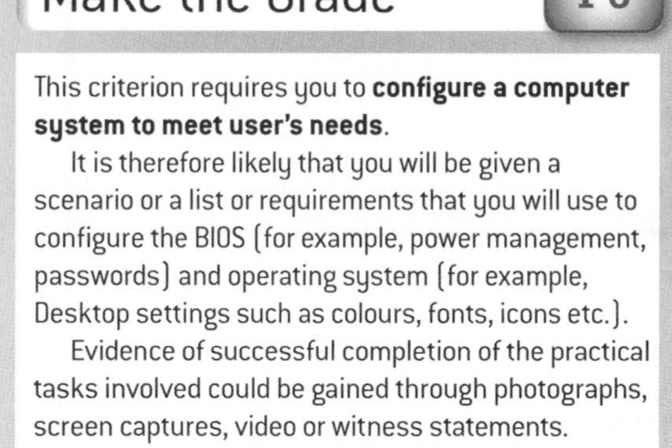

Make the Grade P6

This criterion requires you to **configure a computer system to meet user's needs**.

It is therefore likely that you will be given a scenario or a list or requirements that you will use to configure the BIOS (for example, power management, passwords) and operating system (for example, Desktop settings such as colours, fonts, icons etc.).

Evidence of successful completion of the practical tasks involved could be gained through photographs, screen captures, video or witness statements.

Although most end users will eventually fully customise their computer system to reflect their own preferences, there are a number of settings that can initially be made to personalise the system:

BIOS password

A **BIOS password** can be added to the computer system to prevent either unauthorised use of the computer (a BIOS **user password**) or unauthorised changes to the CMOS settings (a BIOS **supervisor password**).

A user password must be entered before the computer system will boot the operating system (Figure 2.70).

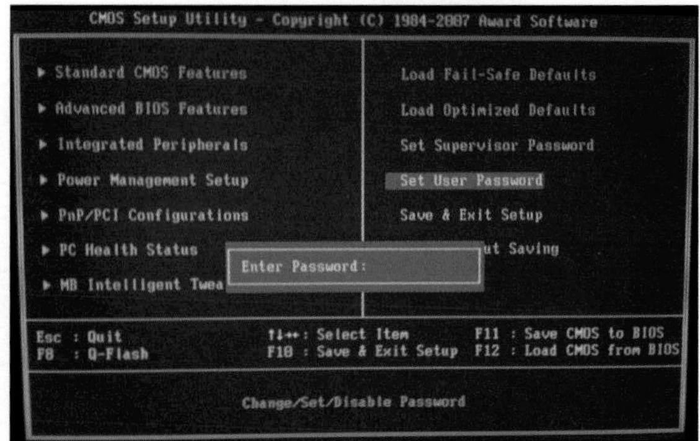

Figure 2.70 Setting a BIOS password

However, BIOS passwords can be removed by either clearing the CMOS jumper or removing the CMOS battery (and power supply) for 2–3 minutes.

Power management options

Modern operating systems control the way the computer system manages its electrical power. Power management settings are available in most BIOS versions. They are particularly useful on notebooks and netbooks to conserve valuable battery power.

Common options include:

- **Video standby mode**: The video card stops sending signals to the monitor.
- **Hard drive standby mode**: The hard drive spins down.
- **Suspend mode**: The system goes inactive, awaiting a 'wake' signal.

The user will typically specify for each option how many minutes of inactivity must elapse before these power management operations are acted upon. Wake signals can be generated by the power button, keyboard, mouse or network card.

Most operating systems also have compatible power management options that can control hardware and software. In most versions of Microsoft® Windows®, these are usually accessed via the Control Panel (Figure 2.71).

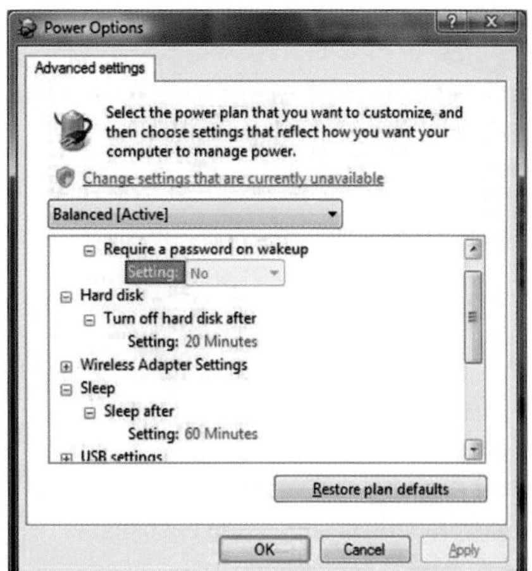

Figure 2.71 Power management options in Microsoft Windows Vista®

Editing the Desktop

A computer system's Desktop is fully customisable through options in the operating system's GUI. In most versions of Microsoft Windows®, various options can be accessed and set through the Control Panel (Figure 2.72).

Common options include: icon size, font size and colour (include high-contrast colour sets for visually impaired users), background wallpaper and icon choices for certain objects (for example, what the 'recycle bin' looks like).

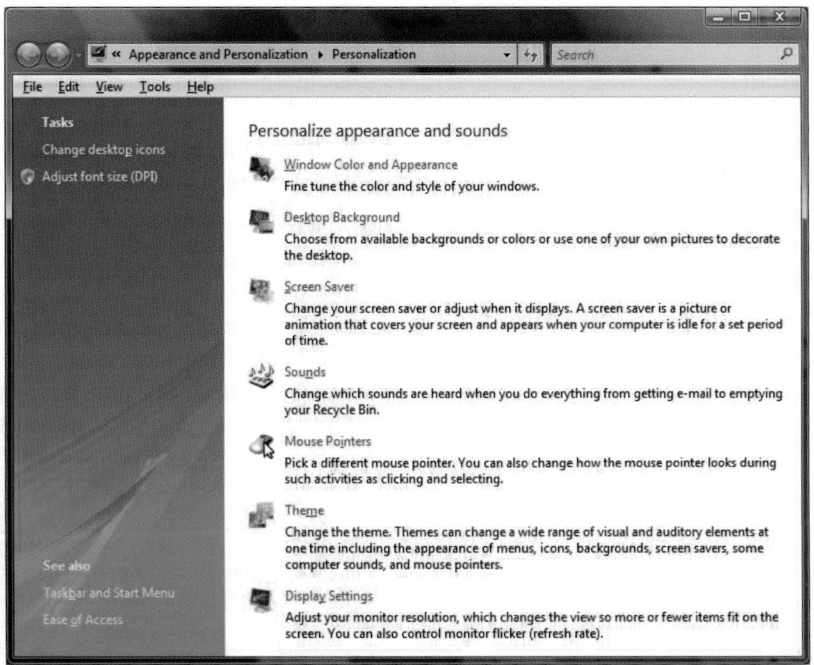

Figure 2.72 The Desktop options in Microsoft Windows Vista®

2.3.5 Testing

The following sections will cover the following grading criteria:

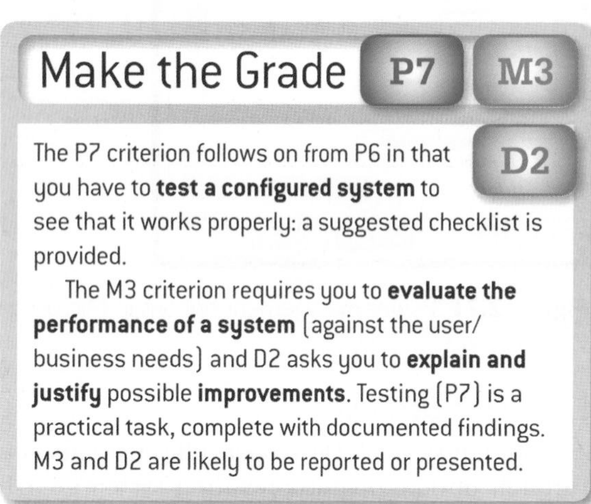

Make the Grade P7 M3 D2

The P7 criterion follows on from P6 in that you have to **test a configured system** to see that it works properly: a suggested checklist is provided.

The M3 criterion requires you to **evaluate the performance of a system** (against the user/business needs) and D2 asks you to **explain and justify** possible **improvements**. Testing (P7) is a practical task, complete with documented findings. M3 and D2 are likely to be reported or presented.

Testing the functionality of an installation and configuration of a computer system is vital.

The checklist in Table 2.10 is divided into hardware, software and system settings categories. Use it to test your own set up and maintenance.

Note: This list is not intended to be exhaustive but should represent a broad, but representative, example of those aspects that should be tested by a technician before release to the target user.

Evaluating a system

Thorough testing of an assembled computer system will allow the IT technician to make judgements about its effectiveness and, more importantly, how well it meets the identified business purpose. (An important factor, in addition to functionality, is **value for money**.)

As discussed in Section 2.2.1, there are several considerations that should be made when deciding on the selection of components for a computer system. We can use these to judge the effectiveness of an assembled computer system under four broad headings.

Hardware

- Is the processing power capable of supporting software processing?
- Is the hardware correctly installed and configured?
- Is the storage capacity sufficient for user data and software needs?
- How will the hardware be maintained?
- Is the hardware future-proofed as much as possible?

Software

- Is the required software installed and working correctly?
- Does the software produce the outputs required by the user/business?
- Has appropriate security software been installed and configured?
- Does the software support network sharing of data etc?

System settings

- Are the system settings correctly configured and optimised for currently installed hardware and software?
- Can the system be easily integrated with other systems?
- Are routine tasks scheduled to assist routine maintenance?

User competence

- Does the current system reflect the IT competence of the intended user?
- Does the current system take account of the accessibility needs of users?
- Have you discovered any training needs for the target user?

It should be possible to construct a good evaluation of a system by examining these questions and answering them honestly.

Explaining and justifying possible improvements

During the evaluation of a computer system, it should be possible to identify areas that could be improved through the use of better hardware components, better software or improved installation and configuration. Figure 2.73 shows how to arrive at the right decision for every weak aspect discovered.

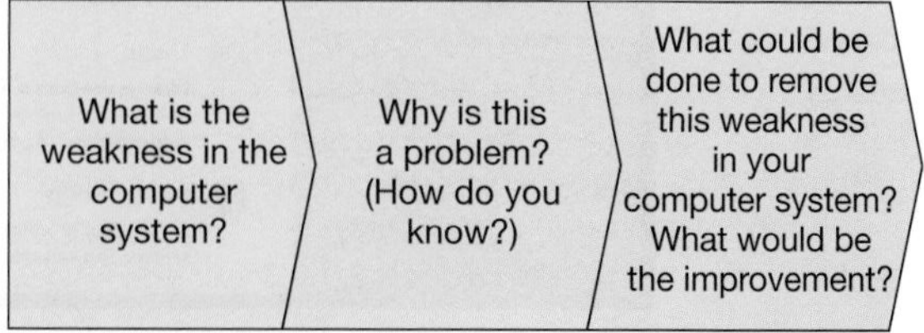

Figure 2.73 Testing checklist

Table 2.10

Category	What you are testing	Check?
Hardware	Hardware is correctly connected	☐
	All hardware powers up correctly	☐
	All hardware is recognised by the computer system (BIOS) during POST	☐
	All hardware is recognised by the computer system (operating system)	☐
	All devices are reported as working correctly by the operating system	☐
	Test operations for hardware peripherals work correctly (for example, producing a test page on a printer, sound plays through speakers)	☐
Software	Application shortcuts are present	☐
	Applications start when selected	☐
	Applications work as expected (open and save files)	☐
	Applications close as expected	☐
	Operating system updates are correctly installed and up to date	☐
	Drivers for hardware are correctly installed and working	☐
	Appropriate security software (for example, antivirus, firewall etc.) is installed and working	☐
	All user requirements (in terms of software needs) have been met	☐
System settings	System date and time is correct	☐
	Power management options are optimal	☐
	Passwords are correctly set	☐
	Desktop is correctly configured for user	☐
	Accessibility options for disabled users have been considered and acted on as required	☐
	All required Desktop shortcuts are present and work as expected	☐
	Regular processes required are correctly scheduled (for example, clean up, defragmentation etc.)	☐
	Printer settings are correct (for example, correct paper size, print quality etc. are set as default for application use)	☐
	Required folders are created and users have correct file shares and permissions	☐

2.3.6 Routine maintenance

This section will cover the following grading criterion:

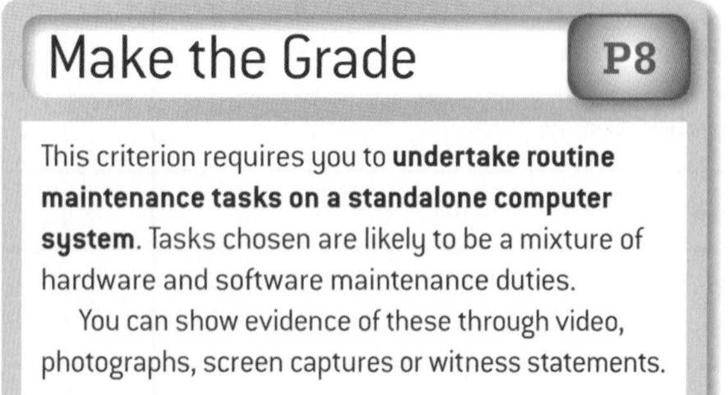

Make the Grade P8

This criterion requires you to **undertake routine maintenance tasks on a standalone computer system**. Tasks chosen are likely to be a mixture of hardware and software maintenance duties.

You can show evidence of these through video, photographs, screen captures or witness statements.

Maintenance can generally be broken down into hardware and software maintenance.

Software maintenance

Here are some of the most common software maintenance tasks for an IT professional:

- **Upgrade software**: Software often has to be upgraded to fix identified bugs, improve performance or add new functionality. An example of this would be updating **virus definition files (virus signatures)** on an antivirus suite (Figure 2.74).
- **Backup procedures**: Most operating systems have built-in backup utilities that will copy programs and data (or specific folders as required) to either another hard drive, a remote network drive or off-line backing storage such as CD or DVD.

  Microsoft Windows® has a **Backup and Restore Center** (accessed from the Control Panel) which will lead the technician through the steps necessary to backup and restore specific files to selected backing storage options (Figure 2.75).
- Scheduling maintenance tasks: The majority of operating systems have automatic scheduling facilities. Although the mechanics of these differ between operating systems, Figure 2.76 shows three basic aspects.

A typical example of this is to run an antivirus scan **(Action)** when the computer system has been idle for more than 30 minutes **(Condition)** every week **(Trigger=regular schedule)**.

Scheduled tasks (Figure 2.77) could include such operations as:

- backup of user data (archiving);
- deletion of unwanted data;
- deletion of temporary files;
- run antivirus or spyware scan or update their definitions;
- disk defragmentation;
- checking for new versions of software or patches.

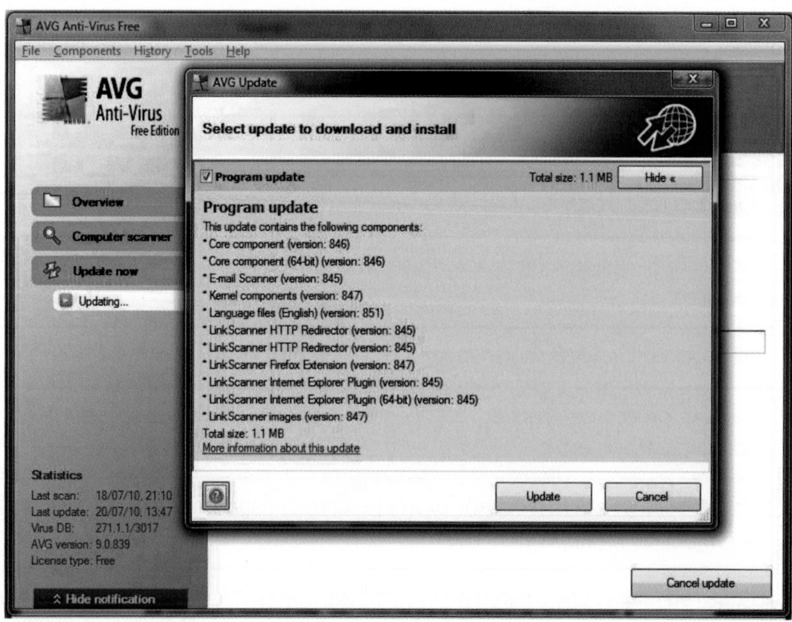

Figure 2.74 AVG update option for virus definition files

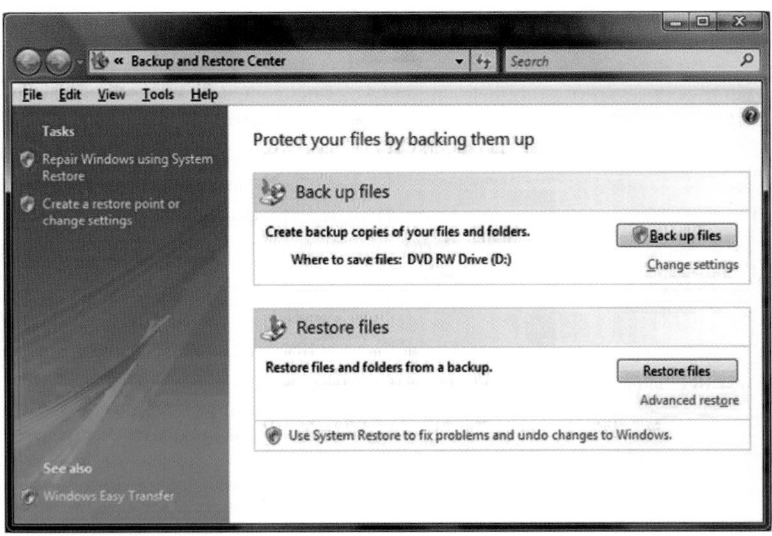

Figure 2.75 Microsoft Windows® Backup and Restore Center

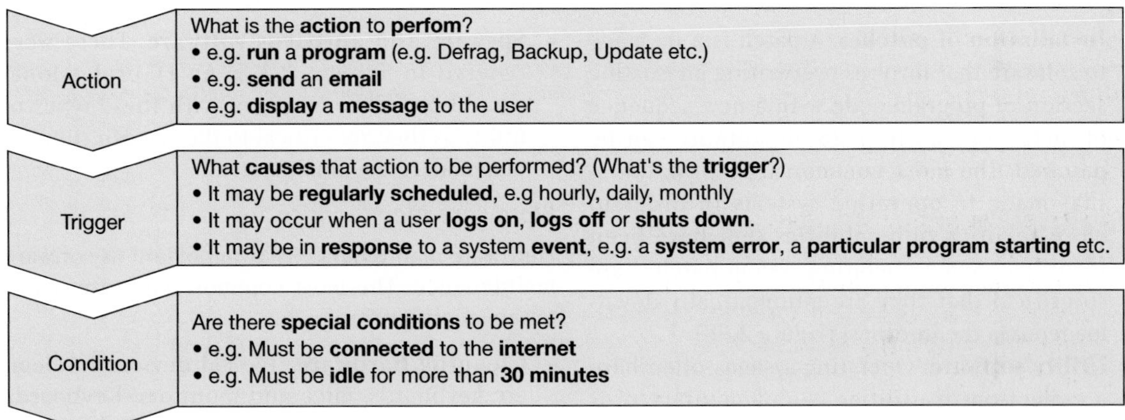

Figure 2.76 Scheduling maintenance tasks

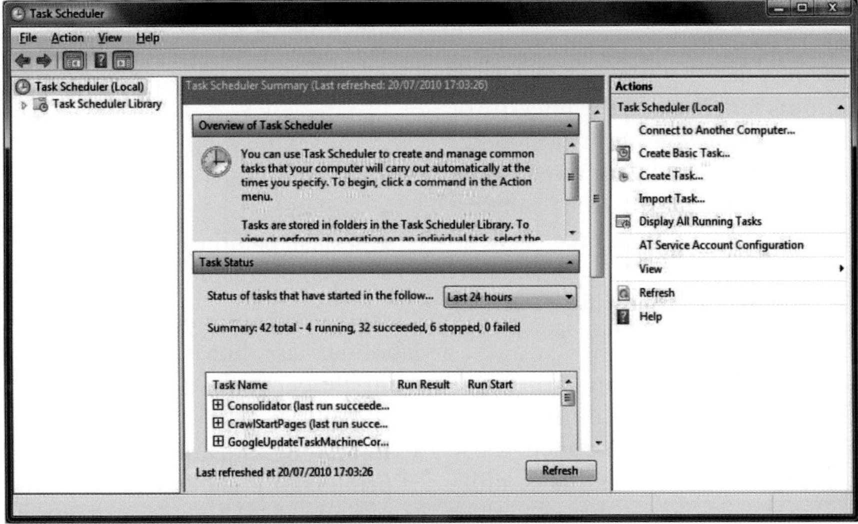

Figure 2.77 Scheduling maintenance tasks in Windows Vista®

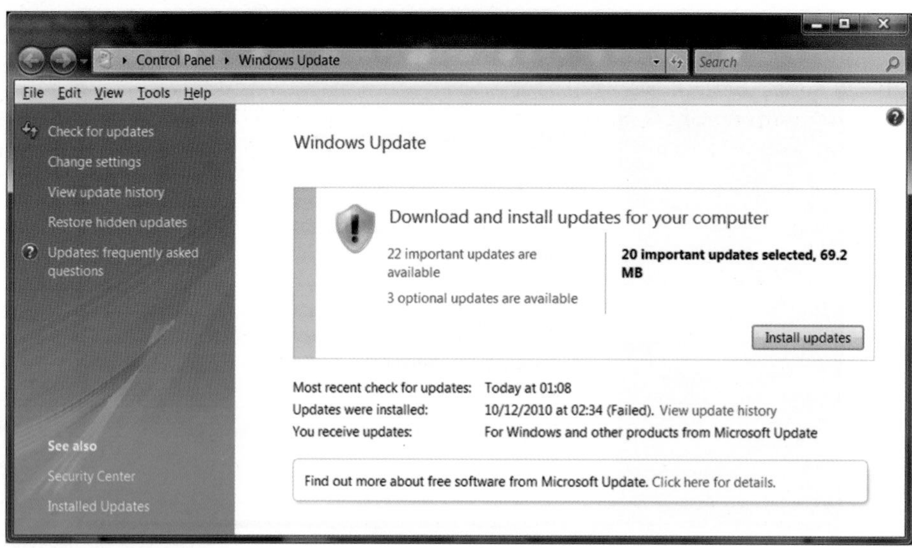

Figure 2.78 Updates for Microsoft Windows Vista® related products

- **Installation of patches**: A patch is a fix made to software that involves overwriting an existing section of program code with a new sequence of instructions. Although all software can be patched, the most common type of patch is that made to operating systems in order to close security vulnerabilities that have been identified. Some operating system patches are so critical that they are automatically downloaded (via the internet) (Figure 2.78).
- **Utility software**: Operating systems often have a collection of utilities (supplementary programs designed to carry out a specific function, usually performing regular housekeeping tasks). Common utilities include:
  - **defragmentation tools**;
  - **disk clean-up tools** for getting rid of unnecessary temporary files that may accumulate;
  - **disk scan tools** for checking the integrity of backing storage and fixing any errors found;
  - **system profiler** for creating an inventory of hardware components and installed software – system profilers are often in organisations for auditing software licences and calculating the **T**otal **C**ost of **O**wnership (**TCO**) of current IT systems.
- **Compression utilities**: Most operating systems support compression, but utilities such as WinZip® and WinRar® are also popular. Most third-party compression utilities have additional options that make the process much less time consuming.
- **Spyware and antivirus software**: These were covered in Section 2.1.5. An IT professional should be fully conversant with these types of utility as they are critical to the smooth running of a modern computer system.

Hardware maintenance

Hardware maintenance is as important as software maintenance. The most common hardware maintenance jobs are:

- **Cleaning hardware**: Typical devices to clean are keyboards, mice and monitors. Keyboards and mice get especially dirty (and unhygienic) after prolonged use and screen displays can easily be smeared by fingerprints. Exhaust vents (used for cooling) should be blasted with compressed air to displace dust, which may clog up fans and cause systems to overheat. Standard tools for this type of maintenance include:
  - dry cloth or duster;
  - recommended cleaning fluid;
  - cotton buds;
  - a small paintbrush;
  - a can of compressed air or a vacuum cleaner.

Cleaning computer equipment is often seen as a laborious task, but is important to extend equipment lifespan and contribute to good standards of health and safety.

- **Replacing consumables**: Peripherals, such as printers, use materials that need replacement periodically. These are collectively called consumables. Common **consumables** include paper, ink or toner cartridges. Always refer to the manufacturer's documentation to correctly replace consumables in order to prevent damage to the equipment. Some printers require calibration after consumables have been replaced (for example, to align printer heads in order to assure good-quality printing). In addition, some ink and toner cartridges can be reused and refilled in order to keep costs down and help to lessen environmental concerns.

Unit Links

Unit 2 is a **Mandatory** unit for all qualifications and pathways of this Level 3 IT family.

Qualification (pathway)	Mandatory	Optional	Specialist optional
Edexcel BTEC Level 3 National Certificate in Information Technology	✓		
Edexcel BTEC Level 3 National Subsidiary Diploma in Information Technology	✓		
Edexcel BTEC Level 3 National Diploma in Information Technology	✓		
Edexcel BTEC Level 3 National Extended Diploma in Information Technology	✓		
Edexcel BTEC Level 3 National Diploma in IT (Business)	✓		
Edexcel BTEC Level 3 National Extended Diploma in IT (Business)	✓		
Edexcel BTEC Level 3 National Diploma in IT (Networking and System Support)	✓		
Edexcel BTEC Level 3 National Extended Diploma in IT (Networking and System Support)	✓		
Edexcel BTEC Level 3 National Diploma in IT (Software Development)	✓		
Edexcel BTEC Level 3 National Extended Diploma in IT (Software Development)	✓		

There are specific links to the following units in the scheme:
Unit 9 – Computer networks
Unit 25 – Maintaining computer systems

Achieving success

This particular unit has 13 criteria to meet: 8 Pass, 3 Merit and 2 Distinction.

For a Pass: You must achieve all 8 Pass criteria.

For a Merit: You must achieve all 8 Pass and all 3 Merit criteria.

For a Distinction: You must achieve all 8 Pass, all 3 Merit and both Distinction criteria.

Further reading

Anderson, H. and Yull, S. – *BTEC Nationals IT Practitioners: Core Units for Computing and IT* (Newnes, 2002) ISBN-10 0750656840, ISBN-13 978-0750656849

Knott, G. and Waites, N. – *BTEC Nationals for IT Practitioners* (Brancepeth Computer Publications, 2002) ISBN-10 0953884821, ISBN-13 978-0953884827

Fulton, J. – *Complete Idiot's Guide to Upgrading and Repairing PCs, 4th edition* (Alpha, 1999) ISBN-10 0789722062, ISBN-13 978-0789722065

White, R. and Downs, T. – *How Computers Work, 9th edition* (Que, 2007) ISBN-10 0789736136, ISBN-13 978-0789736130

By the end of this unit you should be able to:

1. Understand how organisations use business information
2. Understand the issues related to the use of information
3. Know the features and functions of information systems
4. Be able to use IT tools to produce management information

Whether you are in school or college, passing this unit will involve being assessed. As with most BTEC schemes, the successful completion of various assessment criteria demonstrates your evidence of learning and the skills you have developed.

This unit has a mixture of pass, merit and distinction criteria. Generally you will find that merit and distinction criteria require a little more thought and evaluation before they can be completed.

The colour-coded grid below shows you the pass, merit and distinction criteria for this unit.

To achieve a pass grade you need to:	To achieve a merit grade you also need to:	To achieve a distinction grade you also need to:
P1 Explain how organisations use information	**M1** Illustrate the information flow between different functional areas	**D1** Explain how an organisation could improve the quality of its business information
P2 Discuss the characteristics of good information		
P3 Explain the issues related to the use of information	**M2** Assess how issues related to the use of information affect an organisation	
P4 Describe the features and functions of information systems		
P5 Identify the information systems used in a specified organisation		
P6 Select information to support a business decision-making process		**D2** Justify the information selected to support a business decision-making process
P7 Use IT tools to produce management information	**M3** Generate valid, accurate and useful information	

Introduction

Information systems is a 10-credit unit that helps you to develop an understanding of how computers and information technologies are used within business.

You will be introduced to the concepts of business information and you will learn how information is generated through business activities and how it is drawn in from external sources so that it can be used to support the activities of organisations.

Being able to produce business information within defined constraints is another essential skill that will be assessed through this unit.

How to read this chapter

This chapter is organised to match the content of the BTEC unit it represents. The following diagram shows the grading criteria that relate to each learning outcome.

You'll find colour-matching notes in each chapter about completing each grading criterion.

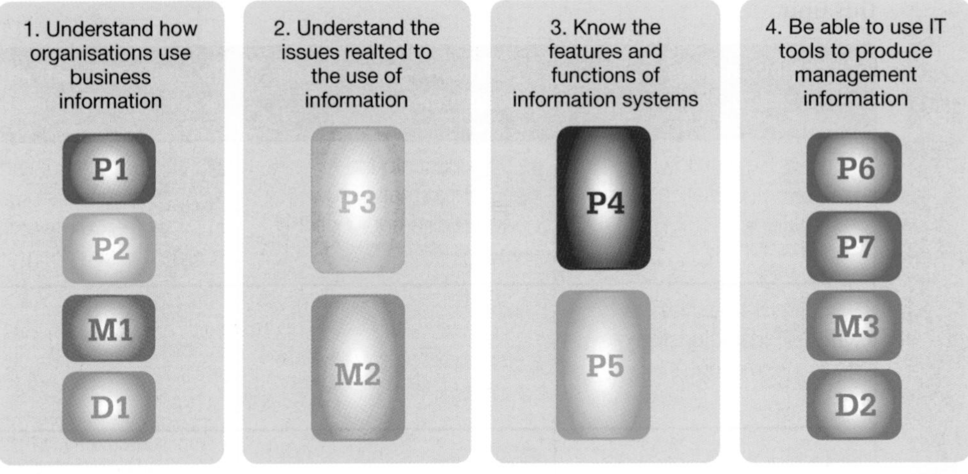

Figure 3.00

3.1 Understand how organisations use business information

This section will cover the following grading criterion:

P1

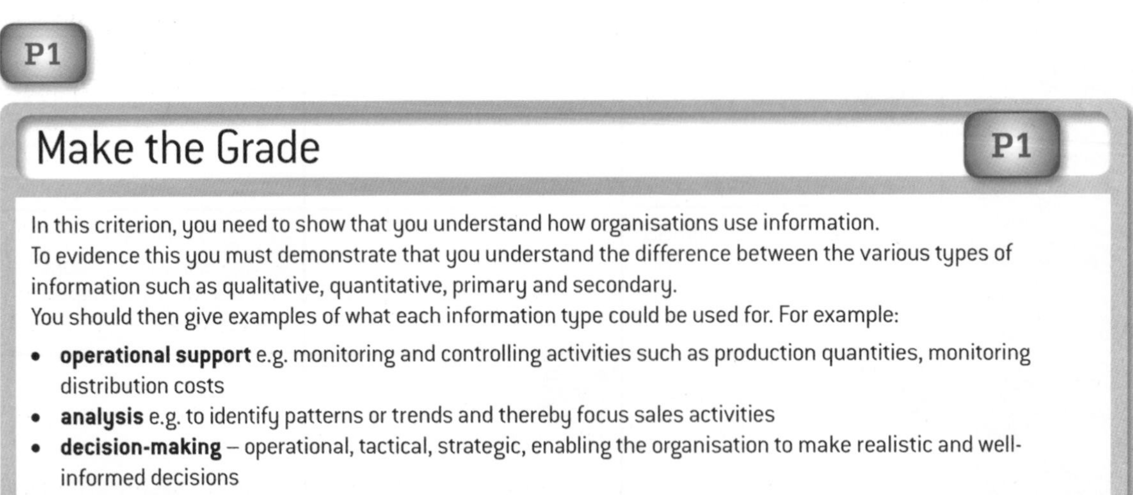

Make the Grade

P1

In this criterion, you need to show that you understand how organisations use information.
To evidence this you must demonstrate that you understand the difference between the various types of information such as qualitative, quantitative, primary and secondary.
You should then give examples of what each information type could be used for. For example:

- **operational support** e.g. monitoring and controlling activities such as production quantities, monitoring distribution costs
- **analysis** e.g. to identify patterns or trends and thereby focus sales activities
- **decision-making** – operational, tactical, strategic, enabling the organisation to make realistic and well-informed decisions
- using competitor information to gain commercial advantage .

When considering this type of topic it is sometimes useful to begin with a series of definitions.

Key terms

Data is raw facts and/or figures that have not yet been processed, manipulated or interpreted into useful information, such as times, weights, measurements, sales.

Information is data that has been manipulated into something meaningful and usable, such as TV listings, bus timetables, top 40 singles download chart.

3.1.1 Types of information

Key terms

Qualitative data – Involves data/information that cannot be measured in the usual way. As such, it is usually in some sort of narrative form (spoken or written). An example might be 'customers generally feel product X represents good value for money'.

Quantitative data – Data or information that can be measured numerically and can be proven as fact. For example, the girls' height information included previously would be an example of quantitative data – each girl's height would have been measured to provide the actual figure. If we take the qualitative data example and revise it to be an example of quantitative data, we would say '76 per cent of customers said that they believed product X to be good value for money'. In this instance, the percentage can be proven (assuming that the raw data were available).

Primary data – Data that you (or your organisation) gathers and interprets itself, such as a survey amongst your customers about the quality of service your organisation offers.

Secondary data – Data that is collected and then passed to another organisation for interpretation (for example in a comparison of customer satisfaction for a number of organisations offering the same type of service).

3.1.2 Purposes of information

It is essential that organisations have access to business information in order for them to be able to function. This section discusses some of the ways in which information can be used to sustain ongoing business activities.

Operational support (e.g. monitoring and controlling activity)

To support its daily activities, all organisations need to have access to information. Operational information can be divided into two sub-categories: **monitoring** and **controlling.**

The types of information that an organisation will use in order to help it monitor its activities could include:

- how much stock of each product it has to sell;
- how many hours overtime were needed to complete a particular order.

Control information is much more obvious, and may well include:

- production schedules (what the organisation will be making today)
- what deliveries need to be made.

Without the records of day-to-day activities, organisations will find it very difficult to function normally. An organisation needs to constantly monitor its own performance and control its activities so that precious resources are not wasted.

Analysis (e.g. to identify patterns or trends)

To be effective, managers must understand their own data. They must be able to look at tables or charts of performance data and be able to explain any **anomalous** values (these are values that are unusual and not expected). Take Figure 3.01 as an example (note that the lowest value is 200, not zero, so that the lines are better emphasised).

It is clear that there is something unusual about August, where widget production has been repetitively low. The production manager would probably be able to explain this with relative ease because it is a recurring event. The possible explanations are:

a) Significant staff are on annual leave and so production is affected.

b) The company always closes down for two weeks in August, so no widgets are produced.

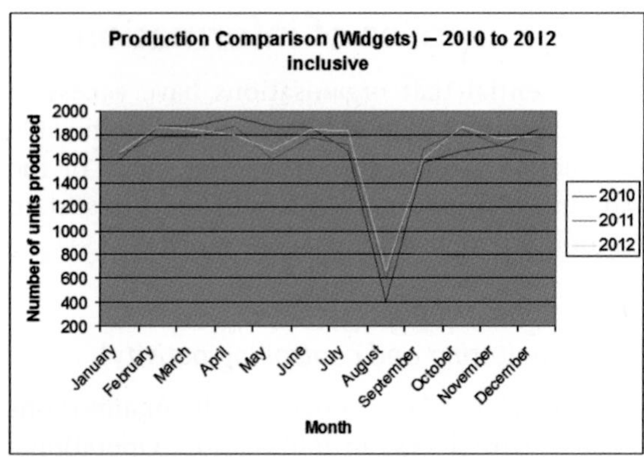

Figure 3.01 Trend analysis with a predictable event

Compare these results with those in Figure 3.02.

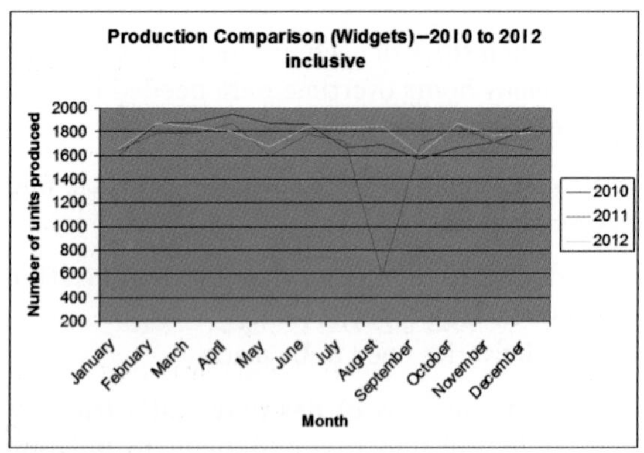

Figure 3.02 Trend analysis with an exceptional event

In this case the production figure only dropped in 2011, and was more or less normal in August 2010 and August 2012. Now the event is even more puzzling. What could have happened in August 2011? Here are some possible explanations:

a) The organisation was let down by its suppliers and did not have the raw materials to produce the widgets.

b) There were major problems with machinery – significant breakdowns caused a delay in production.

c) There were major problems with machinery – the organisation couldn't get spares when one of the primary machines developed a fault and needed a new part.

Clearly there will be other possible explanations.

What should be noted here is that the data has been presented visually as a chart. Here is the raw data on which the chart was based:

	2010	2011	2012
January	1601	1636	1654
February	1872	1784	1871
March	1877	1789	1843
April	1952	1871	1799
May	1874	1598	1671
June	1863	1774	1844
July	1667	1721	1838
August	1694	587	1844
September	1572	1686	1610
October	1662	1845	1872
November	1711	1706	1766
December	1842	1648	1791

Would it have been quite as easy to identify the anomaly if the data had been presented in this way? Probably not, other than the fact that the number 587 has only three figures and the rest of the numbers have four! What would have happened if the anomaly had been 1001? It wouldn't have stood out!

Analysing data is a complex subject area, and people who do this type of work have traditionally had to be highly trained. Today, however, software is available that can monitor your data and can flag unusual events (known as **exception reporting**) as and when they occur. This has made it much easier for organisations to monitor their activities.

Decision making (operational, tactical, strategic)

Information gained from the organisation's usual activities, together with information that can be **projected** (estimated, based on previous trends), will be used to help the organisation make decisions. Each type of decision has different characteristics, which will be explained here:

Operational decisions – These are decisions about the establishment's activities now and within the next 6 to 12 months. For example:

1. A number of production employees are off sick – what do you do in the short term to ensure that production is not affected?
2. What raw materials will we need today?

3. Can we organise ourselves differently and speed up operations?

To enable them to make these decisions, organisations need the following sorts of information:

1. Who has called in sick today, and how long are they likely to be away from work?
2. What is going to be produced today (we will assume that the raw material stock was checked a few days prior to today) and do we have assurance that the raw materials have been moved to the production area?
3. A floor plan and production flow information (looking at how the goods move through the production line).

Tactical decisions – These are decisions about what will happen within the organisation in the next five years or so. These decisions are often informed by market research, to ensure that the company remains safe in the medium term. For example:

1. Are there any new products that we should be making?
2. Are there any existing products that we should stop making?
3. Do we need to make any capital investment to meet the organisation's longer-term strategy?
4. Does our workforce need any training to enable us to meet our longer-term goals?

To enable them to make these decisions, they need the following sorts of information:

1. Information about what competitors are making. Information about what customers' changing wants are.
2. Stock information on existing products and information about stock movement (if the stock is not moving, then it is not selling, in which case it might well be selected as a product that should be discontinued).
3. What our current capital reserves are. If there is insufficient finance available, should we be taking out a business loan to finance future strategies?
4. What training does our workforce have? Will this training be sufficient and suitable to enable us to meet our mid-term goals, or do we need to have some staff trained? What training courses are available?

Strategic decisions – These are decisions that have a long time frame and require organisations to look well into the future (in excess of about five years). For example:

1. Should we expand?
2. Should we buy larger premises?
3. How should the organisation be structured?

To enable them to make these decisions, they need the following sorts of information:

1. Estimates of how our organisation will develop over the next five to ten years.
2. The costs of larger premises, including the anticipated overheads on such a property (such as council tax, average heating and lighting costs), so that they can be compared with current expenditure on these items.
3. The current organisational structure should be identified and written down, so that managers can discuss whether changes in the hierarchy could be achieved and how they see these changes being implemented.

Clearly in all three cases the list is not extensive, or definitive, but the lists are representative of the types of decisions that the management of organisations need to make at various points. They should give you a flavour of business decision-making issues.

Gaining commercial advantage

Clearly it is in an organisation's interests to find ways of gaining an advantage over its competitors. To this end, those individuals working for the company who have marketing responsibilities will be closely monitoring what competitors are doing. They will be watching pricing strategies, looking at what products competitors are offering for sale, and what they have withdrawn. They can gain operational information about companies by looking at a competitor's accounts. This is only possible if the company is a **PLC** or **Public Limited Company** (a company whose shares are offered for general sale on the stock exchange) or a **Limited Company** (one owned by shareholders but not floated on the stock exchange, where shareholders are usually invited to purchase shares as an investment in the organisation's future). These types of companies have to register their operational accounts at the end of each financial year with Companies House. These can be accessed by any individual who is interested.

Charities also publish their accounts, to assure the public that the monies they donate are being used properly for the purpose for which they were intended.

Clearly the growth of information technology has given many companies information at their fingertips that they might have struggled to gather and interpret five years ago. However, as a note of caution, organisations must remember that while they can now gain information about the competitors more easily, their competitors can equally gain information more easily about their organisation too!

Case Study

Paul Lee, the Chief Executive of Lee Business Supplies, has been on holiday for a few weeks and he has returned to discover that a number of decisions need to be made. Clearly the company has been busy in his absence!

Paul has given you a list of problems and issues and asked you to prioritise them for him. To do this, you have been asked to identify whether these problems or issues are **operational** (require immediate resolution), **tactical** (could wait, but need to be done relatively soon) or **strategic** (need to be done in the longer term).

B Braincheck 1

Complete the following grid. In each case, say whether the issue is operational, strategic or tactical.

Number	Issue or problem	Operational? Strategic? Tactical?
1	One of your managers has heard that a competitor is dropping prices on his main stock items next month.	
2	You seem to have a large amount of stock of product X that doesn't appear to be selling very well. Should you continue to stock the product or consider deleting it?	
3	Most of the staff from the distribution area (primarily drivers) have called in sick with stomach upsets (suspected food poisoning). Out of a team of six staff, only two people are in.	
4	Our vehicle fleet is old and in need of significant investment. Do we want to replace the vehicles or maybe outsource this part of the organisation to a courier?	
5	A supplier was not paid at the end of last month and is refusing to provide any more stock.	
6	A supplier has told you that he will be bringing out a whole new range of business products in about 18 months time and has asked you whether you think your customers might be interested.	
7	The distribution manager has said that we are increasingly running out of storage space in the warehouse. As there is no opportunity for physical expansion at our current premises, should we consider moving operations elsewhere?	

How well did you do? See the supporting website for answers.

3.1.3 Sources of information

Organisations have a range of information sources at their disposal. This section explores some of these.

Internal information (e.g. finance, personnel, marketing, purchasing, sales, manufacturing, administration)

Internal information is information that is generated through the normal business activities of an organisation. This information tends to be generated by a specific **functional area** within the organisation, but can often be used by more than one other business function. This list of functional areas of an organisation is not exhaustive, and in some companies these functional areas might have different titles.

Finance

This area of an organisation deals with all aspects of the company's monetary activities. It will include the **accounting** department, which is responsible for recording activities such as purchase invoices and sales invoices, monitoring **debtors** (those to whom the organisation owes money) and **creditors** (those who owe the organisation money), and handling VAT payments. Based on the activities of this area, other departments will be given **working budgets** (amounts of money that the managers of functional areas can use as they see fit, to support their own area of the organisation).

The **payroll** functional area is responsible for administrating the salaries (money usually paid monthly) and wages (money usually paid weekly) of all employees. Payroll will calculate how much is to be paid, it will make deductions for tax, NI (National Insurance) and pension contributions, and will pay these amounts to the Inland Revenue when required to do so.

Both of the areas defined within the **financial** operating area will be using information generated by other departments, and will be providing information to those departments in return.

Internal information inside this function will include:

- invoices
- lists of debtors and creditors
- VAT returns
- purchase and sales ledgers
- budgetary information
- wage records
- National Insurance and tax contribution information
- Inland Revenue returns.

Personnel

The **personnel** function of an organisation is concerned with the general recruitment and selection of employees. The personnel department will help managers to write job specifications, organise interviews, generate letters offering employment and ultimately administrate the records of employees while they remain in service. This is usually a reactive function, which jumps into action when a department's needs have been identified (for example, when someone has resigned).

The **HR (human resource**) functional part of this area is concerned with helping the organisation to plan its people needs. Usually proactive (involved in planning and in the decision-making process), HR managers assist the organisation at a strategic level, defining recruitment strategies to meet the organisation's long-term goals, or suggesting training schemes for existing employees (whichever is more cost effective and appropriate).

Internal information inside these functions will include:

- job specifications
- interview lists
- training records
- sickness and holiday records
- disciplinary records.

Marketing

As with finance and personnel, the marketing function also has two strands: **marketing** and **advertising**. The terms are often used interchangeably, but in actual fact, the roles are very different!

The marketing function of an organisation is responsible for devising a strategy to make customers aware of an organisation and its products. It is about researching the market (gathering information about potential customers and their buying habits) and planning how and when to advertise. In some cases, marketing executives will get involved with product design as they may well have information about what features customers want from products.

Advertising is more about the physical promotion of the service or product. Specialists in this field will design the posters, leaflets, radio jingles and so on. That will help to bring the product or service into the public arena. They will find the best deals to get the most exposure for the company's money, may organise slots on TV or radio, could purchase newspaper or magazine space, and may well find distributors for the leaflets and posters.

In a nutshell, marketing is about planning and strategy, advertising is about doing.

Internal information inside this function will include:

- market research information
- strategic plans
- advertising costs and comparisons.

Purchasing

The **purchasing** department is responsible for buying goods and services on behalf of the whole organisation. For example, the purchasing staff will find the best deals on raw materials used in production, they will negotiate contracts with distributors (such as couriers) and they will monitor their buying strategies to ensure that they always buy at the best price. This might mean that the company will need to buy materials in bulk (more than they require to reduce the price), or that there is an opportunity for a composite purchasing strategy (where making up a large combined order for a number of products will bring down the price of the individual items because costs such as transportation can be reduced).

Where appropriate, the purchasing department will raise purchase orders and, in liaison with the relevant departments, will set delivery deadlines for suppliers.

Internal information inside this function will include:

- purchase orders
- manufacturing schedules
- composite or bulk deal information.

Sales and customer services

It is important to be aware that not all organisations have a **sales** department. Some have **customer services** instead, while other companies may have both!

The sales function is usually the face of the organisation and is made up of individuals with excellent product knowledge and a good understanding of customers and their needs. Sometimes this face is actually a voice, as increasing numbers of companies are investing in **telesales** staff. These staff usually make first contact with prospective customers, which is often followed up by a sales representative.

The function of the sales team is to secure actual business, selling the organisation's products and services to customers. In addition, they are responsible for expanding the organisation's existing customer base.

Institutions such as the NHS (National Health Service) don't have a sales function in the traditional sense. This is because customers (as patients) tend to come directly to them. However, the individual parts of the NHS will want to know what their customers think about the services they provide, and, to fulfil this role, they have a customer services function. Staff in this area will handle enquiries, offer advice and deal with any complaints or criticisms that are made of the service.

Internal information inside this function will include:

- product lists, price lists and brochures
- customer questionnaires
- sales targets.

Manufacturing (also known as the production department)

Only companies that make a product will have a **manufacturing** department. Manufacturing, by definition, is a function that changes raw materials into products, which might be used in the manufacture of other products or into customer-ready finished goods.

Internal information inside this function will include:

- product plans/recipes/designs
- production schedules
- staff rotas (particularly important if the organisation operates a 24/7 manufacturing operation)
- machine maintenance records
- production records (including batch numbering information where relevant).

Distribution (also known as the dispatch department)

The **distribution** function of an organisation is responsible for ensuring that the products and services supplied by the company get to its customers when intended. They will organise the physical transport, whether this is using the company's own vehicles or using transport companies or courier services. They will also take responsibility for any export issues that may arise if goods are to be sent overseas.

Internal information inside this function will include:

- any hazard information that will affect either the transportation or handling of the products
- emergency details for alternative transport should any issues arise that prevent the company working in the usual way.

It is not unusual for the **stock** or **warehouse** functions to be included under the distribution umbrella. Whether the items that need to be distributed have been manufactured by the organisation or have been purchased by the organisation for resale, they will need to be stored prior to dispatch. Goods are then removed as and when sold, and delivery notes are raised to accompany the goods to their destination. These delivery notes are often then used by companies to generate invoices. However, sometimes goods are sold **COD (Cash on Delivery)**, which means that the customer has to pay for the goods when they are delivered.

Administration

Considering **administration** as a discrete function can be a bit misleading. In some organisations, administration is undertaken by clerical staff who work within each functional area (purchasing clerks or sales clerks for example). In other organisations the administration activity is more **centralised**, where the clerks will undertake any administration tasks, as and when required. In this situation, whoever is free will undertake the task. Sometimes this functional area will also have responsibility for the company's estate (buildings,

B Braincheck 2

Match the departments to their key functions.

Letter	Department	Number	Functions
A	Purchasing	1	Recruitment and selection of employees
B	HR (Human Resources)	2	Recording business activities, monitoring debtors and creditors
C	Manufacturing or Production	3	Making contact with customers and presenting the company's portfolio of products and services
D	Marketing	4	Physical promotion of goods and services with campaigns
E	Distribution	5	Developing new products and improving current ones
F	Finance	6	Handling enquiries, offering advice and support, and dealing with complaints
G	Sales	7	Buying goods and services from suppliers and negotiating contracts for stock or materials
H	Research and Development	8	Ensuring products and services get to customers
I	Personnel	9	Making the products that the company will sell
J	Customer Services	10	Planning the use of staff
K	Advertising	11	Strategic planning based on market research; product re-design

How well did you do? See the supporting website for answers.

car parking arrangements, security). It will depend very much on the individual organisation as to what the administration function will do.

Research and development

Where organisations work with physical products, they may very well have a **research and development** department, whose job it is to develop new products and find enhancements for existing ones. Working with customer feedback, the staff in this area will try to estimate what we, as consumers, will want to buy in the future. For obvious reasons, this functional area will work very closely with the marketing and sales departments in trying to establish what customers may want in the future.

Internal information inside this function will include:

- strategic plans
- product design information
- customer feedback.

Ultimately, as suggested much earlier in this unit, it is likely that most departments will share information, or will generate information that must be passed between them to support the activities of the business. Some of the information will need to be sent outside the organisation, while other information from outside will need to be brought in.

External information (e.g. government, trade groupings, commercially provided, databases, research)

Most organisations also interact with external agencies (those outside the company), receiving and providing information as required. Some of these external organisations are investigated here.

Government

All companies, whether they are limited companies, partnerships, sole traders or charities, must pass information to the Government. Equally, some information will be passed into the company.

The organisation must supply the following:

- VAT information
- tax and National Insurance information about amounts deducted from employees
- pensions information
- information about the company's turnover (for company tax purposes, as companies are taxed as well as their employees).

The organisation must receive and respond to the following:

- legislation
- gathering and paying of VAT (Value Added Tax).

Trade groupings

Some industrial and service sectors have **trade groupings**. These groupings are usually made up of companies operating in the same sector, which come together to raise standards, set prices and develop policies.

An extreme example of a trade grouping is OPEC (Organisation of the Petroleum Exporting Countries). Formed in 1960, OPEC was intended to make the petrol companies fairer in their dealings with the oil-consuming countries. This was partly because there are countries in the world that do not have oil resources, but who need the oil and petroleum products to fuel their cars and other associated services. OPEC was designed to ensure that the oil-rich nations would not treat oil-poor nations unfavourably, charging them high prices because they did not have any alternatives.

More recent developments have seen the creation of OFID (OPEC Fund for International Development), an OPEC-led organisation that is investing some of OPEC's revenues in health and social concerns across the world.

Commercially provided

If an organisation isn't able to generate its own information (for example, customer feedback on its products), it may well need to buy in such information from outside agencies. There are agencies, for example, who gather information and sell it to anyone who wants to purchase it. Other agencies are specialists and will help an organisation to secure the information by helping them to devise a data gathering and analysis strategy. Of course, this is done for a fee.

Databases

It is well known that information about us is stored by many organisations and institutions for various purposes. In order to store such data, these organisations need to comply with the legislation set out in the Data Protection Act 1998 and the Freedom of Information Act 2000 (both of which will be covered later in this unit).

There was a time, however, when it was not uncommon for one organisation to sell its customer list to another organisation that was not in direct competition. For example, a sports company could sell its customer list to a CD outlet. While this does still happen, many organisations are more reluctant to pass this information on, particularly because in some cases, there has been negative feedback from customers about organisations that have done so.

Research

In the process of carrying out research on a particular subject, other information may come to light that is not necessarily relevant to the original research aims. In such cases, this data may be sold on to other organisations that might find it useful, thereby recovering some of the cost for the originator of the research.

Reliability of data sources

Data users need to be confident about the sources of the data they use. Clearly, if information is gathered within the organisation, then it is reasonable to consider this data reliable. The reliability of data obtained from external sources is more uncertain, although books are more likely to be reliable than some other published sources. The internet is very difficult to monitor and police and there is potentially a huge amount of unreliable information. Did you know, for example, that Wikipedia entries can be made by anyone and that no one checks these entries for accuracy? As a result, erroneous entries can easily be added to the service.

To ensure that data and information obtained from the internet is reliable:

1. Check the information against a number of websites.
2. Try to use well-established, reliable websites.

3.1.4 Good information

This section will cover the following grading criterion:

Make the Grade P2

For P2 you will need to discuss the characteristics of good information such as the need to present information in a logical sequence, to ensure the information is accurate, comes from reliable sources, is available when needed, is valid and is of the right level of detail.

Your tutor might choose to evidence this through a fact sheet or leaflet, possibly supported by a poster.

Characteristics

Information is clearly of little use or value unless it is fit for the purpose for which it was intended. Below are some of the characteristics that good information has.

Validity

Data being **valid** is the most fundamental characteristic of good data/information. This means that the data must be completely accurate. It is the responsibility of the data or information gatherer to make sure that all aspects of the information are correct. This means that the information should have been properly checked before being used.

Reliability

The worst situation when using information or data would be to find out after you had finished using it that the data was not **reliable**.

Firstly, the data should have come from a source that you feel you can trust. In general you should feel that you can trust books and publications, as these will largely have been checked for you. This would also apply to organisational websites. However, there are likely to be some websites that would not be considered reliable. This is because the website originator might not be keeping the data and information on the website updated. He or she might not have fully checked the validity of the data or information when it was put on the website, and ultimately, no one has queried it.

Another way to check that information is reliable is to check the data a number of times, ensuring that the result is the same. An example is given below.

Three salesmen work in the same geographical area. Their monthly sales have been worked out and then both a computer and a calculator have been used to find the average monthly total. The results are given in Table 3.01.

Table 3.01

	January	February	March
Chris	1653.25	1958.47	1744.23
Matthew	1954.77	1362.38	1659.48
John	1083.42	1124.61	1367.14
Average (calculated by computer)	1563.81	1481.82	1590.28
Average (calculated with calculator)	1563.81	1481.82	1590.28

According to the computer, the average for January is 1563.81. The calculator also averages the result at 1563.81. Having used the calculator to check the result, we can now consider the result as reliable. It has been checked using alternative means, and if the calculation was done again and again using the same data, the result would still be the same. As such, we can say that the data is reliable.

Timeliness

The concept of **timely** information is a simple one. Timely information is information that was prepared and ready at the point where it needed to be used. In most organisations, managers hold regular meetings where information is checked and shared with other managers. As an example, we will use the idea of a quarterly sales meeting. The first meeting for this year will be on 15 April 2010. At this meeting all the sales statistics and corresponding information for the months of January to March 2010 (inclusive) will be discussed. If the information is ready for use at the 15 April meeting, the information will be said to have been timely. If, however, only information for January and February has been prepared, then clearly the meeting will not have had the intended opportunities for discussion, because the purpose of that meeting on 15 April was to discuss *all* sales information for the first three months of the year.

Fitness-for-purpose

In order to establish whether information is **fit-for-purpose**, we first need to set criteria against which this can be measured! These criteria will obviously vary from situation to situation, but here are some generalisations:

Figure 3.03 has been created using the same sales data as provided earlier in this chapter.

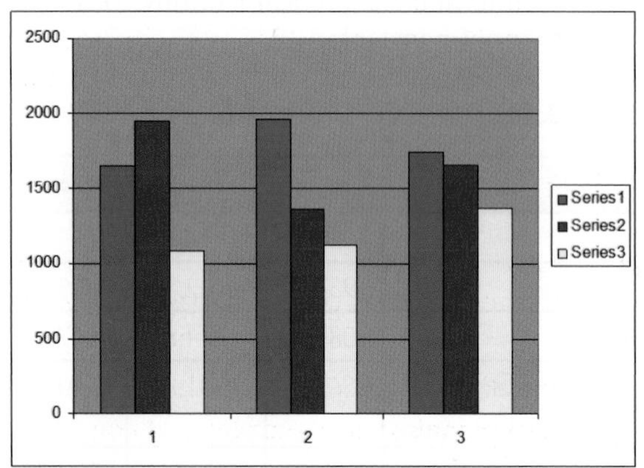

Figure 3.03 Sales performance chart

We are now going to ask the question 'how fit-for-purpose is this'? Firstly we need to decide what the chart is trying to display.

The chart is intended to show graphically sales performance for the months from January to March 2010, inclusive.

If you look at this chart, can you get the required information? No!

So what is wrong with the above chart?

- The chart has no title.
- The X-axis has no title.
- The Y-axis has no title and has a scale top value that is unnecessary (the figures do not go above 2000, so why have a top value of 2500?).
- The columns cannot be identified (e.g. you cannot identify which column reflects the sales of which representative).
- Although there is a legend (a key to the different column colours), it doesn't provide any useful information!
- The chart needs to be modified to make it fit-for-purpose. Figure 3.04 shows the modified version. Is it better?

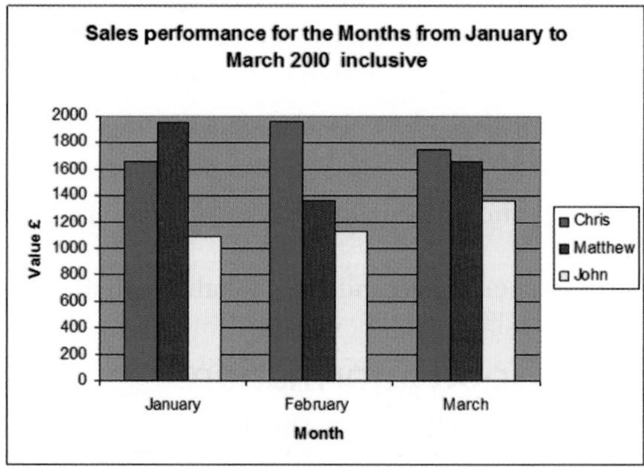

Figure 3.04 Annotated sales performance chart

The second version of the column chart is clearly much more usable than the first attempt.

Key terms

Sometimes learners find it difficult to remember which is the X-axis and which is the Y-axis on a chart. The easiest way to remember is to say X is '**a cross**', or **across**.

By a process of elimination, that would mean that the Y-axis must be 'down'.

Table 3.02

Category	Amount 2007	Amount 2008	Amount 2009
Average weekly commission based on average sales	260.1	295.875	304.8756
Average sales per week	5600.34	6780.34	2002.25
Weekly commission as percentage of sales	0.046443609	0.043637192	0.025401537

Table 3.03

Category	Amount 2007	Amount 2008	Amount 2009
Average weekly commission based on average sales	£260.10	£295.88	£304.88
Average sales per week	£5,600.34	£6,780.34	£2,002.25
Weekly commission as percentage of sales	5%	4%	3%

Table 3.02 shows an example from KAM (Kris Arts & Media) Limited that is intending to show their agent's sales commission based on recorded sales.

In this instance, there are various numbers that are accurate, but are difficult to read because of the way they have been formatted. Table 3.03 shows an improved version.

This should now be easier to read. The currency figures have been formatted to two decimal places, which forces the decimal points to align. In addition, rather than just stating that the weekly commission is being represented as a 'percentage of sales', the figure has been formatted as a percentage.

In Table 3.03 it is easier to see that the weekly commission has reduced significantly over the last three years. Should KAM's agents be worried?

Table 3.03 would be considered fit-for-purpose, depending on the importance of some of the other criteria in this section (such as having the right level of detail or sufficient accuracy) which follow.

Accessibility

We would all agree that it would be pointless for a functional area of an organisation to generate data and information that it would then be unwilling to share with other areas, particularly when you consider that all parts of an organisation should be working together towards a common goal.

Each department will need to take responsibility for preparing its data in such a way that it will be **accessible** to other parts of the organisation.

Cost-effectiveness

There are times when the costs of gathering data are too high in comparison to the advantages to be gained from having the data available. Let's look at an example:

An organisation wants to find out how many males and females there are in the UK, and where they live, broken down by country.

While there are a number of ways to gather this data, there are two obvious avenues to explore:

1. Pay a consultancy or data agency to gather the information for you (which will cost a significant amount of money)
2. Look up the population information on www.statistics.gov.uk/

There are times, however, when first-hand research is an absolute necessity, either because the information doesn't already exist or because it is in a format inappropriate for the uses to which it is going to be put. Sometimes the cost is not in physical money, but in the time it will take to gather the information required.

Sufficient accuracy

It is possible that there will be occasions when you will be able to use data that is not 100 per cent accurate, but is almost accurate. It will then be up to you to decide how usable a piece of data is.

The following is an example:

> You have a bank savings account that contains £130.76.

How accurate you need to be about this information will depend on what you are using the information for.

a) If you want to buy an item that costs £130.76, then clearly the whole value is very important (if you had less, you wouldn't be able to buy the item).
b) If you are telling a friend about your savings account, you could say 'I have just over £130', which is still relatively accurate. Or you could say 'I have over £100'; after all, does the friend really have to know how much you have in the account to the penny? Ultimately, all these statements are true, they are just increasingly inaccurate!

As another example, imagine that you have secured a job working 5 hours per week. You would need to know exactly how much you get paid for each hour you work (e.g. £4.75). It is unlikely that you would be satisfied to know that you will earn approximately £5 per hour. In this case, you would want the information to be exact.

How accurate information needs to be will depend on what it is going to be used for. That is a decision that can only be made by the person who is going to use the information.

Activity 1

The concept of **relevance** in information is relatively easy to understand, and is probably best explained using a series of questions and answers. In each case, read the question and decide which information would be most relevant.

1 You are looking at the price of an item you wish to purchase in the next few days. Which of these is likely to be the most relevant?

a. The price of the item last week.

b. The price of the item next month.

c. The price of the item today.

2 You need the sales information for the first quarter of 2011. Which figures would be most relevant?

a. January to March 2011 information

b. April to June 2011 information

c. January to May 2011 information

3 You are going to travel in Europe. Which of the following would be relevant?

a. The US Dollar to UK pound exchange rate

b. The Euro to US Dollar exchange rate

c. The UK pound to Euro exchange rate

4 You are travelling to the USA. Which of the following would be relevant?

a. Weather report for Kingston

b. Weather report for New York

c. Weather report for New Delhi

5 You need some production information about widgets. Which of the following would be relevant?

a. Number of widgets being produced each month

b. When current widget was designed

c. Colour of the widgets in the workplace

How well did you do? See the supporting website for answers.

Relevance

In each case, while you might like to know the other information offered, only one piece of information in each situation would be wholly relevant to the issue being investigated.

So, relevant information is information that is needed to investigate an issue or answer a particular question. Irrelevant information is, in effect, useless in its contribution to the investigation or search for an answer.

Having the right level of detail

In some situations, having a level of detail down to thousands of a millimetre may be appropriate. An example of this would be in engineering where measurements have to be incredibly accurate.

Take the following number: 5.81333333cm

An engineer might need to work with the figure 5.8133cm, while a salesman might well say that the item is 5.81cm.

There is another perspective on this, and to explain, we will once again refer to the monthly sales results. It might well be sufficient to give the monthly results, without giving the individual figures for each week. It will very much depend on how the information will be used, and why. Equally, there may be occasions when only the weekly sales information will suffice.

From a source in which the user has confidence

While we can be relatively confident about the content of books, journals and newspapers (because the activities of publishers are policed and checked), the same is not true of internet sites. For this reason, users should be careful about trusting the reliability of websites unless they feel sure that their content is up-to-date and accurate.

Take the following websites as an example:

www.bigjimscomputerhardwarewebsite.com/

www.microsoft.com/

Which of the two websites is likely to be more reliable? We would clearly say Microsoft® because the organisation polices its website and ensures that it stays up-to-date. The reason it does this is that it wants to present a professional image. Ultimately its reputation is at stake. This will be the same for any organisation. However, bigjim might actually be an anonymous person who just happens to like computers. He might well believe that the information he has on his site is accurate. This might not, however, be the case. As such, it is unreliable.

Understandable by the user

Part of the reason why we include titles and legends on graphs and charts is to make information more understandable by the user. Clearly, if information cannot be understood, then it can't be considered information in the first place. When developing information, ensure that it is what your user ultimately wants.

3.1.5 Business functional areas

This section will cover the following grading criterion:

Make the Grade M1

It is essential for M1 that you can demonstrate an understanding of how the functional areas of an organisation interact. You will produce an information flow diagram, which should include at least three internal and two external functional areas that should be addressed to provide sufficient complexity in your evidence.

This topic has been covered extensively earlier in this unit. Table 3.04 opposite provides a brief overview of each functional area.

Table 3.04

Department/ Functional area	Description
Accounts (Finance)	The functional area concerned with recording the financial transactions of the organisation, both income and expenditure (payments in and out). This area will chase creditors (those who owe the company money) for late payments and ensure that sufficient funds are available to pay staff and debtors (those to whom the company owes money).
Payroll (Finance)	Coming under the umbrella of accounts or finance, the payroll function is solely responsible for ensuring that employees are correctly paid for their services. Payroll employees will calculate gross wage (the total amount you earn), and will take off any deductions for tax, National Insurance or pension contributions as appropriate. The employee will then be given a pay slip reflecting this information, and the net pay due (calculated as the gross salary less any deductions).

Table 3.04 continued

Department/ Functional area	Description
Personnel	This area is responsible for recruiting staff and, in some cases, terminating employment contracts. They will undertake the general administration of staff records, including sickness records and holiday entitlement, and will monitor training expiry dates to ensure that recertification is achieved in good time. An example of this would be forklift truck (FLT) drivers. Each FLT driver has to have a specialist licence, which needs to be renewed on a regular basis. If the licence is allowed to expire, then the employee will not be able to drive a fork lift truck until such time as he or she has re-sat the test. This is also true of first aid officers who must renew their practising licences on a regular basis.
HR (Human Resources)	Looking at staff as a resource like any other organisational resource, the HR function will help managers plan how the resource will be used most effectively.
Marketing	Employees who work in marketing will be gathering and analysing information – including customer feedback, product information, development information – to enable them to design strategies for promoting new products in the marketplace.
Advertising	As suggested previously, advertising is about the physical promotion of the service or product provided by the organisation. Employees in this functional area will be creating the leaflets, posters etc. that we see each day.
Purchasing	This area is responsible for buying the products and services that the organisation will use to support its activities.
Sales	Staff in this functional area secure business for the organisation by selling its goods or services to customers. In addition, sales representatives are responsible for growing (expanding) the organisation's customer base.
Customer Services	Customer Services generally handle complaints and concerns that are being directed at the organisation. But this area also has a positive side – staff in Customer Services will also provide product support or advice and guidance.
Manufacturing or Production	This is the functional area that is responsible for physically making the products sold by the company.
Distribution or Dispatch	The Distribution function ensures that the goods and services provided to customers arrive at their destination. In some organisations, this department also has responsibility for stock.
Administration	An administrative department will be very different within each organisation in terms of what it actually does. Administration will include many different types of clerical work, but can also include responsibility for the estate of the organisation (buildings, maintenance, security etc.).
Research and Development	Research and Development is an important functional area as it is the 'think tank' for new products and services that the company might want to sell in the future. In addition, this department will constantly revisit existing products to see whether they can be improved.

3.1.6 Information flows

To fully understand how functional areas within an organisation interact and exchange information, it is necessary to analyse the types of information that flow between them. It is clear from content earlier in this unit that information generated by functional areas can either be shared with other functional areas within the organisation (**internal information flow**) or passed to agencies outside the organisation (**external information flow**).

It is becoming increasingly common for departments in an organisation to share information; it is now considered that a company's information belongs to the whole company, not to a particular department. Figure 3.05 represents some company information broken down by departments.

Internal information flows

Even as late as the 1980s, it was common for departments in an organisation to communicate using internal phone systems or memos if they needed to have a paper copy of a communication. These days, however, it is more common for employees to communicate via **email** or, in some cases, an organisational messaging system (a little bit like a company chat programme). Many organisations also have an **intranet**, which is a website created and managed internally for the benefit of the employees, usually containing links to organisational policies, news and important events. Clearly there are now multiple ways of communicating that do not necessarily require moving paper between departments!

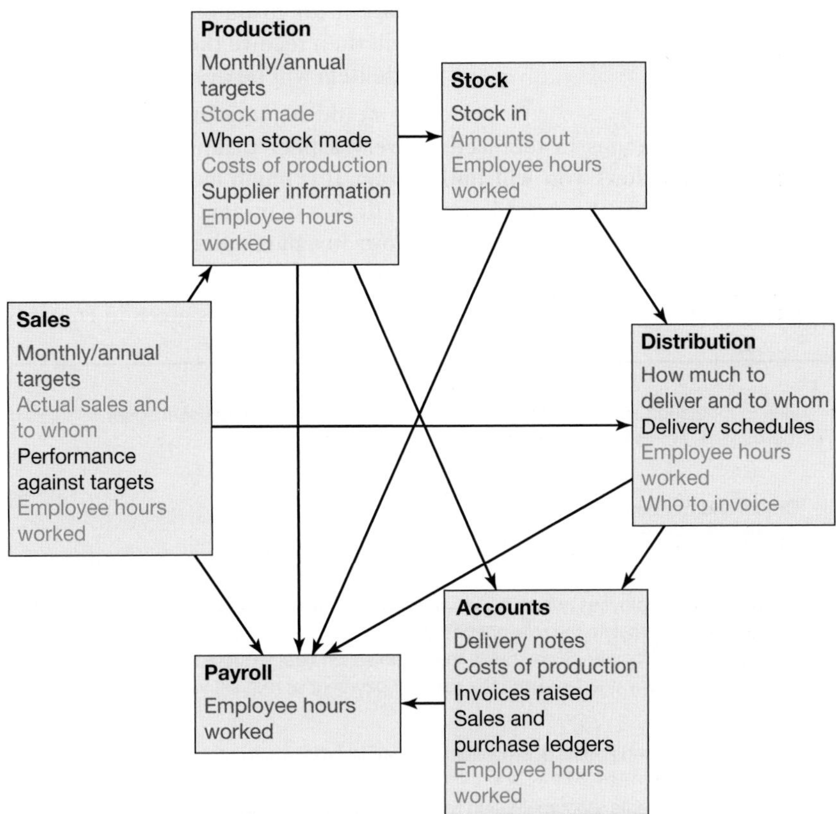

Figure 3.05 Flow of data between departments

All information shown in **green** is generated by the department and passed to another area.
All information shown in **blue** is passed into the department from outside.
All information shown in **black** is generated within the section, but might not be used by any other area.

Notice that the Management function is over *all* other areas. This implies that managers will have access to all information generated by the organisation.

Having focused largely on communication between departments, we need to consider that the information also flows vertically (up and down) within the organisation. Managers will set targets for departments and will provide instructions about how various activities should be undertaken. The employees will then carry out the tasks and send back relevant information to the managers that confirms that targets have been met or that instructions have been followed.

Information flows to external bodies

There are a number of important external agencies or bodies with which organisations will need to communicate. Sometimes the communication can be **unidirectional** (one way), while on other occasions it will be **bidirectional** (both ways).

The common agencies with which most organisations will communicate are shown in Figure 3.06, together with examples of the sorts of information that are exchanged.

Information flow diagrams

When it comes to drawing diagrams to represent an organisation's information flows you will find many different diagram styles in the books you read and on the websites you visit. There are no hard and fast rules as to which technique is best or which technique you should use.

What you should remember, however, is that whatever style of diagram you apply, you must do it consistently! Figure 3.07 on page 97 represents an e-business organisation like amazon.co.uk or PLAY.com (both of whom trade solely online).

The figure includes representations for both internal functions or departments, and external agencies with which the organisation will communicate. In each case, the arrow showing the information being passed also shows the direction of the information flow (the originator and the recipient).

In general this is a very straightforward process:

The customer places an order – he or she could pay the company directly or could instruct an intermediary such as PayPal to pay the organisation.

Once the organisation has both the order and confirmation of payment, it will pass the order to the distribution function that will pack it and prepare it for dispatch. A courier or delivery service will then receive the item and documentation, and the item will be delivered to the customer.

It would be very unusual to attempt to represent every aspect of an organisation in a single diagram. It is much more likely that you will be asked to draw a diagram that represents the information flows in a particular functional area, or for a specified process.

Another example is given in Figure 3.08.

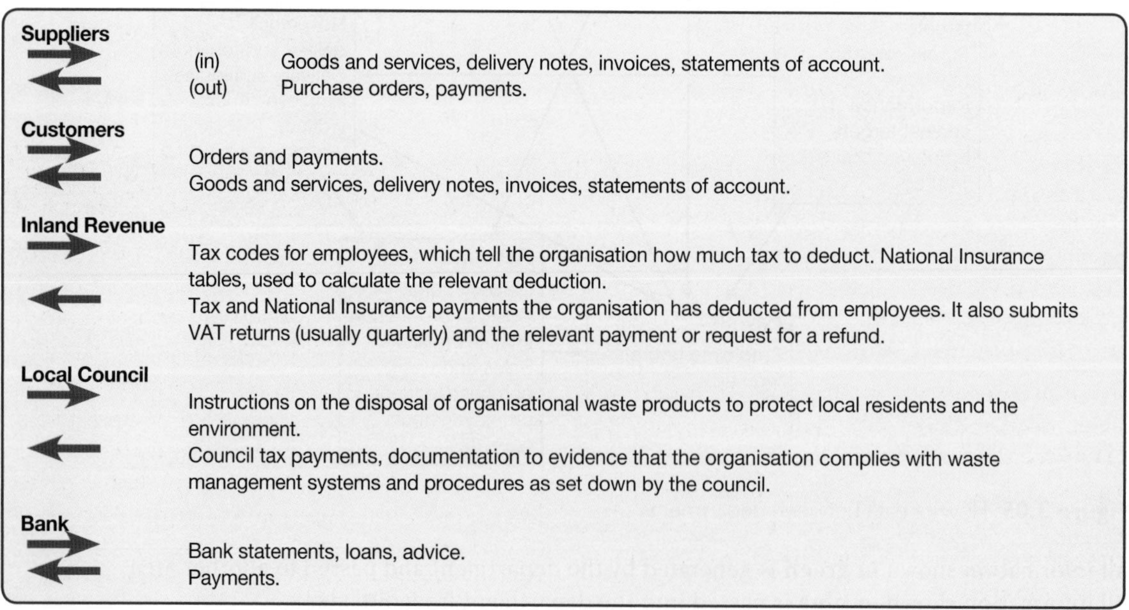

Figure 3.06 Typical information exchanged externally

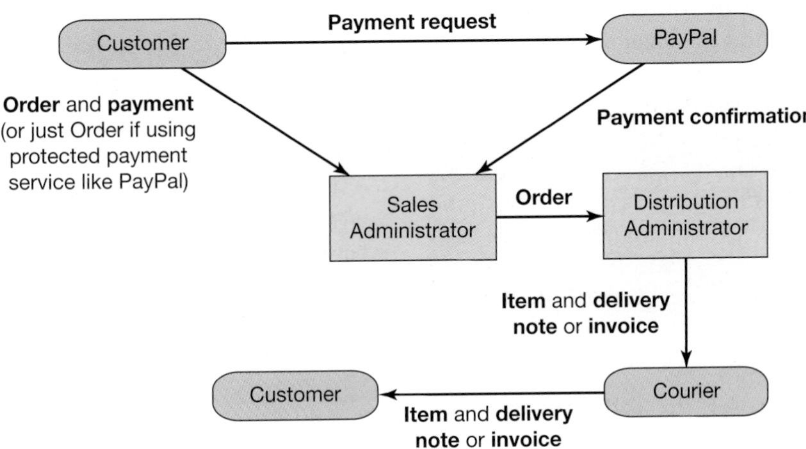

Figure 3.07 Customer order information flow

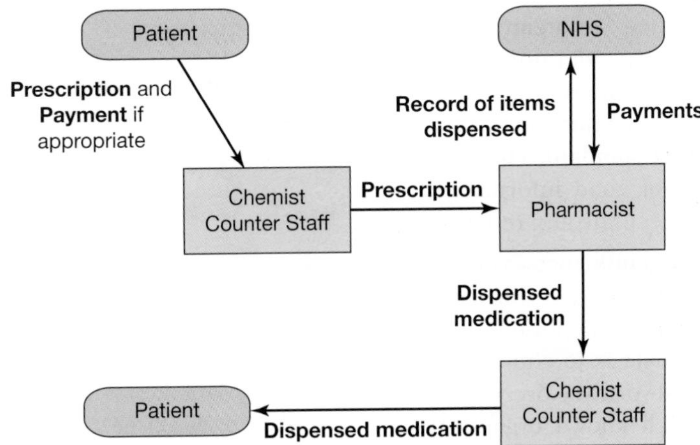

Figure 3.08 Medical prescription information flow

In this example, the patient gives a prescription to the counter staff in a chemist. If they have to pay for their prescriptions they will also provide payment. The prescription goes to the pharmacist who dispenses the medication. The medication is then given to the counter staff, who hand it to the patient.

If the patient does not pay for prescriptions, the items dispensed are recorded and the money is claimed from the NHS.

The most important factor about drawing information flow diagrams is that both the originator and the reader can both fully understand what is being communicated.

Case Study

Rington College is a sixth form college that offers a range of level 2 and 3 vocational courses in ICT, Engineering, Health and Social Care, Hair and Beauty and Land-based studies.

In order to properly advise prospective students about these courses, the Course Teams in each area provide course information to the Academic Advisors. This information is then passed to schools in the area or directly to prospective students on request.

If you look at the recommended solution, it would seem that the course information going to schools does not seem to have been requested. It is likely that the Academic Advisors send the information to the schools as a matter of routine. If it was only sent when requested, there would be an additional line going the other way between the Academic Advisors and the local schools.

> Activity 2
>
> Using the case study for Rington College, draw a simple information flow diagram that represents the processes as described. Answers are included on the supporting website.

This section will cover the following grading criterion:

There are a number of areas an organisation can explore to improve the quality of information and both external sources and internal management of information should be examined to ensure that it is always of the highest standard. The most important characteristics of good information are that the information is accurate and reliable.

External data is difficult to influence as clearly the organisation will have little control over data generated elsewhere. The only real option the organisation has in selecting data is to choose sources that are likely to be trustworthy. Government statistical websites and well known organisational websites are expected to be good sources. If it is possible to check the information with various sources this will help the organisation have confidence.

Internal data and information should be regularly checked to make sure it is up to date. Old data should be purged (deleted) if no longer required. Data should be carefully structured and stored to ensure that there is no data duplication (otherwise one record could be changed While the other remains unchanged causing a potential mismatch).

Many organisations have data management policies for their internal information – largely to comply with the Data Protection Act (see section 3.2.1) which sets out guidelines on how information should be stored.

> **Make the Grade** 
>
> The better the quality of organisational information, the more reliable decision making will be.
>
> For D1 you will need to explain how an organisation could improve the quality of its business information, for example how could information drawn from organisations externally be improved? Why is it important for an organisation to clean or purge its own data?

3.2 Understand the issues related to the use of information

This section will cover the following grading criteria:

> **Make the Grade** 
>
> For P3 you will need to identify some of the issues that are related to the use of information. You will need to discuss at least two items from each of the three issues outlined in the unit content (legal, ethical and operational).
>
> For M2 you will also need to reflect how each of the issues you identified could affect the organisation – this really examines the impact of the issues, for example, through additional costs (see 3.2.3).
>
> To evidence these criteria, your teacher may well use a case study.

3.2.1 Legal issues

In general it is fair to say that there is significant legislation with which an organisation must comply. In this next section we consider the legal issues related to the use of information.

Relevant data protection legislation (e.g. Data Protection Act 1998, Freedom of Information Act 2000)

The first two acts we will consider are the **Data Protection Act** and the **Freedom of Information Act**. Both of these acts are designed to protect individuals and organisations by setting out guidelines that must be strictly adhered to. Failure to do so can result in prosecution (and imprisonment), because breaching these acts is a criminal offence.

Data Protection Act 1998

Both individuals and organisations holding personal information about individuals must inform the **Office of the Information Commissioner** that they are in possession of such data. In other words, organisations must register the fact that they are holding personal data, and they must pay a small annual fee. According to the British Computer Society:

'The eight principles require personal data to be:

- fairly and lawfully obtained;
- held only for specific and lawful purposes and not processed in any manner incompatible with those purposes;
- adequate, relevant and not excessive for those purposes;
- accurate and where necessary kept up-to-date, not kept for longer than necessary;
- processed in accordance with the rights of the person to whom the data refers;
- kept securely to ensure data is not lost, disposed of or misused;
- not transferred out of the European Economic Area unless the destination has an adequate level of data protection.'

Source: www.bcs.org

There are also a number of direct offences for which organisations and individuals can be fined; for example, selling data is against the law.

Freedom of Information Act 2000

Although the Freedom of Information Act was passed in the autumn of 2000, it was not fully implemented until January 2005. With the knowledge and understanding that more and more data was being held about us as individuals, the Government passed this act to give us improved access to our individual records.

In order to gain such access, individuals need to make a direct request to the organisation holding the information. The act actually stipulates how such requests should be made. Again drawing on information gained from the British Computer Society:

'The act sets out that public requests must be managed as follows:

- Requests must be written; no set format or justification is defined.
- The request must be processed within 20 days of receipt.
- The body must inform the requester if the information is not available or cannot be supplied with full justification.
- The body must contact the requester and discuss the requirement, if the request for information is vague or complex, so that the request can be met.
- The requester can appeal if the information is not made available.'

Source: www.bcs.org

As long as individuals comply with the request guidance, the organisation is obligated to provide the relevant evidence.

There are, even so, a number of exceptions where the Freedom of Information Act **does not** apply:

'FOIA does not authorise the disclosure of the following:

- information more than 50 years old;
- commercial secrets;
- national security information;
- information that would prejudice commercial and/or public affairs;
- court records;
- personal data, as this is regulated by the Data Protection Act 1998.'

Source: www.bcs.org

The information given above is merely an overview. For more detail on the Freedom of Information Act 2000 or the Data Protection Act 1998, see the British Computer Society website (www.bcs.org).

Other relevant legislation (e.g. Computer Misuse Act 1990)

The following legislation does not apply directly to data, but to the use of computers in general.

Activity 3

Match the act to its correct description.

Act	Description
Data Protection Act 1998	An act intended to reduce the instances of unsolicited communication using electronic means.
Freedom of Information Act 2000	This act is designed to prevent groups and individuals from intimidating others for political ends.
Computer Misuse Act 1990	This act gives us the right to know what data is being kept about us.
Terrorism Act 2000	The principles in this act define how data about us is captured, used and stored.
Privacy and Electronic Communications Regulations 2003	An act designed to discourage individuals from using computers to support criminal activities.

Answers are included on the supporting website.

Computer Misuse Act 1990

The **Computer Misuse Act** came into being to attempt to resolve a surge in criminal activity surrounding computers and their use – primarily the increase in instances of **computer hacking**. Hacking is the intentional accessing of computer systems to illegally gain access to data (for the purposes of theft) or with other malicious (and sometimes quite serious) intent. The legislation covers activities such as the **denial of service (DOS) attack**.

A denial of service attack is where the intention is to prevent legitimate users from using their systems by disabling ports or dramatically increasing network traffic to slow down or simply prevent access.

According the Department for Education and Skills, the Computer Misuse Act recognises 'three key offences:

- Unauthorised access to computer material.
- Unauthorised access with intent to commit or facilitate commission of further offences.
- Unauthorised acts with intent to impair the operation of computer.'

Source: www.legislation.gov.uk/ukpga/1990/18/contents

Terrorism Act 2000

The **Terrorism Act 2000** also has implications for computing and ICT in that it is now an offence to use computers to intimidate individuals and groups, particularly from a political perspective, or to hack into or block any websites for political reasons. For further information see www.homeoffice.gov.uk.

Privacy and Electronic Communications (EC Directive) Regulations 2003

Another act is the **Privacy and Electronic Communications (EC Directive) Regulations 2003**.

'The Directive primarily required the EU Member States to introduce new laws regulating the use of:

- unsolicited commercial communications (spam);
- cookies;
- location and traffic data; and
- publicly available directories.'

Source: www.junk-mail.org.uk

3.2.2 Ethical issues

In the previous section you were introduced to legislation that can be enforced by law. In addition to this legislation, organisations and institutions can develop their own policies with which employees or service users must comply. Failure to do so will not result in criminal prosecution, but the outcome will probably be a sanction of some sort that is imposed by the organisation. Some of these sanctions will be more serious than others. These issues are **ethical** rather than criminal, where the term '**ethical**' means a **generally accepted type of behaviour**.

Ethical behaviour requirements are usually set through **Codes of Practice** or **Organisational Policies**. While these terms are frequently used interchangeably, Organisational Policies tend to be set by the organisation itself, while Codes of Practice are usually set by external bodies (for example, the British Computer Society has developed a suite of behavioural codes including the **Code of Good Conduct** and the **Code of Good Practice** when applied to ICT). Many **trade bodies** develop Codes of Practice designed to be used and adhered to by members of their industry. In some cases, failure to comply with these codes may well see the organisation or individual excluded from the trade body.

Codes of Practice are frequently adopted by organisations as a basis for expected behaviour, with policies added that are designed around the needs of the organisation. It should also be remembered that the codes and policies you have to observe with one employer will probably be different with a subsequent employer.

Some examples of codes and policies will be investigated below.

Use of email and the internet

Generally, employers expect employees to use email and the internet for business purposes only. This will include emailing colleagues about business-related issues, emailing suppliers and customers and other external agencies. Employers do not usually allow employees to use email to send personal correspondence or to surf the internet during the working day. This is largely because if employees are sending personal mail or surfing the net, they can't possibly be working! However, many employers will accept limited use of these services during work breaks.

Whistle blowing

When applied to ICT, **whistle blowing** means employees having a responsibility to their employers for reporting their colleagues for any inappropriate behaviour that they witness in relation to the use of the organisation's systems. While employees are more likely to report their colleagues for **serious misuse** (such as hacking into the organisation's systems or data theft), most will not report others for **excessive emailing** and **inappropriate internet use**. Ethically, they should, particularly if it is part of the organisation's policy or code of practice. Failure to do so could be seen by the employer as **complicity** (you will effectively be considered an accomplice to the offence).

Information ownership

The interesting part about the concept of **information ownership** is that morally if you own something you should take responsibility for looking after it. Some organisations have an information ownership policy or a set of guidelines for employees. Hampshire County Council, for example, set out their own information ownership policy on their website, where they state that each page on their website:

'has to be owned by a nominated person. They are responsible for:

- the accuracy and currency of the information provided
- ensuring that if the information has come from another source, the source is clearly identified
- providing the name (or job title/team name) along with an email address (or preferably an online form) and a telephone number to whom a visitor can address any queries.'

Source: www3.hants.gov.uk/webstandards/web-information-ownership.htm

This is an example of responsible information ownership.

We have also previously suggested that departments in an organisation should take responsibility for the information they generate and distribute. This means that they are particularly responsible for the accuracy of its content.

When it comes to the ownership of information stored about individuals, many organisations will require employees to sign **non-disclosure agreements** (NDAs), which means that the staff member will promise not to pass on any information belonging to the organisation to a third party. This includes information about the organisation's activities in general, not just information about individuals.

3.2.3 Operational issues

From an operational perspective, the company initially needs to ensure that its data and information are secure and can be recovered in the event of a disaster. It also needs to be aware that there will be additional costs incurred in working with data, and ensure that employees working with ever more complex systems are suitably trained.

Security of information

Computer security is a very important issue for any organisation that uses ICT to support their business activities. The physical loss of the computer system or its data can be damaging for organisations and for this reason there should always be systems in place to protect both the data and the systems as far as possible. What are the potential security threats to the data?

The main threats are:

- Theft of data
- Damage to data.

Theft of data

This includes the intentional removal of data using physical means such as floppy disks, USB devices or copies burned to CD or DVD, or electronic transfer of all or parts of the data using email.

Clearly, theft is an intentional act, and as such it is a criminal offence. Individuals who take part in such activity may not only lose their employment, but could well lose their liberty.

Data that can be targeted by thieves includes personal information to be used in identity theft, research information, diagrams of products under development, ideas for new products and services. These might be offered for sale to competitors.

Damage to data

Data can be damaged in two ways:

1. A physical part of the system could be damaged. In extreme circumstances, intentional damage can be done to physical aspects of the system (intentional damage is known as **malicious** damage). This could include the insertion of foreign objects into open parts of the machine, such as the cooling fan or the DVD or CD drives. Physical damage can also happen accidentally, for example because the machine gets wet. If parts of the physical system become damaged, the data could also become damaged. In addition, parts of the machine could simply break down (such as hard drive failure).
2. Alternatively, the data files themselves could become damaged. For example, **viruses** could be introduced through external media such as USB devices or as attachments to emails. Again, this could be intentional or accidental. Data can also be damaged due to simple human error!

To reduce the likelihood of data becoming damaged, there are a number of software solutions that organisations can consider installing.

The most common ones are anti virus software, firewalls, spyware and adware protection and data encryption. These will be considered in more detail on page 103.

Backups

There is now a range of options available to enable organisations to make backups of their data.

Storage media include removable backup storage devices, as shown in Figure 3.09.

Figure 3.09 Removable backup storage devices, such as DVD multi recorder drives

If backup files are made they should be stored off-site or in a secure medium such as a fire-proof safe, otherwise there will be little point in having the backup (it could potentially be destroyed along with the original).

Some organisations that have multiple branches use a round-robin style approach to data backup. Figure 3.10 represents a group of four outlets that are using each others' systems to keep their data safe.

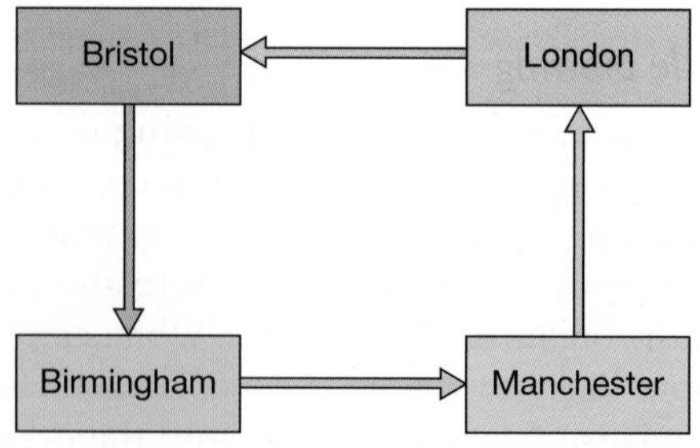

Figure 3.10 Backup strategy between branches of the same organisation

Key terms

Anti virus software can be installed on a network or on individual PCs and is intended to screen the system regularly, while monitoring the file content of any input devices. Commercial software is available from companies such as Norton, McAfee, Sophos and Grisoft AVG (who offer a free anti virus solution for home and individual use). This software serves two purposes: detection and destruction.

A **firewall** is a program that monitors a computer's data communications (both incoming and outgoing). This software can reject data transfer based on the fact that the destination has a particular **IP address**, that a **specific port** is being used or because a program is trying to transmit data to the outside world. Alternatively, if the user wishes this transfer to take place, the user can allow the transmission.

Firewall software can take time to configure, as when first installed, every communication will be questioned by the software and the user will have to make one of the following choices each time he or she is asked:

- Yes, always allow
- Yes, allow just this once
- No, never allow
- No, deny just this once.

Any firewall settings can be modified at a later date. For this reason it is better to deny rather than allow any communications you are unsure of.

Spyware programs covertly gather information about a system and send the information to a third party via an internet connection, usually without the knowledge of the user. **Adware programs** are designed to constantly display advertisements whether a user wishes them to be displayed or not.

The following products are examples of software designed to handle this type of irritant.

- XoftSpySe
- Spyware Nuker
- NoAdware
- AdWare ALERT
- Microsoft Defender®

Data encryption is where the data will be scrambled in some way so that it makes it unusable, even if it is intercepted. In order to read the data, it will need to be **decrypted** using some sort of **algorithmic process** – a little bit like a key. Loss of the key or the ability to decrypt the data will make the data useless.

Destruction can occur in two ways – the infected file can simply be **deleted** from the system or the virus can be **healed**. In the event that the software is unable to heal the virus, it can isolate it by putting it into a **virus vault.** The vault essentially separates the virus from the remainder of the system, to prevent it from doing any damage (or any further damage).

Anti virus software has to be updated regularly to ensure that it stays up-to-date. New viruses are being written all the time and as such, **anti virus signatures** (identification and destruction protocols) need to be downloaded to tackle these new viruses. If you have purchased anti virus software, these updates are generally free.

Popular forms of encryption include:

- **PGP** (**P**retty **G**ood **P**rivacy). Invented by Phil Zimmermann, PGP is popular for encrypting data files and email. It is often described as a **military-grade** encryption algorithm because of its complexity.
- **RSA** (named after the inventors **R**ivest, **S**hamir and **A**dleman). RSA is often used in **electronic commerce**.
- **WEP** (**W**ired **E**quivalent **P**rivacy) and **WPA** (**W**i-Fi **P**rotected **A**ccess) for encrypting **wireless communications**.

Whether attempting to counteract potential data loss through physical or logical means, one recommended solution is for the organisation to keep regular backups of the data.

In Figure 3.10, the data is backed up to another branch or outlet:

- Bristol's data is copied to Birmingham.
- Birmingham's data is copied to Manchester.
- Manchester's data is copied to London.
- London's data is copied to Bristol.

In the event that any of the outlets lose their data, it can be recovered by being copied back from the second location.

How often backups should be taken depends on the volume of transactions that would be lost in the event that the data was lost. With some companies once a week will be sufficient; other organisations may need to backup data two or three times a week. In some instances, such as truly high-volume situations where systems may be running in real time (transactions are processed instantly), this could be done hourly or even after each transaction!

Health and safety

When considering this topic area we need to look at the subject matter from two perspectives – firstly in terms of **using systems** within the workplace and secondly from the perspective of **responsibility** for monitoring and maintaining the working environment in situations where computers are used.

Using systems

There is now increasing legislation on the use of computers in the workplace, including specific guidance on what individuals can do (in addition to what employers can do) to ensure that risks are minimised.

Common conditions that can develop as a result of computer use are eye-related conditions such as headaches, visual fatigue and blurred or watery vision. Musculoskeletal problems can also become exacerbated including stiffness, aching joints and muscles from sitting in the same position for extended periods of time and **RSI** (**R**epetitive **S**train **I**njury), which is usually experienced in the wrists or hands.

The following websites give extensive guidance on health and safety issues when working with computers:

- icthubknowledgebase.org.uk/healthandsafety (general guidance on working with computers and associated technologies)
- www.hse.gov.uk/pubns/indg36.pdf (guidance on working with VDUs)

What should be mentioned here, however, is that this guidance is based on current legislation surrounding computers and their use. As such legislation can change, this information was correct at the time of printing.

The main laws associated with this issue are:

- Health & Safety (Display Screen Equipment) Regulations 1992
- Management of Health & Safety at Work Regulations 1992
- Provision and Use of Work Equipment Regulations 1992
- Workplace (Health, Safety and Welfare) Regulations 1992

To enable employees to work as safely as possible, employers should:

- Ensure that employees can have breaks or change their activities to vary what they do.
- Ensure that employees have up-to-date health and safety information (and training if required).
- Arrange for eye tests for those employees whose job requires them to have prolonged contact with computer systems.
- Analyse and monitor an individual user's requirements in terms of the workstation they are using (including furniture and equipment considerations, special chairs if appropriate).
- Ensure that the workstation that the employee is using meets the minimum requirements, which include considerations such as suitable lighting, screen type and positioning, keyboards, desks, chairs and footrests (if required).

Employees should also attempt to work safely by:

- Ensuring firstly that there is sufficient space to work.
- Adjusting any equipment where positions and heights, for example, can be altered, until the user feels fully at ease (for example, the chair height and back support).
- Positioning VDU equipment where glare is reduced, away from bright light, adjusting contrast and brightness of the display as required.
- Experimenting with the layout of the keyboard, mouse, screen and documents to find the most suitable positions for these items.
- Taking regular breaks (frequent short breaks are better than longer, less frequent breaks).
- Trying to change their seating position rather than sitting in the same position for extended periods of time.

Responsibility

As you can see, working safely is considered today to be a shared responsibility for both employer and employee. An **employer** must:

- Keep up-to-date with legislation and comply with it.
- Ensure that the working environment is monitored.
- Resolve any problems identified either by staff in general or employees designated to monitor the health and safety of the working environment.
- Respond to employee needs (and accept that these may change).
- Provide relevant equipment.

The **employee** must:

- Comply with legislation.
- Help the employer by monitoring his or her own working environment and report any problems.
- Be generally aware of the working environment and report any issues identified.
- Be realistic and give employers sufficient warning to allow them time to respond.
- Work safely.

Ultimately, if the employer fails in his or her responsibilities, this might result in the employee being able to take legal action. If, however, the employee fails to monitor his or her own environment and report any safety issues, there are no grounds for complaint!

Organisational policies

As suggested earlier in this unit, organisations may well create policies in line with external agency Codes of Practice or to reflect **legislative requirements**. In addition, they may create policies that dictate how data will be accessed, used and managed. In terms of accessing the data, for example, some organisations dictate that screens must be positioned in a way that unauthorised users will have limited visibility. This is to promote confidentiality.

In addition, some organisations make employees sign **non-disclosure agreements**, which will prevent staff from discussing any information gained from within the organisation, outside. This will usually cover all types of information, from information about suppliers, customers and employees to information about products and services.

Other policies have been covered earlier in this unit.

Business continuance plans

When you consider that many organisations today are heavily reliant on computer technology, any organisation that does not plan a strategy for overcoming a catastrophic event could well be destroyed by such an occurrence. The incident could be man-made (for example an arson attack) or could be the result of a natural disaster such as a flood.

Apart from anything else, formalising such a plan will ensure that, should there be a disruptive incident, the organisation and staff will have a well-defined plan to follow.

The key to successful **business continuance** planning is:

- identifying potential risks
- fully understanding how the organisation will be affected
- identifying factors and implementing resolutions as far as possible to minimise the risks in the first place
- implementing safety strategies (such as backing up data regularly)
- testing the plan by simulating a disaster and seeing whether the organisation can recover (if not, why not, and what can be done)
- ensuring that staff understand the role they will play in the recovery process (ensuring that they receive any appropriate training)
- reviewing the plan at regular intervals, to ensure that it is still current when you consider that the organisation and its needs may have changed over time.

As this is such an important facet of business, there are many companies that specialise in helping organisations to plan for disaster recovery.

Costs (e.g. additional resources required, cost of development)

In order to respond to every eventuality, whether it be the need for change within the organisation or business continuance strategies, organisations need to understand that they will need to invest in the resources that will facilitate these needs.

Disaster planning, for example, takes time that in itself is an indirect cost of developing such a strategy. Usually teams made up of key personnel meet regularly to monitor the organisation's situation and advise if appropriate. Clearly, if staff are involved in such activities, they will not be doing their own jobs! However, from a company perspective, this type of investment is important to ensure the longevity of the organisation. Many companies will spend hundreds of thousands of pounds over the years developing strategies to overcome catastrophe, when in fact catastrophe never strikes. Some would argue that this was a waste of money.

Think about it in these terms – why does a business pay any type of insurance (because essentially that is what business continuance planning really is)? Because one day, it could be them!

Impact of increasing sophistication of systems (e.g. more trained personnel, more complex software)

As ICT systems develop, many are becoming more **integrated** (working together and relying on each other). This in turn means that systems and software are becoming increasingly complex. In order to work with the systems:

- More staff with the right skills will be required, and these may well need to be brought in from outside the organisation.
- Existing staff may need to receive further training to ensure that they understand and can confidently and competently work with more of the system.

Again, this is an investment issue for most organisations, but their failure to seriously consider these issues may see systems that they have purchased at great expense not being used as efficiently as they should or could be.

3.3 Know the features and functions of information systems

This section will cover the following grading criteria:

Make the Grade P4 P5

For P4 and P5 you will need to show that you understand information systems by describing their features and functions. You will also need to identify information systems that are used in a specific organisation.

This might be evidenced by describing the features of information systems and explaining which ones you might use in a mini-enterprise and why.

3.3.1 Features of information systems

In order to be an effective information system, the following key elements should be in place:

Data – data must first be introduced to the system as inputs, before it can be processed and output as useful information. This data will be generated by all functional parts of an organisation, as well as being received into the system from outside the company.

People – staff must have the right skills to enable them to get the best out of an information system.

Hardware – the computer hardware must be capable of running the software and handling the volumes of data that are put through the system. Large volumes of data being interrogated (searched through) by a computer system that is old and slow will cause significant frustration to users.

Software – the software that is installed must have the features and functionality to produce the information required by the organisation. In some instances, staff using the software must have relevant training.

Telecommunications – if information output from systems is required in multiple locations, the telecommunications infrastructure must be in place to enable the data to be distributed.

3.3.2 Functions of information systems

In basic terms, the functions of an information system are simple:

- take and store inputs
- process them
- output them.

Input and storage, processing and output

Figure 3.11 is a good representation of the nature and source of inputs, typical processing functions and potential outputs.

Control and feedback loops and closed and open systems

The functionality of information systems can be defined as being:

- closed
- open.

The definition will reflect how the system interacts with the environment in which it exists.

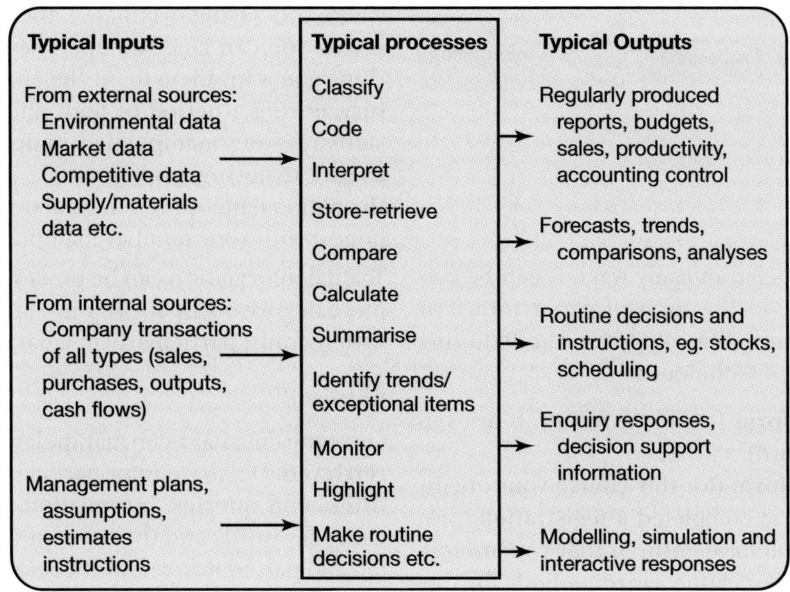

Figure 3.11 A typical information-processing system
(*Source*: Terry Lucey (2000), *Management Information Systems* (8th Edition), page 39)

A **closed system**:

- Is largely isolated from its environment.
- Means that any interaction will be totally predictable and probably automated.
- Does not influence the external environment in any way.

Examples:

A refrigerator or central heating system is an example of a closed system.

The refrigerator cools when triggered to do so by a sensor. When the correct temperature has been reached, the machine switches off.

A central heating system is triggered by a thermostat and timer. The timer ensures that the system becomes active at specific times each day, and that the radiators are heated if the temperature is lower than a set value.

In actual fact, this is an example of a **control and feedback loop**. The system constantly repeats the same sequences, activated by the same triggers.

An **open system**:

- Is fully capable of interacting with its environment.
  - The system will receive inputs and other influences from the environment.
  - It will pass back outputs and influences to its environment.
  - It is capable of handling unexpected events because it is constantly monitoring and anticipating the environment.

Example:

Most functional areas of organisations are effectively open systems, because they interact with the other functional areas around them, and also with factors outside the organisation. Take the example of the marketing function in an organisation.

- They investigate the market, having contact with the public and/or other organisations.
- They have to react to legislative changes.
- They must respond to changes in user needs.
- They must respond to developments in technology.

3.3.3 Transformation of data into information

We have already considered what is often called the data processing cycle.

Figure 3.12 represents this activity and shows how data collected or gathered will need to be processed into information. In reality, however, this is really much more complex as we need to take additional features into consideration.

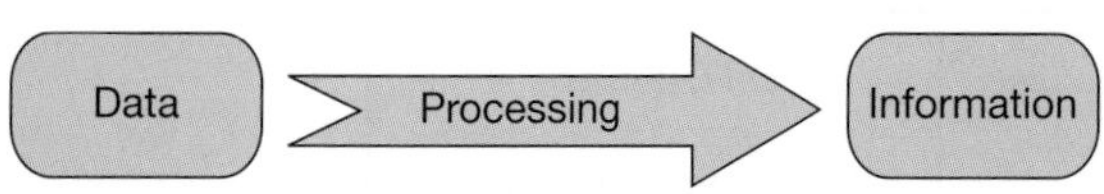

Figure 3.12 Data processing cycle

Collection

Data can be collected in many ways. It can be collected physically, in the form of paper forms, or electronically, through a computer. The following are data collection techniques:

- **Application form** (could be for a job or even for a library card)
- **Registration form** (for this course your organisation will have completed a registration form for you that will have ensured that you are registered with Edexcel, the awarding body for this qualification)
- **Questionnaire** (you might create one or you might be asked to complete one)
- **Interview** (this could be recorded on paper or using an electronic device such as a tape recorder)
- **Observation** (this will be where you watch something to gain information)
- **Discussion**
- **Online website form**

Storage

Once data has been collected or gathered, it will need to be organised in some way so that it can be stored. Failure to organise data successfully may make it more difficult to process and manipulate.

Data can be stored electronically in files, in paper archives such as A4 files, or on videotape or cassette. How the data is stored is important not only in terms of how it will subsequently be used, but how it will be protected. The main advantage of data stored electronically is that it can be copied and stored elsewhere. It is more difficult to achieve this with A4 paper files, videotapes or cassettes.

Processing and manipulation

How data is processed will depend on what the data is and what it will be used for.

Data containing numbers may well be subjected to a variety of **calculations**. The data can be categorised, sorted and manipulated. There is a well-known saying, 'lies, damned lies and statistics'. While there is still significant argument over where this saying originated, the implication of it is that you can make numbers say just about anything you want them to. At the end of the last century, during a period of high unemployment, the statistics were manipulated to appear more positive by removing 'young people in training' from the national figure. You must always take care to be honest with your number manipulation.

Textual information can be processed by, for example, categorising or sorting it. This is usually done with records, particularly in a database.

Retrieval

Once the data has been manipulated, it needs to be **retrieved**. Database information is retrieved using **filters** and **queries**. Information will be searched using key words and the relevant information copied and pasted into relevant documents. If the data moves outside its original source (such as a paragraph from a book), the source should be **attributed**. As the data user, you are responsible for saying where the original data or information came from.

Presentation

Ultimately, all information that has been retrieved from systems will need to be presented.

There is significant presentation software on the market today. Table 3.05 shows a small range of the software you can use to help you to effectively present information you have gathered.

Whichever software is used to present information, the user should endeavour to make the information as professional as possible.

3.3.4 Types of information systems

In general terms the information produced by information systems is used in the following activities:

- Planning
- Decision making
- Controlling operations
- Forecasting the future

All these features are necessary in good **management information systems** (this is considered in section 3.3.5 on page 110).

Realistically, these activities will be undertaken in all functional areas of an organisation. Table 3.06 on page 110 gives some examples of the sorts of information that can be extracted from a

Table 3.05 Presentation software

Software manufacturer	Application purpose
Microsoft Word®	Word-processing package for presenting text
Corel WordPerfect®	Word-processing package for presenting text
Microsoft Excel®	Spreadsheet package for working with and presenting numbers, and with functionality to help users create graphical representations such as charts and graphs
IBM Lotus 1-2-3®	Once the world's most popular spreadsheet package, now part of IBM's integrated suite of office productivity software.
Microsoft Publisher®	Presentation package that can be used to create leaflets, newsletters, advertisements, menus, business cards etc.
Microsoft PowerPoint®	Presentation software that creates slide shows for use when presenting information to large groups of people
OpenOffice®	A multi-platform (Microsoft Windows®, Linux and Mac OSX) based open source free product that has some of the functionality of Microsoft Office®

B Braincheck 3

Try the following crossword based on what we have covered so far. The grid and clues are provided, along with the answers on the supporting website (if you get stuck).

ACROSS

3 Information that is gained from another source
4 Extracting information to prepare for presentation
5 Raw facts that have not yet been interpreted
8 The Microsoft spreadsheet package
9 Data or information that can be measured
10 Combined term for facts and figures
11 Key on a chart or graph that aids interpretation
12 Is data that has been processed and manipulated
13 Data or information that an organisation collects itself
14 Data or information that is ready when it is needed

DOWN

1 A software package that is for text processing, published by Microsoft®
2 An electronic device for making voice recordings of information
6 The orientation of the X-axis
7 Data or information that is subjective and can not be measured

Table 3.06

Type of information	Functional area	Business use
Sales performance (e.g. comparing one sales area against another, comparing one year's sales against another, comparing the sales of particular products across a number of years or financial quarters)	Marketing	Being able to react to business opportunities and threats will be dependent on the ability of an organisation to fully understand the environment in which it operates. When information is compared, any anomalies will be highlighted and investigated so that the company can understand why a particular event occurred.
Competitor (e.g. prices, delivery, terms and conditions)	Marketing	Knowing the pricing information of competitors will help an organisation to set its own prices.
Development (e.g. new products or services)	Marketing	Information about the technological developments in the real world will help an organisation plan its own developmental strategies.
Financial costs (e.g. budgets and targets)	Financial	Setting budgets is essential to ensure that no area of the organisation spends more money than it should. Similarly, setting targets enables functional areas of a business to know what is expected of them.
Investment returns	Financial	Any money invested by the organisation should be monitored – for example, an organisation could have invested in new production machinery, and it needs to establish whether the investment was worthwhile (has production throughput increased?).
Financial performance (e.g. profit and loss)	Financial	The organisation overall needs to know how profitable it is – this will help it to plan its expenditure, expansion and possible investment.
Staffing (records)	Human resources	The organisation must hold extensive information on its employees, including such standard information as personal details, next of kin, bank details. They must know which functional area individual staff belong to and how many staff overall work in each part of the organisation.
Professional development	Human resources	The needs of each area must be met by the staff that work in that area – if those needs change, then the organisation must endeavour to develop the staff accordingly through training programmes.

good information system. Also shown is the business reason why an organisation would want the information.

3.3.5 Management information systems (MIS)

Essentially, a **management information system** is a system that is designed to help executives to manage an organisation, by giving them sufficient information to help them control the overall direction and the day-to-day activities.

Features

While the key elements of an MIS can be seen in the next section of this unit, it might be appropriate at this stage to explain that all information systems are said to have a **behaviour** – this behaviour is defined by the level of predictability the system is said to have.

Terry Lucey in *Management Information Systems* (8th Edition, 2000), page 38, defines a series of information system behaviours, of which these are the most notable:

Deterministic – Where the exact outputs of the system can be predicted because the inputs are known in advance. For example, a manufacturing process where a number of predetermined inputs go into the system so that a particular product can be output.

Probabilistic – Using prior knowledge about the system, the likely outputs can be predicted. For example, the overall number of hours of downtime on a piece of production machinery can be estimated based on previous breakdown history, but the actual number of hours that it will be out of action (it could be higher or lower than previously) will not be known in advance.

Self organising – These systems are by nature reactive: the inputs are unknown and unpredictable and the potential outputs would be variable and also unpredictable. For example, a social work department may have a series of 'routine responses' for given situations, but the response actually taken will need to be adapted to accommodate factors not necessarily known in advance.

Benefits

The business benefits of information systems have already been stated repeatedly through this unit, but as an overview these systems provide information that is:

- up to date
- timely
- accurate
- reliable
- valid
- fit for purpose
- accessible
- cost effective.

The additional benefit is that the content of information can be backed up with relative ease to ensure that recovery from organisational disaster is more likely.

Effectiveness criteria (e.g. accuracy, sustainability, timelines, confidence)

How effective any information system is will be determined by a number of factors, some of which are **measurable** and others that are **subjective**. The same system could be used by two competing companies and one might say the system is effective while the other might disagree.

Measurable criteria:

- **Accuracy** – This is easy to measure: were the outputs correct or incorrect? It is not unusual for organisations to have checked the outputs of systems by other means, such as using a calculator!
- **Sustainability** – The system is said to be sustainable if the quality of the outputs from the system can be maintained on an ongoing basis.
- **Timeliness** – The system needs to be able to respond with appropriate outputs at the right time (information that is produced too late is clearly not very useful).

Subjective criterion:

- **Confidence** – This is difficult to measure and will largely depend on the personal judgements of the individuals using the information output by the system. If the users' experiences have been largely positive, they will be said to have confidence in the system.

3.4 Be able to use IT tools to produce management information

This section will cover the following grading criteria:

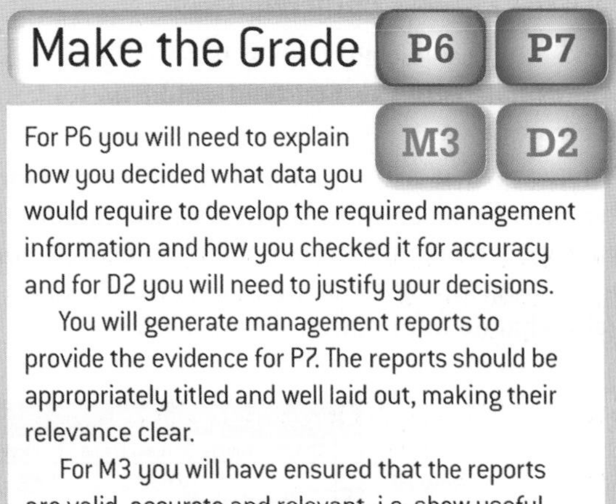

For P6 you will need to explain how you decided what data you would require to develop the required management information and how you checked it for accuracy and for D2 you will need to justify your decisions.

You will generate management reports to provide the evidence for P7. The reports should be appropriately titled and well laid out, making their relevance clear.

For M3 you will have ensured that the reports are valid, accurate and relevant, i.e. show useful information that is ultimately fit for purpose.

3.4.1 Tools

What is the difference between a computer with data and an information system? The distinction is much as it would be if we defined the difference between data and information.

> **Activity 4**
>
> Can you remember and write down the definitions for data and information?

In reality, information systems are made up of a number of components. Which components a particular information system will have will depend on what the system is supposed to do.

Many information systems are built on **databases**. This is because data needs to be stored electronically before it can be converted into information. In most cases this will be in a database, although on occasions you will see a spreadsheet used instead (because spreadsheets also have limited database functionality).

> **Key terms**
>
> A **database** is a collection of records that has been organised in a logical way.

From Figure 3.13, you will see that each **column** of information (known as a **field**) will hold a different piece of **like** information for a number of students. Each **row** will hold a **different** record.

If we were to add a subsequent record, the (AutoNumber) in the first field would **increment** (increase) to 2.

Databases that are structured in this way form the basis for most information systems, and other software can be used to manipulate, interrogate or make judgements about this data. This is essentially what an information system does.

There are a number of examples of information systems. These will be explored here.

Artificial intelligence, expert systems

Artificial intelligence is a huge developmental area at present, where scientists attempt to programme machines that can mimic human thought processes and react accordingly. Robots that can learn are a good example.

Let's think about this in real terms. The CleanMate 365 QQ1® is an intelligent vacuum cleaner that, once set up, can vacuum a room without any human intervention. To see this in action use the following link:

www.youtube.com/watch?v=QvxXFtOeUmA

Another example of an intelligent solution is the Robomow® which, like the CleanMate®, needs to be configured (see Figure 3.14).

The Robomow® requires a one-time simple set up, which can easily be done by the consumer. A standard electric wire is laid around the edges of the lawn, and attached to the surface of the lawn with pegs every few metres. The wire and pegs are supplied with the unit in the same box. The wire is connected to a small battery-powered current source called Perimeter Switch (also supplied in the box). Typically the wire will be covered by grass and become unnoticeable in a matter of 2–3 weeks. Robomow® recognises the wire using a special sensor and makes sure it always stays inside. In this instance the sensors help the machine to **mimic** thought processes and react accordingly and so the lawnmower will only mow the grass where there is in fact grass, staying away from objects such as bushes and borders.

Another example of using expert systems is **NHS Direct**. This service is designed as a first port-of-call for patients and their families when they have urgent queries regarding medical conditions. It is a **medical diagnosis tool**. This is how it works:

The patient or family member calls the designated phone number.

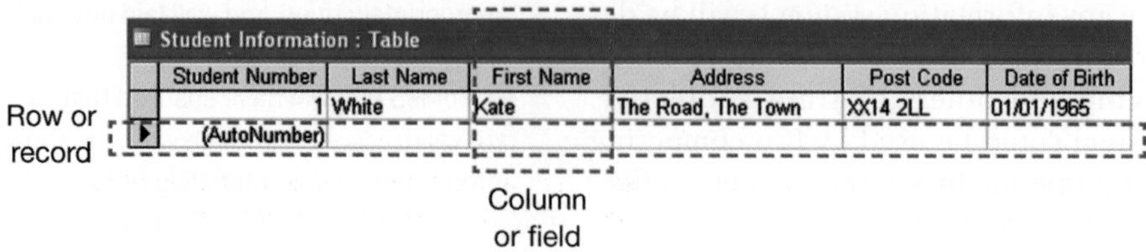
Student Information : Table

Student Number	Last Name	First Name	Address	Post Code	Date of Birth
1	White	Kate	The Road, The Town	XX14 2LL	01/01/1965
(AutoNumber)					

Figure 3.13 Database table

Figure 3.14 How the Robomow® works (images and text used with the kind permission of www.mower-magic.co.uk)

The phone is answered by a trained nurse who runs through a series of set questions.

Depending on each answer that the caller gives, the next question is activated. See Figure 3.15 to see how this works.

The expert system is effectively **rule-based** (forming a **decision 'tree'**), and it depends on how each condition is resolved as to the action the system then takes.

Other professionals will also use industry-related expert systems – for example engineers, geologists and chemists will use such software.

The main advantages of these systems is firstly that they can be easily updated and secondly that relatively inexperienced professionals can use them effectively. Expert systems, particularly, will be based on the concepts of a database.

Predictive modelling

Predictive modelling is a process of using and manipulating ranges of variables to **forecast potential outcomes** or **behaviours**. For example, to be able confidently to create a range of clothing for different markets around the world, data about the relevant population, such as heights, weights, colour preferences, would be used to adapt each item in the right way to make it suitable for the intended market.

Internet

With the significant growth in recent years of **e-commerce** (doing business online), many organisations rely on websites, supported by databases, to manage and record their business transactions. In fact, some organisations trade solely online. Many companies with high-street outlets have created websites as an additional means of selling their goods and services.

Data mining

Data mining software provides specific types of functionality that are not usually available in

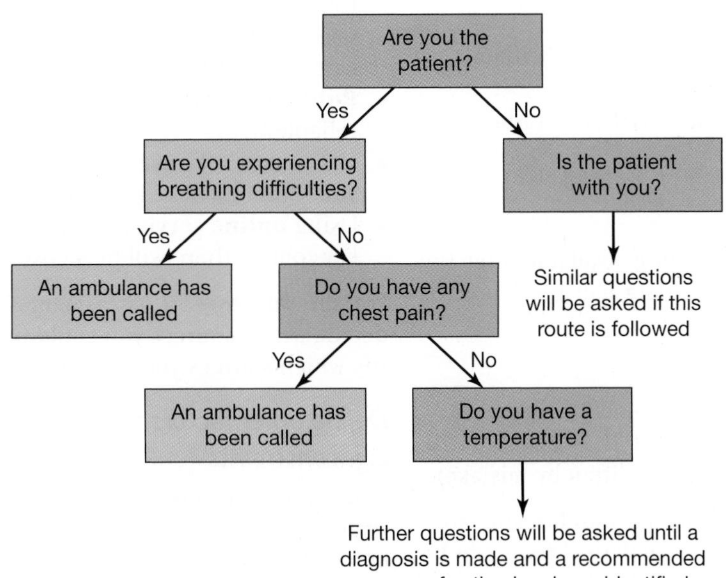

Figure 3.15 NHS Direct

regular software, without intervention and activity from the user. Earlier in this unit we looked at the line graph shown in Figure 3.16.

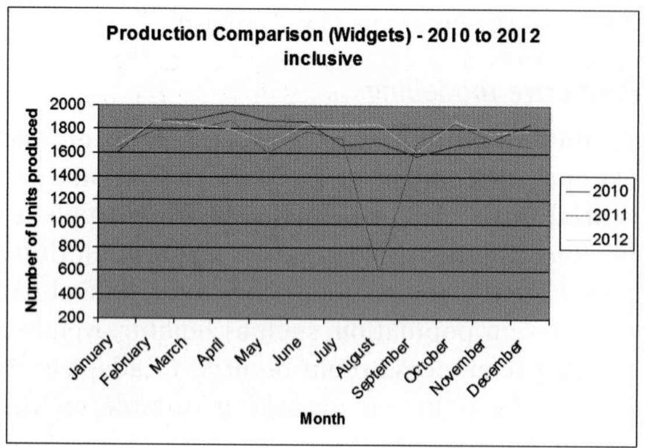

Figure 3.16 Exception report

In order to identify that there was a problem with the data, it required the user firstly to make the chart, then to interpret whether there was anything **exceptional** about it.

Data mining software can not only identify unusual events, but has **drill-down** functionality so that the data can be investigated at lower and lower levels until the exception is found and can be understood.

Typical data mining software has:

- number crunching and statistical functionality not usually found in software like Microsoft Access®
- the ability to analyse sub-levels in the data
- report-writing functionality
- the ability to be used with most database software.

Data warehousing

In order that historical data is available after the trading year has finished, data can be deposited into **data warehousing** software.

The data must be:

- well organised (often by subject or theme)
- stored in such a way that it is non-volatile (cannot be deleted or over-written by mistake).

Once the data is stored in the warehousing software, data mining or other analytical tools can be used to interrogate the data and make comparisons.

Producing management information

To complete the unit you will have to produce management information using IT tools and it is likely that the evidence will be generated through assessment based on a simulation. Spreadsheets and/or database software will probably feature heavily.

3.4.2 Gather information

Define the requirements

Before beginning any management information exercise, you should ensure that you really do understand exactly what it is you are trying to find out.

Let's consider that you want to launch a new product that will be targeted at the general public. What do you need to know?

- Who will buy the product?
- In what quantities will they buy it?
- How often will they buy it?

In this instance, these are the requirements for information gathering – they define what you want and need to know.

Establish sources of information

You now need to decide the sources you will use to gather the information. Let's consider some examples that could be used:

- **Questionnaires** – return rate of completed questionnaires can be low
- **Focus groups** (groups of individuals gathered together to discuss a new product) – can be useful for fully exploring a new product, but can also be time consuming to run
- **Published information** – is the information reliable?
- Use a **market research consultancy** to help you – there will be a cost involved
- Using **online services** such as www.surveymonkey.com/ – there will be a cost involved

For the purposes of assessment you will need to decide which sources you could use, and then justify which sources you did use.

Define other factors to be considered, e.g. constraints

Is the product only to be launched nationally or regionally? In this case, you might not want to know about the views and buying habits of individuals and groups elsewhere in the UK.

Are there time constraints? For example, if the product is seasonal, is there time to gather information and implement the project?

Select information

Having gathered the information, it should be carefully screened to make sure that only the most relevant information is selected. For the assessment, you will need to justify which information you do use and which you choose to discard.

3.4.3 Analyse information

Establishing the quality of the information chosen for analysis is straightforward if you consider the data from the following perspectives:

- Is it valid? Is the information logical and reasonable?
- Is it accurate? Could the information have been compromised? Could some of it be incorrect?
- Is it current? How old is the information? Is more up-to-date information available?
- Is it relevant? Is it the right information for our needs?

In the event that the answer to any of the above is no, then you should also consider what alternatives are available.

3.4.4 Management information

You will need to produce management information to meet a defined requirement. This could include creating reports such as sales reports, but could also include analysing college enrolment statistics or marketing analysis. It may well involve creating charts and graphs that identify trends or the information could be used to make predictions through a cash flow forecast. In terms of brick versus click – a comparative analysis of buying trends when purchasing on the internet or on the high street will certainly give organisations a focus for where they should be selling their products.

As an example, the sales figures in Figure 3.17 could be used to make predictions about ice cream sales for 2011.

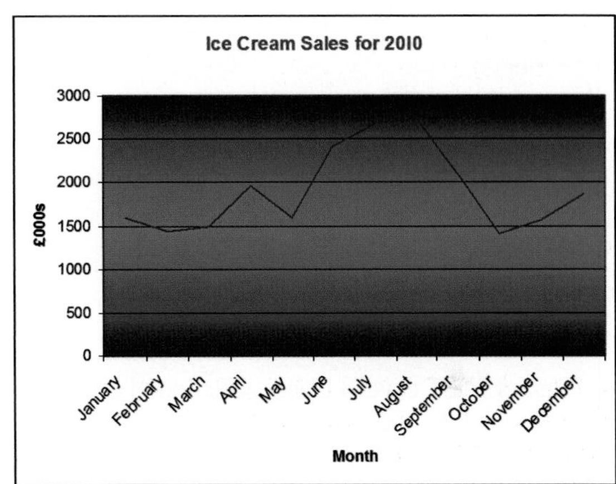

Figure 3.17 Sales report for ice cream for 2010

These predictions could then be used to plan production. Once production is established, the production figures will be used to plan purchasing activities. In order to be able to pay the suppliers, the finance department will need to ensure that sufficient finance will be available.

All this information needs to be available to be used to make the right decisions. To achieve a distinction, you will need to be able to justify the information you selected and explain how you used it to support a decision-making process.

Unit link

Unit 3 is a **mandatory unit** for all **open** and **named** pathways for National Diploma and National Extended Diploma on this Level 3 IT family. It is also **optional** for the National Certificate and National Subsidiary Diploma.

Qualification (pathway)	Mandatory	Optional	Specialist optional
Edexcel BTEC Level 3 National Certificate in Information Technology		✓	
Edexcel BTEC Level 3 National Subsidiary Diploma in Information Technology		✓	

Qualification (pathway)	Mandatory	Optional	Specialist optional
Edexcel BTEC Level 3 National Diploma in Information Technology	✓		
Edexcel BTEC Level 3 National Extended Diploma in Information Technology	✓		
Edexcel BTEC Level 3 National Diploma in IT (Business)	✓		
Edexcel BTEC Level 3 National Extended Diploma in IT (Business)	✓		
Edexcel BTEC Level 3 National Diploma in IT (Networking and System Support)	✓		
Edexcel BTEC Level 3 National Extended Diploma in IT (Networking and System Support)	✓		
Edexcel BTEC Level 3 National Diploma in IT (Software Development)	✓		
Edexcel BTEC Level 3 National Extended Diploma in IT (Software Development)	✓		

There are specific links to the following units in the scheme:
Unit 21 – Data analysis and design

Achieving success

In order to achieve each unit, you will complete a series of coursework activities. Each time you hand in work, your tutor will return this to you with a record of your achievement.

This particular unit has 12 criteria to meet: 7 Pass, 3 Merit and 2 Distinction.

For a Pass: You must achieve all 7 Pass criteria.

For a Merit: You must achieve all 7 Pass and all 3 Merit criteria.

For a Distinction: You must achieve all 7 Pass, all 3 Merit and both Distinction criteria.

Further reading

Lucey, T. – *Management Information Systems, 8th* Edition (Continuum Press, London, 2000) ISBN 0826454070

Bocij, P., Cheffey, D., Greasley, A. and Hickie, S. – *Business Information Systems: Technology Development and Management* (FT Prentice Hall, 2005) ISBN 027388146

Anderson, H. and Yull, S. – *BTEC Nationals IT Practitioners: Core Units for Computing and IT* (Newnes, 2002) ISBN 0750656840

Knott, G. and Waites, N. – *BTEC Nationals for IT Practitioners* (Brancepeth Computer Publications, 2002) ISBN 0953884821

Website

www.comp.glam.ac.uk/pages/staff/tdhutchings/chapter1.html,

Unit 4: Impact of the use of IT on business systems

By the end of this unit you should be able to:

1. Understand the effect of developments in information technology on organisations
2. Understand how organisations respond to information technology developments
3. Be able to propose improvements to business systems using IT

Whether you are in school or college, passing this unit will involve being assessed. As with most BTEC schemes, successful completion of various assessment criteria demonstrates your evidence of learning and the skills you have developed.

This unit has a mixture of pass, merit and distinction criteria. Generally you will find that merit and distinction criteria require a little more thought and evaluation before they can be completed.

The colour-coded grid below shows you the pass, merit and distinction criteria for this unit.

To achieve a pass grade you need to:	To achieve a merit grade you also need to:	To achieve a distinction grade you also need to:
P1 Explain the reasons for upgrading IT systems in an organisation	**M1** Examine why an organisation needs to keep pace with IT developments	
P2 Explain the impact of IT developments on an organisation		**D1** Evaluate the impact of IT developments on an organisation
P3 Explain how organisations respond to information technology developments		
P4 Explain how an organisation can manage risk when using IT technology		
P5 Describe recent IT developments	**M2** Suggest how recent developments may improve a business system	
P6 Produce a proposal for an IT-enabled improvement to a business system	**M3** Demonstrate originality in proposing an IT-enabled improvement	**D2** Fully justify proposals for an IT-enabled improvement

Introduction

IT-related products and services are under constant development, so this 10-credit unit focuses on technological change and its impact on the face of business today. Whether or not organisations explore and embrace new technologies will be their choice. If, however, they do such systems will have on the business. They will also need to understand the potential costs of not investing.

How to read this chapter

This chapter is organised to match the content of the BTEC unit it represents. The following diagram shows the grading criteria that relate to each learning outcome.

You'll find colour-matching notes in each chapter about completing each grading criterion.

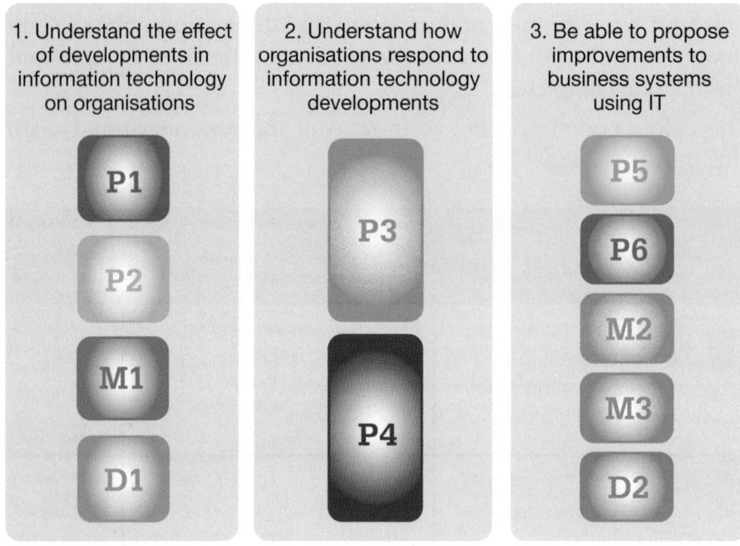

Figure 04.00

4.1 Examine the reasons for upgrading IT systems

The following sections will cover the following grading criterion:

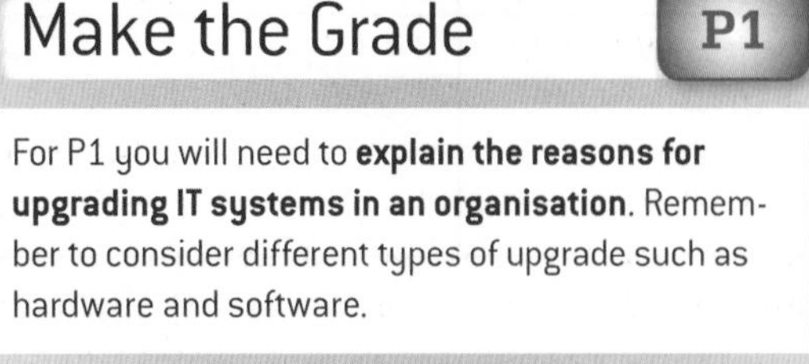

Extensive technological developments made over the last three decades have seen:

- a wider range of software;
- more business functionality support;
- the resolution of compatibility issues between different packages;
- better integration of products.

Organisations use this improved technology:

- through better information management;
- improved presentation;
- increased ability to manipulate data in different ways;
- better communication.

4.1.1 Hardware developments

Anyone who has been technologically aware since the late 1980s or early 1990s can give you lots of anecdotes about how slow computers used to be and how you had time to go and make a cup of coffee and a sandwich while the machine went through its boot sequence or attempted to open an application!

Computers at this time ran on Intel® 80286 or 80386 processors which, when compared with modern processors, is like comparing the tortoise and the hare (Figure 4.01).

Having said that, however, users would not really have considered the speed of a 386 16 MHz processor particularly slow because at that time there was nothing faster to compare it with. It was only as new technology (in this case the 80486 processor) came into the public arena, that the 80386 technology began to look jaded. So it is with any technological advancement.

Figure 4.01 Old technology

The increased power and speed of modern hardware has opened up a whole range of technological possibilities from robotic manufacturing to interactive learning and computer-assisted medical procedures. The upsurge in **C**omputer-**A**ided **D**esign/**C**omputer-**A**ided **M**anufacturing (CAD/CAM) technologies, for example, has triggered huge changes in the way that goods are produced.

Automated car production (Figure 4.02) is now commonplace, with the knock-on effect that jobs traditionally done by people are now being done by machine. The advantage of using machines over human workers is obvious: machines do not take holidays and can work long hours without breaks. While you might initially want to say that machines don't get sick, you would have to bear in mind that machines, like humans, can go wrong. However, if machines are regularly maintained and serviced, rather than being allowed to run until they break, then even downtime can be largely avoided.

Figure 4.02 Automated car plant

The automotive industry is not the only one that has been affected by advances in technology. Plastics production, bottling plants, food production, distribution, logistics and many more have seen a rise in technology investment, with a corresponding fall in the use of human workers.

Education, too, has been changed beyond all recognition through **I**nformation **L**earning **T**echnology (**ILT**). Computers in the classroom have improved learners' access to information to gain knowledge, with the advantage (unlike with books) that this resource is nearly always up to date.

There are some obvious exceptions to this trend. Many of the service industries (for example, nursing, hairdressing) and the trades (for example, plumbing, building, car maintenance) rely on human interactions. They have remained largely unaffected, although they increasingly use computerised equipment as part of their jobs (for example, programmed **knowledge systems** like those used by NHS Direct are also being developed for other diagnostic uses).

Some people believe that advances in technology will slow down in the next few years as companies run out of invention ideas. Others, however, believe the opposite – that continued investment in development will see even more progress being made.

Today, areas of major investment include robotics (specifically artificial intelligence), medicine (such as smart limbs, which are capable of interfacing with the body's own nervous system) and communications (mobile telephones with even more functionality than at present).

Increasing capacity and sophistication of platforms

There are three main advances here:

- Increased hard-drive capacity allows organisations to store more of their historic data than previously possible, giving them access to larger datasets for analysis.
- Faster processors allow much more complex tasks to be undertaken more quickly.
- Operating systems have improved functionality, enabling systems and networks to work together more efficiently, including allowing users to share resources and offering a wider range of utilities for system management.

Increasing sophistication of communication technologies

The developments in communications technology have probably had the most impact on the way in which organisations operate.

Modern mobile phones ensure that working teams, customers, suppliers and distributors maintain contact much more easily than was ever really thought possible. The ability to access the internet and thus a range of information via mobile phone technology has also revolutionised our responsiveness.

Electronic systems that track goods in transit have enabled businesses to demand a better service from their delivery agents, and ensure that customers' needs are met more effectively.

Networks have ensured that individuals inside companies can have access to and can share information more easily: information can be quickly updated improving response times, timeliness of information and generally making up-to-date facts and figures available at the touch of a button. In addition, many organisations have their own intranet through which they share news and event information.

Wireless networking and wireless broadband technologies have enabled employees to work from just about anywhere.

Prior to email, almost all companies had busy internal mail systems, where memos and other documents were physically moved between departments, even across sites. While this still happens (as there will be instances where documents can not be sent electronically), more and more internal communication is now supported through the use of email, and in some cases, organisational online messaging systems.

Electronic data interchange

> **Key terms**
>
> **Electronic data interchange (EDI)** Essentially, an EDI is a method of exchanging controlled information between companies using information technology.

EDI is a system that allows inter-organisational communication of business documents, such as orders and invoices, and that through its use has reduced the amount of paperwork needed to support most business activities. Boeing, for example, schedule their manufacture of aircraft well in advance, and as they are unable to stock many of the components that go into aircraft building (specifically because of the size of an engine, set of wings, fuselage pieces), they need these components to be delivered to them immediately, the components prior to being installed into an aeroplane. They use EDI-style systems to communicate with their suppliers, who then produce the components and get them to the Boeing factory, immediately before they are needed (**JIT – Just In Time**).

The advantage of all of the above communications technologies is that many of them are effectively **time-independent**. Using a computer to track a parcel through an electronic system can be done at any time of the day or night. Email from customers in different time zones can be sent to you while your company is closed, and will be held until your workers return. EDI systems can operate day and night because any documents sent through such a system will be stored until the employees are there to respond to them.

4.1.2 Software developments

Software is becoming increasingly complex, but is also offering more and more advanced functionality over its predecessors.

Increased complexity and integration of application software

The main difficulty for software manufacturers when developing new applications software has always been the issue of backward compatibility (that is being able to open and upgrade files created in previous versions of a product). Files created in the original Microsoft Access® database software, for example, were not usable when Microsoft® upgraded to Microsoft Access® 2.0. Many companies had to find ways of exporting huge quantities of data from the old version, changing its format and then importing it into the newer version. Microsoft® was aware of the problems it cause for companies, and has endeavoured not to cause the same problems with subsequent releases of software.

It has also long been recognised that being able to export tables of information from a database package, and maybe graphs or charts from a spreadsheet, would create better presented, more interesting and professional word-processed reports. However, until recently, simple copying and pasting was not an option, because there was a level of incompatibility between the products. Microsoft Office® is a truly integrated package, where copy, paste and embedded editing of different data sources is readily available. This has been followed by a number of similar integrated software packages (see Table 4.01).

Many of these products have also been created for multiple platforms (for example, Microsoft Windows®, Mac OSX® and Linux).

Integrated software has also enabled organisations to produce consistent documentation across multiple applications, further enhancing their professional image.

Specialised support software

It should also come as no surprise that there are more and more specialist products on the market that have specific uses (for example, management information systems, decision-support software, expert systems). **Middleware**, for example, is specialist communications software that enables applications to integrate across networked systems and environments.

Management Information Systems

A **M**anagement **I**nformation **S**ystem (**MIS**) is designed to help executives manage an organisation by giving them sufficient information to help them control the overall direction and the day-to-day activities. The information the system produces must be in the right format and must be available at the right time to provide the required support.

Decision-support software

Decision-support software is used to help managers predict the future, using 'what if?' scenarios, so that they can, as far as possible, see the consequences of decisions that they make. The software is able to use what is known about a previous decision of the same type, plus a range of other known or estimated factors, to simulate the likely outcome.

Table 4.01

Name of product	Manufacturer	Functionality
Oracle Open Office	Oracle®	Word processing, spreadsheet, presentation, drawing and database www.oracle.com/us/products/applications/open-office/index.html
WordPerfect® Office X5	Corel®	Word processing, spreadsheet, database, presentation, PDF tools www.corel.com/servlet/Satellite/gb/en/Product/1207676528492
Open Office Suite	OpenOffice.org	Word processing, presentation, drawing, spreadsheet, database, Advanced calculator, PDF creator www.openoffice.org/

Expert systems

Using a pre-programmed knowledge base and a set of rules, an expert system is designed to act as an expert in a given situation. One of the best-known expert systems is used by NHS Direct to help medical staff diagnose medical conditions and offer recommendations on treatment. It should be noted, however, that this particular system is monitored by qualified staff, particularly as the decisions it makes could literally mean life or death for the caller.

Security software

The increased ability to communicate electronically has increased an organisation's need for better security of systems, both in terms of physical security (for example, locking rooms and employing security staff) and logical security (tools that are largely software based). In fact, this has become such an important issue that this course has dedicated an entire unit to it – Unit 7.

E-commerce

The face of business changed forever with the development of the internet and the World Wide Web. Suddenly products and services were easier to find, the range and choice expanded beyond anything previously experienced, and businesses suddenly had more opportunities. In fact, some would say that organisations that fail to exploit e-commerce might be in danger of losing business to those organisations that are willing to invest in the relevant technologies.

Key terms

Internet – The internet was originally developed in 1969. It is effectively a huge network of networks, containing millions of computers. The internet is used to communicate, inform and gather information. Two of the most widely used facilities that use the internet are email and the World Wide Web.

Intranet – An intranet is a private network inside an organisation. The organisation uses the intranet to share information or advise staff of training courses or upcoming events. Some organisational intranets also have messaging or chat software that allow staff to communicate in an instant electronically.

Extranet – an extranet is a cross between an intranet and the internet in that it is still a private network, but it uses standard communications systems that are open to the public to securely share organisational information with selected external parties (such as customers or suppliers).

The three services work to provide improved communication throughout the organisation, between the organisation and its stakeholders and the world in general.

Unit link

Please refer to **Unit 8** for a much more detailed look at e-Commerce.

4.1.3 Reasons for upgrading systems

Why do organisations need to change? Why can't they just go on in the same way that they have been for years?

- **Customers make demands for new products and services.** Companies that fail to respond to these demands will (a) not receive any new business and, (b) more importantly, could lose their existing business as customers go elsewhere to buy the new products and find the other products also available.
- **Companies need to grow.** Money put into companies is basically an investment, so investors will want to see an improved return over a period of time. If this does not occur, then they will simply withdraw their money and invest it somewhere else, where they anticipate that the returns will be greater. Eventually, as more and more demands are made on systems, they become increasingly inefficient (for example, the volumes of data they handle get larger, the tasks the computers are expected to perform become more complex).
- **Competitors' activities see them becoming proportionally more successful.** Anything that weakens an organisation's position in the market will be detrimental to the ultimate survival of the organisation.

Key terms

Globalisation – This can be more or less defined from a number of different viewpoints. The following perspectives are all part of the globalisation framework:

- Internationalism
- Liberalism
- Universalism

Internationalism – This is the concept that international barriers are being overcome and accepted as normal. Part of this is because of improved communications between most nations in the world. World travel is also much easier. Taking Europe as an example, the countries within it were originally extremely well defined and separated. Each had its own boundaries, language(s) and currency. In the last three or four decades, however, the European Union (EU) has been formed and the divisions between the member countries has begun to diminish. While each country still has clear physical borders, English is becoming the main language, and the euro has replaced the traditional currency of many of the member countries. Britain has chosen to retain its own currency, although this decisions is under constant review.

Liberalism – In order to benefit from an improved world economy, many countries (but not all) are becoming more lenient about their borders, encouraging trade and the migration of individuals, and in general there is more acceptance of other traditions and cultures. The world is, in many respects, becoming a much more integrated society. Similarly, in the UK we are required to comply with legislation created by the European Parliament (significant work-related legislation has come to UK this way).

Universalism – This is the fact that goods that had once been hard to buy in some countries are now easier to purchase than ever before.

Globalisation has resulted in some technologies becoming more generic so that they fit with other technologies in different parts of the world. Consider the concept of the home entertainment system. Some manufacturers have had to make agreements on standards, formats and physical connections of certain types of device. Other companies have been reluctant to do this as they fear losing sales and competitiveness if they forego their unique position.

Case Study

Keeping up with competitors

Some years ago, Benetton® (the clothing manufacturing group) invested heavily in new computerised CAD/CAM and logistics systems, which let it get products to the marketplace three weeks earlier than it had done before. This let the group increase its competitive advantage over its rivals and reduce the amount of manpower required. It effectively increased efficiency and throughput, while decreasing the need for human workers. The impact of new CAD/CAM technologies in clothing businesses has greatly improved the industry's ability to respond to new markets, and those competitors that have the funding have found themselves having to invest in similar technologies just to keep up.

Activity 1

Investigate software used in the clothing and fashion industry. Name five different software products and explain what they do. You might find the following URL useful: www.apparelsearch.com/computer_assisted_design.htm

Managers, particularly, should fully appreciate where the organisation is positioned in relation to its customers, investors and competitors and should be prepared to respond to the challenges posed.

There are many reasons why organisations find themselves having to upgrade their systems. They will, for example, have to react to external pressures such as **changes in the law**, and they will also need to explore internal data trying to **find enhanced business opportunities**. This section considers some of these factors.

Changes in regulatory and legal frameworks

Unit 3 Information systems discusses in depth the legal implications of using information, and considers the responsibilities of employers and employees in relation to Health and Safety in the workplace when using IT. Other legislation also has a direct impact on organisations and employees, particular in terms of IT-related issues.

As markets have become more global, then organisations have more legislation to contend with because they will also need to observe and comply with any regulations in countries with whom they trade. The **I**nternational **O**rganization for **S**tandardization (**ISO**) is a body that seeks to regulate standards. It has a large number of member states with different levels of membership. Their level of membership has a bearing on the voting rights of each state country. A full list of the member states can be found at http://www.iso.org/iso/about/iso_members.htm.

The member countries work together to ensure that issues, such as safety standards and product standards, are set, adhered to and policed in those countries. Clearly, membership of any multinational organisation is going to be optional.

The ISO is essentially trying to make the economic environment much fairer for all. If an organisation trades with one of the member states, then it can take reassurance that the rules and regulations will be the same. However, the list of countries has some interesting omissions! For this reason, organisations must protect themselves by ensuring that they are not breaking any regional laws when trading in external environments.

Enhanced business opportunities

No one would disagree that perspectives are increasingly important and companies that wish to succeed in the global market must accept these concepts, and be willing to work with them, rather than trying to avoid or work against them!

Potential for outsourcing and geosourcing

Companies that are willing to take advantage (and a little risk) by outsourcing or geosourcing will probably find that they can purchase good quality solutions much more cheaply.

Improving customer service

Some might say that using technology in customer service and support is a negative step. Technology has, for example, enabled companies to outsource their customer support functionality (usually known as **call centres**) to other countries around the world (Figure 4.03). This is currently a controversial debate, because some customers are irritated by the fact that they find themselves speaking to someone in a foreign country when the business has premises geographically close by.

Figure 4.03 Customer service adviser

Key terms

Outsourcing – This is the practice of buying in skills (that are not core to the revenue-earning side of the business, for example, IT skills) from outside the organisation when they are needed on a fixed-term basis. This can be cheaper than employing and training staff who may not have sufficient work to do to make their employment viable.

Geosourcing – This is similar to outsourcing, but the implication is that organisations can seek these skills outside the UK or the usual partner countries. For example, at the moment there is a surplus of available games programming skills in Eastern Europe (in places like Poland, the Czech Republic and Serbia and Montenegro), with a similar surplus of skills in general applications programming in parts of Asia. The advantage here is that employees in these regions have the skills, but are willing to work for significantly less money than their European counterparts would demand.

One of the main advantages, however, is that using internet technologies, for instance, lets an organisation give customer support 24 hours per day.

Technology can be used to support customers by providing:

- online user manuals;
- health and safety information;
- product specifications;
- Frequently Asked Questions (FAQs), where queries by other users are logged and the answers given recorded for all to see;
- complaints handling systems;
- customer feedback opportunities.

With the exception of the last item in the above list, most of us are always ready to accept this type of online support. In fact, many of us prefer to use websites to access this kind of information because it allows us to view the content in our own time. However, many of us become frustrated if we have to make complaints in the same way because we often want a quick response.

An organisation offering excellent customer support will respond almost immediately to an unhappy customer. Another organisation, however, may choose not to do this and continue to handle the complaint via email. There are times when this strategy is successful, but equally there are times when it is not. Good customer service is when a company knows the difference!

4.1.4 Benefits of developments in information technology

The following sections will cover the following grading criterion:

Make the Grade — M1

For M1 you will **examine why an organisation needs to keep pace with IT developments** and the reasons for upgrading, such as external pressure. You will consider some of the benefits. You will effectively be explaining why an organisation might feel that upgrading is necessary.

From a performance perspective, the implementation and wider use of improved IT systems has had a positive impact on the fortunes of organisations. Generally, this impact can be seen as a series of undeniable benefits.

Productivity gains

The use of IT systems:

- facilitates longer production periods;
- more or less guarantees a consistently better quality of product;
- makes processes more efficient;
- enables processes to occur faster.

Cost reduction and increased profitability

If you can reduce operating (day-to-day running) costs, production costs, distribution costs and so on, then you will automatically see an increase in profitability. Examples of how IT has enabled these costs to be reduced are:

- fewer staff are required as processes become automated, saving wages and salaries;
- the use of EDI, thereby removing the need for sundry expenses (such as postage);
- less wastage of raw material if more of it is successfully turned into the finished product.

Efficiency

IT solutions provide opportunities for greater efficiency, particularly as the profit margin (the difference between the cost of making or doing something and how much you can sell it for) increases. This means:

- Better stock efficiency, with less stock tying up capital because it can be ordered closer to when it will be sold or used.
- Queries are handled more quickly.
- Enhance ability to respond to opportunities and threats.

Improved management information and control

This is such an important aspect of the use of IT in business that Unit 3 **Information Systems** is dedicated solely to this subject area. In brief:

- More information is available because greater quantities of data are being stored.
- Data and information are more accessible.
- Data is more easily manipulated and viewed from various perspectives.

- Information can be made available more quickly.
- Information will be more accurate.
- Historic data can be effectively used to make comparisons about performance.
- Decision-making will be enhanced because information to support the process will be readily available.
- Control over activities is enhanced because information from all areas can be shared to improve the quality of activities across the whole organisation.

Customer service

Customer service benefits from:

- seemingly being available for longer periods of time (for example, if the service is provided via email);
- using email to quickly distribute queries and concerns to the right individuals within the organisation;
- analysing the types of calls taken to look for particular issues or trends, which could help a proactive organisation (one that anticipates the sorts of problems that customers might face and react accordingly).

Synergy and integration of systems

Well-developed systems, where the issues of data and process integration have been considered and accommodated, will produce systems that have greater **synergy**. This means that the various systems within the organisation will work together to produce better quality data, information and therefore better services to all stakeholders within the organisation.

4.1.5 Impact of developments on organisations

This section will cover the following grading criteria:

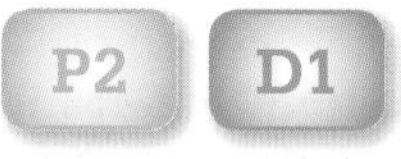

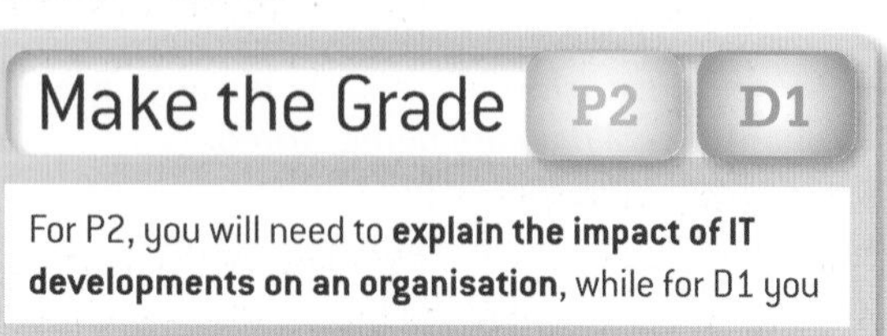

For P2, you will need to **explain the impact of IT developments on an organisation**, while for D1 you should **evaluate the impact of IT developments on an organisation** (that is, evaluate the benefits of change when weighed against the risks).

A cost–benefit analysis, although not specifically required, may provide the evidence to meet the D1 criterion effectively.

Developments in technology can have a widespread impact on organisations and for this reason a company should carefully consider the consequences of the decisions it takes.

Costs of development

An organisation should not make an investment unless it is confident that it can fully recover the cost. At the very least, the company should break even. Here are some examples:

Case Study

Company A has a production line that designs and manufactures plastic products. It has an antiquated CAD/CAM system and a large number of operatives who use the system. The company decides to spend £30,000 upgrading the system and retraining four of the six employees who use the current system. Once implemented, the organisation reduces the workforce by two people who earn £15,000 each per year. This means that at the end of the first year the organisation has been able to break even. In the second year, the implemented system will be helping the organisation to make a profit.

What is the impact on the organisation? Financial outlay is recovered quite quickly, but what about the reduction in staff? Two staff members, in this instance, have been made redundant, so the cost to the organisation is also the loss of two individuals and any other skills that they contributed to the organisation's activities.

Company B spends £50,000 developing and implementing a new online presence (website and sales system). It anticipates that if it can increase sales by £10,000 per year over the next five years, the investment will have been worthwhile. In actual fact, because the organisation is now entering markets that were previously inaccessible, it improves sales by £30,000 in the first year and by a further £36,000 in the second year.

What is the impact on the organisation? In this instance it is likely that the organisation will have had to employ extra staff (at extra cost) to help them managed the increased sales.

Impact on procedures and staff

The implementation of technology will almost always have an impact on organisational procedures. Staff will find themselves having to do things in a new way, with new equipment and tools. They may also find themselves working differently because some of the tasks they would normally have undertaken are now executed by computers or machines.

Upskilling and training staff

One of the most important **consequences** of the increased use of IT in the workplace has been the constant need for organisations to 'upskill' their workforce through **appropriate training**. From an organisational perspective, this dramatically increases the cost of implementing new systems.

Nearly all further education (FE) colleges provide a wide range of IT courses, many of which may suit the needs of employees. In addition, college-supported venues and commercial training providers will also offer a similar, possibly more limited, range. For those employees working with computer technology, such as hardware and systems, any of the following courses might be appropriate:

- Computer hardware qualifications (maybe from the CompTIA® suite, such as A+, Security+ or Network+).
- Higher National Certificates, Diplomas and Foundation Degrees in Software Development (computer programming), Networking or IT Systems.
- Specialist courses such as Microsoft® Certified Systems Engineer (MCSE) courses for managing servers and networks.
- Cisco® Certified Network Associate (CCNA) courses for organisations that use Cisco systems.

Alternatively, if organisations need to provide user-level qualifications the range offered might include:

- word processing;
- database;
- Microsoft Outlook Express®;
- desktop publishing;
- Sage Accounting®.
- spreadsheets;
- internet and email;
- webpage design;
- presentation graphics;

If, however, the systems implemented use bespoke (purpose-built) software, then it would be unlikely that any training would be available from the usual sources. At these times, it is customary for the developers to provide some level of training as part of the development package.

Organisations must always weigh up the cost implications of training, which can be wider than simply the costs of courses.

Scorecard – Training

+ Training on generic software, such as word-processing, internet or desktop publishing, is likely to be relatively inexpensive, particularly if the courses are done in a college or community venue.
+ Using cascade training (such as training one or two individuals from an organisation, who in turn train others) can be an inexpensive way of teaching staff.
+ Staff feel valued if organisations invest in their skills.
+ If appropriate, training can be made specific (tailored) to the needs of organisations, and it can be delivered at the organisation's premises, to ensure that it exactly meets the needs of the organisation.
– Generic training might not always fully address the needs of users.
– When employees are being trained, they will not be doing their usual jobs and organisations either need to put cover arrangements in place or accept that work will fall a little behind (this costs additional money and can put other people under pressure).
– Tailored training can be expensive, although most organisations would say that they feel the investment in such training is worthwhile in the long run.

Identifying training needs

Sometimes a need is easy to identify because new systems are being implemented and, as such, it is obvious that users will need to be trained to use these systems.

It is more likely, however, that training needs will be identified through the annual appraisals that most employees undergo. This is when the employee's performance over a period of time (usually one year) is discussed and evaluated. Employees are encouraged to identify their own training needs, but managers also may make suggestions.

What is most important about this concept is that an organisation's failure to train employees to use systems correctly will merely result in staff not working efficiently, which ultimately will be to a company's detriment and to the benefit of its competitors.

Dealing with redundancies

Another consequence of improvements in technology has been that some employee skills have become unnecessary or redundant. For example, engineering parts once manufactured by highly skilled lathe workers are now produced by programmed machines. One of the main advantages of this is that there are fewer parts rejected because machines can work more consistently with very accurate machining tolerances.

The company has a number of choices for what it does with employees whose skills are no longer needed:

- Use employees elsewhere – it is possible that some employees will have other skills that could be further developed to make them useful elsewhere in the organisation.
- Retrain employees – most organisations will have implemented new systems as the result of a strategic plan that was developed some time earlier, so they will have decided what to do with employees whose skills are no longer needed. Some employees will be completely retrained to do something fundamentally different from the job they were doing previously.
- Make employees redundant – this means to actually ask the employees to leave the organisation (see the case study below). An organisation might be reluctant to do this because it could lose a significant amount of knowledge about its business which it might not be able to replace very easily or which could fall into the hands of competitors.

Even so, there are times when the organisation actually has no choice other than to make employees redundant. This was certainly the case in the 1980s when unemployment in the United Kingdom rose higher than it had in previous decades.

Balancing core employees with contractors and outsourced staff

Increasingly, if an organisation is unable to afford to employ staff with particular skills or abilities, it may well have to resort to buying in these skills and experiences from contractors or other outsourced staff. However, it is likely that the organisation itself will maintain a number of key (or core) staff, primarily because of the disadvantages of using staff or services secured from outside the organisation.

Case Study

In the early part of the 1980s, when the manufacturing industry in the United Kingdom was highly affected by the recession at that time, one of the world's most well-known and largest photocopier manufacturers was forced to make most of the employees at a manufacturing plant redundant.

As a responsible employer, however, the senior management decided to do all that they could to help employees find alternative employment and, to this end, they set up their own employment agency where a group of personnel consultants were employed with the remit of contacting other local companies to try to relocate any staff who wanted that level of support. Although not all employees found new employment quickly, in general this strategy was successful because in addition to finding new opportunities for the majority, it ensured that the reputation of the manufacturer as a professional and caring company was maintained.

Scorecard – Contractors

+ You pay for contractors when you need them.
+ You don't have to train contractors.
+ You will always have a service, because if a contracted member of staff is off sick, another one will normally be provided by the external agency – there would be no reason for you to continue to pay for the service if staff were unavailable because it's not your problem.

- Contract staff may have little or no knowledge of your organisation, its products or services.
- External staff have no stake in the organisation and therefore might be less motivated and could walk away from the situation at any time.
- Staff turnover can be high as the parent organisation pulls experienced staff off one job and puts them on another.
- The organisation effectively has little control over the individuals, it must trust the agency (at the end of the day, it can always fire a contractor if the job isn't being done satisfactorily).

It would be extremely unwise for any organisation to outsource or contract staff into key positions within the organisation for the reasons listed in the scorecard.

Companies are more likely to retain their own core staff who they will continue to develop in order to ensure that the activities of contractors and agency staff are monitored.

Enabling home and remote working

A major advance in employment was made when it became technically possible for workers to work from home or from other remote locations, either as an employee of a company or by setting up a business on their own. (Figure 4.04). This had two distinct advantages:

- Organisations had a larger skills pool to choose from (because it could employ individuals outside its usual recruitment area).
- It now became possible for individuals who had not traditionally been able to enter mainstream employment to take up job opportunities.

Figure 4.04 Working from home

Types of work that individuals could now do remotely as freelancers or as a small business, or as an employee of a mainstream company, included:

- consultancy;
- writing;
- teaching (for example, The Open University uses tutors who work from home);
- graphic design;
- specialist mail order;
- product design;
- web design;
- programming;
- telesales;
- web publishing.

Most home workers simply need a computer, internet connection, appropriate software and the time and skills to be able to do the job, so it is possible for those with the skills to run a small business alone. This in itself has many advantages and disadvantages, some of which are common to the advantages and disadvantages of home working as an employee of a company.

Scorecard – Home working: the employer's perspective

+ Employers have better access to a more diverse skills set.
+ Employees might be less stressed (for example, travelling to and from work is effectively avoided).
+ There is less need to rent large amounts of office space.
+ It is usually easier to contact your employees because they are likely to be in one fixed location.
+ Some employers believe that those who work from home are more productive because they will often work slightly longer hours (travel time is avoided) and because they (possibly) experience fewer distractions or interruptions in the working day.
- Employees might become unhappy with their working situation and be difficult to motivate, for example, initially an employer might be unaware that there is a problem, so one or two minor problems that might have been resolvable could grow into much bigger issues.
- Getting employees together for meetings is more difficult because they are not all working in the same location.

– The potential for ad hoc interaction is completely diminished (no bumping into each other in the corridor, no opportunity to have a quick meeting because a project is facing a sudden crisis).
– In order to monitor an employee's activities (and productivity), an employer might have to resort to using activity monitoring software, which, in itself will have a detrimental effect on staff morale who will feel that they are not trusted.

Scorecard – Home working: the employee's perspective

+ Employees can work at a time that suits them, which accommodates those who are better at working at a specific time of the day.
+ There is a sense of freedom and the feeling of trust that employers are not watching every move.
+ The job becomes more flexible as employees are able to work around commitments (such as children or other family responsibilities).
+ Home workers can work as many, or as few, hours as they choose (so long as they meet deadlines).
– They might be tempted to work at times that are inappropriate, and where they might not be giving their employer a level of productivity that has any real quality.
– Many home workers become isolated because they have little or no direct contact with others apart from via email or the occasional phone call.
– Employees need to have a good level of self-discipline to work effectively from home because they might be easily distracted and the work might not get done.

Working from home can be exceptionally rewarding, particularly if all the systems are in place to enable an individual to do it effectively.

Dealing with the impact of regular restructuring on staff

Implementing technology can quite often result in the need for an organisation to be restructured. There are some organisations that are able to do this with a minimum of fuss, and where there is no real evidence of resistance from employees. Other organisations, however, often due to their size and structure, will find restructuring very difficult and consequently demoralising and destabilising for staff.

In many respects, the way that an organisation responds to the concept of change will be representative of the culture of the organisation.

Organisations that are unwilling to respond to change are generally autocratic and rooted in tradition and the past. This makes any restructuring, particularly due to implementation of new technology, a difficult and costly experience:

- Employees may well be resistant to restructuring or change, particularly if they feel that their own jobs and livelihoods are under threat (this is a natural reaction).
- Key employees may leave the organisation because they fear that technology or a new organisational structure might ultimately push them out.
- A lack of change management skills may make managers reluctant to implement change, and poor planning may endanger the organisation's activities.
- Unless all parts and levels of the organisation buy into the change process, success will be patchy, making it difficult for the organisation to work effectively.
- Staff may well feel demotivated and demoralised because they do not feel valued (or consulted).

This kind of response is often referred to as a **closed culture**.

Conversely, organisations that are open to the prospect of change, are more likely to see change as a natural and important part of organisational development:

- Change means new opportunities (for promotion or learning new skills).
- New employees might join the organisation (often referred to as 'bringing in new blood').
- It is a healthy consequence of an organisation that is growing and that is becoming more prosperous.
- Generally, individuals see themselves as part of the greater whole (as an important part of the organisation).
- People will feel valued and thus motivated.

This is often referred to as an **open culture**.

Successful implementation of technology will be dependent on the culture of the organisation being an enabling one – this is a culture that effectively makes things possible.

Integration of legacy systems

It is common for organisations to have multiple databases, sometimes containing the same data.

For example, in Figure 4.05, the manufacturing database is likely to hold data about which personnel worked on production. The suppliers database will have details about the raw materials that were purchased, and the manufacturing database will store how those materials were used. The customer database will have records of which personnel have been in contact (for example, sales representatives who have visited).

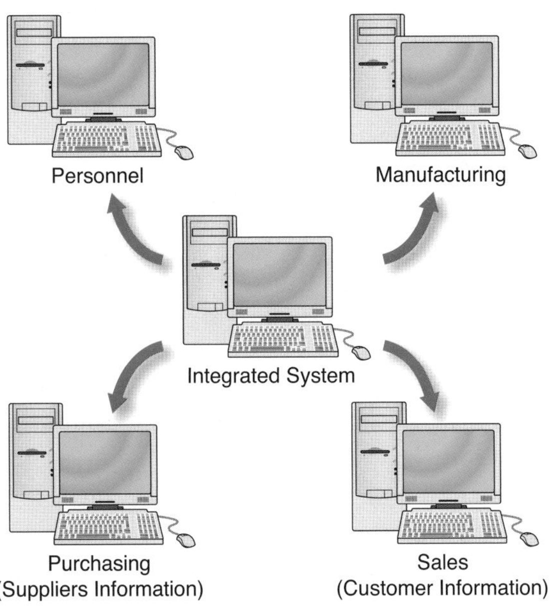

Figure 4.05 Legacy systems

These databases seem to have been created individually in order to respond to an organisational need. None of these systems are linked in any way and it is likely that identical data will be held in more than one of them at the same time.

In IT terms, these different databases would be known as **legacy systems**. This is because they are likely to be using old technology and software, but they continue to be used by the organisation because there is no alternative without investing in an integrated system which will hold all the data for the organisation and share it with the functional areas.

Although there would be a need to convert the data from legacy systems to import it into an **integrated system** (which can take time and money), the advantages of shared data, free of errors and needless duplication, far outweigh the costs (Figure 4.06).

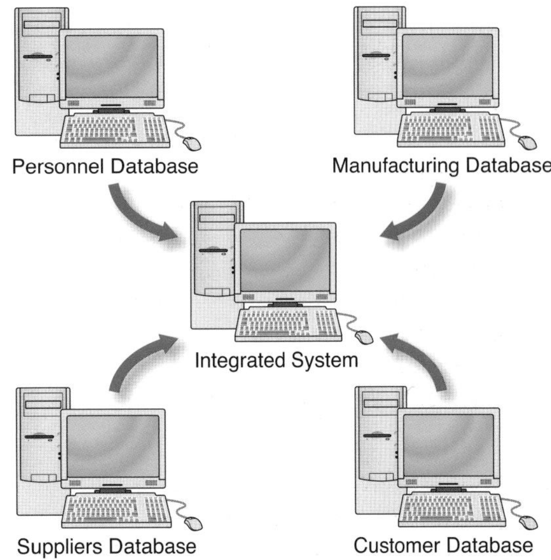

Figure 4.06 Integrated systems

Security

Advances in security technology have enabled organisations to be more confident about the safety and security of their sensitive and confidential data.

Figure 4.07 Laptop with fingerprint scanner

These technologies include a range of both physical and logical techniques.

Physical techniques will include locks on doors and alarm systems to prevent unauthorised access to computers and/or paper files. It could also include laptops that have to be accessed through a fingerprint scanner as well as a password (Figure 4.07).

Many organisations also prohibit staff from using USB flash drives in their systems (some even removing these to reduce the temptation) and from making CD or DVD copies of data (so again some computers do not have CD/DVD devices for this reason).

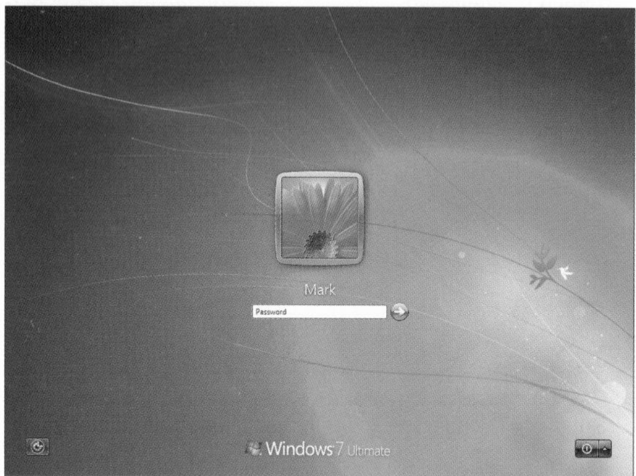

Figure 4.08 Windows® 7 Welcome screen requiring a user password

Logical techniques include password protection (Figure 4.08) and encryption protocols designed to scramble the data and make it useless to anyone that does not have the decryption keys.

Legal requirements

There is significant legislation with which an organisation must comply. This section only briefly considers the major legal issues because Unit 3 covers the requirements more thoroughly. Two important laws are:

- **Data Protection Act 1998 (DPA)**: This details the rules and regulations that govern the storage and use of personal data. Both individuals and organisations that hold personal data about individuals must inform the Office of the Information Commissioner that they are in possession of such data. There are also a number of other direct offences for which organisations and individuals can be fined, for example, selling data is against the law.
- **Copyright, Designs and Patents Act 1988**: There are strict rules around issues of copyright. In terms of this unit, you will consider it from two perspectives:
  - Copyright of data or information – information that has been copyrighted cannot be used or quoted by third parties without permission.
  - Copyright of software – unless classified as freeware or shareware (where there is a small charge), software cannot be indiscriminately copied to multiple machines. This is because the manufacturer retains ownership of the software. An organisation or individual buys a licence to use it as individual copies for individual machines or as a site licence that allows multiple installations from a single CD.

Failure to comply with either the Data Protection Act 1998 (and its amendments) or the Copyright, Designs and Patents Act 1988 (and its amendments) can result in heavy fines and, in extreme cases, imprisonment.

4.2 Understand how organisations respond to information technology developments

This section will cover the following grading criterion:

Make the Grade P3

In order to **respond to information technology developments**, organisations need to make some very complex decisions.

For P3, you should **explain** some of these responses (for example, changing the way they receive payments or how they respond to implementation of new technology in terms of changing needs for staff).

A presentation or report could be a useful way of generating this evidence.

4.2.1 Adapting business processes

Sales and marketing strategies

Sales and marketing has always been a 'data-hungry' part of any organisation. In order to understand markets, buying patterns, service users, peaks and troughs in demand, activities of competitors and so on, large quantities of data must first be gathered and then analysed and interpreted as usable information so that predictions about the future can be made, to which the organisation can respond, perhaps capitalising on global opportunities.

Gathering data has never been easier. A wealth of information is collected about us on a regular basis (some of which we might not even be aware of):

- Organisations gather data about us through media (such as loyalty cards, credit and debit cards) and through Electronic Point Of Sale (EPOS) systems (such as supermarket checkouts).
- Websites record data about our purchases and, through the additional use of hit counters, companies can calculate the sorts of websites that have the most activity.
- Demographic statistics (such as age groups populating particular towns or villages, and information about employment status) are freely available through government websites.
- Data is not restricted to particular locations.

Manipulating data is more straightforward:

- There is better functionality in database and spreadsheet software.
- New products are specifically designed to work with and interpret data.
- Identifying trends is easier, particularly with the development of graphical tools.
- 'Drill down' functionality allows users to interrogate data at lower levels.
- The use of computer systems to undertake tasks has seen quicker availability of information.

Interpreting data is easier:

- Information is presented in a more user-friendly way.
- Exceptional events are easier to identify.
- Managers will have more confidence in the outcomes of analysis.

Organisations can adapt their sales and marketing strategies because of the way that information can now be managed. They can:

- gather and analyse data more promptly;
- respond more quickly to opportunities;
- manage sales teams more effectively;
- provide information more successfully.

Purchasing strategies for automated ordering

Some organisations now refuse to do business with other organisations if they do not have access to EDI (Figure 4.12) automated ordering systems and supply chain management. Certainly some of the larger supermarkets will not trade with smaller companies who have not invested in this technology because they do not feel that these companies will be able to respond quickly enough to meet their needs. There is also less opportunity for error if information is digitally transmitted.

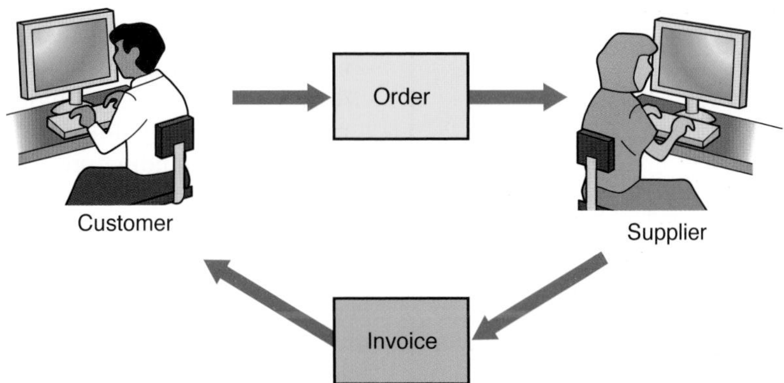

Figure 4.9 Typical EDI

A number of different types of EDI currently exist:

- **An Applicability Statement 2 (AS2)** EDI allows organisations to transmit electronic documents via the internet. The AS2 standard dictates the way that the connection is created and the way that the data is actually transferred.
- A **web-based EDI** uses a web browser to handle the data exchange process.
- **A Value Added Network (VAN) EDI** is usually set up using private networks to allow the secure exchange of information between business associates. An investment into this type of EDI, particularly with all the security requirements to ensure that systems are fully protected, would be more likely with a large company involved in regular transactions with one of its trading partners.

As with other technical aspects of systems, an organisation's EDI requirements can also be outsourced.

Case Study

Boeing use a carefully orchestrated supply system to provide the parts and materials for their aircraft manufacture.

Using a system based on **Just In Time (JIT)** principles, the company publishes its production schedules up to a year in advance on a secure system that links Boeing with its suppliers.

The suppliers can then see when particular parts will be needed, and it becomes the suppliers' responsibility to ensure that the relevant parts are delivered to the factory floor just before they are needed.

From a suppliers' perspective, this system is useful because, in addition to effectively being an ordering system, it can be used to help them plan their own production schedules.

Boeing uses JIT because the large size of parts (aircraft engines, bodies, wings etc.) means it would need to spend a large amount of money on storing these items prior to using them in production. Using JIT technology means that Boeing only has to store these items for a very short time (sometimes only a matter of a day or two).

Customer support processes for online systems

Many customers are reluctant to buy goods online, particularly if they feel that the seller is remote and they will have no comeback if any items break or arrive damaged.

It is therefore very important that an organisation planning an online trading presence should ensure that there is a human voice on the end of a telephone who will provide a contact point to handle customer concerns. An organisation that trades online has to have very high standards of customer service, replacing and repairing goods as appropriate (with a minimum of fuss), because a reputation for being uncaring and remote will definitely have a detrimental effect on their business.

Financial systems for secure funds transfer

These systems have been available for many years and are commonly used to transfer money between organisations, between organisations and individuals, and even between individuals. Here are some examples:

- **Bankers Automated Clearing Service (BACS)** is the most common money transfer method. For example, it is often used by companies to pay salaries into employee bank accounts. Similarly, it is often the preferred method of handling credit and debit card payments, and regular payments such as direct debits and standing orders.
- **Direct debit** is an amount that you pay out of your bank account to an organisation on a regular basis. An example is a monthly charge for your home utilities, where you complete documentation and present it to your utilities company, who then present to your bank with notification of the amount of money it needs to pay on your behalf, and when.
- A **standing order**, on the other hand, is generally set up by the bank account holder, direct with his or her bank. An example is making a monthly donation to charity, where you set up a standing order that to pay a fixed amount into the charity's bank account on a regular basis.

The key issue with any funds transfer system is its security. This is why it is extremely important that you check how any system you use is protected. Unless you are fully satisfied that your personal information is safe, find another service!

Automated manufacturing processes

These processes are now common where manufacturing requires the creation of identical objects or outcomes that can be clearly defined, and where these processes are predictably repetitive.

This doesn't only include manufacturing the products themselves, but can also include packaging activities such as bottle filling (Figure 4.10).

Figure 4.10 Automated bottling process

Scorecard – Automated manufacturing

+ Can be active for longer hours.
+ Less potential downtime if regular maintenance is undertaken.
+ Better quality and consistent product.
– Some systems will need an available programmer capable of handling any programming anomalies or problems.
– Fewer staff are required, so more unemployment.

No response

An organisation can choose not to respond to information technology developments. A large financial outlay to invest in technologies might not be cost effective if it will take many years to recover the initial costs.

Similarly, an organisation may not have employees with the right combination of skills, so the hidden cost of new technology could be a large outlay in terms of training costs.

There is no hard and fast answer when it comes to investing or not investing. Each organisation has to carefully consider the advantages and disadvantages of investing and reach its own conclusions. This will also mean that they may have to justify any decisions to shareholders and other organisational stakeholders.

4.2.2 Managing risk

This section will cover the following grading criterion:

P4

Make the Grade P4

The biggest issue with technology is understanding that there are **risks that need to be managed**, and developing and implementing strategies to reduce those risks.

For P4, you will need to consider a number of risks and suggest how these risks can be minimised (such as back-up plans etc.).

This could be achieved as a wiki, a presentation, a podcast or as a review of possible risks and strategies in a magazine or web page article.

Cyber crime

Cyber crime (crime using computers and the internet) is probably the fastest growing platform for criminal activity across the world.

Typical examples include:

- diverting financial assets;
- sabotaging communications;
- stealing intellectual property.

Diverting financial assets

The most obvious criminal activity that uses computers is theft. This includes identity theft, where the criminal acquires someone else's personal financial details to pose as the rightful owner and gain access to their bank accounts). Other crimes include attempting to use the general public in illegal money movement activities. An example of this occurred where a used car was put on sale on a website: the seller was contacted by a prospective buyer who insisted that they wanted to buy the car to ship abroad. The process seemed straightforward (see Figure 4.11 on page 136)

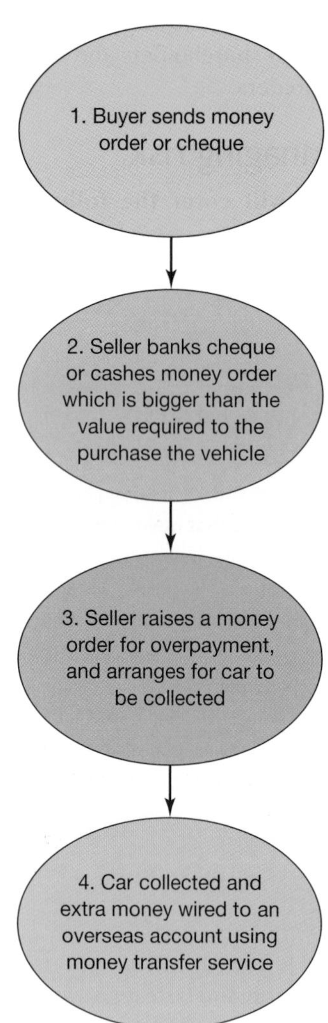

Figure 4.11 Diverting funds

Suspicious about this, the seller contacted the police and discovered that this is not an uncommon activity, and it would be likely that the car would either never be collected, or would be collected and then dumped! Clearly the objective of the whole transaction was to move the money from A to B, making the tracking of the various transactions more difficult to untangle.

Sabotaging communications

Sometimes unlawful activities that result in communications being sabotaged (by being either diverted or deleted) are merely the actions of pranksters who simply want to cause mischief. They can also instigate **denial-of-service (DOS)** attacks where they bombard networks with activity to effectively slow down processing, thereby denying users the usual quality of service (Figure 4.12).

However, there are more serious criminal acts, such as preventing organisations from trading by disrupting their ability to do so, or diverting business transactions to other sources.

From a legal standpoint, it doesn't make any difference in law whether the crime had serious intentions or was a prank. The law will punish both activities with equal severity.

Stealing intellectual property

Most people agree that stealing from others is unacceptable. We all understand that copying CDs or DVDs is a criminal offence. We are appalled by street crime, vehicle theft and violence. Have you considered, however, that directly copying information from the internet, using copy and paste functionality, or taking information from books, word for word to use in your coursework, is also a form of stealing known as plagiarism? If you use information from particular sources you must reveal the original source of the material, by including a reference to its origin in a bibliography. A bibliography is a list of authors, documents or web pages that have been used in the preparation of published text (which, as suggested, includes your coursework). Sometimes, because of copyright restrictions, you might also need to obtain permission before you can use the material directly.

Many institutions consider deliberate plagiarism as gross misconduct and this can lead to exclusion from a course or expulsion from a college. In Higher Education, the punishments can be even more serious (for example, legal action).

For this reason you should begin fully accrediting your sources now!

Activity 2

Find out about the Harvard Method of Referencing, which is a common referencing method used in Higher Education institutions.

Discuss your findings with your tutor, and find out whether your organisation has its own method of referencing information in coursework.

Hint: http://libweb.anglia.ac.uk/referencing/files/Harvard_referencing.pdf

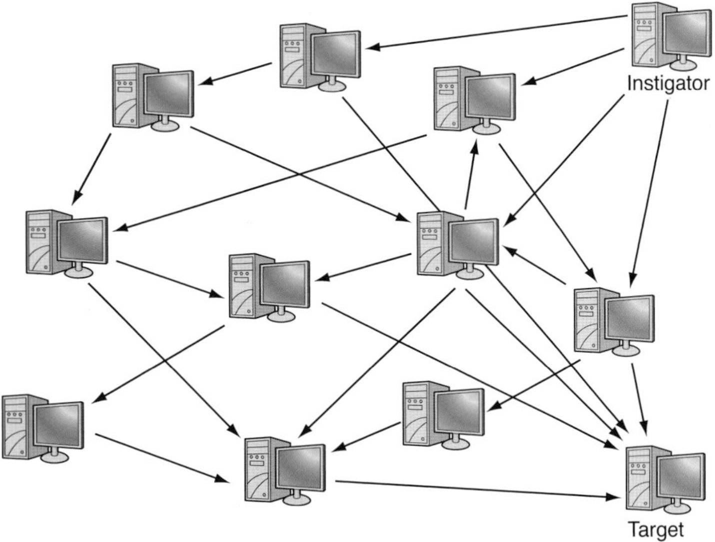

Figure 4.12 Denial-of-service attack

Preventive technologies

A wide range of physical and logical technologies exist to help organisations prevent criminal activity.

Physical technologies include:

- surveillance systems, which discourage inappropriate behaviours because they could be seen and recorded (CCTV systems);
- locked rooms, accessed through the use of swipe cards, key pads and keys;
- dongles, which are physical devices that are plugged into systems, and without which a user will have no access to certain software or data.

Unit links

Please refer to Section 7.3 Software and Network Security in **Unit 7** (Organisational Systems Security) for a complete look at crime preventative technologies.

Section 2.3 Software Utilities in **Unit 2** (Computer Systems) provides a full overview of antivirus, anti-spyware and firewall software.

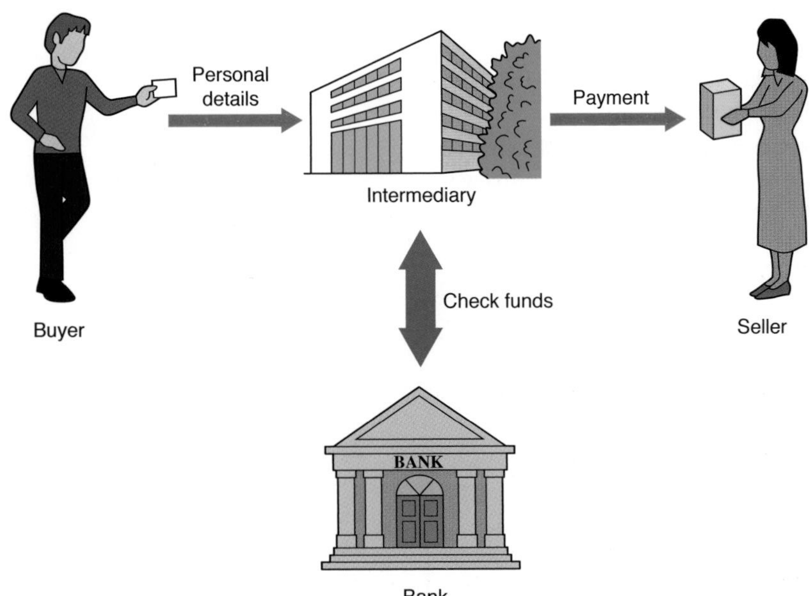

Figure 4.13 Using an online intermediary payments system

In addition, there are other software-controlled solutions that provide logical security, such as passwords and encryption.

Secure payment systems

Most people will, quite rightly, warn you about making payments for goods and services online using bank cards, particularly if you are not completely sure that the website is genuine. For such eventualities, intermediary organisations like PayPal® and NoChex® exist. Figure 4.13 on page 137 shows how they work.

This system protects both the buyer and the seller:

- The buyer's information is not passed on.
- The seller has confirmation that the buyer is genuine because he or she knows the funds are available.

The intermediary takes a small payment from the buyer for the service.

Before you use an intermediary, you should always ensure that you have checked it out.

Disaster recovery

Organisations today rely heavily on computer technology to undertake and record their activities, so businesses must ensure that their activities are not affected from data loss should their systems be hacked, or if a disaster, such as fire or flood, should occur. An organisation should have a carefully considered back-up plan so data can be recovered and business can continue as normal.

In many respects, since the development of IT systems, it has become much easier to prevent data loss, particularly as larger storage devices have come onto the market and the price of this technology has come down significantly.

There is really no excuse for data loss in this age of technology. This includes the loss of coursework because you have failed to take a backup!

Help

Disaster recovery – what you need to know

- Potential risks have been identified.
- The organisation fully understands how it will be affected in the event of a disaster.
- Resolutions will have been sought in advance, including strategies such as backing up data in other locations to ensure that the minimum possible amount of data is lost.
- The organisation will be implementing safety strategies (such as backing up data regularly).
- Disaster will have been simulated to test the plan, ensuring that the plan works and is modified if required.
- The organisation will ensure that staff understand the role they will play in the recovery process and that they receive any appropriate training).
- The plan will be reviewed at regular intervals to ensure that it remains up to date.

Unit link

Unit 7 Organisational Systems Security provides a more detailed insight into disaster recovery in section 7.3.

4.3 Be able to propose improvements to business systems using IT

This section will cover the following grading criteria:

P5 P6 M2 M3 D2

Make the Grade

P5 P6 M2 M3 D2

Assessment of the remaining criteria in this unit would be well suited to a newsletter, magazine or newspaper style approach. For P5, for example, you will need to use online and published sources of information that **describe the recent developments in IT**.

As part of that process, and to meet the needs of M2, you will need to suggest **how recent developments may improve a business system**, linking to real contextualised examples.

The final outcomes require you to produce **a proposal for an IT-enabled improvement** and this is an ideal opportunity to present your proposal to a virtual client. To meet P6, your proposal should be fit for purpose and should be in sufficient detail to show how the improvement would fit in with the existing system.

You will probably be presented with a scenario or case study and you will develop your ideas on a possible business improvement. You should include details such as the costs, inputs, outputs, effect on staff and other knock-on effects as appropriate. You will need to demonstrate **originality** (to meet criterion M3), which could be through the introduction of more than one improvement or by the suggestion of a series of improvements over time.

For D2, you will need to **fully justify your proposed improvement** including any positive and negative aspects. A cost–benefit analysis could be included to help focus your answer.

In order to propose improvements to business systems it is essential that you understand how business works, how functional areas operate and the types of tasks they perform (this was covered in Unit 3).

In addition, you need to keep up-to-date with developments. You need to find out about technology and new technological advancements by reading news articles and journals.

Understanding businesses needs and understanding technology solutions will enable you to put both together! Let's consider some recent developments.

4.3.1 IT developments

New applications

New software is coming onto the market all the time. Applications software is updated regularly. For example:

- Microsoft Office® 2010 is the most recent version of the successful Office® integration suite.
- Norton Ghost® (Version 15) was recently launched and provides functionality for backup and recovery.
- The market share that Google Chrome® (Figure 4.14) has achieved since its launch is rising all the time.

Activity 3

Find **five** different examples of new software applications that have been launched during the last 12 months.

Name them and briefly describe what they do.

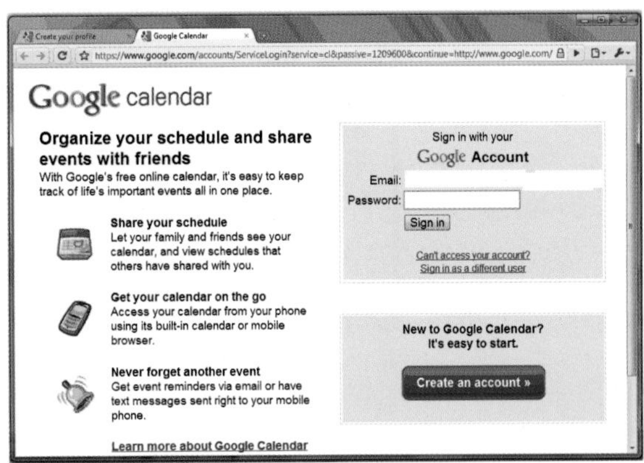

Figure 4.14 Google Chrome®

Wireless technologies

Wireless technology has enabled homes to have cable-free networks (**wi-fi**). Wireless technology has become so cheap and reliable that you will find it built into notebooks, netbooks, portable game consoles and MP3 players. This means that all family members can effectively access the internet from anywhere in the home.

In addition, many restaurants, pubs and hotels provide free hot-spot internet access to encourage people to come in during the day because this service will usually see them buying food and drink while they browse. McDonalds, for example, advertises free wi-fi for customers.

Activity 4

Using your own wireless devices or one or more of the following websites, discover three free wireless hotspots near your home and three near your school or college.

www.hotspot-locations.co.uk/

btopenzone.hotspot-directory.com/

Operating systems

We have come a long way since the days of Microsoft Windows® 3.1, which was one of the first truly graphical user interfaces (Figure 4.15). Even though this interface in its time was state of the art, it was still cumbersome to use and had little true functionality of its own. It was more a portal for accessing other software and did not function as an operating system.

Windows® 7, the most recently released version of Microsoft®'s GUI has some of the most advanced

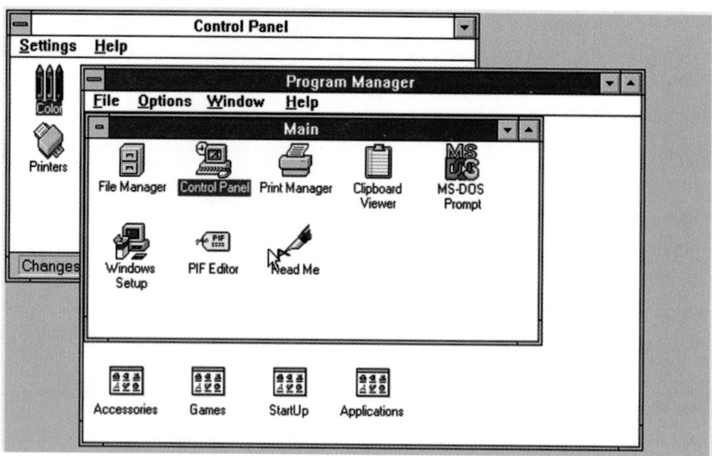

Figure 4.15 Microsoft Windows® 3.1

features seen so far in an operating system (like the Snap function that allows users to view and work with two documents side by side).

Innovative software platforms

A **software platform** typically 'sits' on top of an operating system, acting as an environment (with a user interface) in which other applications can run.

Perhaps the greatest growth of innovative software platforms at the moment is connected to **mobile devices** and, specifically **smart phones**. The following software platforms offer innovative support for application development, particularly in terms of touchscreen interfaces with haptic feedback, accelerometer and tilt-sensitivity (to detect movement):

- S60 (formerly System 60) running on the Symbian OS;
- Android (from Google®);
- Cocoa Touch as part of iOS (from Apple®);
- Java ME (Java Platform, Micro Edition from Sun/Oracle®).

Changing market leaders

Although Microsoft® is still a market leader, other software manufacturers are beginning to get a larger share of the market. The most prolific web browser, Internet Explorer®, which was unrivalled for many years and which is still the market leader, is being challenged by Mozilla Firefox® and Google Chrome® (see statistics released by www.w3counter.com in 2010, Figure 4.16).

In May 2010, Apple®'s market value was worth \$222 billion dollars compared with Microsoft®'s \$219 billion. This made it the world's biggest technology company – not bad for a company whose fortunes have rapidly risen since it nearly went out of business over a decade ago. Of course, Apple® has its Mac OSX®, iPod®, iPad® and iPhone® technologies to thank for its turnaround – all new products which continue to change customer perceptions and help to shape the fortunes of market leaders.

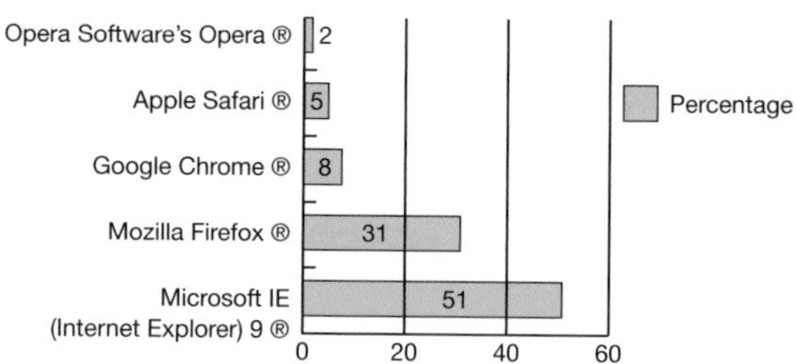

Figure 4.16 Popularity of web browsers
Source: Median values derived from W3Counter, StatOwl

4.3.2 IT improvements

With the availability of faster processing technology, combining the functionality of multiple systems into larger, single integrated systems, should not diminish a system's capabilities.

Integrated systems

The advantages of integrated systems are obvious:

- Fewer systems make data easier to back up.
- Fewer systems mean better security because there will be fewer loopholes.
- It makes it easier to share data across an organisation.
- Data is more likely to be up to date and reliable.

Databases

Improved data storage capacity and the ability to set up and use search indexes has made it much easier to have larger databases. In addition, new data-mining software and tools that work with existing databases have made it easier to drill down into statistical and trend data to find unusual events and trace aspects like fraud.

Networks

The development of a virtual **LAN (VLAN)** will allow a network to be divided up in different ways, regardless of the physical infrastructure. This is particularly useful for mobile devices that are able to maintain a logical connection even if physically moving.

Communication technologies

Mobile broadband now plays an important role for staff who work remotely. Using a laptop or netbook and a mobile broadband USB dongle (Figure 4.17), these staff can now send emails, process orders and check stock levels and prices without having to carry large volumes of paper. It also means that the information that they gather will be up to date.

Figure 4.17 Mobile broadband dongle

Web presence

Many high-street shops are finding sales dropping as customers increasingly favour the use of catalogues and online services, so some feel that they are being forced to establish an internet presence.

At a minimum, organisations could merely set up an **online brochure**, which would show prospective customers what goods or services they provided, but without any possibility for the user to interact with the website (so no orders could be placed). In this instance, the company would be hopeful that that customer will see a good deal and then be prepared to come to the shop to make the actual purchase.

Case Study

Kris Arts & Media (KAM) Ltd has decided to develop a website to bring its name and its products to the attention of businesses and the general public.

However, unlike Lee Office Supplies or Frankoni T-shirts Limited, KAM has no stock for sale, so the usual online ordering functionality would be inappropriate.

KAM effectively creates an online brochure, with an interactive gallery of images acting as a portfolio of their previous commercial work. As graphics projects tend to be bespoke (made to the specifications of the client), it would not even be appropriate to have a price list (such information would be client confidential).

In reality, as the population becomes more **IT literate** (able to use the technology), the expectation is for companies to increasingly offer online services. Even so, some organisations are understandably reluctant to give up their high-street visibility.

In some cases, having an online presence would not really be feasible. For example, if your business is car maintenance, the most that you could actually do would be to put an advertisement and maybe a price list online. You would not be able to sell using this medium. In this case, you may well pay a small fee to a directory listing service that would include your organisation, along with other similar organisations in your area.

Management reports

Providing timely and up-to-date **management reports** that summarise a company's operations and activities is essential to support effective decision-making in any organisation.

The most common management report is probably the **sales report** for a given period, which shows how much of a product or service an organisation has sold.

Similarly a gross and net profit report will be used to measure the effectiveness of the organisation in terms of **cost of sales** (what it has to buy in order to make the sale) and **net profits** (profits after other costs have been taken into consideration).

It is the role of the IT professional to understand the organisation's data well enough to be able to say whether the data that is required for a new management report exists and is even accessible through the system.

4.3.3 Business systems

The introduction of any new technology can be met with **resistance** by employees. For this reason it is essential that IT professionals understand what different business systems do, so that they can discuss implementation with users both to introduce them to the technology and to share with them how the system will support their role. Ideally, any new technology should complement the workflows (that is, how employees do their jobs) that employees have already developed.

Customer relationship management

Customer Relationship Management (CRM) is used by the sales department(s). It is used to manage the relationship between the organisation and its customers. For example, the system will record the nature of each contact, recording who the contact was with and what was discussed. Data stored in the system will also enable the organisation to target marketing campaigns because they can identify customer buying trends, which will mean that they can target advertising more effectively.

These systems will also monitor the relationship with the customer to help the organisation improve its customer service. Most importantly, the data held in a CRM will help **all** employees within the organisation understand each customer more fully, which in itself will help to build a good working relationship. Clearly this will benefit the organisation as a whole.

Supplier management

Supplier management software is frequently used by manufacturing companies to help purchasing and manufacturing departments to maximise their relationship with their suppliers. It means that they will be more efficient in ordering stock because it will be possible to order items closer to when they will be needed as a result of understanding their suppliers lead time and other behaviours, thereby saving on storage costs.

This software is essential for organisations running manufacturing processes using JIT techniques.

Product development

Product development software is used in a combined way by product development and marketing functions to analyse concepts, screen ideas, define products and produce marketing strategies.

The software uses large amounts of historic data from which it extracts trends and exceptions. It then compares the new product against elements of this data to predict how successful it will be in the marketplace.

Stock control

Monitoring stock to manage it successfully and reduce wastage is essential for any organisation looking for greater efficiency. Even setting simple reorder quantities that automatically highlight stock items that are running low will, in particular, protect production lines from running out of raw materials.

Analysing stock usage will also help to ensure that slow-moving stock is kept in smaller quantities, while fast-moving stock could be ordered more often or ordered in larger quantities to take advantage of better buying deals.

These are tasks that have, in the past, been done manually through the examination of card index systems, which was time consuming and prone to error.

Finance system

Almost all organisations have a finance system of some sort.

These systems generate sales invoices, statements and credit notes, support credit controllers by highlighting outstanding invoices based on pre-defined parameters, process payments to suppliers, record payroll payments, record the day-to-day transactions of the organisation and calculate amounts due to government bodies such as HM Revenue and Customs (to whom VAT, National Insurance contributions and tax are paid).

In the past, these activities have largely been done manually using ledger books, pens and calculators!

Clearly this type of system will also allow managers to analyse the organisation's financial performance to help with decision-making.

Activity 5

Your company has decided to invest in new technology to replace the current sales and stock systems. It is quite clear that the staff in these areas, who are generally not IT literate, are concerned about how these systems will affect their activities.

Create a short electronic slideshow to show how the enhanced technologies will support their areas.

Once completed, present this to your tutor.

Unit link

Unit 4 is a Mandatory unit for the Edexcel BTEC Level 3 National Diploma and National Extended Diploma in IT (Business) pathway and optional for all other qualifications and pathways of this Level 3 IT family.

Qualification (pathway)	Mandatory	Optional	Specialist optional
Edexcel BTEC Level 3 National Certificate in Information Technology		✓	
Edexcel BTEC Level 3 National Subsidiary Diploma in Information Technology		✓	
Edexcel BTEC Level 3 National Diploma in Information Technology		✓	
Edexcel BTEC Level 3 National Extended Diploma in Information Technology		✓	
Edexcel BTEC Level 3 National Diploma in IT (Business)	✓		
Edexcel BTEC Level 3 National Extended Diploma in IT (Business)	✓		
Edexcel BTEC Level 3 National Diploma in IT (Networking and System Support)		✓	
Edexcel BTEC Level 3 National Extended Diploma in IT (Networking and System Support)		✓	
Edexcel BTEC Level 3 National Diploma in IT (Software Development)		✓	
Edexcel BTEC Level 3 National Extended Diploma in IT (Software Development)		✓	

There are specific links to the following units in the scheme:
Unit 8 – e-Commerce
Unit 33 – Exploring Business Activity

Achieving success

In order to achieve this unit you will complete a series of coursework activities. Each time you hand in work, your tutor will return this to you with a record of your achievement.

This particular unit has 11 criteria to meet: 6 Pass, 3 Merit and 2 Distinction.

For a Pass: You must achieve all 6 Pass criteria

For a Merit: You must achieve all 6 Pass and all 3 Merit criteria

For a Distinction: You must achieve all 6 Pass, all 3 Merit and both Distinction criteria.

Further reading

Bocij, P., Greasley, A. and Hickie, S. – *Business Information Systems: Technology Development and Management for the e-business. Edition 4* (FT Prentice Hall, 2008) ISBN-10 027371662X, ISBN-13 978-0273716624

Reynolds, J. – *E-Business: A Management Perspective* (OUP Oxford, 2009) ISBN-10 0199216487, ISBN-13 978-0199216482

Websites

www.oncallgeeks.com

www.teach-ict.com

Unit 6: Software design and development

By the end of this unit you should be able to:

1. Know the features of programming languages
2. Understand the principles of software design
3. Be able to use tools to demonstrate software designs

Whether you are in school or college, passing this unit will involve being assessed. As with most BTEC schemes, successful completion of various assessment criteria demonstrates your evidence of learning and the skills you have developed.

This unit has a mixture of pass, merit and distinction criteria. Generally you will find that merit and distinction criteria require a little more thought and evaluation before they can be completed.

The colour-coded grid below shows you the pass, merit and distinction criteria for this unit.

To achieve a pass grade you need to:	To achieve a merit grade you also need to:	To achieve a distinction grade you also need to:
P1 Describe the application and limits of procedural, object-oriented and event-driven programming paradigms		
P2 Describe the factors influencing the choice of programming language		
P3 Explain sequence, selection and iteration as used in computer programming		
P4 Outline the benefits of having a variety of data types available to the programmer		
P5 Explain the role of software design principles and software structures in the IT systems development life cycle	**M1** Explain the importance of the quality of code	**D1** Discuss the factors that can improve the readability of code
P6 Use appropriate tools to design a solution to a defined requirement	**M2** Justify the choice of data types and software structures used in a design solution	**D2** Develop algorithms to represent a design solution

Introduction

Software design and development is a 10-credit unit designed to introduce the learner to the processes involved in creating a bespoke (or tailor-made) program for a business client.

It focuses on the steps required to get the job done properly, from understanding the client's initial request, to selecting an appropriate programming language and then proceeding to create a workable solution that meets the client's needs.

Although this unit does not specify a target programming language, this book focuses on those languages that are most likely to be used in both a learning and commercial environment. It is through examining such examples that the world of programming will open up to you!

How to read this chapter

This chapter is organised to match the content of the BTEC unit it represents. The following diagram shows the grading criteria that relate to each learning outcome.

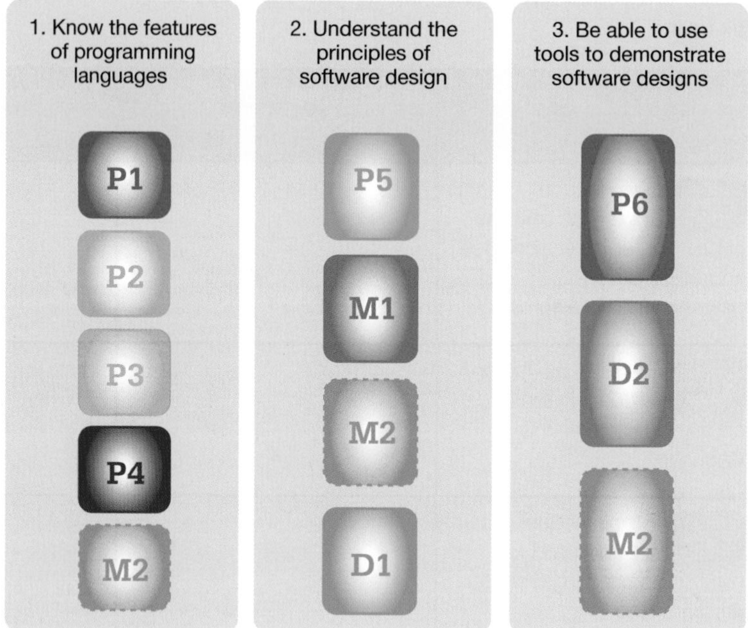

Figure 6.00

You'll find colour-matching notes in each chapter about completing each grading criterion. Please also note that criterion M2 assesses aspects from three different learning outcomes.

6.1 Know the features of programming languages

Before we can examine different features of programming languages it is worthwhile explaining what a programming language actually is!

Computers only understand binary instructions: sequences of 1s and 0s that open and close electronic circuits inside the CPU. Programming a computer in binary is often referred to as **machine-code programming** or **low-level programming**. In the earliest days of computing, this was the only option.

Modern programming languages (**high-level languages**) are designed to be more readable by humans than binary. Therefore, high-level languages require translation into their machine code equivalents before the CPU can execute it. Figure 6.01 illustrates this point.

Scorecard – Low-level languages

+ Need no translation before a CPU can understand it, so it is very fast.
+ Gives full control over CPU.
– Difficult to write.
– Difficult to read.
– Difficult to 'debug' (find errors and correct them).
– Are specific to the CPU being used – this means that low-level program code is not 'portable' from one type of CPU to another.

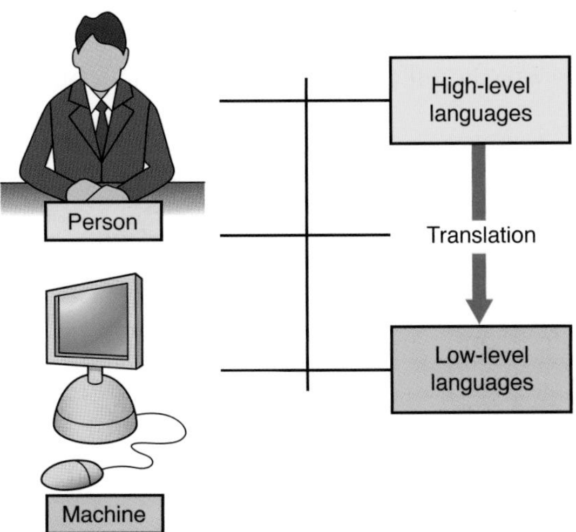

Figure 6.01 High and low-level languages

Scorecard – High-level languages

+ Are easier to learn because they are more like a natural language.
+ Are easier to debug.
+ Translators are available for many different CPUs, so the code is portable.
+ Modern translators (commercial compilers) are very advanced and can generate low-level program code that is as efficient as low-level code written by hand.

The following gives a comparison between high- and low-level languages.

High-level language

```
cout << "BTEC National Diploma";
```

Low-level language

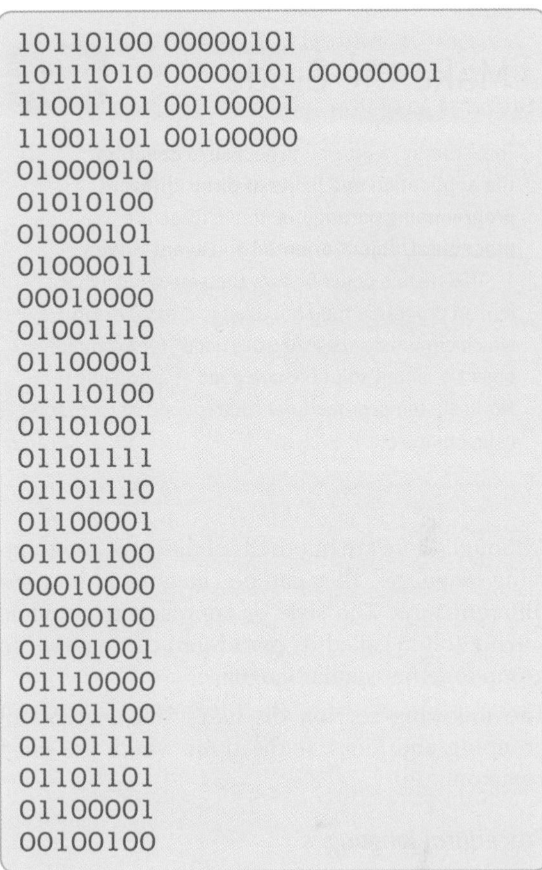

```
10110100 00000101
10111010 00000101 00000001
11001101 00100001
11001101 00100000
01000010
01010100
01000101
01000011
00010000
01001110
01100001
01110100
01101001
01101111
01101110
01100001
01101100
00010000
01000100
01101001
01110000
01101100
01101111
01101101
01100001
00100100
```

Both programs output the phrase 'BTEC National Diploma' on an PC using an x86 compatible processor (that is, a modern Intel® or AMD® processor). The high-level example is written in **C++**, a popular language developed in 1983 as an extension to an earlier language called C.

The low-level example is **machine code** (in binary). Although both samples of code do the same thing, the C++ code would need to be translated **into** the machine code **before it** can work on the CPU. Of course, if we had written the code in binary originally then no such translation needs to take place. Which *would* you prefer to learn? Which do you think is more *commercially productive*?

6.1.1 Programming paradigms

This section will cover the following grading criterion:

Make the Grade P1

This criterion asks you to be able to **describe the application and limits of three different programming paradigms**. These three are **procedural, object-oriented** and **event-driven**.

This means describe how they are used, what kind of programs they are used to create and in which circumstances they are used (for example, object-oriented solutions are good at modelling real-world systems, procedural code is good at recreating calculations etc.).

Although there are hundreds of different programming languages, they can be categorised in a few different ways. The style or approach to problem solving (often called its **paradigm**) can be used to group together similar languages.

The following section discusses this method of grouping and looks at the three which are most common.

Procedural languages

Procedural languages, developed from the 1960s onwards, are still popular today. They rely on the programmer writing the solution to a problem as an algorithm or, put simply, a logical series of steps that provide an answer. It is seen as a very traditional approach to programming and as such, it is highly likely that the majority of today's commercial programmers started their careers working this way. Here are some common procedural languages.

BASIC

During the 1970s and 1980s, BASIC (**B**eginners **A**ll-purpose **S**ymbolic **I**nstruction **C**ode) was the preferred language. Originally it relied on line numbers and was home to the infamous 'goto' statement whose misuse resulted in horribly complicated 'spaghetti' code.

Early BASIC (e.g. Microsoft's 'Gee-Whiz' GW-BASIC®)

```
10 let stars = 0
20 let count = 0
30 print "How many stars would you
like?"
40 input stars
50 for count = 1 to stars
60 print "*"
70 next count
80 end
```

Later versions removed the line numbers and use a more structured approach.

Modern BASIC (e.g. Rockerfer BASIC, online at www.pachesoft.com/rockerferbasic/index.html)

```
declare variable integer count
declare variable integer stars
print "How many stars would you
like?"
input stars
for count from 1 to stars do
 print "*"
end for
end
```

BASIC came in many different (and non-compatible) dialects, many of which were developed by Microsoft® in the 1980s.

Though no longer popular as a commercial option, as we will see later in this book, Microsoft® used BASIC as the foundation for its popular Visual Basic® and Visual Basic.NET® products.

Pascal

Pascal is named after the seventeeth-century mathematician and philosopher, Blaise Pascal.

Although over 30 years old, Pascal remains a popular language for teaching programming in schools and colleges because it encourages good planning and a structured approach to problem-solving. It was created in 1970 by Niklaus Wirth.

Today, many different versions of Pascal exist for many different operating systems and platforms, although there is a standard dialect defined by the International Organization for Standardization (ISO).

```
Program mystars (input,output);
  {A short program to demonstrate the
  use of a for loop in Pascal.
  Author: M Fishpool
  Date : July 2010
  Ref  : BND             }
Var
  stars: integer; {How many stars
  the user wants to see}
  count: integer; {The for loop
  counter}
Begin
  writeln('How many stars would
  you like?');
  readln(stars);
  for count := 1 to stars do
  writeln('*');
  {endfor}
  readln;
End.
```

Borland's 'Turbo Pascal' was a popular version, leading to its object-oriented extension, 'Delphi', challenging Microsoft's Visual Basic® for quick Windows® development.

A modern implementation of the language, called 'Free Pascal' is functionally similar to Turbo Pascal and can be freely downloaded from www.freepascal.org/

C

C is considered to be a general-purpose, work-horse language ideal for creating applications, operating systems and interfacing with electronic control systems. It was developed in 1972 by Dennis Ritchie at the Bell Telephone Laboratories.

Unlike languages such as BASIC and Pascal, C relies on symbols rather than friendlier keywords. As such, it is often described as being 'terse' and more difficult to learn, but typically offer more powerful solutions in fewer lines of code.

```
/* mystars.c
  A short program to demonstrate the
  use of a for loop in C.
  Author: M Fishpool
  Date : July 2010
  Ref  : BND          */
// header files
#include <stdio.h>
#include <stdlib.h>
// main function
int main(int argc, char *argv[])
{
  int stars; // How many stars the
  user wants to see
  int count; // The for loop counter
  printf("How many stars would
  you like?");
  scanf("%d",&stars);
  for (count=0; count<stars;
  count++)
  printf("*\n");
  //endfor
  system("PAUSE");
  return 0;
}
```

By 1989, the American National Standards Institute (ANSI) had decided on an agreed dialect of the language (now commonly known as ANSI C®), followed a year later by ISO.

Many versions of C® exist, both commercially and as downloadable freeware.

The C® example was written and tested using Bloodshed's Dev-C++®, a modern development suite which is freely available from http://www.bloodshed.net/

Finally, it is worth mentioning that procedural languages are often referred to as **imperative** langauges.

> Activity 1
>
> Use the links given in the text to download and/or try freeware procedural languages on machines for which you have administrator rights.
>
> Try to get the simple programs running.

Object-oriented languages

Object-**O**riented **D**esign **(OOD)** and **O**bject-**O**riented **P**rogramming **(OOP)** are not new ideas. They have been around in one form or another since the late 1960s. However, in the 1980s, the OOP approach to programming became popular and has since been a common feature of most current commercial programming languages.

The following popular programming languages all use object-oriented (**OO**) techniques:

- C++®
- Microsoft C#® (C sharp)
- Sun Java®
- Microsoft Visual Basic® .NET

In object-oriented programming, the programmer has to examine the problem in a less traditional way. Instead of writing an algorithm, they seek to break down elements of the problem into a number of **classes**.

Key terms

Classes and **objects**: In procedural programming, **data** and **functions** (functions **process** the data) are usually **kept separate**. The object-oriented approach does things a little differently by packaging the data and its functions **together**. This is called **encapsulation**.

The collection of data and functions is called a **class**.

These classes act like a template, a mould or a stencil for creating solid **objects**.

Objects are created through a process called **instantiation**. This sounds complex, but in reality it simply means making **solid instances** (objects) from a class.

Here's an example:

If I wanted to create **circle objects**, I first need to design a **circle class** (Figure 6.02).

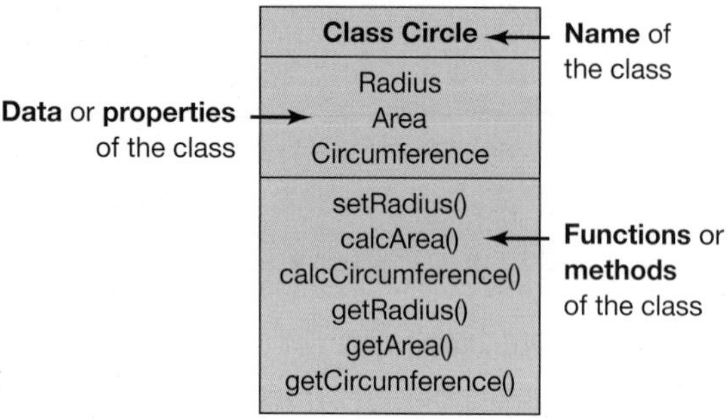

Figure 6.02 Example of a schema

This type of diagram is called a **schema**. In the example, it shows the **name** of the class, the **data** (or **properties**) of a circle and a number of **functions** (or **methods**). A design tool present within Unified Modelling Language (UML) is very similar: it's simply called a UML class diagram.

In this class we imagine that it will store three items of **data** (the radius, the calculated area and circumference).

Also, we think that we will need six **functions**:

setRadius()	to give the circle its radius
calcArea()	to calculate the area using the formula: **Area = Pi × Radius²**
calcCircumference()	to calculate the circumference using the formula: Circumference = **2 × Pi × Radius**
getRadius()	to get the radius value
getArea()	to get the calculated area value
getCircumference()	to get the calculated circumference value

The order in which the functions (or methods) are coded in the class is not really important.

If we examine this as a Microsoft C#® solution, the class code becomes:

```
class Circle
{
  private float radius;
  private float area;
  private float circumference;
  public void setRadius(int r)
  {
   radius = r;
  }
  public void calcArea()
  {
   area = 3.14f * radius * radius;
  }
  public void calcCircumference()
  {
   circumference = 2 * 3.14f *
   radius;
  }
  public float getRadius()
  {
   return radius;
  }
  public float getArea()
```

```
  {
   return area;
  }
  public float getCircumference()
  {
   return circumference;
  }
}
```

However, in order to make it work, we must create some objects and use the methods in a logical order:

```
class CircleTest
{
 public static void Main()
 {
   Circle Circle1 = new Circle();
   // create 1st object
   Circle1.setRadius(10);          //
   give it a radius
   Circle1.calcCircumference();
   Circle1.calcArea();

   Console.WriteLine("1st Circle");
   Console.WriteLine("Radius of Circle
is {0:F}", Circle1.getRadius());
   Console.WriteLine("Circumference is
{0:F}", Circle1.getCircumference());
   Console.WriteLine("Area is {0:F}",
Circle1.getArea());

   Circle Circle2 = new Circle();     //
create 2nd object
   Circle2.setRadius(15);          //
give it a radius
   Circle2.calcCircumference();
   Circle2.calcArea();

   Console.WriteLine("\n2nd Circle");
   Console.WriteLine("Radius of Circle
is {0:F}", Circle2.getRadius());
   Console. WriteLine("Circumference
is {0:F}", Circle2.getCircumference());
   Console.WriteLine("Area is {0:F}",
Circle2.getArea());

   Console.ReadLine();
 }
}
```

In this example, **two objects** are created (**Circle1** and **Circle2**). The program gives each object a radius (10 and 15, respectively) and then uses their functions (or methods) to **calculate** and **return** the resulting values.

This C#® program would generate the output in Figure 6.03.

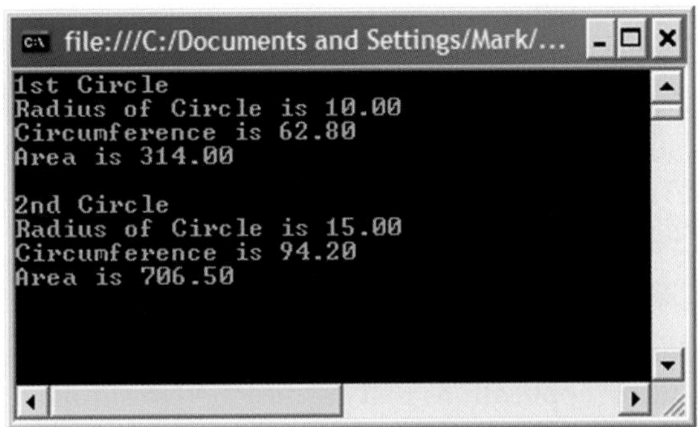

Figure 6.03 Output from the example Microsoft C#® program

Object-oriented programming works in a similar fashion in other OOP languages.

One thing to remember though is that classes may represent anything, such as an operating system 'window', a folder on a hard drive or even a type of opponent in an online game.

> Activity 2
>
> Using the schema and the Circle class examples as shown on pages 150–1, design the following class:
>
> **Rectangle class**
>
> A rectangle has a long side and a short side measurement.
>
> Its perimeter is measured by adding up the two long sides and the two short sides.
>
> It also has an area calculated by multiplying the length of the long side by the length of the short side.

Event-driven languages

In event-driven programming, the code that is executed is not determined by a fixed procedural order or by the planned calling of methods/functions (as is the case in object-oriented solutions). In this paradigm, code is executed based on triggers, which occur when certain events happen (for example, a button is clicked, a form is loaded on a screen or another process triggers an error).

Unit link

Unit 14 Event-Driven Programming explores this programming paradigm in great detail.

Supporting tools and environments

Modern software development tools are varied and help the developer quickly build, test and deploy a programmed solution. Common tools include the following:

CASE tools

Computer-aided Software Engineering (CASE) is a suite of applications that are designed to automate the process of building reliable, robust and maintainable program code.

Key terms

CASE tools: There are many different CASE tools available and each covers different aspects of the software design and development process. Perhaps the easiest distinction is to consider what the CASE tool creates.

Tools that create DFD diagrams, ER diagrams and screen forms are called **upper-case** tools – they generate high-level elements of the solution.

Tools that generate actual program code, data files etc. are called **lower-case** tools – they generate low-level elements of the solution.

CASE tools that do both are often called **integrated-case** tools. Rational Rose, from IBM, is one of the best examples of this type of CASE suite and can be found at:

www-01.ibm.com/software/rational/

IDE

An **Integrated Development Environment (IDE)** is, as the name suggests, **a piece of software that combines a** number of software development tools that were once separate utilities into a **single interface** for the developer's convenience.

Most modern programming languages are used via an IDE.

Key terms

IDE: An IDE typically consists of the following software development tools:

- **a visual editor**, to provide 'drag and drop' functionality for form-based design
- **a text editor**, to key in program code – usually has syntax highlighting (different language elements appear in different colours)
- **a compiler**, to produce object code (that is, machine code) and report errors
- **a linker**, to package object code into a standalone executable program
- **debug facilities** (for example, trace, breakpoints and watch)
- **a help system**, to give language specific support.

6.1.2 Types of language

This section will cover the following grading criterion:

P2

Make the Grade **P2**

This criterion asks you think about the different types of language available. In order to achieve this criterion, you'll need to be able to name at least three language types (including visual) and match these to particular factors you might use for selection. For example, if you have little programming skill but can assemble a solution using graphical elements, a visual language may help.

You will also have to name specific programming languages.

A number of other types of programming languages exist in addition to procedural and object-oriented languages. The following details the types you are most likely to encounter on your course.

Visual languages

Visual languages use graphical development tools to create software. The user can often create simple programs by **dragging and dropping** icons, logic pathways and special symbols. Thus every visual component (its appearance and function) may represent many thousands of lines of traditional program code in a non-visual language.

A typical visual language is **VisSim** (Figure 6.04).

Other languages such as Visual Basic.NET® and Visual C#® have visual development environments but are not truly visual programming languages as they still rely on traditional text-based program code to make them work. Many books make this error however, and as a result, it has become commonly accepted as fact. This distinction is often misunderstood, so be careful!

Scripting

Scripting (or **script**) languages are usually formed from short, meaningful instructions that are used to automate processes in a computer system. **Batch files** and **Job Control Languages (JCL)** are typical examples of scripting.

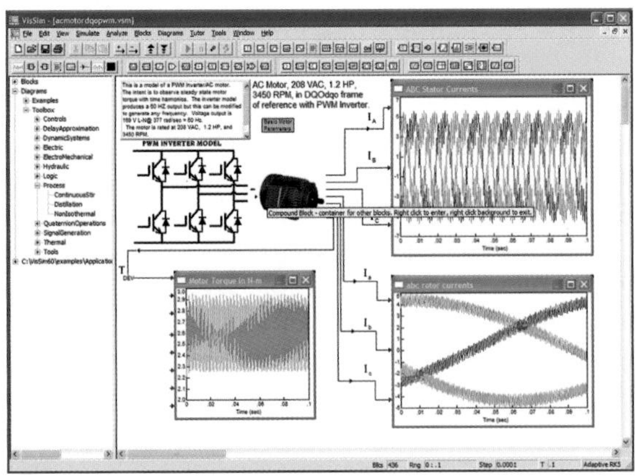

Figure 6.04 VisSim ©2007 Visual Solutions Inc.

PHP

PHP (PHP Hypertext Pre-processor or **Personal Home Page)** is a server-side scripting language that works on a number of different hardware platforms **(cross-platform)** and operating systems.

PHP's job is to create **dynamic web page content**. What this means is that the actual HTML sent to the client PC requesting the page is written by a PHP script rather than being coded manually by a person. The generated HTML often comes from live database queries so the information sent to the client's web browser should be up to date. The client PC only receives the generated HTML document, so the end user never gets to see the PHP scripts involved.

```
<?php
 echo "<b>BTEC</b> National
Extended Diploma";
?>
```

Figure 6.05 shows the steps in a typical PHP scenario.

1. The user's web browser makes a request for a particular piece of information. This request is sent via the internet to a remote host running a web server.
2. The PHP script queries (usually with a Data Manipulation Language such as SQL) a linked 'back-end' database and a **results set** (of data) is created.
3. The results set is returned to the PHP engine.
4. The PHP engine converts the data in the results set into valid HTML, adding formatting as necessary.
5. The web server 'serves' the dynamically created HTML page back to the client PC's web browser.

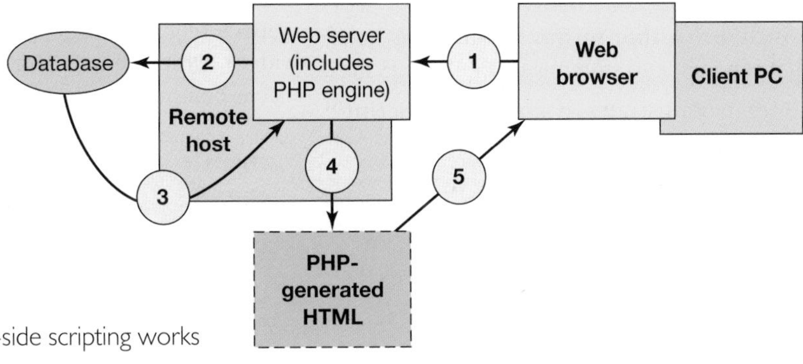

Figure 6.05 How server-side scripting works

A common use of such scripting is in search engines, particularly those used to check stock in an online shop. Message boards and forums may also use PHP.

ASP.NET

ASP.NET is the follow-up to Microsoft®'s earlier Active Server Pages (ASP). As with PHP, it can be used to create dynamic web page content. Unlike PHP, which is available on a number of different computer platforms, ASP.NET is designed to run specifically on Microsoft Windows® operating systems.

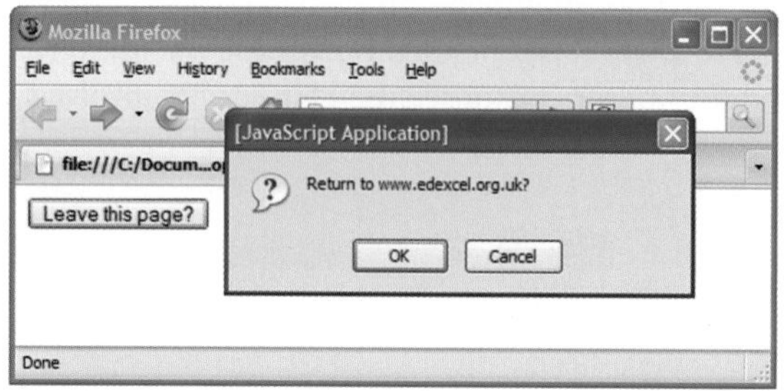

Figure 6.06 JavaScript™ working in a web page

ASP.NET is part of Microsoft®'s larger .NET platform: a framework of software components built onto the Windows® operating system. The .NET framework provides a large collection of reusable classes which are ideal for creating new Windows® applications.

```
Response.Write("<b>BTEC</b>
National Extended Diploma");
```

JavaScript™

JavaScript™ and Java™ are not the same. Although the name is similar, JavaScript™ is only distantly related to Sun®'s full object-oriented programming language. JavaScript™ is Netscape Communications' name for its own ECMAscript dialect.

JavaScript's primary purpose is to provide automation and interactivity for existing web pages, so it is often included within in the HTML page itself, although it is possible to store it separately in .JS files.

Figure 6.06 demonstrates a simple JavaScript™ automation of a web page.

```
<html>
<head>
<script = "JavaScript">
function check()
{
 var reply = confirm("Return to
 www.edexcel.org.uk?")
 if (reply)
 {
  window.location = "http://
  www.edexcel.org.uk";
 }
}
</script>
</head>
<body>
<form>
<input type="button"
onclick="check()" value="Leave this
page?">
</form>
</body>
</html>
```

Mark-up languages

Mark-up languages are used to describe the way in which text is **presented** to a reader. A number of mark-up languages exist and, while they are **not** programming languages in the truest sense, they **do** provide solutions to set problems.

HTML

Hyper**t**ext **M**ark-up **L**anguage (**HTML**) is currently the most popular way of creating web pages for publishing on the World Wide Web (WWW). It was created by Tim Berners-Lee, the director of the **World Wide Web Consortium (WC3)**, which regularly publishes standards for web page creation to ensure that pages remain interoperable (that is, they work together) on different computer systems.

HTML uses a series of **block** tags to indicate the **start** and **end** of structured text and web page elements (e.g., images, tables, bulleted lists).

The central idea of HTML is the **hyperlink**: a link that, when clicked, takes the user to another **resource** (e.g., an image, piece of music, document or video), which may be on the same page or on another computer system located somewhere else.

```
<html>
<head>
<title>BTEC National Extended
Diploma in IT</title>
<META name="Author" content="M
Fishpool">
```

```
</head>
<body>
<p>Welcome to the BTEC National
Extended Diploma in IT!
<IMG src="computer.jpg"
alt="Computer System">
</p>
</body>
</html>
```

Cascading Style Sheets

Cascading Style Sheets (CSS) are the preferred technique for **formatting the appearance** of modern web pages (e.g., fonts, colours, alignment, text effects such as bold, underline, italics).

The following example shows an example of embedded CSS, using the <style>> tag to set the format of the HTML <h>> elements.

```
<html>
<head>
<style type="text/css">
h1 {color: #ff0000}
h2 {color: rgb(0,0,255)}
</style>
</head>
<body>
<h1>Welcome to BTEC National
Extended Diploma</h1>
<h2>Welcome to BTEC National
Extended Diploma</h2>
</body>
</html>
```

This would produce the formatted content shown here.

Welcome to BTEC National Extended Diploma

Welcome to BTEC National Extended Diploma

It is preferable to keep the content of a web page in one file (the .HTML file) and the formatting in another (a .CSS file).

XML

XML is the abbreviation for E**x**tensible **M**ark-up **L**anguage, a specification also developed by the W3C. XML that allows programmers to create their own personalised tags. As such, .XML documents are exceptionally portable across different systems.

```
<!--
 Written by M Fishpool, 2010
-->
<announcement>
<to>BTEC Students</to>
<from>M Fishpool</from>
<heading>Welcome</heading>
<body>Enjoy your BTEC National
Extended Diploma!</body>
</announcement>
```

Formatting (or **style information**) for .XML documents can be achieved by using .CSS.

6.1.3 Reasons for choice of language

The reasons why a programmer chooses a particular language are varied. If the programmer is able to choose which language to use, it may simply be a case of familiarity: a tendency to use the language that they know best. However, there are other important factors to take into consideration. These include:

- cost
- organisational policy
- availability
- reliability
- suitability
- expandability.

Cost

The **development** costs (incurred during producton) and **maintenance** costs (incurred after the solution has been delivered) will differ between languages. An unreliable solution will probably mean high maintenance costs. Additionally, the price of IDEs differs depending on the programming language it supports.

Organisational policy

Some organisations specify both the language and development environment to be used (e.g. Ada might be specified for govermental security projects).

Availability

Programming languages need to be learned and practised to gain proficiency, so an organisation must have sufficient numbers of staff who are trained and experienced with a particualar language. In addition, the language chosen must be compatible with the hardware used in the organisation.

Reliability

Some languages may be seen to be more reliable than others. A language with a dependability of less than 10 per cent is unlikely to be chosen for a **mission critical** system.

Suitability

It is essential that a chosen programming language is suitable for the task in hand, particularly taking account its features and tools. For example, Java™ is very useful for web-based applications, but is not so suitable for controlling real-time systems when a rapid response to real-world events is crucial.

Expandability

A critical part of ongoing maintainability of a system is the ability to expand an existing solution. Some programming languages, particularly object-oriented languages, are good at this.

B Braincheck

1. Name **three** different programming paradigms.
2. Name **two** organisations responsible for establishing standards for languages.
3. How do **HTML** and **CSS** differ?
4. What is a **script** language?
5. What is another name for a **procedural** language?

How well did you do? See supporting website for answers.

6.1.3 Features

This section will cover the following grading criterion:

Make the Grade P3

This criterion focuses on the three main programming constructs: **sequence, selection** and **iteration**. Explaining what each is, why it is used and providing a specific coding sample of each should be sufficient to achieve this criterion. Each coding sample is likely to use other programming features.

Although it is fair to say that all programming languages were created as tools to solve problems, they don't all approach this job in the same way. Languages vary in their **syntax** (the rules governing how statements are written) but, fortunately, they are built from a collection of similar features.

In this section, we'll examine some of these common building blocks, using Microsoft C#® as our reference language.

Variables, data types and naming conventions

A **variable** is a form of identifier. It is **name** that represents a **value**.

In programming, a variable is used to store and retrieve data from the computer's RAM. Every variable should have a unique (and meaningful) name. In order to reserve enough RAM for the variable, we must select an appropriate **data type** (see 171). For example, if we want to store our user's age in a variable:

```
int iAge;
```

This line of code is called a **declaration**. It essentially reserves enough RAM to store an **integer** (a whole number) and lets us refer to that reserved RAM by the **name** we have picked: **iAge**

Professional programmers often **prefix** the name of their variables with an **initial letter** that indicates the variable's **data type**. This is considered to be good practice: it's known as using a **naming convention**, this particular one is called **Hungarian notation**.

Even better practice would be to add a comment as well:

```
int iAge; // Will store the user's age
```

Local and global variables

In simple terms, the terms **local** and **global variable** define how visible the variable is. In a large program split into a number of different modules (see section 2.2), a global variable would be visible to all modules, whereas a local variable would only be visible within the module it was declared.

Professional programmers prefer to use local variables where possible because any faults with the variable have to be in a particular module. This makes a program easier to debug.

Constants

In addition to variables, it is possible to create another type of identifier: a **constant**. As the name suggests, it does not change its value once the program starts running.

```
const int MAXAGE = 125; // oldest allowable age
```

In this example, **MAXAGE** is declared as a constant and given the value of 125.

A program using this declaration will now use the constant **MAXAGE** whenever we want to refer to the value **125**. There are two advantages of this: it improves the readability of the program code; and, if we want to change the maximum age we only have to alter the constant's declaration, not find every occurrence of **125** in the code.

Assignment statements

An **assignment statement** is used to give a variable a value.

When an assignment is successfully performed, the previous value stored in the variable is overwritten.

```
iAge = 16; // set user's age
```

In most languages an **equals sign** (=) is used for the assignment operator.

If the variable is being assigned for the first time, the process is called **initialisation**. Some programming languages do not automatically set new variables to sensible starting values (e.g. 0), so initialisation must occur to ensure that the variables are ready for use.

Output statements

All programming languages have a method for generating output, normally to screen.

In C#® the **Write** or **WriteLine** method can be used:

```
Console.Write("Please enter your age: ");
```

```
Console.WriteLine("Please enter your age: ");
```

Each of these methods will output text to the console (or command line interface). The only difference is that the second method (**WriteLine**) will move the cursor to the start of the next line once the text has been displayed.

A more advanced version of **Write** allows us to output the contents of a variable:

```
Console.Write("Do you still feel young at {0}?", iAge);
```

If **iAge** currently had the integer value 16, the associated screen output would be:

```
Do you still feel young at 16?
```

The content (**16**) of the variable (**iAge**) is inserted into the correct part of the message.

Input statements

There are many different ways of obtaining input. For now we'll just focus on basic **keyboard** input.

The following code **prompts** the user for a value (their name) and **stores** it in a variable (**username**).

The stored **string** (their name) is then repeated to the user, complete with a greeting.

```
string username;

Console.WriteLine("What is your name?");
username = Console.ReadLine();

Console.WriteLine("Hello, {0}!", username);
```

Arithmetic operators

These are the basic building blocks for forming **arithmetic expressions** (that is, number calculations).

The number of arithmetic operators in programming languages varies greatly but there are some that are absolutely fundamental. Table 6.01 shows these with their C#® symbols.

Table 6.01

Arithmetic operation	C# implementation
Add	+
Subtract	-
Multiply	* (asterisk)
Divide	/ (forward slash)
Modulus (obtains the remainder)	% (percentage)
Increment (increase by 1)	++
Decrement (decrease by 1)	--

In addition, parentheses (brackets) may be used to alter the natural order of operations (Division, Multiplication, Addition and Subtraction), for example:

num1 + num2 + num3 / 3

isn't the same as

(num1 + num2 + num3) / 3

Logical operators

Most programming languages have **keywords** or **operators** to process logical operations.

Table 6.02 lists these **logical operations** and their C#® implementations.

Table 6.02

Logical operation	C# implementation
AND	&&
OR	||
NOT	!

Logical operators can be used to create more complex compound conditions.

Relational operators

In most languages, **relational operators** are a set of operators that make direct comparisons between values. The result of this type of comparison can only be **true** or **false**.

Table 6.03 lists these **relational operations** and their C#® implementations.

Table 6.03

Relational operation	C# implementation
Equal to (test for equality)	==
Not equal to (test for inequality)	!=
Greater than	>
Less than	<
Greater than *or* equal to	>=
Less than *or* equal to	<=

B Braincheck

Work out whether these expressions evaluate to TRUE or FALSE.

1. 10 > 5
2. 6 < 6.1
3. 'A' != 'B'
4. FALSE == FALSE
5. 7 > 2 && 5 >= 5
6. 3 < 10 || 99 < 67
7. "REBEKAH" == "rebekah"
8. (10 + 2) >= (60/5)

How well did you do? See supporting website for answers.

Conditional statements

Although programs can be built from a simple sequence (one event following another), these only provide limited solutions (Figure 6.07). In this example, the solution follows steps 1, 2 and 3. No step is missed, no step is repeated.

Figure 6.07 Example of a simple sequence

More complex solutions require the ability to make choices (Figure 6.08). In this example, a condition is made after step 2: if the condition is true, step 3 is performed; if the condition is false, step 4 is performed instead. It isn't possible to perform both steps 3 and 4: the program has a choice to make.

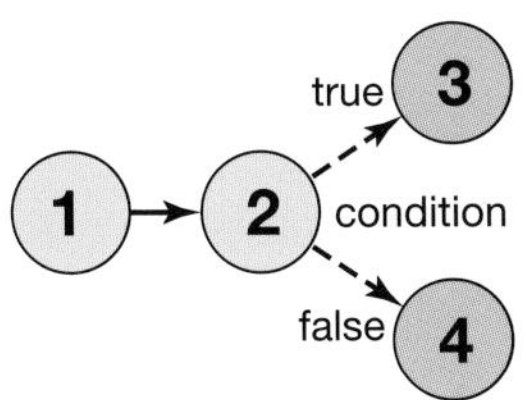

Figure 6.08 Example of a conditional sequence

If...Else statement

Most programming languages, including C#®, perform these types of decision using an **If...Else** statement:

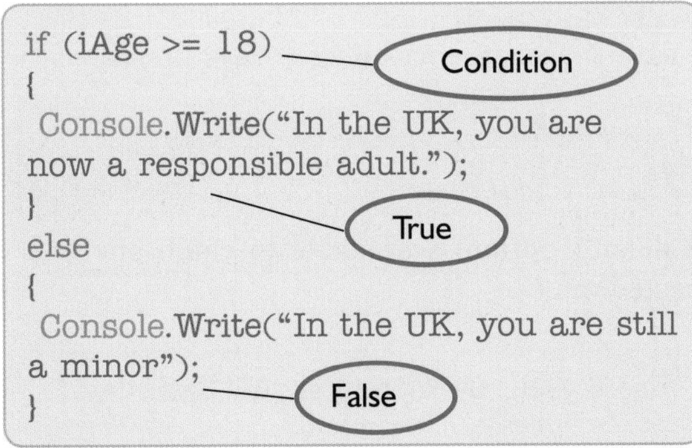

```
if (iAge >= 18)
{
 Console.Write("In the UK, you are
now a responsible adult.");
}
else
{
 Console.Write("In the UK, you are still
a minor");
}
```


In this example, any **iAge** value of 18 (or more) would cause the ...**responsible adult** message to be output. Any **iAge** value less than 18 would cause the ...**minor** message to be output.

The **Else** part of the **If...Else** statement is optional in most programming languages. If you don't have any action for the **false** part, you don't need an **Else**.

Case statements

Sometimes a programmer might wish to check for multiple possibilities.

Two main techniques are available, first the **'nested'** If...Else statement (Figure 6.09).

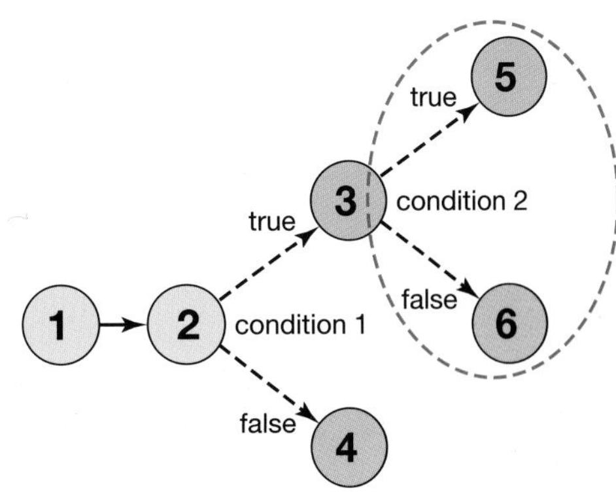

Figure 6.09 Example of a nested conditional sequence

Here, the second **If...Else** is nested into the 'true' part of the first **If...Else** statement.

The use of nested **If...Else** statements is common but can lead to unnecessary over-complication. **Case** (or **switch**) statements simplify things by being able to pick a single matching value from a list of possibilities (Figure 6.10).

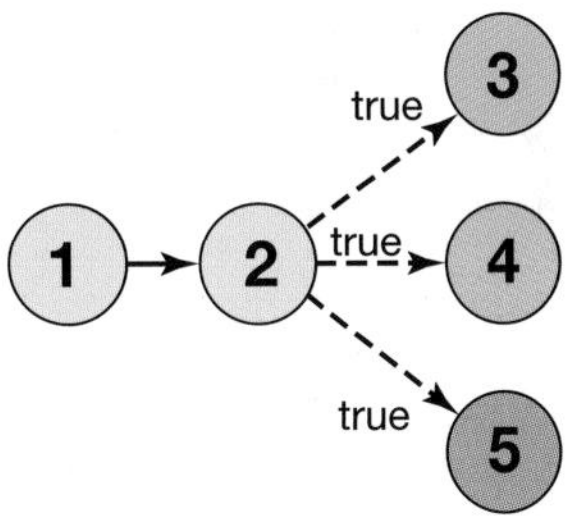

Figure 6.10 Example of a case statement

The case statement works more effectively because it can make individual comparisons against each possible matching value. If the comparison is true (they match), the resulting action (3, 4 or 5) is performed.

Here is an example of case statement use in C#. Imagine that we have stored the day of the week as an integer variable (1 is Sunday, 2 is Monday etc.). What we'd like to do is examine the variable and be able to output the correct day of the week in text (for example, "It's Monday!").

Examine the following C#® example, which is coded using nested If...Else statements.

```
if (iDayofWeek == 1)  (A)
{
  Console.WriteLine("It's Monday!");
}
else  (A)
{
  if (iDayofWeek == 2)  (B)
  {
    Console.WriteLine("It's Tuesday!");
  }
  else  (B)
  {
    if (iDayofWeek == 3)  (C)
    {
      Console.WriteLine("It's Wednesday!");
    }
    else  (C)
    {
      if (iDayofWeek == 4)  (D)
      {
        Console.WriteLine("It's Thursday!");
      }
      else  (D)
      {
        if (iDayofWeek == 5)  (E)
        {
          Console.WriteLine("It's Friday!");
        }
        else  (E)
        {
          if (iDayofWeek == 6)  (F)
          {
            Console.WriteLine("It's Saturday!");
          }
          else  (F)
          {
            if (iDayofWeek == 7)  (G)
            {
              Console.WriteLine("It's Sunday!");
            }
          }
        }
      }
    }
  }
}
```

As you can see, even though the matching pairs of If...Else statements have been identified, this code looks rather untidy and inefficient.

The case (switch) statement version of this in C#® looks a bit more straightforward.

```
switch (iDayofWeek)
{
 case 1: Console.WriteLine("It's Monday!");
         break;

 case 2: Console.WriteLine("It's Tuesday!");
         break;

 case 3: Console.WriteLine("It's Wednesday!");
         break;

 case 4: Console.WriteLine("It's Thursday!");
         break;

 case 5: Console.WriteLine("It's Friday!");
         break;

 case 6: Console.WriteLine("It's Saturday!");
         break;

 case 7: Console.WriteLine("It's Sunday!");
         break;
}
```

Case statements can also handle multiple matches, for example if we want to cheer on the weekend a minor modification is needed.

```
case 6:
case 7: Console.WriteLine("Yay! It's the
        weekend!!!");
        break;
  }
```

A default option is available to catch any unexpected values.

```
case 6: Console.WriteLine("It's Saturday!");
        break;

case 7: Console.WriteLine("It's Sunday!");
        break;

default: Console.WriteLine("That isn't a
        valid day");
        break;
}
```

Loops

Loops (or **iterations**) let the programmer make something happen repeatedly.

Normally loops will repeat until they are told to stop. This is achieved by using a conditional statement (for example, **reply == 'Y'** will repeat the loop while a reply is **Y** for Yes).

Post-check conditioning occurs when the conditional statement is placed after the actions (Figure 6.11). The actions in a post-check conditioned loop will always work at least once.

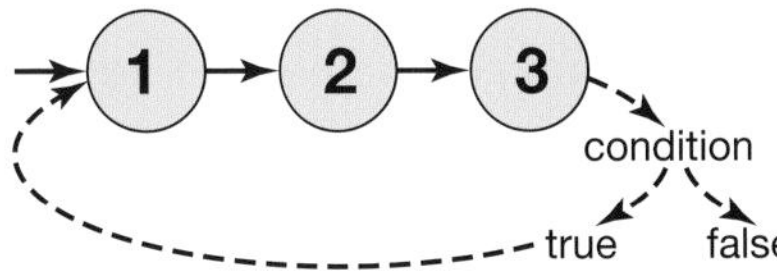

Figure 6.11 Example of a post-check loop

In C#®, a post-check loop can be created by using a **Do...While** statement:

```
int counter;

counter = 1;

do
{
  Console.WriteLine("Counter is
  currently {0}", counter);
  counter++;
} while (counter <= 10);
```

In this example, a post-check condition is used to repeat the loop while the counter is less than or equal to 10. Each cycle of the loop outputs the counter's current value (starting from 1) and increments the counter. The loop stops when the condition is no longer true: When the counter gets to 11.The resulting screen output is shown in Figure 6.12.

```
file:///C:/Documents and Settings/Mark/...
Counter is currently 1
Counter is currently 2
Counter is currently 3
Counter is currently 4
Counter is currently 5
Counter is currently 6
Counter is currently 7
Counter is currently 8
Counter is currently 9
Counter is currently 10
```

Figure 6.12 Output from the example Do...While loop

Pre-check conditioning is when the conditional statement is placed before the actions (Figure 6.13).

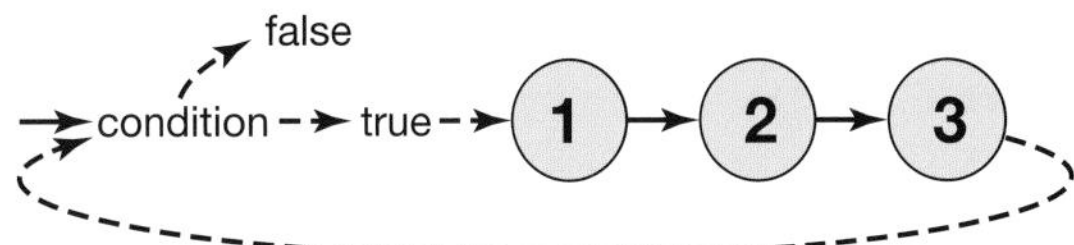

Figure 6.13 Example of a pre-check loop

Placing the condition at the start of the loop has an interesting effect. If the loop condition is found to be false to begin with, its actions will never be processed.

In C#®, a pre-check loop can be created by using a **While** statement:

```
int counter;

counter = 1;

while (counter <=10)
{
  Console.WriteLine("Counter is
  currently {0}", counter);
  counter++;
}
```

The resulting screen output is shown in Figure 6.14.

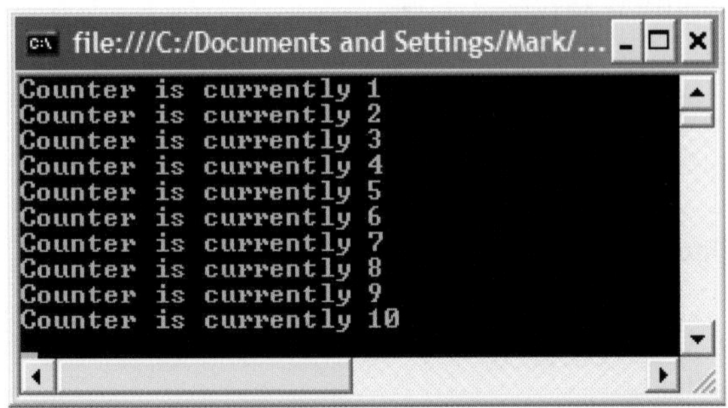

Figure 6.14 Output from the example While loop

Array

In programming, an **array** is a form of **data structure**, that is, it is a way of collecting together data items of the same type.

An array can be one dimensional (1D) or multi-dimensional. (Figures 6.15–6.17). Higher dimensional arrays are possible, but these are more difficult to represent on paper.

Figure 6.15 One-dimensional array

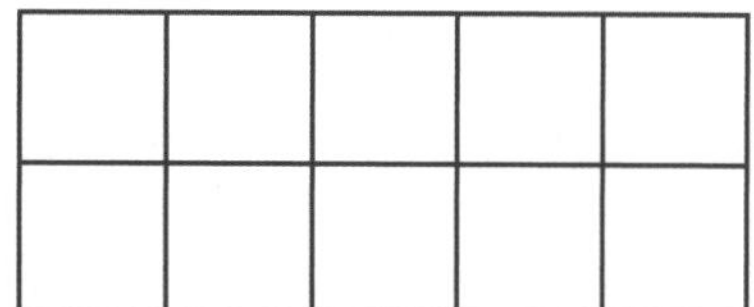

Figure 6.16 Two-dimensional array

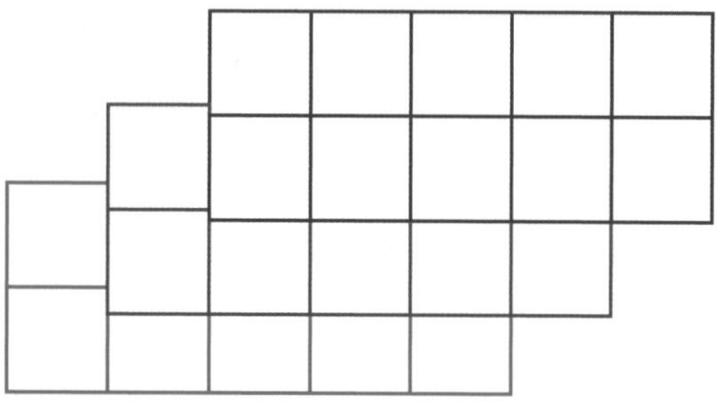

Figure 6.17 Three-dimensional array

Programmers use arrays to help solve complex problems because they provide an easy way to access similar data values in a specific order.

Let's start by examining a 1D array of integers (Figure 6.18).

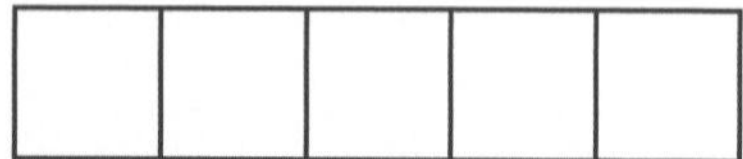

Figure 6.18 One-dimensional array

In C#®, this can be created by a simple line of code:

```
int[] iaMyNumbers = new int[5];
```

This code will create an array of five integers. Notice that it doesn't say which integer values we wish to use. C# will handle this automatically, giving each **box** (or **element**) its default value. For an integer, this is the value **0** (Figure 6.19). Not all programming languages are this helpful.

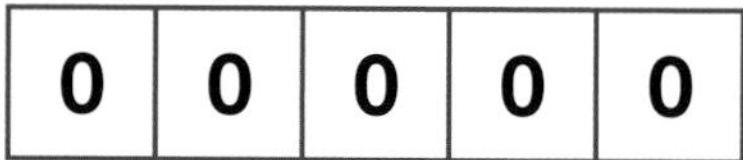

Figure 6.19 One-dimensional array of five integers

The code would have been slightly different if we had wanted to give each element an initial value:

```
int[] iaMyNumbers = new int[5] { 9, -2,
8, 4, 3};
```

Notice that the integers values are added to the end of the declaration.

This will create a slightly different array (Figure 6.20):

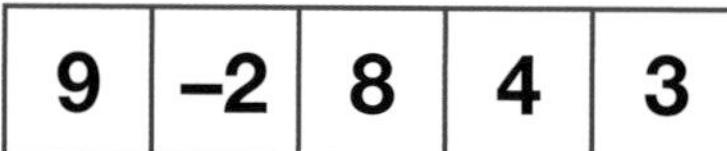

Figure 6.20 One-dimensional array of five integers with their initial value set

Once the array has been created, it typically stays this size (five elements) in the majority of programming languages. It is called a **static data structure** (that is, it doesn't shrink or grow).

Another point to remember is that elements are numbered with the first element (the left-most) being element 0 (Figure 6.21):

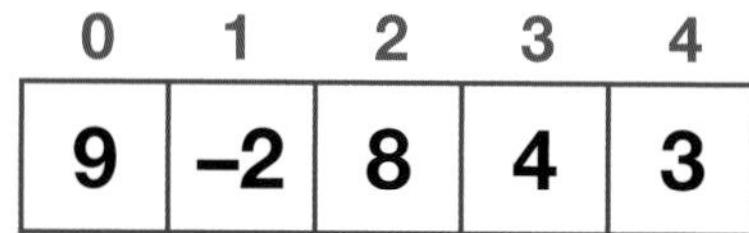

Figure 6.21 One-dimensional array showing element numbers

Programmers often use a special form of pre-check loop, called a For loop, because of an array's fixed size. Here's an example **For** loop in C# being used to 'walk along' the array and output each element's value:

The resulting screen output is shown in Figure 6.22.

```
int counter;
 int[] iaMyNumbers = new int[5] {
 9, -2, 8, 4, 3 };

 for (counter=0;counter <5;counter++)
 {
  Console.Write("The value in
  element ");
  Console.WriteLine("{0} is {1}.",
  counter,iaMyNumbers[counter]);
 }
```

```
file:///C:/Documents and Settings/...
The value in element 0 is 9.
The value in element 1 is -2.
The value in element 2 is 8.
The value in element 3 is 4.
The value in element 4 is 3.
```

Figure 6.22 Output from the example For loop to 'walk' an array

Key terms

Data type – These are the essential building blocks for programming. They are used to specify the kind of values the programmer needs to store.

6.1.4 Data types

This section will cover the following grading criteria:

Make the Grade P4 M2

The P4 criterion asks you (as a programmer) to be able to outline the **benefits of having different data types**.

The easiest way to do this is to identify a problem that requires the storage and manipulation of (at least) six different types of data as variables. Create a **data table**, listing each identifier, showing its name, the chosen type, storage requirement, a typical value and a comment from you about the rationale for the **data type** selected, for example, 'I need to store a name, so a **string** is the most appropriate choice because that can store multiple alphabetic characters'.

The M2 criterion requires you to read Sections 6.2.2 and 6.3.2. However, in terms of **data types**, you will partially meet M2 by **justifying the types you have used in a design solution**. For example, if the input is 'age', an **integer** (possibly a small integer) would be most appropriate in order to **store the data efficiently**.

The actual names of the data types available will vary from language to language but common categories are typically found (Figure 6.23)

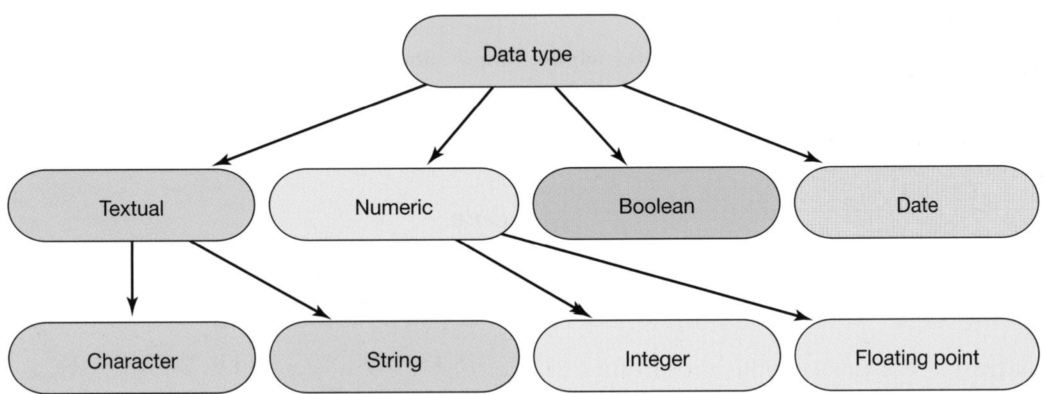

Figure 6.23 Common data types 'family'

The following describes the data types.

Character

Sometimes abbreviated to **char**, this can store one character (that is, any symbol in the computer system's character set, such as alphabet, digit, punctuation, currency symbols etc.). A character normally needs 1 byte of RAM storage.

Character examples are: A & " @ 9 #

String

This is a number of characters joined together. The string can be composed of any number of valid symbols. Some languages may define a limit for the length of the string (e.g. 255 characters or bytes).

String examples are: "BTEC National Diploma" "01412 989922" "Jane Smith" "#123"

Some languages use what are called ASCIIZ strings. These use a zero (0) value to mark the end of a string (Figure 6.24).

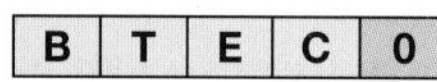

Figure 6.24 An example of an ASCIIZ string

Other languages place the length of the string in the first byte (Figure 6.25).

Figure 6.25 An example of string with a pre-defined length

Integer

Often abbreviated to **int**, an **integer** is a whole number (that is, it has no decimal part). Integers can be positive, negative or neither ('unsigned').

Integer examples are: 2814 +52 −7

> **Unit link**
> See also: Unit 11 Systems analysis and design

Languages place a limit on the size of integers. However, this usually depends on how much RAM an integer is allocated and whether the integer is signed (positive or negative) or unsigned. Some languages have **short** (or **small**) **int** variables which use less RAM.

For example, for an 8-bit signed integer (Figure 6.26):

Signed range (max & min)

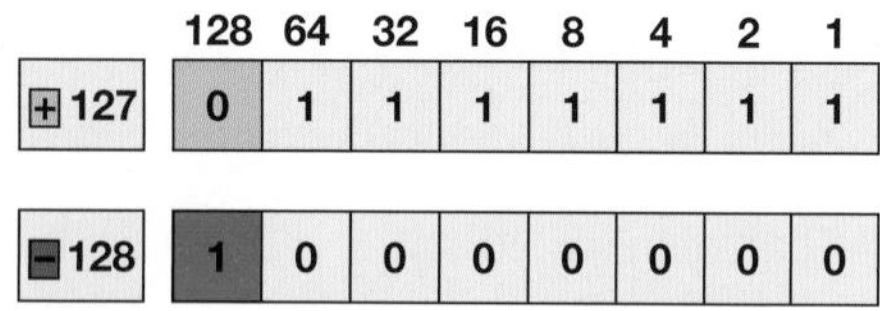

Figure 6.26 Ranges for 8-bit signed integers

Integer sizes, in most modern programming languages, are at least 16 bit.

Floating point

These are 'real' numbers (that is, ones that have a decimal point and fractional part).

Floating point examples are:
+1025.34 −117.1234 +0.4

Floating point numbers have two components: the **mantissa** and the **exponent**.

For example, +1.34 E + 2 or 1.34×10^2

In this example, both values equal 134.

The exponent **E + 2** means move the decimal point two places to the right.

1.34×10^2 means multiply 1.34×100 (10 squared).

The mantissa represents the **accuracy** of the number where the exponent represents the **magnitude**.

In programming languages, the floating point data type comes in various sizes. Larger floating point numbers offer greater magnitude and accuracy of numerical data.

Boolean

The name recognises the field of mathematical logic developed by nineteenth-century English mathematician George Boole. A Boolean value is either **true** or **false** (yes or no), reflecting the 0 and 1 binary values used by computer systems.

Date

Date data types may be stored in different ways, for example:

YYYY-MM-DD
16 August 2010 would be 2010-08-16

DD-MM-YYYY
16 August 2010 would be 16-08-2010

Data table

Although data tables are design considerations, it is appropriate to introduce their concept here.

Table 6.04 Data table for Program name

Identifier name	Variable or constant	Data type	Typical value	Storage	Local or global	Description
iRadius	Variable	Integer	10	32 bits	Local	Radius is specified as a whole number so I have used a standard integer.
fPI	Constant	Float	3.14	64 bits	Local	PI is fixed so I have created a constant based on a float.
fArea	Variable	Float	314	64 bits	Local	fArea is calculated by: fArea = fPI × fRadius * fRadius Its result will be a float for accuracy.
fCircumference	Variable	Float	62.8	64 bits	Local	fCircumference is calculated by: fCircumference = 2 × fPI × fRadius Its result will be a float for accuracy.

They fulfil a similar function to a **data dictionary** (typically when working with databases). A **data table** is a simple method for **documenting identifiers** (e.g. variables and constants) and **data types** used in a solution.

The usual convention is to draw a table with the headings shown in Table 6.04.

A separate row is then used for each identifier used in the solution.

Your description can be used as the comments for each declaration if you want.

Unit link

Chapter 11 – Systems analysis and design, section 3.1 has complete coverage of data dictionaries.

Activity 3: Investigating data types

Select **one** of the following popular programming languages:

C++® C#® Pascal® Visual Basic.NET®

Investigate which data types the language would use to store the following data values:

400 'C' 6.7 false "Saturn"

Data types in an example language

Table 6.05 shows actual primitive data types available in Oracle's Java™ programming language.

Other programming languages have data types with different names. When you start to program in a specific language, an important first step should be to familiarise yourself with the data types available.

Benefits of appropriate choice of data type

Selecting the correct data type for a value is vitally important. Choosing badly can generate serious run-time problems. A number of benefits are associated with picking the correct data type:

- **Accurate storage:** This is vitally important for numeric values. If the data type is too small to store a value it becomes **truncated** (chopped) and **accuracy is lost**. Using a data type of the right size prevents this happening.
- **Efficiency of storage:** Although cheaper RAM has reduced the need for programmers to be as efficient as they once were, there are still occasions when using data types efficiently is recommended. This can be particularly important in **embedded computer systems** where free RAM or processing power may be **limited**.
- **Additional validation:** Entering non-numeric data into a numeric data type can cause a program to **crash** at run-time. One simple technique is to enter all data as a text data type, **validate** the characters and then only convert to a true numeric data type if the contents are correct.

Table 6.05

Java™ data type	Range	RAM requirement
byte	+127 to −128	8 bits (1 byte)
short	+ 32,767 to −32,768	16 bits (2 bytes)
int	+2,147,483,647 to −2,147,483,648	32 bits (4 bytes)
long	+9,223,372,036,854,775,807 to −9,223,372,036,854,775,808	64 bits (8 bytes)
float	1.40129846432481707 E−45 to 3.40282346638528860 E+38 (positive or negative)	32 bits (4 bytes)
double	4.94065645841246544 E−324 to 1.79769313486231570 E308 (positive or negative)	64 bits (8 bytes)
Boolean	True/False	1 bit
char	Any Unicode character, the theoretical range being any one of 65,536 different global symbols	16 bits (2 bytes)

B Braincheck

1. What are the **four** basic categories of data type?
2. **Numeric** data types can be __________ or __________.
3. How many characters can be stored in a **char** data type?
4. What kind of number does a **floating point** data type store?
5. Which part of a floating point number does the **mantissa** represent?
6. What is a typical maximum length of a **string** data type?
7. What is the difference between **signed** and **unsigned** numbers?
8. Which data type can only store **True** and **False** values?
9. What is the real value of 0.1963 E + 3?
10. Select appropriate data types for the following values:

    −5.8 A +7800 (0120) 101000 04/09/2012 Miss Helena Wayne

How well did you do? See supporting website for answers.

Activity 4

Frankoni T-shirts Ltd needs a program that will calculate the production cost and projected sales price of a designer T-shirt.

Frankoni buy blank shirts at the following rates: Small (£3 each), Medium (£4 each), Large (£6 each) and eXtra Large (£7 each).

It costs Frankoni £2.50 to print the customer's design on the T-shirt.

Frankoni aims to make a 30 per cent profit on each T-shirt sold.

Write a program that will calculate and output production costs, projected sales and the profit of selling a user-specified quantity of each type of T-shirt.

6.2 Understand the principles of software design

This section will cover the following grading criterion:

Make the Grade P5

This criterion asks you to **explain the role of software design principles and software structures in the IT systems development life cycle**. What does this mean? Essentially it is asking you to link the steps needed to design software (the cycle) with the structures used in each step. For example, testing is easier if the code is modular (that is, written in functions/procedures), consequently this will make the code more **robust** (quality of code).

6.2.1 Software development life cycle

Program development forms part of a natural life cycle. New solutions are designed and implemented because:

- an older system is failing (**system decay**)
- user needs have changed.

It is important to put the design and implementation of a new solution into a wider context to see what part of the overall process it represents (Figure 6.27).

The following examines each stage of this cycle in more detail.

Stage 1: Determining the scope of the problem

Scope is a term used to describe the boundaries of the problem (sometimes called the **problem domain**). In particular, it is a definition of what is and what is not covered by the identified problem. It also includes those who are affected by the problem (e.g. people, organisations) and how they are affected.

Understanding the scope is vital in order to understand the nature of the problem.

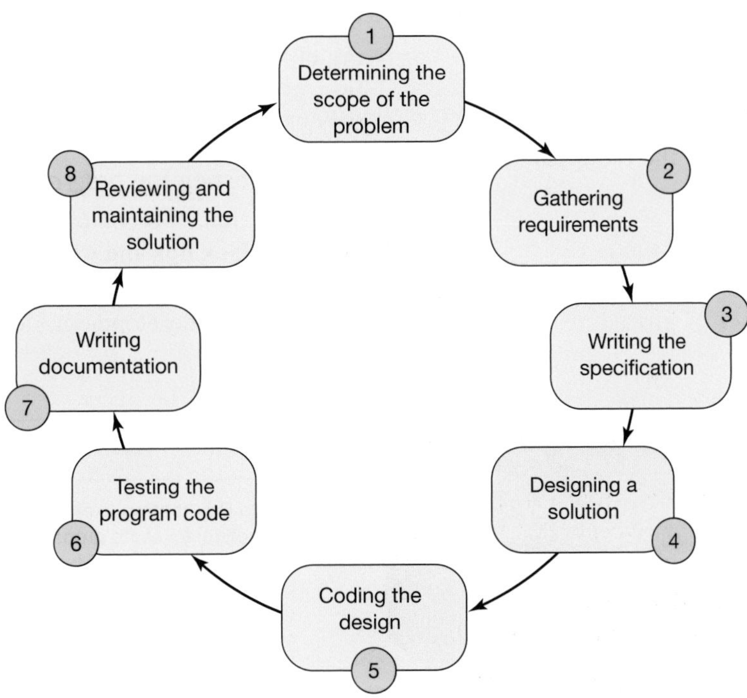

Figure 6.27 Software development life cycle

Stage 2: Gathering requirements

Before the problem is tackled it is vital that the **functional requirements** (what is wanted from the solution by those who are affected) are clearly known. Those affected by the problem are commonly referred to as **stakeholders**.

This will absolutely specify what the solution **does** and **does not** cover. A staggeringly high number of commercial solutions fail because these requirements are poorly researched; it is a common failure of IT projects worldwide.

Functional requirements may be collected in the form of **use cases**; a use case is simply a way of describing how a single task is achieved.

> **Unit link**
>
> **Unit 11** – Systems analysis and design, section 2.1 has more information on gathering techniques.

Stage 3: Writing the specification

This is a categorised list of the elements required in order to start designing a solution that includes:

- inputs
- outputs
- processing
- storage
- user interface
- constraints.

Section 6.3.1 examines the requirements specification in greater detail.

Stage 4: Designing a solution

A solution is built using a suitable **design tool** or **methodology** (a set of procedures or methods). This may be paper based or electronic depending on the design tools being used.

Modern IT solutions can be partly solved by software tools; programs effectively writing new solutions.

Avoid the temptation to rush ahead into the coding, many mistakes are made this way and a lot of time is needlessly wasted!

A number of different design tools are examined in Section 6.3.2.

Stage 5: Coding the design

At this stage, designs are converted into program code by experienced **software developers**. The programming language will have been selected before they start as some design features will lend themselves to particular languages.

It is common for software developers to work in a team. If this is the case, it is important that they are all clear about their individual responsibilities and adopt similar working practices and an 'in-house' style.

Programs written in a modular way (broken into smaller modules such as procedures and unctions) ensure reusability through shared libraries. Use of classes will also permit easy code reuse and speed up the development process.

Ideally, all developers need to have an understanding of how their modules fit into the larger solution, even if they do not know how modules that they have not written actually work.

Stage 6: Testing the program code

Testing is vital. Two common testing methods are used are **black box** and **white box** (Figure 6.28).

Testing is the part of the quality assurance process in the software development life cycle.

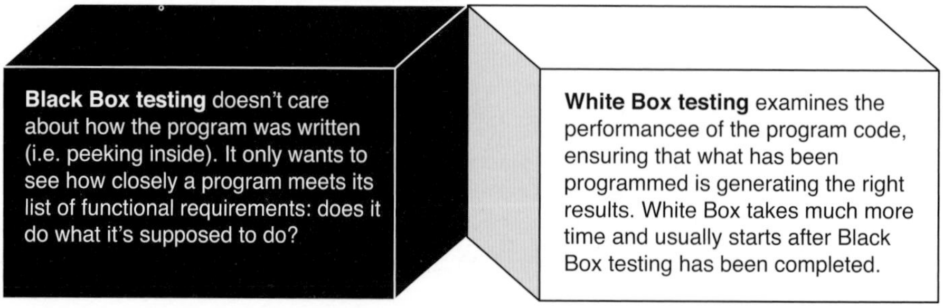

Black Box testing doesn't care about how the program was written (i.e. peeking inside). It only wants to see how closely a program meets its list of functional requirements: does it do what it's supposed to do?

White Box testing examines the performancee of the program code, ensuring that what has been programmed is generating the right results. White Box takes much more time and usually starts after Black Box testing has been completed.

Figure 6.28 Black box and white box testing

Thorough testing guarantees that the solution should work properly and meet the identified needs of the stakeholders (as detailed in the requirements specification).

A **test plan** is used to explain the testing strategy being used. It should attempt to check the following:

- **Logical pathways:** For example, does the test check both halves (True and False) of a conditional statement or all possible outcomes of a case statement? Have all the loops been successfully tested? Flowcharts are particularly good for this as the logical pathways are easy to see: The tests should represent all the flow arrows on the diagram.
- **Normal data:** The program needs to be tested with data that is within a sensible range and with data that is likely to be input.
- **Extreme data:** The program should also be tested with values that, although still within a sensible range, are less likely to be input. These are the values on the extremes (both high and low). For example, an age over 115 years isn't impossible, but it is extreme (approximately 1 in 2.1 billion).
- **Erroneous data:** Not all data entered into a program will be sensible. In order to ensure that it is robust, spurious data should be tested. This typically includes values outside valid ranges and wrong types of value (e.g. alphabetic when a number is expected).

Collecting suitable test data is important, both in quantity and quality of spread.

The test plan structure should include:

- **Test:** what is being tested; which part of the program is being tested.
- **Date:** when the test is taking place; this is important as it may link to a particular version of the program.
- **Expected result:** what results are expected out of the program by tracing through first on paper.
- **Actual result:** the results generated by the computer using supplied test data.
- **Corrective action:** if a problem is discovered, what was done to the program to fix it.

Many test plan formats exist. A **trace table** is often seen as a simple way of tabulating and comparing the results. An example is shown in Table 6.06.

The trace table allows us to record the values entered and logical pathways used when a program runs both on paper (the 'dry run') or live.

The comparison between the actual and expected results will quickly show how accurate the programmed solution is and also, given the variables involved in any particularly test, where any possible problem will be found.

Screen captures are a good addition to any trace table because they reinforce the actual results of the program running.

Error messages

The process of finding and removing errors from program code is known as **debugging** (Figure 6.29).

Some errors occur when the code is compiled (as the high-level language is translated into low-level language). Statements that break the language's syntax generate compilation errors.

Table 6.06

Trace table for program 'Water mover'								
Date: 12 September 2010								
Test: Calculation of water mass based on volume								
#	Box H	Box W	Box L	Vol cm cubed expected	Vol cm cubed actual	Calculated mass expected kg	Calculated mass actual kg	Corrective action
1	10	20	30	6,000	6,000.0	0.001 × 6,000 = 6 kg	6.0	None
2	20	40	60	48,000	48,000.0	0.001 × 48,000 = 48 kg	12.0	Fix data type problem

When errors occur while the programming is running, they are referred to as **run-time errors**.

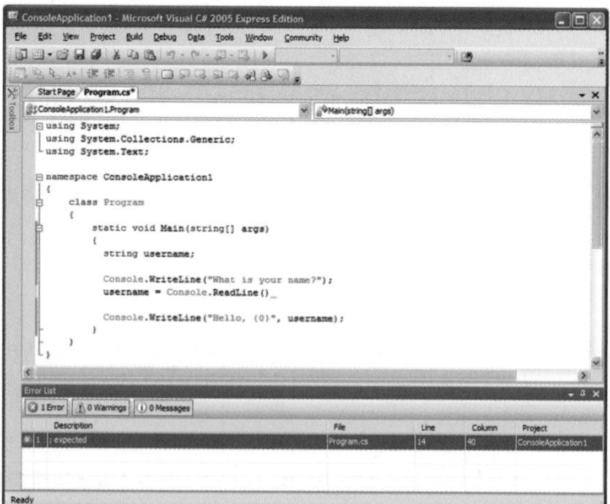

Figure 6.29 The C# IDE highlights a certain error (a missing semicolon)

Warnings are minor issues discovered during translation. They are not **fatal** (like an error), but may indicate possible run-time errors. A common example is using a data type that is too small to hold a calculated result. The run-time effect would be truncation and, therefore, inaccurate results.

Specialist software tools

Modern programming software has feature-rich tools to help the specialist debug a program solution. In a typical IDE, the three most commonly used debug tools (Figure 6.30) are:

- **trace:** This lets the programmer follow a program line-by-line as it executes, walking through the different logical pathways as the program progresses. Tracing is very useful when conditional statements are present. If the trace shows an unexpected behaviour (going down the wrong logical pathway, for example) the programmer will need to check the logic to see where things have gone wrong.
- **watches:** This lets the programmer spy on the contents of a variable while the program is running, usually during a trace. One of the most common programming problems is a variable storing unexpected values. The watch feature lets the programmer see the changes in a variable's contents as different lines of the program code are executed. The appearance of an unexpected value in a watched variable will let the programmer narrow the search to just a few lines of program code.
- **breakpoint:** This is a debugging feature which lets the programmer mark a line of code with a physical breakpoint. When the program runs, it will halt temporarily at this point. From the stop point, the programmer can decide to trace the remaining code and/or inspect variable watches he or she has set. The clear advantage is that parts of the program that are functioning correctly need not be traced; the breakpoint can be placed after these sections have finished.

Stage 7: Writing documentation

Documentation is also vital! Generally there will be three types of documentation:

- internal documentation
- technical documentation
- user documentation.

Internal documentation is documentation that is actually inside the program's code.

All good programs should be self-explanatory. There are some easy ways to achieve this:

- the use of meaningful and sensible variable names
- the good use of comments, written to describe the code's purpose in the solution, not the syntax of the actual code itself
- good use of indentation and a tidy layout. Most modern IDEs do this automatically for the programmer).

Technical documentation is written by developers for other developers to read. This means that programming terminology (jargon) may be freely used, as long as it is sufficiently explained.

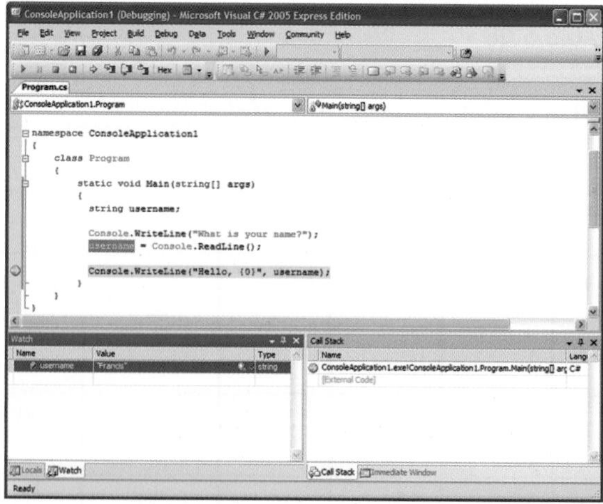

Figure 6.30 The C# IDE demonstrates tracing, watches and breakpoint

Depending on how the design was developed, technical documentation may often include:

- the requirements specification
- forms design (manual or electronic, particularly for data entry)
- flowcharts
- JSP diagrams
- UML diagrams
- DFDs, ERMs
- the data dictionary (a table listing data items and data types used in the solution)
- class schemas.

It should also contain:

- the test strategy
- the test results (predicted and actual)
- error messages (and corrective actions)
- the fully commented program code
- recommendations for future enhancements.

Perhaps the most important factor to consider is that software needs to be maintained. Even with the best programming it is unlikely to have covered all potential outcomes, so the technical document is the ultimate handbook, which tells another programmer how the program was created and why things were written certain ways. This is particularly important when maintenance has to be performed by another programmer when the original programmers of a solution are unavailable after a period of time (that is, they may have changed job or be busy on other projects). Additionally, over time, it easy to forget details.

In addition, the technical document is also live documentation. It should be updated to show any changes made to the program code.

User code is meant to be read by a typical end-user, not a developer. As a result, the user instructions should avoid the use of technical terms or jargon where possible.

Typical content may include:

- how to install the program (including 'loading' instructions and hardware/operating system requirements)
- how to safely uninstall the program
- how to start and end the program
- how to use the program properly
- how to resolve problems that might occur (also known as a 'troubleshooting' guide)
- how to get further help (online forums, files on disk, telephone support etc.).

Effectively, user documentation should 'hold the user's hand' by taking them through a typical example of the program working. In addition, instructions should be brief (step-by-step are ideal), with accurate screen, mouse or keyboard diagrams or screen captures to show the program running.

The move from paper

Over the last 15 years or so there has been a shift from producing printed program documentation to electronic distribution:

- **Text files** (for example, Readme.txt): An ASCII (American Standard Code for Information Interchange) text file containing basic information about the program. This is usually stored as a file on a disk or in a downloaded archive (such as .ZIP or .RAR). Text files can be created and read using a text editor such as Microsoft Windows® Notepad.
- **PDF file**: Adobe's Portable Document Format file is a popular, secure and reliable way of sharing electronic documents. A copy of the freely downloadable Adobe Acrobat Reader application is required in order to read a PDF file (www.adobe.com/products/reader/). Acro Software's CutePDF is a freely downloadable PDF creation tool (www.cutepdf.com).
- **Screencast videos and animations**: Why describe how something works when you can show it? Applications such as Wink (www.debugmode.com/wink/) and Adobe Captivate (www.adobe.com/products/captivate/) can be used to create recordings of programs being used. These recorded tutorials (**screencasts**) often have additional highlighting and narration to help explain what is being shown on a screen.

Stage 8: Reviewing and maintaining the solution

Reviewing is a reflective process: looking at the solution and comparing it with the stakeholders' original requirements. Have they been met? And if so, how well is the solution working?

Maintenance is an ongoing process. Programs are written to solve a problem that exists at a particular point in time. As business or personal needs change, the solution might seem less ideal. It is the process of keeping the solution working, fixing minor errors that occur, and making small adjustments, which expand the scope of the program to add extra features and functionality.

If the maintenance requirements become too severe, it may be necessary to redevelop (that is, to start the cycle again).

6.2.2 Software structures, readability and quality

This section will cover the following grading criteria:

Make the Grade M1 M2 D1

Criterion M1 requires you to be able to explain the importance of the quality of code, for instance, if the code quality is poor, then it might operate unreliably giving inconsistent or inaccurate results.

For D1, you need to be able to discuss the readability of code and the factors that affect it. In order to achieve this, you may link back to the complexity of the programming language being used, the choice of appropriate software structures, and the use of comments, meaningful variable names and indentation to highlight the code structure.

Software structures

Software is built from a number of different **structures and elements** (that include the variables and data types we have already seen). Table 6.07 opposite shows some other terms you should be aware of.

Most programs are built from combining these different elements in various patterns and quantities.

Readability

We have already discussed readability of the software design through the use of internal documentation' as part of Stage 7 of the software development life cycle (see section 6.2.1).

Quality of code

The quality of code is judged through several criteria. Let us look at the most obvious ones you should consider using when making decisions about the quality of your solutions:

- Portability: code can be recompiled for different hardware and software platforms with minimal modification.
- Efficiency: the code calculates results and performs operations as quickly as possible.
- Accuracy: the code produces results with an acceptable level of accuracy.
- Robustness: the code does not crash when given bad or silly input.
- Reliability: the code works the same way every time it is used: there are no unexpected surprises.
- Usability: the code is intuitive for the end user to operate.
- Maintainability: the code is easy to modify and improve (as needed).

6.3 Be able to use tools to demonstrate software designs

This section will cover the following grading criteria:

Make the Grade P6 D2

These criteria are linked and you will be awarded them when you complete the basic solution's design (preferably using a recognised design tool) to a defined need (that is, a problem set by the tutor) and when you **develop the necessary algorithm for a design solution** (for example, pseudo code).

The use of **tools** and **algorithms** (note the plural) in these criteria suggests that you'll be creating at least **two** different solutions.

6.3.1 Requirements specification

As previously discussed, the requirements specification starts to identify the following area before a full design is produced.

- **Inputs:** Essentially any data that is entered into the system by its target user. Every input will need to be separately identified and listed. This can take some time to investigate fully.

Table 6.07

Software structure	Overview
Sequence	Any collection of program statements that are performed one after the other.
Selection	A decision or conditional statement whose result lets the program execute one set of program statements or another. These form the program's logical pathways.
Iteration	A block of statements that are repeated based on some conditional statement evaluating to true.
Modules	In programming, a term used to describe different parts of a program. The implementation of a module (size, layout etc.) will vary from language to language.
Functions	A practical example of a module. Functions generally are used to calculate a value, although some may perform actions instead. Re-usable.
Procedures	Another practical example of a module. Procedures tend to perform actions. As with functions, these are re-usable.
Classes	Part of the object-oriented programming paradigm, a class contains both data and functions that describe a real-world 'thing'.
Objects	A concrete instance of a class, complete with its personal data.
Data abstraction	One of the key principle ideas behind the creation of classes. In data abstraction, the data type is less important than the operations that can be performed on it; in a sense the data type is hidden behind a limited number of functions/methods.
Pre-defined code	Generally a term describing code that is already written and that can be used in a developer's solution (with permission). This may take the form of a compiled module, a 'call' to the operating system or a 'snippet' of ready-made code that can be inserted into their solution.

- **Outputs:** This is the output required from the system as requested by the user. In order to program the solution correctly the designer will need to know:
  - what the outputs are needed
  - how the outputs should be displayed
  - when the outputs should be generated.
- **Processing:** These should be basic descriptions of the processing that is required, such as 'Calculate tax', 'Verify user account', 'Print customer report'.

These process descriptions can then be decomposed (broken down) into more detailed algorithms as part of the design phase. Remember: the processing required should convert the inputs into the desired outputs.

- **Storage:** This typically means two things:
  - Temporary data stored in RAM (variables).
  - Permanent data stored on backing storage (for example, hard disk) in a data file.

Any identified data should include:

- any piece of data mentioned in the problem
- any calculated value needed to solve the problem
- any value that will be output.

At this point it is worthwhile identifying whether these storage items are numeric, text, date or Boolean. More complex types such as arrays could also be considered.

- **User interface**: This is a separate study in itself (HCI – Human Computer Interface/Interaction). There should be a detailed look at how the end user will interact with the program. Mouse or keyboard only? Which colours to use? Size of font? How is the screen laid out? Forms design is an important part of this aspect.
- **Constraints**: A constraint is some kind of limiting factor: something that could prevent you completing the task satisfactorily. Common constraints to plan for are:

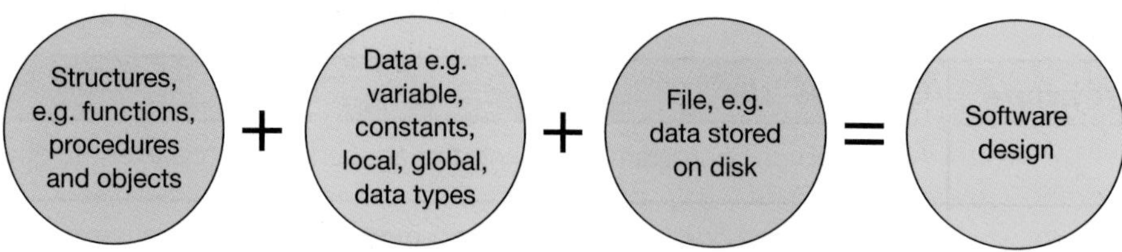

Figure 6.31 Design solution

- operating system software availability and compatibility
- hardware availability and compatibility
- timescale for development (e.g. is there enough time?)
- funding (e.g. is there enough money available?)
- workforce (availability of trained developers, quality assurance testers etc.).

6.3.2 Design

Once the requirements specification has been created (and agreed by all stakeholders), it is time to design a solution that takes account of all of the factors discussed so far. Figure 6.31 shows what this is likely to involve.

The next step is to use an appropriate tool to represent the planned solution.

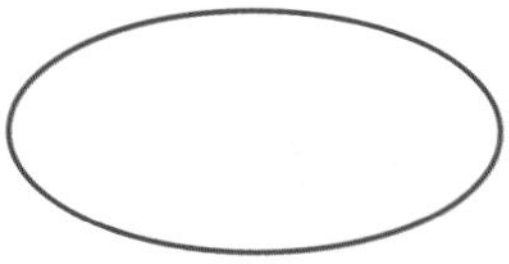

Figure 6.32 Terminator An oval symbol which is used to start or end the flowchart.	**Figure 6.33** Decision A diamond symbol used for indicating a choice (for example, If...Else etc.
Figure 6.34 Process A rectangle which is used to show an action or calculation that must be performed.	**Figure 6.35** Input or output A parallelogram can either be used to specify a user's input or the desired output.
Figure 6.36 Connector A circle that is used to connect different sections of a flowchart together, particularly when drawing flow arrows would be difficult.	**Figure 6.37** Flow arrow Arrowed lines used to indicate the flow of logic in the solution. Logic, by default, goes top-to-bottom, left-to-right.

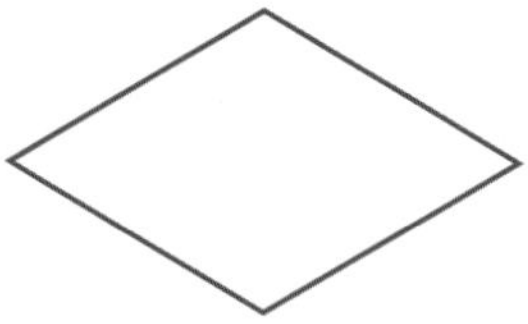

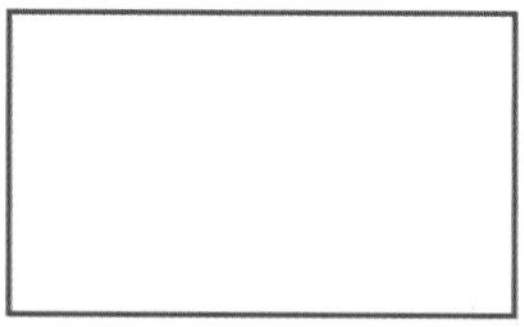

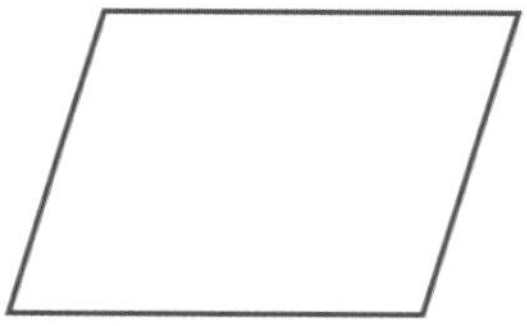

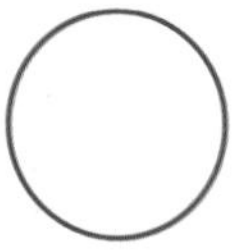

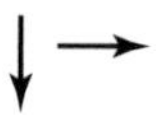

6.3.3 Tools

There are a number of **design tools** available. In order to use the tool effectively, it has to be appropriate to the type of solution in hand. For example, coding a scientific solution often requires different design tools than a solution that involves a database.

The most common techniques are listed as follows. Familiarise yourself with them.

Flowchart

Flowcharts are a familiar visual tool for describing the logical steps needed to solve a problem. Many user manuals use them to explain complex sequences of instruction.

Flowcharts use a standard set of drawn symbols as shown in Figures 6.32–6.37:

As with any design tool, the flowchart should not contain any programming language, only natural language (e.g. English). A limited use of general symbols is acceptable.

An example flowchart that checks an inputted password is shown in Figure 6.38. The user has three opportunities to type the password correctly before the program identifies them as an 'Unauthorised user'.

```
String guess;
int tries;
bool userok; (A)
tries = 0;
do (G)
{
 Console.Write("{0} attempt(s)", 3 - tries);
 Console.Write("Enter your password:"); (B)
 guess = Console.ReadLine(); (C)
 userok = guess. Equals ("secret"); (D)
 if (userok == false) (E)
 {
  Console.WriteLine ("Incorrect!"); (F)
  tries++;
 }
} while (tries < 3 && userok == false); (G)
if (userok == true) (H)
{
 Console.WriteLine("Welcome!"); (I)
}
else
{
 Console.WriteLine("Unauthorised User!");
}                                        (J)
```

The C# solution is arrived at by using the flowchart:

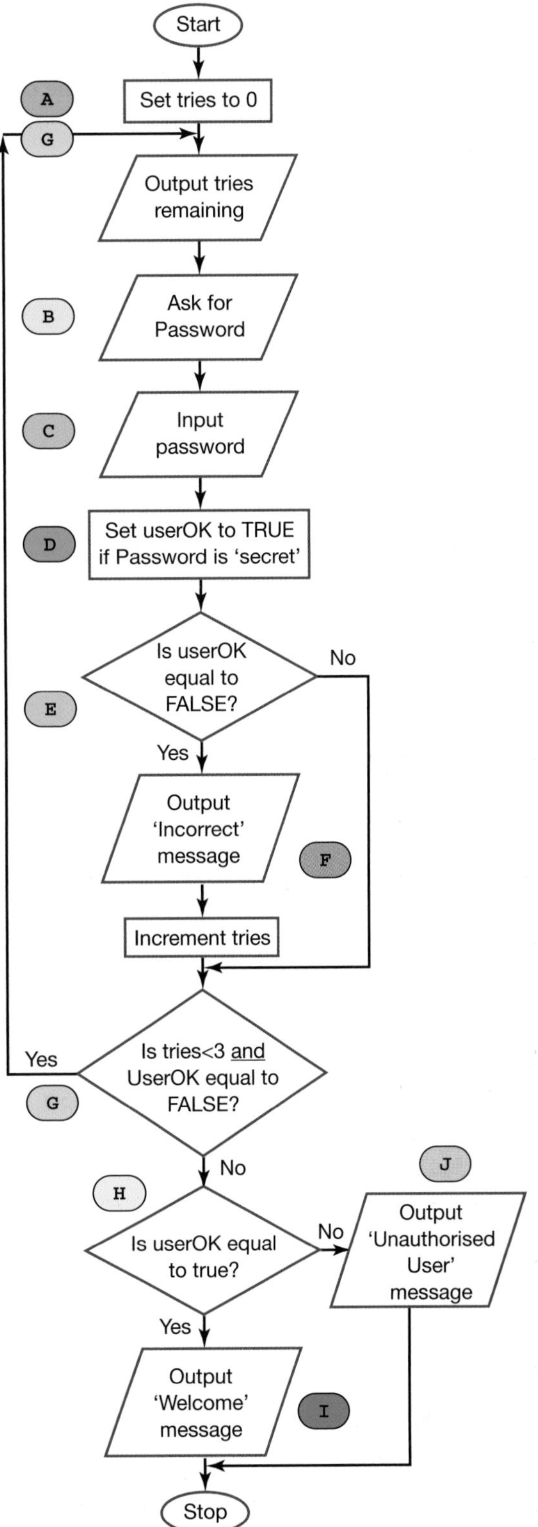

Figure 6.38 Example flowchart

JSP

As you have seen, a flowchart is good at demonstrating the logical flow of a solution.

Unfortunately, even short solutions quickly become large and confusing, preventing the reader from grasping the underlying structure of the code (for example, where the conditional statements or loops actually are).

Jackson Structured Programming **(JSP)** uses a simple system that breaks solutions down into three basic building blocks: **sequence**, **selection** and **iteration**.

Sequence

Figure 6.39 shows a sequence: first action A, then action B, followed by action C.

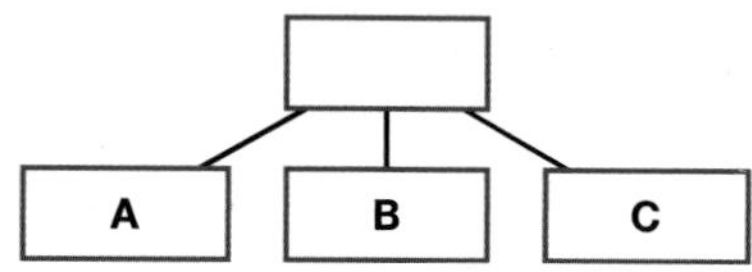

Figure 6.39 JSP sequence

Selection

Unlike the sequence, the selection (Figure 6.40) uses a condition to perform either A or B, but not both. If the condition is true, A is performed, else B is performed.

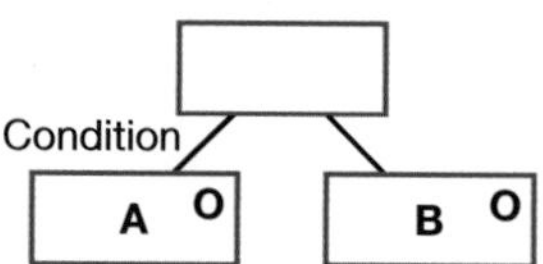

Figure 6.40 JSP selection (the letter O in the top-right corner of a box shows that it is a selection rather than a sequence)

Iteration

An iteration is shown by a pair of boxes (Figure 6.42). The parent box indicates a plural, built from the lower box repeating 0 or more times (as specified by the condition).

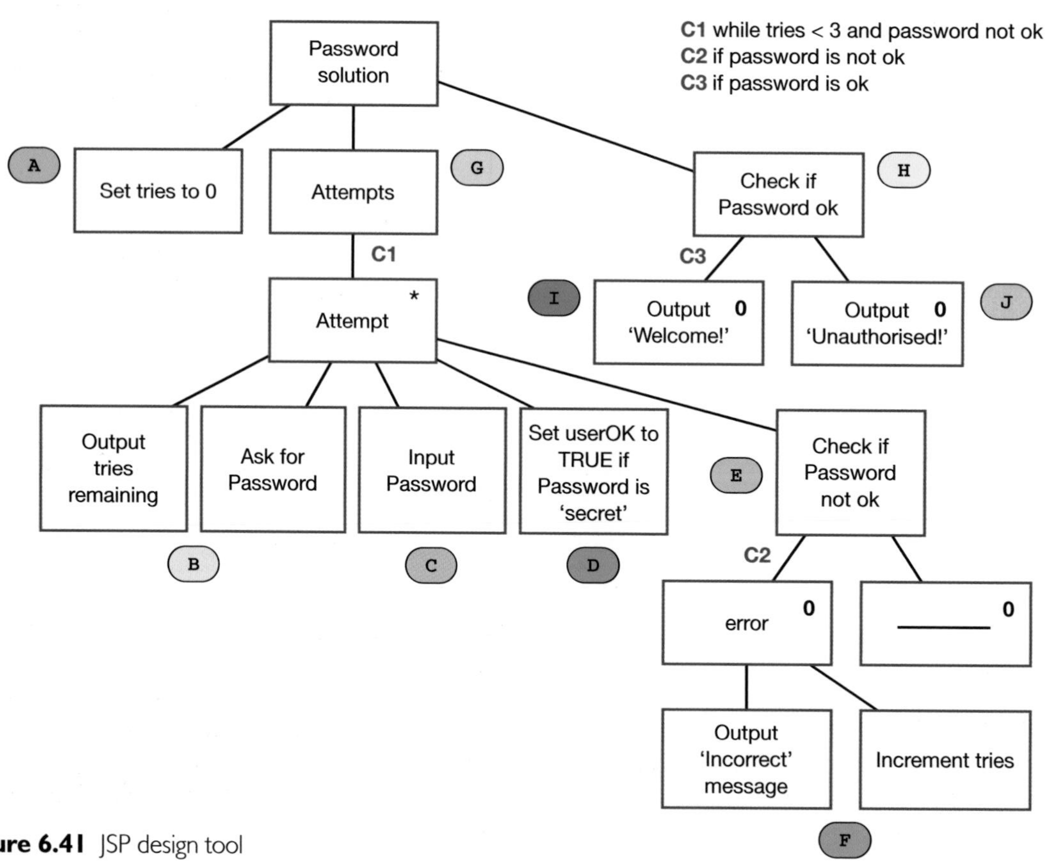

Figure 6.41 JSP design tool

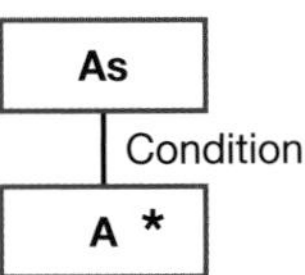

Figure 6.42 JSP iteration (the * (asterisk) in the top-right corner of the lower box indicates that the box will occur a number of times)

Let's examine that 'Password' solution again, but this time using the JSP design tool (Figure 6.42).

```
String guess;
int tries;  (A)
bool userok;
tries = 0;
do (G)
{
 Console.Write("{0} attempt(s)", 3 - tries);
 Console.Write("Enter your                     (B)
 password:");
 guess = Console.ReadLine(); (C)
 userok = guess.
 Equals("secret"); (D)
 if (userok == false) (E)
 {
  Console.WriteLine("Incorrect!"); (F)
  tries++;
 }
} while (tries < 3 && userok == false); (G)
if (userok == true) (H)
{
 Console.WriteLine("Welcome!"); (I)
}
else
{                                          (J)
 Console.WriteLine("Unauthorised User!");
```

Figure 6.43 shows the output for the JSP example.

Other tools

Some other tools you might encounter are:

- Unified Modelling Language (UML), first mentioned as part of the object-oriented programming section.
- Data Flow Diagram (DFD).
- Entity Relationship Model (ERM).

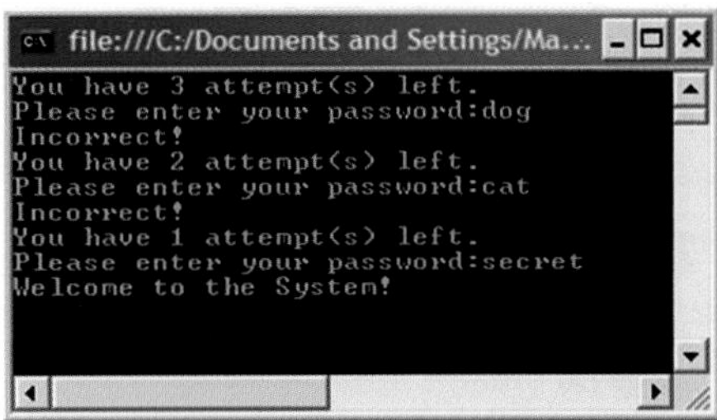

Figure 6.43 Sample output from the Password program

> ## Help
>
> **Reading JSP diagrams**
>
> Some students find JSP diagrams difficult at first. Perhaps the most important thing to remember is that JSP diagrams are read top-to-bottom, left-to-right.
>
> Examine the mapping labels shown on the JSP diagram and the C#® program code. Here, you can clearly see that actions B, C, D, E and F are all within loop G. It should also be easy to spot that condition H occurs after loop G has finished.

> ## Unit link
>
> Unit 11 – Systems analysis and design has extended coverage of DFD and ERM.

Algorithms

An **algorithm** is a set of **step-by-step instructions** designed to solve a problem. Algorithms can be developed from design tools (or be used instead of them). A common way to represent an algorithm is by using **pseudo code**.

Pseudo code

Pseudo code, literally meaning 'false code' (from the Greek), is a way of writing the outline steps required in an algorithm without having to write any real programming language code. The pseudo code is written in a natural language (e.g. English). For the 'password' solution, the following pseudo code would be adequate:

```
Set tries to 0.
Do loop
  Show number of attempts left
  Ask user for password
  Input password
  If password is not equal to 'secret' then
    Output 'Incorrect!'
    Add 1 to tries
  End if
While tries less than 3 and password not correct
If password correct then
Output 'Welcome!'
Else
Output 'Unauthorised User!'
End if
```

You will occasionally see some pseudo code with line numbers. This is fine. What you should **not see** is anything specific to any particular programming language.

6.3.4 Review

You should review your solution during development and on completion. A review is a formal, reflective procedure that should clearly identify:

- the program's strengths
- the program's weaknesses
- how well the program meets the stakeholders' needs.

A review is essentially a comparison of the final product and the requirements specification. You will need the cooperation of all the stakeholders in order to get the necessary feedback, and this could take time.

End-users of the software can be interviewed, observed or be given a questionnaire to complete. The use of focus groups to dig down into your solution from a user's viewpoint is also valuable.

In addition, it is likely that a section on further developments will be required. This should list:

- an overview of corrections made (to resolve errors)
- **improvements** (to existing performance) that could be made
- **expansions** (to existing functionality) that could be invested in.

The review process should be ongoing, exploring **program performance** and **end-user satisfaction** at regular intervals. The software development life cycle (as seen in Section 6.2.1) will have to be started again if faults are found that cannot be remedied using minor maintenance.

B Braincheck

1. Name **seven** qualities a good program should possess.
2. Name **four** properties that a test strategy should cover.
3. Explain the difference between an error and a warning.
4. Name **three** specialist tools that help the debugging process.
5. Name **four** different aspects a user guide should cover.
6. Name **three** different forms of documentation media.
7. Which **three** points should a formal program review identify?
8. What is **pseudo code**?
9. What should user documentation avoid?
10. What is an **algorithm**?

How well did you do? See supporting website for answers.

Unit link

Unit 6 is a Mandatory unit for the Edexcel BTEC Level 3 National Diploma and National Extended Diploma in IT (Software Development) pathway and optional for all other qualifications and pathways of this Level 3 IT family.

Qualification (pathway)	Mandatory	Optional	Specialist optional
Edexcel BTEC Level 3 National Certificate in Information Technology		✓	
Edexcel BTEC Level 3 National Subsidiary Diploma in Information Technology		✓	
Edexcel BTEC Level 3 National Diploma in Information Technology		✓	
Edexcel BTEC Level 3 National Extended Diploma in Information Technology		✓	
Edexcel BTEC Level 3 National Diploma in IT (Business)		✓	
Edexcel BTEC Level 3 National Extended Diploma in IT (Business)		✓	
Edexcel BTEC Level 3 National Diploma in IT (Networking and System Support)		✓	
Edexcel BTEC Level 3 National Extended Diploma in IT (Networking and System Support)		✓	
Edexcel BTEC Level 3 National Diploma in IT (Software Development)	✓		
Edexcel BTEC Level 3 National Extended Diploma in IT (Software Development)	✓		

There are specific links to the following units in the scheme:
Unit 14 – Event Driven Programming
Unit 15 – Object-oriented Programming
Unit 16 – Procedural Programming

Achieving success

In order to achieve this unit you will complete a series of coursework activities. Each time you hand in work, your tutor will return this to you with a record of your achievement.

This particular unit has 10 criteria to meet: 6 Pass, 2 Merit and 2 Distinction.

For a Pass: You must achieve all 6 Pass criteria

For a Merit: You must achieve all 6 Pass and all 2 Merit criteria

For a Distinction: You must achieve all 6 Pass, all 2 Merit and both Distinction criteria.

Further reading?

Bowman, K. – *Systems Analysis: A Beginners Guide* (Palgrave Macmillan, 2003) ISBN-10 033398630X, ISBN-13 978-0333986301

Flanagan, D. – *JavaScript Pocket Reference, 2nd edition* (O'Reilly, 2002) ISBN-10 0596004117, ISBN-13 978-0596004118

Knuth, D. – *The Art of Computer Programming: Volumes 1–3, 2nd Edition* (Addison Wesley, 1998) ISBN-10 0201485419, ISBN-13 978-0201485417

Wang, W. – *Visual Basic 6 for Dummies* (John Wiley & Sons, 1998) ISBN-10 0764503707, ISBN-13 978-0764503702

Wender, K. – *Cognition and Computer Programming* (Ablex Publishing Corporation, 1995) ISBN-10 1567500951, ISBN-13 978-1567500950

Willis. T., Crossland, J. and Blair, R. – *Beginning VB.NET, 3rd edition* (John Wiley & Sons, 2004) ISBN-10 0764556584, ISBN-13 978-0764556586

Websites

www.guidetoprogramming.com/joomla153

www.profsr.com

visualbasic.about.com

www.vbexplorer.com/VBExplorer/VBExplorer.asp

By the end of this unit you should be able to:

1. Understand the impact of potential threats to IT systems
2. Know how organisations can keep systems and data secure
3. Understand the organisational issues affecting the security of IT systems

Whether you are in school or college, passing this unit will involve being assessed. As with most BTEC schemes, successful completion of various assessment criteria demonstrates your evidence of learning and the skills you have developed.

This unit has a mixture of pass, merit and distinction criteria. Generally you will find that merit and distinction criteria require a little more thought and evaluation before they can be completed.

The colour-coded grid below shows you the pass, merit and distinction criteria for this unit.

To achieve a pass grade you need to:	To achieve a merit grade you also need to:	To achieve a distinction grade you also need to:
P1 Explain the impact of different types of threat on an organisation	**M1** Discuss information security	
P2 Describe how physical security measures can help keep systems secure	**M2** Explain the operation and use of an encryption technique in ensuring security of transmitted information	**D1** Discuss different ways of recovering from a disaster
P3 Describe how software and network security can keep systems and data secure		
P4 Explain the policies and guidelines for managing organisational IT security issues		
P5 Explain how employment contracts can affect security		
P6 Review the laws related to security and privacy of data	**M3** Explain the role of ethical decision-making in organisational IT security	**D2** Evaluate the security policies used in an organisation

Introduction

Organisational systems security is a 10-credit unit that focuses on the dangers that modern enterprise faces in the up-to-the-minute digital age.

Looking at both internal and external threats, this unit chapter describes the most common forms of attack, the best forms of defence and the resulting costs to an organisation of being poorly protected.

Additional themes will tackle moral and ethical use of ICT systems, the balance between individual freedoms, organisational needs and the professional bodies that are there to help strike a balance.

How to read this chapter

This chapter is organised to match the content of the BTEC unit it represents. The following diagram shows the grading criteria that relate to each learning outcome.

You'll find colour-matching notes in each chapter about completing each grading criterion.

7.1 Impact of threats to IT systems and organisations potential

This section will cover the following grading criterion:

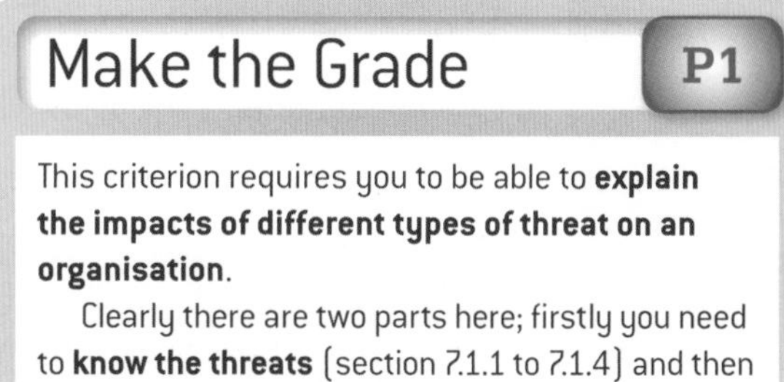

This criterion requires you to be able to **explain the impacts of different types of threat on an organisation**.

Clearly there are two parts here; firstly you need to **know the threats** (section 7.1.1 to 7.1.4) and then how each impacts the organisation (section 7.1.5).

Assessment is likely through a quiz, discussion, leaflet, poster, report or presentation.

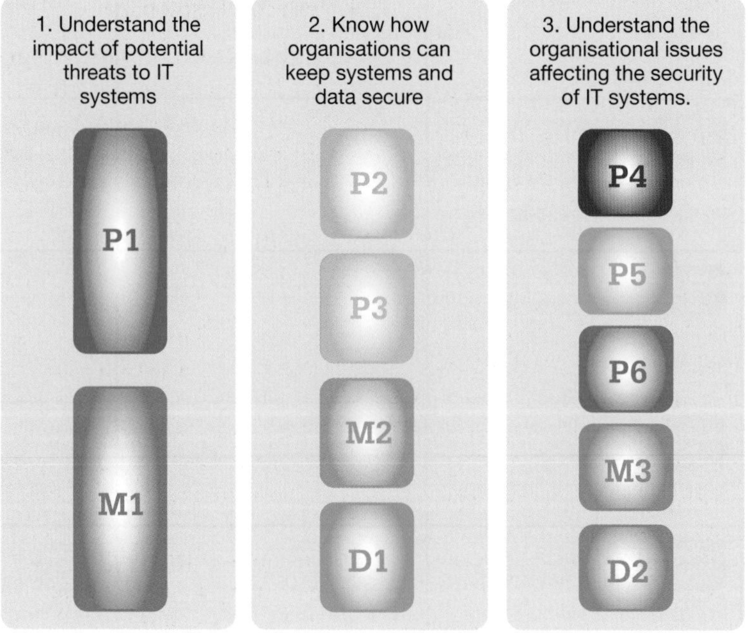

Figure 7.00

7.1.1 Potential threats

Threats to ICT systems and organisations are many and varied.

Common types of threat include:

- malicious damage (see 7.1.2)
- those specifically targeted at e-commerce organisations (see 7.1.3)
- counterfeit goods (see 7.1.4).

Technical failure

All devices have a point of failure. They will inevitably fail at some point in the future.

Generally, as devices become more complex, so does the act of predicting all of the possible failures that may occur.

Avoid technical failures by:

- thorough user training, so equipment is used properly and safely
- regular preventative maintenance that spots faults early
- investment in new, more reliable (or replacement) technology
- using well-developed systems that use good quality components and techniques.

A back-up plan (another way of doing things when technology fails) safeguards an organisation from lost business. Although important in day-to-day running, it is especially important if new, untried technologies are being implemented.

Human error

It is a basic fact that people make mistakes. Moreover, they can make silly mistakes (which may have little impact) and colossal errors of judgement, which may be life threatening to themselves or others.

In an organisation, it is helpful if employees feel that they can reveal any errors made without fear of immediate disciplinary action.

Organisations where employees fear making errors often lead to them to cover mistakes up, making matters worse when the problem is discovered.

Theft

IT thefts constitute about a third of all insurance claims for losses in the commercial sector. It is one of the fastest growing crimes in the UK. At the very least, theft might mean that a replacement item needs to be purchased, but more seriously, day-to-day business might be affected. The cost to a business of replacing hardware or software will affect its profit (see section 7.1.5). Data and ideas can also be stolen. These might be key to an organisation's success in the marketplace, and the loss of such intellectual property can seriously affect its ability to compete successfully.

7.1.2 Malicious damage

Malicious damage can occur through internal or external means.

Internal malicious damage means that it comes from within an organisation, perhaps as a result of a disgruntled employee:

- **breaking** or **sabotaging** equipment
- **deleting**, **altering** or **making public** business-sensitive or embarrassing data.

External malicious damage means that the threat has emanated from outside of an organisation, perhaps for self-gain or self-satisfaction, or maybe for a competitor company. Examples are:

- hacking
- theft
- criminal damage
- industrial espionage.

However, the distinction between internal and external malicious damage is not black and white: the four external damage examples listed here could also result from within an organisation and so could be classed as internal.

Key terms

Hacking This was once a term used to describe programmers causing harmless changes to existing programs. More commonly these days, it is a term used to identify the illegal practice of an individual accessing other people's computer systems (without their permission) for the purpose of destroying, copying or modifying the data they find there, usually for fun, spite or financial gain.

Unauthorised internal or external access can cause damage to data or the **blocking** of important **resources** (e.g. a virus scrambling vital data) or services (e.g. email being disabled).

Key terms

Unauthorised access This is when a person or group of individuals gain admission to a location or use a piece of equipment, data or information for which they have no permission.

It is possible to access a system without authorisation and create no (or little) damage (e.g. to look at data or obtain passwords). When this happens, it may take some time before the infiltration has been noticed.

Key terms

Phishing (Pronounced 'fishing'.) This is a type of financial fraud committed over the internet that tries to steal valuable personal information (PIN, passwords, credit card numbers) by simply asking the user to reveal them.

The fraudulent tactic is that an email received (or website visited) by a user is designed to look real, imitating a legitimate business the user may really have business with (e.g. a bank, insurance company or an online shop).

Phishing relies on the user trusting the email or website and responding to requests for personal details (as such it is a means to **identity theft**). Modern web-browsing software such as Microsoft® Internet Explorer® and Mozilla® Firefox® have a phishing **filter**, which aims to protect users against such threats (Figure 7.01).

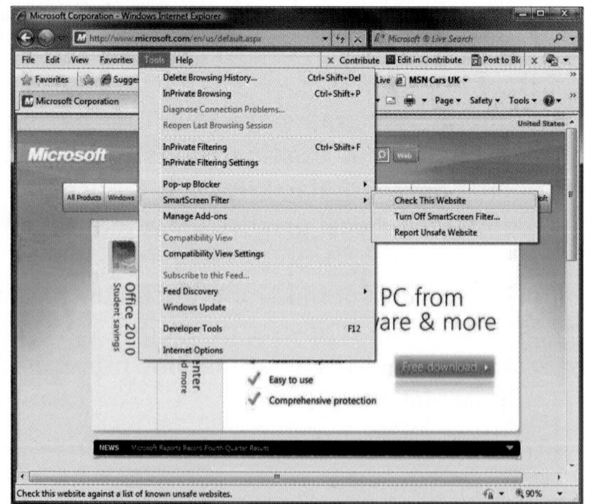

Figure 7.01 Microsoft® Internet Explorer® 8's SmartScreen 'phishing' filter

Phishing filters usually work by keeping lists of reported phishing websites on a remote server, which the browser can check against. Flagged sites can then be blocked and the user informed of the danger.

Identity theft This is not a new threat, but it is a fast growing crime worldwide. A survey in 2005 by *Which?* magazine discovered that 25 per cent of UK adults have either had their identity stolen or know someone else who had.

Traditional techniques typically involve interception or theft of personal items, for example:

- a wallet, purse or handbag
- discarded bank statements, invoices, personal letters etc. (which a thief might find in a rubbish bin)
- post deliveries.

A thief can pose as a legitimate individual by using the stolen personal details to access bank accounts, commit fraud, start loans or buy expensive items using credit agreements.

The increase in electronic data storage and transfer, and the advent of IT and the internet, have meant that it is easier than ever to use another person's identity to perpetrate such illegal acts.

The introduction of successful schemes (such as Chip and PIN) and the previous Government's attempt to introduce National Identity cards are seen as methods that can be used to protect an individual's identity and make it harder for thieves to commit criminal acts in their name (with their money).

Piggybacking This is generally seen to be the act of using a legitimate user's credentials to follow them into a building or system.

Some common examples of unauthorised access include:

- hacking
- phishing
- identify theft
- piggybacking.

Activity 1: Forms of identity

Find out what forms of identity are required to:

- open a typical current account at a bank or building society in the UK
- purchase a car from a showroom in the UK
- apply for a UK passport
- open an email account such as Gmail, AIM Mail or MSN Hotmail.

7.1.3 Threats related to e-commerce

Organisations that rely on e-commerce solutions are open to threats through their IT systems. Although traditional organisations may be able to function during the loss of an IT service, the impact on e-commerce-reliant organisations is much greater and can completely stop any interaction with their customers.

Common threats to IT systems include:

- website tampering/web page defacement
- loss of access to data for third-party suppliers
- Denial of Service (DoS) attacks
- customer phishing
- theft of customer information.

Any unauthorised change to a website or web page is a serious threat because an e-commerce organisation relies on its web presence to attract custom. Any disruption to this can be crippling to sales.

Most web server attacks are speculative, taking advantage of weak administration security (guessable passwords or unencrypted files) or security flaws in the software itself. Most web page defacement is done for fun, acting as a modern form of personal expression akin to street graffiti with hackers leaving their distinctive 'tags' behind as a mark of achievement and expression. More damaging attacks are made to express political or personal views about an organisation or its services. Some case could be made that such attacks are highlighting the (sometimes) serious security flaws that exist in commercial websites that process sensitive customer information. However, any such defacement undermines both an organisation's professional image and its current clients' (and potential clients') trust in them.

Organisations who have been the victims of website tampering include:

- Panasonic
- Xerox
- The Samaritans
- The US Army
- Virgin Records.

Unit link

Unit 8 – e-Commerce provides a more detailed insight into this relatively new and popular form of business and the organisations that use it.

7.1.4 Counterfeit goods

Counterfeit goods are those that are illegal copies of an original. They are often inferior to the original and they may be unsafe for use. They are advertised and sold as the genuine article, so this is a form of fraud (an illegal act). The incentive to the fraudster is that the counterfeit article is cheap to make, but it can be sold for the high prices associated with an original.

Common consumer products that are often counterfeited include:

- commercial software applications
- DVDs (films, television, concerts)
- computer games
- music
- clothes (especially designer labels).

Common distribution mechanisms for counterfeit goods include:

- online auction sites (for example, eBay), although this is against these sites' codes of practice and their administrators police the items being auctioned (Figure 7.02).
- car boot sales;
- classified advertisements in newspapers
- personal contact
- peer-to-peer networks.

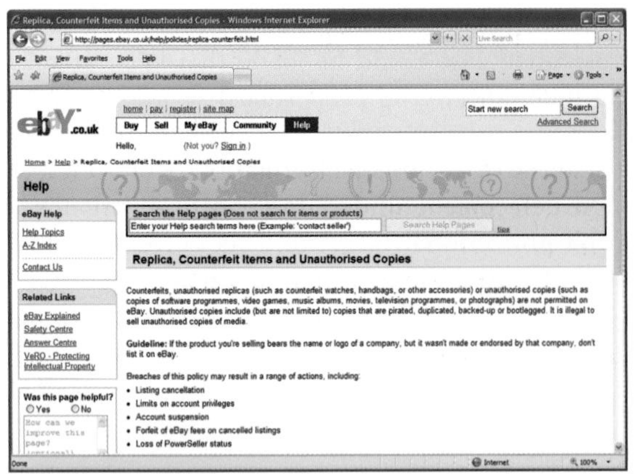

Figure 7.02 eBay policy on replica, counterfeit items and unauthorised copies

Local **Trading Standards** in the UK are tasked with protecting customer interests when it comes to traditionally purchased counterfeit goods. They are guided by various pieces of legislation, but primarily refer to:

- the Sale of Goods Act 1979 (as amended)
- the Supply of Goods and Services Act 1982.

Jurisdiction over goods purchased online can sometimes be more difficult to decide, often because the internet allows goods to be sold globally.

7.1.5 Organisational impact

The impact of weak systems' security on an organisation can be severe. Common problems that occur as a result of security breaches include:

- **Loss of service**: for example, services such as email, customer order processing, finance processing etc. no longer work.
- **Loss of business or income**: for example, customer records, payments, orders etc. are lost because they have been deleted or corrupted.
- **Increased cost**: for example, because damaged systems need repairing, lost data needs to be recovered or recreated.
- **Poor image**: a poor reputation might be earned because of customers' adverse reactions to poor service.

It is not unknown for some organisations to become bankrupt (that is, go out of business) through the impact of a security breach.

The above goes some way to explain why organisations take security of both IT and non-IT systems seriously and are willing to invest money in the installation and maintenance of preventative measures. Education and training of employees and better vetting of new applicants is also important.

Key terms

Peer-to-peer networks (P2P) (For example, BitTorrent, eDonkey, Gnutella etc.). A peer-to-peer network operates by relying on the distributed bandwidth and processing power of a number of different computer systems. When a file (such as an MP3 music track or game) is announced, a number of 'hosts' can be accessed that each have small chunks of the file.

These chunks are then glued together to re-form the complete file. While these chunks are being downloaded (in any order), the user's computer system becomes a host itself, serving the file chunks it already has to other users. This process continues until all users have the files they want (Figure 7.03).

Although peer-to-peer networks have a legitimate purpose, a lot of copied (and therefore counterfeit) electronic data (images, video, music and software) is illegally swapped this way.

The difficultly in policing this type of network is that it is decentralised. Therefore it is very robust, making it complicated to track. It is precisely this threat that the introduction of Digital Rights Management (DRM) in the music industry aims to tackle.

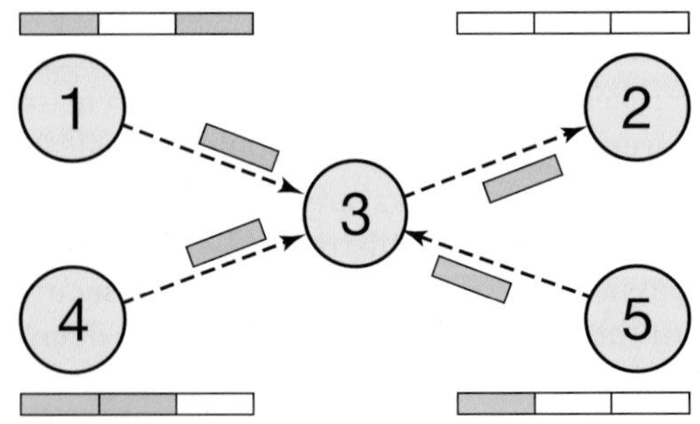

Figure 7.03 P2P network (computer 3 downloads from hosts 1, 4 and 5 and serves computer 2)

7.1.6 Information security

This section will cover the following grading criterion:

M1

Make the Grade M1

This criterion requires you to be able to **discuss information security**.

There is a natural tie to criterion P1, which looks at potential threats, so you may link these two criteria at assessment time as a presentation or report.

In order to achieve M1 you need to be able to **relate** the organisation's **four key responsibilities** to its customers.

It is an organisation's legal responsibility (see section 7.3.3) to ensure that information and data is:

- kept **confidentially** (access is given only to those who have a right and need to know)
- with **integrity** (kept safely and in a state of **completeness**)
- and made **available** (when asked for, with appropriate permission, as needed).

7.2 How organisations keep systems and data secure

This section will cover the following grading criterion:

P2

Make the Grade P2

This criterion requires you to be able to **describe how physical methods can help keep systems secure**.

The methods are listed throughout the section and they cover both traditional methods (e.g. locks and cameras) and newer technologies (such as biometrics).

It is likely that a presentation or report will be required to assess your knowledge of these tactics.

7.2.1 Physical security

Physical security measures are those things that you can see and touch. They include:

- **locked doors** (manual or timed)
- **visitor identification passes** (ideally with a photograph)
- **visitor or employee sign in/out logs**
- **closed-circuit television** (CCTV)
- **security guards** and regular patrols
- **cable shielding** to prevent unwanted signal transmission that may be intercepted.

Additional security may be achieved through the use of biometric devices.

Key terms

Biometrics A term used to describe systems that authenticate users by the use of physical characteristics such as facial structure, hand geometry, fingerprints, retina patterns, DNA (deoxyribonucleic acid) signature or voice recognition.

Biometric systems are generally expensive (because they require complex scanning equipment and processing software), but they do provide highly reliable results.

Although simple fingerprint scanning is now available on upper-end notebooks (Figure 7.04), biometrics is usually reserved for high-security applications where costs of installing such systems are far outweighed by the risk of compromised system security.

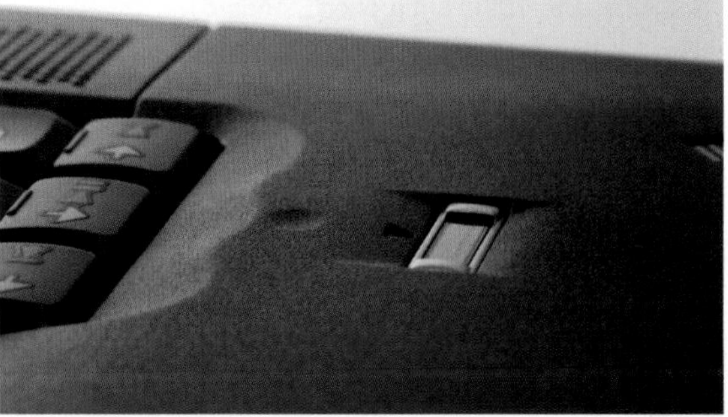

Figure 7.04 Fingerprint biometric device on Sony notebook

Activity 2: Biometric security

Find out which commercial biometric systems and devices are currently available for:

- fingerprints
- voice pattern
- signature
- retina pattern.

Try to keep within a budget of £200 for each device. Is this possible for each type of biometric device?

7.2.2 Software and network security

This section will cover the following grading criteria:

Make the Grade P3 M2 D1

The P3 criterion requires you to be able to **describe how software and network security can keep systems and data secure.**

Familiarise yourself with the techniques described in section 7.2.2 and be prepared to produce a report, poster, leaflet or presentation on these.

The M2 criterion requires you to be able to **explain the operation and use of an encryption technique**. There are many different ones to choose, from a simple XOR algorithm to more complex techniques such as DES (Data Encryption Standard).

A presentation or demonstration can be used to demonstrate your knowledge of these techniques.

The D1 criterion requires you to be able to **discuss different ways of recovering from a disaster**. This should focus on back-up systems, possible replacement of whole systems and the concept of tiered recovery.

A group discussion, presentation, leaflet or poster are typical ways of being assessed for this criterion.

A mixture of different techniques can (and should) be used to improve security in any organisation that uses IT systems. Some of these techniques are hardware- and software-based, some are procedural (steps to be followed) and some are physical (actions that must be performed).

Hardware-based security

In addition to biometric devices (see Section 7.2.1), there are other hardware-based security measures that can be implemented. These include:

- **Diskless workstations**: These are computer systems that have no removable storage media. This prevents employees from accidentally introducing viruses to a system or from physically taking sensitive data out of the organisation.
- **Disabling ports**: USB and firewall ports have metal cover plates or hard resin plugs installed to prevent access.
- **Diskless networks**: These use a thin client network to load the operating system and applications over a local area network into RAM. This ensures that all software is controlled centrally and that employees are always using the most up-to-date and secure versions of all products.

Software-based security

The most common types of software that can be used to improve security are:

- the operating system itself (with setting of appropriate **user rights** and **privileges**)
- antivirus suite
- anti-spyware suite
- firewall, to screen incoming and outgoing network traffic
- audit logs to record application use, websites visited, emails sent etc.
- transparent back-up tools to ensure that local data is always copied to another volume (possibly off-site) at scheduled intervals.

Unit link

Section 2.3.1 Software utilities in Unit 2 – Computer Systems provides an overview of antivirus, anti-spyware and firewall software.

In addition, the importance of keeping software correctly updated cannot be understated. Hackers will often exploit known security flaws in an application or operating system. Patches, which address these identified security loopholes, are released regularly by software developers and publishers.

They should be downloaded and installed as a matter of organisational policy.

Encryption

Encryption is the computing process of converting readable text ('plaintext') into unreadable, meaningless text ('cyphertext'). Encryption can be used prevent documents, emails and network data being read by prying eyes.

Key terms

Encryption A software-based technique for improving an organisation's IT security on both local workstations and on networks (particularly those that are wirelessly connected).

Encryption uses the pairing of a private key and a public key to create digital signatures. Both must be known in order to encode and decode data successfully. The public key is made freely available to 'lock' the data. The private key is kept safely in order to decrypt the data.

Procedural

Procedural aspects of an organisation include some elements that we will see in section 7.3.1 (Security policies and guidelines).

Procedures may include the installation and routine running of certain software and network tools, including:

- a scheduler for routine data backup (e.g. each night)
- the creation of audit logs to detail software and network usage
- intruder detection systems (IDS) to spot **unusual activity** or attempts at accessing particular network addresses or ports
- the creation and use of passwords
- the creation and use of user accounts that define levels of access to sensitive data.

The creation of Virtual Private Networks (VPNs) is also a common technique that is used by organisations to secure their data.

The main advantage to a VPN is that the organisation can safely (and securely) extend its private network across a much larger geographic area. It can do this exceptionally cheaply by using a publicly available infrastructure.

It is a particularly popular method for connecting distant branch offices and teleworkers (employees working from home) who rely on telephone and computer access to perform their everyday job function).

Disaster recovery

Organisations may encounter disaster through natural (e.g. flood, fire) or unnatural means (e.g. theft, vandalism). They will typically have a **disaster recovery policy** (see section 7.3.1) to deal with this occurrence. This is often called **recovery management**.

From a network and software perspective an organisation may:

- recover from backup, or
- use whole system replacement.

Key terms

Virtual Private Network (VPN) A VPN works by transmitting private network data over a public telecommunication infrastructure (such as the internet). It does this by using a connection formed by a **tunnelling** protocol.

Tunnelling works by placing packets of data inside other data packets. The infrastructure network deals with (and routes) the 'outer' packet, leaving the 'inner' payload (the VPN data) alone until it reaches its destination where the 'outer' packet is removed.

VPNs also make use of encryption, firewalls and authentication services to secure both ends of the VPN connection (that is, the remote end user and the organisation's network). See Figure 7.05.

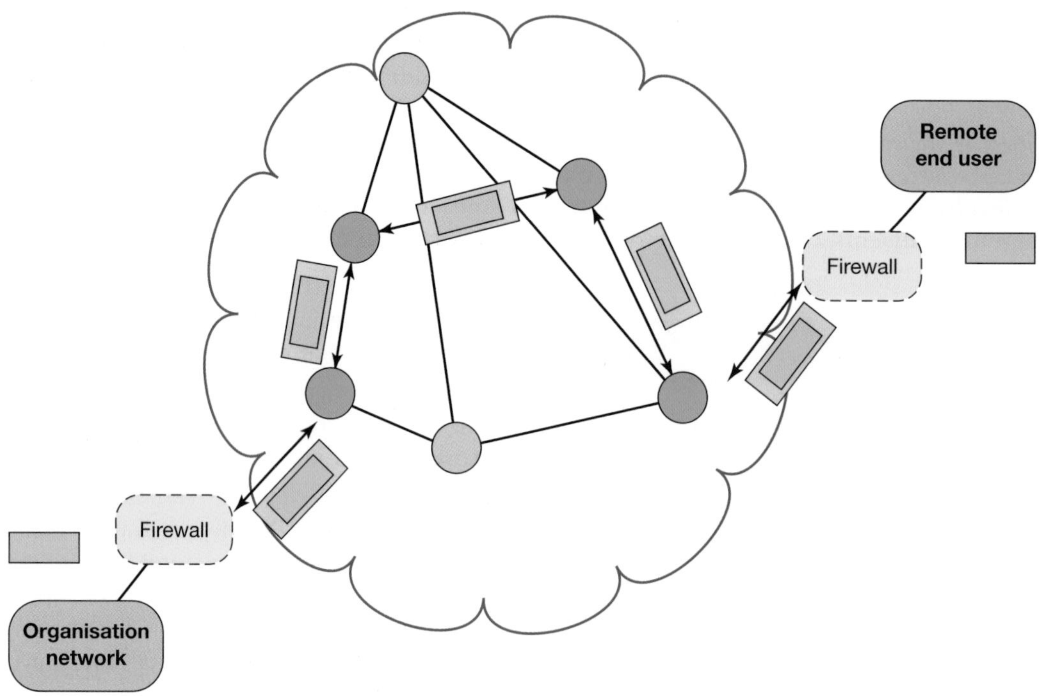

Figure 7.05 Using tunnelling to send packets over a public network

Recover from backup

Backup of data and software can either be:

- phased, that is performed at specific times (e.g. at the end of each business day)
- continuous or real-time, that is as (and when) data changes.

While phased backup is more common, the latter is more intensive, expensive and accurate. It is usual to have remote (off-site) backup of such data, whether through networked transmission or physical removal of disks/tapes to another building. However, the use of on-site fireproof data safes, placed in structurally sound locations, is still common.

Whole system replacement

When IT systems have been damaged or irreparably broken, the only option available may be to replace a whole system. This is particularly true with equipment and software because the pace of technology development often makes spares increasingly difficult to find at a reasonable price and compatibility issues arise.

7.4 Organisational issues affecting the use of IT systems

This section will cover the following grading criterion:

Make the Grade P4

This criterion requires you to be able to **explain the policies and guidelines for managing organisational IT security issues**.

There are a number of ways to achieve this. A good way to practise your understanding of this is to create a **security policy** for your **own fictional organisation**. A **template** that you can adapt and customise can be found at www.sans.org/security-resources/policies/Acceptable_Use_Policy.pdf

7.3.1 Security policies and guidelines

Any organisation with substantial IT system coverage will have a number of policies in place that specify the actions required to deal with problems, in routine or non-routine circumstances, that occur. These are categorised as follows:

- **Disaster recovery policy**: This is a statement or plan of what to do if things go wrong through acts of theft, destruction (by natural causes such as fire, flood, earthquake etc. or by vandalism) or loss of data, which severely impacts on the business function (or security) of an organisation.
- **Security procedures**: Security features must evolve with the IT technology used in an organisation. Security procedures should be reviewed regularly (usually by an organisation's head of IT security or IT services, sometimes in conjunction with outside agencies).
- **Security audits**: Audits on procedures, physical resources, equipment, software and logical protections need to take place regularly. These will highlight opportunities and potential threats that can be dealt with effectively by strategic planning.

In addition, many organisations ask employees to sign a **communications policy** as part of their contract of employment. It will detail their permissions and rights when interacting with an organisation's IT Systems and may form part of a larger **code of conduct**.

A **code of conduct**, aiming to improve IT system security, may include policies on:

- **use of email**:
  - what personal views (and language) can be used in an email
  - what can be emailed externally (that is, sent to clients and external entities)
  - printing restrictions (sustainability, privacy etc.)
  - inbox restrictions
  - frequency of reading and replying to email communication
  - attachments
  - acceptable response time to queries
  - forwarding of spoofs, jokes or chain mail
- **use of the internet**:
  - which websites can be visited (appropriate content)
  - when the World Wide Web can be used for personal use (e.g. lunchtime only)
  - what can be uploaded to/downloaded from a website

Key terms

Seven-tier recovery In terms of disaster recovery and ensuring business continuity, many subscribe to the principles of the seven tiers of recovery (though arguably there are really eight!).

The seven tiers of recovery

(Ideal practice, with less disruption and less delay, but it is expensive in terms of technology invested.)

↑

Tier 7 – Building on tier 6, but recovery procedures are automated to reduce delays.

Tier 6 – Data is mirrored in real-time using various forms of disk technology.

Tier 5 – Critical data is kept synchronised between business and its recovery centre.

Tier 4 – Uses disk technology to make more frequent 'snapshot' copies of data.

Tier 3 – Backups are transmitted to electronic tape or disk vaults.

Tier 2 – Backups are sent to an off-site location, which acts as a recovery centre.

Tier 1 – Backups are transported to an off-site storage location, takes time for recovery.

Tier 0 – No data or systems backup; disaster recovery has not been considered.

(Not ideal, expensive in terms of data loss, disruptive, takes longer to recover data.)

The higher tiers promise almost uninterrupted business continuity through almost real-time duplication and recovery of systems and data; this can be exceptionally costly.

  - what can be posted on an online message board, forum or newsgroup
- **software acquisition**:
  - what software can and cannot be used on a company's system
  - how to officially request new software
- **use of user areas**;
  - how much storage space a user has in their personal area
  - what can be stored in the allocated storage space
  - who has access to the storage space
  - backing up sensitive data
- **account management**:
  - regular updates of password (e.g., every 30 days)
  - robustness of password (e.g., alphanumeric, minimum six letters, upper and lower case)
  - letting others know you password to use your account
  - rights and privileges given to a user account based on role in organisation
- **reporting**:
  - reporting of system errors
  - reporting of security breaches.

Non-compliance with such policies will undoubtedly lead to disciplinary action.

Key terms

Risk management Risk occurs when you are uncertain about an outcome (that is, what will happen). It is the tolerance between impact of failure and the likelihood of problems occurring (that is, risks are taken if the benefits are thought to outnumber the possible difficulties).

Every organisation needs a **risk management strategy**, and this should address all levels, (for example, high-level strategic planning, where new ideas are explored, to operational needs, where these ideas are implemented). Risk management strategies will always identify those individuals who are responsible for any strategic or operational action.

Risk management protects an organisation, its employees and customers by:

- **identifying** possible threats
- **limiting** those threats to acceptable levels
- helping to make **informed decisions** about opportunities presented
- giving **increased confidence** in the likelihood of achieving the desired outcomes.

Identified risks must be investigated to discover:

- **what** will happen if the desired outcome fails
- **how** the risk can be limited when events can be controlled
- **how** to plan contingency for when events cannot be controlled.

These risks can be identified through external risk review or by self-assessment. Although outside the scope of this unit, visit www.strategy.gov.uk for information on the **PESTLE** (Political, Economic, Social, Technological, Legal and Environmental) analysis model.

In addition, **surveillance** and **monitoring** policies may be in place: the exact details of these may or may not be made known to general employees.

Risk management (particularly financial and health and safety related) is also examined and documented.

Ad hoc (as and when needed) improvements to security through the use of incremental software updates will be considered routine and will not require separate policies because this would be impractical based on their high frequency of occurrence.

7.3.2 Employment contracts and security

This section will cover the following grading criterion:

Make the Grade P5

This criterion requires you to be able to **explain how employment contracts affect security**.

You may be asked to present this in a report, as a model contract or as an employee leaflet.

Hiring policies

Hiring policies will specify different levels of background checks on a potential employee depending on the sensitivity of the nature of the organisation's business.

For example, a sensitive Government organisation might interview family, friends and previous employers rather than just relying on information written on an application form.

Generally, the following information may be requested and checked to help screen out undesirable applicants:

- previous employment
- criminal record (convictions and cautions)
- health records (particularly in terms of absence records)
- qualifications.

Employees who are later found to have lied (or deliberately misled their employers through failing to mention pertinent facts about themselves) may find themselves dismissed.

Separation of duties

This is an internal security tool used by organisations to ensure that no one employee has 100 per cent control of a process from start to finish (Figure 7.06).

Separation of duties typically works by giving checking duties to another employee who can catch deliberate (that is, fraudulent or malicious) actions or genuine mistakes in a system. The availability of detailed audit tools and activity logs makes this process much easier.

Training and communication

Regular training is part of an organisation's commitment to its staff. This is known as **Continuing and Professional Development (CPD)**. In addition, it ensures that the employee is both capable of performing the tasks required of them and aware of recent changes to policy that may affect them or their role.

Internal communication is also a vital tool to improve security, helping employees to understand their personal and professional responsibilities within the organisation and the overall strategic aims that are being pursued.

Ensuring compliance

Compliance is generally assumed in an organisation, but employees are usually made aware of the penalties of not working to agreed policies. This will obviously include security-related issues. Employees are therefore held to an organisation's code of conduct, especially when dealing with IT systems.

A code of conduct, as laid down in the employee's contract of employment (and usually in an organisation's handbook), will detail the disciplinary steps that will be taken for unacceptable breaches. These breaches may typically include (in ascending order of severity):

- a verbal warning
- a written warning
- a final interview
- dismissal (the 'sack').

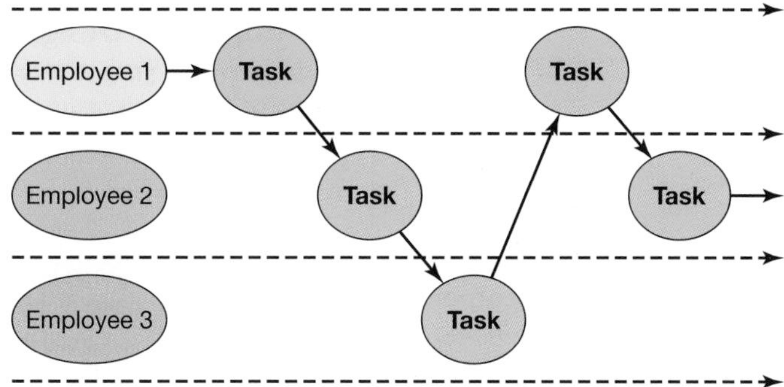

Figure 7.06 Splitting a task between three employees, with each tasked with checking

7.3.3 Laws

This section will cover the following grading criterion:

Make the Grade P6

This criterion requires you to be able to **review the laws related to security and privacy of data**.

Read through the summaries provided here to prepare for this. In practical terms, assessment may be linked to M3 and D2.

Security-related legislation can vary from country to country and this can cause problems for organisations that operate globally. In the UK, however, familiarisation with the following areas and associated legislation is a good starting point.

Protecting the organisation and the customer

Help

UK Data Protection Act 1998 (DPA) – what you need to know

This legislation ensures that any personal data is:

- processed fairly and lawfully
- obtained for specified and lawful purposes
- adequate, relevant and not excessive
- accurate and kept up to date
- not kept any longer than necessary
- processed in accordance with the **data subject's** (the individual's) rights
- kept reasonably secure
- not transferred to any other country without adequate protection.

The original Data Protection Act was published in 1984 with revisions in 1998 designed to incorporate the European Union's (EU) Directive 95/46/EC on the protection of individuals with regard to the processing of personal data and on the free movement of such data.

About privacy and you

You are allowed, under Section 7(1) of the Data Protection Act 1998, to know whether information is being held about you and what it may be. This is called making a **subject access request**. It is likely to cost a maximum of £10 and must be replied to within 40 days.

About compensation and you

As the data subject you have a general right to compensation for any damage caused and any distress associated. This is usually claimed from the **data controller** (the individual or organisation who decides what data to keep and how it is processed). Compensation may be claimed directly from the organisation or through the courts.

Activity 3: Computer Misuse Act 1990

The following website lists real cases where individuals have been taken to court for charges associated with the Computer Misuse Act 1990.

www.computerevidence.co.uk/Cases/CMA.htm

Explore this resource (and its news site links) and determine which parts of the Act are most commonly broken and the types of security breach which have been attempted.

Help

UK Copyright Designs and Patents Act 1988 – what you need to know

In simple terms, a copyright is the exclusive legal right to use an expression or idea (known as **intellectual property** (IP)). It is indicated by use of the familiar © symbol. In British law, the initial owner of a copyright is assumed to be the original creator of the IP. However, in many cases, any work that is created by an employee in the course of their employment, gives the employer copyright ownership. This is usually part of the employee's contract.

In addition, the owner of the work may not be the actual copyright holder, for example a letter sent from Person A to Person B is owned by Person B, but cannot be published without the permission of Person A (as the creator, they are the copyright holder). The purpose of copyright is to give the creator protection against unauthorised duplication of their IP. IP covered by copyright can include such creative works as books, films, music, photographs, paintings, software and ideas (see FAST, Section 7.3.6). The duration that copyright applies varies with the work. When copyright expires, the IP is said to have lapsed into the public domain.

In 1996, the EU extended the period of copyright to 70 years after the year in which the creator died (although there are some exceptions). This is often referred to as **post mortem auctoris** (PMA). In the UK, a concept called 'fair dealing' grants some exclusions to copyright for the purposes of academic or review purposes, particularly where the IP is used in a non-profit making venture. As a matter of courtesy, an acknowledgement of the copyright holder's permission should be publicly made.

Help

Computer Misuse Act 1990 – what you need to know

This Act helps organisations by providing three basic protections against:

- unauthorised access to computer material
- unauthorised access to a computer system with intent to commit or facilitate the commission of a further offence
- unauthorised modification of computer material.

Of particular interest are the first and third parts. Part 1 targets hacking (whether the unauthorised access is internal or external). Part 3 targets deliberate damage caused to programs or data. This would include deliberate virus infection or deletion and alteration of data.

Offenders caught breaking these laws would be subject to either a Magistrates or Crown Court. Penalties could range from substantial fines, community service or one or two years in prison, depending on the severity of the offence and damage incurred.

Help

Freedom of Information Act 2000 (Scotland 2002) – what you need to know

A part of this legislation gives citizens right of access to any information that is held about them by public bodies. The range of public bodies is quite broad, but notable examples include:

- local authorities (e.g. council departments)
- police authorities
- National Health Service (NHS) authorities
- schools and colleges.

Release of information is subject to some exceptions, but generally a written request for information should force the authority to confirm whether they have information, what it is and require them to provide a copy of it.

See: www.opsi.gov.uk/acts/acts2000/20000036.htm for further information.

Key terms

Open source This can be freely distributed and users can make changes to the program's source code and modify it as they see fit as long as they make their amendments freely accessible. Well-known examples of open source software include Linux and the Apache HTTP Web Server.

Freeware This is copyrighted software offered 'as is' with no charge to the user. Some commercial software is offered as scaled-down, fully functional freeware in an attempt to encourage users to buy the fuller versions. Freeware may be limited to non-commercial use (that is, for students or personal use only).

Shareware This is typically a 'try before you buy' time-limited trial or function-limited version of commercial software. Users who are happy with the software then purchase the full version when the evaluation period has expired.

Commercial software This is software purchased (usually at retail) from a software publisher that has extensive legal protection in the form of an End User License Agreement (EULA) which prohibits illegal duplication, reverse engineering and modification of the program's code. Source code is not usually made available. Well-known examples include Microsoft® Windows®.

Activity 4: Software ownership

Investigate the following software applications and operating systems and decide whether they are available as open source, freeware, shareware or commercially.

- OpenOffice suite
- WinZip®
- CutePDF Writer
- AVG Antivirus
- Apple® QuickTime®
- FreeBSD

7.3.4 Copyrights on software

In addition to being aware of the various laws related to security, organisations that deal with operating systems and applications software must be clear on the distinction between their different legal categorisations. See key terms on page 195.

7.3.5 Ethical decision-making

This section will cover the following grading criterion:

Make the Grade M3 D2

M3 requires you to be able to **explain the role of ethical decision-making in organisational IT security**.

D2 requires you to **evaluate the security policies used in an organisation**.

Although D2 could be seen as an extension of P4, it is more useful to think about these two criteria in terms of the **balance** between the **law**, the **needs** of the organisation and the **rights** of the individual. D2 is more difficult as it requires you to make some **supported judgements**. Does the security policy meet the needs of the organisation? Does it break the law? Does it treat customers and employees in an ethical manner?

A report or presentation is the most likely tool to use to communicate your ideas.

Ethical considerations

Security concerns often clash with the concept of personal privacy and the rights of the individual in society. For example, information about where an individual lives can be easily pieced together through examination of a local council's electoral roll, the telephone book and available street maps.

It is perhaps fair to say that ethical decision-making takes over where the legislation stops, forcing the organisation or individual to examine whether what they are doing is crossing any moral or ethical boundaries. Examples of this may include:

- the use of photographs in an appropriate way
- the placement and use of video captured by CCTV cameras
- logging of employee activities.

In most cases it may be sufficient to simply ask for permission to commit such actions or at least make people aware that it is happening (and why).

7.3.6 Professional bodies

Professional bodies exist that offer organisations advice and guidance on security issues. As an IT student, you should be familiar with the following bodies:

- The Business Software Alliance (BSA)
- The Federation Against Software Theft (FAST)
- BCS, The Chartered Institute for IT
- The Association for Computing Machinery (ACM)

Let's examine each one in a little more detail (Table 7.01).

Table 7.01

Professional body	Description
Business Software Alliance (BSA) www.bsa.org/uk/	Established in 1988, the BSA is the leading voice of the software industry around the world. It serves to educate business owners and IT decision-makers about software management and intellectual property rights in order to encourage the use of legitimate software and reduce software piracy. BSA programmes also advocate technology innovation through education and public policy to promote copyright protection, cyber-security trade and e-commerce.
Federation Against Software Theft (FAST) www.fast.org.uk/	Established in 1984, FAST was the UK's first software anti-piracy organisation that worked to protect developers' / publishers' intellectual property. In the mid 1980s, it succeeded in lobbying the UK Parliament to include the phrase 'computer program' in the Copyright (Computer Software) Amendment Act 1985, thereby formally including computer software as a literary work in law, and as a result, providing it identical copyright protection attributable to a book, magazine or journal. The Copyright, Designs and Patents Act 1988 incorporated these changes. FAST focuses on reducing software theft by pursuing software copyright infringements using the UK's civil and criminal procedures. FAST is convinced of the need to educate to ensure comprehension of the high value in digital product.
BCS, The Chartered Institute for IT www.bcs.org	BCS, The Chartered Institute for IT, promotes wider social and economic progress through the advancement of information technology science and practice. It brings together industry, academics, practitioners and government to share knowledge, promote new thinking, inform the design of new curricula, shape public policy and inform the public. The Institute has over 70,000 members including practitioners, businesses, academics and students in the UK and internationally. The Institute delivers a range of professional development tools for practitioners and employees and as a leading IT qualification body, offers a range of widely recognised qualifications.
Association for Computing Machinery (ACM) www.acm.org	ACM was established in 1947. It is an educational and scientific society uniting the world's computing educators, researchers and professionals to inspire dialogue, share resources and address the field's most pressing challenges. ACM strengthens the profession's collective voice through strong leadership, promotion of the highest standards and recognition of technical excellence. ACM supports the professional growth of its members (84,000 from more than 140 countries) by providing opportunities for life-long learning, career development, and professional networking.

Activity 5: Professional IT bodies

Using an internet connection and access to World Wide Web, find out about the following professional bodies:

- Investors in Software (IIS)
- Software & Information Industry Association (SIIA)
- Institute of Information Security Professionals (IISP)

What does each organisation do? Who runs it? Who is it for? Is it profit making?

B Braincheck

1. Name **two** techniques for accessing systems without damage.
2. What is **phishing**?
3. What is **identity theft**?
4. How do you protect against human errors?
5. How do you provide information security?
6. What is website defacement?
7. What is a **P2P** network?
8. Give **three** impacts on an organisation from security breaches.
9. Give **three** forms of physical security.
10. What are **biometrics**?
11. Name **three** forms of biometric measurement.
12. What is a **VPN**?
13. Give **two** advantages for having diskless workstations.
14. What might be in a **communications policy**?
15. What is '**separation of duties**'?
16. Which **three** security aspects does the Computer Misuse Act 1990 cover?
17. What are you most uniquely going to get in open source programs?
18. **Ethical decision-making** is a balance between ________ and ___________.
19. What is **FAST**?

How well did you do? See supporting website for answers.

Unit links

Unit 7 is a Mandatory unit for the Edexcel BTEC Level 3 National Extended Diploma in IT (Business) pathway and optional for all other qualifications and pathways of this Level 3 IT family.

Qualification (pathway)	Mandatory	Optional	Specialist optional
Edexcel BTEC Level 3 National Certificate in Information Technology		✓	
Edexcel BTEC Level 3 National Subsidiary Diploma in Information Technology		✓	
Edexcel BTEC Level 3 National Diploma in Information Technology		✓	
Edexcel BTEC Level 3 National Extended Diploma in Information Technology		✓	
Edexcel BTEC Level 3 National Diploma in IT (Business)		✓	
Edexcel BTEC Level 3 National Extended Diploma in IT (Business)	✓		

Qualification (pathway)	Mandatory	Optional	Specialist optional
Edexcel BTEC Level 3 National Diploma in IT (Networking and System Support)		✓	
Edexcel BTEC Level 3 National Extended Diploma in IT (Networking and System Support)		✓	
Edexcel BTEC Level 3 National Diploma in IT (Software Development)		✓	
Edexcel BTEC Level 3 National Extended Diploma in IT (Software Development)		✓	

There are specific links to the following units in the scheme:
Unit 32 – Networked Systems Security

Achieving success

In order to achieve this unit you will complete a series of coursework activities. Each time you hand in work, your tutor will return this to you with a record of your achievement.

This particular unit has 11 criteria to meet: 6 Pass, 3 Merit and 2 Distinction.

For a Pass:	You must achieve all 6 Pass criteria
For a Merit:	You must achieve all 6 Pass and all 3 Merit criteria
For a Distinction:	You must achieve all 6 Pass, all 3 Merit and both Distinction criteria.

Further reading

Beekman, G. and Quinn. M.J. – *Computer Confluence Complete: and Student CD – 1st international edition* (Pearson Education, 2005) ISBN-10 1405835796, ISBN-13 978-1405835794

Heathcote, P. – *A Level ICT – revised edition* (Payne Gallway, 2004) ISBN-10 0953249085, ISBN-13 978-0953249084

Websites

www.acm.org

www.bcs.org

www.bsa.org.uk

www.fast.org.uk

www.ico.gov.uk

www.patent.gov.uk

Unit 8: e-Commerce

By the end of this unit you should be able to:

1. Know the technologies required for an e-commerce system
2. Understand the impact of e-commerce on organisations
3. Understand the effects of e-commerce on society
4. Be able to plan e-commerce strategies

Whether you are in school or college, passing this unit will involve being assessed. As with most BTEC schemes, the successful completion of various assessment criteria demonstrates your evidence of learning and the skills you have developed.

This unit has a mixture of pass, merit and distinction criteria. Generally you will find that merit and distinction criteria require a little more thought and evaluation before they can be completed.

The colour-coded grid below shows you the pass, merit and distinction criteria for this unit.

To achieve a pass grade you need to:	To achieve a merit grade you also need to:	To achieve a distinction grade you also need to:
P1 Describe the technologies required for e-commerce		
P2 Explain the impact of introducing an e-commerce system to an organisation	**M1** Recommend methods to promote an e-commerce system	**D1** Evaluate the use of e-commerce in a 'brick and click' organisation
P3 Explain the potential risks to an organisation of committing to an e-commerce system	**M2** Discuss how security issues in e-commerce can be overcome	
P4 Review the regulations governing e-commerce		
P5 Examine the social implications of e-commerce on society		**D2** Compare different payment systems used by e-commerce systems
P6 Plan an e-commerce strategy	**M3** Design an interface for an e-commerce business	

Introduction

e-Commerce is a 10-credit unit that explores how businesses have been revolutionised through technology. It will investigate the range of technologies that are needed for an e-commerce system.

The social implications of this alternative form of trading will also be examined and the impact on the business itself will be considered.

The practical aspect of this unit will be to plan an e-commerce strategy for a given situation and scenario.

How to read this chapter

This chapter is organised to match the content of the BTEC unit it represents. The following diagram shows the grading criteria that relate to each learning outcome.

You'll find colour-matching notes in each chapter about completing each grading criterion.

8.1 Know the technologies required for an e-commerce system

This section will cover the following grading criterion:

Make the Grade P1

To evidence P1 you will need to describe the technologies required for e-commerce. You will need to consider hardware and software issues, networking and registration of domains, download speeds and compatibility.

This criterion would be best assessed through a presentation, short report or an information video.

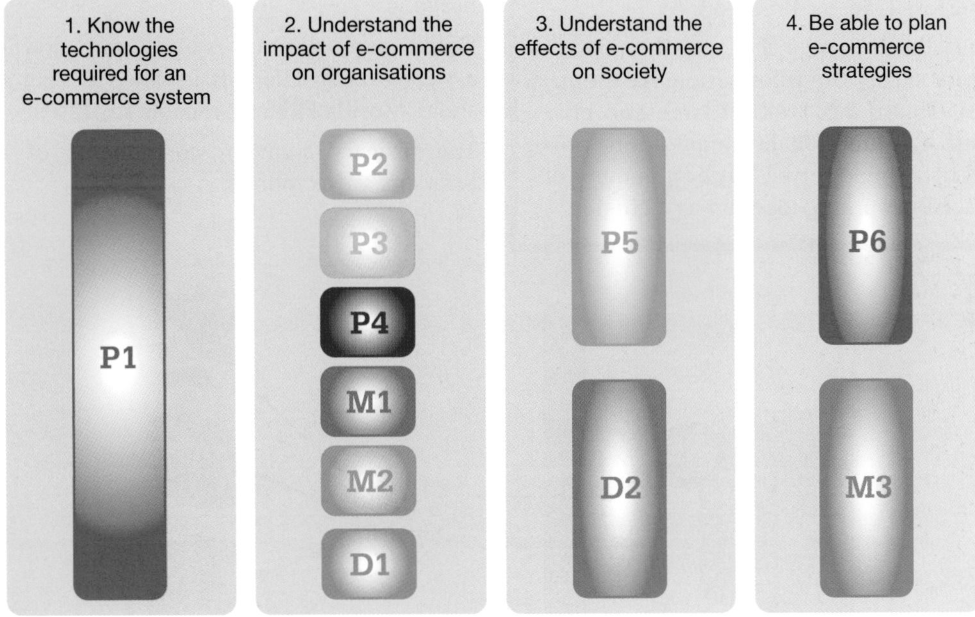

Figure 8.00

8.1.1 Technologies

Hardware and software

Firstly it should be noted that this section is intended to help you understand what e-commerce is, the security and legal implications of trading via e-commerce and give you an overview of the technologies involved. Your programme has other units that concentrate on the practical server scripting, website production and management and customisation of web pages that implement your e-commerce ideas; these may be linked by your tutor.

Web servers

> **Key terms**
>
> A **web server** is essentially a specialist computer that stores, organises and serves website content written in **HTML** (**H**yper **T**ext **M**arkup **L**anguage). Users will access this material via a **web browser** using **HTTP** (**H**ypertext **T**ransfer **P**rotocol).
>
> Essentially, the server manages the process as users access the information via the internet (Figure 8.01) with a large and busy website, this functionality might not be provided by a single server, but by a number of web servers working together as a **cluster.**

The web server, which is made up of the usual computer components such as a motherboard, memory and one or more hard drives, depending on the capacity required, will be controlled by designated software such as Microsoft OEM Windows Server 2003 Web Edition®, which has versions for both Mac- and Windows-based hardware.

The software, supplemented and supported by security utilities such as firewalls, virus protection, spyware and adware products, controls user access to the content stored on the server.

Browsers

In order to access the content of internet sites, users need to have a **web browser client.** A browser is a specialist software application that requests web pages (and their assets e.g. images) from a remote web server, downloads them and then renders them onto your computer system's (or mobile device's) screen. It is through the browser that the user is then able to interact with the web content.

Figure 8.02 shows some web browsers, arranged by usage.

Unlike many other types of software, downloading a web browser client is usually free. Figure 8.03 shows Mozilla Firefox® version 3.6.12.

The primary common components of all web browsers are as follows:

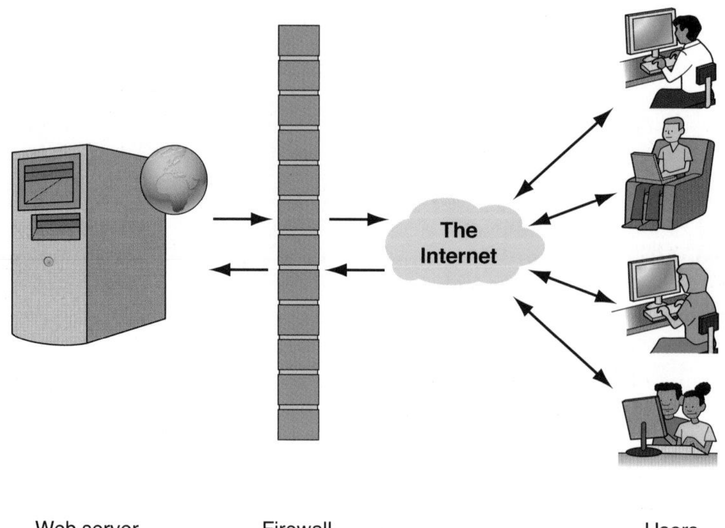

Figure 8.01 How a web server communicates with the outside world

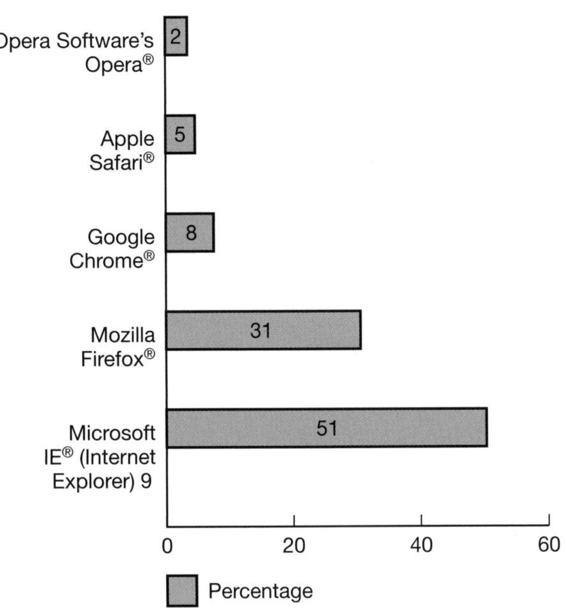

Figure 8.02 Web browsers by usage, July 2010 (Data source: median values derived from W3Counter, StatOwl)

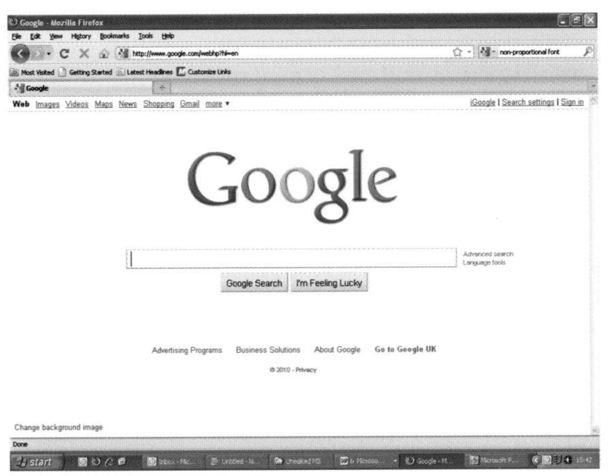

Figure 8.03 A typical web browser

1. The **address bar** – this is where the user can type in the **URL** (**U**niform **R**esource **L**ocator) of the page he or she would like to view. The address is translated to a server's **IP** (**I**nternet **P**rotocol) **network address** by a **DNS** (**D**omain **N**ame **S**erver). Alternatively the user can key some search terms into the search bar and choose from a list of addresses which, when clicked, will automatically move into the address bar.
2. The **search engine** – this is the tool that can be used to find specific web content. These search engines are created by organisations and, in some cases, they offer a free service, where in others there can be a small indirect charge. Most search engines through advertising and sponsored links.

There are a large number of charity-based web search engines currently active on the internet, such as the Everyclick website shown in Figure 8.04.

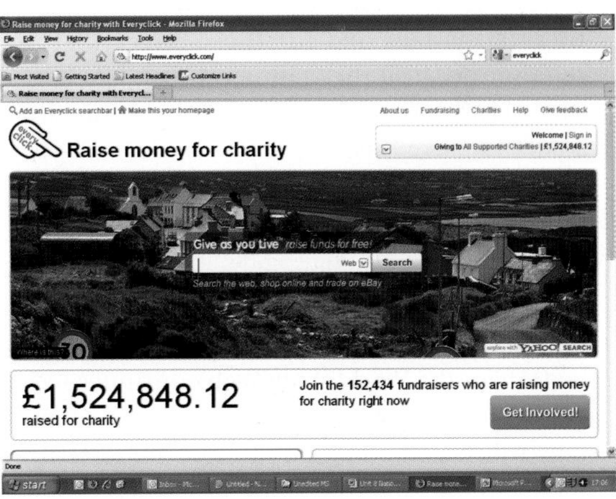

Figure 8.04 Everyclick website and charity search engine

Through advertising revenue received from companies who use this service as one of the mediums for users to access their web pages, the organisation donates money to the charity of the user's choice. This is one way to donate passively to charity.

3. The **search bar** – this is where the user keys in one or more search terms that will be used to explore the content of websites looking for particular subject matter. Where the subject matter is found, the system will filter out the relevant hits and list them. The user can then look through the list to find the exact content required.

Key terms

A **meta tag** is data that is included in code at the beginning of a web page that contains information on which a user might search. For example, the name of an author, a company name, a list of key words. The more matches there are between the detail in the meta tag and the search criteria input by the user, the higher up the results list the page is likely to be. Not all web pages, however, contain meta tags.

The principle is relatively straightforward: authors of web pages can create a **meta tag**. This is not visible to the user but it bears a description of the page's contents and a number of key words. When the user enters the relevant search terms into the browser, the software will search these mega tags and list those pages that are relevant because they contain those key terms. The HTML script for a meta tag would look something like this:

<META name="Web Browsers" content= "Everyclick">

Not all internet documents contain meta tags and not all search engines are set up to use this information. However, as the quantity of information on the World Wide Web continues to increase, it will be more likely that the use of meta tags will become more and more important to reduce the search time (rather than search each page manually).

4. **Bookmarks** are a useful tool if you find that you have found a website you might wish to return to at a later date (see Figure 8.05).

Figure 8.05 Bookmarking a page

Once you have found a page, you simply click on the bookmark menu on the toolbar, and then click on **Bookmark This Page**. As part of the process the browser will offer you a suggested title for the bookmark. You may, however, choose your own.

5. **Done** – while it might seem odd to draw your attention to this data item on the bottom toolbar, it is actually an important one. There will be times, for example, where a website loads and it appears blank. If the word 'Done' appears in the toolbar, then it means that as far as the computer is concerned, it has downloaded the requested web page content. If it is not yet done, there will be other messages in the toolbar, like the one shown in Figure 8.06.

Waiting for www.google.co.uk...

Figure 8.06 Internet activity guidance

As long as the word 'Done' is not visible, the page loading is still active.

Around the **search bar** you will see a number of options (see Figure 8.07).

Figure 8.07 Google's search bar

Table 8.01 takes these in order (top row first).

Table 8.01

Option	Description
Web	This option or category is the most general term. In fact, if this option is selected, the search engine will explore the content of most of the other categories as well! The hits are displayed in order of relevance – an item is deemed more or less relevant depending on the number of matching words there are between the search terms and the article. If the search terms were: New York Hotel Offers then the pages that would be listed first would contain all the search terms; following that, pages where two of the search terms occur, following that pages where only one of the search terms occurs. There are other ways of refining a search by using symbols to influence how the search is executed, for example the inclusion of a '+' symbol between two words will ensure that the only hits returned are those that include both search terms.
Images	Clicking on the images tab before entering the relevant key word will ensure that the search only returns image files that contain the keyword(s) in the file name as shown in Figure 8.08.  The hits returned when 'e-commerce' was keyed into the search bar with the image tab selected were a range of photographic images and diagrams, although these searches can often also return clipart illustrations. **Figure 8.08** Images search
Groups	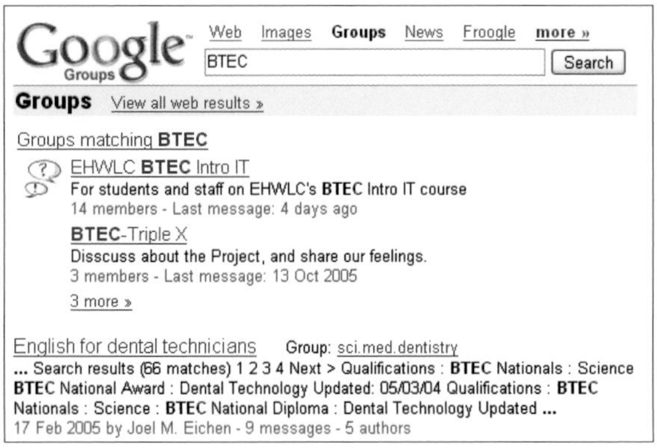 Selecting the groups option will search for message boards for groups interested in a particular subject. Inserting BTEC into the search bar found the pages shown in Figure 8.09. **Figure 8.09** Groups search

Table 8.01 Continued

Option	Description
News	 Google News UK **News results** **Browse Top Stories** Last hour Last day Past week **Past month** Archives New! News Alerts **Figure 8.10** News search interface menu options A news search will filter for articles associated with a given topic. As articles will be published at a specific time point, users can filter in different time periods. As you can see from Figure 8.10, Google News UK® has now also added an Archive feature.
Froogle	 Froogle™ UK BETA Web Images Groups News **Froogle** **more »** Search Froogle Advanced Froogle Search Preferences Froogle Help froo·gle (fru'gal) *n.* Smart shopping through Google. **Figure 8.11** Froogle interface The Froogle tab is a portal that gives you access to pages about products you can buy. You will also notice that the website even provides you with a definition of what it is!
More>>	 Alerts Receive news and search results via email Blog Search Find blogs on your favorite topics Book Search Search the full text of books Calendar Organise your schedule and share events with friends Directory Browse the web by topic Docs & Spreadsheets Create and share documents online and access them from anywhere Earth Explore the world from your PC **Figure 8.12** Other Google utilities and services This contains a number of other features available through the browser, including those shown in Figure 8.12.

Below the search bar are four additional options. These are straightforward:

- Google Search button – clicking on this button will search the net and return a list of matches that the user can then browse.
- I'm feeling lucky button – clicking this button, however, will simply take the user to what would have been the first hit on the list had the user chosen the Google Search option, and will open up the page. There are times when this is a very useful feature, but then you must be very careful to choose your keywords accurately!
- Search the web radio button – if selected, this option will search the web for information based on the key words or search terms the user input, and may include pages from anywhere in the world.
- Search pages from the UK button – this option will only return pages from the UK.

To use browsers and search engines effectively is a skill, and the more you use and experiment with them, the better you will become.

Server software

The two main server software solutions are **Microsoft IIS®** (Internet Information Services) and **Apache HTTP Server®**, which is usually simply referred to as just **Apache®**.

Both products contain a series of utilities and services specifically directed at managing the serving of web page content to remote clients.

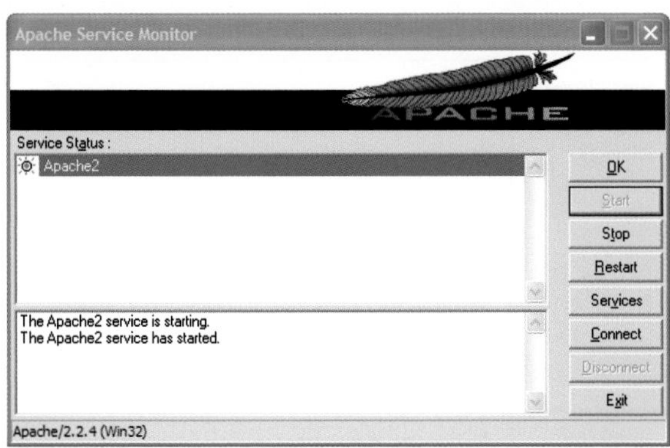

Figure 8.13 Apache® Service Monitor – a simple front end to start and stop Apache®

This may include:

- organising multiple websites
- logging requests and resources successfully served to clients
- logging faults and errors
- filtering requests based on client IP addresses
- interfacing with **server-side scripting** languages to provide automation and user interaction
- interfacing with **server-side database systems** to provide dynamic content.

Web authoring tools

A **web authoring tool** is basically a software application that is used to generate web pages. This software includes HTML/Text editors such as:

CoffeeCup's CoffeeCup HTML Editor	www.coffeecup.com
Don Ho's Notepad++	www.notepad-plus-plus.org
Chami.com's HTML-Kit	www.chami.com/html-kit

and **combined** site management and editing products such as:

Adobe Dreamweaver®	www.adobe.com/products/dreamweaver/
Microsoft Expression Web®	www.microsoft.com/expression/products/Web_Overview.aspx
NetObjects, Inc. NetObjects Fusion®	http://netobjects.com/

Many of these products are defined as being either **WYSIWYG** or **non-WYSIWYG**, although some of the authoring tools have combined functionality and allow the developer to work in either way.

Some more traditional text editors have developers working with descriptive codes known as **markup** (e.g. HTML), which describe the text (for example 'text colour blue' or 'text bold' immediately prior to the text that will ultimately be output will ensure that the relevant text when viewed will be blue and emboldened).

As with most software types today, some products can be downloaded free from the internet, although it is unlikely that they will have all the features and functionality of their commercially available alternatives!

Key terms

WYSIWYG stands for **W**hat **Y**ou **S**ee **I**s **W**hat **Y**ou **G**et, which is a term that applies to any software that allows the user or developer to physically see the end product of documents, internet pages or interfaces while they are being developed.

In terms of web authoring, WYSIWYG authoring tools let the developer design the web pages visually, generating the underlying HTML code and CSS formatting automatically. This permits the creation of web pages with very little technical skill, placing emphasis more on traditional graphic design aspects.

Database systems

Developers of websites, where database functionality is essential, have a number of options in terms of how this functionality can be achieved.

Although not ideal, the simplest and probably most easily understandable solution would be to create a database using proprietary Enterprise-level software like Microsoft SQL Server®, then manipulate the database using, for example, Adobe Dreamweaver®. Basically, Dreamweaver® will be using the database purely as a data source to generate its dynamic content.

Alternatively, the database can be developed using combinations of **open source** tools like **PHP®** and **MYSQL®**, where PHP® (PHP Hypertext Preprocessor), which is a server-side scripting language that can be used across different platforms (e.g. Microsoft Windows® or Linux), is typically used alongside MYSQL® (SQL stands for **S**tructured **Q**uery **L**anguage), which is a database system based on relational principles. Requiring heavy coding, these products are generally classified as non-WYSIWYG.

The range of alternatives for creating dynamic web-based database solutions are shown in Table 8.02.

Clearly which options are chosen will depend on the skills and abilities of the developer or the development team.

Table 8.02

Tool	Description
ASP® ASP .Net	Active Server Page From the Microsoft® stable, ASP creates web pages dynamically using scripts, HTML and ActiveX® components.
JSP®	JavaTM Server Page Developed by the Sun Corporation, this uses servlets to modify the HTML content of a web page once it has been requested and before it is sent down to the user.
CGI®	Common Gateway Interface CGI is a standard rather than a specific technology that defines how web servers generate web page content through the use of programming (e.g. C) or scripting languages (e.g. PERL).

Networking

TCP/IP addresses, ports and protocols

The **prefix** in an URL provides a clue to the **protocols** being used. Table 8.03 gives some common examples.

Table 8.03

Protocol	Accesses
http://	Web servers
https://	Secure web servers (often used when you are trying to gain remote access to secure web content) for example when someone accesses their organisation's email systems remotely, transmitting credit card information or logon details.
news://	Accesses newsgroups providing the user has subscribed
ftp://	File Transfer Protocol servers and related files
file://	This will access HTML documents stored on your local hard drive (although the full path does need to be defined)

Considerations

Domain names

Like any computer system connected to the internet, a web server is identified by a **unique IP address.** However, asking customers to remember an address such as 123.12.7.8 is obviously unrealistic! This is the reason why user-friendly domain names are used instead.

A domain name acts as a type of alias to the actual IP address. The domain has to be unique, should be memorable and be registered with a domain authority. These domain and IP address pairs can then be linked so that when a customer looks for a particular domain, it is converted to a target IP address by a **domain name server (DNS)**, typically at the customer's **internet services provider (ISP)**. This process is completely transparent to the user.

For example:

www.google.com is really IP address 64.233.183.103

www.apple.com is really IP address 17.112.152.32

www.microsoft.com is really IP address 207.46.170.123

> Activity 1
>
> You can usually access a website by typing its IP address directly into the address bar of your web browser.
>
> Try this for the examples provided.

Domain registration companies (e.g. www.UKreg.com) can reserve domains for customers and will usually charge on an annual basis for the right of an organisation to use that name. Different types of domain exist, usually indicating the country of origin (e.g. UK = United Kingdom, FR = France) and the type of organisation (e.g. .co is a company, .org is an organisation, .gov is a government department etc.). The .com (commercial domain) is typically used by multinational organisations. Apart from cost, there is nothing stopping a company from registering multiple domains.

For example:

www.google.co.uk	(Google, company, UK)
www.google.com	(Google, company, multinational)
www.ford.com	(Ford, commercial, multinational)
www.ford.co.uk	(Ford, same company but UK only)

Multiple registration of domains

Some organisations, like amazon® for example, multiply register domains for **contextualised** (i.e. culturally and language specific) and **adapted content**:

www.amazon.com (United States)

www.amazon.fr (France)

www.amazon.co.uk (United Kingdom)

www.amazon.de (Germany)

Programming requirements

e-Commerce solutions rely on programmed solutions in order to function correctly. In terms of technologies used and likely programmed content, Figure 8.14 (overleaf) represents a good checklist of the programming requirements a typical commerce solution could need.

Green requirements will require use of:

- Backend database such as MySQL® Server or Microsoft® SQL Server with SQL to interrogate the data.
- Server-side scripting to automate the processes (e.g. PHP, ASP.Net)
- Client-side scripting to process and validate input in HTML forms (e.g. JavaScript™)
- e-Commerce content will be written in HTML, formatting in CSS.

Orange requirements will require use of a specific **API** (**A**pplication **P**rogramming **I**nterface) as supplied by the third party payment system.

Blue requirements may require use of automated script technologies such as Perl, Microsoft Windows® Script Host (WSH).

Purple indicates those aspects where security concerns are paramount, i.e. everything – in order to fully protect the company and its customers!

Download speeds

When websites are being built, developers should ensure that the system that is produced can be used on a variety of hardware specifications. For example, the download speed of **narrowband** solutions like dial-up will be much slower than for **broadband** access through **cable** or **ADSL**. Some websites achieve this by providing graphic and text-only versions of their content, enabling customers to choose which is most appropriate to their download capabilities.

The growth of portable platforms, that is web-enabled mobile telephones, PDAs and netbooks, should also be considered – these have more limited screen dimensions, processing capabilities (for rendering complex content) and connections.

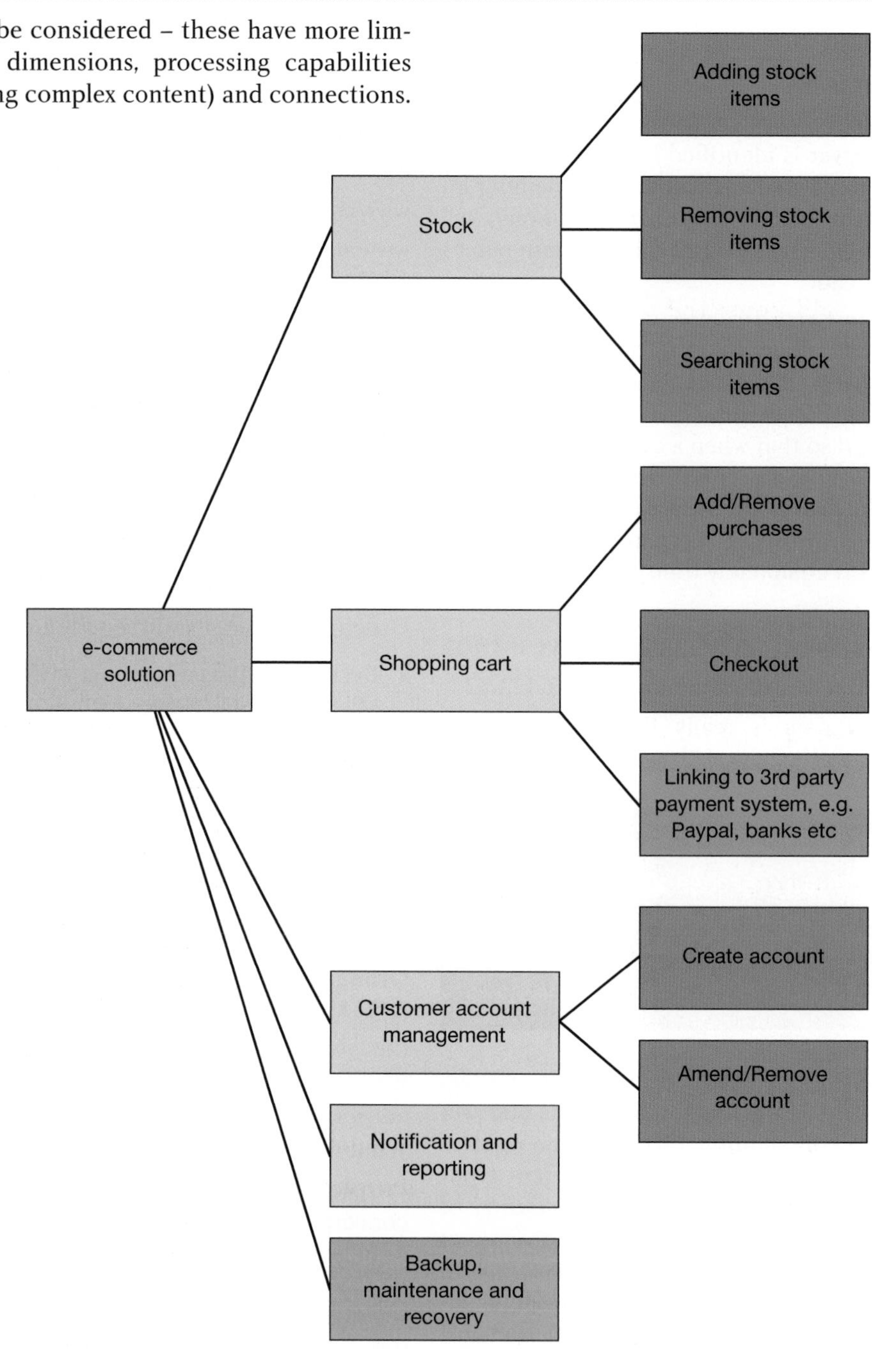

Figure 8.14

Essentially, developers must ensure that all of the technical aspects of the system have been fully considered in terms of the volumes of data that the system will need to handle, but more importantly, in terms of the potential number of simultaneous users that may want to access the website, download specific resources or query underlying 'back end' databases.

Browser and platform compatibility

Care should be taken when building websites as, despite firm standards being laid down by the **World Wide Web Consortium (W3C)**, many browsers interpret and render HTML and **Cascading Style Sheets (CSS)** differently.

Although Microsoft's Internet Explorer for Windows® is by far the most popular browser used, potential web page content should be tested with other browsers (such as those listed earlier) and on different computer platforms (i.e. hardware and operating system combinations).

8.2 Understand the impact of e-commerce on organisations

This section will cover the following grading criteria:

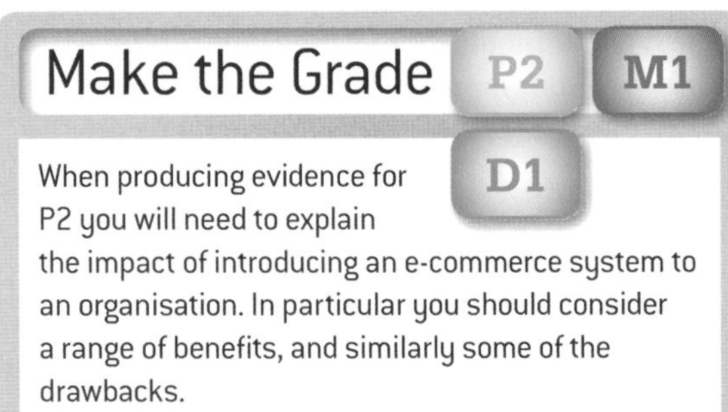

When producing evidence for P2 you will need to explain the impact of introducing an e-commerce system to an organisation. In particular you should consider a range of benefits, and similarly some of the drawbacks.

For M1 you will need to recommend methods to promote an e-commerce system and should consider how using search engines can be made effective as well as some of the other promotion options such as banners and pop-ups and developing customer loyalty.

For D1 you must evaluate the use of e-commerce in a 'brick and click' organisation looking at what the 'click' part of the operation will give the organisation over and above their high-street presence, and what disadvantages it might bring.

8.2.1 Benefits

Global marketplace and alternative income sources

For some time now we have all accepted that our world is getting smaller! With advances in transportation, we now go further on holiday than most of our grandparents would have done. This is because faster planes, cars and trains have enabled us to go further, more quickly, which has truly opened up new horizons for all of us.

Similarly, we might now consider buying a CD, DVD or computer game from Japan or the USA, particularly if it wasn't available in the UK (as long as we have region-free machines to play DVDs and computer games from other regions on – it doesn't apply with CDs).

We can buy textiles from Asia and South America, we can buy sculptures from Italy and Africa . . . the list goes on.

Similarly, as businesses, we can find our own products and services being purchased by individuals living or working outside our usual trading regions, adding to our sources of income.

Today we really can say that the world is our **global marketplace**; our customers can be situated anywhere in the world, and so can our suppliers.

Providing and selling advertising space on websites can offer additional income streams for organisations. Alternatively, exploiting good working relationships with complementary organisations and including each others' links on both websites will probably result in increased business for both.

24/7 trading

Another advantage of trading online is that we do not have to have any particular opening or closing times. If customers order online, orders are stored in a database until they are processed. At the point of ordering, no human intervention is required. If customers have queries, they will send an email, which can then be answered when the staff are at work. For this reason it doesn't actually matter whether the customer is buying at 9.00 am, 3.00 pm, 8.00 pm or midnight.

This means that, effectively, the online shop is open 24 hours a day, seven days a week (24/7), and restrictive time-zones no longer have an impact on an organisation's ability to trade.

Relatively low start-up and running costs

The emergence of companies offering web-hosting services to small businesses has ensured that the start-up and running costs of having a website can be very low indeed. This is an option that many organisations pursue, specifically because it means that they do not have find the money for hardware and software, but more importantly, they do not have to employ skilled staff to maintain the website and hardware if they are using the services of a web-hosting company.

Competitive edge and pricing opportunities (e.g. differences, fluid pricing)

Any organisation that has an online presence is going to have a competitive advantage over any company that does not. In the simplest terms, this will be because e-commerce offers increased trading opportunities, and those companies that do not have this facility will clearly have the potential for less business.

The other aspect to the concept of securing a competitive edge is that if your competitors are advertising their goods and services online, including prices, delivery services and so on., your organisation will be able to see the type and level of service your competitors are offering their customers. This will enable you to find ways of making your own offers more attractive to customers (lowering prices, or offering cheaper or no delivery costs). Because it is easy to change the prices you display on your website, you can respond easily to the activities of your competitors and apply **fluid pricing** principles, which are to adjust your prices quickly in response to competitor activity.

Always remember that if you can do this to your competitors, they can do it to you!

Search facilities

Most websites have search facilities built into them. This is to help users to find information, products or website services quickly and efficiently.

Figure 8.15 HMV online search facility

Using a search facility requires the user to input key words, which the system will then use to look for matches in its product database. The matches are then listed for the user, but if the user then decides that this was not what he or she was looking for, the search can be done again.

Gathering customer information

Software now exists that can report on the **visitor traffic** experienced by a website, detailing which products or web pages they viewed, and how many times they returned to the website and so on. This information, stored in log form, is then analysed to build up a picture of the site usage.

The simplest log is a **hit counter**, which can be made visible, or kept invisible, on the site as shown in Figure 8.16.

Count: 1 3 4 5 9 9

Figure 8.16 A hit counter

This allows companies to compare the number of hits they receive with the number of orders generated. If the hit count is high, but the number of orders is low, the company should be trying to establish why this has occurred.

Is there something unsatisfactory about the website?

- Are the prices too high?
- Are delivery times too long?
- Is it too difficult to find the right product?
- Is not enough product information given?
- Are checkout procedures too time consuming?

Another positive aspect of gathering customer information is that if your organisation knows that particular products are selling better than others, it can change the stock levels of less popular items, ensure that they have increased numbers of the more popular items, and even look for other similar items that could be equally popular. This is **online supply and demand**.

Clearly, the advantages of trading online are extensive. There are however, also drawbacks.

8.2.2 Drawbacks

Consumer trust

Gaining the trust of your customers is paramount if you are trading in remote locations and do not have the potential for **face-to-face contact**. Companies must therefore place a great importance on the customer service function.

The two main concerns for customers who buy goods online are:

- How will the company respond to complaints if goods are faulty when purchased, become faulty within their guarantee period or if they became damaged in transit?
- Will my goods actually ever arrive?

Certainly there will be unscrupulous companies that will attempt to avoid their legal obligations in such situations, and if this is experienced by customers they would: a) have the right to take action against the organisation and b) they would be unlikely to recommend the organisation to others, or more importantly, would be unlikely to use them again.

If an organisation is determined to behave badly towards its customers, then it will do so, regardless of whether it is trading online or on the high street. The only difference is that on the high street the company is more visible than it is online.

In the long run, the best way of ensuring that an organisation will earn the trust of its customers is by keeping its promises:

- delivering on time
- keeping prices low
- dealing with queries quickly and effectively
- handling complaints without a fuss.

Lack of human contact

One of the main problems of trading through an online medium is the lack of human contact you will experience, because your suppliers and customers will feel extremely remote. If you are a very small business, maybe even a sole trader, you might, therefore, not have any contact with the outside world at all, other than by post or email. What are the implications of this?

Consider Figure 8.17.

Figure 8.17 Isolation

This image might look peaceful and inviting – but consider the one person in the image. What happens if anything goes wrong? What can that one person do? Who can he or she turn to for support? As with the person in this image, an online trader could be reliant only on themselves. This can be a stressful situation.

According to published theory, human beings are fundamentally social animals – we generally live in groups and we form relationships. Failure to have this kind of interaction can make individuals socially isolated. This is a serious issue and anyone who works alone, or works from home should be aware of the problems that this could cause.

Delivery issues

Before the growth of e-commerce, when companies traded with individuals and organisations in more or less the same location, the delivery costs were relatively straightforward and largely inexpensive.

Now, with the global market, it is not unusual for organisations to trade with businesses and individuals in other countries. This has presented a number of issues:

- The first is that there will be greater costs in getting goods to their destination. Companies have two choices:
  - absorb the cost and reduce their own profit
  - add the costs of delivery and risk losing the sale if these costs make the purchase unattractive.
- Secondly, in some countries there are regulations about packaging – not only product packaging, but delivery packaging – sometimes this must be of a specific type. In the first instance, the company should be fully aware of the legislation in the destination country. Then the company has three choices:
  - Use specialist packaging and absorb the cost (so as not to pass it on to the customer), thereby reducing profit.
  - Add the costs of specialist packaging and risk losing the sale if these costs make the purchase unattractive.
  - Send the goods in standard packaging and risk being caught breaking the law – which clearly isn't a serious option.

Clearly, increased costs to customers might make sales unattractive. Organisations with specialist or rare products may have no difficulty adding delivery costs, because in this instance it would be a **seller's market** (this means that the buyer has limited choice about where he or she can obtain the product – so the seller is really in control of the transaction). In the event that the product is more easily accessible, it would be considered a **buyer's market** (where the buyer has a large choice about where he or she can obtain the product, and so can be choosy about trying to find the best deal).

This will have implications for the overall success of the business.

International legislation

As organisations and businesses are now increasingly able to access global markets, they will have a growing number of laws to contend with. In recognition of these issues, the **ISO** (**I**nternational **O**rganisation for **S**tandardisation) was formed, and working as a combined body with a large number of member states, they have attempted to ensure that issues such as legally defined safety standards and product standards are set, adhered to and policed.

Product description problems

Once you begin to cross country boundaries, the issues of language and understanding have an impact on the success of communication! This is because sometimes when sentences are transferred from one language to another, something can be lost in translation – maybe the spirit in which something was said, maybe the actual meaning. Even when countries share a common language, there can still be misunderstandings (see Table 8.04).

It is also worth remembering that in some countries the same words can be spelled in different ways, but still mean the same thing.

Table 8.05

UK	USA
Organisation	Organization
Colour	Color
Centre	Center
Analogue	Analog
Theatre	Theater

Interestingly, the word organization, spelled with a z, is now in the UK dictionary as an acceptable alternative spelling.

Similarly, there can be issues even within the same country!

Table 8.04

Term	UK	USA
AC	Alternating current – an electrical term to do with domestic and industrial power supply	Air conditioning
Chips	Sliced and fried potatoes	Crisps
ER	The Queen, e.g. Elizabeth II	Emergency Room, which is usually known as A & E – Accident and Emergency – in the UK!
Holiday	Time taken away from normal routine – a day off school, college or work, often associated with spending time away from home, in a resort for example	A public festival like Christmas or Thanksgiving
NHS	The National Health Service	National Historic Site
Pants	Underwear	Trousers
Subway	A pedestrian underpass, under a road for example	The underground rail network
The tube	UK terminology for the underground rail network – primarily in London	The television
Vest	An undergarment like a sleeveless T-shirt worn under main clothes	A waistcoat – part of a three-piece suit!
Vet	Abbreviation of veterinarian (a doctor for animals)	Abbreviation of veteran (someone who has served in the armed forces during a conflict or war is said to be a veteran of that conflict)

Security issues

One of the fundamental problems with distributing goods over large areas is the amount of time that passes between the goods leaving the supplier and being received by the purchaser. During this period any number of things could happen, including:

- damage (the item could be damaged in transit)
- theft (although with modern tracking systems this is less likely as losses are identified more quickly)
- loss (there have been many instances of letters arriving a considerable time after they were posted).

Activity 2

Using the internet, see how many instances you can find of letters, postcards and parcels arriving years after they were posted:

news.bbc.co.uk/1/hi/england/1934116.stm

news.bbc.co.uk/1/hi/world/europe/2221882.stm

The above news items are an interesting place to start!

Overland transit is likely to be the least secure as goods will tend to change transportation vehicles a number of times between origin and destination.

Air freight will probably be the quickest and least likely to be open to difficulties that could be experienced. It is usually, however, the most expensive method of delivery.

Essentially, companies need to be aware that as much as there is a major benefit from e-commerce, there can also be significant disadvantages, which can, usually, be overcome once organisations have become aware of them and have put some sort of remedial action in place!

8.2.3 Promotion

Effective use of search engines

In order to promote their own websites, organisations can use a series of techniques to ensure that their sites are among the first in the list when a search is run. The options are:

- using **meta tags**
- **spiders**
- **paying for prominence** in a search result listing (a sponsored link).

Key terms

A **spider** is a program within a search engine that accesses and reads web page content to extract information that will be used in a search engine index. It will also 'crawl' through web links in a web page to find other pages, hence the name!

Some organisations are prepared to pay for the privilege of being one of the first hits in a search list (see Figure 8.18).

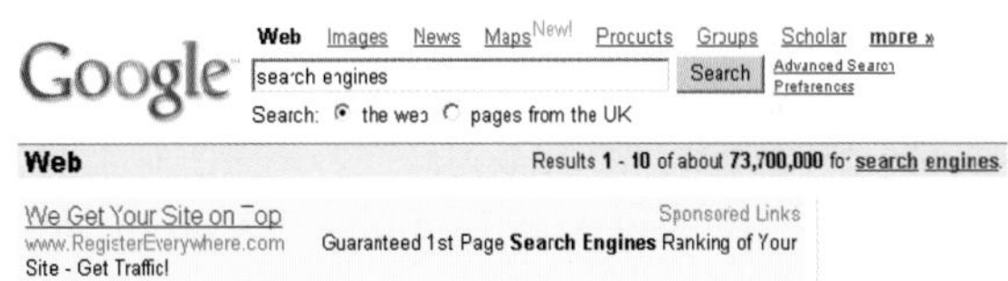

Figure 8.18 Search engine ranking providers

So as not to give free advertising through this book, the name of the organisation offering the ranking service has been removed. However, it is clear from their claim that companies can buy guaranteed first- page ranking relatively cheaply. With a current exchange rate of $1.54 to each £ sterling, the $2.75 per day converts to about £1.83.

Newsgroups and forums

Newsgroups and forums are **discussion groups** that concentrate on specific subjects.

As you can see from Figure 8.19, there are 206 newsgroups that when clicked separate into different aspects of science and technology. Not surprisingly, perhaps, the largest topic grouping is computers!

What you will notice is that Google has created some main categories for the groups:

- groups by topic or interest
- groups by geographical region
- groups by the level of activity
- groups by the number of members they contain.

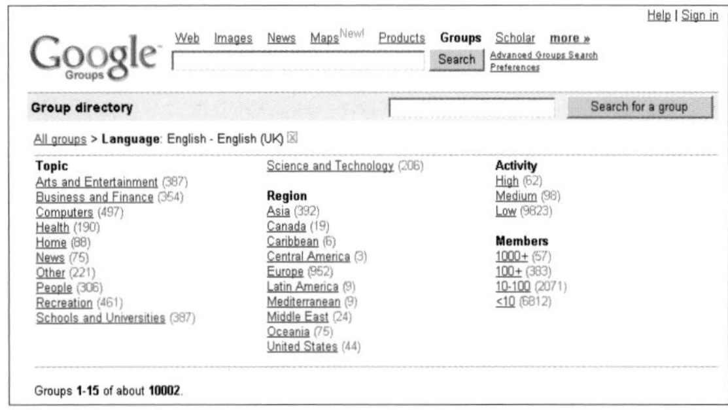

Figure 8.19 Google group categories

Banners and pop-ups

Banners and **pop-ups** are used very effectively to promote organisations, goods or services to users. Sometimes these can be really useful – for example, a company could add a pop-up or banner to their website containing special offers. At times these are likely to generate impulse purchases.

Sometimes, however, these can be extremely irritating. For this reason, most web browsers contain options to suppress pop-ups ('**pop-up blockers**'), as can be seen in Figure 8.20.

In this case the user would simply click on the relevant checkbox to block pop-up windows; the user does then have the option to allow particular sites if he or she chooses.

Figure 8.20 Mozilla Firefox® options window

Banners are useful for free advertising, although they do not always publicise chargeable products (Figure 8.21)!

Spam

Spam is another term for junk email. It is basically **unsolicited email** (mail that you did not request or want), that can be sent to you from a variety of sources.

In order to partially protect yourself against spam, you should always ensure that if you are keying your email address into a web page, you look for the check box that so often exists that usually looks something like the one shown in Figure 8.22.

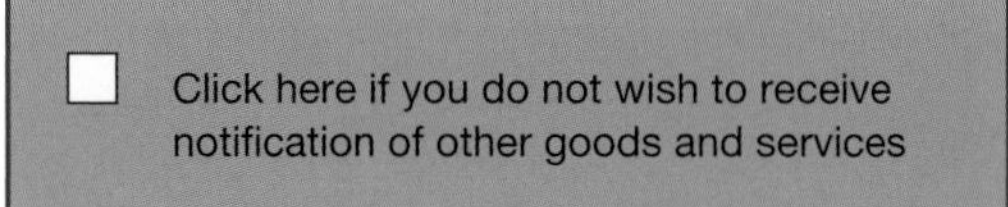

Figure 8.22 Check box

Quite often this is written in a very small font, and if you fail to click where required, your email address will undoubtedly be added to a **mailing list**!

There are times, however, where if you want to access particular information you have to submit an email address. Another strategy that might help you to avoid excessive spam is to have two email accounts: your main account and a second junk account which bears a different email address. If you then have to submit an email address, you can input your junk account address and any spam will be sent to your alternative mailbox.

Clearly there are also software utilities that help you manage your account against spam.

One solution is to add each spam address to a **banned list** – but as spam regularly comes from addresses you will not yet have added, you may reduce the amount of spam you get, but you won't eradicate it.

The second solution is to activate a **spam filter**. This filter will instantly divert any emails it believes to be spam to a particular directory and folder. However, this is not foolproof as it relies on being able to scan the subject line on the email,

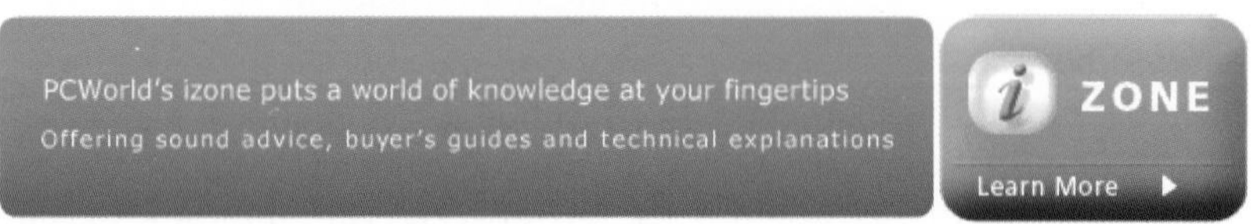

Figure 8.21 Advertising banner from PC World's website

comparing the content to a list of particular words. If the subject contains any of these words, the email will be filtered. There will be times that a particular word will be included in the subject line legitimately and in this instance the email might be incorrectly identified as spam.

Spam is clearly a growing problem and organisations are constantly looking for new ways to block and eradicate it!

Site name

Choosing an appropriate site name can be a challenge, particularly when you consider the millions of names that have already been used around the world.

In choosing a name you should carry out as many checks as possible to make sure that the name:

- is available as a domain (domain '**cybersquatting**' can be legally challenged if you have a significant trading history and someone else has registered your preferred name)
- does not mean something rude in another language, particularly in a country where you would like to do business
- is not similar to that of a competitor (otherwise you could lose business)
- is not similar to another website that has dubious content.

Direct marketing

Most commercial enterprises that have an online presence will have a **direct marketing** strategy, but depending on the organisation, the strategy will be implemented differently. Some companies may send regular emails to existing customers (those who have purchased goods previously) or potential customers, which could be those who have previously requested information from a website and, in some cases, those who have visited a website.

This could result in monthly, weekly or ad hoc emails, or could even result in traditional snail mail! It is certainly true that many mail order companies, who now have websites, frequently follow up online orders by sending printed catalogues to customers.

Ensuring an effective user interface

One of the key principles of web page design has to be understanding the importance of the interface design. Websites that are too crowded (have too much information in a confined space), are too sparse (have too little information) or require too much navigation (movement between pages and around the screen) will be unattractive to the user, and the user will be less likely to visit the website again.

In addition, there are aspects such as colour combination, font choices and so on that have an impact on the effectiveness of any website.

You should also be aware that the **D**isability **D**iscrimination **A**ct (**DDA**) has been modified to cover accessibility issues, to specifically ensure that physically less able users will not be disadvantaged because of the way that websites are constructed.

The **RNIB** (**R**oyal **N**ational **I**nstitute of the **B**lind) website provides a good overview of how the October 2004 changes to the DDA directly relate to websites, among other things (see Figure 8.23).

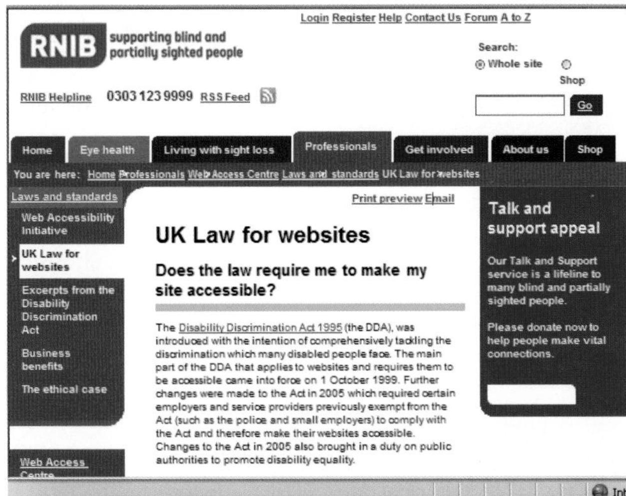

Figure 8.23 DDA modifications from the RNIB website

The DDA and its requirements can be viewed on the RNIB website at www.rnib.org.uk.

In addition to laws such as the DDA, the **WAI** (**W**eb **A**ccessibility **I**nitiative) developed by the **World Wide Web Consortium** (**W3C**) provides advice, guidance, strategies and resources to help organisations who might be new to understand the concepts of accessibility, which will enable these organisations to make sites more accessible to those with disabilities.

For further information see:

www.w3.org/WAI/gettingstarted/Overview.html

> **Activity 3**
>
> This legislation is clearly very important. To ensure that you understand and appreciate its intricacies, log on to the URL shown above and write a short set of revision notes for the questions listed. The information is readily available and is easy to understand.
>
> 1 Explain the obligations of organisations as defined by the DDA.
>
> 2 Explain how these obligations apply specifically to websites.
>
> 3 The term **reasonable adjustments** has been used to guide organisations – what does this mean?
>
> 4 Explain what can happen if companies do not adhere to the legislation and its requirements.
>
> Once you have completed your revision notes, discuss them with your tutor.

Establishing customer loyalty in a virtual environment

While customer loyalty is what most companies strive for, many find it very difficult to achieve as customers will ultimately shop around to find the best deals.

As a result, enterprises have had to find new ways of encouraging customers to stay with them. The two main ways that they have done this demonstrate examples of both commercial and social strategies:

- One current **commercial strategy** has come directly from high-street retail, which is the concept of **loyalty points**. The customer will be given a proportional number of points against the money that he or she spends through the website. The points can then either be exchanged for gifts or can be converted into money, which will be deducted from a subsequent order. The online retailer amazon® has incorporated this concept into its own credit card, where users will earn double points if they use the card to purchase goods from the amazon website, but single points if they use the card in other outlets.
- On a slightly different tack, one of the major **social strategies** is where organisations give to charity when their search engines are used. This is known as a **passive donation**. Two examples are **GoodSearch** and **charitycafe**, which can be seen in Figures 8.24 and 8.25, respectively.

Figure 8.24 The GoodSearch website

Figure 8.25 Charitycafe.com

Unlike some charity search engines, GoodSearch allows the user to choose the charity to which he or she would like to contribute. Prior to using the search facilities, the charity is entered and verified. Users are able to enter a category like AIDS for example, and they will then be presented with a list from which to choose. You should be aware, however, that the beneficiaries will largely be US charities.

This website donates 100 per cent of its profits to major charities that have worldwide activities.

8.2.4 Security

This section will cover the following grading criteria:

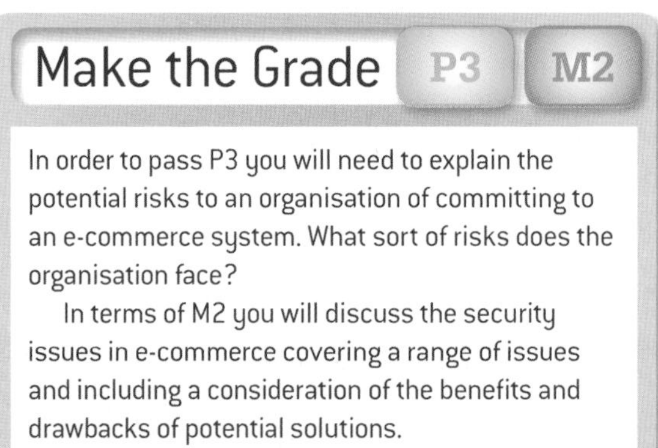

In order to pass P3 you will need to explain the potential risks to an organisation of committing to an e-commerce system. What sort of risks does the organisation face?

In terms of M2 you will discuss the security issues in e-commerce covering a range of issues and including a consideration of the benefits and drawbacks of potential solutions.

Key terms

A **virus** is mini program that is attached to a genuine executable file and which is intended to damage the carrier file or other files on the system. The intended damage may be very severe, such as destroying folders or particular types of file, or it can be more of an irritant, like generating pop-up messages that have to be closed down.

Some viruses have **time delays**, in other words some time may elapse between your machine becoming infected and the virus activating.

There are a number of potential threats and other issues that affect e-commerce, some of which will be explored here.

Prevention of hacking

Hacking is the unauthorised access of a computer system via a network. It is the intentional accessing of computer systems to gain access illegally to data (for the purposes of theft) or with other malicious (and sometimes quite serious) intent.

Some hackers are merely pranksters who will attempt to access systems they know to be secure just to see if they can.

The intention of the activity is irrelevant when it comes to the consequences in law. It is an illegal and criminal activity and can result in imprisonment.

Common hacking techniques include **SQL injection** and **XSS (Cross-site Scripting)**.

Viruses

Categories of virus include:

- **Email viruses**, which enter your system as attachments to emails you receive, and may well be passed on by you inadvertently as part of the virus **payload** (the action the virus is intended to perform). The virus may then be sent to every contact in your address book.
- **Worm viruses** are designed to **reproduce** and they are capable of transmitting themselves across networks so that they can infect other systems. They do not need any help to reproduce; they can do this without any user intervention. Worm viruses are designed to harm networks, sometimes contributing to DOS (denial of service) attacks by reducing bandwidth, and some viruses will corrupt and destroy files.
- **Macro viruses** usually cause the least damage. They are only activated when the host program is activated and largely their payload will include irritants like inserting unwanted phrases or words in documents and changing font types, styles and colours.
- **Trojans** are hidden inside other programs and are designed to cause as much destruction as possible, including hiding files and directories, or encrypting system files with the intention of rendering systems unusable. The main problem with Trojans is that they can be difficult to find and difficult to destroy.

If detected, most viruses can either be **healed** or **deleted**. However, this is only possible if you have installed a good quality antivirus product *and* you keep the software up-to-date.

Identity theft

Identity theft is a serious issue worldwide. It occurs where individuals or groups intentionally gain unauthorised access to information, particularly financial information, and use this to support criminal activity. This can include directly accessing someone's bank account to divert funds and using someone's account numbers and codes to purchase goods (often online).

To make sure that your details are safe you should avoid giving any information unless you are absolutely sure that you know who you are giving it to.

Firewall impact on site performance

Firewalls are programs that monitor a computer's **traffic** (which is the incoming and outgoing data communication that takes place when the user is online). The software needs to be **configured** to **permit** or **deny** communication with websites, as chosen by the user.

In general, once configured, there is no real impact on the performance of websites, but it can take time to set up the relevant permissions between the site and the user's computer.

Firewall software includes products such as those shown in Table 8.06.

Table 8.06

Check Point's ZoneAlarm® firewall (and related products)	www.zonealarm.com/security/en-gb/home.htm
McAfee® internet protection products	www.mcafee.com/uk/
Norton® internet security products from Symantec	www.symantec.com/index.jsp
Sophos Security Suite	www.sophos.com/products/

Unit link

Unit 2 – Computer systems, section 2.3.1, Software utilities, provides a full overview of anti-virus, anti-spyware and firewall software.

SSL (Secure Socket Layer)

Originally developed by the Netscape Corporation, this technology is a protocol that manages the confidentiality and security of transmissions. Data that is being transmitted is effectively encrypted, and then decrypted at its destination.

HTTPS

HTTPS uses SSL technologies to make web servers more secure. This is frequently used when accessing private data (organisational email or personal bank account information that is accessed remotely is usually accessed through an HTTPS secure web server).

RSA certificates

This is a security method that is used for encryption, decryption and authentication, and which is based on mathematical principles – specifically the pairing of prime numbers.

Strong passwords

To demonstrate password strength, we will set up a **Hotmail account** for Frankoni T-Shirts Limited.

Activity 4

Activate Hotmail and select the option that allows you to create a free email account.

You will be asked to select your country from a drop-down list, then create an email address.

Figure 8.26 Creating the email address

In this instance, frankoni@hotmail.co.uk is available, although it is likely that when you undertake this activity it will not be, so you might need to add some numbers on the end to create a potential account.

You will then need to choose a password – this is where the guide to password strength is visible. To see how it works we will now enter three different passwords and look at the response we receive from the interface.

The first password is **pickles**.

Create your password

Please type a password, and then retype it to confirm.

Password: *******

The password must contain at least six characters and is case sensitive.

Password strength: Weak | Medium | Strong

Retype password:

Figure 8.27 A weak password

The system has estimated that 'pickles' is probably not a very secure choice. This is because simple dictionary words that have a recognisable structure are relatively easy to guess. Some individuals, for example, use the names of boyfriends, girlfriends, wives, husbands or children, which will clearly not be difficult to find out.

Let's try again!

The second password is **pickles1992**.

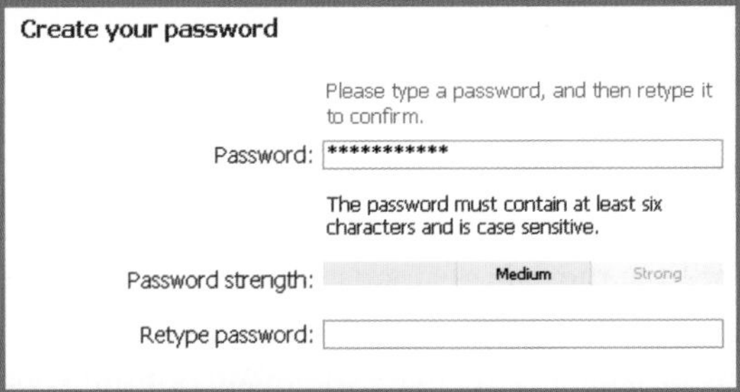

Create your password

Please type a password, and then retype it to confirm.

Password: ***********

The password must contain at least six characters and is case sensitive.

Password strength: Medium | Strong

Retype password:

Figure 8.28 A medium password

Now we have added some numbers to the password (this can be done before or after any text), which means that this password would be considered more secure.

How can we make this even more secure?

The third password is **P1ckles 1992** (where the **P** is a capital and the **I** becomes the number **1** and so is numeric).

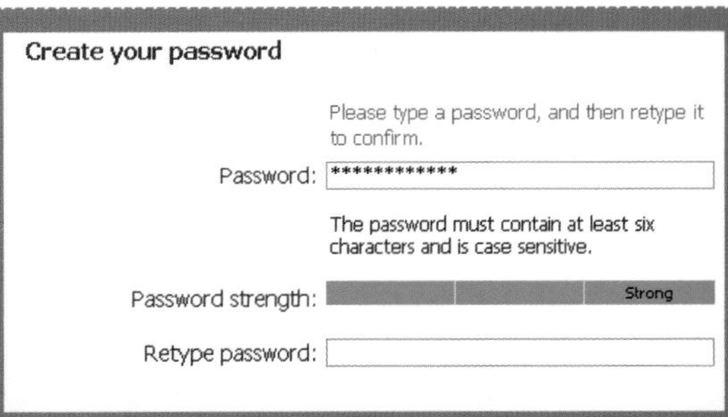

Create your password

Please type a password, and then retype it to confirm.

Password: ************

The password must contain at least six characters and is case sensitive.

Password strength: Strong

Retype password:

Figure 8.29 A very strong password

The more secure a password is, the less likely it is that someone else will be able to guess it or crack it using hacking tools.

Now that you have seen this in action, close down the setup process without creating the account!

Activity 5

Create a series of passwords for the following:

Lee Office Supplies

Frankoni T-shirts

Kris Arts and Media

In each case, create a weak, medium and strong password, using words that you would associate with the activities of each organisation.

Once you have done this, reconsider your own system passwords and create a new strong password for your own account. Implement the new password.

Alternative authentication methods

There are clearly alternative authentication methods for systems including **biometrics** (such as fingerprints, retinal scans or voice patterns) that can be used in preference (or in addition) to traditional username and password combinations. The hardware required to facilitate this type of authentication is, however, not yet in the general public domain. As a result, organisations would be unable to use this to authenticate access to their websites.

8.2.5 Legislation

This section will cover the following grading criterion:

> **Unit link**
> Unit 7 – Organisational systems security, section 7.6, Laws, provides a more detailed overview of the DPA, Computer Misuse Act and the Freedom of Information Act.

Make the Grade P4

This criterion requires you to consider e-commerce from a wider perspective and to do this you will need to show that you have an understanding of the regulations governing e-commerce.

You will need to reference the relevant legislation and regulations and could present your evidence as a table of information that you could then use as an aide-memoire. You might like to consider using headings such as:

Legislation/ Regulation	Description	Website

Legislation in general is so important that is it mentioned many times in different units. Why is it mentioned quite so often? Simply to ensure that one way or another it will be studied, regardless of which qualification pathway you follow and which units you choose.

Relevant legislation

Data Protection Act 1998

The **Data Protection Act (DPA)** sets out enforceable guidelines on how data about us is stored and used. It also makes organisations responsible for ensuring that the data being stored is accurate. Organisations that fail to implement the regulations as laid out in this act can be prosecuted by both individuals and organisations.

Computer Misuse Act 1990

Essentially, this legislation is designed to prevent users from using computer systems intentionally for criminal activities such as theft, pornography and terrorism.

Consumer Credit Act 1974

This act was designed to protect individuals against being drawn into credit agreements, in many cases, without the full facts.

Under the terms of the law, companies must (in addition to other aspects of the law):

- Set out the repayment expectations (both the repayment amounts and dates when payments should be received).
- Explain what will happen if payments are missed.
- Explain how the contract can be terminated.
- Explain the charges that will be applicable (including the interest rate and any penalties).

Also, to protect individuals who feel coerced into signing credit agreements in their own homes, the amendments to this legislation offer additional protection known as a **cool-off period** (usually seven days) during which you can withdraw from the agreement if you change your mind.

For more information about this important law see the following website:

www.compactlaw.co.uk/free_legal_information/consumer_law/consumf4.html

Trading standards

Trading standards legislation is made up of content from the Sale of Goods Act 1979 (as amended) and The Supply of Goods and Services Act 1982.

It is designed to regulate the quality of the goods and services we buy and fundamentally decrees that these should be fit for purpose and safe to use.

Freedom of Information Act 2000

Clearly a relatively new law, having only been passed in 2000, this act enables individuals to see the information that is being stored about them.

This is an important step forward, particularly if you find you are one of those unfortunate individuals who are being disadvantaged by data that may not be correct.

Copyright legislation

Interestingly, when it comes to website content, there is no need for specific legislation, as current legislation will still apply. Simply put, this legislation deals with the ownership of visual content, whether that be through books, magazines, journals, music, images or, indeed, websites.

For further information you can also see:

www.copyrightservice.co.uk/copyright/p01_uk_copyright_law

E-Commerce Regulations

The **E-Commerce Regulations** (officially called Electronic Commerce (EC Directive) Regulations 2002) came into effect in August 2002 and almost all commercial websites in the UK must comply.

The following are directly affected:

- businesses that sell goods and services to the public or other businesses via the internet (but the regulations also cover any goods or services sold via email or text messages)
- businesses that advertise via the internet, by email or via text messages
- businesses that store electronic content for their customers or whose websites provide access to communications networks.

The regulations do not cover direct marketing that is undertaken via fax or phone.

The regulations cover the use of spam (unsolicited email), as well as setting out what information about the organisation must be provided to customers and how any contracts entered into via a website will be managed and stored.

For full information see:

www.businesslink.gov.uk/bdotg/action/detail?itemId=1075385095&type=RESOURCES

8.3 Understand the effects of e-commerce on society

This section will cover the following grading criterion:

Make the Grade P5

There are a wide range of implications in relation to e-commerce and for P5 you need to show that you have examined some of the social implications and the impact of e-commerce on society as a whole.

You should begin by considering the range of e-tailers and the products and services now available remotely. You should consider the benefits of remote shopping while contrasting it against the problems of making complaints. You should also consider the impact on employment.

A Microsoft PowerPoint® presentation or short report or information leaflet would provide a good opportunity for covering this criterion.

8.3.1 e-Commerce entities

In section 8.1 we considered some of the organisations that have an online presence, and some of the services we can now find online. In section 8.2 we investigated the ways in which organisations can use the internet as part of their activities and the impact this has had on the way businesses function. Now we will look at the range of entities that have online activity (see Table 8.07).

Table 8.07

Category and definition	Name of entity	What they do!
e-tailers – these are companies that trade solely online. The term probably comes from the abbreviation of e-commerce and retailers.	amazon.com	amazon began by selling books, CDs and DVDs to the general public, largely for less than customers would expect to pay on the high street (as a result of lower overheads with not having a high-street presence). Initially trading only in the USA, an English .co.uk site soon followed. The company now deals in a large range of products including electronics.
	ebuyer.com	ebuyer sells a wide range of goods, including computer products and accessories and audio-visual products such as TVs and cameras.

Table 8.07 Continued

Category and definition	Name of entity	What they do!
Manufacturers – companies that produce goods for sale either direct to the general public or through other outlets.	dell.com	Unlike most other brands of computer, Dell computers can only be purchased through online retailers. As such, Dell is a rare example of a manufacturer that trades solely online.
Existing retailers – this is where companies originated in other formats, either on the high street or as mail-order companies that have now opted to have an online presence.	tesco.com	A clever concept as an extension to a supermarket, customers can now do their weekly shopping online, from the comfort of their own computers. One of the advantages of this particular service is that you can configure your account to order specific items that you purchase regularly as part of your order, with you only then having to add the items that would not form part of your usual shopping list. One huge benefit for the customer of shopping this way is that you tend to spend less money overall, and you are less likely to succumb to impulse purchases. In addition, you can check whether you have pasta in the cupboard before you buy another bag to add to the four you forgot you had! Subsequently, Tesco has diversified their business by providing other services such as insurance, entertainment products such as CD, book and DVD sales, loans and personal finance products and mobile communications.
	argos.co.uk	As Argos is a High Street catalogue shop, customers are generally unable to browse the actual products prior to buying them. They are only able to look at pictures in a catalogue. However, because it is a lower price store, the shops themselves are often full of customers, particularly around Christmas. When Argos opened its online shop, its range expanded dramatically because products that would ordinarily be too costly to store or too heavy for staff to move, could be held by the store and delivered to the customer directly to their front door.
	trutex.com	Originally a mail-order only distributor for school uniforms, this organisation has now invested in a website, although it still publishes its printed catalogue for those customers who have no internet access.
Consumer led – an online site that is largely controlled by the activities of consumers.	eBay.co.uk	At its outset eBay was simply an online auction site, where individuals could sell products they no longer wanted. Rather than throwing them away, they were now able to offer them for sale. Examples might include baby products that were still in good condition but which children had outgrown, unwanted gifts, old records and books. More recently, however, many small businessmen and businesswomen have used eBay as an outlet for their own goods and services via online shops.
Informative – generally these are websites that are intended to provide information, although as in the case of National Rail, this can also include providing services such as ticket sales.	bbc.co.uk	As an online news service, the BBC is extremely successful and is accessed around the world. The advantage of a news website is that information can be accurately and quickly updated, prior to any general TV news update. Other services include: www.bbc.co.uk/learning/ where students can access learning and revision materials for a variety of subjects. www.bbc.co.uk/health/ which contains health-related information including physical and mental health. www.bbc.co.uk/relationships/ which has pages containing general relationship advice. The assortment of information available on the BBC website is expanding all the time.

Category and definition	Name of entity	What they do!
Informative continued	nationalrail.co.uk	This website is useful for the traveller as it contains all the information you might need for planning a rail journey. Train times, ticket prices (including offers as a result of different pricing bands), journey stops etc. can all be viewed online, then printed for reference purposes. If there is sufficient time when you plan your journey, you can ask for the tickets to be sent to you. If there is insufficient time, you can print out the information and book the tickets at a station ticket office.
Service providers – companies that provide low-cost services or act as agents for third parties	easyjet.co.uk	A low-cost airline, Easyjet was one of the first companies that traded solely online to offer cheap flights to the general public. The website also allows you to book hotels independently of the flights, thereby allowing you to customise your own trip.
	lastminute.com	Lastminute.com is also a travel organisation, although it offers more to its service as it also allows customers to book car hire, restaurants and theatre tickets in their destination location.
	seetickets.com	An event tickets service – once you have purchased gig or concert tickets from this website, you can register to receive regular updates. As new gigs, concerts and tours are added, you can be automatically notified. The company acts as an agent for ticket sales for venues across the UK. The events are listed, the tickets are then ordered and paid for online, before being delivered to your front door.
Financial – this category would include internet banks, loan providers and online insurers.	esure.com	Essentially an insurance company, esure.com now provides a range of insurance and subsidiary services. Customers can purchase car, home, pet and travel insurance from one website, along with securing a personal loan.
	egg.com	Egg.com was one of the first banks to be created that traded solely online. While most high-street branch services can be obtained from an online bank, clearly one major problem remains: the technology does not yet exist that will allow you to use your computer base unit as a cash dispenser!

Activity 6

You have been asked to consult for Frankoni T-Shirts Limited regarding the value to their business of trading through e-commerce.

Create an A5 booklet that will be distributed to Frankoni employees about the notion of trading online.

N.B. Make sure you discuss the benefits and the drawbacks that the organisation would experience, and that you link your discussion directly to Frankoni and its activities.

Show the leaflet to your tutor.

8.3.2 Social implications

Changing customer perspectives (e.g. providing added value, providing service, ease and security)

The growth of internet trading has been of great benefit to customers throughout the world. Quite apart from the obvious advantage of being able to buy a wider range of products at increasingly competitive prices, improved business efficiency and distribution logistics have ensured that online purchases do not take weeks to arrive. There was a time when if you bought anything over the phone or by completing order forms or coupons from magazines or newspapers, you would be advised that you should 'allow 28 days for delivery'. In those days, a 28-day wait was standard practice.

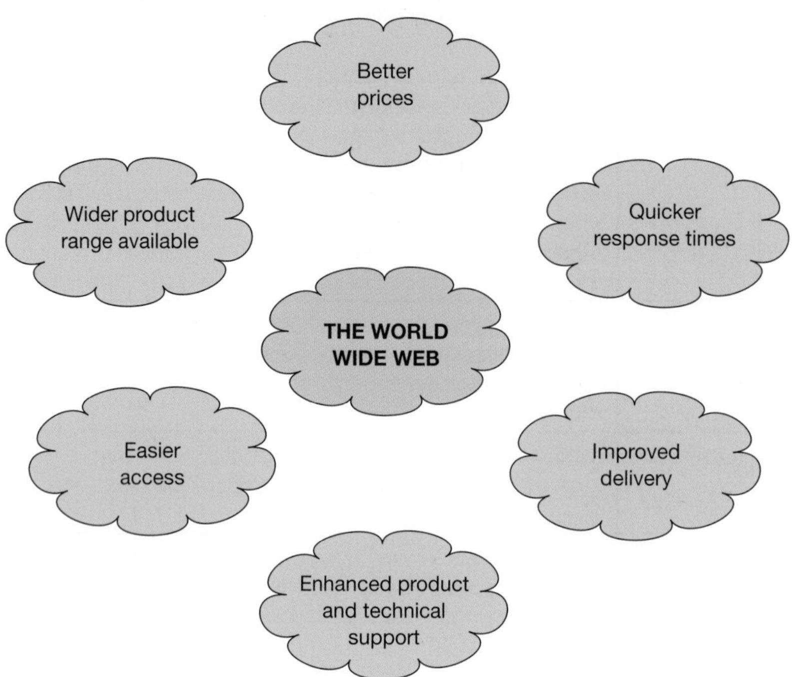

Figure 8.30 Added value for consumers

Today, however, it is not unusual for you to receive goods you have purchased around 24–72 hours after payment to the seller has been confirmed.

What has the internet really done for us as consumers?

The internet has widened consumer participation by giving those who might not easily be able to access goods and services the opportunities to do so, particularly those who are ill, housebound or who are caring for others. Equally, it has offered businesses new customers to whom they would previously have had little or no access, so potentially increasing sales revenue.

Customers can now explore wider product ranges because they are not limited to the items on display in high-street outlets, but can effectively choose from a whole range of companies. The days where you would have to walk from shop to shop with a notebook, comparing products and prices are long gone. This can all now be done from the comfort of your own home, using a keyboard, mouse and screen. Some websites even do it for you! In Figure 8.31, a price comparison website, PriceRunner®, compares the costs of a DVD box set and as you can see, prices range from £17.99 to £39.99 – quite a difference.

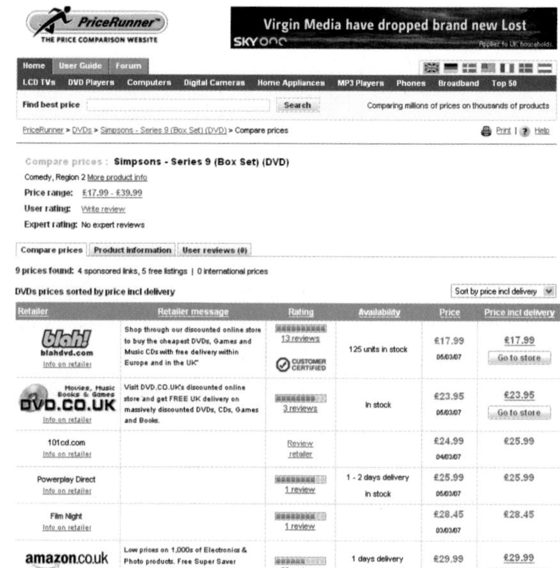

Figure 8.31 A price comparison website

Consumers are now better informed, and this has encouraged other consumers to take that little bit of extra time to shop for better prices.

Customers are not satisfied unless they receive quick response times from the organisations with

Figure 8.32 The Royal Mail website

whom they trade. As a result, businesses have had to find ways to become more efficient. The use of email in business has ensured that dialogue between the consumer and the trader has improved.

Equally, better technology has ensured that customers can receive their goods more quickly, and has offered them the ability to track their orders through business systems and with the delivery company through online **track and trace** facilities like the one provided by the Royal Mail (see Figure 8.32 above).

Organisations can now provide enhanced product and technical support by, for example, having product manuals available online.

Keying the words **'iphone manual'** into a search engine can provide the manual for the iphone.

Initial customer fears that trading with organisations online would tend to make them more remote and less likely to provide a good service have not been realised, although, as with anything, there are exceptions to this and clearly there has been significant internet-facilitated fraud over the last few years.

In general, businesses have seen the rise of the internet as an opportunity, and they have embraced this fully. As a footnote, however, there are organisations who have failed to take advantage of the internet, and who have, as a result, seen a large part of their customer base disappear.

Economic and social impact due to speed of changes

The emergence of the internet created an economic impact on organisations, who initially found they had to invest heavily in new technology, as well as paying website designers and other specialists for website services, particularly while these technologies were new. In general, those who invested felt they had seen a good return on their investment. For some **SME**s (**S**mall and **M**edium **E**nterprises), however, the situation was less favourable and many were unable to invest, particularly in the hardware that would be required to have a website managed in-house. The result of this was that small website companies were founded which offered **outsourced services** to those organisations that did not have the technical skills or the money to acquire these.

The speed of change also caused problems for many because of the constant requirement to upgrade, particularly hardware, to improve download speeds and remain competitive.

In terms of society at large, it would be fair to say that most of us choose *not* to stay 100 per cent up to date with every technological advance that comes along. Inevitably, there are people who do. Some individuals feel that not keeping up with such changes would be equivalent to failing, and they do not see that as an option.

Technology will continue to change, but the cyclical nature of change (it speeds up, it slows down) will mean that alongside the times of heavy transformation, there will be periods of relative calm.

From a business perspective, companies must try as hard as possible to stay ahead of their competitors, and investing in new technology is one way to do this. Individuals are less likely to see the need for constantly staying up to date as important.

Bricks and clicks (integrating high-street and online presence)

One of the biggest dilemmas for companies that have a high-street presence is whether or not to set up online trading facilities. In the early days of e-commerce, company websites were effectively nothing more than online brochures, providing images and descriptions of products and services, but they were not interactive and the user was unable to purchase any of the goods or services directly. This quickly became unsatisfactory for consumers and most of the major high-street companies, who were already in the **brick** world, joined the **click** world.

Conversely, some companies who begin with an online presence later make the decision to open a high-street shop.

Benefits for customers

What are the benefits of e-commerce to customers?

Remote shopping

In June 2010, the Expat Info Desk (a website that provides news, blogs and community services to UK citizens living abroad) ran the following article:

www.expatinfodesk.com/news/2010/06/14/sterling-shopping-how-expatriates-in-france-can-reduce-cost-of-living/

In the article it claims that due to the state of the exchange rate between the pound and the euro, UK citizens living in countries like France had begun buying their groceries from online outlets like Asda®, Sainsbury's® and Marks & Spencer® and had been using courier services to have the goods delivered to France. It appears that this is a cheaper option than buying food in the supermarkets in France.

Access to goods and services for the housebound

Through e-commerce, those of us who are housebound can access a wide range of goods and services that might previously have been difficult to access. For example, we have already established that the range of products that can now be bought online is vast, including food, cosmetics, shoes and clothing, health products, white goods and technology. In addition, however, the internet has also made accessing services much easier. It is not uncommon to find businesses like plumbers, electricians and builders advertising online. The list shown in Figure 8.33 (an extract from a larger list) was the result of a search in Google for a 'plumber' in 'Bedford uk'.

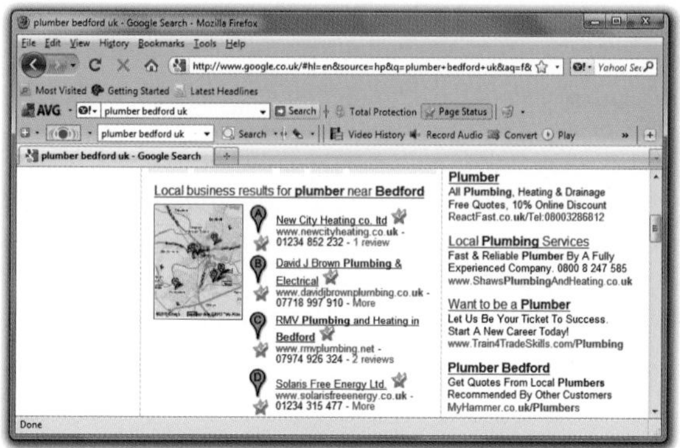

Figure 8.33 Search for a service

Dentists, solicitors, insurance companies, complementary therapy providers and a whole range of other services can also be sourced online. This is a real help to those unable to leave their homes. They really can bring both goods and services to them.

Remember to include 'UK' after your town if you are searching for a service because many UK town names also exist abroad. Birmingham is one such example as there is a Birmingham in the West Midlands and there is also a Birmingham in Alabama, USA.

Anytime access

The internet enables goods and services to be accessed 24/7 (24 hours a day, 7 days a week, 365 days a year). This is of particular benefit to those individuals who work shifts or who have unusual working patterns.

Internet discounts

Some organisations give additional discounts for goods and services bought online. For example, PC World® has a number of web-exclusive deals and offers that are not available if you purchase the item in a store (see Figure 8.34).

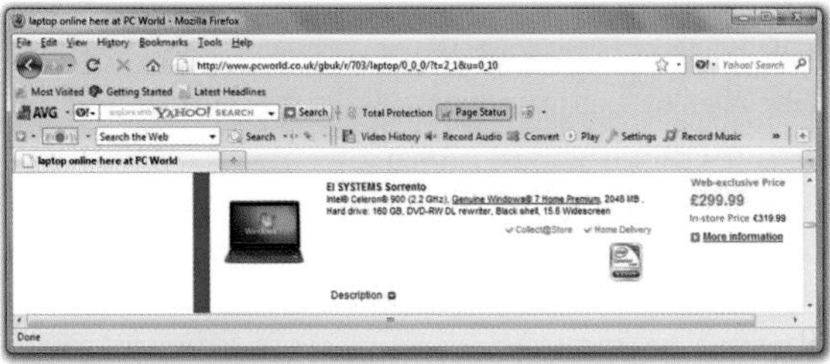

Figure 8.34 Internet discounts

Why can businesses offer internet discounts? If you have purchased an item online, it has probably cost the business less to make that sale to you. The costs of premises are lower for retail units than for shops. You don't need any sales staff in an online business because the orders and payments largely come in electronically, while in a shop you need people to take the orders and process the payments. In an online business you generally find that there are fewer staff overall. This reduction in costs is then passed on to the consumer through discounts and special offers.

Drawbacks

With all its benefits, trading on the internet can also have drawbacks. Here are some examples:

Payment security

Unless you feel confident that a website is legitimate, you should always be very cautious about giving out payment information such as your bank details. This is because data can be accessed by third parties who might make use of your data for criminal activities.

> Activity 7
>
> *Payment security*
>
> Working with a partner, create an A3 poster that highlights some of the issues of payment security and how these issues can be overcome.

This is the reason why secure payment service providers like NoChex® and PayPal® came into being. These are covered in greater detail in the next section.

Assessing quality/fit without actual product

It is incredibly difficult to be sure of the quality of products when they are purchased online. Although it is against the law to **digitally enhance** photographs of products so that they no longer reflect their true state in an obvious attempt to **defraud**, digital enhancement and airbrushing (commonly used to manipulate images, particularly of models and celebrities) can be used to make things look better than they truly are.

The dent in a car bonnet, the crack in a plastic casing or the tear in the fabric of a sofa can all be digitally removed. So in the case of internet shopping, what you see is not necessarily always what you get.

> Activity 8
>
> *Digital enhancement*
>
> Working with a partner, investigate the following website and discuss the before and after pictures of products and people.
>
> http://homepage.mac.com/gapodaca/digital/digital.html

Similarly, clothes and shoes purchased online might not fit. When we buy trousers, for example, in a store, we can try before we buy. This clearly isn't the case with online purchases, although many companies do provide a returns service so that customers can return goods in these circumstances.

Reliance on delivery services

There are two main drawbacks of buying goods online.

The first is that you are at the mercy of delivery services. If you do not work or you work to an unusual pattern, it may be possible to schedule the delivery of your purchases at a time when you can be there to receive them. Unfortunately, in reality, most delivery services will not be able to provide exact information about when the goods will be delivered. This can mean that someone needs to wait in for long periods of time until deliveries are made.

The other drawback is that if you buy products online, you have to wait to receive them – unlike buying something in a shop where you can literally leave the shop with your purchase. The exceptions to this are insurance, where the cover can start immediately, downloading music, and buying and registering downloaded software, where the key code can be emailed to you to activate your program as soon as your payment has been processed.

Enquiries and complaints

Most organisations will actively promote an enquiries service, but often will not have an obvious route for directing complaints, perhaps because they do not really want to encourage complaints by highlighting this as a possible activity! Enquiries and complaints are usually made via email and may initially result in an automated email response.

The automated response shown in Figure 8.35 was to an enquiry, and not to a complaint, but the principle should be the same.

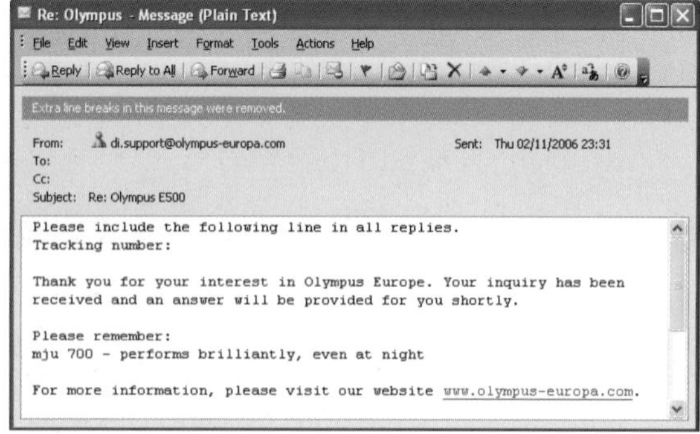

Figure 8.35 Olympus automated response to an enquiry

Organisations should acknowledge the receipt of emails; most do this by returning a simple email that acknowledges receipt of the email and allocates a tracking number, which recipients are asked to quote in future communications. In some situations, the company may respond with a telephone call – it will usually depend on the nature of the enquiry or complaint. Companies that really don't want to deal with your complaint, however, can simply ignore you and in this situation it can be difficult to find a resolution.

Impact on employment

The rise of e-commerce has had a significant impact on employment as a result of the reduction in need for high-street sales staff. However, there has been a considerable increase in the need for back-office staff such as warehouse staff, order processing and payment processing staff. Effectively, the job market has been influenced by the necessity for employees to have different skill-sets to complement the skills needed by e-commerce.

The other major impact, and, in fact, a benefit to society as a whole, has been the rise in opportunities for home working. Specifically, many individuals have become self-employed because they can advertise and sell their products and services more easily online.

Social divide

Some people believe that e-commerce has widened the social divide, particularly in terms of those who can access and who have the benefit of these technologies and those who do not.

Activity 9

Social divide

Working with a small group, research how internet technologies, in particular e-commerce, have contributed to the widening social divide.

As a group you will need to research the arguments from both sides, and draw a group conclusion or conclusions.

8.3.3 Payment systems

This section will cover the following grading criterion:

Make the Grade

As an IT professional, you should be able to demonstrate that you fully understand the different payment methods used by e-commerce systems, and that you understand some of the pros and cons of these systems.

To evidence D2 you will need to carry out a comparison between the different systems. 'Different' means 'different type' thus debit card and credit card are regarded as a single type, that is, payment by card. Comparisons must include good and bad points. A suitably labelled table is an efficient way of showing this information.

Services available

Clearly, with so many commercial enterprises selling their goods and services through online sites, finding ways for customers to pay quickly is essential in maintaining the throughput of orders through any system. If companies had to wait for traditional cheques to arrive, then allow time for them to be cashed through banking systems, it would create a backlog of orders awaiting distribution. Not a satisfactory situation! For this reason a number of **electronic payments systems** have been created over the last few years.

Electronic cheque

In many respects the electronic cheque is very similar to its paper counterpart because it communicates to a bank or building society that funds should be transferred from an account holder to a third party.

The main benefit of this technology, however, is that aspects of the cheque can be encrypted so that these will not be known to the payee, and the system can also provide an additional level of security in that payments can be validated and confirmed as genuine.

Already used extensively in the US, the following websites contain images of this technology:

www.mods4u.net/images/uploads/eCheck.JPG

www.kansas.gov/corp_search/prototype/city/kan-pay_check.gif

PayPal® and NoChex®

Both of these organisations are intermediaries. They provide a secure service between sellers and buyers that allows money to be transferred safely.

The main selling point of such a service is that the intermediary promises a secure service where the buyer can register his or her card details. When the buyer then needs to make an online payment, the buyer authorises the transaction with the intermediary and using buyer and seller identification numbers, and information about the amount of money to be transferred, the transaction takes place with *no other information* being exchanged. Therefore, the seller does not receive the buyer's personal financial information.

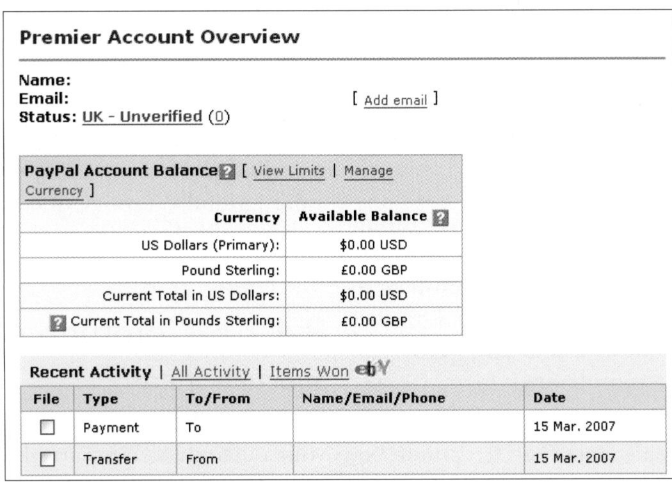

Premier Account Overview

Name:
Email: [Add email]
Status: UK - Unverified (0)

PayPal Account Balance [View Limits | Manage Currency]

Currency	Available Balance
US Dollars (Primary):	$0.00 USD
Pound Sterling:	£0.00 GBP
Current Total in US Dollars:	$0.00 USD
Current Total in Pounds Sterling:	£0.00 GBP

Recent Activity | All Activity | Items Won

File	Type	To/From	Name/Email/Phone	Date
☐	Payment	To		15 Mar. 2007
☐	Transfer	From		15 Mar. 2007

Figure 8.36 PayPal® Account Overview interface

The account holder can manage his or her account through the **account interface**.

1. The user's name is displayed, along with his or her email address. You will notice that the user can add email addresses meaning that s/he can use a single PayPal® account to pay for items that might have been purchased through different email accounts.
2. Each transaction will be listed and will include the name of the recipient or the contributor, depending on whether a payment was made or a transfer was received.
3. An additional column will list the amount of the transaction.

Both PayPal® and NoChex® are advertised as being fully secure methods of transferring funds online.

Debit and credit cards

Using a credit or debit card is a relatively straightforward process. The buyer keys in his or her account number, card start and expiry dates, and a security number taken from the reverse of the card.

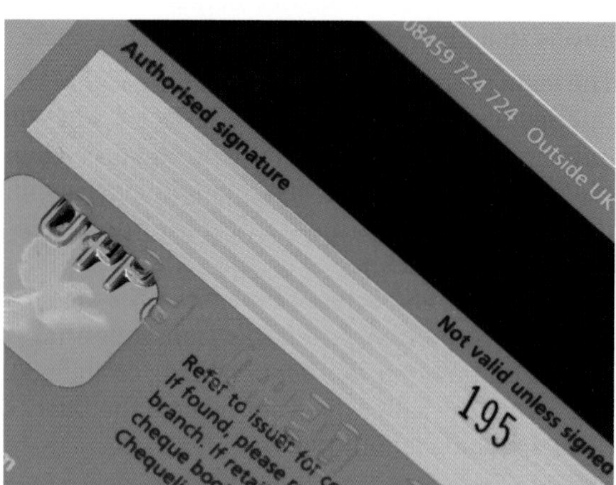

Figure 8.37 Reverse of credit or debit card

The transaction is then electronically authorised by the bank (or credit card company) before the seller will despatch the goods.

Remember, however, that you should never input personal information into a website unless you are absolutely certain that the website is genuine and is secure. The small closed padlock symbol on the status bar at the bottom of a web page gives an indication that the site is probably safe.

Customers will want reassurance that their personal information is safe and that it cannot be accessed by unscrupulous individuals who might want to use it for fraudulent purposes. This is known as identity theft. Not only will the criminal be able to access bank, building society or credit card accounts, but with this type of personal information they will be able to purchase goods or services in someone else's name with someone else's money.

8.4 Be able to plan e-commerce strategies

This section will cover the following grading criteria:

Make the Grade P6 M3

To evidence the final criteria (P6 and M3) you will probably be asked to produce a report linked to a specific business for which you will design an e-commerce strategy.

Before developing your own strategy, you will benefit from reviewing current commercial interfaces to gather some ideas and give you something to aim at.

Your tutor might decide to give you complete freedom to decide on the nature of the business you will choose as a focus or they may provide a list of alternatives.

Your strategy should include ideas for promoting the site, a discussion on what costs will be involved (actual figures are not required), the security measures to be put in place and how the site will be hosted.

To achieve M3 you will also need to include a customer interface design to support your strategy.

The key to a good e-commerce website is an effective plan or strategy. The developer needs to consider carefully a range of issues with the client, to ensure that the needs of the business are met and that the website will draw in business.

8.4.1 e-Commerce strategy

Structure of site

How your website is structured will depend on your customers. Who are they? The design of the website cannot begin until this is known. Once this is established, you can then make a decision as to whether the website will be an interactive online store where customers can order and pay for goods, an auction site where customers bid on products, or simply a brochureware site that provides information such as product specifications and images of products with a price list and a contact email address. Brochureware sites are not updated very regularly.

You will be able to think about the user interface and what you need it to achieve.

Hosting

Decisions will need to be made about how the website will be kept active so that it can be viewed and accessed by others via the internet.

Promotion

Websites need to be promoted, otherwise how will potential customers know that they exist? How this will be achieved needs to be planned in advance to make sure that any expenditure is used effectively. The site will need to be advertised in such a way that it will attract a large audience and this can be achieved through careful placing in search engines, tags to message boards and chat rooms.

Issues

The main issues involved in setting up an e-commerce site are usually the cost of setting up the website in the first place and then the ongoing costs of maintenance, security and the leasing of the web-hosting services. These are examined in a little more detail later in this unit.

8.4.2 Structure

Customer or user interface

The website designer will need to use his or her skills and expertise to design and create a website that fulfils the various criteria detailed below.

Ease of use

As previously suggested, the careful design of the customer interface is essential if the organisation wishes to widen participation (that is to encourage the widest range of people to use the website). As part of their efforts to do this, they should ensure that they ask regularly for user feedback and should be prepared to act on this feedback when it is received.

Adapting and modifying the customer interface to improve its usability should be a standard maintenance activity for any good website. Online customer feedback forms are the obvious way to achieve this.

Display of products

How will the products be displayed?

- Simple text descriptions?
- Individual images?
- Images of groups of products?
- Images of groups of complementary products?
- Images showing the products being used?
- A combination of all these?

In an effort to represent all the necessary information, some web developers can be guilty of creating overly cluttered websites that have too much going on. They can also be a complete mixture of styles that don't necessarily look good together. These types of sites can be overwhelming for users and could lose the organisation customers and business.

Designers should not be afraid to use white space!

Providing customer account/profile

If you have an account with any online organisation, you will have options about how you set up your own account. This will include you keying in and possibly storing personal details, credit card details and delivery information (such as your address).

Under normal circumstances, you will input all the relevant information at the start when creating the profile, but you may need to change some of your settings from time to time. For example, you may need to change your password. You would usually do this through some sort of Self Care, Profile or Account Settings interface, much like the one shown in Figure 8.38 on page 234.

Order tracking

Similarly, part of the customer interface/profile will include functionality to track orders. Figure 8.39 on page 234 shows such an interface.

You should always remember, however, that some of the functionality is no longer available depending on where the item is in the despatch system (for example, you cannot change a delivery address after the item(s) have been despatched)!

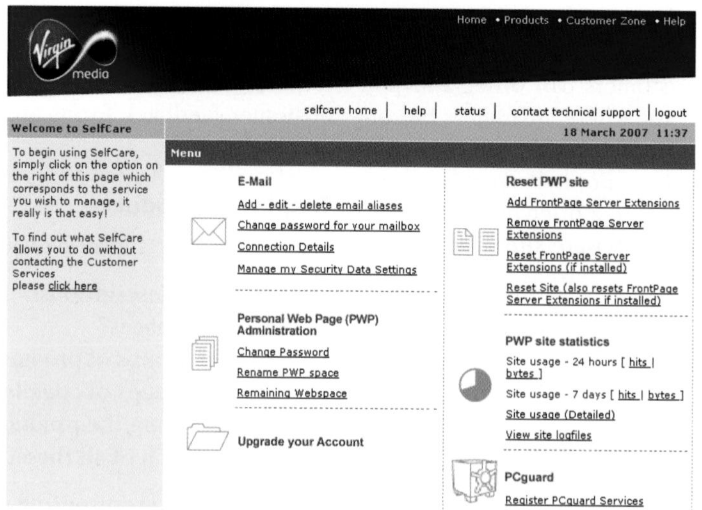

Figure 8.38 Virgin Media SelfCare interface

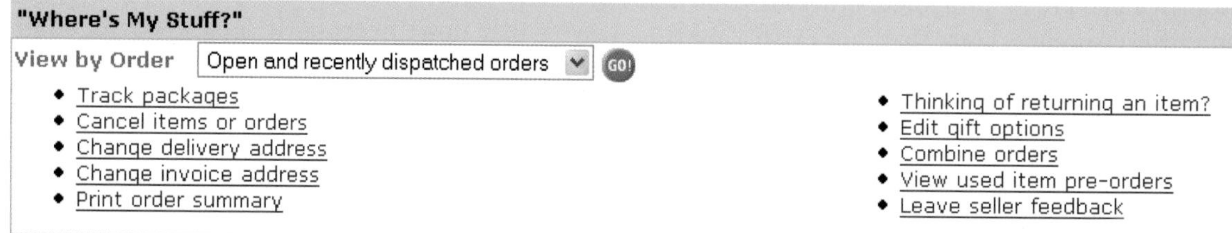

Figure 8.39 Amazon order tracking interface © 2010 Amazon.com Inc. and its affiliates. All rights reserved.

Image and style

Without really examining the notion of stereotyping, the image and style of a website will need to be manipulated to suit the target customer base.

www.barbie.com/

Largely designed in shades of pink, the Barbie website has medium-sized text and both video and audio streaming and includes a link to the Barbie shop. The target audience is girls aged 7 to 12.

www.sesamestreet.org/

Designed with large fonts and lots of colours, this website again has both video and audio streaming and includes a link to the Sesame Street store. The target audience is youngsters of both sexes aged approximately 3 to 8.

Connexions-direct.com (Figure 8.40) is an information website for young people aged about 15 and upwards that explores a range of issues that affect young people. The design of this website is bright and logical and the positioning of the 'Want Advice?' banner draws attention to the different technologies that young people can use to access some of the services.

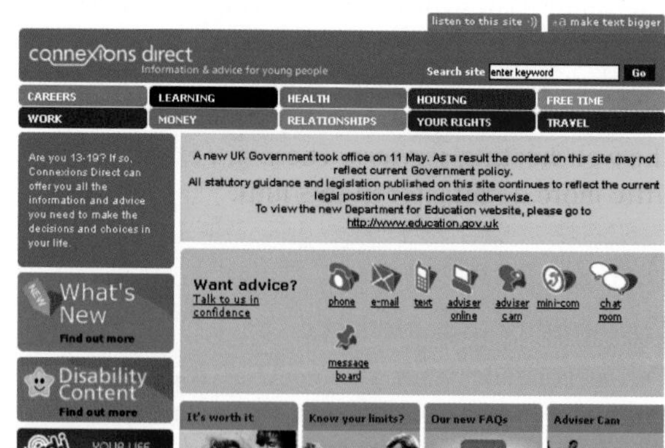

Figure 8.40 Connexions http://www.connexions-direct.com/

The final example is the website for Saga® (Figure 8.41), an organisation that provides a range of services for older people – specifically the over-50s. This website is calm, uses pastel colours and has obvious tabs for different sections of information. Interestingly, it also has a 'Text too small' feature that allows the user to make the fonts bigger!

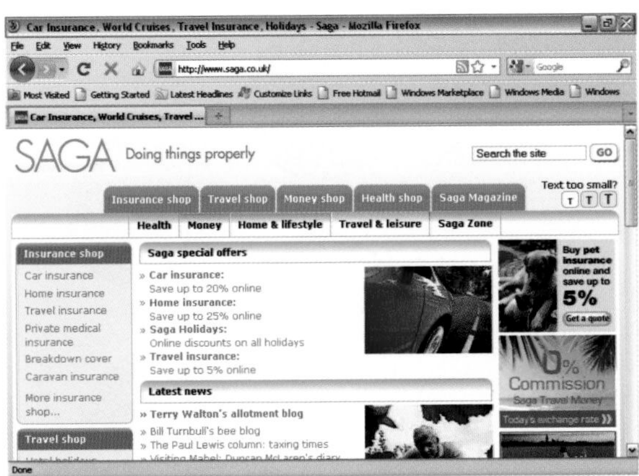

Figure 8.41 Saga

Whatever image and style is chosen, it needs to be appropriate for the end user, and fully researching the market (also talking directly to the target customer base) will enable the designer to ensure that the site meets the needs of its anticipated customers.

8.4.3 Hosting

Key terms

A **web-hosting service** is where you pay a third party to use disk space on its server. This means that access to the web pages will be looked after by someone else and this usually results in a contract being drawn up between the business and the web-hosting service that fully defines the levels of expected service in terms of bandwidth totals, storage space, scripting, database support, concurrent user limits and so on.

Choice of ISP

Choosing your **ISP** (**I**nternet **S**ervice **P**rovider) can be quite complex, particularly as there are so many to choose from. You will need to decide whether you need a service that allows you to have:

- **metered access** – access up to a particular limit and then disconnect
- **pay as you go** – pay only for what you use
- **monthly subscription** – pay a set amount each month but have open access.

The most important thing to bear in mind is that you should *not* make the decision based solely on cost. This is because a cheap service might have limitations or restrictions, which could mean that you outgrow the service quickly and it ceases to be able to meet your needs. For example:

- They might not be up front with setup charges.
- Their service might limit file sizes.
- They could have daily transfer limits.
- They might not publish emergency phone numbers or in fact any phone numbers on their materials.
- They could ask you to sign up to a long-term agreement.
- They might not provide any technical out-of-hours support (particularly at weekends).

For guidance on choosing an ISP see the following:

www.thegoodwebguide.co.uk/?PAGEID=010675 for a list of unmetered, free and broadband ISPs

www.ehow.com/how_108530_choose-internet-service.html – for a step-by-step guide to choosing an ISP.

In-house or sub-contracted

Depending on the size of a business, some organisations will choose to manage their websites **in-house**. This means that they will employ their own specialist staff to maintain their website(s). This will cost more than **sub-contracting** (buying in support from outside the organisation), but at least gives the business complete control. Sub-contracting is cheaper as the web-hosting services will be handling more than one website at a time.

8.4.4 Promotion

Marketing

There is a huge range of marketing methods available to web developers and designers, and the designer/developer will need to work with the client to decide on a marketing strategy that will grow the website's visitor numbers quickly.

Advertising the site

Banner advertisements on other people's websites are a good way of generating interest (Figure 8.42). Other website owners will charge you for this privilege, but as your website becomes more well known, you could enter into reciprocal arrangements where you place a banner on someone else's website and in turn you allow them to have a banner on yours.

Figure 8.42 Banner advertising

Alternatively, the inclusion of a simple hyperlink on a third-party website can cost significantly less.

Placing in search engines

How does a particular website come in the first ten hits in a search engine? In order to have your website appear in the top 10, top 50 or top 100 search hits, most search engine companies like Google®, Bing® and Yahoo® charge a fee. It is largely through these types of activities, along with the sale of advertising space, that these types of organisations are funded.

For a comprehensive list of search engine providers see:

www.thesearchenginelist.com/

Message boards and chat rooms

Different types of organisations may have a message board or a chat room where a new business might be able to advertise. Clearly, finding the right ones may be a time-consuming activity, but in the long term it will probably be a good investment!

8.4.5 Costs

The costs connected to a website are varied and not always obvious (see Figure 8.43).

Setup

A business can keep down its setup costs if it already has web-development skills and expertise within its own organisation, or if it can find someone who is prepared to develop the website for nothing. To gain experience in web development, it is not uncommon for students to offer their services to local businesses for free. The alternative is to train staff with the appropriate skills.

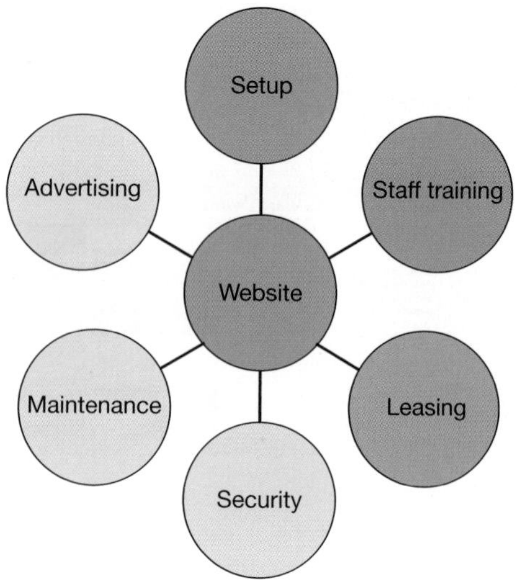

Figure 8.43 Possible costs

It currently costs around £500 to develop a website, although this figure can increase into the thousands if the developer is experienced.

Maintenance

Maintenance is an ongoing cost; even brochureware websites will have to be maintained. Maintenance activities could include:

- error removal (remember some software errors can surface once the software is in use)
- checking that links are still valid
- checking that navigation is still active
- updating content such as images and prices.

Security

Websites can be targets for malicious acts by others. This can include intentional sabotage or even defacement of the website itself. User accounts and profiles can also be hacked into and personal information stolen.

Furthermore, websites can be infected by viruses such as Trojan or the backdoor virus.

To prevent this kind of threat, it is essential that websites are run with up-to-date virus and firewall protection.

Leasing

As an alternative to paying for and maintaining a website, businesses can now lease or rent a website instead. Although this will create an ongoing monthly commitment, the business benefits from not having to find hundreds or thousands of pounds to get the project off the ground.

Activity 10

Website leasing

Lee Office Supplies has decided to lease a website. You have been asked to carry out a short investigation to establish the likely costs of such a lease.

Investigate website leasing and write a short email to the manager at Lee Office Supplies that gives an overview of costs and levels of service.

You may use the following website as a starting point:

www.cpcmarketing.co.uk/website-leasing/

Advertising

As suggested earlier in this unit, there are a range of advertising opportunities that can be explored. Each has a different cost implication. With some the cost might be a one-off fee, while for others there may be a monthly commitment. This cost should be carefully investigated to ensure that the business gets value for money.

Delivery strategy

Businesses must carefully consider the costs of getting their products to their customers, particularly if they are planning on trading internationally. They should also have investigated any restrictions on trading with businesses or individuals overseas (products banned from a particular country for example), and they should be aware of any special packaging requirements for certain types of products, to make sure that they meet the destination country's regulations.

Staff training

The costs of staff training can come from two perspectives. Firstly, the actual cost of any training course or courses. Secondly, if an employee is away from his or her job to attend training, either the job will not get done (which obviously has a business implication), or other staff will have to cover aspects of the job, thereby diluting their ability to do their own job over that period. Temporary staff could also be engaged, but that will also have a direct cost.

8.4.6 Security

Fraud protection

To reduce the likelihood of fraud, many websites carry **encryption protocols** to protect credit card details. Transaction encryption is facilitated using **SSL** (**S**ecure **S**ockets **L**ayer), which is the recognised standard for secure data transmission.

Another possible fraud is one that can only be detected through the vigilance of individuals and employees. The email shown in Figure 8.44 *appears* to have been received from egg.com, the internet bank. An employee in a busy accounts department might well click on the link as instructed and input the details requested without realising that this is actually a bogus request.

Look at the email. What do *you* think?

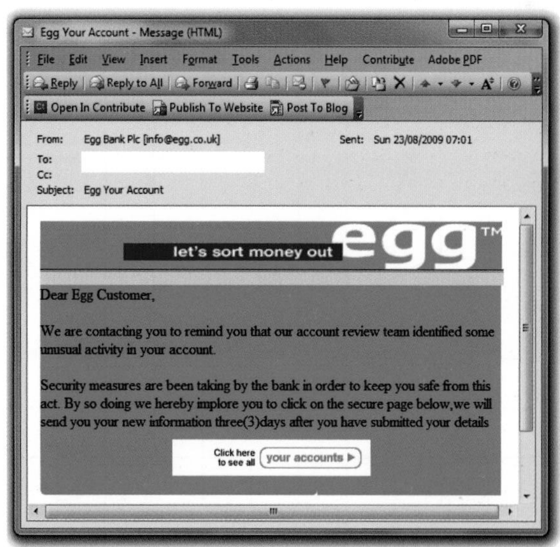

Figure 8.44 egg.com

The poor standard of spelling and grammar should be an immediate indicator that all is not as it seems, even if the fraudster has attempted to make the email appear genuine by copying the actual egg® logo (see their website: www.egg.com).

In this instance, however, it should have been very obvious that the email was fraudulent. Why? Because the person who received it didn't have an egg® account! This kind of email is known as **phishing**.

Hackers

The objective of a hacker is generally to steal data or to perform some sort of malicious act. Businesses must make sure that their customers' data is as safe as possible and that their website is secure.

Unit link

Unit 7 – Organisational systems security provides a complementary look at concepts such as phishing and threats related to e-commerce (section 7.1.1).

Viruses

Virus software, including firewall technology, is essential to protect websites against threats like an undiscovered backdoor virus, which logs user keystrokes, downloads personal information and spies on user activity.

This software also needs to be kept up-to-date, so there is likely to be more financial commitment than purely the initial cost. You may find that there is an annual fee on top.

To reduce the effects of breaches in security, the website should be backed up on a planned and regular basis.

B Braincheck 1

Test your understanding of what we have covered in this unit by completing this crossword. Answers are provided on the supporting website.

ACROSS

4 An email that is immediately generated in response to an enquiry or complaint

5 One of the two common web server software solutions

6 Unsolicited email

8 The A in FAQ

11 Information about a user that can be changed

12 What you see is what you get?

13 A Google facility for accessing shopping websites

DOWN

1 A link to a page saved by the user to enable quicker page access

2 Information at the beginning of a website that contains keywords

3 An organisation that acts as an agent between two companies to facilitate transactions

7 The interface for accessing web pages

9 A program within a search engine that accesses, reads and extracts key information to add to an index

10 A window that appears when accessing and which often includes advertising material

Unit link

Unit 8 is a **mandatory unit** for the Edexcel BTEC Level 3 National Extended Diploma in IT (Business) pathway and **optional** for all other qualifications and pathways of this Level 3 IT family.

Qualification (pathway)	Mandatory	Optional	Specialist optional
Edexcel BTEC Level 3 National Certificate in Information Technology		✓	
Edexcel BTEC Level 3 National Subsidiary Diploma in Information Technology		✓	
Edexcel BTEC Level 3 National Diploma in Information Technology		✓	
Edexcel BTEC Level 3 National Extended Diploma in Information Technology		✓	
Edexcel BTEC Level 3 National Diploma in IT (Business)		✓	
Edexcel BTEC Level 3 National Extended Diploma in IT (Business)	✓		
Edexcel BTEC Level 3 National Diploma in IT (Networking and System Support)		✓	
Edexcel BTEC Level 3 National Extended Diploma in IT (Networking and System Support)		✓	
Edexcel BTEC Level 3 National Diploma in IT (Software Development)		✓	
Edexcel BTEC Level 3 National Extended Diploma in IT (Software Development)		✓	

There are specific links to the following units in the scheme:
Unit 4 – Impact of the use of IT on business systems
Unit 33 – Exploring business activity

Achieving success

This particular unit has 11 criteria to meet: 6 Pass, 3 Merit and 2 Distinction.

For a Pass: You must achieve all 6 Pass criteria

For a Merit: You must achieve all 6 Pass and all 3 Merit criteria

For a Distinction: You must achieve all 6 Pass, all 3 Merit and both Distinction criteria.

Further reading

Chaffey, D. – *E-business and E-Commerce Management, Second Edition* (FT Prentice Hall, 2003) ISBN-10 0273683780, ISBN-13 978-0273683780

Malmsten, E., Leander, K., Portanger, E. and Drazin, C. – *Boo Hoo: A Dot.com Story* (Random House Business Books, 2002) ISBN-10 0099418371, ISBN-13 978-0099418375

Vise, D. – *The Google Story* (Pan, 2008) ISBN-10 0330508121, ISBN-13 978-0330508124

Websites

www.ico.gov.uk International Commissioner's Office

www.w3.org World Wide Web Consortium

Unit 9: Computer networks

By the end of this unit you should be able to:

1. Know types of network systems and protocols
2. Understand the key components used in networking
3. Know the services provided by network systems
4. Be able to make networked systems secure

Whether you are in school or college, passing this unit will involve being assessed. As with most BTEC schemes, the successful completion of various assessment criteria demonstrates your evidence of learning and the skills you have developed.

This unit has a mixture of pass, merit and distinction criteria. Generally you will find that merit and distinction criteria require a little more thought and evaluation before they can be completed.

The colour-coded grid below shows you the pass, merit and distinction criteria for this unit.

To achieve a pass grade you need to:	To achieve a merit grade you also need to:	To achieve a distinction grade you also need to:
P1 Describe the types of networks available and how they relate to particular network standards and protocol resources	**M1** Compare the benefits and disadvantages of peer-to-peer network and client/server networks	
P2 Describe why different network standards and protocols are necessary		
P3 Explain the key components required for client workstations to connect to a network and access network	**M2** Design a networked solution to meet a particular situation with specific requirements	**D1** Justify the design and choice of components used in a particular networked solution
P4 Explain the function of interconnection devices		
P5 Describe typical services provided by networks		**D2** Evaluate typical services available from a network operating system directory service
P6 Make a networked system secure	**M3** Report on the business risks of insecure networks and how they can be minimised	

Introduction

Computer networks is a 10-credit unit that expands upon (and reinforces) elements introduced in Unit 10 (Communication technologies) and gives additional support for Unit 5 (Managing networks).

In contrast to the other units, there is a distinct focus here on the complete network 'package', including the sizes of networks, their connectivity, devices, services and security concerns. This is reflected in the assessment criteria, which encourage practical design and awareness of the different elements that form modern networks.

How to read this chapter

This chapter is organised to match the content of the BTEC unit it represents. The following diagram shows the grading criteria that relate to each learning outcome.

You'll find colour-matching notes in each chapter about completing each grading criterion.

Unit links

For more on LANs and WANs please refer to Unit 10 – Communication technologies, section 10.1.1.

9.1 Know types of network systems and protocols

This section will cover the following grading criteria:

Make the Grade P1

P1 requires you to be able to describe different types of network available and be able to relate these to different network standards and protocols. A table linking the network type, standards and protocols is the easiest way to represent this information.

9.1.1 Types of network

As we have seen in other units, networks can be of different sizes and complexities.

The most common types are **L**ocal **A**rea **N**etworks (**LAN**) and **W**ide **A**rea **N**etworks (**WAN**) although the rise of wireless technologies and mobile devices has seen an increase in **P**ersonal **A**rea **N**etworks (**PAN**).

As noted, the primary difference between PANs, LANs, WANs and the internet is the size of the geographical area they cover.

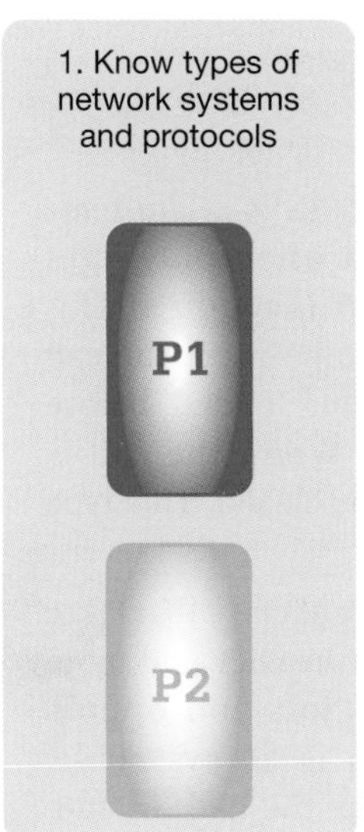

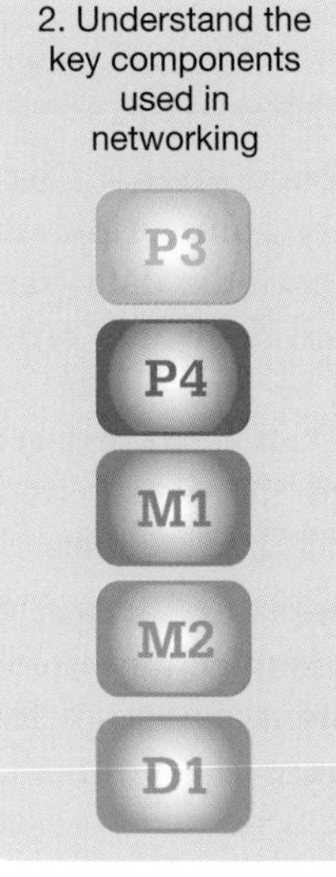

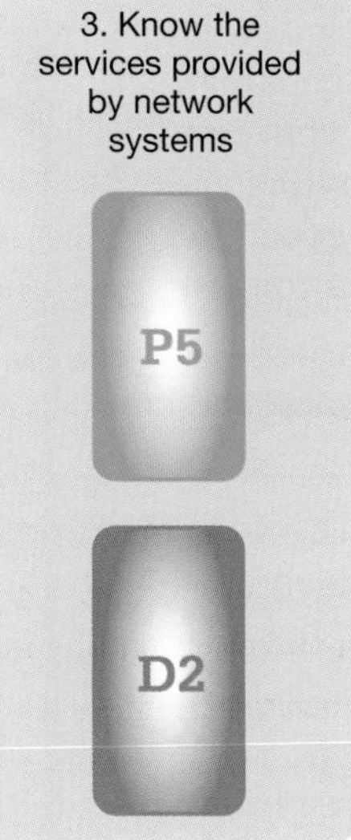

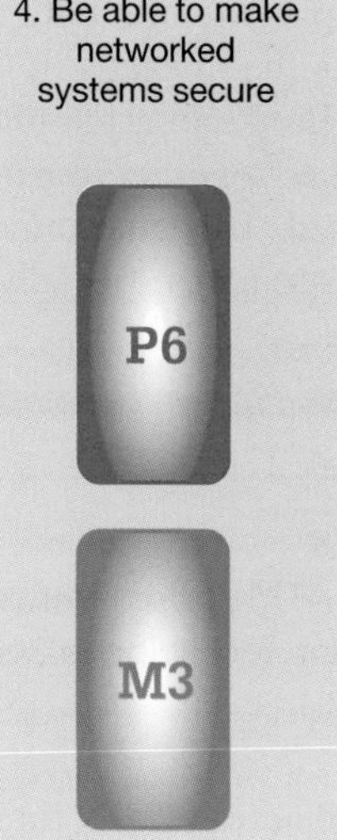

Figure 9.00

Often factors include those shown in Table 9.01:

Table 9.01

	PAN	**LAN**	**WAN**	**Internet**
Accessibility	Private or public depending on access provided and within a few metres of a person	Private (within an organisation)	Public (e.g. internet) or private (to connect an organisation's LANs together)	Public but requires access via an ISP (Internet Services Provider)
Transmission media	Typically wireless	Wired or wireless	Wired although satellite communication can be used	Mixed
Set-up costs	Relatively cheap	Relatively cheap	Can be very expensive as it may typically require leased connections	Expensive
Technologies used	Bluetooth iRDA Wi-Fi	Ethernet (commonly)	Frame Relay **M**ulti**p**rotocol **L**abel **S**witching (**MPLS**) **A**synchronous **T**ransfer **M**ode (**ATM**)	Mixed

Key terms

Multiprotocol Label Switching (MPLS) is a clever enhancement of the standard packet-switching Internet Protocol (IP), which can 'label' packets of a data stream so that related data (e.g. images in a video stream or sound chunks in a telephone conversation) can stay 'together' during routing and be prioritised. This guarantees a good **QoS** (**q**uality **o**f **s**ervice), especially on a congested network.

Unit links

For more on ATM please refer to Unit 10 – Communication technologies, section 10.1.1.

Originally used across **ISDN** interfaces, **frame relay** is a standardised packet-based protocol that is designed for high-speed data-only transfer.

It is generally used to connect LANs together to form a WAN. Connections must be made before data can be transferred between two pieces of **D**ata **T**erminating **E**quipment (**DTE**). The connection made is said to be a **V**irtual **C**ircuit (**VC**) and two types exist as shown in 'key terms'.

Key terms

Switched Virtual Circuits (SVCs) are temporary connections used when only light and periodic data transfer is required ('little and rarely'). In order to be used, the call must be formally 'set up' and 'ended' before data can be transferred. When the call is ended, the virtual circuit is closed. This type of VC is less popular.

Permanent Virtual Circuits (PVCs) are fixed connections used for heavier and more frequent data transfers ('lots and often'). Because the connection is always made, there is no need to 'set up' the call or 'end' it; the PVC is always ready to accept data.

Logical and physical topologies

Topologies (the network's shape or form) can be **physical** (how they are actually connected together) or **logical** (how they communicate, e.g. their network access methods).

Each point on a network is called a **node**. In theory a node could be any **network device** (e.g. a workstation) or an **interconnection device** (e.g. a network switch).

Unit links
To see graphical representations of common network topologies please refer to Unit 10 – Communication technologies, section 10.1.1.

There are a number of points to remember when selecting a topology:

- LAN or WAN?
- costs involved
- type of media (e.g. cable type)
- length of cable needed
- maximum run length of a cabled media
- expansion (accommodating future growth)
- level of reliability required
- ease of management
- ease of troubleshooting (faultfinding and repair)

In addition, a quick examination of each topology can reveal some significant advantages and disadvantages as shown in Table 9.02.

Common topology scorecard

Table 9.02

Topology	Advantages	Disadvantages
Star	+ Central management + Suitable for LAN or WAN + Easy to install + Easy to expand + One outer node breaking down will not affect others' connectivity	– Reliance on central node for communication
Ring	+ Data travels in one direction only + Helps to avoid data collisions ('deterministic') + Suitable for LAN	– One node breaking down will affect the network – Data passes through all nodes (can be slower)
Mesh	+ Very fault tolerant (keeps working when many nodes have failed) + Suitable for LAN or WAN (albeit very expensive)	– Expensive – lots of cabling! – Difficult to troubleshoot – Complicated to install
Tree	+ Can be a mixture of different network equipment and topologies (bus and star) + Different branches of the tree can be treated as separate segments (reducing data collision)	– If a backbone cable is used, separate branches will lose connectivity if it is damaged
Bus	+ Easy to install + Easy to expand + Low cost (less cable) + Suitable for LAN	– Older technology – A cable break could down entire network – Troubleshooting is difficult – Backbone cable must be terminated at both ends

Network access methods

Depending on the topology, different types of **network access methods** exist, with perhaps **CSMA** and **Token Passing** being the most common.

> **Unit links**
> For more on Carrier Sense Multiple Access (CSMA) and Token Passing please refer to Unit 10 – Communication technologies, section 10.1.1.

The network access method defines (to an extent) the logical topology of the network.

Network models

Worldwide networking standards are encouraged through the adoption of the **OSI** (**O**pen **S**ystem **I**nterconnect) model as pioneered by **ISO** (**I**nternational **S**tandards **O**rganization).

> **Unit links**
> For more on the ISO OSI Model please refer to Unit 10 – Communication technologies, section 10.1.4.

9.1.2 Network protocols and standards

A number of different network protocols and standards exist in order to meet different environments, jobs and technological demands. It is likely that you will have already encountered some of these from other networking units, particularly those covered in Units 5 or 10.

Examples include:

- **Transmission Control Protocol/Internet Protocol suite (TCP/IP)**

> **Unit links**
> For more on TCP/IP please refer to Unit 10 – Communication technologies, section 10.1.4.

- **AppleTalk®**
  This was the collective name for a suite of networking protocols developed by Apple Computers, Inc. in the 1980s for communicating data between Apple® Computer products (such as the famous Apple® Macintosh) and other compatible systems.

  It could be used on a number of different topologies including **token ring, Ethernet-style bus** and **star** as it had protocols to support data traffic and routing over each type.

  Common **OSI-layer compatible** protocols inside the AppleTalk suite include:

  - **Session** Layer: AppleTalk **D**ata **S**tream **P**rotocol (**ADSP**)
  - **Network** Layer: **D**atagram **D**elivery **P**rotocol (**DDP**)
  - **Physical** Layer: **Ethernet driver**

  Modern Apple computer systems have largely moved towards TCP/IP as their preferred protocol solution although AppleTalk® remains '**deprecated**' (outdated but still present) to ensure **backwards compatibility** in newer Apple® Mac Operating Systems for older hardware and applications that still require it.

> **Make the Grade** P2
>
> P2 requires you to be able describe why different standards and protocols are necessary. Read through sections 9.1.2 and 9.1.3 in order to gain an overview of these. In terms of working through this, the recommended approach is to think about practical concerns, e.g. wireless networking requires different standards to those for wired solutions because they involve radio frequencies and data being transmitted speeds; in order for all wireless devices to be able to talk to each other, a minimum standard must be created.

- **U**ser **D**atagram **P**rotocol **(UDP)**

Key terms

UDP is part of the TCP/IP suite of protocols and can be used when guarantee of reliable delivery of data is not necessary.

It is more efficient in data transfer then TCP/IP but its inability to confirm that data packets were successfully received is a hindrance. As a result it is often used for time-critical but not mission-critical applications such as multimedia streaming, DNS and SNMP.

- 802.2
- **802.3** (more commonly known as **Ethernet**)
- **F**ibre **D**istributed **D**ata **I**nterface **(FDDI)**

Key terms

FDDI is a transmission protocol that uses a token ring topology to achieve a data bandwidth of 100 Mbps using optical fibre.

Its unique feature is its **double rings** (called **primary** and **secondary**).

FDDI uses its double ring to good effect; it can detect a **broken node** (i.e. a malfunctioning workstation) and can divert the data to the other ring where data travels in the opposite direction, thereby 'closing off' the affected part of the network.

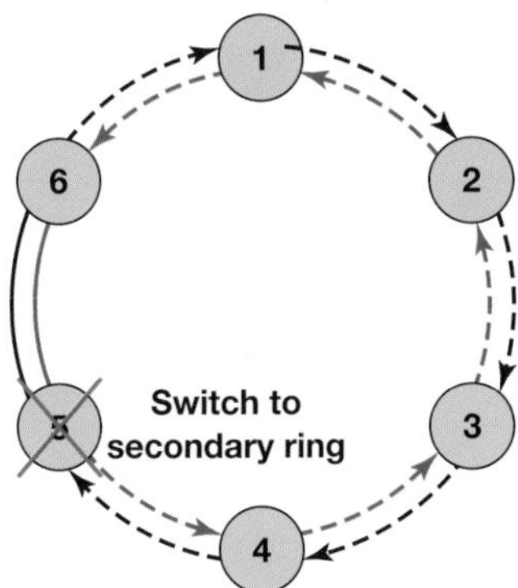

Figure 9.01 Double-ring FDDI network

This process is called '**self healing**'. The secondary (inner) ring is often called the '**backup**' ring. While the backup ring allows the network to continue functioning, node 5 can be safely repaired.

For this system to work, each node (e.g. server or workstation) would need **DAS** (**D**ual **A**ttach **S**tation) connections to each ring (see Figure 9.02).

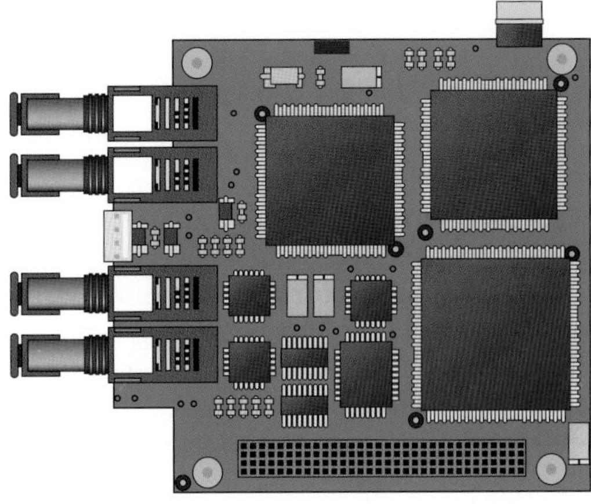

Figure 9.02 Double-ring FDDI network adaptor

- **802.5** (Token ring)

Unit links

For more on 802.2, 802.3 (Ethernet) and 802.5 (Token ring) please refer to Unit 10 – Communication technologies, section 10.1.1 and 10.1.2.

In addition, a number of **wireless technologies** are also worth revisiting:

- **802.11** (more commonly known as '**Wi-Fi**')
- **Infrared**
- **Bluetooth**
- **3G (3rd Generation)**.

  3G is a third generation wireless service that is often associated with mobile phones and their high data speeds, which support faster internet access and streaming full motion video on websites such as Youtube.

  3G data rates vary but typically fall between 144Kbps and 14Mbps. Well-known 3G technologies you may have encountered include:
  - **G**eneral **P**acket **R**adio **S**ervice **(GPRS)** – 114 Kbps
  - **E**nhanced **D**ata rates for **G**lobal **E**volution **(EDGE)** – 384 Kbps
  - **UMTS** **W**ideband **CDMA** **(WCDMA)** – 1.92 Mbps (download only)
  - **H**igh **S**peed **D**ownlink **P**acket **A**ccess **(HSDPA)** – 14 Mbps (download only).

> **Unit links**
> For more on wireless technologies please refer to Unit 10 – Communication technologies, sections 10.1.3, 10.1.5, 10.2.5 and 10.2.6.

Wireless technologies – factors affecting their range and speed

The main factors are:

- **signal strength** from antennae
- **security settings** (e.g. use of encryption)
- **environmental factors** (e.g. adverse weather, walls) that block or absorb signals
- **interference** from other wireless systems that share the same frequency range (e.g. microwaves, household cordless telephones).

In addition range and speed are interrelated; slower connections may be more sustainable over longer distances or a weaker strength of signal.

9.1.3 Application layer protocols

A number of different protocols are used at the **application layer** of the **ISO OSI model**.

Some of the common ones are detailed below.

DNS (Domain Name Service)

It should be remembered that domain names are a **human convenience** – computer systems are happy with just their numerical identification!

A simple example would be tracking a request made from a web browser such as Mozilla Firefox® (see Figure 9.03).

Figure 9.03 URL

When a **U**niform **R**esource **L**ocator (**URL**) such as 'news.bbc.co.uk' is keyed into a web browser's address window, a long, complicated process is started.

Part of this process includes resolving the IP address of the remote BBC HTTP server using a DNS. This is achieved via a **DNS query**.

DNS works like a distributed database, with a number of DNS servers worldwide each holding part of the overall picture. They are arranged in a hierarchical fashion, with each level responsible for resolving different levels of the URL from top-level domains (e.g. UK) to the name of the actual server itself (e.g. NEWS).

When a DNS server receives an URL to resolve it has three possible choices (see Figure 9.04).

> **Key terms**
>
> **DNS** is best defined as a program running on a server (often called a **D**omain **N**ame **S**erver) that translates domain names (e.g. www.google.com) into their correct IP addresses (e.g. 173.194.36.104) so that the request can be correctly routed. This makes use of **UDP** and **port 53**.

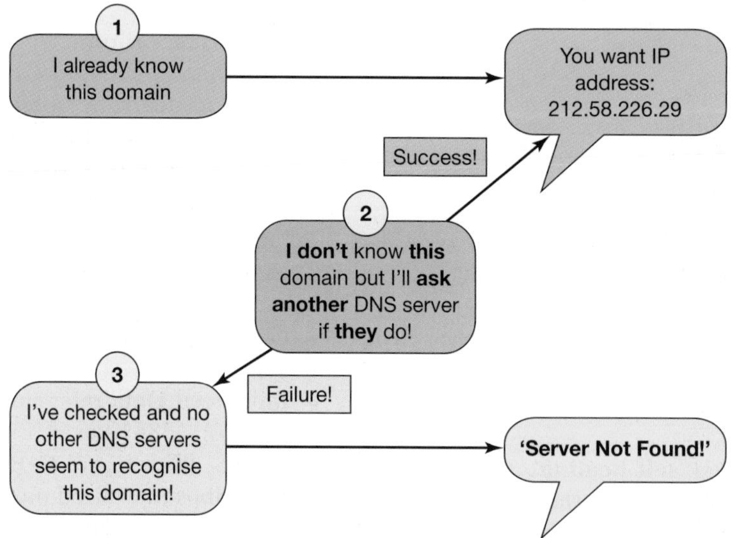

Figure 9.04 What happens when a DNS server receives a URL

Fortunately a DNS server will **cache** (store temporarily) a number of recent requests (and their resolved IPs) so it is possible that the query can be resolved without the need of further help. When this fails, the DNS will ask another DNS server. This second DNS server will also either be able to resolve the query or be able to give the IP of yet another DNS server that may be able to help – so the process goes on until a resolution is found (or not – if the domain is invalid).

To give maximum **redundancy**, a number of DNS servers will have the same domain and IP addresses, essentially still providing coverage when some may fail.

DHCP (Dynamic Host Configuration Protocol)

On a TCP/IP network, a client PC or device (e.g. a networked printer) requires a unique IP address even though its **NIC** (**N**etwork **I**nterface **C**ard) will already provide a unique **MAC** (**M**edia **A**ccess **C**ontrol) 'physical' address.

There are two types of IP address that can be used: static and dynamic.

- **Static** – As the name suggests this is a **fixed IP address** that is always set by the device itself, without a request to a DHCP service.
- **Dynamic** – This a '**leased**' IP address that is provided by another device (typically a server or a router) that is running a **DHCP service.** As the IP address is leased, it will only last a finite period of time before it **expires** and another must be **requested and assigned.** As such, devices receiving a dynamically assigned IP address may receive several different ones (in the same network range) over a period of time.

As noted, a server or device on the network must be running a DHCP service on ports 67 and 68. This is typically achieved as part of a server's configuration or in a router's settings (see Figure 9.05 for an example).

Typically, the DHCP will set the 'pool' of available IP addresses (e.g. 192.168.123.2 to 192.168.123.100) by specifying a start and end address. Some exclusions in this range (e.g. 192.168.123.50) may also be possible.

In addition, certain addresses may be reserved for particular devices (as seen in Figure 9.05, the Print Server is always assigned 192.168.123.11).

Filtering of IP requests is also possible by banning DHCP requests coming from certain clients without authorised MAC addresses. This is particularly useful when dealing with security issues on wireless networks although '**spoofing**' (forging) MAC addresses will circumvent the protection.

In order to use DHCP, the client's OS must be configured so that it enables a DHCP request rather than setting its own static IP address.

Figure 9.06 overleaf shows the user setting a DHCP requested IP address in its IP Properties dialogue in Microsoft Windows Vista®.

The other section ('Use the following IP address') can be used to set a **static IP address.**

The resulting leased IP can be viewed by examining the properties of the appropriate network connection (see Figure 9.07 on page 248).

Other common protocols include:

- **FTP** (**F**ile **T**ransfer **P**rotocol)
- **HTTP** (**H**yper**t**ext **T**ransfer **P**rotocol)
- **SMTP** (**S**imple **M**ail **T**ransfer **P**rotocol)

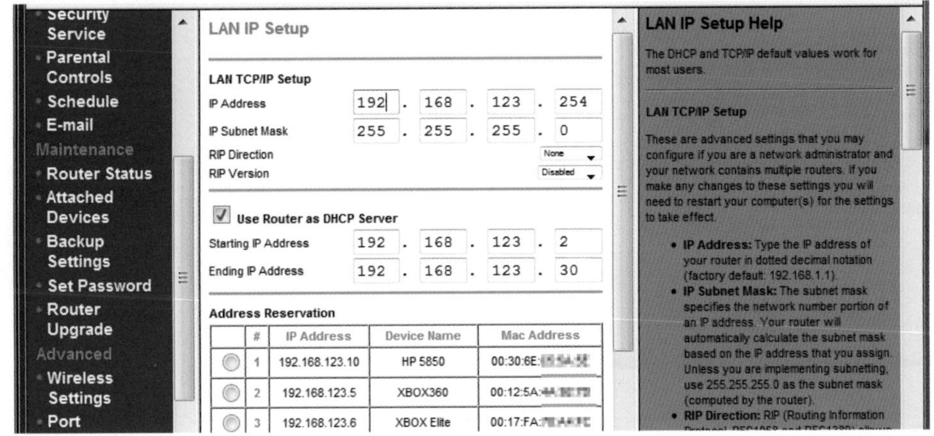

Figure 9.05 A Netgear Router's DHCP service with an address pool and reservations

Unit links

For more on FTP, HTTP, SMTP and other protocols please refer to Unit 10 – Communication technologies, section 10.3.1, and Unit 5 – Managing networks, section 5.1.1.

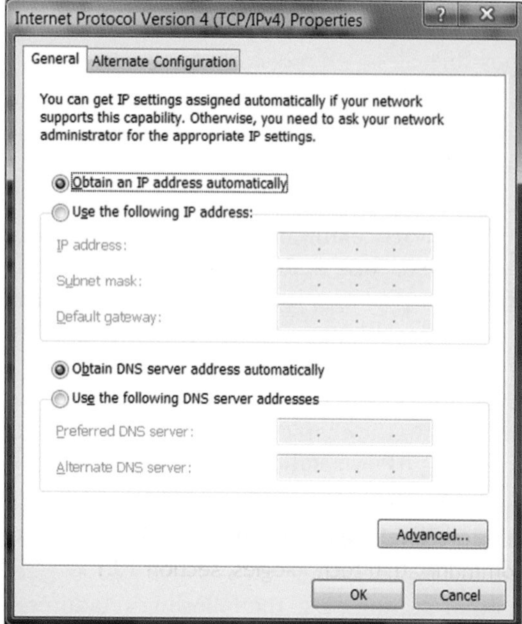

Figure 9.06 Windows Vista® IP Properties dialogue

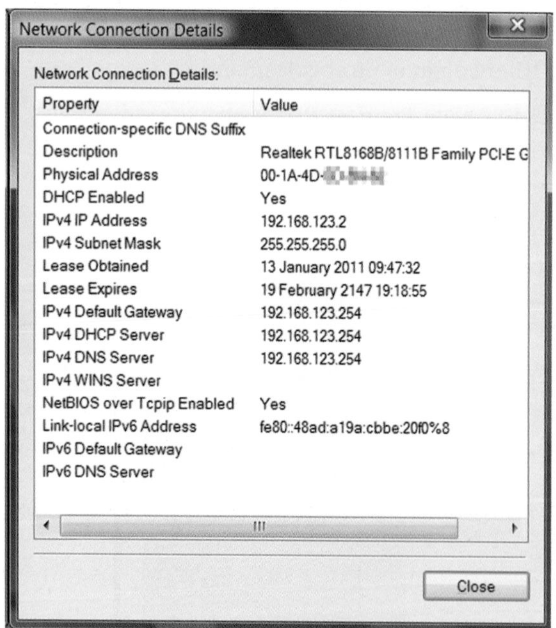

Figure 9.07 Windows Vista® showing its DHCP-assigned IP address

Help

DHCP – information returned by the DHCP service

- IP address
- Lease expiration date/time
- DNS (Domain Name Service) server's IP address
- Gateway IP address
- Name of the network domain (e.g. '.business.co.uk')

B Braincheck 1

Match the application layer protocol description to its correct name!

A	For posting electronic mail between mail servers or from a client to a mail server	**1**	DNS
B	For requesting and serving web pages	**2**	SMTP
C	For performing file transfers	**3**	DHCP
D	For resolving domain names to their IP addresses	**4**	FTP
E	For assigning an IP address to a network client	**5**	HTTP

Activity 1

Use a router or server running a DHCP service to assign a pool of IP addresses of your choosing.

See whether the DHCP service can a) reserve IPs for specific MAC addresses and b) filter IP requests for unauthorised MAC addresses (particularly for a wireless router).

9.2 Understand the key components used in networking

This section will cover the following grading criteria:

Make the Grade M1

M1 asks you to compare the benefits of peer-to-peer and client/server networks.

Key points to remember for peer-to-peer:

+ Cheap and easy to set up.
+ No need for network administrator.
+ Resources (e.g. printing, files etc.) are easily shared.
+ Most operating systems are capable of supporting basic peer-to-peer networking out of the box.

Key points to remember for client/server:

+ Security can be controlled centrally.
+ Dedicated services can be provided to all clients and be updated centrally.
+ Copes with network growth better as the server can cope with increased demands.
– Requires specific server version of the operating system.

Although a network's topology may remain the same, it can be configured as either **peer-to-peer** or **client/server** in its operation depending on the hardware and software used.

Key terms

Peer-to-peer (P2P) is where all workstations on a network have equal importance and control over the network's management.

Client/server occurs where control of the network and its services is overseen and driven by a server computer 'talking' to less powerful workstations (known as network clients). The server responds to processing or resource requests made by its clients.

Many of the hardware and software elements occurring on these types of network have already been detailed in Units 5 and 10. Please refer to the associated link boxes for more information.

9.2.1 Key components

There are several categories of key components that fit together to form a typical network:

- **network devices** (see 9.2.2)
- **interconnection devices** (see 9.2.3)
- **connectors and cabling** (see 9.2.4)
- **software** (see 9.2.5).

Let us examine each in turn.

9.2.2 Network devices

Network devices typically include the following items of hardware:

- **n**etwork **i**nterface **c**ard (**NIC**)
- **servers** (e.g. print, mail, file, web, proxy).

Unit links

For more on these please refer to Unit 10 – Communication technologies, section 10.1.2.

9.2.3 Interconnection devices

Hardware that permits interconnection of different network devices includes:

- bridge
- gateway
- hub
- **mod**ulator-**dem**odulator (modem)
- repeater
- router
- switch
- **W**ireless **A**ccess **P**oint (**WAP**)

Make the Grade P4

P4 is a relatively straightforward criterion asking you to explain the function of interconnection devices. A table, poster or leaflet may be appropriate to demonstrate what job each of the devices in 9.2.3 actually does.

Unit links

For more on different interconnection devices please refer to Unit 10 – Communication technologies, section 10.1.3.

9.2.4 Connectors and cabling

In networking terms, external (i.e. WAN) cabling may be leased or dedicated.

Key terms

A **leased line** is a permanent, high speed telecommunication line between two points that is always 'on' (i.e. requires no 'dial up'). It normally has high installation costs and requires a monthly rental fee.

In contrast, a **dedicated line** is often seen as a form of leased line that is specifically designed to be used for a single purpose (e.g. data or voice communication, not both). Most organisations use leased lines to connect their premises together if they are spread over a large geographic area. Line names are usually referred to by their **bandwidth,** e.g. a '10 Meg' (10Mbps) line would cost around £7,000 per year but would be suitable for most business applications.

Make the Grade

D1

These criteria may be linked into a single task. M2 requires you to design a network to meet a specific requirement (likely to be set by your tutor). You may design this on paper or using network design software. It is likely as part of this task that you will need to explain the key components that you have used to build your network – that's P3. This is likely to include some network devices (9.2.2), interconnection devices (9.2.3), connectors and cabling (9.2.4) and software (9.2.5). D1 asks you to justify your choice of components. The key here will be to say why you used specific devices in your network design, for example, 'Traditional UTP cables were used as thick walls absorbed too much wireless signal.'

A number of different types of **media** may be used to connect two network **nodes**:

- coaxial
- fibre optic
- microwave
- satellite
- **S**hielded **T**wisted **P**air **(STP)**
- **U**nshielded **T**wisted **P**air **(UTP)**
- wireless ('Wi-Fi')

Unit links

For more on these connection media please refer to Unit 10 – Communication technologies, section 10.2.6, and Unit 5 – Managing networks, section 5.1.1

9.2.5 Software

A number of different systems and application software can be used on a network.

These include, categorised by type:

Systems software (including utilities):

- anti virus
- anti-spyware
- firewall
- Network Operating System (NOS).

Application software:

- email client (e.g. Microsoft Outlook®, Mozilla Thunderbird®)
- instant messaging client (e.g. MSN Messenger®)
- monitoring software client
- server software (e.g. HTTP server such as Microsoft® Internet Information Services or Apache® HTTPD server)
- web browser client (e.g. Microsoft Internet Explorer®, Mozilla Firebird®)

All of these require a network stack of protocols in order to operate and as a consequence both receive and generate their own network traffic.

9.2.6 Commercial systems

Elements of the following operating systems are 'network aware', effectively NOS (network operating systems), and are therefore key components of the network:

- **AppleShare®** (as part of Apple's Mac OS, discussed in 9.1.2)
- **Linux** (both server and client implementations)
- **Microsoft Windows®** (both server and client implementations)
- **Novell Netware®**
- **Unix®** (both server and client implementations)

Unit links

For more on Linux and Novell Netware®, please refer to Unit 5 – Managing networks, section 5.1.2.

9.3 Know the services provided by network systems

This section will cover the following grading criteria:

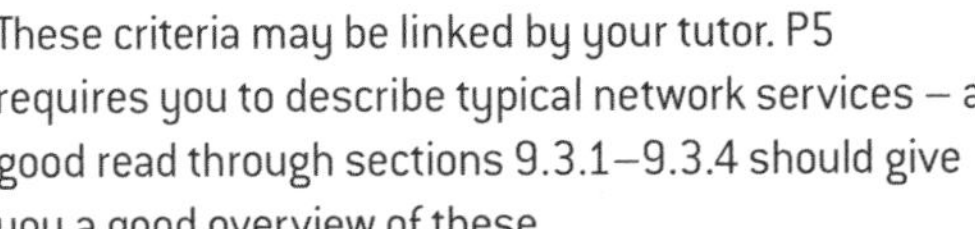

These criteria may be linked by your tutor. P5 requires you to describe typical network services – a good read through sections 9.3.1–9.3.4 should give you a good overview of these.

D2 asks you to evaluate different sections available from a network operating system's directory services. Read through the descriptions in section 9.3 and then examine Figure 9.09, which focuses on Microsoft®'s well-known Active Directory. A recommended section to focus on would be the account management of different Windows® users. What features are there? Which functions work well? What could be improved?

9.3.1 Directory services

The range of directory services can be viewed as network objects or entities; they are managed in abstract form (i.e. all the technical background details are safely hidden) and may simply be represented by clickable icons with drag and drop functionality. In addition, these complexities are also hidden from end users who can navigate their part of the network with little understanding of how the assets or functions are managed. This makes working with networked assets much simpler, whatever the individual's role in the organisation.

Part of a network manager's (or network administrator's) job is to create entries for each entity type by mapping it against a real 'live' asset that exists in the organisation. The simplest example of this would be creating a user account for an employee.

Example of commercial directory services include:

- **Microsoft Active Directory®** (Windows 2000® server onwards)
- **Novell eDirectory®** (formerly known as Novell Directory Service – NDS)
- **Sun's Java™ System Directory Server**

All of these include implementations (or interfaces) for the **Lightweight Directory Access Protocol (LDAP)**, a **TCP/IP compliant protocol** that enables users to locate resources on public or private networks, given suitable access permissions.

Some of the different functions that exist within a typical directory services:

- **Account management**
  - Add/delete/amend network domains.
  - Add/delete/amend network groups.
  - Add/delete/amend network users.
- **Authentication management**
  - Add/delete/amend policies.
  - Grant/revoke permissions for groups/users/applications/devices.
- **Asset management**
  - Perform critical network updates.
  - Add/remove network devices.
  - Add/remove network applications.
  - Add/remove network services (e.g. FTP).

Key terms

Directory services represent a way to provide an organised method for identifying assets on a networked computer system (whether it is a WAN or LAN).

Acting like a database, it contains information about networked hardware, applications, services, data files, folders, users, groups (of users), address books, permissions and the relationships that connect them.

It can be seen as a trusted partner of the network operating system.

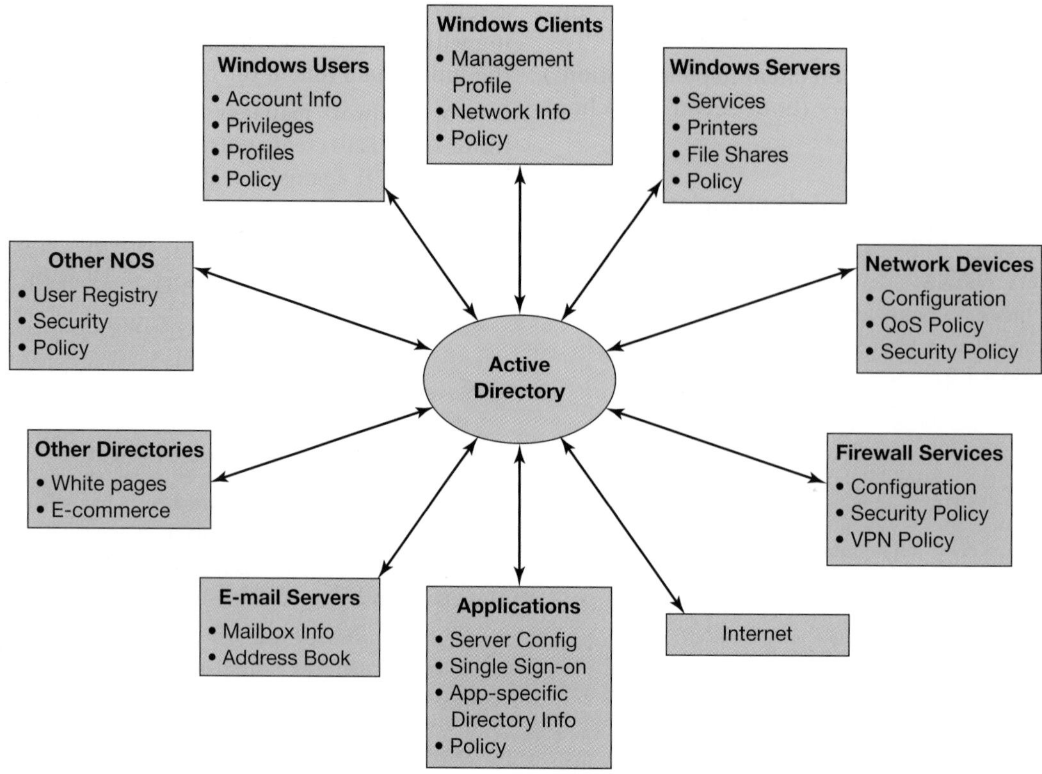

Figure 9.08 Microsoft's Active Directory® and its central role
(*Source*: http://www.microsoft.com/technet/technetmag/issues/2005/01/ActiveDirectory/fig03.gif)

Most directory services interfaces appear in the form of **collapsible hierarchical trees** in which network objects can be grouped and ordered for easy access and management.

Figure 9.09 shows a typical, but smaller, LDAP tree.

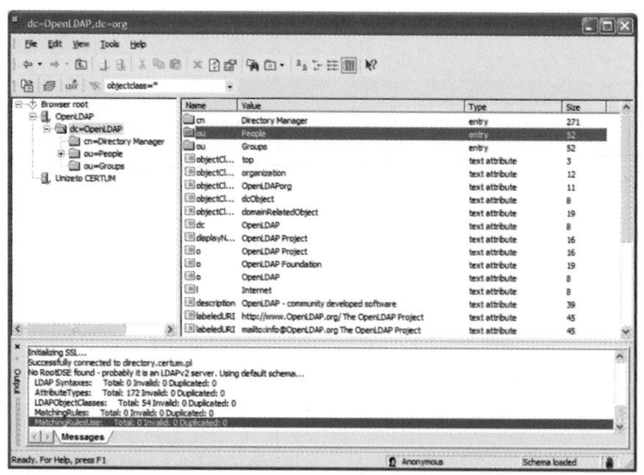

Figure 9.09 Browsing an open LDAP resource with Softerra's free LDAP Browser

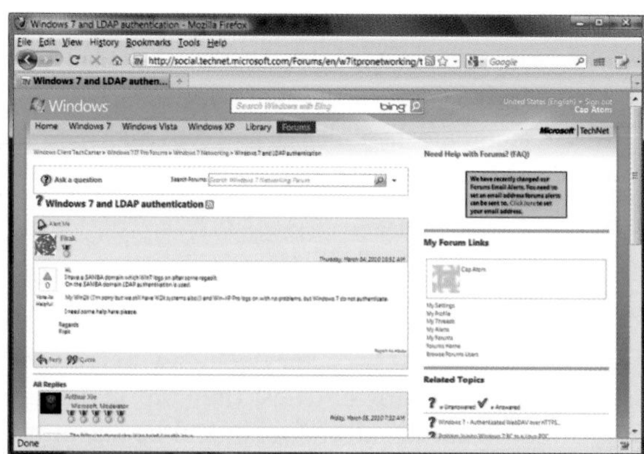

Figure 9.10 A user poses a problem in Microsoft's Windows Forum

9.3.2 Telecommunication services

A network provides a number of different communication services.

Communication

Perhaps the most well known and commonly used are:

- **Discussion boards** (also known as on-line forums or message boards)

  Typically accessed via a web browser, this is an online service that allows registered users to post specific questions and responses to other users' posted questions that they have seen.

  Forums are a popular communication tool among IT professionals.
- **Email**
- **Instant Messaging (IM)**

> **Unit links**
> For more detail on instant messaging, please refer to Unit 10 – Communication technology, section 10.3.1.

- **Internet Relay Chat (IRC)**
- Dating back to 1988, **IRC** is a text-based service on the internet where real-time conversations among multiple users take place in virtual rooms ('channels') via special IRC-clients. It uses ports in the range 6660–6669 and 7000.

  Users can subscribe to a number of different channels (each begins with a # symbol), which are dedicated to a specific area of interest.

  In order to use IRC, the user must install a suitable IRC client on their computer system; these are generally available for most operating systems. IRC client software can connect to remote IRC servers that are part of a larger IRC network, which in turn represents a small part of the internet itself.

  A commonly used IRC client is **mIRC** (see Figure 9.11).

  IRC also uses **bots** (a collection of automated scripts or a program) that can perform special actions like disconnecting users who use bad language or break the channels' published rules!
- **Social networking**

  Websites such as **Facebook** and **MySpace** are **portals** for users to express themselves and socialise with others, often including self-selected or hyperlinked content such as music, pictures, messages, blogs and video.

  Most social networking sites specialise in certain topics, for example:

  - **Bebo** – school and college
  - **Flickr** – photo sharing
  - **FriendsReunited** – school, college and work friends.

  Care should be exercised when using such websites, particularly with regard to the level of personal information provided. Some social networking sites refuse entry for users below a certain age (although this is easy to circumvent).

  Due to the common access method (HTTP), social networking sites are best monitored or filtered through the use of their IP addresses or URLs.
- **Usenet** (Newsgroups)

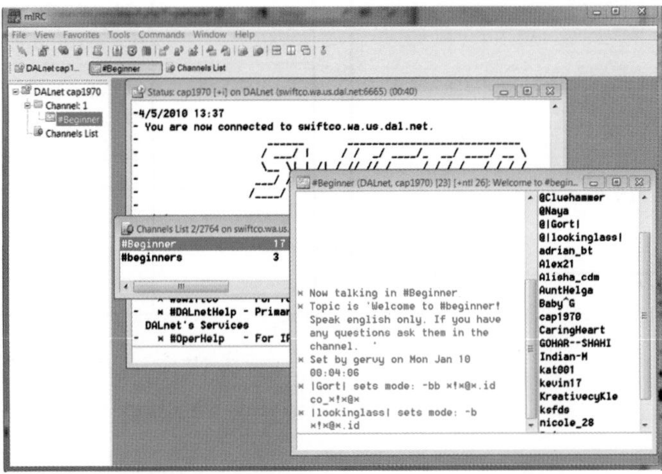

Figure 9.11 mIRC client visits the #Beginner channel

Key terms

Usenet is a distributed discussion system that operates worldwide, consisting of a number of different newsgroups.

Each newsgroup belongs to a particular hierarchy, organised by subject. Users log-in, download new messages and message threads and can decide whether they would like to post a reply via email.

There are over 30,000 different newsgroups available although few news servers will carry them all.

The following is an extract from a typical Usenet hierarchy:

alt.tv.cartoon-network
alt.tv.cartoon-network.toonami
alt.tv.casper
alt.tv.charmed
alt.tv.comedy-central
alt.tv.comedy-central.daily-show

In order to access Usenet, the user must have a suitable Usenet client (such as Forté Agent in Figure 9.12) application, a Usenet account and the IP address (or URL) of a Usenet server.

Although some newsgroups are moderated for content (views, bad language etc.), most aren't so caution is advised. In addition, some groups in the **alt.bin** hierarchy have **binary attachments**, which when decoded could contain viruses or spyware.

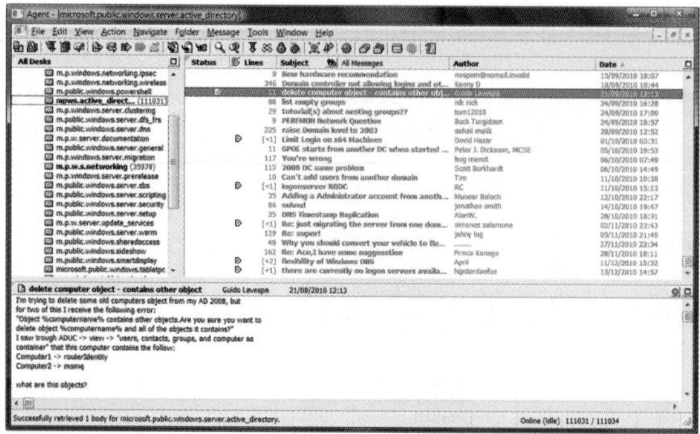

Figure 9.12 Usenet client Forté Agent accessing a newsgroup

Usenet works by using **port 119** for **Network News Transfer Protocol (NTTP)**, the protocol that is used between the news client and news server to read or post messages.

9.3.3 File services

Network file services include:

- **file transfer**
- **file sharing**.

As such the network operating system must have mechanisms to support the **transfer** (movement) of files across the network (from computer to computer) and also the **sharing** of a file (or folder) with other users and computers.

File sharing operating systems such as Microsoft Windows® can also make use of **A**ccess **C**ontrol **L**ists (**ACLs**), which specify not only which users (or groups) have access to a particular file, but also what type of access they have.

Permissions for Everyone	Allow	Deny
Full Control	☑	☐
Change	☑	☐
Read	☑	☐

Figure 9.13 Access control List

As you can see from Figure 9.13, users in the 'Everyone' group have 'Allow' for all three permissions (Full Control, Change and Read).

Permission	For a file, allows the user to...	Danger level
Full control	Read the file Re-write the file with new contents Delete the file	
Change	Read the file Re-write the file with new contents	
Read	Read the file only	

In an ACL, the file's owner (or network administrator who will have access) can change the

permissions for each group or single user.
More permission types are common, including the ability to **execute** (run) an application.

Activity 2

Sharing files

On an available computer system, explore the File Share functions offered by the network operating system.

Which types of permissions are listed?

9.3.4 Application services

The network can also be responsible for providing application services.

These could include:

- **relational databases**, e.g. Microsoft® SQL Server or MySQL®
- **web applications**
- **proxy**.

It can also be tasked with:

- **shared resources** (e.g. printing)
- **storage space** (e.g. network drives)
- Voice**over IP (VoIP)**
- providing **mobile working** via **VPN**
- **authentication** (e.g. of users via **LDAP**)

Unit links

For more on VoIP, please refer to Unit 10 – Communication technology, section 10.3.3.

B Braincheck 2

1. Name any two network devices.
2. Name any two interconnection devices.
3. What is a leased line?
4. Name three different types of network media?
5. What is LDAP?
6. Name three types of services provided by a network.
7. What is IRC?
8. What is Usenet?
9. Which network service uses ports 6660–6669 and 7000?
10. What is an ACL?

How well did you do? See answers on supporting website.

Activity 3

Linux file services

Linux also uses permissions to control user access to files.

Three specific commands can be used to manage these:

chmod

chown

chgrp

Use a suitable web-enabled computer system to find out what each command does and how it can affect Linux file permissions.

9.4 Be able to make networked systems secure

This section will cover the following grading criteria:

P6 M3

Make the Grade P6 M3

P6 is really a practical task requiring you to make a network secure. In order to do this, you must have identified the threats and installed and configured the necessary software and settings in order to secure your network. This could range from adding WPA2 encryption on a wireless network to having scheduled backups of user data. This will lead onto M3.

9.4.1 Securing a system

Networked systems can be secured in a number of different ways.

Common techniques include:

- **disaster planning** and **recovery**
- **authorisation permissions** and **ACLs** (see 9.3.3)
- **backup schedules** and **restore policies**
- **passwords policies**
- **biometrics**

- **encryption** (documents, passwords or data transmissions)
- **physical security** such as **Closed Circuit Television (CC-TV)** and simple locks
- **regular updates** of **security patches** to applications and the network operating system.

Various software products can be used to protect a network. These include those shown in Table 9.03:

Unit links

For more on biometrics and encryption, please refer to Unit 7 – Organisational systems security, sections 7.2.1 and 7.2.2.
An example of creating strong passwords is demonstrated in Unit 8 – e-Commerce, section 8.2.4.

Table 9.03

Products	To protect the network against...
Firewall	...unwanted network traffic entering or leaving the network. A firewall can filter network traffic by application, protocol, IP address or port being used.
Antivirus	...**malware** (malicious software) that may be hostile, intrusive or annoying. This typically includes: viruses, Trojan horses and Worms. A **virus** is a section of malicious code that is usually integrated into an executable file that infects a network client when it attempts to 'open' it. A **Trojan horse** is a malicious program that, while pretending to be something innocent (and useful), installs a virus onto a network client. A **Worm** is a specialised form of virus that self-replicates itself and propagates over a network connection, travelling from networked client to networked client. An **antivirus program** will detect and remove these forms of malicious code.
Anti-spyware	...malware that is typically an annoyance but which can represent a security risk. Some spyware will log keystrokes ('keyloggers') made by the users, some will report browsing habits or forcefully display unwanted adverts that are connected to search queries.
Intrusion detection systems	...attacks on a network from outside forces (e.g. hackers) to gain access to sensitive data or applications. Intrusion detection systems are usually able to: • detect unusual network traffic • alert a network administrator or manager to the problem • log the suspect activity. More proactive IDS software may be able to autonomously adjust the settings on the network or the firewall to protect against an identified threat.

Unit links

For more on firewalls, antivirus and anti-spyware please refer to Unit 2 – Computer systems, section 2.3.

Braincheck 3

Match the network software's protection to its correct name!

A	Protects against **unwanted network traffic**	**1**	**Anti-spyware**
B	Protects against **malware that may be hostile, intrusive or annoying**	**2**	**Firewall**
C	Protects against **attacks on a network**	**3**	**Antivirus**
D	Protects against **malware that is typically an annoyance**	**4**	**IDS**

Make the Grade M3

An extension of themes explored in P6, M3 asks you to report on the risks to a business that are posed by insecure networks and how these risks can be minimised.

You will already have made a network secure for P6 so you should have a good idea of how to reduce the vulnerability of a business through poor network security. Reflect on section 9.4.2 and try to link these issues to the risks listed in section 9.4.1, e.g. 'We can reduce costs from data recovery of corrupted network data by having a comprehensive backup schedule.'

9.4.2 Risk-related business issues

Insecure networks pose a risk to the businesses that use them and their customers.

Risks that may occur include:

- loss of customer faith (leading to...)
- loss of business (impacting its income)
- legal implications (sensitive information being compromised)
- increased costs (e.g. repairs, compensation, data recovery)
- loss of confidentiality (implications for the Data Protection Act)
- loss of data integrity (implications for the Data Protection Act and everyday business operations)
- security issues (caused by malicious software, see 9.4.1)

It is vital that businesses have systems and procedures in place to deal with potential problems.

Unit links

Unit 9 is a **mandatory unit** for the Edexcel BTEC Level 3 National Diploma and National Extended Diploma in IT (Networking and Systems Support pathway) and **optional** for all other qualifications and pathways of this Level 3 IT family.

Qualification (pathway)	Mandatory	Optional	Specialist optional
Edexcel BTEC Level 3 National Certificate in Information Technology		✓	
Edexcel BTEC Level 3 National Subsidiary Diploma in Information Technology		✓	
Edexcel BTEC Level 3 National Diploma in Information Technology		✓	
Edexcel BTEC Level 3 National Extended Diploma in Information Technology		✓	
Edexcel BTEC Level 3 National Diploma in IT (Business)		✓	
Edexcel BTEC Level 3 National Extended Diploma in IT (Business)		✓	
Edexcel BTEC Level 3 National Diploma in IT (Networking and System Support)	✓		
Edexcel BTEC Level 3 National Extended Diploma in IT (Networking and System Support)	✓		
Edexcel BTEC Level 3 National Diploma in IT (Software Development)		✓	
Edexcel BTEC Level 3 National Extended Diploma in IT (Software Development)		✓	

There are specific links to the following units in the scheme:

Unit 5 – Managing networks
Unit 10 – Communication technologies
Unit 32 – Networked systems security

Achieving success

This particular unit has 11 criteria to meet: 6 Pass, 3 Merit and 2 Distinction.

For a Pass: You must achieve all 6 Pass criteria

For a Merit: You must achieve all 6 Pass and all 3 Merit criteria

For a Distinction: You must achieve all 6 Pass, all 3 Merit and both Distinction criteria.

Further reading

Dodd, A. Z. – *The Essential Guide to Telecommunications, 4th edition* (Prentice Hall, 2005) ISBN-10 0131487256, ISBN-13 978-0131487253

Hallberg, B. – *Networking: A Beginner's Guide, 5th Edition* (Osborne/McGraw-Hill US, 2009) ISBN-10 0071633553, ISBN-13 978-0071633550

Lowe, D. – *Networking All-in-One Desk Reference for Dummies,* 3rd Edition (John Wiley & Sons, 2008) ISBN-10 0470179155, ISBN-13 978-0470179154

Schiller, J. – *Mobile Communications, 2nd Edition* (Addison Wesley, 2003) ISBN-10 0321123816, ISBN-13 978-0321123817

Websites

www.howstuffworks.com	How Stuff Works
www.webopedia.com	Webopedia

Unit 10: Communication technologies

By the end of this unit you should be able to:

1. Understand the communication principles of computer networks
2. Know the main elements of data communications systems
3. Be able to implement different forms of network communications

Whether you are in school or college, passing this unit will involve being assessed. As with most BTEC schemes, the successful completion of various assessment criteria demonstrates your evidence of learning and the skills you have developed.

This unit has a mixture of pass, merit and distinction criteria. Generally you will find that merit and distinction criteria require a little more thought and evaluation before they can be completed.

The colour-coded grid below shows you the pass, merit and distinction criteria for this unit.

To achieve a pass grade you need to:	To achieve a merit grade you also need to:	To achieve a distinction grade you also need to:
P1 Explain how networks communicate		
P2 Identify communication protocols and models	**M1** Explain why communication protocols are important	**D1** Compare the OSI seven layer model and the TCP/IP model
P3 Identify different types of communication devices		
P4 Describe what data elements are and why they are important		
P5 Describe the principles of signal theory		
P6 Describe different transmission methods used	**M2** Explain why particular transmission methods are chosen in particular situations	**D2** Compare the effectiveness of different transmission methods
P7 Create direct network communication between two users	**M3** Assess the effectiveness of data transfer over wired and wireless networks	
P8 Set up interconnection devices for direct communication		

Introduction

Communication technologies is a 10-credit unit designed to introduce the learner to the theoretical and practical challenges of planning and using emerging communication technology to improve business productivity and performance.

The unit focuses on both the underlying communication technology and the principles that make it work and interoperate seamlessly with different systems worldwide.

How to read this chapter

This chapter is organised to match the content of the BTEC unit it represents. The following diagram shows the grading criteria that relate to each learning outcome.

You'll find colour-matching notes in each chapter about completing each grading criterion.

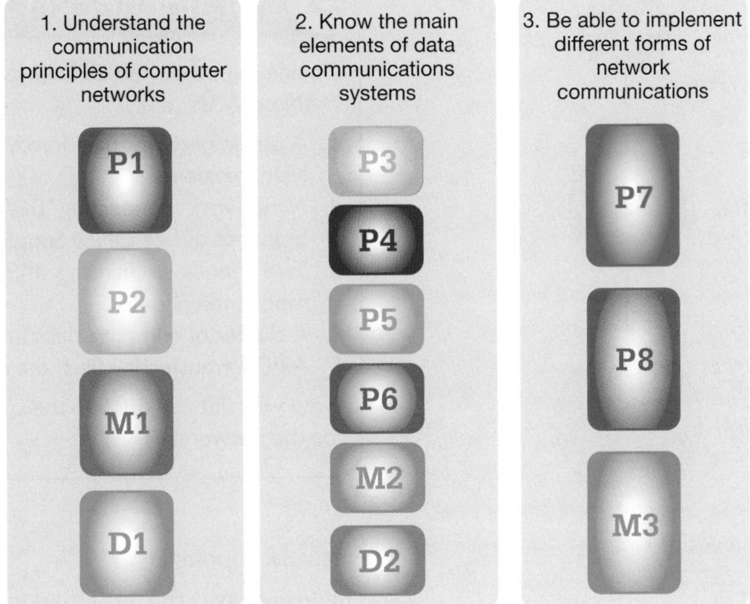

Figure 10.00

10.1 Understand the communication principles of computer networks

This section will cover the following grading criteria:

Make the Grade P1

P1 requires you to explain how networks communicate. This really links to the content in sections 10.1.1 through 10.1.5, inclusive. Your explanation will need to cover core concepts such as different network types, components and interconnection devices and the protocols required.

10.1.1 Computer networks

Network size

Every network has a determined size. Common network sizes include (in ascending order of size):

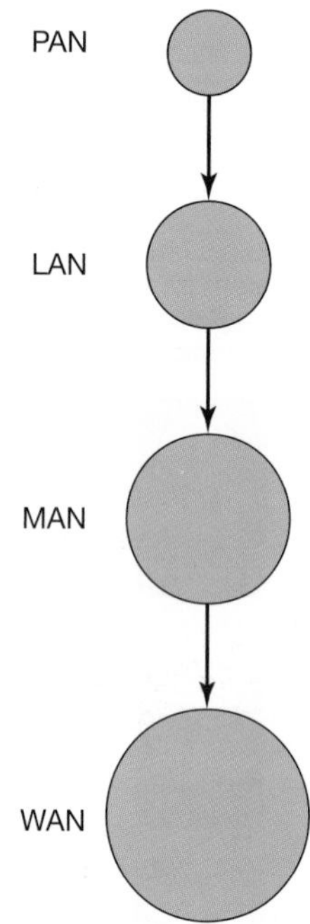

Figure 10.01 Network size

PAN (or Piconet)

A **Piconet** or **PAN** (**P**ersonal **A**rea **N**etwork) is a network of computing devices that use Bluetooth technology protocols to allow one master device to interconnect with up to seven slave devices. See IEEE 802.15.

LAN

A **LAN** (**L**ocal **A**rea **N**etwork) is a computer network that covers a local area, typically like a home, connecting nearby offices or small clusters of buildings such as a college. These typically use wired Ethernet (IEEE 802.3) or wireless Radio Frequency (RF) technology (IEEE 802.11).

MAN

A **MAN** (**M**etropolitan **A**rea **N**etwork) is a computer network that covers a town or city. This type of solution often relies on fibre-optic solutions.

Wireless **MAN**s (**WMAN**s using microwave technology) are becoming increasingly popular, see IEEE 802.16.

WAN

A **WAN** (**W**ide **A**rea **N**etwork) is a computer network (public or privately owned) that uses high-speed, long-distance communications technology (e.g. telephone lines and satellite links) to connect computers over long distances.

WANs can be used to connect LANs together, e.g. geographically distant branches of the same organisation.

B Braincheck 1

Decide whether the following are PAN, LAN, MAN or WAN:

1. A public network paid for by a city council for all its residents.
2. A network connecting the various national branches of Lee Office Supplies.
3. Two friends exchanging .MP3 songs via their mobile telephones.
4. A cluster of computer labs in a local school.
5. A PDA transferring files to a notebook.

How well did you do? See the supporting website for the answers!

Network topologies

The **topology** is the term used to describe the network's shape or form.

In simple terms, this is how the **nodes** (servers, workstations etc.) are physically or logically connected.

Common topologies include:

Star

One **central node** with **outlying** nodes.

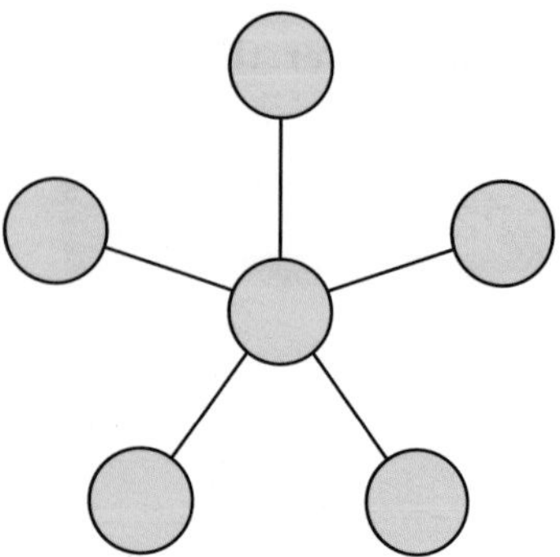

Figure 10.02 Star

Ring

A series of nodes connected **daisy-chain** style.

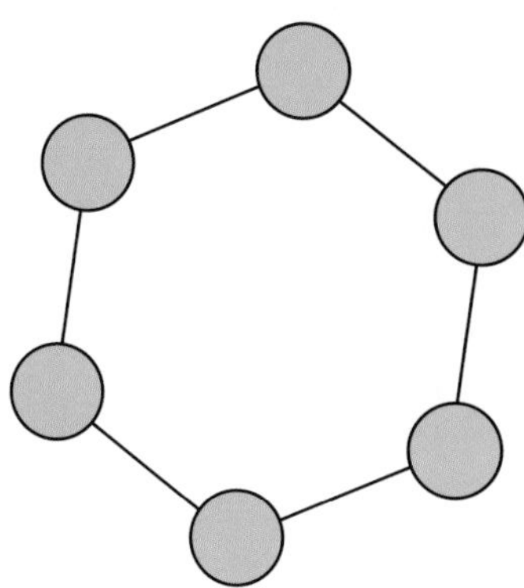

Figure 10.03 Ring

Mesh (fully connected)

Each node **interconnected** with others.

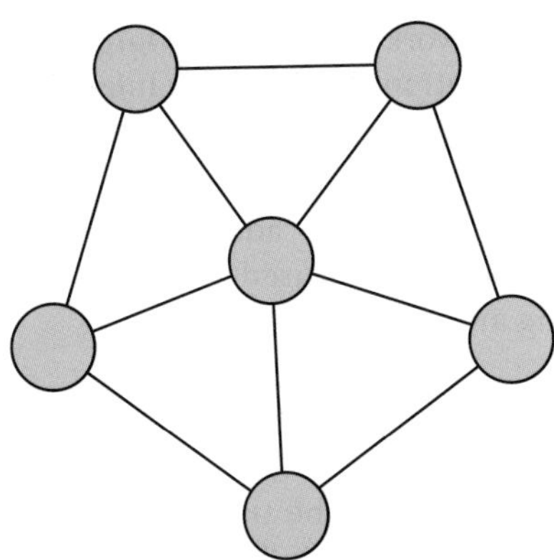

Figure 10.04 Mesh

Tree

Nodes are linked in a **hierarchical structure**.

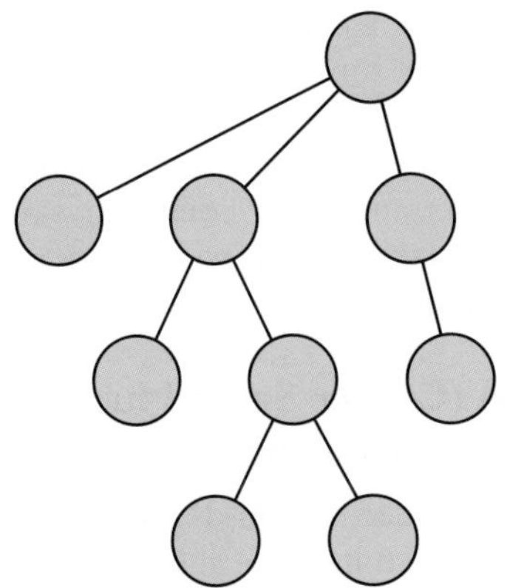

Figure 10.05 Tree

Bus

Different devices connected from a **common backbone** (a single run of cable)

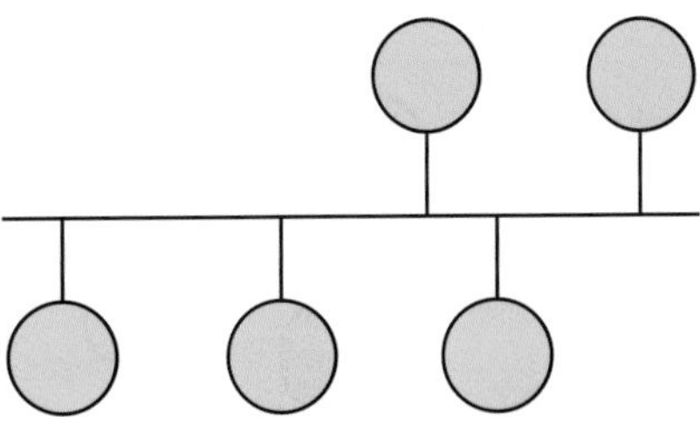

Figure 10.06 Bus

Network services

A number of different network services are available. These will be detailed in turn below.

Packet-switched

This is the opposite of a **circuit-switched network** (where a permanent circuit is made between two nodes before communication can take place).

In a **packet-switched network**, data is divided into packets (see 10.2.3) and then moved from source node to destination node through a number of different nodes (see Figure 10.07).

Depending on the nodes available, each packet may take a different route (see section 10.2.3).

ISDN

ISDN or **I**ntegrated **S**ervices **D**igital **N**etwork is a standard devised by the **CCITT/ITU** (**C**omité **C**onsultatif **I**nternational **T**élégraphique et **T**éléphonique/**I**nternational **T**elecommunication **U**nion) for digital data transmission. This type of network service occurs over ordinary telephone copper wire and thus is still popular where faster DSL and cable services are not available.

ISDN represented an upgrade from dial-up narrowband services (which relied on modems). Any home or businesses customers wanting to use this early broadband service would need to install an **ISDN adapter**.

Typical ISDN connections gave a bandwidth of about 128 Kbps. At the time (mid- to late 1990s) this was much faster than the best modem speed of 28.8 Kbps so proved an attractive option.

ISDN has been mainly superseded in the UK through the mass availability of relatively inexpensive DSL and cable services.

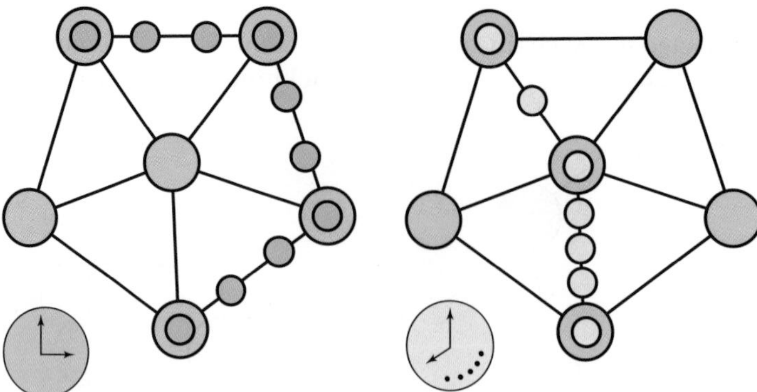

Figure 10.07 Packet-switched network

ATM

ATM or **A**synchronous **T**ransfer **M**ode is the international standard for dedicated-connection switching technology; a connection between source and destination nodes must be made before any data can be sent.

It organises digital data (voice, video and data) into fixed-length 53-byte cell units. This is different to packet-switched networks where the size of the data packets may vary.

Fixed-length cells allow processing to be easily implemented by hardware, resulting in faster processing and reductions in transit delay.

Broadband (e.g. DSL)

Traditional telephone lines carrying voice conversations in an analogue signal form don't make full use of the transmission medium's available bandwidth.

Digital-signal based **DSL** (**D**igital **S**ubscriber **L**ine) uses the unused frequencies available on the copper wire to transmit data traffic in addition to voice. This means that DSL allows voice and high-speed data to be sent simultaneously over the same connection.

A DSL **splitter** (also known as a **micro-filter**), located at the customer's end, separates voice and data signals.

WAP (see section 10.1.3)

Network software (e.g. NOS)

A **NOS** (**N**etwork **O**perating **S**ystem) is written specifically to support networking (especially LANs).

Its functions can include:

- networking protocols (e.g. TCP/IP)
- mechanisms for sharing files and resources such as printers
- facilities for managing administrative functions such as security.

NetBIOS (**Net**work **B**asic **I**nput/**O**utput **S**ystem) is an **API** (**A**pplication **P**rogramming **I**nterface) that allows other applications to communicate with a LAN.

Originally created by IBM (International Business Machines) it was later adopted by Novell and Microsoft. NetBIOS is used in modern Ethernet, Token ring and Windows® networks.

Access methods (e.g. CSMA/CD, CSMA/CA, Token passing)

Access methods describe the ways in which a device knows **when** it can talk on a network.

CSMA/CD (**C**arrier **S**ense **M**ultiple **A**ccess **C**ollision **D**etection)

This works as follows:

1. Device '1' wants to transmit data so first checks the channel for a carrier.
2. If no carrier is sensed, device '1' can transmit, however. . .
3. . . .if two devices transmit simultaneously, a collision occurs and each computer stands back and waits a random interval before attempting to transmit again.

CSMA/CA (**C**arrier **S**ense **M**ultiple **A**ccess with **C**ollision **A**voidance)

CSMA/CA is similar but sends a **R**equest-**T**o-**S**end (**RTS**) signal, which must be acknowledged by other nodes before it transmits.

Token passing

Token passing is a network access method particular to **token-ring networks**.

Token-ring networks are a form of LAN developed and supported by IBM. They typically run at 4.16 or 16 Mbps over a ring topology (see section 10.1.1).

In a token-ring network, access is very orderly as it is based on the possession of a small frame called a **token**. Having a token gives a node the 'right' to talk.

In order to talk, a node:

1. Captures a token as it moves around the ring (see Figure 10.08):

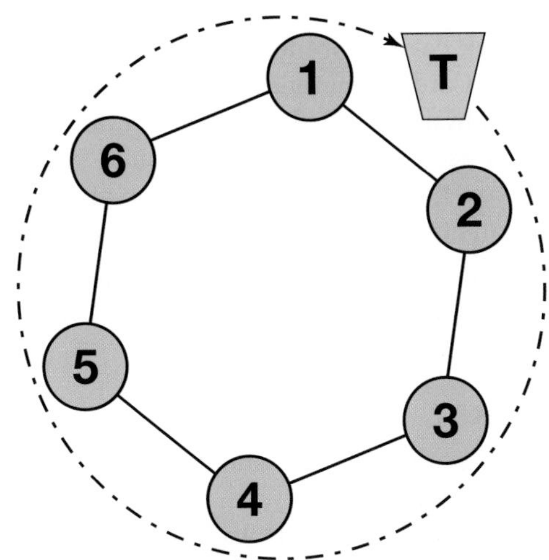

Figure 10.08 Token passing

2. Inserts its data, target node address and control information into the token frame (see Figure 10.09):
3. Changes the token frame to a data frame (see Figure 10.10):

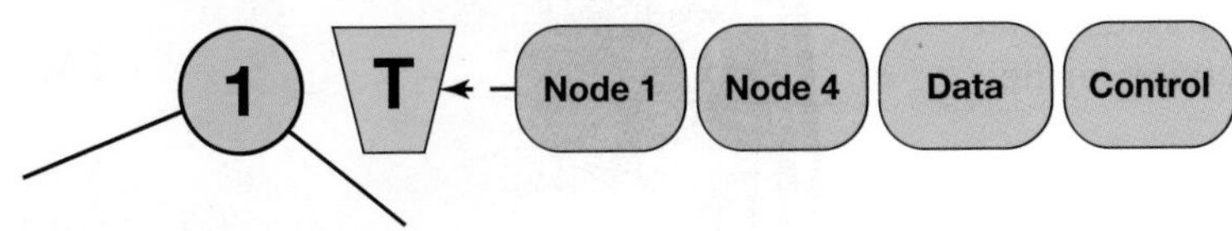

Figure 10.09 Token frame

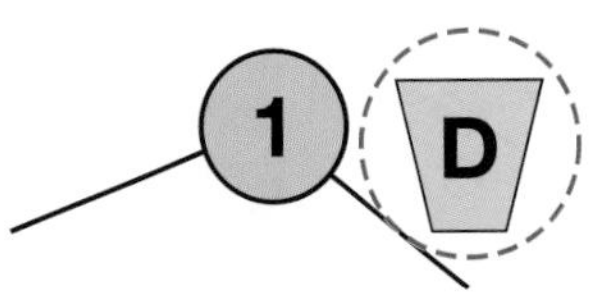

Figure 10.10 Data frame

4. Node 1 then transmits the frame around the token ring towards the destination node.

   Nodes not targeted by the data frame just pass the token on.

   The target node opens the data frame and reads the data stored inside (see Figure 10.11).

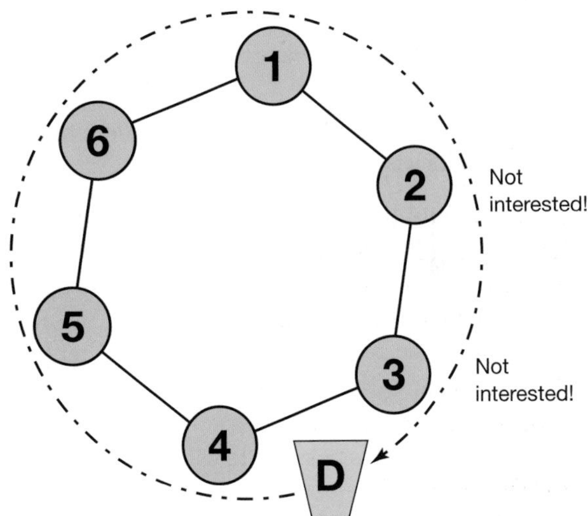

Figure 10.11 Destination node

5. After processing its data, the target node releases the data frame, and after a complete circuit, it finds itself back at its sending node. The sender node removes the frame and generates a new token (see Figure 10.12):

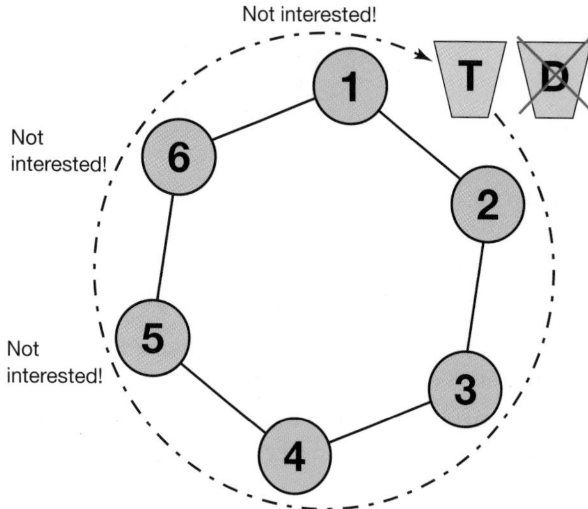

Figure 10.12 Generating a new token

6. This new token is then passed around to the next node wishing to talk.

The important thing to remember about the token passing access method is that collisions cannot occur.

While the data frame is circling the ring, no free token is on the network, meaning that other stations wanting to transmit just have to wait until a new one is generated.

Because of this, it is possible to calculate the maximum amount of time a node will have to wait to transmit; this is referred to as being **deterministic**.

Token rings and token passing are laid down in the IEEE 802.5 standards.

10.1.2 Network components

Aside from cables and connectors (see 10.2.6), a network consists of a number of typical components. These include the components detailed below.

Server

A **server** is typically a power computer system that provides some form of processing service for network clients (or other servers).

Servers tend to be well specified (powerful CPU(s), large RAM and hard drive capacity) and have **U**ninterruptible **P**ower **S**upplies (**UPS**) to keep them going during an electrical power cut.

Typical services provided by a server include:

- **mail server** for processing email (electronic mail) requests
- **web server** for processing **HTTP** (**H**yper**t**ext **T**ransfer **P**rotocol) requests for **HTML** (**H**yper**t**ext **M**arkup **L**anguage) files and associated assets (images, video, sound etc.)
- **file server** for managing access to shared network drives and folders.
- **print server** for managing print queues to network printing facilities.

Workstation

A **workstation** is a common name for a computer system, particularly one operating within a business environment and connected to a network.

Network cards

A **network card** (more formally a **NIC** – **N**etwork **I**nterface **C**ard), sometimes called a network adaptor, is a physical layer device (see section 10.1.4) which is used to transmit data from a computer system to a target node via some form of transmission media (Figure 10.13).

Depending on the type of transmission media, a number of different types of network card are available.

Ethernet

Ethernet is a wired card, offering a RJ45 connection. Ethernet cards may be plugged into older **ISA** (**I**ndustry **S**tandard **A**rchitecture) or **PCI** (**P**eripheral **C**omponent **I**nterconnect) slots on a motherboard. Like any other device, drivers for the operating system installed will be required before the card will work properly.

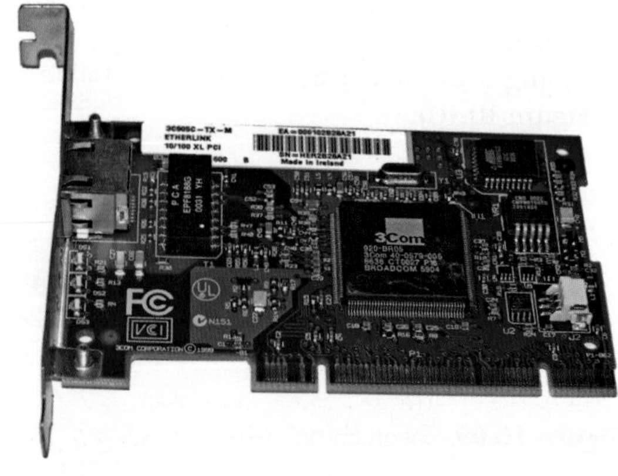

Figure 10.13 PCI Network interface card

Modern motherboards have **onboard LAN** – Ethernet technology built into the motherboard as a single microprocessor (Figure 10.14).

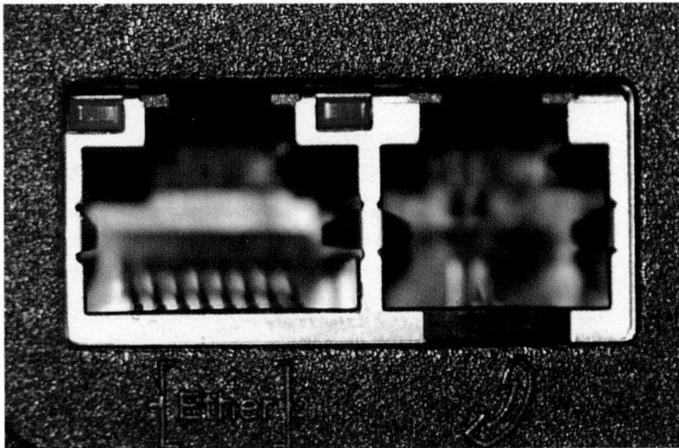

Figure 10.14 Onboard Ethernet (RJ45) and smaller modem (RJ11) port

PCMCIA (**P**ersonal **C**omputer **M**emory **C**ard **I**nternational **A**ssociation) Ethernet adaptors are also available for notebooks although onboard LAN is now more commonplace (see Figure 10.15).

Wireless

Wireless connectivity is very often built into modern portable devices such as PDAs and notebooks. Where wireless functionality isn't available, PCI, USB and PCMCIA wireless adaptors are commercially available.

Figure 10.15 PCMCIA wireless NIC adaptor

Token ring

Token-ring networks (see section 10.1.1) are not compatible with Ethernet networks. As a result, specific network cards must be used which process data in a way that is compatible with the **deterministic approach** used on a token ring. Physically, they are not dissimilar from their Ethernet counterparts (Figure 10.16).

Figure 10.16 PCMCIA token ring adaptor

10.1.3 Interconnection devices

A number of different devices are used to connect together different aspects of a network.

These are detailed below.

Repeater

A **repeater** is a device that can be used to extend cable runs and, as a result, the physical size of a network. One of the biggest problems with long cables is **signal attenuation** – the decrease in the signal's strength as it travels over distance.

A repeater is simply an electronic device containing a **transceiver** (transmitter and receiver) that receives, **amplifies** ('boosts') and then **retransmits** the signal. At no point is it aware of what the signal actually represents (it doesn't know that it's network data).

Hub

Also known as a **multiport repeater**, a **hub** performs the same basic function as the repeater. The number of ports (which typically can be up to 16) allows a number of different network devices to be connected together.

Because hubs are not 'intelligent' (they are not interested in the data, only the electrical signals), any incoming signal is retransmitted to all ports of the hub, whether the transmission is targeted to its connected device or not.

Hubs are generally cheaper than switches and therefore, after a **cross-over cable**, present the most inexpensive way of creating a simple LAN.

Hubs extend the **collision domain** – the network segment in which transmitted signals may clash (see section 10.1.1 CSMA/CD).

Switch

Switches are aesthetically similar to a hub, however this is just superficial. Inside, a switch can filter and forward packets between different LAN segments. Because of this segmentation, a switch can improve network performance by reducing competition for available bandwidth (see Figure 10.17).

When a packet of data is received, it is only forwarded onto the appropriate port for the intended recipient (by examining the target node's **MAC address**), thereby reducing unnecessary network traffic – compare this to the 'boost and repeat it all' tactic of the hub.

A switch can therefore be used to **reduce** the collision domain through segmentation.

Figure 10.17 USB powered 5 port 10/100 Mbit switch (RJ45 sockets at the rear)

Router

A **router** (Figure 10.18) is a complex device, making decisions about which of several possible paths should be used to relay network data (see mesh topology, section 10.1.1).

Figure 10.18 A router. 7 x RJ45 connectors for the LAN, 1 x RJ45 for a WAN

It does this by using a **routing protocol** to learn about the network, and has **algorithms** to help it select the best route based on several criteria (its **routing metrics**).

Sometimes the metric may be **time-based** (which is quicker), sometimes the metric may be **reliability-based**. Uniquely, routes are regularly updated and, as part of a packet-switching solution, two consecutive packets could travel completely different routes.

Most network operating systems have a **traceroute** command or utility, which provides information about the route being taken by a sample test packet (Figure 10.19).

Each node along the route is called a **hop**.

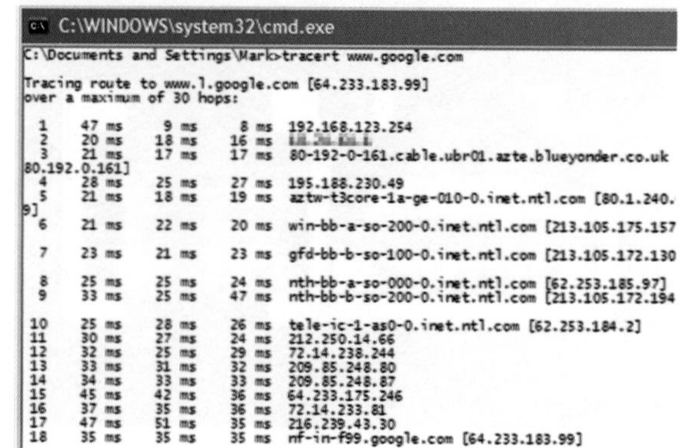

Figure 10.19 A traceroute – following 18 hops from gateway to remote host

Bridge

A **bridge** is a network device that is used to connect two different network segments, usually ones that use the same communication protocol (though not always).

Unlike a repeater, the bridge is usually intelligent (it learns) and can make decisions about which packets of data should move from one segment to another by examining the target MAC address. In this regard, they are similar to a switch and indeed are often described as a switch on an Ethernet network. In addition, they can remove targets from their 'forward' list if they haven't had contact with the destination for some time; this lets the segment on the other side of the bridge remain fluid (i.e. devices can be added and removed without incident). A **wireless bridge**, a more recent invention, allows wired extension of a wireless network.

Gateway

A **gateway** is a device that acts as a direct interface between two different networks.

It is the gateway's job to translate from one network's set of protocols to those of the other network so that its data can be relayed out of the network.

It also performs a routing function so acts like a router; on a TCP/IP network, any data that is destined for a host not on the current network is forwarded to the gateway for processing.

A gateway may be a dedicated device or a computer that has suitable hardware (two network interface cards, one for connecting to each network) and appropriate routing software.

WAP (Wireless Access Point)

A **wireless access point** may be used to connect wireless nodes to a wired network, forming what is described as an **Infrastructure Mode** (Figure 10.21).

Figure 10.20 A wireless access point showing external antenna and RJ45 socket

A WAP is wired traditionally into a switch or router to gain access to the wider network (see Figure 10.21).

From this point, the WAP usually broadcasts an **SSID** (Service **S**et **Id**entifier) – a name (up to 32 characters) that is used to identify itself to listening wireless devices. Broadcasting an SSID is a common practice, but not ideal from a security point of view.

In order to prevent unauthorised connection, wireless access points typically feature security **(MAC filtering)** and **encryption** facilities (WEP, WPA, WPA2 etc.).

The MAC filtering prevents devices with non-approved MAC addresses from connecting wirelessly. This **access device** list is set up via the WAP's web-based user interface (Figure 10.22).

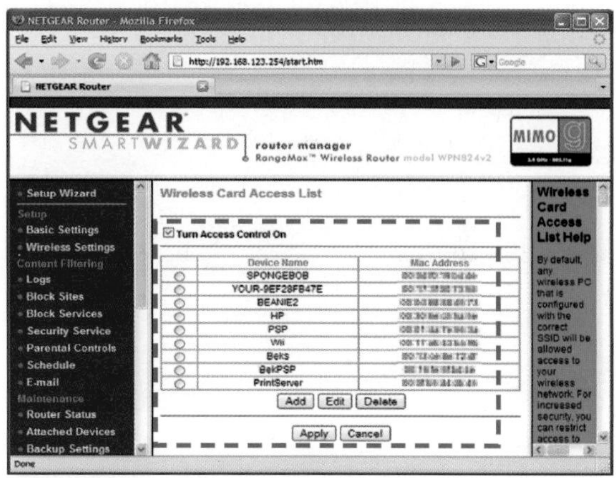

Figure 10.22 Filtering wireless devices by their MAC address

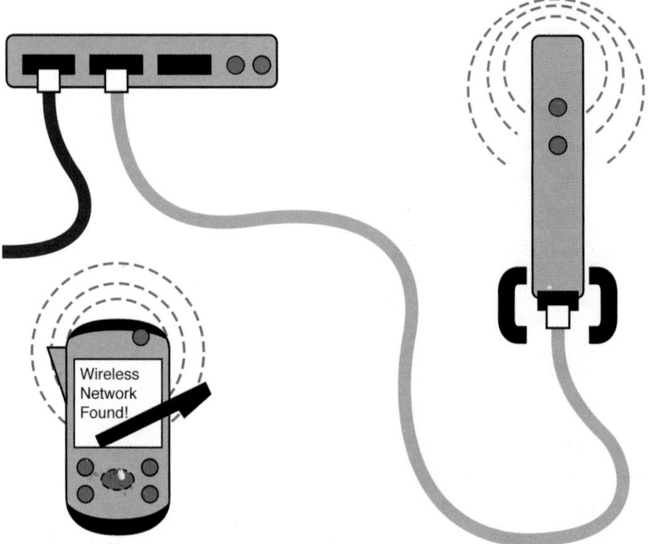

Figure 10.21 A PDA with wireless access connects to a WAP

In addition, if encryption is enabled (and it really should be), a connecting device would need to have the correct text or hexadecimal key code in order to decrypt the transmitted data packets.

Activity 1

Planning a SoHo network

Your employer, Lee Office Supplies, is planning to network their current premises and has asked you to purchase equipment necessary to complete the task.

The building has a main office (ten PCs plus one printer), reception (one PC), the manager's office (one PC) and a storeroom (two PCs).

You have been asked to:

- supply all PCs with internet access
- share the office printer with all ten PCs.

Draw up plans for this network, including costs for any network devices that must be purchased.

Activity 2

Building a simple LAN

Use the network diagram in Figure 10.23 as a blueprint to build a small LAN in a computer lab.

Shopping list:

4 × PCs with network operating systems (e.g. Microsoft Windows®)

2 × wireless network cards (PCI)

1 × wireless access point (WAP)

1 × switch (minimum four port)

2 × wired network cards (PCI)

3 × Cat 5 UTP cables

The best way of checking your LAN is to assign each PC an IP address in the range 192.168.123.X where X can be any value between 5 and 10. No IP must be duplicated. Use a ping command to check connectivity.

Make the Grade P2

P2 requires you to be able to identify different connection models (e.g. OSI, TCP/IP) and different protocols, so familiarise yourself with sections 10.1.4 and 10.1.5.

A leaflet or a few presentation slides could help evidence your understanding.

10.1.4 Models

Network technology comes in many different shapes, sizes and configurations and from many different manufacturers worldwide. Originally manufacturers drew up their own proprietary standards, which understandably generated compatibility issues.

In order to ensure **interoperability**, models were developed to provide guidance standards for creating seamless network communication, even though equipment and software would be created by different companies.

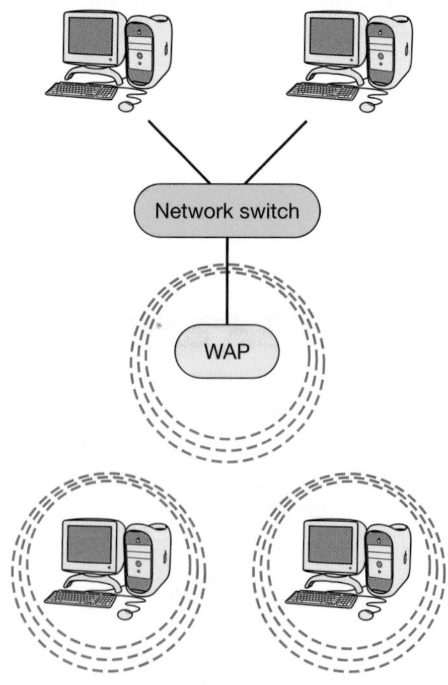

Figure 10.23

Perhaps the most well-known standard in communication technology is the **OSI** (**O**pen **S**ystem **I**nterconnect) model as pioneered by **ISO** (**I**nternational **S**tandards **O**rganization) back in 1984.

OSI

Commonly known as the **seven layer model**, OSI is shown in Figure 10.24.

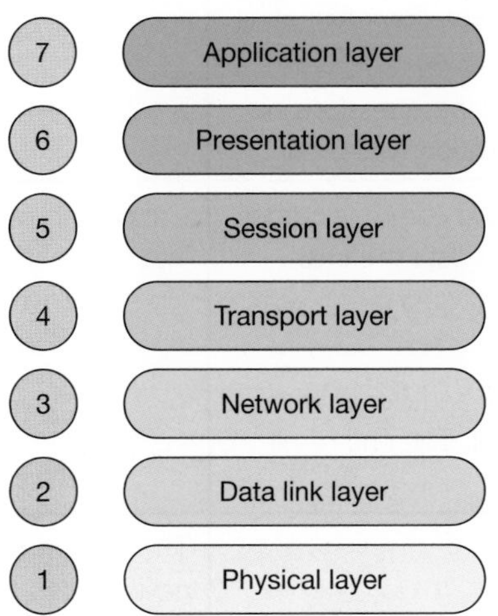

Figure 10.24

What does OSI do?

As a conceptual framework, OSI defines all of the basic services a network should provide.

As noted, the model is divided into seven layers, each of which plays a key role in processing data and requests, enabling data to be transmitted between any two points in a network. Each layer interacts directly with the one beneath it and provides functionality for the layer above it.

> **Help**
>
> *How to remember the OSI model*
>
> Many **mnemonics** (memory aids) exist to help IT practitioners remember the seven layer names and their correct order. Here are two common ones that may help:
>
> **(P)**lease **(D)**o **(N)**ot **(T)**hrow **(S)**ausage **(P)**izza **(A)**way
>
> **(A)**ll **(P)**eople **(S)**eem **(T)**o **(N)**eed **(D)**ata **(P)**rocessing

What does each stage do?

Table 10.01 describes the purpose of each layer and notes any DCE or DTE that are associated.

Table 10.01

Layer#	Layer Name	Purpose	Features
7	Application	A layer providing network access for applications (e.g. web browser) A number of specific network protocols may occur here: • FTP (File Transfer Protocol) • HTTP (Hypertext Transfer Protocol) • SMTP (Simple Mail Transfer Protocol) • DNS (Domain Name Server) • TFTP (Tiny File Transfer Protocol), • NFS (Network File System) • Telnet (Terminal Emulation) • Rlogin (Remote login)	Data
6	Presentation	This layer translates data into a format usable by the application layer above. In particular it is responsible for: • Translation • Encryption • Data compression	Data (file formats include ASCII, .BMP, .JPG, .MPEG etc.)

Layer#	Layer Name	Purpose	Features
5	Session	This layer allows applications on connecting systems to establish a session. It also provides synchronisation between communicating computers. In addition it manages and terminates these sessions as needed, determining how communications will occur.	Data
4	Transport	This layer is responsible for end-to-end communications. It segments and reassembles data into data streams. It establishes, maintains and ensures orderly termination of virtual circuits. It can also detect faults in data transfer and can provide recovery and information flow control. The end result needs to be a reliable service.	Data is encapsulated into segments.
3	Network	The layer manages: • IP (Internet Protocol) addressing • Path selection • Packet routing	The most important device at this level is the router. Data is encapsulated into packets.
2	Data link	Provides point-to-point data transmission services by managing the physical layer below. This layer has two sub-layers: • Logical Link Control (LLC) • Media Access Control (MAC)	Devices such as network interface cards, switches and bridges. Data is encapsulated into frames.
1	Physical	The lowest level, it is concerned with the 'nuts & bolts' of the network; the electrical, the mechanical and timing issues etc.	Transmission media, e.g. cables and connectors, hubs, repeaters, DCE and DTE. Data is in bits.

Help

What are the advantages of breaking the model into separate layers?

There are many, but the main advantages are:

- easier to develop network components
- easier to develop full networks
- easier to troubleshoot network problems
- easier to successfully manage a network and its resources
- layers can be improved in isolation without affecting others

TCP/IP model

As its name suggests, the popular TCP/IP model consists of two separate, but connected, parts.

Both TCP and IP were developed by the United States' Department of **D**efense **A**dvanced **R**esearch **P**rojects **A**gency **(DARPA)** to connect a number of different networks together to form a much larger inter-network ('Arpanet', which became the 'Internet').

The inter-network had to be reliable as, even though it was envisaged that network links would be broken in times of armed conflict, communication and services would still be required.

As a result DARPA designed TCP/IP to be robust, automatically recovering from any node failure; data would just get routed to the destination another way.

Let's examine each in a bit more detail:

TCP (Transmission Control Protocol)

Transmission Control Protocol is a **connection-oriented** transport protocol.

TCP's primary job is to verify that data has been correctly delivered from source node to destination node.

In addition TCP can:

- detect errors
- detect duplicate messages, discarding them as necessary
- detect lost data
- request retransmission of data until satisfied that it is both correct and complete
- use flow control to slow data transfer if the receiving node can't keep up.

TCP works in conjunction with IBM's NETBIOS (Network Basic Input/Output System) to complete this task.

IP (Internet Protocol)

As defined by IETF RFC791, IP's primary job is to **move data packets** from one node to the next node.

IP forwards each data packet based on a four octet (8 bits) destination address (called the IP address). For example:

Sender IP 192.168.123.**10**

Destination IP 192.168.123.**20**

Gateway IP 192.168.123.**254**

In this example, host '10' wants to send data to host '20'. All is fine as both machines are on the same network (192.168.123.0).

However, if a different destination IP (e.g. 64.233.183.99) had been encountered, it would have been forwarded to the **Gateway IP** (192.168.123.254) for routing out to another network.

Although the best-known version of IP is **IPv4**, it has its problems – too few available IP addresses! A newer version, **IPv6** resolves this by having **128-bit addresses** (instead of 32 bits).

IP classes

Although IPv6 has been defined (increasing the addressing space to accommodate greater numbers of network aware devices), it is version IPv4 that is still in widespread use.

There are a number of IP classes currently in use. These are shown in Table 10.02.

Table 10.02

Class A	Network addresses 1.0.0.0 through 127.0.0.0.	N.H.H.H A 24-bit host part, allows for 1.6 million hosts per network.
Class B	Network addresses 128.0.0.0 through 191.255.0.0	N.N.H.H A 16-bit host part, allows for 16,320 nets with 65,024 hosts each.
Class C	Network addresses 192.0.0.0 through 223.255.255.0	N.N.N.H An 8-bit host part, allows for nearly 2 million networks with up to 254 hosts.
Classes D, E and F	These network addresses, in the range 224.0.0.0 through 254.0.0.0, are either experimental or are reserved for special purposes (e.g. IP Multicast).	

Some addresses are **reserved**, e.g. 127.0.0.1 is assigned as the '**Loopback**' interface.

This lets a networked computer system act like a closed circuit; any IP data packets sent to this address are returned to the client just as if they had just arrived from some other network (Figure 10.25).

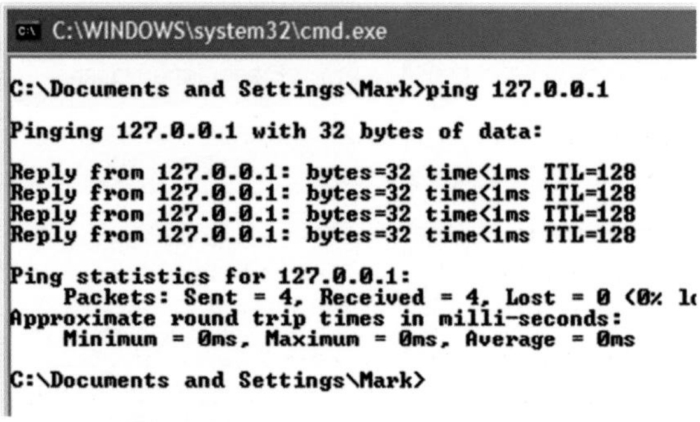

```
C:\WINDOWS\system32\cmd.exe

C:\Documents and Settings\Mark>ping 127.0.0.1

Pinging 127.0.0.1 with 32 bytes of data:

Reply from 127.0.0.1: bytes=32 time<1ms TTL=128
Reply from 127.0.0.1: bytes=32 time<1ms TTL=128
Reply from 127.0.0.1: bytes=32 time<1ms TTL=128
Reply from 127.0.0.1: bytes=32 time<1ms TTL=128

Ping statistics for 127.0.0.1:
    Packets: Sent = 4, Received = 4, Lost = 0 (0% l
Approximate round trip times in milli-seconds:
    Minimum = 0ms, Maximum = 0ms, Average = 0ms

C:\Documents and Settings\Mark>
```

Figure 10.25 A ping is used to successfully test the Loopback interface

> **Make the Grade** D1
>
> D1 asks you to compare the OSI seven layer model with the TCP/IP model.
>
> Clearly, although they have some noticeable differences, Figure 10.26 shows which layers in each model act as rough equivalents (performing similar functions).
>
> Use this diagram as a basis to create your own evidence; a poster or leaflet would be ideal.

This lets the user develop and test networking software without ever using a 'live' network.

In addition, **hosts '0'** and **'255'** are not permitted as these represent the number and broadcast address of the network, respectively.

An introduction to the subnet mask

The **subnet mask** is used to determine which parts of an IP address belong to the network (N) and which parts belong to the host (H).

In an example such as 192.168.123.45 (which is a class C address) the subnet mask (by default) will be: 255.255.255.0.

This would indicate that the first three octets (192.168.123) are the network address and the connected device is host number 45.

The TCP/IP model

The TCP/IP model has fewer levels than the ISO OSI. However, there is clear mapping between the TCP/IP and the ISO OSI as shown by Figure 10.26.

Table 10.03 summarises this in more detail.

Table 10.03

TCP layer #	Purpose
1	Defines the device driver and network hardware (NIC – Network Interface Card).
2	This layer handles basic communication, addressing and routing. Protocols seen here include **IP** (as discussed), **ARP** (**A**ddress **R**esolution **P**rotocol), **ICMP** (**I**nternet **C**ontrol **M**essage **P**rotocol) and **IGMP** (**I**nternet **G**roup **M**anagement **P**rotocol).
3	This layer segments data into packets for transporting over the network. Both **TCP** and **UDP** (**U**ser **D**atagram **P**rotocol) work at this layer. UDP is similar to TCP but less reliable; it doesn't acknowledge or guarantee safe delivery of data.
4	This layer deals with TCP/IP applications such as **Telnet, FTP, SMTP, Traceroute** etc.

10.1.5 Protocols

A number of different communication protocols may be found in a modern data communications network. Protocols are essential as they lay down

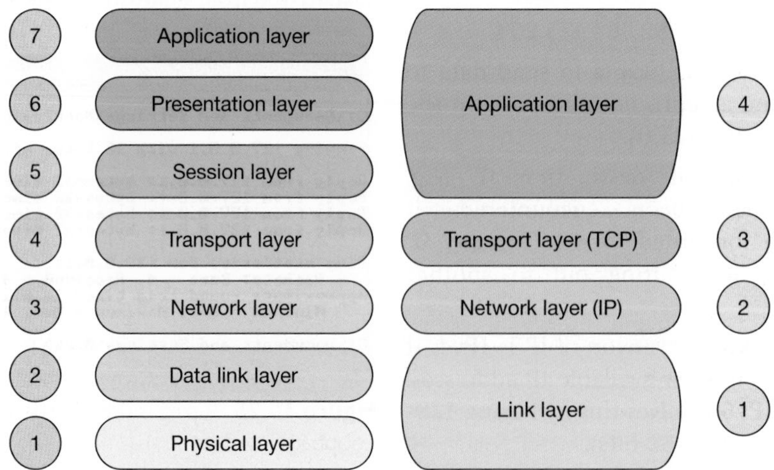

Figure 10.26

rules of communication **between** devices, and are specifically designed for the environments, media types and hardware limitations present. The following section describes a number of common technologies, some wired, some wireless.

Bluetooth

Bluetooth is a wireless communication technology that was originally developed by Ericsson back in 1997.

Named after King Harald Bluetooth (Harald I of Denmark), Bluetooth is a popular IT industry specification for exchanging data between portable devices (mobile telephones, PDAs), printers and notebook PCs. Although some computer systems have onboard Bluetooth, inexpensive third party USB Bluetooth adaptors are common and relatively inexpensive, adding the facility to any PC.

Bluetooth technology uses the short-range, unlicensed radio frequency of 2.45 GHz.

As noted in section 10.1.1, Bluetooth can create secure PANs (Personal Area Networks or Piconet); connecting PCs together for the purpose of exchanging data and sharing resources and services.

Figure 10.27 A Belkin Bluetooth USB adaptor

Make the Grade — M1

M1 asks you to explain why communication protocols are important.

This is not a question requiring you to list all relevant protocols. Instead, you should try to focus on why different protocols are needed (e.g. Bluetooth for low-power consumption data transfer on mobile devices). This could be evidenced through a simple viva, presentation or leaflet.

Each Bluetooth device is identified by its own unique 48-bit number. Upon discovery, a Bluetooth device will reveal: its name (manufacturer and model), its device class (e.g. a PDA) and a list of services it can provide – the latter being supplied by the **S**ervice **D**iscovery **P**rotocol **(SDP)**.

In order to share these services, devices have to become **trusted**, this means sharing a **PIN** (**P**ersonal **I**dentification **N**umber). The PIN is typically **alphanumeric** and up to 16 characters long.

Scorecard – *Bluetooth*

– Bluetooth supports data transfer rates of up to 2.1 Mbps.
– **Limited range** on low power (<10 metres is common).
+ Bluetooth **can penetrate** walls.
+ **Omni-directional** – no direct **Line of Sight** (**LOS**) needed between devices.
+ Has **low-power consumption**; ideal for mobile devices.
+ Use of **trusted pairs** to form secure connections.
+ **Configuration** is fairly simple.

IrDA

IrDA, which is a registered term for the **I**nf**r**ared **D**ata **A**ssociation, a non-profit organisation, specifies worldwide standards for infrared (IR) data transmission.

Members of the IrDA include a number of well-known 'household name' companies that specialise in consumer electronics and telecommunications.

Infrared (often abbreviated to 'IR') is a form of electromagnetic radiation that has a wavelength longer than visible light but shorter than that of microwaves and was discovered in the early nineteenth century.

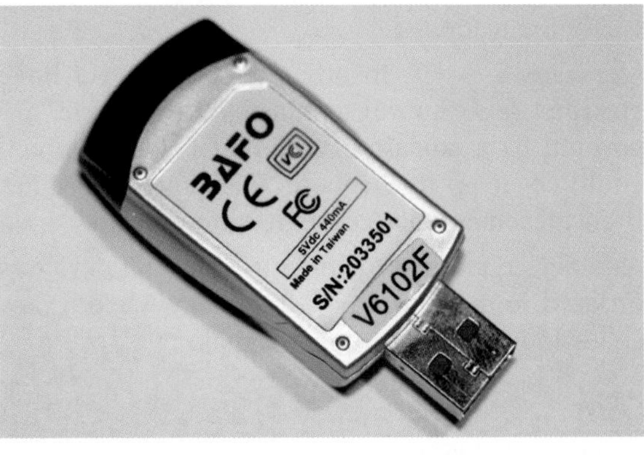

Figure 10.28 A BAFO irDA USB adaptor

Among its modern applications is short-range data communication, typically between portable devices such as mobile telephones and PDAs. You may be more familiar with IR as the method used to change TV channels via a remote control handset.

Infrared works by device 1 firing **L**ight **E**mitting **D**iodes (**LEDs**) to create **data pulses**, which are then received by **photodiodes** in a second device.

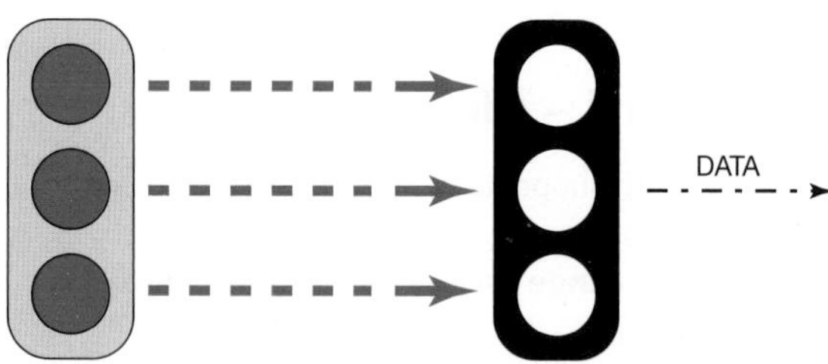

Figure 10.29 How infrared works

Excited by the light pulses received, the photodiodes generate electrical current, which becomes an electronic signal for device 2 to process.

Scorecard – *Infrared*

- IrDA-Data standard has speeds of up to 16 Mbps but is usually much slower.
- IR typically has a **short range** (limited to a few metres).
- IR **cannot penetrate** walls or solid objects.
- **Line of sight** (**LOS**) is required for IR to work effectively.

\+ It's a tried and tested technology – it has been used for many years.

Cellular radio (e.g. GSM/UMTS, WAP, WML)

Mobile telephones act as **radio transceivers**, meaning that they can both transmit and receive radio waves. These waves can be converted into voice or data messages depending on the type of call being made.

Messages are sent to other telephones via **base stations** (also known as **masts**). Large areas are covered by a **mosaic** of different cells. Each cell could cover up to 5 square miles and sometimes their placement may cause them to overlap.

As a device moves from area to area, the device is ordered to move to a new frequency when a new cell is found with a stronger signal.

GSM

GSM (**G**lobal **S**ystem for **M**obile communications) is a popular standard for mobile telephones in Europe and the rest of the world, providing a customer base of over 1.5 billion people. GSM communication has a narrow bandwidth and, as a result, is primarily used for voice communication.

GSM standards are referred to as **2G** (or **2nd generation**) because they use **digital signals** to communicate; earlier devices had used **analogue signals** and are now retroactively referred to as 1G, although this term was never used then.

UMTS

UMTS (**U**niversal **M**obile **T**elecommunications **S**ystem) is a **3G** (or **3rd generation**) standard that supports broadband, data packet-based transmission of text, music, video and digitised voice.

An extension of GSM, it supports data rates up to a theoretical 2 Mbps; fast enough to support live video streaming for films, television, sports events and video telephony.

WAP

WAP (**W**ireless **A**pplication **P**rotocol) is a set of communication protocols that allows mobile telephones to access online services and in particularly the world wide web (Figure 10.30).

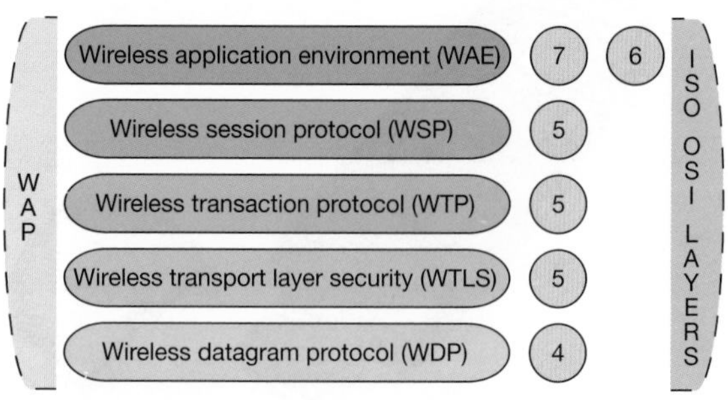

Figure 10.30 WAP

WAP was originated by four companies: Phone.com, Ericsson, Motorola and Nokia.

WAP content is created in **WML** (**W**ireless **M**arkup **L**anguage), similar to HTML and XML-compliant, which is specifically designed for portable devices which have:

- limited bandwidth
- small screen size
- modest memory (RAM)
- short battery life
- low-powered CPU
- limited user interface controls.

```
<?xml version="1.0"?>
<wml>
<card id="Card1" title="WAP WML ">
<p>
This is basic WML.
</p>
</card>
</wml>
```

WML divides contents into cards (like a HTML page) and has various tags which permit fairly comprehensive user interfaces to be created.

WAP has not been overly successful, particularly in its early days when mobile telephone WAP access (charged by the minute) proved expensive and delivered, compared to its PC + WWW 'big brother' a rather lacklustre experience. Changes in WAP billing (measured by the downloaded data), improved content and cell provider subsidised WAP minutes have increased its popularity to a degree but it struggles to compete with 3G services.

Wi-Fi (including 802.11x standards and security)

Wi-Fi (commonly and erroneously referred to as 'wireless fidelity') is the name given to the IEEE 802.11b standards that cover 11 Mbps bandwidth wireless networks operating in the 2.4 GHz (unlicensed) frequency.

The **IEEE** (**I**nstitute of **E**lectrical and **E**lectronic **E**ngineers) is an international organisation that develops standards for many different types of modern technology.

The **802 committee** develops standards for local area networks (**LANs**) and wide area networks (**WANs**). A subsection of these standards, called **802.11**, concerns the use of wireless networks.

Table 10.04 gives details about other notable 802.11 standards.

Perhaps the biggest threat to wireless networking is security. In contrast to wired solutions, wireless networks are particularly vulnerable to infiltration and data theft.

It is possible to gain unlawful access to a wireless connection using appropriate hardware and software. '**Wardriving**', the art of driving around looking for free, unguarded wireless signals, is well known, as is '**warchalking**' – marking locations of free wireless networks for others to exploit.

Table 10.04

Standard	Year	Description
802.11	1997	Original 2 Mbps standard. Now obsolete.
802.11a	1999	Operates in 5 GHz frequency range, attracting less interference at a faster 54 Mbps. Shorter range than 802.11b and not compatible.
802.11d	2001	Standards for country-to-country roaming. Also known at the **Global Harmonisation** standard. It permits location-sensitive adjustments for frequency, power levels and bandwidth.
802.11e	2005 (delayed)	Incorporation of **Q**uality **o**f **S**ervice (**QoS**) to wireless network transmissions. QoS is vitally important for time-critical applications such as **VoIP** (**V**oice **o**ver **IP**) and streaming multimedia.
802.11g	2003	Primarily for wireless LANs operating in 2.4 GHz range but at a faster 54 Mbps. Popular for **SoHo** (**S**mall **O**ffice, **H**ome **O**ffice) applications in the UK. Also backwardly compatible with 802.11b equipment.
802.11i	2004	The introduction of enhanced security features (including **WPA2**).
802.11n	2004–2009	Includes the introduction of **MIMO** (**M**ultiple-**I**nput and **M**ultiple-**O**utput); essentially, uses multiple antennae to improve communication performance.

Security protocols used in 802.11

Table 10.05

Security protocol	Year	Description	Strength
WEP (**W**ired **E**quivalence **P**rivacy)	1999	Part of 802.11b standard. Optional security; not enabled on equipment by default. Weak encryption that can be cracked through network observation due to recycled use of encryption keys.	
WPA (**W**i-Fi **P**rotection **A**ccess)	2003	Released before 802.11i finalised. Replaces WEP; introduces **TKIP** (**T**emporal **K**ey **I**ntegrity **P**rotocol) which ensures that each data packet has a unique encryption key (see Figure 10.31).	
WPA2 (**W**i-Fi **P**rotection **A**ccess 2)	2004	Part of 802.11i standard. An enhanced form of WPA using **AES** (**A**dvanced **E**ncryption **S**tandard) rather than TKIP. AES is a US Federal standard for the encryption of commercial and government data.	

Setting security on a wireless router

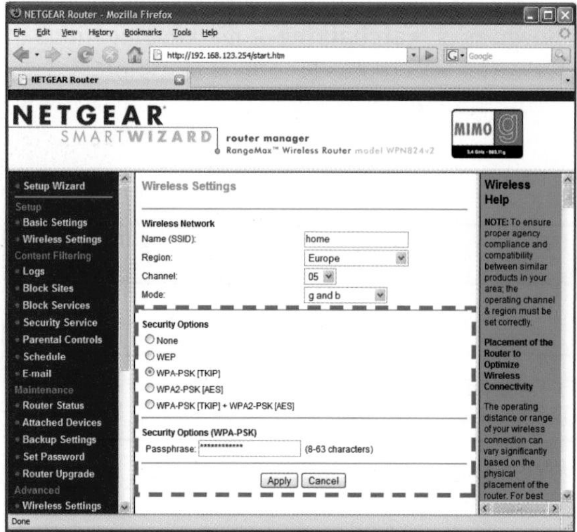

Figure 10.31 Enabling WPA passkey with TKIP (Temporal Key Integrity Protocol)

Scorecard – *Wi-Fi*

+ Wi-Fi standards ensure global **interoperability** between different manufacturers' devices.
+ Wi-Fi signals can penetrate walls.
+ Enables easy, inexpensive networking in the home or small office where wired solutions are prohibitive.
+ **Ad hoc** or **infrastructure** modes available. Ad hoc mode allows wireless devices to connect to each other without a WAP. Infrastructure mode requires wireless devices to connect through a WAP.

– Normally uses unlicensed frequency of 2.4 GHz so **interference** can occur.
– Slower than a physically wired solution.
– Security can be weak if equipment is obsolete (WEP) or badly configured.
– Three times more expensive than Bluetooth.
– Uses five times more power than Bluetooth.

10.2 Know the main elements of data communications systems

This section will cover the following grading criteria:

10.2.1 Main elements

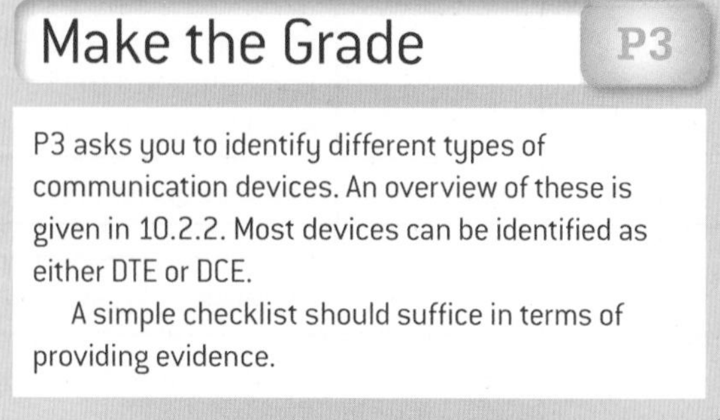

Make the Grade P3

P3 asks you to identify different types of communication devices. An overview of these is given in 10.2.2. Most devices can be identified as either DTE or DCE.

A simple checklist should suffice in terms of providing evidence.

The main elements of a computer network can be separated into four different categories:

- communication devices
- data elements
- electronic communication methods
- transmission media and methods.

10.2.2 Communication devices

Communication devices are often grouped into categories that either describe their purpose or their underlying technology.

Data Terminal Equipment (DTE)

Data Terminal Equipment is any device that generates data (as a sender) or is (as the receiver) the final destination.

An example of DTE is a computer system acting as a **terminal** (Figure 10.32).

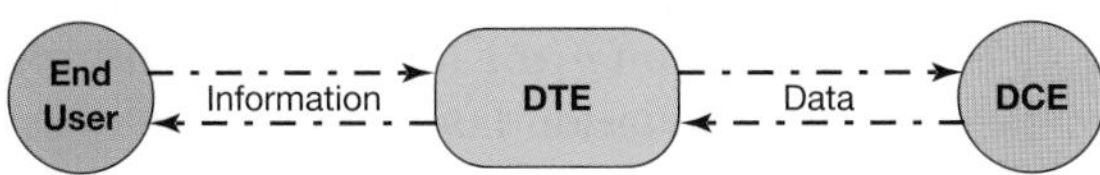

Figure 10.32 DTE

The DTE is normally seen as the end point in a data communication link. The terminal's job as a DTE is to convert incoming data into information for the end user and convert information provided by the user back into data for transport (achieved by a **DCE**).

Data Communications Equipment (DCE)

Data Communications Equipment (or, in some sources, **D**ata **C**ircuit-terminating **E**quipment) is a term that is used to describe a device that provides a communications link for a DTE.

An example of a DCE would be a modem (modulator-demodulator), a device that can convert a computer's digital signals into analogue signals for use over a telephone line (and back again when receiving).

Originally these terms were exclusively used with **serial data transmission** as part of the **RS-232 standard** (see 10.1.4). In more recent years the definitions are much more loosely used.

Traditionally, DTE and DCE devices are wired. More modern technologies such as the cellular telephone, PDAs and notebooks use wireless connections, relying on various radio frequencies to make connections.

Wireless devices might include:

- mobile telephones using **3G** or **GPRS**
- laptops
- netbooks
- PDAs etc.

10.2.3 Signal theory

Data is represented in a digital format based on binary (base 2) principles (Figure 10.33):

Figure 10.33 Binary data

Digital signals are said to be **discrete** – they offer no continuous graduation between values; the values are stepped.

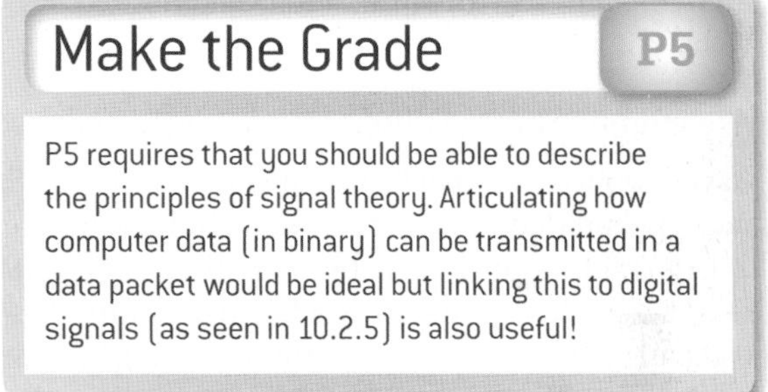

Data

The smallest element of data is the **bit** or **bi**nary digi**t**.

This can represent either a **1** or a **0** (Figure 10.34).

Figure 10.34 Bits

When bits are grouped together they form more useful units of data, e.g. eight bits forms a **byte** (Figure 10.35).

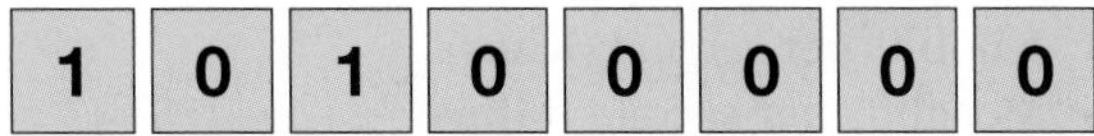

Figure 10.35 A byte

Concept of a packet

In networking, data has to be **encapsulated** into a suitable 'package' for transport.

The actual format of this package changes between different types of network, however the term **data packet** is generically used to describe this package.

Figure 10.36 shows what a data packet should minimally contain.

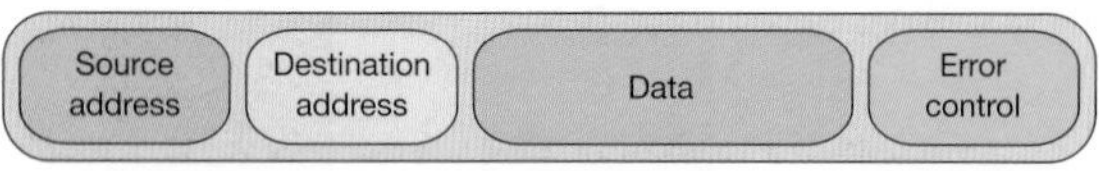

Figure 10.36

The source address is sent so that the recipient knows who has sent the data. The destination address is used to find the right recipient. Data is the actual 'message' being sent. **Error control** is added to the packet to help identify problems with the data once it has been received.

A common error-control method is the concept of a **checksum**. You'll read more about these in section 10.2.4.

Asynchronous vs synchronous transmission

Asynchronous transmission means that device 2 must acknowledge receipt of data **before** device 1 will send more. This is because there is no attempt by either device to synchronise before data transfer starts. They rely on the receiving device recognising that a stream of data is beginning or ending. This is usually achieved with **start** and **stop bits** (see section 10.2.5).

In **synchronous transmission**, both devices will synchronise with each other before any data is sent. When no transmissions are being sent, the two devices will transmit special characters to each other to keep each other 'in sync'.

Bandwidth

Bandwidth is generally defined as the quantity of data that can be sent through a data transmission medium over a specified period of time.

Bandwidth is usually quoted in (from slow to fast):

- **B**its **p**er **s**econd (**bps**)
- **K**ilo**b**its **p**er **s**econd (**Kbps**)
- **M**ega**b**its **p**er **s**econd (**Mbps**)
- **G**iga**b**its **p**er **s**econd (**Gbps**).

Data compression

Data compression is the process of removing unnecessary padding from data so that it takes up less physical or electronic 'space'. Compressing data makes more efficient use of available bandwidth.

10.2.4 Data elements

Checksum

Part of the error control mechanism, a checksum is a calculated value based on the **contents** of the data packet. When the packet is received at the destination node, the packet's checksum value is recalculated based on the data packet's received contents. The new checksum is compared against the one sent.

If the checksums *match*, it is assumed that the data sent was received successfully (good data integrity).

If the checksums *don't match*, the destination node suspects that an error has occurred during transport. The destination node can then request a retransmission of the data from the source node.

Some checksums may simply be a total of the bits sent in the packet. In this case, the checksum is merely confirming safe quantities of data rather than the quality of the data.

CRC

A **Cyclic Redundancy Check (CRC)** is a more thorough form of checksum used for checking errors in data transmission (on the motherboard, in data files and in networking).

CRC error checking involves a very complex **algorithm** that generates a numerical sequence based on the data that was transmitted. CRCs are therefore able to guarantee (beyond a reasonable doubt) the accuracy and quality of the data transmitted; even a **transposed data sequence** (data in the wrong order) would be identified.

Make the Grade **P4**

P4 requires that you should be able describe what data elements are (section 10.2.4 has a list) and why they are important.

Again, this is a small criterion and could be achieved using a viva, a simple table of definitions, a few electronic slides or a poster.

Sequence numbers

In systems where data is split up into a number of packets, it is important to know in which order a series of packets should be read.

This is especially important as it is possible that they may arrive out of sequence; a consequence of packet-switched routes.

e.g. Source node sends packets: 1, 2, 3, 4 and 5

Destination node receives packets: 2, 4, 1 and 5.

Verdict: The packets are in the wrong order and the message cannot be read until 3 (currently missing) is resent. Please resend packet 3.

Packets, datagrams and frames

Unfortunately these terms – all meaning something slightly different – are often used interchangeably. In reality, they are very often grouped together as **PDU (Protocol Data Units)** – collections of data that occur at different layers of the **ISO OSI model** (see section 10.1.4) as shown in Table 10.06.

10.2.5 Electronic communication

Let us examine how data gets from point-to-point.

Simplex

Simplex describes data transmission which is **one-way** only (Figure 10.37).

Figure 10.37 Simplex transmission

Half-duplex

Half-duplex describes data transmission that is **two-way**, but not simultaneous (Figure 10.38). Each device must wait until the other has finished in order to transmit successfully.

Figure 10.38 Half-duplex transmission

Full-duplex

Full-duplex describes data transmission that can be **simultaneously two-way** (Figure 10.39).

Each device is capable of transmitting and receiving at the same time.

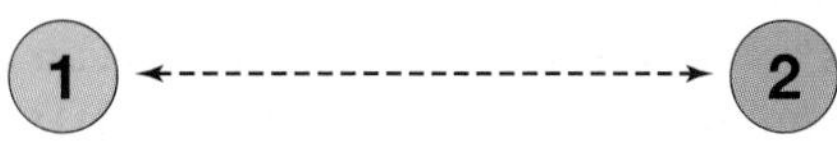

Figure 10.39 Full-duplex transmission

Sometimes this is referred to as just '**duplex**'.

Serial communication

Serial communication occurs when data is sent along a channel bit-by-bit, that is, in a sequence (Figure 10.40).

Table 10.06

Packet	A **packet** is a collection of data that has been created by software, not by a hardware device. For example, chunks of data created by Internet Protocol are called **IP packets**. Crucially (and here's the important point), a packet contains **logical addressing** (e.g. IP addresses) for its data.
Frame	The term **frame** is normally used to describe a collection of data that has been created by network hardware (e.g. network interface cards (NIC) or routers). A frame contains **physical addresses** (e.g. MAC addresses). Examples of frame types include **Ethernet frames** and **token ring frames**.
Datagram	A **datagram** is an independent, self-contained collection of data that is sent over the network. Whether it arrives, what time it arrives and what it will contain are not guaranteed. **UDP (User Datagram Protocol)** is a transport layer protocol used on IP networks. Unlike TCP (see 10.1.4), it is a simple, connectionless protocol. As such it cannot guarantee successful delivery nor does it have much functionality to detect errors or data loss. The terms 'packet' and 'datagram' are often used interchangeably.

In reality, this can simply be the case of sending an electronic signal along a single wire.

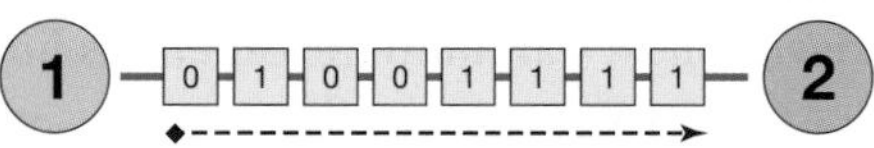

Figure 10.40 Serial communication

Examples of forms of serial communication include the following:

RS-232

Dating back to 1962, the **R**ecommended **S**tandard **232 (RS-232)** is an electrical signalling specification that was originally published by the **E**lectronic **I**ndustries **A**ssociation **(EIA)**. It also has standards laid down by the **I**nternational **T**elecommunication **U**nion **(ITU)** known as **V.24** and **V.28**.

RS-232 is synonymous with serial data transfer; the earlier 25-pin (DB25) and more recent 9-pin serial connectors are still reasonably common on a motherboard's backplane (Figure 10.41). RS-232C offers a **full duplex connection** and can be used to connect **DTE-to-DTE** and **DTE-to-DTC**.

Figure 10.41 A 9-pin serial connector (male)

The communication protocol between two devices using a RS-232 connection has to agree:

- **start bit**
- **data bits** (usually 7 or 8)
- **parity bit** (odd, even or none)
- **stop bits** (usually 1 or 2).

The data packet itself is typically stored in an **ASCII** (**A**merican **S**tandard **C**ode for **I**nformation **I**nterchange) format.

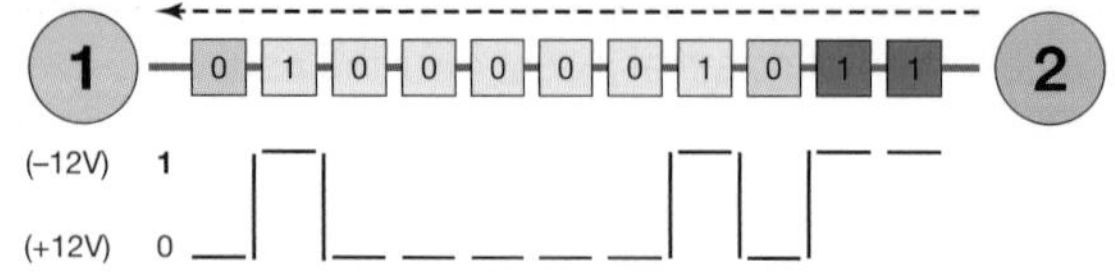

Figure 10.42

The transmission shown in Figure 10.42 is sending the ASCII character 'A' (65_{10} or 1000001_2) with even parity and two stop bits from device 2 to device 1.

Common RS-232 data transmission speeds are up to 1.5 Mbps on the newest devices, with 20 Kbps being the specified standard.

Parallel communication

In direct contrast to serial communication, **parallel communication** permits data transfer to occur in groups, across a number of wires (Figure 10.43).

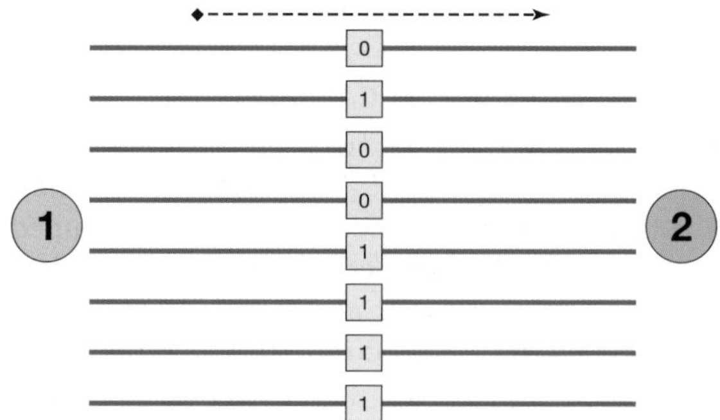

Figure 10.43

Care has to be taken that data is reassembled in the correct order at the receiving end.

Examples of forms of parallel communication include IEEE 1284.

Figure 10.44 A 25-pin parallel connector (female)

Although now rapidly being overtaken in favour of faster serial USB connection, the older IEEE 1284 is a good example of parallel data transmission, used to connect printers and scanners.

The IEEE 1284 standard supports a number of different modes, as seen in Table 10.07.

Table 10.07

Mode	Description
Centronics (SPP)	**S**tandard **P**arallel **P**ort – unidirectional mode, providing backward compatibility
Nibble mode	Unidirectional mode, transmitting 4 bits per pulse
Byte mode	Transmit of 8 bits per pulse
EPP	**E**nhanced **P**arallel **P**ort – half-duplex transmission up to 2 Mbps
ECP	**E**xtended **C**apability **P**ort – supports compressed data and up to 1 Mbps

10.2.6 Transmission

Modern communication systems use an array of different transmission media (the physical method used to get signals from point to point). Detailed below are the most common media used.

Coaxial

Although you are probably more familiar with these from television aerials and cable equipment, **coaxial** cables are used to connect telecommunication devices that use high-frequency, broadband connections.

A typical coaxial cable has a number of components (see Figure 10.45).

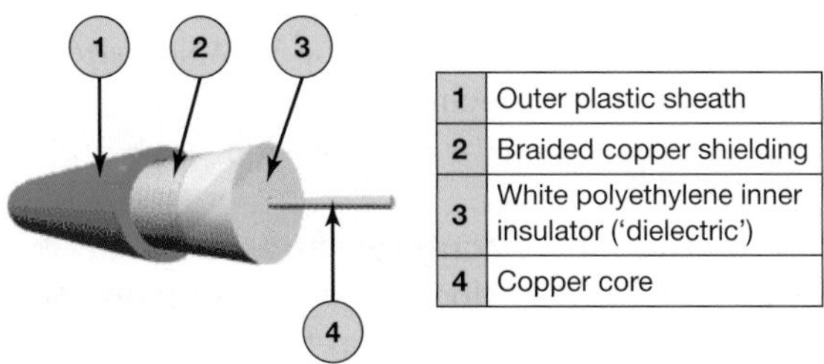

Figure 10.45 Coaxial cable

A separate copper braided shield (also known as a screen) surrounds the insulator. This shield provides a barrier from electromagnetic interference. This also makes the cable quite stiff and hard to work with.

> **Make the Grade** P6
>
> P6 requires that you should be able to describe different transmission methods – this is covered in section 10.2.6.
>
> Again, this is a small criterion and could be achieved using a viva, a simple table of definitions, a few electronic slides or a poster.

Coaxial cable has a much higher capacity than a standard copper wire, which explains its use for carrying Radio Frequency (RF) Television signals.

Various different types of coaxial cable exist and are used for:

- **Thin Ethernet** (10 Base 2)
- **Thick Ethernet** (10 Base 5)
- **Amateur** ('Ham') **radio**

Coaxial's use in building computer networks (Thin or Thick Ethernet) has mainly been superseded by **Unshielded Twisted Pair (UTP)**.

Optical fibre

Optical fibres use light for data transmission; **LEDs** (**l**ight **e**mitting **d**iodes) or a **laser** (**l**ight **am**plification by **s**timulated **e**mission **r**adiation) generate light pulses, which are sent down the fibre (actually a thin strand of glass). **Photodiodes** detect the light pulses at the far end.

Each fibre is about 2 microns in diameter – about 15 times thinner than a single human hair.

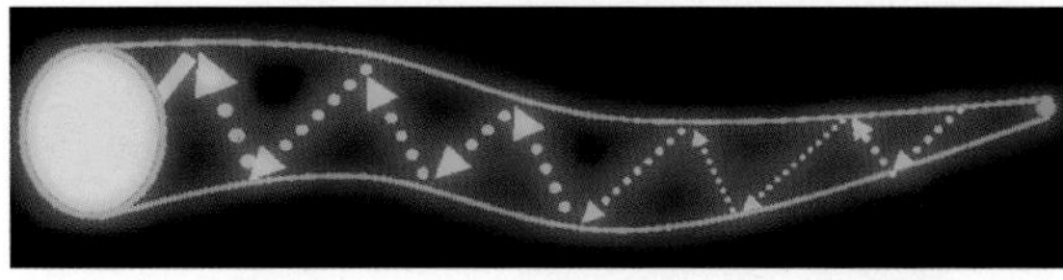

Figure 10.46 An optical fibre

Total internal reflection (about 41 or 42 degrees) prevents the majority of the beam's light from being absorbed by the outer cladding, leaving the remainder to safely reflect back along the fibre from one end to the other.

Optical fibres are not affected by stray electromagnetic interference (unlike copper cables). In addition, they are capable of sustaining high transmission rates, ideal for broadband applications such as voice, music and video.

Optical fibres can be manufactured into:

- **single mode** – used for longer distances (3 km), carrying a single beam of light
- **multimode** – used for shorter distances (2 km), normally has a single LED light, carrying multiple beams of light (and therefore more data simultaneously).

Make the Grade M2 D2

M2 and D2 are linked as they ask you to explain why certain transmission methods (media) are chosen in certain circumstances and to compare their effectiveness.

A table of comparison with some suitable case studies may be an appropriate way of evidencing these criteria successfully.

UTP and STP

Unshielded and **shielded twisted pair** (**UTP** and **STP**, respectively) both use copper wires (the oldest type of transmission medium) (Figure 10.47).

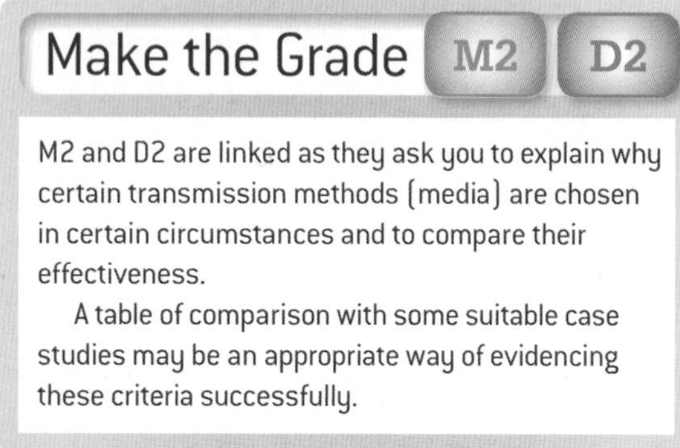

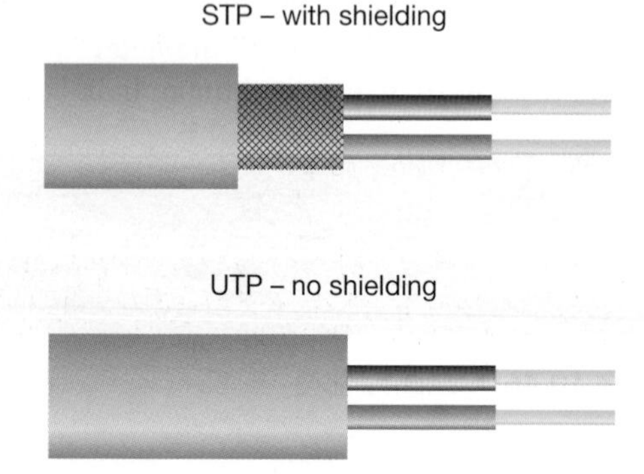

Figure 10.47 STP and UTP

STP has a metallic-coated plastic foil within the plastic sheath that is used to screen out electromagnetic interference. Because of this, STP is generally more expensive than its UTP counterpart.

Cross-talk can occur between two wires that run in **parallel**. In both UTP and STP cables, the individual wires are twisted in order to cancel out this form of interference (see Figure 10.48).

Figure 10.48

The core of STP and UTP wires is copper. Copper is an excellent conductor (having low electrical resistance), is an easy material to work with and is very flexible (which makes cabling in narrow spaces very simple).

Wireless solutions

Wireless solutions use infrared (discussed in section 10.1.5), radio, microwaves and satellite.

Radio

It is possible to convert the computer's digital signals into **radio waves**.

The transmitting device uses an antenna to generate radio signals, which spread out in a straight line. Signals can be reflected, absorbed or refracted as they travel through different materials (e.g. wood, brick, moisture in the air). As such, radio signals weaken over distance, necessitating the receiving device using an antenna to amplify the weak electrical signals.

Radio waves form the basis for WLANs (wireless LANs) and wireless technologies.

Microwaves

Microwaves are electromagnetic waves in the range 1 to 30 GHz. Modern microwave-based networks are becoming popular as the technology improves. They offer high bandwidth at a relatively low cost.

Satellites

Satellites are artificial orbiting devices that relay data between multiple Earth-based stations. Satellites provide high-bandwidth solutions (at least downloading data).

Comparing transmission media

Table 10.08

Transmission medium	Strengths	Weaknesses
Coaxial	Long runs (500 m) Relatively inexpensive Immunity to stray signals ('noise') Tried and trusted technology 10–100 Mbps	Rigid; difficult to install Expensive to install
Optical fibre	Very long runs (2,000–3,000 m) depending on the mode Not susceptible to electromagnetic interference Does not generate noise	Light signal strength diminishes over distance due to scattering and absorption Expensive to install
UTP	Reasonable runs (100 m) before repeating needed Inexpensive (cheapest per metre for LAN installation) Small – easy to install 10–1000 Mbps	Prone to interference from stray signals
STP	Reasonable runs (100 m) before repeating needed Shielded 10–100 Mbps	Moderately expensive (due to extra weight and size)
Infrared	No wires Quick to install	Must have direct LoS (line of sight) Limited in range Easy to disrupt
Radio	No wires No LoS required Greater range possible	Signals become weaker over distance Wireless signals can be intercepted so security is an issue

B Braincheck 2

1. How many levels are there in the ISO OSI model?
2. Which level deals with end-to-end communication?
3. Name three data processes that the presentation is responsible for.
4. Which layer sees data in bits?
5. Which layer sees data encapsulated into segments?
6. Which layer sees data encapsulated into packets?
7. Which layer sees data encapsulated into frames?
8. Which layer would a router operate at?
9. Which layer would a NIC operate at?
10. When was the OSI created?

How well did you do? See the supporting website for the answers!

10.3 Be able to implement different forms of network communications

This section will cover the following grading criteria:

10.3.1 Internet communication

Internet communication relies on a number of different technologies, each bringing its own terminology and jargon.

The more common ones are listed below:

HTTP (*H*ypertext *T*ransfer *P*rotocol)

Part of the internet suite of protocols, HTTP performs the requests and retrieval functions when a web browser tries to load a particular web page. This means that it is HTTP that is responsible for asking the remote web server for .html, images and sounds when they are specified by the URL input by the user in the address bar as in Figure 10.49.

Figure 10.49

By default, HTTP operates through port 80. This is the same port that a remote web server would listen to (for requests). In addition, any firewall would need to permit traffic on this port.

The HTTP protocol is commonly seen as the prefix before the desired website address.

In the example shown in Figure 10.50, a PC is set up as a web server (using Apache®) and is simulating HTTP requests to itself.

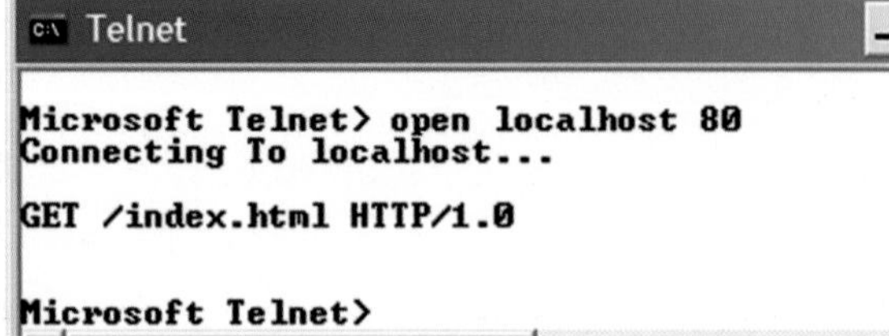

Figure 10.50 Telnet connects to the web server on port 80 and sends a HTTP request

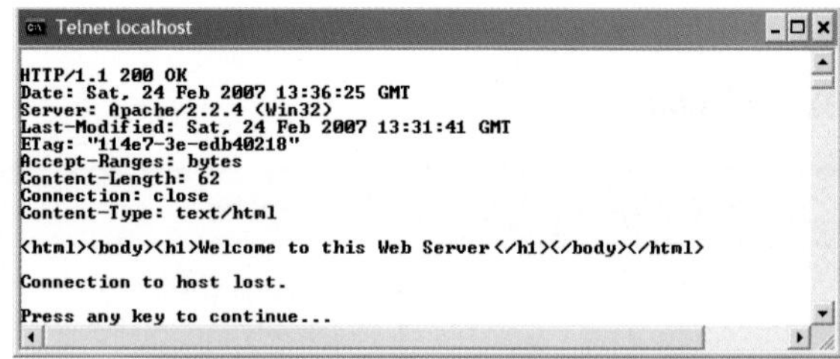

Figure 10.51 The web server responds to the HTTP request by returning the HTML file

Figure 10.52 shows what is happening in the background when the same request is made from the web browser application.

Figure 10.52 The web browser client receives .HTML from the web server (localhost)

It should be noted that 'localhost' – the name being used for the web server – is actually the internal name for the loopback address (see section 10.1.4).

URL

As we have seen, the **URL** (**U**niform **R**esource **L**ocator) is the address of a resource available on the internet.

Examples include:

BBC News – World News main page http://news.bbc.co.uk/1/hi/world/default.stm

Doctor Who website www.bbc.co.uk/doctorwho/dw

Drunken Sailor midi sound file www.contemplator.com/tunebook/midimusic/drnksailor.mid

HTTPS

HTTPS (**HTTP** **S**ecured) is similar to HTTP, but it uses port 443 instead of the more familiar HTTP port 80.

This port change permits the use of an additional encryption/authentication layer between HTTP and TCP. It is often used for security sensitive communications such as:

Activity 5

Do-it-yourself: installing a web server to test HTTP requests

What you will need:

- PC
- Windows operating system (e.g. Windows XP®, Vista®, Windows 7®, etc.)
- Administrator rights to the operating system
- A copy of Apache® HTTP Web Server (source: http://httpd.apache.org/)

Instructions

1 Download and install the Apache® HTTP Web Server.

2 Configure the Web Server correctly.

3 If firewalled, open port 80 for HTTP requests (likely to be open already).

4 Start the Apache® Web Server service.

5 Open a CMD prompt.

6 Start Telnet.

7 Connect to localhost.

8 Issue the HTTP request (ensure uppercase).

The Web Server should process the request and issue a 200 code ('OK – the requested resources have been sent').

Examine the HTTP header and HTML file returned.

Congratulations, you are now a very basic web browser!

Please remember to stop and uninstall the Web Server when you have finished!

- on-line payment transactions
- on-line banking
- corporate logons.

Because the data being transmitted (e.g. credit cards, passwords) is encrypted during transport to and from the server, any attempt to intercept the packets will be pointless; the data will be meaningless without the decryption key. The term **SSL** (**S**ecure **S**ockets **L**ayer) is often used in conjunction with this technology.

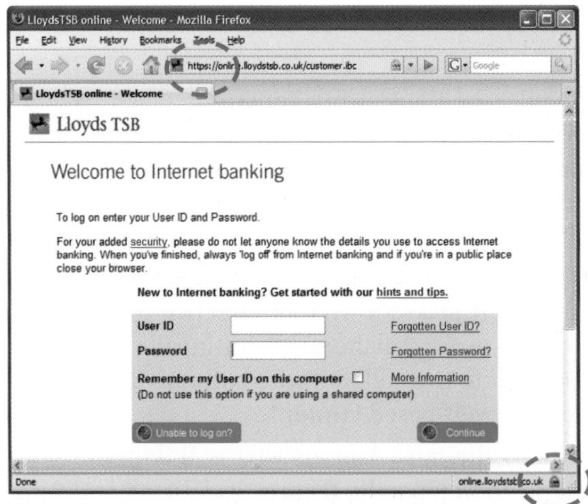

Figure 10.53 Lloyds TSB internet banking, secured by HTTPS

The HTTPS system was designed by Netscape Communications Corporation and is still in popular use today (see Figure 10.53). However, it should be remembered that this technology only protects data in transit, not at either end. Both client and web server would still need to be protected from hackers.

FTP

FTP (**F**ile **T**ransfer **P**rotocol) is a common method for moving files over a network system, from one computer system to another (see Figure 10.54).

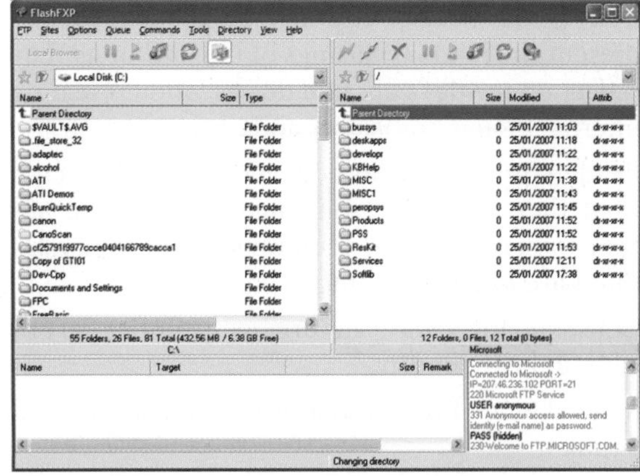

Figure 10.54 FlashFXP FTP client connects anonymously to the Microsoft® FTP site

FTP predates the World Wide Web and has been popularised through the use of **anonymous FTP** – a file transfer between locations where the user does not need to specify a username or password.

FTP clients connect to an FTP server using port 21. The server responds on the same port, usually prompting for a username and password (unless it is anonymous FTP, of course).

Port 21 is only used for **server-side control**; the server and client would nominate another port for the actual data transfer itself.

FTP is generally seen as a fast and reliable file transfer protocol.

SMTP

SMTP (**S**imple **M**ail **T**ransfer **P**rotocol) is a protocol used to send and receive email messages between servers. Another protocol (either **POP**, **P**ost **O**ffice **P**rotocol, or the newer, more flexible **IMAP**, **I**nternet **M**essage **A**ccess **P**rotocol) is used by email client programs to retrieve the mail from a mail server.

SMTP is also used to send messages from a mail client to a mail server.

Mail client software needs to have server names specified for both incoming and outgoing mail. The incoming will be either POP or IMAP. The outgoing is likely to be SMTP.

Other forms of internet communication include:

Blogs

A **weblog** or just '**blog**' is a journal (or newsletter), frequently updated and intended for public consumption on the World Wide Web.

Blogs generally mirror the personality of the author or the website and may be themed or just present the random musings of the author as they reflect on the day's ups and downs, often revealing internal thought processes and ideas.

Readers are invited to comment on and discuss what they have read, sometimes helping the author to make sense of the events and life puzzles that have been perplexing them.

Consequently, blogs can form an essential part of a **virtual community**.

A number of **blog communities** are active and popular:

LiveJournal www.livejournal.com/
(See Figure 10.55)

MySpace blog.myspace.com/
Blogger www.blogger.com/
TypePad www.sixapart.com/typepad/

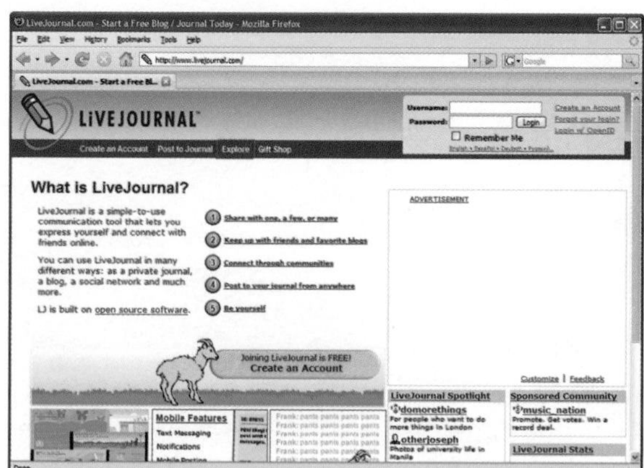

Figure 10.55 LiveJournal – a popular blogging community

Wikis

A **wiki** is a web-based application that lets everyday users add new content to existing online resources. In addition, it allows others to edit the content (though some user registration may be required).

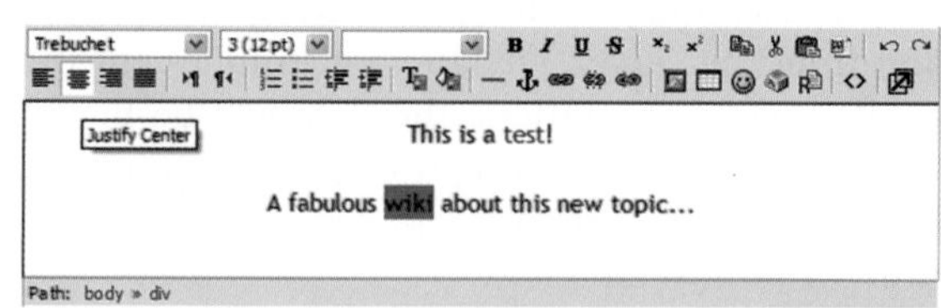

Figure 10.56 A wiki in progress...

Complex web-authoring functions (such as font, formatting, alignment, links and images) are made simpler through a basic user interface that encourages rapid creation and editing. With the removal of technical demands from the process, the user can feel creatively released and enjoy the experience.

As such, it makes a wiki an effective tool for performing mass collaborative authoring. Wiki can also refer to the collaborative software used to create such web-based content.

Perhaps the most famous wiki is **Wikipedia** – an online encyclopaedia (Figure 10.57).

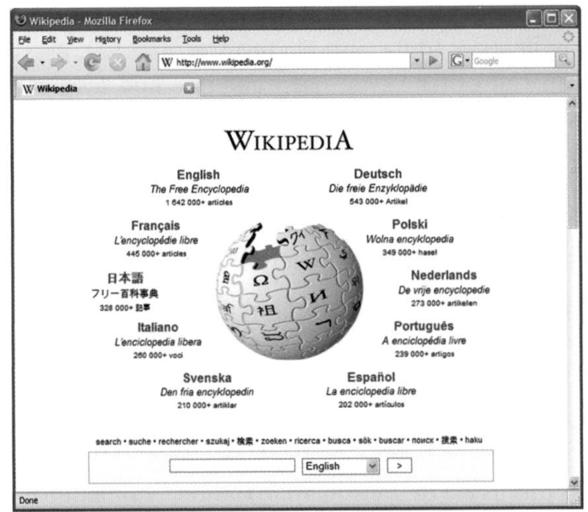

Figure 10.57 Wikipedia searchable front-end

Video conferencing

Video conferencing is a system that uses a computer, a video camera and a broadband network connection to conduct a live conference between two or more people, usually geographically distant.

It is a useful technique as it saves people the expense and time-consuming travel needed to accomplish face-to-face communication.

Instant messaging

Instant Messaging (IM) is primarily a text-based interface that lets users communicate in real time over a network connection (including the internet).

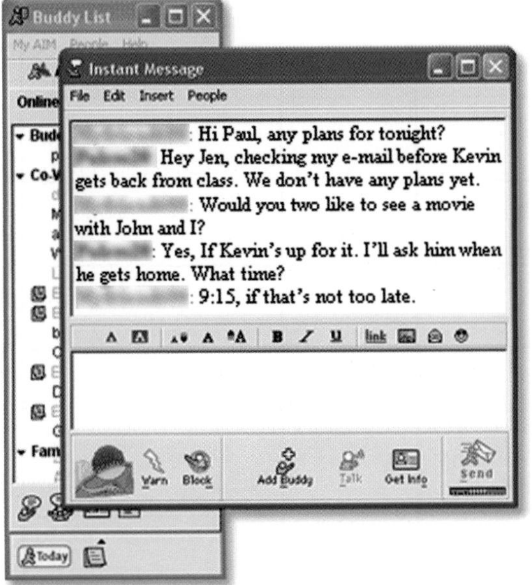

Figure 10.58 AOL Instant Messenger

When a message is received, the receiver is instantly notified and can choose to respond to the sender (see Figure 10.58).

IM software and the IM network is generally free to use, often being supported through the use of advertisements. More advanced IM software permits group messaging and the use of **webcams** to provide **real-time video feeds**.

Functions such as file transfer are useful but can provide ways and means for viruses to enter a computer system, so care should be taken when accepting downloads.

Other popular IM software applications include:

AIM (America on-line Instant Messenger) http://info.aol.co.uk/aim/

ICQ ('I seek you') www.icq.com/

Yahoo! Messenger http://messenger.yahoo.com

VoIP

VoIP (**V**oice **o**ver **I**nternet **P**rotocol) is a technology that carries voice communication over an existing IP network; the specification includes the digitisation of the analogue voice signals and the conversion of the signals into packets for transport.

VoIP is part of a larger scheme known as **IP Telephony**.

Figure 10.59 Cisco VoIP telephones

VoIP has become popular with larger business corporations and internet-enabled home users.

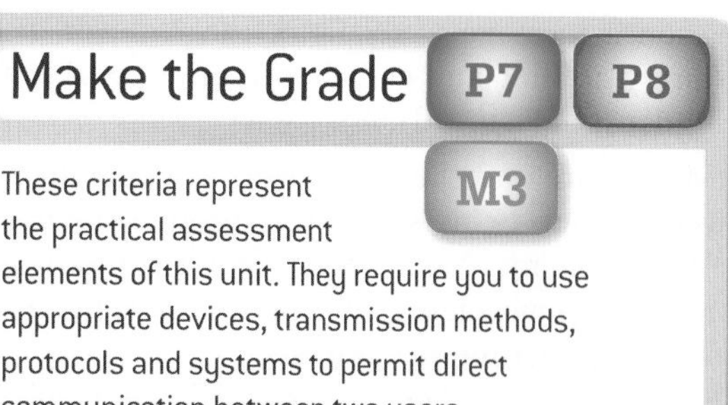

Make the Grade P7 P8 M3

These criteria represent the practical assessment elements of this unit. They require you to use appropriate devices, transmission methods, protocols and systems to permit direct communication between two users.

M3, slightly more complex, asks you to assess the effectiveness of data transfer over wired and wireless networks. If you set up a wired and wireless solution, you will be able to compare data transfer rates by performing a data transfer operation from one user to another (e.g. sending a large file).

These criteria are likely to be evidenced by observation records, photographs and video.

The major advantage to businesses is that VoIP helps reduce running costs because its telephone calls travel over its own data network rather than the **tel**ephone **co**mpany's (**Telco**). In addition, this also means that a company using VoIP has better control over security and voice quality.

Skype, a free VoIP solution, was founded by Kazaa (peer-to-peer file-sharing suite) creators Niklas Zennström and Janus Friis. With the free Skype application and a suitable headset/handset, users can call other Skype users for free and also call (SkypeOut) and receive calls (SkypeIn) from POTS numbers for a fee.

Skype: www.skype.com/

10.3.2 System requirements

Hardware and software requirements for wired and wireless services are discussed in sections 10.1.2, 10.1.3 and 10.1.5.

10.3.3 Direct communication

As discussed in section 10.3.1, direct communication can be achieved using video communication (webcams), instant messaging, email and VoIP.

Each of these electronic methods has a social impact – some good (distance is no longer a barrier to communication), some bad (not all forms of communication can be accurately duplicated using electronic means, e.g. body language).

10.3.4 Interconnection devices

You should feel able to use a combination of the different interconnection devices seen in section 10.1.3 to enable network communication.

Unit link

Unit 10 is a **mandatory unit** for the Edexcel BTEC Level 3 National Diploma and Extended Diploma in IT (Networking and Systems Support pathway) and **optional** for all other qualifications and pathways of this Level 3 IT family.

Qualification (pathway)	Mandatory	Optional	Specialist optional
Edexcel BTEC Level 3 National Certificate in Information Technology		✓	
Edexcel BTEC Level 3 National Subsidiary Diploma in Information Technology		✓	
Edexcel BTEC Level 3 National Diploma in Information Technology		✓	
Edexcel BTEC Level 3 National Extended Diploma in Information Technology		✓	
Edexcel BTEC Level 3 National Diploma in IT (Business)		✓	
Edexcel BTEC Level 3 National Extended Diploma in IT (Business)		✓	

Qualification (pathway)	Mandatory	Optional	Specialist optional
Edexcel BTEC Level 3 National Diploma in IT (Networking and System Support)	✓		
Edexcel BTEC Level 3 National Extended Diploma in IT (Networking and System Support)	✓		
Edexcel BTEC Level 3 National Diploma in IT (Software Development)		✓	
Edexcel BTEC Level 3 National Extended Diploma in IT (Software Development)		✓	

There are specific links to the following units in the scheme:
Unit 9 – Computer networks

B Braincheck 3

1. Name the four sizes of network in decreasing size order.
2. Name four different network topologies.
3. Name three different network access methods.
4. Switch, router and hub are all ___________ devices?
5. What is a WAP?
6. What is the purpose of the ISO OSI?
7. Name the layers of the ISO OSI.
8. Who is the IEEE?
9. Which four elements does a data packet contain?
10. What is a checksum?
11. Which point-to-point data communication occurs only one way?
12. What is the difference between HTTP and HTTPS?
13. Which port does FTP use?
14. What is VoIP?
15. What is a Blog?

How well did you do? See the supporting website for the answers!

Achieving success

This particular unit has 13 criteria to meet: 8 Pass, 3 Merit and 2 Distinction.

For a Pass: You must achieve all 8 Pass criteria.

For a Merit: You must achieve all 8 Pass and all 3 Merit criteria.

For a Distinction: You must achieve all 8 Pass, all 3 Merit and both Distinction criteria.

Further reading

Dodd, A. Z. – *The Essential Guide to Telecommunications, 4th edition* (Prentice Hall, 2005) ISBN-10 0131487256, ISBN-13 978-0131487253

Hallberg, B. – *Networking: A Beginner's Guide, 5th Edition* (Osborne/McGraw-Hill US, 2009) ISBN-10 0071633553, ISBN-13 978-0071633550

Lowe, D. – *Networking All-in-One Desk Reference for Dummies, 3rd Edition* (John Wiley & Sons, 2008) ISBN-10 0470179155, ISBN-13 978-0470179154

Schiller, J. – *Mobile Communications, 2nd Edition* (Addison Wesley, 2003) ISBN-10 0321123816, ISBN-13 978-0321123817

Websites

www.howstuffworks.com

www.webopedia.com

Unit 11: Systems analysis and design

By the end of this unit you should be able to:

1. Understand the principles of systems analysis and design
2. Be able to carry out a structured analysis of business systems requirements
3. Be able to design business systems solutions.

Whether you are in school or college, passing this unit will involve being assessed. As with most BTEC schemes, the successful completion of various assessment criteria demonstrates your evidence of learning and the skills you have developed.

This unit has a mixture of pass, merit and distinction criteria. Generally you will find that merit and distinction criteria require a little more thought and evaluation before they can be completed.

The colour-coded grid below shows you the pass, merit and distinction criteria for this unit.

To achieve a pass grade you need to:	To achieve a merit grade you also need to:	To achieve a distinction grade you also need to:
P1 Outline the principles of systems analysis		
P2 Illustrate the stages of a development cycle	**M1** Discuss the most appropriate uses of different development life cycle models	
P3 Explain the benefits of structured analysis		
P4 Carry out a structured analysis of a specified business process		
P5 Produce a requirements specification for a business process	**M2** Suggest alternative solutions	**D1** Analyse costs and benefits
P6 Produce a design for a specified system requirement	**M3** Explain any constraints on the system design	**D2** Generate comprehensive design documentation independently

Introduction

Systems analysis and design is a 10-credit unit that focuses on how new systems are developed.

Understanding the principles of analysis and design, the role of the analyst is to investigate user requirements, offer advice on alternative solutions, and create a design for the chosen solution.

At the end of this process, the solution design will be passed on to system developers (either programmers, network specialists, database designers or even all three) for the physical solution to be built and installed.

In this unit you will investigate and design a system solution for an organisation, to solve a business need.

How to read this chapter

This chapter is organised to match the content of the BTEC unit it represents. The following diagram shows the grading criteria that relate to each learning outcome.

You'll find colour-matching notes in each chapter about completing each grading criterion.

11.1 Understand the principles of systems analysis and design

This section will cover the following grading criteria:

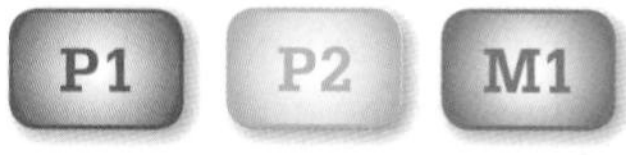

Make the Grade P1 P2 M1

To evidence P1 you will be required to explain the principles of systems analysis by considering what a development life cycle is, the types of tools and techniques that are used and the key drivers for analysing systems.

For P2 you will need to outline the stages of one development life cycle, briefly explaining each stage. Although the choice of which life cycle you explore is yours, your tutor may list some examples from which you can choose.

To achieve M1 you must consider other models and explain why different models are used, supported by examples.

These criteria may be assessed through a series of presentation slides with supporting handouts.

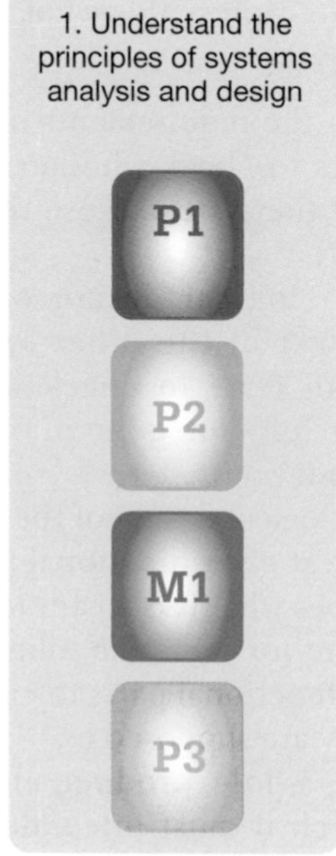

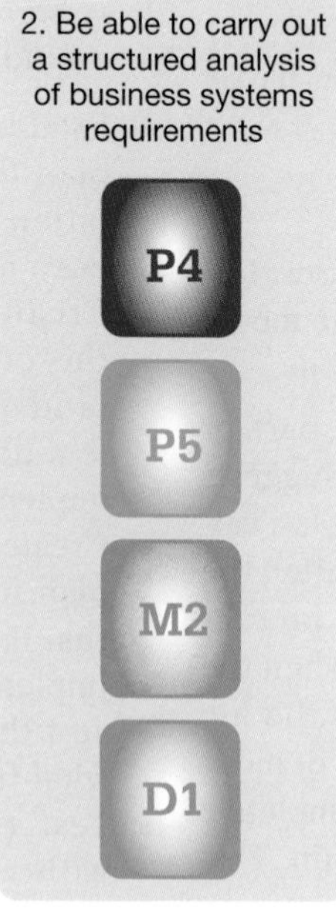

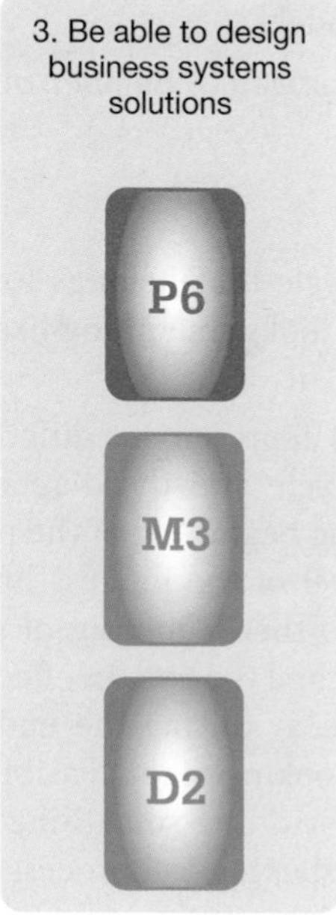

Figure 11.00

11.1.1 Principles

Giving structure to any analytical activity will ensure that the processes required are completed correctly and in the right order to ensure a valid and reliable outcome. Each **development life cycle model** has different components and different tools and techniques including recording mechanisms and diagrams. These will be examined in the next sections.

The **key drivers** for the analysis and redevelopment of business systems will also be explored.

11.1.2 Development life cycle models

Every system, whether it's computerised or not, has a **life cycle** – that means that in order to have been developed the system will have been:

- defined
- investigated
- designed
- implemented and tested
- maintained and reviewed.

Ultimately, over time, the system will **decay** (become less usable and useful as the needs of the users change).

If you look in systems analysis theory books, or on the internet, you will find a huge selection of analysis methodologies, each with their own variation of the life cycle model.

Firstly, we will investigate a number of alternative life cycle models.

Waterfall model

The systems life cycle that belongs to the **waterfall methodology** looks something like the model shown in Figure 11.01.

Each ellipse (oval) represents a different part or stage of the life cycle and the diagram suggests that you start at the beginning of the process, carrying out each level of the process one after the other, returning to the beginning of the process once you have reached the end. In effect, when the system starts to decay during the end of the life cycle, you may be looking at the feasibility of modifying the system or doing something completely different, thereby starting the process again. This will be considered later in this unit.

The key point with this life cycle is that, like a waterfall, the process falls from the top to the bottom. As we all know, water cannot flow upwards. Thus, Figure 11.01 implies that each level or stage will be undertaken after the previous one is finished, with no possibility for going back and revisiting an earlier stage if anything goes wrong.

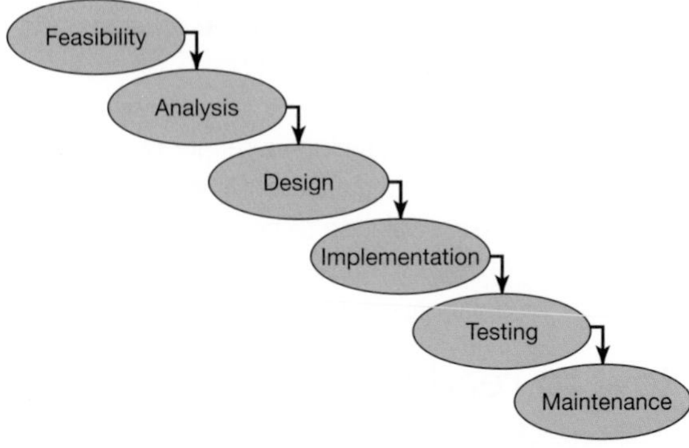

Figure 11.01 Systems life cycle (waterfall)

V-shaped model

Similar to the waterfall model, and containing most of the same stages or levels (even if expressed slightly differently), the **V-shaped model** places a heavy emphasis on the need for testing for the outcomes of the various stages of the development, with tests planned and then executed after implementation. As a diagram, the V-shaped model is expressed as shown in Figure 11.02 on the next page.

If we were to express this whole life cycle as text, we would say:

- Establish the requirements of the system (and plan tests to check whether, after implementation of the system, these requirements have been met).
- Create a logical design of the system in the context of the other systems around it (and plan tests to check whether the system does fully integrate into its context, after implementation).
- Create a logical design of the system itself (and plan to test each functional part to make sure that it does what it is meant to).
- Implement (or code) the solution.
- Test the functional parts to ensure that they do what they are supposed to.
- Test the whole product alongside systems with which it must integrate – does it do so successfully?
- Test the whole system and check that the users' original requirements have been met.

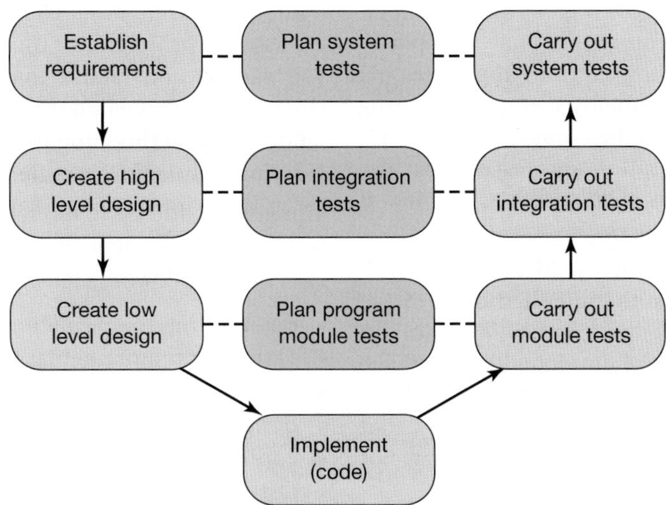

Figure 11.02 Systems life cycle (V-shaped)

Effectively, when using this model, we go down the left-hand side of the diagram, through implementation, which is at the bottom, then up the other side.

Rapid Applications Development (RAD)

RAD has a much simpler life cycle model (see Figure 11.03).

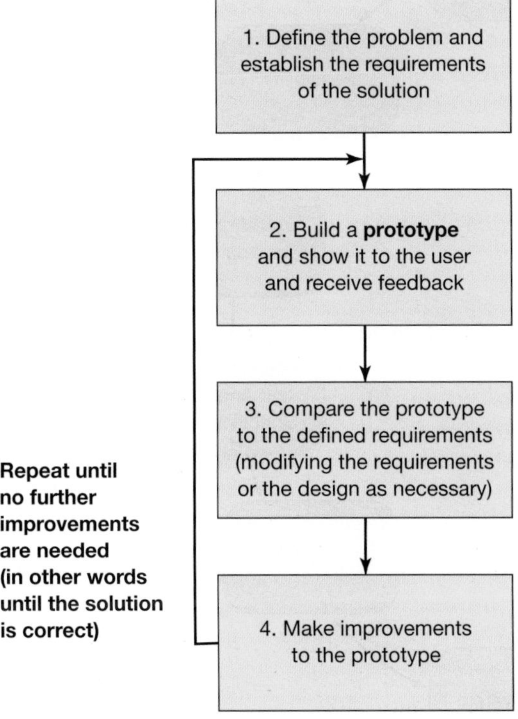

Figure 11.03 Systems life cycle (RAD)

Made up of four basic stages, steps 2 to 4, inclusive, are repeated as many times as required until the user (or users) are satisfied that the problem has been solved. Clearly, this model is reliant on the users being heavily involved in the development process, and this would be an unrealistic model if there were a large number of potential system users – it's difficult to please everyone, opinions can vary too much.

Benefits

What are the benefits of following any of these life cycle models?

Quite simply, choosing not to adopt a recognised development model when designing and implementing a business system is a little like attempting to build flat-pack furniture without any instructions: it's extremely difficult, and could potentially go wrong many times along the way.

These models provide a blueprint which, if followed, should result in a satisfactory system being built. They provide guidance and support for the process.

Considered specifically from the perspective that these are theoretical models, each one has a particular focus, which, if identified and understood, might help users to choose appropriately when developing a solution.

The waterfall model essentially places **equal emphasis** on **each stage** and it recognises that when the process is finished, it may well begin again to ensure that the system continues to meet the needs of the organisation.

The V-shaped model places a great deal of importance on testing and requires the analyst to plan a series of rigorous tests from various angles: testing that the required functionality is in place, testing that the product fits into the context of all the systems inside the organisation and testing that the system meets the needs of the users as defined at the beginning of the process.

Adopting the RAD approach is ideal if the developer has open access to the intended users of the system and can get feedback easily. With this in place, the product will be developed quickly. The only real danger is that the developer could get side tracked as the users add functionality that they might just have thought of, but which was not in the original proposal.

Stages (e.g. initiation and feasibility, investigation, requirements analysis and specification, design (logical and physical), build systems, testing, implementation, maintenance)

With the exception of the RAD model, you will have seen that the life cycle diagrams essentially contain the same basic elements. We now need to explore the principles of these elements, although you should understand that there will be some slight differences when they are applied to specific models and methodologies. We will begin by considering a **generic** life cycle model (Figure 11.04).

The generic life cycle model is very similar to the software development life cycle model, which consists of the following elements:

- determining the problem scope
- gathering requirements
- writing the specification
- designing a solution
- coding the design
- testing the program code
- writing documentation
- reviewing and maintaining the solution.

Initiation or problem definition

The life cycle has to have a beginning. At this point the project is said to be **initiated** or **defined**. How does this happen? Usually one of two ways:

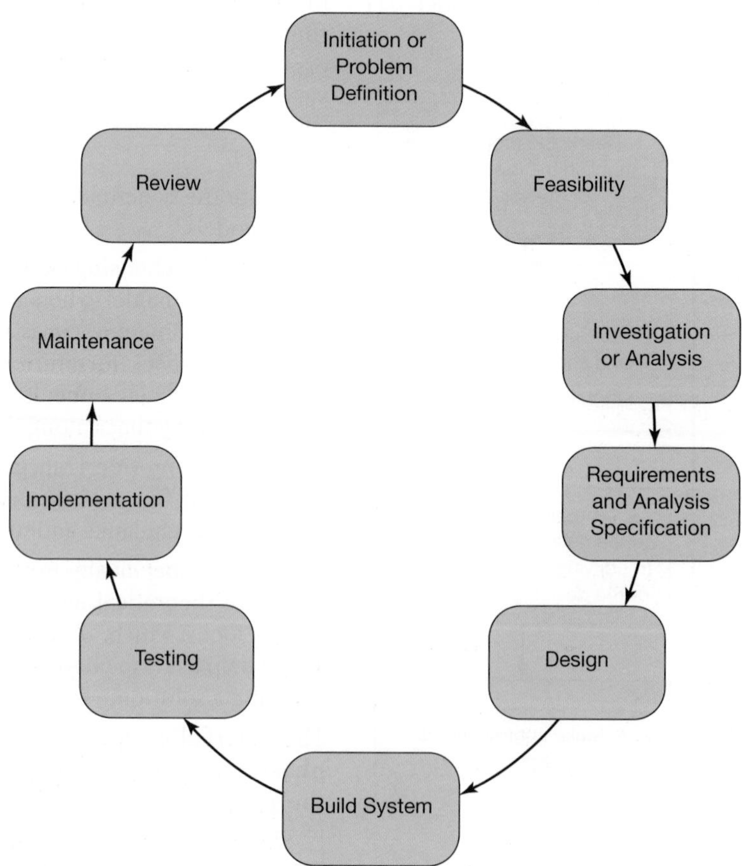

Figure 11.04 A generic life cycle model

1. A user or group of users identifies something that the system needs to do and cannot (or can, but does so slowly)
2. The system needs change for one of the following reasons:
   a. Speed and efficiency can be improved if a manual system is updated to a computerised one (the manual methods are effectively just too slow).
   b. The organisation identifies that functions within it need to process large volumes of similar data (e.g. invoices, payroll, mail-order transactions).
   c. It becomes necessary for the same data or information to be shared in various locations.
   d. It becomes necessary for the data or information to be constantly updated.
   e. There is obvious duplication of effort by a number of users of the system.
   f. More control over activities is needed.
   g. More (or missing) management information is required.

The process may well begin as a result of informal discussions between individuals inside the organisation. Before any formal activity begins, however, it is important that the problem, as understood by all, has been agreed and written down, as this will form a record and provide boundaries for subsequent activity. Although this might be modified during the life cycle of a project, if this is not done formally there is potential for a misunderstanding between users, analysts and developers about what was identified as being needed and what has subsequently been developed.

Feasibility study

Initially, a **feasibility study** is undertaken. This study usually looks at the problem from three perspectives: economic, technical and social.

Economic – will any investment in new systems be cost effective? We should remember here that the costs of a system can be split into two categories – **development costs** (the expenditure to purchase and implement the system) and **running costs** (the on-going expenses that will have to be met once the system is up and running, for example the purchase of consumables such as printer paper and cartridges, or the need for a maintenance contract).

These costs will need to be measured against the potential benefits the system will provide:

- **indirect benefits** – improved customer service, better access to information
- **direct benefits** – reduced costs (less labour expense for example).

Technical – will a new system work in the context of the organisation? If it is to be integrated with other systems, will this be successful? Technical feasibility issues are possibly the easiest to resolve, as it is likely that any discrepancies or technical problems can be overcome with a little more money. Providing that this still remains within the organisation's overall budget, technical issues are unlikely to prevent a project from moving forward.

Social – this involves consideration of how developing a system may affect those that will need to interact with it, for example, staff and customers. One ramification of changing a system from a manual to an electronic will be that the organisation will probably require fewer staff to do the same work. How will the surplus human resource be resolved? Will there need to be redundancies? Will the organisation wish to retain these staff and retrain them or relocate them to other parts of the organisation? Will those staff who will continue to work with the system be effective or will they need training to use it? Will the service to customers be affected in any way?

Ultimately, in a project such as this the cooperation of staff will be paramount. Understanding how the proposals will affect them will be essential in securing their assistance.

Once the feasibility study has been undertaken, it will be written up formally in report format, where ultimately the conclusion will be that it is feasible to move forward with such a project, or the project should be halted immediately.

The report will contain a **cost–benefit analysis**, which will itemise the physical costs of a solution, will draw the organisation's attention to indirect costs of the project and will list the benefits the organisation should receive once the project is implemented.

Finally, any constraints on the project that have been identified will be itemised and recorded. Usually these will include:

- **budget** for the project
- any **organisational policies** that must be considered
- the **timescale** for the project (when is the solution expected to be fully up and running)

- whether the system will have to incorporate any **legacy systems** (the existing systems)
- whether the solution will need to be developed to incorporate any current hardware or software (particularly in terms of compatibility).

In the event that the recommendation is to move forward, the life cycle will move to the investigation or analysis stage.

Investigation or analysis

Before deciding exactly what an organisation needs in terms of a new system, the analyst or team will need to undertake a detailed investigation of the present system. This is so that there will be a full understanding of how the system currently works and how it could change. Each of the following aspects of the existing system needs to be investigated and recorded:

Data

- What data exists?
- How it is used?
- The volume of the data.
- The number of transactions.
- The characteristics of the data.

Procedures

- What processes and procedures are carried out?
- Where are they carried out?
- When?
- How are errors or exceptions intercepted and dealt with?

Future needs

- Does the company have any medium-term plans that might have bearing on a new system?
- Is the company going to expand?
- Does the organisation expect growth in any areas, for example, the number of anticipated users, volumes of data.

Management needs

- What sorts of outputs do managers receive from the existing system?
- What do these outputs contain?
- How often are they required?

Problems with the existing system

- Are there any specific problems that have already been identified by users with any of the above?

In order to carry out the investigation into all the areas highlighted above, the analyst will have to be familiar with and able to use a variety of fact-finding methods. These techniques, which will include observation, looking at **existing documentation**, **interviews**, **questionnaires** and so on, will be investigated in detail later in this unit.

Once the full analysis has been undertaken, the findings are presented to the organisation in report format, supported by diagrams and charts (if appropriate).

Requirements analysis and specification

Having now done sufficient research to understand what the system currently does, a **requirements analysis and specification** are developed.

The requirements analysis focuses on what the new system will need to do to enable users to carry out their individual tasks from a functional perspective. Once the functionality of the system has been established, the necessary inputs can be identified, the processing requirements can be established, and the outputs predicted.

At this stage, however, there are no suggestions on how the functionality will be achieved. In other words, you might have established that a Microsoft Access® or Visual C#® solution is required, but you will not make any attempt to design it.

The specification will contain a list of any identified hardware or software requirements, or anything else that will be needed to facilitate the solution (e.g. network cabling, desks and chairs, four PCs with wireless connections and a wireless router, security software for these machines).

As with previous phases or stages of the life cycle, the analysis and specification must be recorded, often through a report.

Design (logical and physical)

The **design phase** begins with the analyst creating a logical representation of the new system, using a series of diagrams and supporting text. The type of diagram will depend on the solution that has been identified.

Entity relationship models (ERM) and **data flow diagrams (DFD)** are used to express the **logical** design of systems that contain data.

The ERM will provide a design for the tables that will be storing the system's data, in a Microsoft Access® database for example. This design tool will be explored later in this unit.

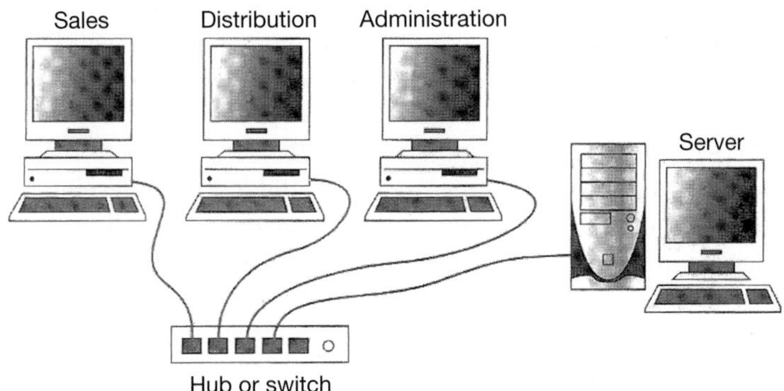

Figure 11.05 Proposed network

In addition a series of DFDs will be developed that will represent the functional areas of the organisation and which will show how the data is used, processed and ultimately output by the system. This diagram will probably have been one of the supporting documents in the system investigation because it can just as easily represent a current system as a future one.

In the event that the solution is (or requires) a network, a **network diagram** will be created that represents the various aspects of the network, as in Figure 11.05.

The logical design will then be supported by the **physical** design, which will include the following information.

For data-intensive systems:

- a data table (or data catalogue) containing the names and data types of each piece of data and showing how data links together
- details of how the data will be sorted or indexed
- explanations of how columns will be ordered
- how each output will be designed (e.g. a management report – the title, data included, any calculations required will be identified and recorded)
- drawings of the user interface.

Where computer programming is involved, there are a range of techniques that may be used to support the design of a programmed solution:

- **JSD (Jackson Structured Diagrams)** are used to represent solutions that will be coded using a procedural language such as Pascal® or C®. (For more on JSD, see Unit 6 – Software design and development.)
- **Pseudocode**, which is based on structured English and laid out like programming code, can be used to support procedural languages. (For more on pseudocode, see Unit 6 – Software design and development.)
- **Storyboards** are used to represent programs that will be written in visual languages such as Microsoft Visual C++® or Visual Basic®.

For network-based solutions, considerations include:

- proposed locations of equipment
- lengths of cabling
- network connectivity
- IP addresses
- security proposals.

Bearing in mind that the developers of the solution might not be the same as the analysts, the analysts' last job will be to develop **test plans** for the finished product, as it is the analyst and his or her team that will have the best understanding of what the system is supposed to do, and they will also know where test data can be obtained and what format it will take. They will establish what data will be available to test the system and they will dictate how the system will be fully tested.

Build the system

This is often where the system developers enter the process, although in some organisations the same team can be responsible for the whole project.

If the previous stages of the project have been correctly and successfully executed, it should be entirely possible for the developers of the system to use the design documentation of a system to produce the actual solution.

As the build process nears completion, the team will also write any documentation that will be required for the system. This will usually include technical documentation and a user guide. However, some theorists believe that this should not be undertaken until after the system testing is fully completed, as the testing itself should also be formalised and included as part of the technical documentation.

In real terms, most systems will be built by a development team rather than an individual person and where this occurs, the team should have regular meetings to ensure that there are no surprises when they finally attempt to integrate all of the developmental work into the final solution!

With a C#® or Visual Basic® solution, for example, a number of programmers might be involved in writing the code. As they will all be writing their own parts, they will need to have established some basic elements prior to starting work:

- names of variables
- data types
- data sizes (if text).

To illustrate:

Two programmers are developing code using the same variable – customer name. Prior to starting the code, they agreed that the customer name would be identified in the code as **tCustomer** as shown in Table 11.01.

Table 11.01

	Programmer 1	Programmer 2
Names it	tCustomer	tCustomer
Data type and size	Text (40)	Text (10)
Outcome	If the data handled by the code is passed at any point to code created by programmer 2, it will be truncated because programmer 2's variable is smaller than the one created by programmer 1.	There will be no problem if the data is passed to programmer 1, because the tCustomer variable is bigger.

It is essential, therefore, that the programmers have agreed not only the identifier or variable name, but also the data type and size.

Once the system is fully complete the formal testing will begin. It should be understood, however, that during development there will be on-going testing – programming code will be checked, as will **validation routines** or **input masking** in databases.

Testing

Using the test plan developed by the analysts, the development team will now test the product on all levels. In some cases the developers will have access to **live test data** belonging to the organisation. Alternatively, the team will need to develop **dummy test data**. This is data that is similar to the actual data that will be used in the system, but which isn't real.

Ultimately, once all aspects have been tested and the results of testing have been documented, the solution will be uploaded to the client's system for live testing, where the users will make use of the system as if they were using it in their usual activities.

Usually, at this stage, the organisation will continue to use the old system as well, so that if any problems in the new system are found, the organisation will be able to continue to function until the problems are resolved.

Implementation

When the system has been tested and is believed to be fully functional, it needs to be formally **implemented**. Users will need to change from the old system to the new. Depending on the situation, one (or a combination) of four possible **changeover** strategies will be used:

1 Direct changeover

This is where on a given date the old system will cease to be used and the new one will begin. A common strategy, this would see the old system used up until the close of business on a Friday, for example, and the users come in and begin using the new system on the following Monday. This is often referred to as the '**big bang**'.

One of the advantages of this is that it is an extremely fast and efficient way to change systems, and the weekend could be used to create the master files. Let's use the example of a stock system.

Prior to changeover, master records will have been created about the stock. This will have included:

Part number

Item description

Item cost

Item price

Now, over the weekend between the old system closing down and the new one beginning, the quantity in stock would have had to be added for each item. This would ensure that the system could be used live on the following Monday.

The main weakness with this strategy would be that in the event that users then experienced problems when they used the system, the old system would no longer be usable because the data would quickly become out of date.

Even so, many organisations take this risk and use a direct changeover strategy.

2 Parallel conversion (or parallel running)

If using a **parallel conversion** strategy, the old and new systems will be allowed to run alongside each other for a period of time. This could be a few days, a few weeks, or even months. **Cautious** organisations will tend to use this strategy, particularly if they feel that the timeframe for parallel system use will be relatively short.

The main advantage of this conversion strategy is that the new system can constantly be checked against the old system to ensure its **accuracy**. Any problems experienced by the user can be addressed as soon as they occur, without having a detrimental effect on the organisation.

The main disadvantage, however, is that this clearly requires **duplication in effort** if every transaction needs to be executed twice. This can put excessive strain on staff and should, for this reason, not be used as a strategy for anything more than a few days, unless the organisation is willing to recruit some temporary workers to help out.

Once the system is seen to be functioning correctly, the old system will be discontinued.

3 Phased conversion

A **phased** strategy is where the system will initially be introduced to one part of the organisation and if the system is then seen to work well, the next part of the system will be added. This will allow the organisation to see how the system works and provide opportunities for resolving any problems before the system is fully rolled out.

A phased changeover can be achieved using parallel or direct principles.

4 Pilot conversion

This strategy is common if an organisation has multiple outlets or sites. For example, a large chain of restaurants wishes to implement a booking system for all outlets where the system will provide managers with statistical analysis on table usage, average customer spend.

It is likely that the product, once developed, will be implemented initially in a single branch of the restaurant, with others added once the system is seen to function correctly.

As with a phased conversion strategy, a pilot strategy can be achieved using parallel or direct principles.

Maintenance

Once the system is in place, maintenance activities will begin – usually in the order shown.

1 Corrective

As problems with the installed system arise, they will need to be dealt with. This could be for any of the following reasons (although this is not an exhaustive list):

1. Something doesn't happen when it should.
2. Totals are missing from reports.
3. The sequence of columns in a report may not be accurate.

While errors (1) and (2) should have been identified and resolved during development, errors can clearly slip through. If this was not the case, then software manufacturers would not have to release **beta versions** of their software in which bugs identified by their clients have been eradicated.

Issue (3) may not have been seen as a problem by the developer, but the organisation might have a particular reason why the content of two data columns should be reversed (it might be an aesthetic preference).

Corrective maintenance is usually required instantly or certainly within a few days.

2 Perfective

Perfective maintenance is usually undertaken where a system does actually run as expected, but it is felt by the organisation that a few aspects could be done **better**. For example:

- Additional management information could be available if a few of the new reports were modified.
- Queries on files or database tables run slowly – modifying parts of the system may improve the speed.
- The tab order (order in which input boxes are accessed) is slightly incorrect – changing the tab order will speed up input.

Table 11.02

	RAD	Spiral	Information engineering	Yourdon structured Method	Soft systems/ multiview	SSADM
Required level of user involvement	Very high	Medium	Medium	Low to medium	Medium to high	Medium
System size	Small	Medium	Large	Any size	Small	Large
Tools and techniques						
Prototyping ERM Normalisation Structure diagrams Low-level diagrams	Yes Possibly Possibly No No	Yes Yes Yes No No	Yes Yes Yes No Yes	Yes Yes Yes Yes Yes	Yes Yes Yes No No	Yes Yes Yes Yes Yes
Additional facts	Good for developing **non-critical systems** such as accounting, graphics or word-processing solutions.	Good for looking at a **potential system** in the **wider context.**	Good for **complex systems** and is proactive as it expects analysts and developers to be included in **strategic planning**, so that **future information needs** can be established early.	This is one of the methodologies that only considers the **feasibility, analysis** and **design** stages of the life cycle and does not concern itself with build, implementation or maintenance.	The smallest methodology as it is only concerned with the analysis and design stages of the life cycle.	The most commonly used methodology. Even though it has many tools and techniques, it is accepted that only those that are **appropriate** will be used during an investigation.

Clearly the perfective maintenance is about making the system work more efficiently and effectively. As such, activities performed as part of perfective maintenance are not as urgent as those required for corrective maintenance and these fixes are a lower priority. There is no fixed timeframe, although it is likely that the organisation (or individual users) will be keen to have some aspects resolved more quickly. As a general rule, however, it is anticipated that these issues will be addressed within weeks, or maybe a few months, depending on the quantity of modifications involved.

3 Adaptive

Adaptive maintenance is a much more long-term concern. This is because the organisation is unlikely to stay still. Its needs will change, sometimes quickly, sometimes more slowly. Either way, the system will need to adapt to these needs. Some possible triggers for adaptive maintenance could include:

- organisational expansion
- more potential users
- larger volumes of data
- technological advances (better hardware or software becomes available)
- activities of competitors – the system might need to be upgraded to ensure that the organisation can maintain a **competitive advantage**.

The timeframe usually involved in adaptive maintenance is very long term and it is often **proactive** as the organisation defines its future strategies and identifies that its information needs may have to change to support new activities. In some instances, however, it will be **reactive**: it will need to react to technological development and the activities of competitors.

Review

The final stage of the life cycle is the review, where all those individuals who were involved in the development of the system will sit down together and evaluate the project, the process and the outcome! This means that each stage of the life cycle will be discussed and good and bad experiences will be explored. It is through this process that analysts, developers and project managers learn. When undertaking the next project, they will feel more confident about what went well and will try to anticipate and avoid anything that went badly.

Eventually, through review activities, a new project may be defined and the whole process will begin again (hence the term life cycle).

11.1.3 Developmental tools and techniques

We have already explored some of the development life cycle models in the previous section and we will fully investigate **SSADM** (one of the most commonly used developmental methodologies) later in this section. To provide an overview of some of the methods we have already considered, shown on page 302 is a table that compares the methodologies by commenting on common elements:

- **Required level of user involvement** – some methodologies require a high level of user involvement in order to allow the project to progress. This is particularly true of RAD, which requires constant input from users as there is likely to be very little design documentation to work with.
- **System size** – some methodologies are best used for investigating and developing a solution for a particular size of system.
- **Tools and techniques** – this is a brief comparison of tools and techniques used by each methodology.
- **Additional facts**.

There are many more methodologies than those listed and described here. Attempting to cover them all in depth would require at least one book in its own right. For this reason, the only methodology that will be covered at this stage will be SSADM.

SSADM (Structured Systems Analysis Design Methodology)

At first glance this methodology can be quite overwhelming, particular to a new analyst. This is because as a **structured** methodology it is quite prescriptive. The defined steps are known as stages and it is recommended that each stage is followed to guarantee a successful outcome to the project.

Stage 0	Feasibility study
Stage 1	Investigation of current requirements
Stage 2	Business systems options
Stage 3	Definition of requirements
Stage 4	Technical systems options
Stage 5	Logical design
Stage 6	Physical design

Notice that the process does not continue to build, implementation, maintenance and review.

With the exception of stages 2 and 4, these stages are as described earlier in this unit.

Business systems options (BSO) are relatively easy to explain – they are the alternative solutions that could be created, viewed from a business perspective. The BSOs are intended to offer business solutions without getting involved in defining specifics about the technical environment. For example, a solution could be an **application**, purchased complete and that just requires data to be input for it to function (e.g. Sage Accounting®). The alternative would be a **tailored** solution using a base program (e.g. Microsoft Access® or Excel®), which needs to be modified and set up before data can be input.

The final business option will be a **bespoke** solution – one programmed from scratch using a programming language such as Visual Basic®, C# or Java™.

Ultimately, a single BSO will be chosen with which the project will move forward.

Technical systems options (TSO) are the physical media on which the business solution will ultimately be installed. Sometimes, particular hardware or software will need to be used, because of functional aspects of the proposed system; at other times there will be much more flexibility. Often a series of TSOs will be developed that will consider different hardware and software configurations, levels of technical support and cost.

As with the BSOs, a single TSO will be chosen and the project will move forward.

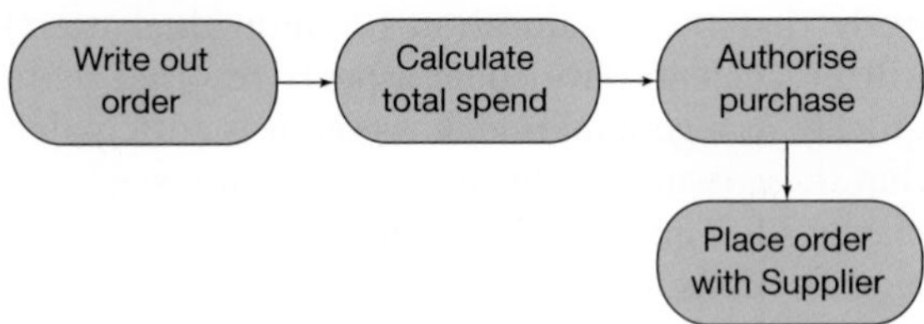

Figure 11.06 Basic activity diagram for purchase order

Bearing in mind that SSADM is a structured methodology, in most circumstances all of the steps will be undertaken (in some form), although the method does accept that inappropriate steps can be missed, or techniques ignored or replaced by suitable alternatives. One example would be the use of data flow diagrams. SSADM uses these at both the investigation and design stages of the life cycle. However, if your system is a website, your solution might not have any data in the conventional sense. As such, using data flow diagramming or normalisation just because they are available techniques in the methodology, would seem to make very little sense.

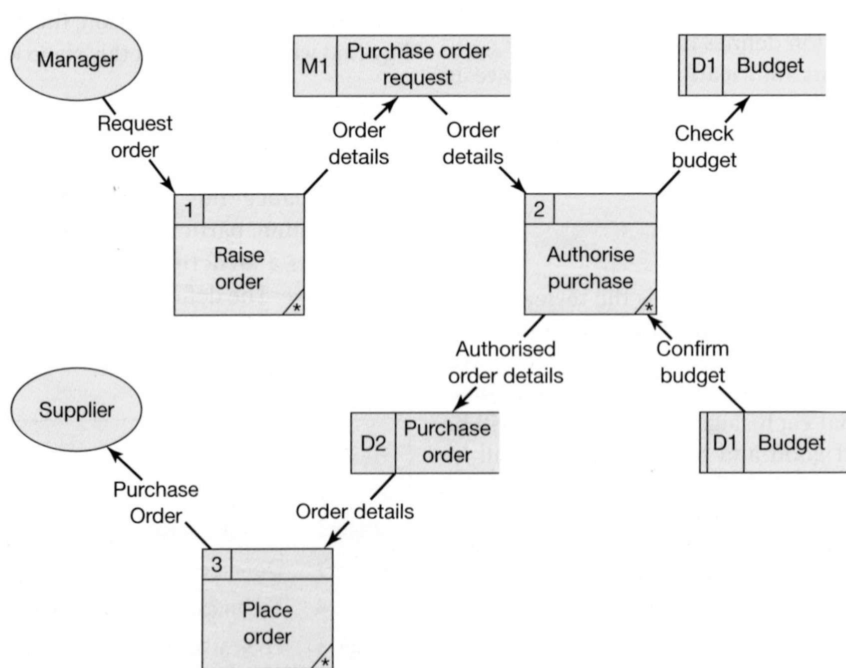

Figure 11.07 Level 1 DFD for purchase order

Typical tools and techniques e.g. activity diagrams, data flow diagrams, computer-aided software engineering tools (CASE)

The text of an analytical report will usually be supported by one or more of a series of diagrams.

Activity diagrams essentially represent the actions of a process, without getting bogged down with data. For example, the production manager asks a purchasing administrator to place an order for a large amount of raw materials (Figure 11.06).

Notice that the following are *not* specified on this diagram:

- what the order is written on
- how the total spend is calculated (or what formula to use)
- how the purchase becomes authorised or by whom.

The same basic process as described in the activity diagram will now be redrawn as a **data flow diagram** (Figure 11.07).

Figure 11.07 represents the same process, but has different elements. The first difference is that the **calculate total spend** activity is missing. This does not imply that it will not be done, it just doesn't need to be represented on this diagram.

The originator of the activity is identified, as is the final recipient.

Physical data stores are identified:

- **Purchase order request** – this could be something as simple as a note on a piece of paper detailing what the manager has requested, or it could be something as formal as an official form that is passed on to be authorised before an actual purchase order is raised.
- **Budget** – the chances are that the manager and department will have a budget. This will need to be checked to see whether the department has enough money to pay for the goods the manager is about to order. The **budget file** is checked.
- **Purchase order** – once authorised, the purchase order is created and sent to the supplier.

Each data store is numbered. You will notice that the purchase order request data store is marked M1, while the budget and the purchase order stores have identifiers that begin with a D – D1 and D2, respectively.

The **M** is the annotation for a **manual** data store. This will be a physical piece of paper. The **D** data stores are **digital**. This means that the information is stored in **electronic files**. It is likely that the budget will be stored in a spreadsheet (D1) and that the purchase order will be stored as a record in a database (D2).

Finally, each line (known as a **data flow**) must be **annotated**. The data flow could, however, be made up of verbal data. For example, when the manager requests that the administrator raises an order, he or she is likely to have made that request verbally. Similarly, the final part of the process, the purchase order flowing to the supplier, will probably be as a document or email.

What is particularly interesting about this diagram is not its content, but the tool that was used to create the diagram. Figure 11.07 was created using a **CASE tool**. CASE stands for Computer-aided Software Engineering, and is a piece of software that is used to assist developers in the creation of software solutions. The software used in this instance (Select SSADM Professional®) is a tool that can easily create the diagrams needed in systems analysis and solution design. Without this tool, developers would need to use tools such as basic shapes and text boxes linked as groups, created in Microsoft Word®. This can be time-consuming to say the least!

Some CASE tools not only create these diagrams, but also have functionality to create the **skeleton program code** at the touch of a button, based on the diagram created by the user. This code really does only have the basic functionality, and will need to be heavily modified by the developer.

11.1.4 Key drivers

We have already considered a number of possible triggers for the need to develop a new system including users identifying a need or an organisation needing to keep up with competitors. A few more drivers are considered here.

Business need (e.g. need for growth, company acquisition, need to increase productivity, legal requirements)

Need for growth

Sometimes businesses can become **stagnant**. This means that they are **not growing** (gaining new business and exploring new opportunities) or they are **shrinking** (losing business). Eventually, businesses that do not have any movement or change will begin to decline, although this can take some time.

Most organisations want to advance – they want to expand, become involved in new markets and increase profits. They need to grow to survive and for this they need to have a **strategic plan**. This is where the company decides what it wants to do and what direction it wants to take. As part of this process, its systems will be examined to ensure that they are capable of supporting the proposed growth. If this is not the case, then the organisation has time to address the issues.

Company acquisition

It is not unusual for one company to buy out another. For example, the media company Telewest was purchased by the larger group NTL a few years ago. Since then, it has been sold again – this time to the Virgin Media Group.

An organisation may well buy another company for any one of or combination of the following reasons:

- **To access new markets** – a company selling sports equipment, for example, buys a sports clothing company so that it can add products and services to its portfolio that it feels will interest its existing customers. Alternatively, an organisation might purchase a company active in a completely different market sector so that it can get involved in new different activities.
- **To increase market share of existing business** – one supermarket chain buys out another supermarket chain, thus having more outlets and business overall.
- **To acquire particular assets** – sometimes the acquisition is because one company needs to purchase the **assets** of another company so that it can use them itself. An example might be a car manufacturer buying an advertising company so that it can reduce its marketing and advertising costs.

If one organisation acquires another, it can do one of two things:

- allow the systems to continue running separately for each company
- find ways of integrating systems so that organisations can work together.

Which route is taken will depend very much on what managers intended when they purchased the company. If the acquiring company does not intend to keep its acquisition, for example, there would be little point in integrating the systems.

Need to increase productivity

When systems have been in place for a period of time, they are said to decay. This means that they become less and less useful to the organisation. Consider Figure 11.08.

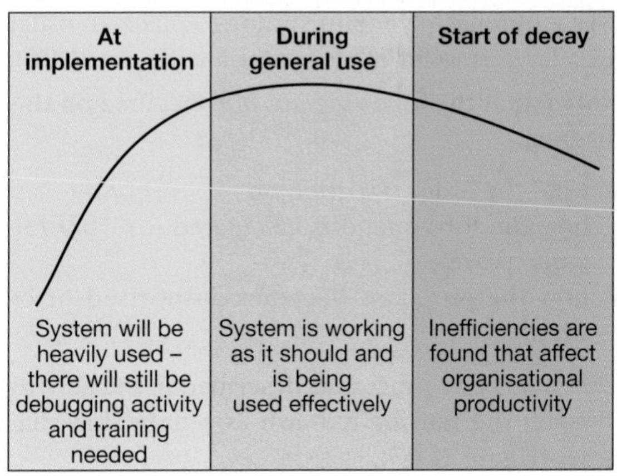

Figure 11.08 Systems decay

What causes systems decay? These are a few examples:

- **New technology** becomes available that would help increase productivity by improving efficiency.
- **Capacity** needs increase because sales have improved and productivity output does not match demand.
- The **activities of competitors** demand that the organisation improves its ability to respond.
- **More users** working on the system can slow it down, thereby making the system less productive overall.

Legal requirements

At times an organisation has no other option but to respond to changes in the law. Responding to and implementing required changes in health and safety legislation is essential if an organisation is going to continue to operate within the law.

The one advantage of changes in legal requirements is that they are usually anticipated. It would not be fair if changes needed to be made immediately that would disadvantage one company over another. When new laws, or changes in existing laws, occur, companies usually have a **grace** period of time to prepare prior to the law coming into force.

11.1.5 Structured analysis

This section will cover the following grading criterion:

Make the Grade

Possibly presented as a complementary poster to the presentation slides and leaflets for P1, P2 and M1, evidence for P3 should centre on an explanation of the benefits of structured analysis, concentrating on the importance of quality analysis to reduce the risk to projects and supporting the notion that competent analysis helps developers to better manage projects as a whole.

The main benefit of using any prescribed process is that carefully following a series of steps that have been tried and tested is more likely to produce a successful outcome or end product than merely guessing your way through the process!

Some of the other benefits are detailed below.

1. **Reduced risk of projects running over-budget** – if projects are not completed within the anticipated budget, it is possible that the project may not be completed at all, even if significant work has already been done. The company may simply not have the money to complete it. As such, meeting deadlines is a priority.
2. **Reduced risk of projects running over-time** – if projects run over the anticipated timeframe, developers might simply run out of time and the project could be shelved. More importantly, with some projects developers might be expected to pay a fine for late completion (a little bit like paying a library fine for not returning a book on time). This means that the development team will effectively earn less for the completed project than they were expecting to because they will end up repaying some of the money. The penalties can be very severe, particularly if the organisation receiving the system is relying on the completion of the system on a given date and other activities will be heavily affected by its non-delivery. Again, meeting deadlines is a priority.
3. **Good quality software is produced that meets requirements** – if each of the steps in the project have been fully and accurately completed, it should ensure that the users receive a good quality product. This point is largely about software, but in real terms it applies to any type of system.
4. **Projects are better managed** – formalised deadlines should be agreed at the beginning of a project. These are usually recorded in a project plan that should contain:
   - **Specific milestones** – these will be points in the process where tasks should have been completed.
   - **Team meetings** – regular team meetings where progress is reviewed should also be planned, as an opportunity for members of the team to get together and discuss any issues that are arising. However, this can become unproductive unless the meetings are kept short and to the point.
   - **Interim review dates** – where the team and the client get together to review progress and discuss any issues.
   - **The final handover date** – this should reflect the date previously agreed with the client.

   All methodologies accept that a poorly managed project will ultimately result in a poor outcome.
5. **Maintainable systems** and code are produced that result in more **resilient systems** – the requirement to document completed systems is part of most methodologies. Good technical documentation will ensure that systems are easy to maintain, because information is available to those whose role it is to carry out the relevant maintenance.
   - Data tables (used for any system that contains data) should be produced that include information about input masking or validation routines.

- Programming code should be fully documented to explain what particular lines of code, functions or procedures do. Variables should be explained.
- Network and cabling diagrams will explain how systems are wired. IP addresses for machines will have been logged.

Ultimately, a system that is well maintained is one that will fail rarely – hence the term 'robustness'. Everything is known and documented in a way that makes the information accessible and complete.

Resilient systems

A resilient system is one that can cope with diversity because it can be **adapted** to accommodate change. It would be little use to develop a system that is only designed to meet existing needs and which would then need to be completely reinvented as new demands on the system come along.

Project planning – useful things to remember

When planning a project, ensure that you allow sufficient **time** to undertake **all aspects** of the project, from analysis, through design to building, testing, implementation and review.

A novice analyst is likely to **underestimate** the time it actually takes to build and test the system. In reality, testing alone can take as much as 50 per cent of the total development time.

B Braincheck 1

Place the following stages of the generic systems life cycle into the correct order:

A) Review	**B)** Feasibility
C) Build system	**D)** Design
E) Testing	**F)** Implementation
G) Investigation or analysis	**H)** Requirements analysis and specification
I) Initiation or problem definition	**J)** Maintenance

11.2 Be able to carry out a structured analysis of business systems requirements

This section will cover the following grading criterion:

Make the Grade P4

For P4 you will be expected to use appropriate tools and techniques to gather the information you need to produce a requirements specification.

You will be given a scenario that will allow you to gather multiple responses (e.g. a customer or staff survey) and you will need to employ a range of information gathering techniques such as questionnaires or interviews (or any other appropriate techniques as defined by the unit).

Evidence can be in the form of witness statements, interview notes and completed questionnaires because at this stage you only need to evidence the information gathering process. The requirements specification is developed for P5.

11.2.1 Investigation

Investigative techniques

There are a variety of investigative techniques at the analyst's disposal. In any situation, one or more of these might be used to ensure that sufficient information about the current system is obtained. These techniques include:

- interview
- questionnaire
- data analysis (examination of records)
- meeting
- document analysis (examination of existing documents)
- observation.

Each method has very different uses and consequently has advantages and disadvantages when applied to analysis activities. How appropriate a specific technique will be depends on a number of factors:

- size of the organisation
- number of staff employed (and who could be potential users of the system)
- location
- distribution.

What now follows is a review of these techniques.

Interviews

An interview is a process where the analyst and user discuss the user's functional role (Figure 11.09). This is usually pre-arranged at a convenient time. In order to ensure that the user will supply the correct information when interviewed, a checklist of points and questions should be created in advance. This checklist should be given to the user prior to the interview, so that the user can think about answers that he or she might need to give.

Scorecard – Interview

+ Interviewing is useful as it will allow the analyst to gather facts and information from those who have experience of the system.
+ Having this level of contact with a user will enable the interviewer to ask additional questions if further information is required.
+ This can have the advantage of highlighting issues that the analyst might not have considered (and not prepared questions for).
– This process can be very time-consuming and expensive as significant time will need to be allocated to interview each user, so it is unlikely that this technique would be used where there is a large body of system users.
– Some users are suspicious of this type of interview and could be uncooperative. This could be illustrated through a refusal to answer questions, changing the subject, getting side tracked by irrelevant information, or just not providing enough detail for the response to be of any use. In extreme cases, the interviewee could intentionally provide incorrect information in an attempt to sabotage the process.

To ensure that this technique has a successful outcome, the interviewer should ideally have received extensive training in interview techniques. He or she will need to be able to build a rapport with the interviewee to ensure that he or she feels at ease and able to give responses that will be of benefit to the design of the new system.

Questions must be carefully written to ensure that they are unambiguous. If the questions are badly worded, they could be misunderstood by the interviewee and the response might not be what was expected.

If the analyst is in any doubt about the validity of questions that have been asked as part of the interview process, s/he should find another method of validating the response (by using another technique for example).

Questionnaires

While lists of relevant questions, formatted as a questionnaire, are an exceedingly useful investigation tool, the success rate in acquiring the right information is lower than for most other techniques. This is because with most other techniques there is either an element of face-to-face contact, or physical documents or records will be used, which will ensure that information gained will be reliable.

Scorecard – Questionnaire

+ Questionnaires are extremely useful when you want to gather small amounts of information from a large number of users, particularly if they are also in multiple locations.
+ Every user will be asked identical questions – which will make the analysis of the responses much easier to facilitate.
+ As there is little personal contact involved, it is likely that the users will be happy to provide responses, particularly if they are reassured that their forms will be anonymous.
+ Questionnaires are good for gathering factual information that can be measured (so is quantifiable). On average, how many records do you think you have to create each week? How many edits are you likely to do? These sorts of questions will help analysts establish volumes of data, for example.
– If a questionnaire has been poorly written, then it will effectively be useless. The users might not have interpreted questions correctly and may have given incorrect or inappropriate answers.
– Sometimes a response might be interesting and it may highlight new, as yet unconsidered, issues. The analyst may want to talk to the user to discuss the

issue further. However, if the responses are anonymous, the analyst has no way of tracing the originator.

- – It can be useful to see a system in action and words on a questionnaire might not adequately explain aspects that the analyst really needs to see to fully understand – it can all be a little remote.
- – With this technique, the analyst can never be sure whether or not the user is being honest. As with interviews, the analyst could intentionally be given incorrect information.

With this technique, preparation is the key.

Meetings

Meetings are a useful way of effectively interviewing a large number of people simultaneously (Figure 11.10). As with the one-to-one interview, this will usually take place at a pre-arranged time that is convenient for all those attending.

Scorecard – Meetings

- + Meetings are useful for gathering facts in an environment where attendees might be able to add useful information, or introduce valuable and constructive new lines of investigation.
- + The personal contact will also enable the analyst to ask additional questions if further information is required.
- + Less time-consuming and expensive than the one-to-one interview, this technique would be used where there is a larger (but not excessively large) body of system users who can be consulted together.
- – Some individuals, might be reluctant to voice opinions and give too much away about what they do with others present.

To ensure that this technique will have a successful outcome, the meeting should have some structure (particularly an agenda and a prescribed timeframe), otherwise useful time could be wasted as those attending get bogged down with irrelevancies.

It would still be useful if the analyst had prepared some specific questions in advance to guide the meeting.

Observations

Like interviews, observations can be extremely informative. One of the main reasons is that during an interview, or even on a questionnaire, a system user will probably have no difficulty recalling and describing activities that he or she does on a regular basis. What is likely, however, is that irregular tasks may be forgotten.

Scorecard – Observation

- + Aspects of the current system that would be difficult to document could be experienced by the analyst – for example, the office layout, the positioning of electrical points, the condition of desks, ventilation, temperature, lighting etc. – which could all have an affect on the productivity and efficiency of both the staff and the current system.
- + The analyst will be able to formally observe the workload that the system user undertakes, comparing it with the estimates of volume, and, more importantly, will be able to identify whether there are any peaks or troughs in the activity, or whether the processes are evenly spaced over the period.
- + Bottlenecks in particular processes will be identified (which the user might not even have been aware of, especially if they are normally busy!).
- – Individuals are often sceptical about being observed and distrustful of the usefulness of this technique.
- – Yet again, this technique is time-consuming as it requires the analyst to spend a reasonable amount of time with users. This would be inappropriate for systems where there are a larger number of users.

To ensure that this technique is used **transparently** (there is nothing hidden about the process) it can be useful if the analyst and user discuss the analyst's findings after the observation, so that the person being observed can feel reassured about the process.

The key with observations is to ensure that all staff being observed are advised in advance, and any concerns they might have should be dealt with prior to the observation taking place.

Document Analysis

This requires the physical examination of the organisation's documents. If current procedures and processes are well documented, then these will provide a convenient source of useful information. The types of source documents that the analyst might be offered include:

- sales invoices
- delivery notes
- purchase orders
- statements
- purchase and sales ledgers
- customer record cards
- supplier record cards
- HR (Human Resource) documents
- production documents.

Scorecard – Document analysis

+ As documents could be considered to be some of the outputs of the system, the analyst should initially ascertain whether the document does actually fulfil some useful purpose.
+ This activity can highlight redundant and repetitive activities the organisation might not have been aware of.
– The difficulty here is that the document may need to be subsequently redesigned.
– As with the examination of records, the analyst can be inundated with documentation that needs to be sorted and analysed.

The analysis of these documents can help the analyst to develop an understanding of how the information flows throughout the organisation, and ultimately to the external entities that interact with the system.

Data analysis

What is required with this technique is that the analyst will examine the organisation's existing records from a data perspective rather than a document perspective. These records could be in many forms. If the organisation currently has a manual system, it will be likely that they will be ledgers, record cards, files of invoices, statements and orders.

If the system is already computerised, even in part, there will be electronic data to consider – possibly using software that is unfamiliar to you.

Scorecard – Data analysis

+ The main advantage of examining current records is that the types of data stored can be physically seen and, to some extent, the volume of data can be estimated.
+ Particular transactions can be traced back through the records to establish the types of processes that are applied to a specific item of data.
+ The main disadvantage of this technique is that analysts can sometimes feel overwhelmed by the quantity of data they are given to look at.
– It is sometimes difficult to be sure that you have all the relevant records.
– It can be difficult trying to decide where to stop!
– Some of the records might be out of date and may not be used any more.

This really is one of the essential techniques that can be used when developing data-driven systems. It doesn't require any input from the users unless the analyst wants to ask particular questions.

Sensitivity in collecting information and observing individuals at work

One of the most difficult aspects of impending change is that most employees will fear the process. This is largely because they do not really understand the procedure, and often have no real comprehension of how the change will affect them on a personal level. In some cases, employees will be worried that their jobs could actually be at risk.

As an analyst, you should be sensitive to this kind of insecurity, particularly when you are collecting information about people and what they do, or when you are observing them in their own working environments. Usually, if the organisation has properly prepared the workforce for such an investigation, by fully explaining the process, the organisation's intentions and how staff will be affected, then most system users will be cooperative, even if you find some will be more reluctant than others.

The analyst and the development team really should ensure that they build up a good rapport with system users.

11.2.2 Analysis

The physical task of undertaking analysis should be linked directly to the chosen methodology to ensure that all relevant processes are examined and recorded adequately, and to make sure that all users who will be involved in using the new system will feel included in the process.

The results will then be reviewed and a **cost–benefit analysis** undertaken to formalise the costs of the implementation in a range of areas.

Cost–benefit analysis

The cost–benefit analysis initially itemises the costs of the project in monetary terms. It will break these costs down in a logical way, so that the organisation is left in no doubt about how much it will need to spend. This breakdown is also useful if the project is running close to budget, as managers and developers can use this information to try to find some savings.

The costs will include the following:

- development – how much it will cost just to develop the solution
- installation – the costs of implementation; e.g. the cost of installing new cabling
- equipment – hardware costs (including peripherals such as printers, routers etc.)
- personnel – e.g. training costs
- projected operating costs – how much the system will cost to run
- indirect costs – the costs of staff time when they are involved in meetings, one-to-one interviews, taking part in training and other developmental activities, and are thus not doing their normal job.

The benefits that the organisation will see are then also listed, for example:

- reduction in staff costs
- savings in other operating costs that the organisation experiences such as consumables
- better sales as marketing information and data analysis improve
- improved cash flow position because invoices and statements go out faster
- better stock control
- enhanced customer service
- happier staff
- better quality and quantities of information for managers.

Through the cost–benefit analysis, the client should be able to see that the project will be worthwhile, even if some of the benefits are also indirect, such as better staff morale.

11.2.3 Requirements specification

This section will cover the following grading criteria:

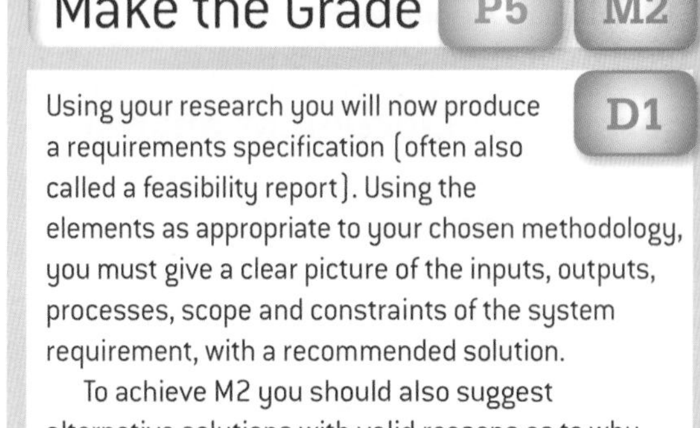

Make the Grade P5 M2 D1

Using your research you will now produce a requirements specification (often also called a feasibility report). Using the elements as appropriate to your chosen methodology, you must give a clear picture of the inputs, outputs, processes, scope and constraints of the system requirement, with a recommended solution.

To achieve M2 you should also suggest alternative solutions with valid reasons as to why you have considered them.

For D1 you will need to include an analysis of the costs and benefits of the solution. This does not need to include precise costs but all elements that should be factored into a cost–benefit analysis must be included.

It is likely that this will be put together as a formal report.

The requirements specification will then need to be prepared, ensuring that the following content is included to give a full picture of the required system.

Scope

Defining the scope of the project by writing the requirements specification will ensure that all those involved in the project will have no doubts about what the system will and will not do.

Initially, the **system boundaries** will be specified. This is a description of the functionality the finished system is intended to have, described in very general terms, and which will specify any limitations that are known in advance. The functionality is broken down into the inputs, outputs and processing it requires.

Inputs

Inputs are what goes into the system. At this stage, the types of information that will be input and stored in the system will be described in general terms. It is also useful to specify how the data will be **captured** (input into the system) For example:

- customer records – keyboard and mouse
- supplier details – keyboard and mouse
- stock – keyboard and mouse
- sales – barcode reader.

Ultimately, data that goes into the system will be processed and will provide the outputs.

Outputs

The specified **outputs** of the system will be a combination of on-screen displays and reports, as necessary to produce the required functionality of the system. At the requirements specification stage, what the analyst will produce will be a list of proposed outputs (the reports and displays will be formally designed later in the process).

Using the example of a stock system, the list might look something like this:

- on-screen displays
  - single stock item
  - all items in a category
  - all items for one supplier
- reports
  - items at or below minimum stock level
  - items not sold in last three months
  - all products with cost and resale price
  - all products with resale price only (for price list).

Clearly this is not a full list, but it does provide a good sample. These outputs will have been chosen through discussions with the users and through looking at the documentation the organisation currently has.

Processes

In order to specify processing, we need to decide how the information that is input will be **transformed** into the outputs, but still in general terms. In the design section that follows, we will look at processing in more detail.

So, how will we process the inputs we have above to provide the outputs? Let's take the on-screen display outputs one by one.

- single stock item – a query allowing the user to search for a single item based on the item code or name
- all items in a category – a query allowing the user to search for all items in a single category (identified by the category input by the user)
- all items for one supplier – a query where all products will be listed for a particular supplier (identified by the supplier code).

Notice that at this stage we have not listed or described what will be physically output (which bits of the records). For example, with the single stock item we have not identified that we will display the stock code, description, cost price, resale price and supplier code(s). That level of detail will be recorded in the design stage.

Costs and benefits

The results of the cost–benefit analysis will also be included in the requirements specification, as this summary will often be used to support the final decision-making process.

Recommendations

At this stage, the recommendation will be to continue with the project or to abandon it. Which solution will be chosen from a range of alternatives will not always have been decided at this point.

Alternative solutions

The final investigative aspect that must be recorded is evidence that alternative solutions were considered by analysts before a single one was recommended to the organisation.

In terms of IT, there are four main alternatives in any situation – three of these solutions are electronic and the remaining one is a manual solution:

1. Bespoke
2. Off-the-shelf application
3. Tailored
4. Improved manual system

Each of the above solutions has advantages and disadvantages for the organisation and the development team.

Bespoke

A **bespoke** solution is one that is created from scratch and which is developed using a programming language such as Microsoft Visual C#®, Visual Basic®, C®, C++® or Java™.

Advantage

+ The organisation will get a system which completely and accurately meets its needs.

Disadvantages

– This is likely to be an expensive solution, in which case it might be outside the financial scope of some organisations.
– It will take a significant amount of time to develop, so the organisation will have to wait.
– The developer will need the right level of programming skill in all the relevant areas.

At times there is no option other than to create a bespoke solution, usually because no current off-the-shelf application exists, and a tailored solution might still not provide all the functionality that is required by the system users.

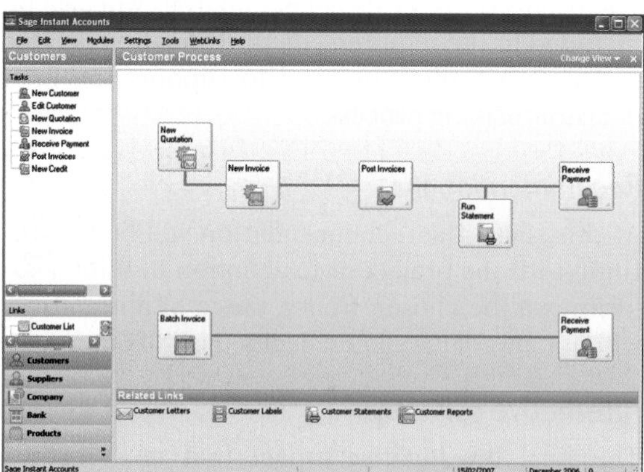

Figure 11.09 Sage Instant Accounts®

Off-the-shelf application

Over the years, many applications solutions have been developed that have specific functionality. Many of these can be purchased as complete solutions, which require only data to be added as all of the functionality is pre-programmed.

Above is an example of an off-the-shelf application. **Sage Instant Accounts®** is an accounting package designed with all the functionality required to run most businesses (see Figure 11.09).

The functionality has been organised into a series of categories. With the 'Customer' category highlighted, the list of possible activities or tasks is as shown in Figure 11.10.

On the customer menu, the usual functionality – such as adding and editing customer records – is present, along with the ability to create quotations, new invoices, process payments as they are received and manage credit levels on customer accounts.

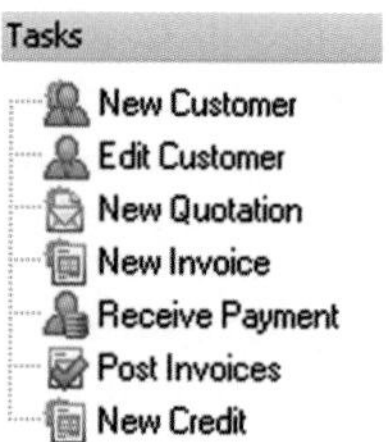

Figure 11.10 Customer tasks

In addition, there are related links, which offer optional functionality, including creating statements, customer letters, mailing labels and reports.

The 'Company' category would clearly require different functionality.

In Figure 11.11, for example, VAT returns are managed and monthly statistics are generated.

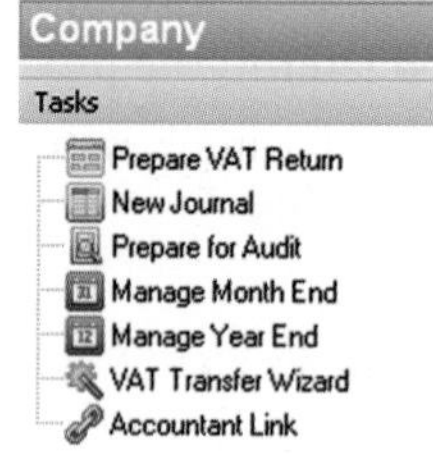

Figure 11.11 Company tasks

Off-the-shelf applications are ideal in most situations, where a specific type of application is required. This software, for example, also has a simple stock system. However, it does not have any distribution management facilities.

Advantage

+ No development time needed (this really is an instant solution!). All that is required is that the master data is input, and the system can be used.

Disadvantages

– Can be expensive, particularly if the software requires organisations to buy and maintain site licenses.
– Might not have all the functionality needed.
– Will require unfamiliar users to be trained.

If the organisation requires functionality that isn't included in a solution, they might need to purchase further software. In these circumstances, there could be a compatibility issue between systems and, as a result, problems sharing their information.

Tailored

A tailored solution uses a generic package or combination of generic packages to build a solution. The Microsoft Office® suite, for example, has spreadsheet, database, word-processing and presentation capabilities. However, it is not quite as straightforward as it is with off-the-shelf solutions, because when using a database package like Microsoft Access® the database itself has no structure.

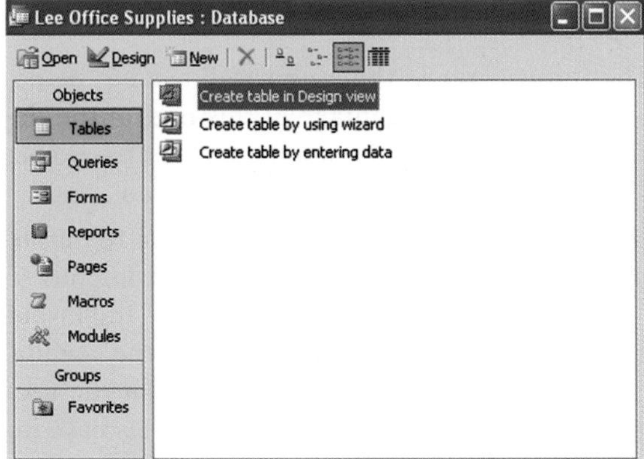

Figure 11.12 An empty database

The database shown in Figure 11.16 has been created for Lee Office Supplies. However, at this stage it is empty – the tables need to be created, data types declared, links between tables established, queries designed, reports developed. Only then will the system users be able to key in the data and begin using the system.

A tailored solution, therefore, is always developed from an existing piece of software that is **modified** or **tweaked** to provide the necessary functionality.

Improved manual system

Analysts and developers should always remember that computerisation is not necessarily going to be the appropriate solution for every situation. There are instances, for example, where it might simply not be cost effective. In the first example below, we are considering a solution for a small business.

> Tony Drogan is a painter and decorator.
>
> He has his company, but as a sole trader he has no employees.
>
> His business is that he sub-contracts his services and expertise to larger companies building houses, offices and factories. As such, they provide his materials.
>
> Contracts are usually a minimum of two weeks, but can be for up to six months.
>
> He is asked to invoice monthly.

From the above scenario the following should be clear:

- Tony only pays his own wages.
- He will not raise more than two invoices at most in a month.
- He does not have to handle any purchase invoices.

As such, a computerised system would probably be considered excessive. Tony is much more likely to maintain a simple record system because he is effectively only charging out his labour.

Consider this second scenario:

> Oldbridge Squash Centre is a five-court squash facility on the outskirts of a medium-sized town. It currently has a manual facilities booking system which they have been using successfully since the centre opened five years ago. A few months ago this system began to become unreliable. There were increased instances of double bookings and the centre lost members. The centre manager is considering implementing a computerised system to eliminate these kinds of problems.
>
> During the investigation, however, the analyst discovers that the problem is largely down to Millie, the new receptionist, who curiously started working at the centre around the time that the problems first developed! Millie came straight from school, has received no training since joining the centre and is often left alone at peak periods when most members are using the centre. She is trying to maintain bookings while handling payments and membership enquiries.

Is a computerised system required? Possibly not, but what may well be required is one of the following solutions:

a) Train Millie to better manage the tasks.

b) Double the reception staff for the peak periods.

As can be seen, there might be occasions when investing in an electronic system might not be necessary, and as such, improvement of the existing manual system should always be considered as an option. However, in the case of the Oldbridge Squash Centre, it is possible that once Millie is trained, and even with reception staff doubled at peak times, the problem might continue or reoccur at a later date. This could be because the volume of transactions that must be dealt with increases as the centre becomes more popular. If this occurs, then the original solutions of training Millie and doubling the staff might simply have delayed the inevitable – that a computerised system ultimately is required!

For the purposes of an analysis, there should be documented evidence that alternative solutions were at least considered as part of the development process. This will reassure the client that the solution that was ultimately recommended was the right one for the situation.

11.3 Be able to design business systems solutions

This section will cover the following grading criteria:

Make the Grade P6 M3 D2

To complete the unit you will need to produce the design documentation to support the solution you have recommended. How this is achieved will again depend on the methodology used and may include, for example, data flow diagrams, ERDs, top-down design or structured English. For P6, it should be clear from the documentation how a basic solution would be implemented.

To evidence M3 you will need to explain any constraints on the system design such as cost constraints, timescales or organisational policies that will need to be worked around or with. You could also have limitations on the hardware platforms available to you.

For D2 you will need to demonstrate that you have worked independently and that you have produced thorough and detailed documentation.

11.3.1 Design

It is only after the existing system has been **fully analysed**, the requirements specification for the new system has been defined and the preferred solution has been identified, that the actual design of the new system **can** be attempted.

Inputs and outputs (e.g. screens and report design)

Inputs

The **input screens** themselves will need to be designed. The one advantage of this part of the design activity is that the analyst usually has something to work from or to use as a template.

If an input screen will be an electronic representation of a form that the organisation intends to continue using, it would make sense if the layout of the online version was similar to the manual form. This is because it will be easier for the user to key in the information if the two forms have inputs in more or less the same places.

Library Membership Request Card

Last Name: ______________ First Name: ______________
Address: ______________
Post Code: ______________ Date of Birth: ______________
Telephone: ______________

Sex (please tick as appropriate): Male ☐ Female ☐

Age group (please tick as appropriate):
Under 5 ☐
5 – 13 ☐
14 – 17 ☐
18 – 59 ☐
60 + ☐

Figure 11.13 Membership card, to be completed by hand

Let's look at the following membership card, which new library members are asked to complete when they join their local library (Figure 11.13).

The design for the on-screen version can be done in many ways.

It could be hand drawn (Figure 11.14).

Or it could be created using a software package (Figure 11.15).

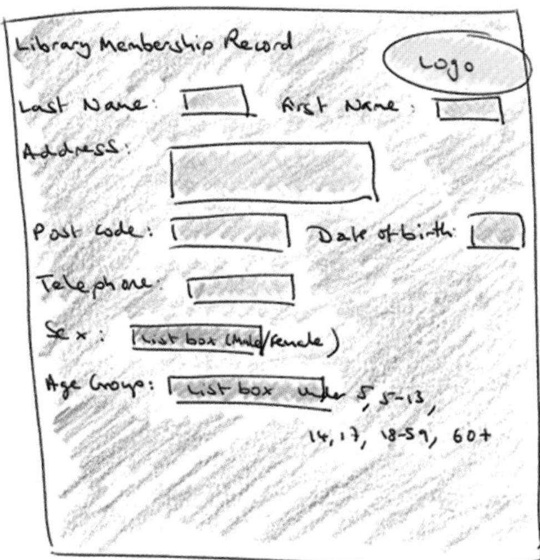

Figure 11.14 Hand-drawn representation of library input form

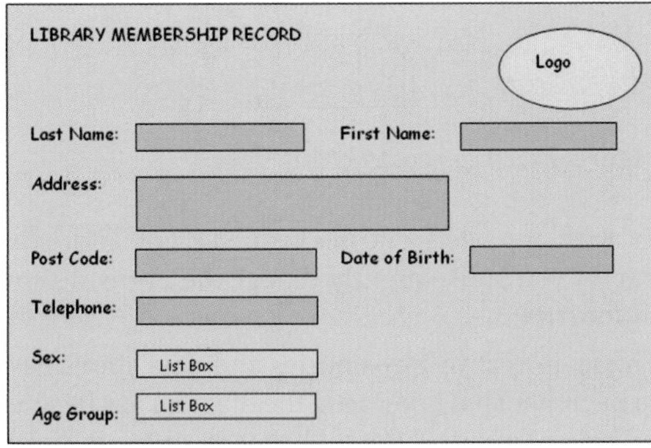

Figure 11.15 Input form reproduced as an electronic design

Tab order and logical flow

Ensure that the **flow** of movement from box to box in an electronic form is identical to the flow on the manual form. This will vastly increase the input speeds achievable by the user. If, however, it is essential for data items to be placed differently in the electronic version of the form, then ensure that the **tab order** remains the same. The tab order is the order in which the input boxes are accessed as the user presses the tab key on completing an input.

Most experienced users will not look at the screen as they input the data, they will merely use the tab key to navigate and key in while looking at the original manual form (this is often called **copy typing**). As such, as long as the order in which the boxes are accessed remains the same, the actual position of the boxes on the screen might not be as critical.

Outputs

Similarly the **outputs** of the system will need to be designed. This will be achieved in a similar way (through hand drawings or computer-generated samples). However, there are likely to be many more outputs designed than there were inputs. This is because the system will give users the opportunity to manipulate and view the data in different ways. While there will usually be some examples of reports that the organisation has that were generated in other ways, many of the outputs defined at this stage will be new. Also, unlike the inputs (which will mostly be computer-based, because sometimes organisations take this type of activity as an opportunity to modify their paper-based forms also), the outputs could be either **screen reports** or **paper-based reports**.

What will need to be defined, in addition to the layout of the form, will be what data will actually be output. Which columns will be used and which titles will be included will need to be decided.

The outputs of the system will need to be justified – in other words, the business purpose of the report will need to be established. This is to ensure that developers don't create reports that the organisation doesn't really need!

Data

Deciding how the data will be stored within the system is an essential component of good design. This must be managed carefully to ensure that the data needed in reports, for example, is accessible and in a format that can be used easily. Using diagrams is a really good way of representing this.

Data flow diagrams

The data flow diagrams created at the analysis stage will now be modified and new ones may be drawn. These diagrams can be drawn at different levels.

Context (or Level 0) and **Level 1** are the most common (although further levels can be drawn if appropriate).

Fundamentally, data flow diagrams are made up of four components.

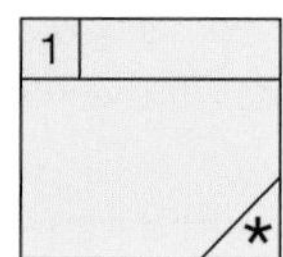

Figure 11.16

Figure 11.16 is a **process box** used to represent a procedure undertaken within a system. If the process consists of a single action (e.g. 'place order'), then the process will be considered to have been defined at its lowest level. The inclusion of the / and * symbols in the bottom right of the box indicates that this is the case. If these symbols are not present, an analyst will know that the process is made up of a series of actions, which might need to be explained on a lower-level diagram (Level 2 for example).

Process boxes are numbered although it should be noted that the numbers do not bear any relevance in the flow of the diagram, they are merely numbered for recording purposes. A process box is never repeated within a diagram.

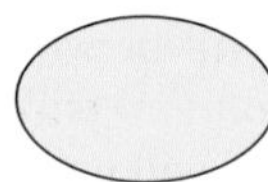

Figure 11.17

Figure 11.17 represents an **entity**. An entity is something that interacts with a process, and it may or may not be external to the organisation. As long as it is not part of the process itself, it will be considered an entity. It can put something into a process, trigger a process or receive something from a process. A customer making an enquiry could trigger a process. The organisation invoicing the customer could be another process from which the customer would receive an invoice. Entities are shown within an ellipse (the oval shape), and these can be repeated within a diagram.

If this occurs, the symbol is modified (including the original instance of the entity) as in Figure 11.18.

Figure 11.18 A repeated entity

You should bear in mind, however, that if an entity is repeated a third time or more, the symbol doesn't change.

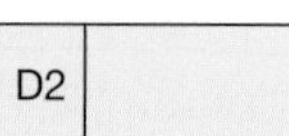

Figure 11.19

Figure 11.19 is a **data store**. A data store represents a file (held in any format). It could be a customer file on a computer or a supplier record held in a card system. Annotating whether a data store is electronic or manual is as simple as changing the letter at the beginning of the data store identifier. A **D** represents a digital (or electronic) store and a **M** a manual store (we discussed this earlier in this unit). As with entities, data stores can be repeated within a diagram. In that eventuality, the notation is modified, by adding an extra bar to the beginning of the box, as in Figure 11.20.

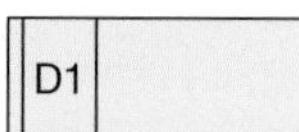

Figure 11.20 A repeated data store

As with repeated entities, you do not add extra bars if you subsequently repeat the entity a third or fourth time.

The main reason why entities and data stores have to be duplicated is because the diagram has become so well **populated** (or full) that in order to link a data store or entity with another process, you would have to cross the data flow lines. This is not allowed.

A data flow (→) denotes the data that is moving between processes, entities and processes, or data stores and processes.

To link or not to link...

You must *never* link the following:

- an entity with another entity
- a data store with another data store
- an entity with a data store.

In *every case* a process will exist and each one will link with another through the process.

Now that we have considered the notation used in data flow diagrams, we will consider the two types and you will be given examples of both.

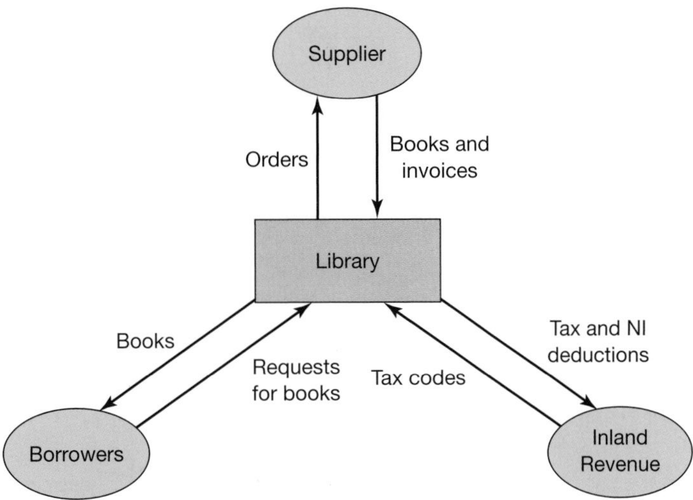

Figure 11.21 A context diagram for the whole library

Context (Level 0) diagram

A context diagram represents the whole system as a single process. If you consider our library example as a whole system, then the diagram might look something like Figure 11.21.

The first thing to notice is that all the **entities** that are shown here are going to be truly **external** to the organisation. **Suppliers**, the **borrowers** (effectively the customers of the library) and the government department known as the **Inland Revenue** will all be interacting with the system. There will be many more that we could have included here.

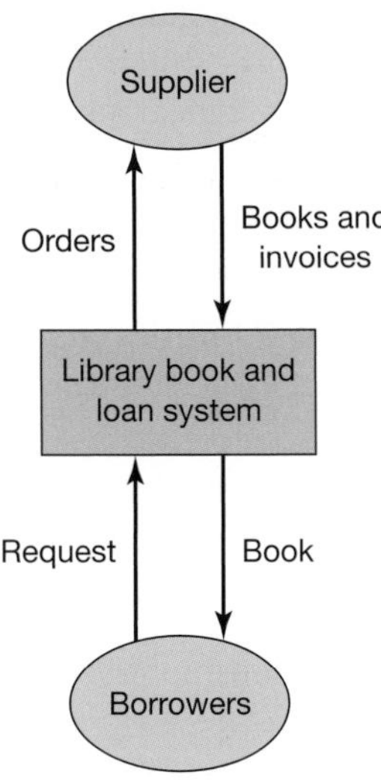

Figure 11.22 Context diagram for the book and loan system

In Figure 11.22, we have refined the system to be concerned only with the book and loan system. As the Inland Revenue has no connection to either the loan of books or their purchase, the Inland Revenue entity **disappears** in this diagram. However, if we were going to include the payroll function of the library (those paying the wages of library staff), the function would have to appear as an external entity as it would be outside the book and loan process.

Level 1 data flow diagram

The Level 1 diagram for Figure 11.21 would now show all the activities that create or use these data flows, and it would also include information about how the data is stored (in what files for example).

When developing diagrams at lower levels you would not expect any entities to be added, although data stores and processes may well be.

This diagram on page 320 (Figure 11.23), while correct in terms of what we were trying to record, does not cover all the possible processes that might exist in a book and loan system. What other functionality could there be?

- Book reservations
- Overdue book reminders
- Fines for overdue books
- Paying suppliers for the books

Whether or not these aspects would be included in the diagram would be dependent on whether the system being designed was going to include that functionality or not.

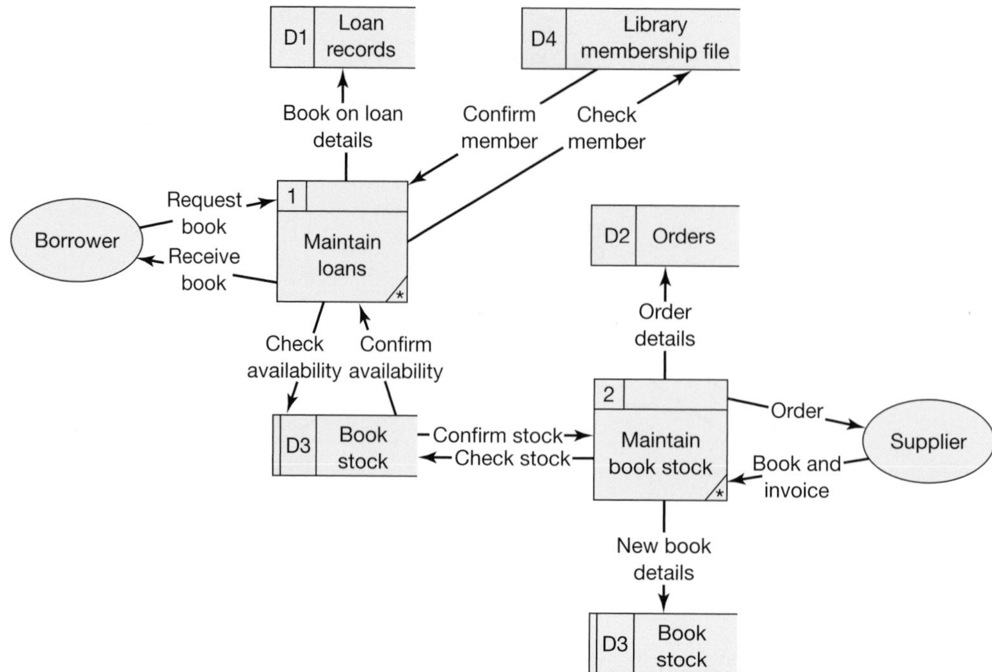

Figure 11.23 Level 1 DFD for our library

During the design phase of the life cycle, one or more diagrams like the one above will be created that will represent what the system will be like and how the data will be processed and used. It is extremely useful for defining what data will be stored, although, at this stage, nothing else about the data is defined.

Entity relationship diagrams (ERD)

Another, complementary method of documenting the design of a system will be to create an **entity relationship diagram**. This is particularly relevant for database systems, although in that particular environment you will probably see the diagram referred to as an ERM (Entity Relationship Model), as it is one of the major database modelling tools currently used in industry.

From a more generic systems design perspective, the basic concept remains the same: in an ERD, we investigate the relationship between the data items and any relevant entities, ignoring the process! This will help us to define what actual data will be held, and how that will be structured.

Entity relationship diagrams are made up of two components, an entity and a relationship (Figure 11.24).

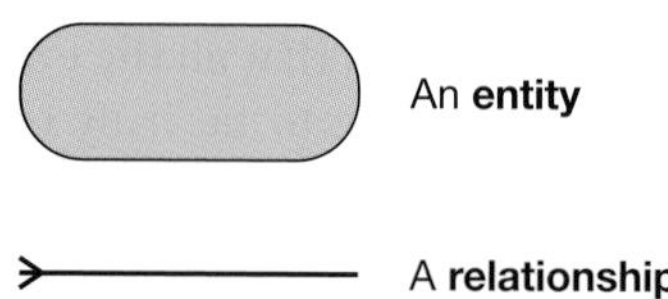

Figure 11.24

The point of an ERD is ultimately to show how all of the data items in a system relate to each other and to establish how the different parts of the data will link together in a logical way.

Key terms

What are **entities**? Entities are things about which we want to store information or data inside a system.

Entities are said to have relationships with each other.

In concept, a relationship will be one of three types (see Figure 11.25):

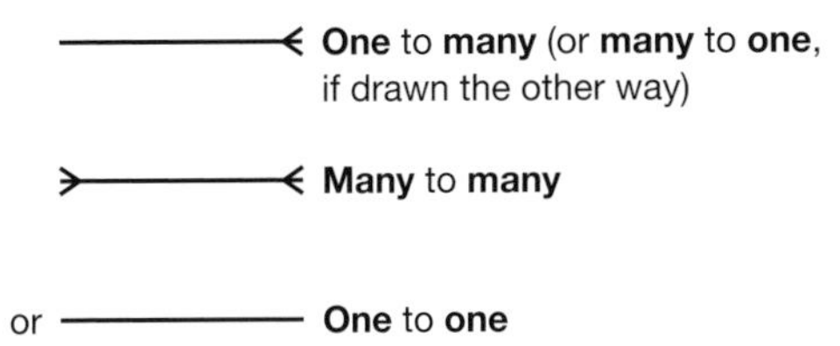

Figure 11.25

But what is a relationship? The relationship is the definition of how the entities are linked. For example:

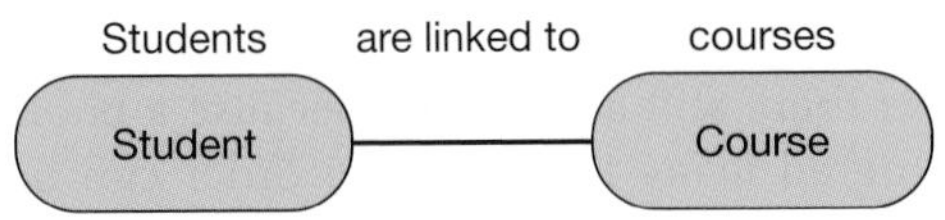

Figure 11.26

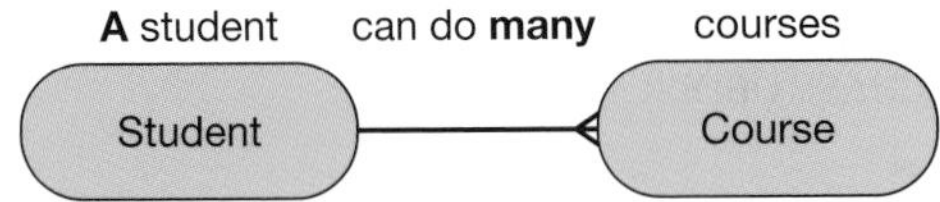

Figure 11.27

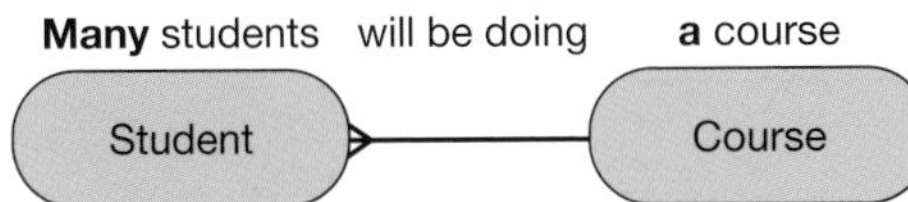

Figure 11.28

The resulting relationship would look like Figure 11.29!

Figure 11.29

Ultimately, for this particular model we need to resolve the many-to-many relationship, as the diagram should contain only one-to-many or many-to-one relationships. Many-to-many and one-to-one relationships should not exist in a well-structured system (although there are exceptions).

So how can we break down the relationship between the student and the course? One possibility might be to consider that students must enrol (register) to attend a course.

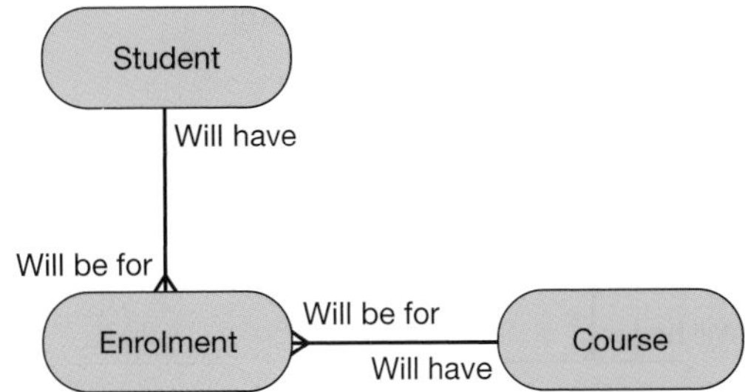

Figure 11.30

This diagram now reads as follows:

- A student will have one or many enrolments.
- An enrolment will be for one student.
- An enrolment will be for one course.
- A course will have one or many enrolments.

In its simplest form: an enrolment will be for one student on one course!

Using the library as an example, we would first consider the following question: what do libraries need to hold information about? Two things are immediately obvious: borrowers and books.

So we begin our diagram:

Figure 11.31

What is the relationship?

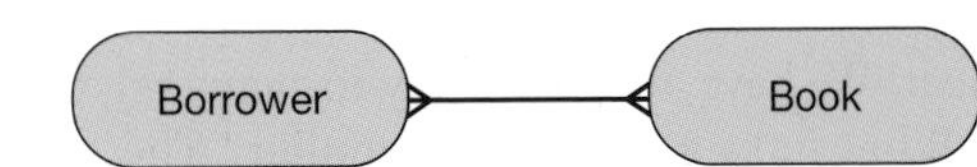

Figure 11.32

A borrower will be able to borrow one or many books and a book can be borrowed by one or many borrowers! A many-to-many relationship is now formed that we now have to go on and resolve.

What is the nature of that relationship? The actual loan of the book. We will obviously want to store data about that!

So, we need to modify the diagram:

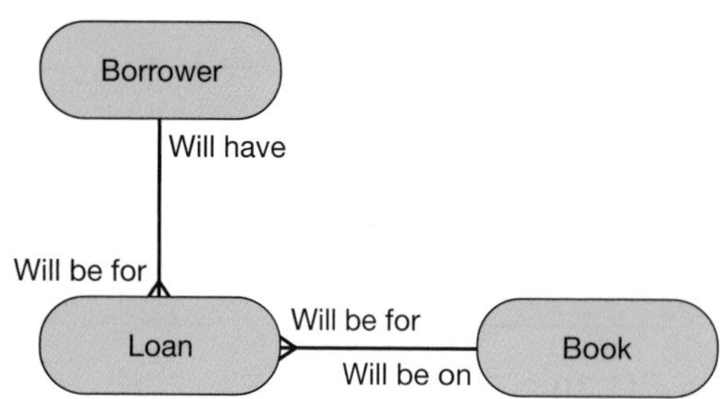

Figure 11.33

Now we can read the diagram as follows:

- A borrower will have one or many books on loan.
- A loan will be for a single borrower.
- A loan will be for one book.
- A book will be on loan one or many times.

We have now resolved this, but we still have more data to store. Clearly, as it is the major part of a library's activities, we might want to store information about the suppliers we get our books from.

We need to add the **supplier** to the diagram. But what are we going to link the new entity to?

Can we link it to the borrower? No, the borrower won't have **any interest in** who supplied the book!

Can we link it to the loan? **No**, because there is **no connection** between the **supplier of a book** and **who** it was loaned to.

Can we link the supplier to the book entity? Yes, because the book will have come originally from a supplier (see Figure 11.34)!

Oh dear! We have another many-to-many relationship. What links a book to a supplier? The order which was placed to get the book in the first place (see Figure 11.35)!

We still don't seem to have fully resolved the problem, because even though we have added an entity, when we think through the relationships logically

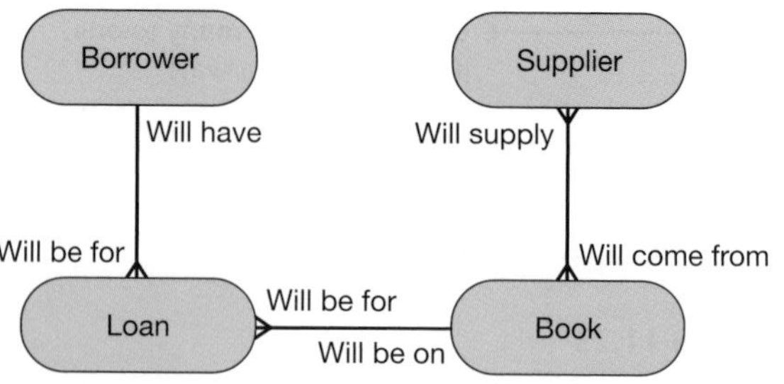

Figure 11.34

the relationship between the book and the order is still many-to-many, even though the one between supplier and order is now fine.

Why is there still a problem? Because a book can be ordered many times and an order can be for many books.

So, how do we take the final step? Let's consider what the order might look like (Figure 11.36).

PURCHASE ORDER

Order Date:

Supplier Details

Delivery Address

Quantity	Title	Author	Price per book	Total

Special Instructions: The books listed are required by 19th January 2011.

Figure 11.36

Where does the book title go on the order? Well, the book title being ordered will be one of one or many books being on that particular order. These

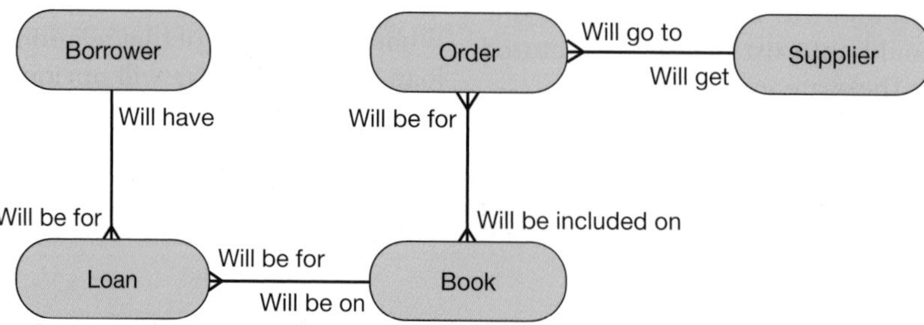

Figure 11.35

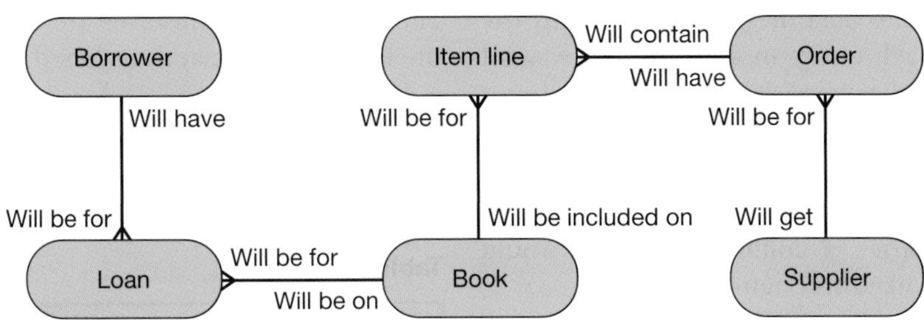

Figure 11.37 Library purchase order form

are listed in the item lines on the order (Figure 11.37). That is the missing entity!

And finally...

- A borrower will have one or many books on loan.
- A loan will be for a single borrower.
- A loan will be for one book.
- A book will be on loan one or many times.
- A book will be included on one or many item lines (for an order).
- An item line will only ever be for one book.
- An item line will only ever exist on one order.
- An order will have one or many item lines.
- An order will only ever go to one supplier.
- A supplier could get one or many orders.

From this model we now know we need to store information on:

- borrowers
- loans
- books
- item lines (which are part of orders)
- suppliers.

Having now created a Level 1 DFD and an ERD for the library problem, you should now be able to compare these two diagrams and identify the fact that you have arrived at the same point, as shown in Table 11.03.

Table 11.03

Entity	Present on DFD?	Present on ERD?
Borrower	Yes (as an entity and a data store)	Yes
Loans	Yes (as a data store)	Yes
Books	Yes (as a data store)	Yes
Orders	Yes (as a data store)	Yes, but further defined to resolve many-to-many relationship
Suppliers	Yes (as an entity)	Yes

The diagrams should ultimately match, and these do, even though the ERD has the additional 'Item lines' entity, which is needed to help define the actual file structure.

The ERD is now used to develop a **data dictionary**.

Data dictionaries

The data dictionary is the formal record of what attributes will be created to hold the data within each entity.

Key terms

An **attribute** is a piece of data that belongs to the entity. Let's take the 'book' entity as an example. What information might the library want to store about a book?

- Book title
- Edition number
- Genre (whether it's a crime book, biography, children's book etc.)
- Author(s)
- Publisher
- Year of publication

Each of the above data items will be an attribute.

It is the job of the data dictionary to record the attributes for each entity in a structured way. At this point the data types, lengths and any input masking or validation that might be applied will also be listed.

Although there are many variations on the subject of data dictionaries, a common template would look something like this (Figure 11.38).

Data Dictionary

Attribute Name	Entity	Data Type	Description	Format or Length	Validation/ Input Mask
Book Title	Book	Text	Title of book	50 characters	Upper case
Edition Number	Book	Integer	Edition number if appropriate		
Genre	Book	Text	Book category eg. Children	25 characters	
Author(s)	Book	Text	Names of all authors	100 characters	
Publisher	Book	Text	Name of publisher	25 characters	
Year of Publication	Book	Integer	Year only, eg. 2007		> 1980

Figure 11.38

Sometimes a single data dictionary is created with all attributes for all entities included in a single document (hence the inclusion of the entity column). The alternative would be to develop a data dictionary for each entity individually. This is also fully acceptable.

You will also see variations on what columns should be included in a data dictionary.

Process descriptors

The final parts of the system that will need to be designed and defined are the processes themselves. What does the system do to make Input A become Output X?

The usual methods of demonstrating the intended design of processes are decision tables, flowcharts and the use of structured English.

Decision tables

In simple terms, a **decision table** is used to represent concisely a process where a number of different actions may be taken, dependent on a range of conditions. It allows the analyst to record all of the possible conditions that might occur and define a suitable action or response. It may be easier to look at a documented example.

The conditions themselves are listed at the top of the table, with the actions listed below.

Staying with our library example, let's look at a decision table (Table 11.04) that records all the **conditions** that need to be tested and the actions that could be taken **when a borrower requests a book**.

Table 11.04

		A	B	C	D
Condition	Is a library member?	Y	Y	N	N
Condition	Book is in stock?	Y	N	Y	N
Action	Loan book	Y	N	N	N
Action	Record loan	Y	N	N	N
Action	Refuse loan	N	Y	Y	Y

Had this tool not been available, we would have had to use either a flow chart or text to represent this process. As text it would have been explained as follows:

Scenario A The borrower is a library member.
The book is in stock.
Loan the book to the borrower.
Record the loan.

Scenario B The borrower is a library member.
The book is not in stock.
Refuse the loan.

Scenario C The borrower is not a library member.
The book is in stock.
Refuse the loan.

Scenario D The borrower is not a library member.
The book is not in stock.
Refuse the loan.

Realistically, we know that with scenario B we would have offered to put a reservation on the book when returned and to notify the borrower at that time.

For scenario C, we would have offered the prospective borrower library membership, then loaned the book and recorded it.

For scenario D, we would have offered the prospective borrower library membership, then we would have put a reservation on the book when returned and notified the borrower.

However, these additional actions **were not required** in this particular decision table because there is nothing in the entity relationship diagram or the data flow diagram to suggest that we have a reservations process or data store, create new member process, or notification process.

Flowcharts

To give you an example here, we again use the 'Maintain Loans' process defined in the data flow diagram in Figure 11.22, and the decision table recorded in the previous section.

This flowchart explains the process, showing how the system should react, but interestingly further explains the decisions. In the decision table, it is implied that if the potential borrower is not available and the book is in stock we refuse the loan. In reality, if the potential borrower was not a member, we would not check the book's availability in the first place! This diagram makes this clear.

Use of structured English

As a final design tool, using **structured English** to describe processes is the closest an analyst can come to writing the actual program code because the process is described and laid out in the way it will ultimately appear in code, but without using any compiler **syntax** (terminology). This is often also called **pseudocode**. Using the process defined in the flowchart in Figure 11.39, the description would look like this:

Maintain loans process

```
Write:  Is a member?
Check:  If Yes
        Write:  Is book available?
        Check:  If Yes
                Record Loan
        Else
                Write: Refuse loan
        Else
                Write: Refuse loan
```

For the purposes of the design, the processes will individually be defined in this way. It is then up to the programmer or developer to interpret this into program specific code.

The absolute key with good solution design is that ultimately all diagrams created, explanations written and decisions made are consistent. Inconsistencies between any of these will cause difficulties when the system is developed, because they will cause developmental errors.

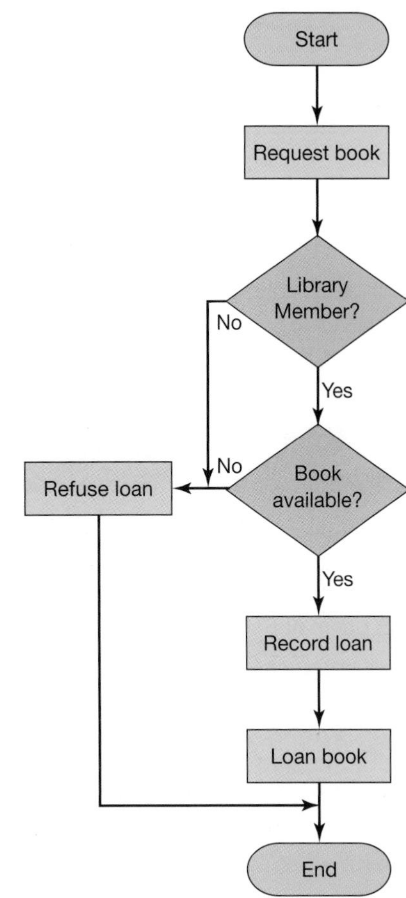

Figure 11.39 Data dictionary example, completed for the book entity

11.3.2 Constraints

From the design perspective, you will take the constraints placed on the development of the system earlier in the systems life cycle, and explain how your design has accommodated these constraints. In other words, you will explain how you have worked around them. Sometimes it can be useful to represent this in a table such as Table 11.05, where all the constraints can be listed, together with the description of how the constraint has been managed.

Table 11.05

Constraint	Accommodation
Costs	Solution will be within budget providing there are no unforeseen issues.
Organisational policies	All organisational procedures and policies have been accommodated as required.
Timescale	Development plan includes 6 weeks of recovery time to accommodate the unforeseen. If these weeks are not required, the project will finish ahead of schedule.
Legacy systems	Existing data files can be converted to provide master data for the new system. Conversion time planned into main schedule.
Available hardware platforms	Existing hardware will be fully upgraded. New equipment should be ordered to ensure that it is available for week 34.

Case Study

The management at Frankoni T-Shirts have asked you to design a new sales and stock system for them, to replace their current manual system, which is becoming increasingly unreliable. What follows here is a write-up of the notes from an interview that one of your colleagues carried out with the main users of the system.

Customers usually place orders as a result of visiting the shop, phoning through an order, or placing an order online using Frankoni's website.

When the order is received, two stocks are checked:

- *T-shirt stock*
- *design stock (the stock of iron-on designs supplied by KAM Limited (Kris Arts & Media)).*

An order is then raised and placed in an order file. This file is then used by the production department to get the information to make up the T-shirts. The order is then stamped as completed and placed in a completed order file. Once a day, the completed order file is accessed by the accounts department who will then use that information to create an invoice.

Once the invoice has been raised, it is sent, along with the relevant order items, to the customer who will then return the payment.

Activity 1

Create the following diagrams based on the scenario described in the Case Study:

- Level 1 DFD
- An ERD that represents the data.

See answers on supporting website.

Unit links

Unit 11 is a **mandatory unit** for the Edexcel BTEC Level 3 National Extended Diploma in IT (Software Development) pathway and **optional** for all other qualifications and pathways of this Level 3 IT family.

Qualification (pathway)	**Mandatory**	**Optional**	**Specialist optional**
Edexcel BTEC Level 3 National Certificate in Information Technology		✓	
Edexcel BTEC Level 3 National Subsidiary Diploma in Information Technology		✓	
Edexcel BTEC Level 3 National Diploma in Information Technology		✓	
Edexcel BTEC Level 3 National Extended Diploma in Information Technology		✓	
Edexcel BTEC Level 3 National Diploma in IT (Business)		✓	
Edexcel BTEC Level 3 National Extended Diploma in IT (Business)		✓	
Edexcel BTEC Level 3 National Diploma in IT (Networking and System Support)		✓	
Edexcel BTEC Level 3 National Extended Diploma in IT (Networking and System Support)		✓	
Edexcel BTEC Level 3 National Diploma in IT (Software Development)		✓	
Edexcel BTEC Level 3 National Extended Diploma in IT (Software Development)	✓		

Although there are no specific links to any other units in the scheme, Systems analysis remains a core skill for those undertaking a Software Development career.

Achieving success

In order to achieve each unit you will complete a series of coursework activities. Each time you hand in work, your tutor will return this to you with a record of your achievement.

This particular unit has 11 criteria to meet: 6 Pass, 3 Merit and 2 Distinction.

For a Pass: You must achieve all 6 Pass criteria.

For a Merit: You must achieve all 6 Pass and all 3 Merit criteria.

For a Distinction: You must achieve all 6 Pass, all 3 Merit and both Distinction criteria.

Further reading

Dennis, A. and Wixom, B. – *Systems Analysis and Design, 4th Edition* (John Wiley and Sons, 2009) ISBN-10 0470400315, ISBN-13 978-0470400319

Yeates, D. and Wakefield, T. – *Systems Analysis and Design, 2nd Edition* (FT Prentice Hall, 2003) ISBN-10 0273655361, ISBN-13 978-0273655367

Websites

www.tutorialized.com/view/tutorial/Systems-Analysis/31659

By the end of this unit you should be able to:

1. Understand the tools and techniques used for technical support
2. Understand how organisational policies and procedures influence technical support
3. Be able to gather information to provide advice and guidance
4. Be able to communicate advice and guidance.

Whether you are in school or college, passing this unit will involve being assessed. As with most BTEC schemes, the successful completion of various assessment criteria demonstrates your evidence of learning and the skills you have developed.

This unit has a mixture of pass, merit and distinction criteria. Generally you will find that merit and distinction criteria require a little more thought and evaluation before they can be completed.

The colour-coded grid below shows you the pass, merit and distinction criteria for this unit.

To achieve a pass grade you need to:	To achieve a merit grade you also need to:	To achieve a distinction grade you also need to:
P1 Explain the tools and techniques used for technical support	**M1** Discuss the importance of keeping fault logs	**D1** Review a recent advance in support systems technology
P2 Explain the impact of organisational policies and procedures on the provision of technical support	**M2** Explain the advantages and disadvantages of outsourcing technical support	
P3 Identify the types of fault that can occur		
P4 Source technical information to provide advice and guidance for a variety of faults	**M3** Judge the value of different sources of support material	
P5 Use different communication routes to provide advice and guidance	**M4** Provide additional support material to users	
P6 Respond appropriately to end users		**D2** Demonstrate effective communication skills with different types of end user
P7 Check solutions and record actions		

Introduction

With most organisations being IT reliant in today's world, providing good IT technical support in the workplace is fundamental to business continuity.

As a result, today's technical staff need to have a wider range of skills than ever before that will better enable them to support both individuals and organisations as a whole, in a multitude of different ways.

This 10-credit unit helps you to develop these skills by introducing you to **techniques** and **strategies** that will help you to become an effective employee in this environment and provides complementary coverage to Unit 13 – IT systems troubleshooting and repair.

How to read this chapter

This chapter is organised to match the content of the BTEC unit it represents. The following diagram shows the grading criteria that relate to each learning outcome.

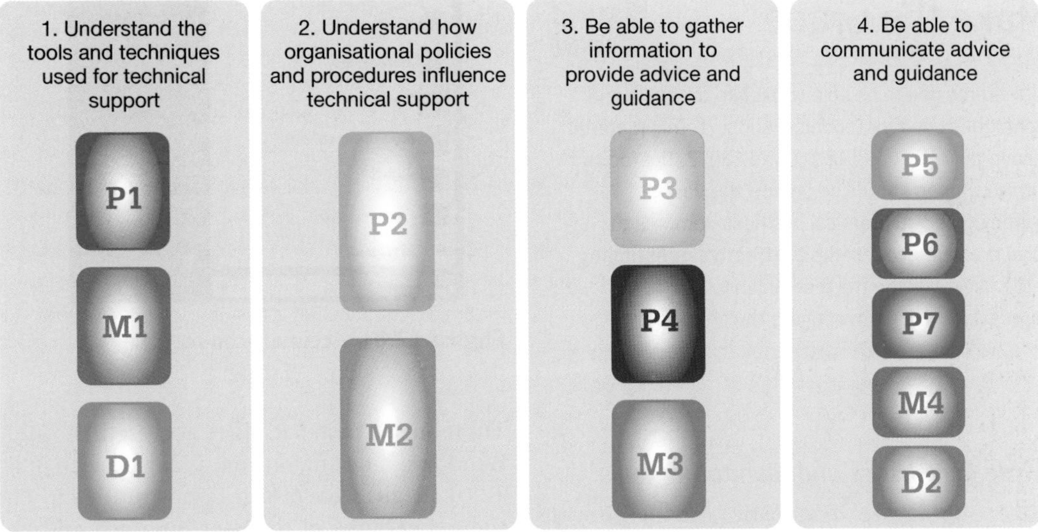

You'll find colour-matching notes in each chapter about completing each grading criterion.

Figure 12.00

12.1 Understand the tools and techniques used for technical support

This section will cover the following grading criteria:

The modern IT technician uses many different tools and techniques in order to diagnose and resolve problems.

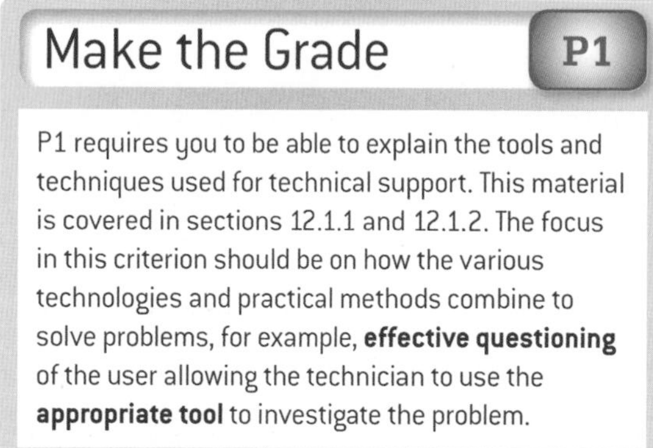

Make the Grade P1

P1 requires you to be able to explain the tools and techniques used for technical support. This material is covered in sections 12.1.1 and 12.1.2. The focus in this criterion should be on how the various technologies and practical methods combine to solve problems, for example, **effective questioning** of the user allowing the technician to use the **appropriate tool** to investigate the problem.

12.1.1 Tools

Software diagnostics and monitoring tools

A range of software diagnostic and monitoring tools is explored in Unit 13 and so will not be discussed here. However, using software to help diagnose and repair faults from or in remote locations has not been covered.

WIN VNC is an abbreviation of **Windows Virtual Network Computing**® and is software that is loaded onto computer systems to enable them to be viewed and manipulated remotely.

For example, it can be used in remote diagnostics and sometimes to facilitate repairs through a **VPN** (**V**irtual **P**rivate **N**etwork) connection. In this situation, the user would be passive, as the machine's activities would be taken over by an engineer or technician in a **remote location**, who would be able to **configure** the machine, add, delete, edit files and settings, and **manipulate** the system in any way that would normally be achieved using a mouse and/or a keyboard. This is an incredibly powerful facility and can be very useful for organisations that employ home workers.

Other (e.g. control panel)

The most common way of accessing set-up and customisation options for Microsoft Windows® operating systems is through the **control panel** (although similar interfaces exist on most GUI-based operating systems).

Figure 12.01 Accessing control panel (Microsoft Windows Vista®)

The control panel itself is accessed through the Windows® Start menu and, as can be seen in Figure 12.01, it gives each user opportunities to change the appearance of the user interface and change aspects of the functionality of the system, depending on the level of user permissions granted by the system administrator.

Through the control panel the behaviours of a whole range of devices and utilities can be easily managed.

Adding or removing hardware or programs, changing mouse, keyboard and sound settings, and automatic updates can all be manipulated through the control panel.

Activity 1

If undertaking this activity on a school or college machine, you will need to establish a) whether you have the relevant permissions to make changes and b) how to restore the default settings. Some systems will always refresh the interface to default settings when users log in, others will save the changes in a user's own profile.

Providing it is acceptable for you to do so, make changes to three of the following:

- Date and time
- Display
- Internet Options
- Keyboard
- Mouse
- Regional and Language Options
- Sounds and Audio Devices

In addition to asking the user to define a particular problem, the technician can also ask the system directly by using diagnostic and monitoring tools such as the BIOS **POST** (**P**ower **O**n **S**elf **T**est) information that is provided by the system at start-up, or by accessing **event logs**, which may be provided as part of the operating system's maintenance suite. In the case of Windows® operating systems, these can be found in the 'Event Viewer' utility.

Key terms

An **event log** contains a list of activities or actions that have been experienced within a system.

The logs are often categorised into three types (application, security and system) and the information stored may cover a set period of time (e.g. last month) rather than just reflecting activities on a single day or during a single situation.

The technician can often select **which items** of information are stored in these logs and **how regularly** they are **purged**.

Essentially there are three types of event logs:

- **Application log** contains a record of events that have occurred when programs have been executed and run.
- **Security log** contains information about log-on attempts or which files have been accessed, edited and deleted.
- **System log** provides a record about system events, for example drivers that have failed to load correctly.

How do you access the 'Event Viewer'? In Microsoft Windows Vista®, you carry out the following process:

Open 'Control Panel' and ensure that 'Category View' is selected (Figure 12.02).

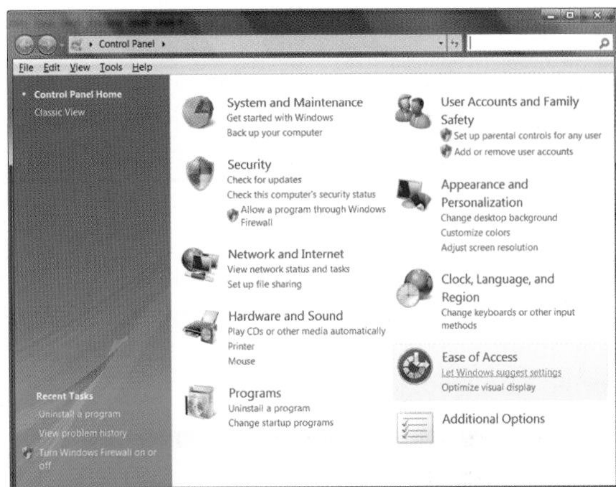

Figure 12.02 Category View

Select 'System and Maintenance' (Figure 12.03).

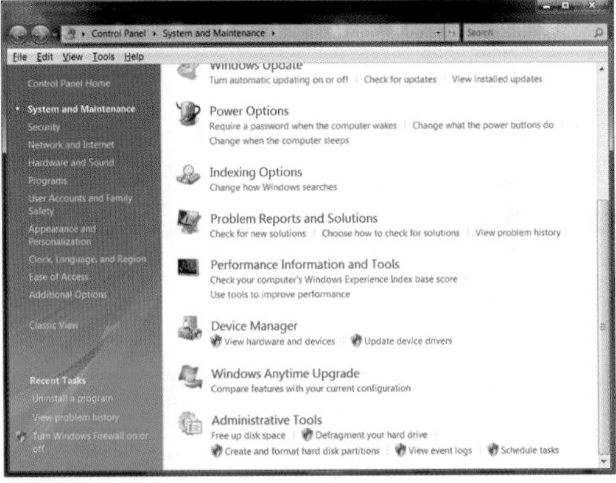

Figure 12.03 System and Maintenance options

Scroll down to 'Administrative Tools' and select 'View event logs'. The 'Event Viewer' interface should appear (see Figure 12.04).

The 'Event Viewer' interface will contain a series of event logs that can be viewed by either a **user** or a **technician**. Selecting one of the logs will focus on a particular aspect of the system's performance.

Try clicking 'Window Logs' then 'Application'.

This should open the 'Application Log' in the central window, showing a series of information,

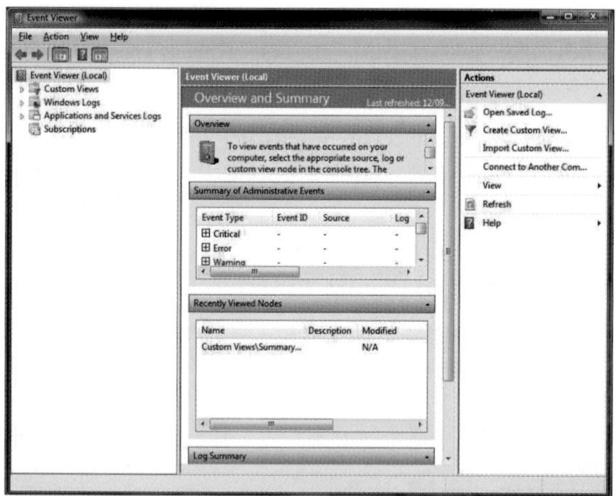

Figure 12.04 Event Viewer interface

warnings and errors related to applications running on the system. Figure 12.05 shows information about a particular error which has been reported with Google Update®.

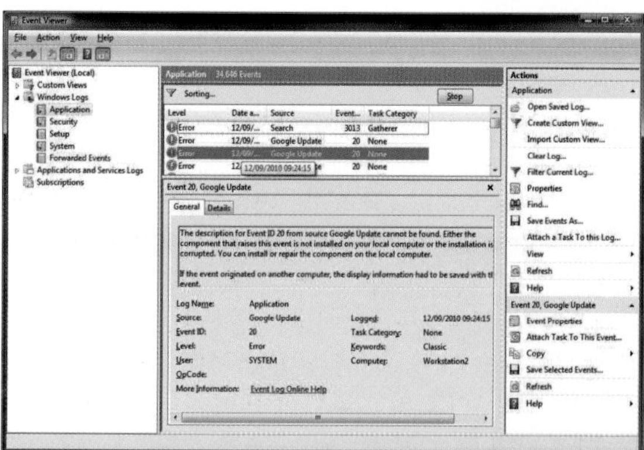

Figure 12.05 Application Log showing a problem with Google Update®

Activity 2

For more on event logs and the event viewer functionality in Windows® operating systems see:

Windows XP® http://support.microsoft.com/kb/308427

Windows Vista® &

Windows 7® http://technet.microsoft.com/en-us/library/cc766042.aspx

In addition to the Event Viewer, Microsoft Windows Vista® also contains a 'Reliability and Performance Monitor' that provides information about aspects of the working system (see Figure 12.06).

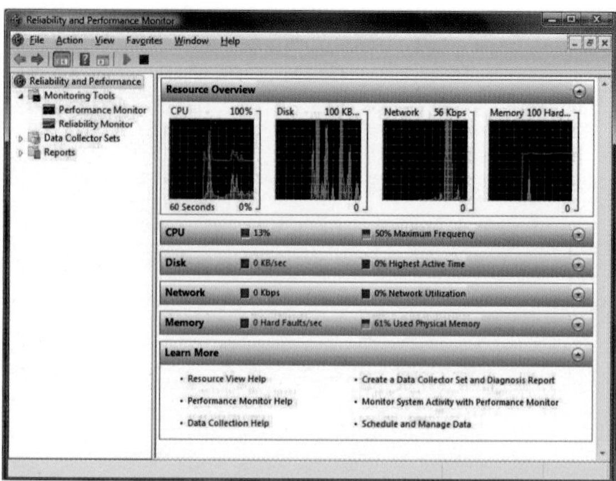

Figure 12.06 Reliability and Performance monitor showing live resource usage

It can be accessed through the control panel via the 'Advanced Tools' option on the 'Performance Information and Tools' screen (see Figure 12.07).

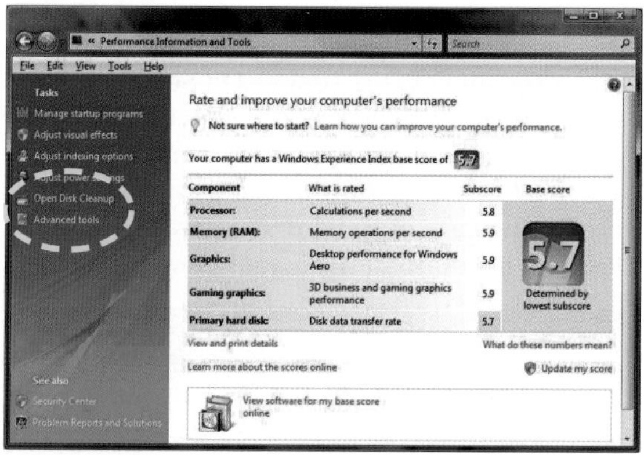

Figure 12.07 Performance Information and Tools

This information is captured in **real time** (i.e. as it happens) and can give the technician useful information about the current loads on the CPU, hard disk, network and RAM.

Activity 3

Investigate the operating system you use most and find the Event Viewer and Performance Monitoring tools (if you are using a version of Microsoft Windows®) or similar utilities in the operating system of the machine you use most regularly.

Unit link

For more on software tools and techniques see Unit 13 – IT systems troubleshooting and repair, section 13.2.2.

12.1.2 Techniques

One of the fundamental principles of being able to provide high-quality advice and guidance is having a good and extensive understanding of the problem in the first place. If you think about it – how can you hope to offer an appropriate solution to any problem, if you don't fully understand what the problem is?

What follows here is a selection of techniques that you can use to gather information about a problem in different ways and from different sources (very important).

Direct questioning

This is probably the most important technique used in information gathering because it is actually the most flexible, particularly if the questioning is carried out verbally. This is because an engineer can ask for clarification or can ask further questions to ensure that he or she has a good understanding of the problem (this is called '**probing**'). In contrast, with a written fault questionnaire, answers may be given that are then not sufficiently expanded to give the technician the level of information that is needed:

Nature of fault? 'Mouse not working'

What does this mean? It could mean any of the following:

- One or more mouse buttons do not work.
- The scroll wheel does not work.
- The mouse pointer 'jumps' around the screen.
- The mouse pointer doesn't move at all.

Each of the above symptoms is obviously different, and each may have a different cause and solution. Therefore, an engineer would be able to probe the statement 'mouse not working' further to establish in what way the mouse fault represents itself.

The most common way of gathering the information is to use a **checklist** as a guide to ensure that the right questions are asked at the outset. Here are some of the most obvious questions:

1. What is the fault?
2. What were you doing when the fault occurred?
3. When the fault occurred, were there any error messages? If so, what were they?
4. Is anything else affected when the fault occurs?
5. Is the fault constant or intermittent?

Clearly this list is not exhaustive as there are many other questions that could be asked depending on the circumstances. For example, if an organisation has a network, questions might be included to investigate how the fault is affected by, or affects, the organisation's network activity. If there is no network, clearly these questions would not be relevant and there would be little point in including them in a checklist.

The other important factor about using questioning is how the question is constructed. Is it an **open question**, a **closed question** or a **probing question**, for example?

The questions above are classified as **open questions**. These are questions where the respondent has control over how much information is given. In answer to 'what is the nature of the fault?', the response could be any combination of the information listed earlier.

Alternatively, with a **closed question**, the question will have been structured in such a way as to limit the possible response:

'Was there an error message when the fault occurred?'

This would require a yes or no answer only.

Probing questions such as 'what else can you tell me about what happened?' would encourage the respondent to think more generally, without giving guidance that might then exclude part of a response.

So, to use direct questioning as a successful tool in gathering information, you must be careful about what questions you ask and which style you ask them.

Unit link

For more on types of questioning see **Unit 1** – Communication and employability skills for IT, section 1.2.4.

Regardless of how the questions are asked (verbally or in writing), the information will usually be recorded on a **fault report sheet** that will stay with the system or peripheral until the problem is resolved.

The report shown in Figure 12.08 is a relatively simple one that could be used to record the key information required to find the fault, diagnose the problem and then record the actions taken to resolve the situation.

This particular example does not include any questions – it merely provides a record. Any information gathered from any source could be recorded here as a permanent record of the activity.

Technical Support

FAULT REPORT

Name of user	
Report date	
Machine identification details	
Nature of fault	
Diagnosis/Faults found	
Remedial action taken	

Figure 12.08 A simple fault report

Ideally, when using direct questioning, the respondent should be the actual user, because this will be the person who has the most experience of the system, the problem and the circumstances during which the problem occurred. If another individual becomes involved in the process (e.g. someone else takes the machine for repair), it is possible that the technician or engineer will not have all the information that might be available!

Make the Grade M1

M1 requires you to discuss the **importance** of keeping fault logs.

Fault logs are used to record problems encountered and this can help future resolutions, identify trends (e.g. faulty components) and be used to create a solutions database. Assessment may occur through a viva or a written overview.

Fault logs

In some organisations, particularly where there are rooms of computers that can be used by many different users over a period of time (e.g. in a school or college), it is common to have a written **fault log** that is regularly checked by technical staff who will identify and remedy any faults that have been reported by users. Clearly this relies on two activities:

Users identify and record faults.

Technical staff make regular checks on fault logs.

A typical fault log may look like that shown in Figure 12.09.

Fault Log

Room 12A

Machine Number	Date	Fault	Remedy	Rectified by	Date
6	4/12/06	Mouse not working	Replaced!	RW	5/12/06
8	16/12/06	KEYBOARD SPACE BAR FAULTY	Replaced!	RW	21/12/06
5	2/1/07	Monitor icons too small	Resolution reset	[illegible]	2/1/07
17	5/1/2007	Loose cables			
12	6/1/07	CD jammed in drive			
1	8/1/07	WON'T BOOT UP!	Motherboard replaced	RW	9/1/07

Figure 12.09 A typical fault log

While a fault log is useful for identifying trends or repeated faults with particular machines, quite often users will not be experienced in **fault reporting** and they may well not provide a sufficient level of detail for the technician to use, without significant further investigation. However, in many cases this is better than no information at all (i.e. that the fault is not even reported in the first place)!

Solutions database

This is typically a commercial product that **stores** and **organises** common **system faults** and their **solutions**. A technician would be able to key error messages, error codes or symptoms into the database and it would produce a report containing likely causes and remedies.

By their very nature, solutions databases tend to be **extensible** – allowing an organisation to add their own 'local' faults and solutions to the knowledge pool. Advanced versions of these systems can resemble an **expert system** with a specialism in IT technical support.

12.1.3 Future trends

Being effective in the times ahead will involve accurately predicting how things will change.

D1 requires you to review a recent advance in support systems technology; this links to material discussed in section 12.1.3.

Think about new hardware, software, concepts or procedures that are new in IT technical support. What impacts have they had? What do they improve?

Assessment may occur through a viva or a written overview.

Increasing reliance on remote support

It is clear that as organisations come to rely more heavily on home and distance workers, there will be a corresponding increase in the demand for remote support. The number of organisations that support the concept of working from home is constantly fluctuating. As a result, it is difficult to predict whether or not there will be a marked increase in this over the next 30 years, even if some websites suggest that we are currently experiencing something of a homeworking revolution (Figure 12.10).

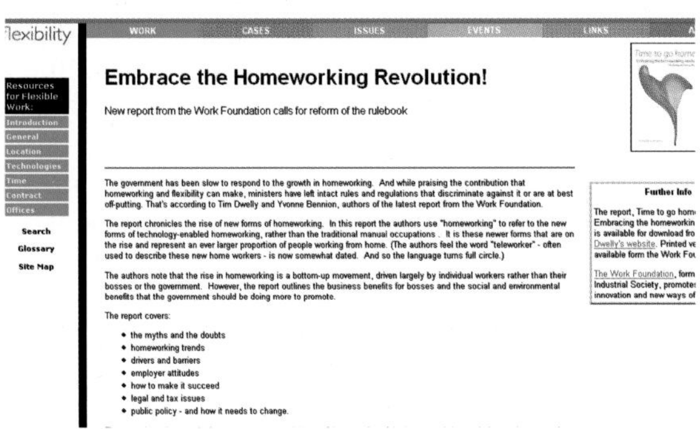

Fig 12.10 The homeworking revolution (Source: http://www.flexibility.co.uk/flexwork/location/homeworking.htm)

However, organisations can, through their own strategic planning, estimate whether they themselves will wish to increase the number of home workers over any given period.

Development of systems that analyse and report on faults

As has been suggested throughout this unit and Unit 13, historic data about faults and fault resolution will be instrumental not only in providing information for the novice technician, but also for providing information that can be used to develop training strategies and programmes.

The programmes themselves will then ensure that users will receive targeted training rather than generic training, where some of the learning might be of little value. Fault and report analysis can therefore make the selection and implementation of training more efficient.

Development of central infrastructures, contracted out and offshore services

More enlightened organisations see IT as central to the infrastructure of the organisation, not as a tool that is merely used to support the organisation's general activities. Therefore, it is not uncommon for information strategies to be considered as part of an organisation's overall strategic plan. Failure to do so may well result in a mismatch between what a system is capable of doing and what the organisation needs it to do.

Equally if an organisation feels that the investment that will accompany an IT strategy is inappropriate, then it may well consider contracting out some or all of its IT needs, whether that is paying external organisations to provide IT support or using external organisations to provide some of the back office administration such as payroll.

Activity 4

Explore TightVNC – a free, fast and reliable tool for remotely controlling another computer system.

1 Visit: www.tightvnc.com/

2 Download the appropriate client for your operating system.

3 Try it!

12.2 Understand how organisational policies and procedures influence technical support

This section will cover the following grading criteria:

12.2.1 Working procedures and policies

Organisational guidelines

The concept of organisational guidelines is vast because in order to control the activities of employees, most companies and institutions will define expected behaviours through formalised procedures and policies that all staff must adhere to. This whole area has been covered in significant depth in a number of other units, and so will not be repeated here. For information on how to find the relevant detail, follow the link below.

It is important to appreciate that there will be fundamental similarities in policies and procedures between organisations, but that most organisations will contextualise the content to suit their own systems and activities.

Unit links

For more on organisational guidelines see Unit 13 – IT systems troubleshooting and repair, section 13.1.1.

In addition, security issues such as internet use have also been covered in depth in a number of units. For more on these subject areas see Unit 7 – Organisational systems security and Unit 8 – e-Commerce.

Service level agreements

The following abbreviated definition has been drawn from Unit 13 – IT systems troubleshooting and repair:

Key terms

A **service level agreement** is a contractual agreement between a customer and a provider of a service that sets out a range of behaviours that the customer will expect:

- speed of response
- maximum repair time
- costs (what is already included, what is not)
- penalties (in some cases customers can inflict penalties on service providers if they fail to provide the level of service described in the SLA).

Confidentiality and sensitivity of information

The concept of confidentiality and the handling of sensitive information is a primary concern for most IT support personnel, primarily as to work effectively with systems, they may well come into contact with information that others working at their level may not be allowed to see, such as salary information, strategic or marketing information, or developmental information on products and services.

For this reason it is not uncommon for employees to be asked to sign non-disclosure agreements (NDAs), which will legally prevent them from sharing such company information with individuals both within and outside the organisation. If outsourcing (see next section) of IT support services is involved, the organisation will have set guidelines on how to ensure that any information will not be accessed by unauthorised personnel.

Other issues

The following definitions have been drawn from Unit 4 – Impact of the use of IT on business systems.

Key terms

Outsourcing is the practice of buying in skills, particularly IT skills, from outside the organisation when they are needed on a fixed-term basis. This can be cheaper than employing and training staff who may not have sufficient work to do to make their employment viable. Outsourced staff may, however, not be with the organisation for long, may not feel 100 per cent committed to the organisation's goals and therefore may employ short-term solutions.

Geosourcing is similar, but the implication is that organisations can seek these skills outside the UK or the usual partner countries. For example, at the moment there is a surplus of available games programming skills in Eastern Europe (in places like Poland, the Czech Republic, Serbia and Montenegro) and a similar surplus of skills in general applications programming in parts of Asia. The advantage here is that employees in these regions have the skills, but are willing to work for significantly less money than their European counterparts would demand.

It is not uncommon for organisations with limited use or requirement for IT systems to outsource the support provision simply to reduce costs. One of the main advantages of outsourcing will be that the company providing the service will be responsible for ensuring that staff are available and are trained to provide the service in the first place.

P2 focuses on material covered in section 12.2.1 requiring you to explain the impact of organisational policies and procedures on IT technical support. A leaflet or poster may be an ideal way of representing this.

M2 asks you to further consider and explain the advantages and disadvantages of outsourcing.

These two criteria are certainly linked as outsourcing services may be a key aspect of the organisation's IT technical support policy. Creating a small 'scorecard' for outsourcing is ideal!

Organisational constraints

Every organisation will be operating within a series of constraints. Successful organisations have learned to manage their activities within these constraints, or have found ways around them.

Costs of resources required

Every organisation, particularly those that are IT reliant, will have a budget that will determine how much is spent on every aspect of the provision from the purchase, installation and maintenance of the systems, to the recruitment and training of the staff who will support these systems.

The importance of the IT system will determine the size of the budget – for example, an organisation that has a computerised manufacturing and distribution system will probably have a larger IT budget than a company that merely uses IT for word processing and invoice creation.

It is essential to remember that costs can be both **direct** and **indirect**.

Direct costs include the cost of equipment, installation and training. **Indirect costs** will occur through, for example, the increased use of electricity as a result of implementing such a system.

Time

An organisation's ability to respond in its market sector can be the difference between success and failure. As a result, an IT department's ability to carry out maintenance and repairs within acceptable timeframes will have a direct impact on whether the organisation will be able to respond in the market!

Long time delays between a fault occurring and the system being fully functional will have a negative impact on the efficiency of the organisation.

User expertise

The only constraint in terms of user expertise will be the amount of money that an organisation is prepared to invest to improve the skills of the workforce. What the organisation should understand is that if simple training will reduce the number of faults that occur due to the activities of inexperienced users, then surely that investment will be worthwhile as the costs of training will be recovered relatively quickly through fewer reported faults.

12.3 Be able to gather information to provide advice and guidance

This section will cover the following grading criteria:

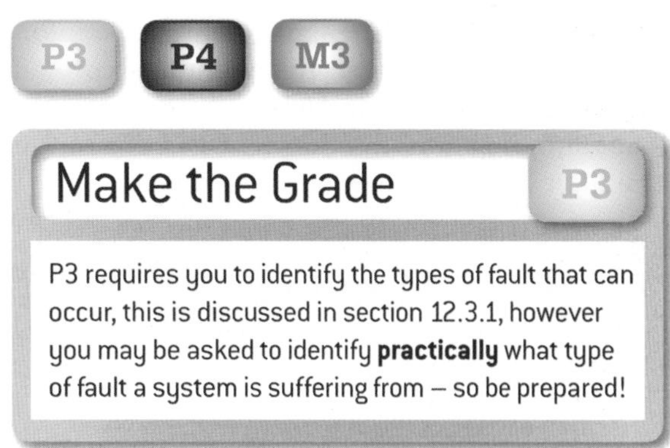

12.3.1 Fault

Fault type

As part of the 'Nature of fault' descriptor in the sample fault report shown in Figure 12.08 on page 334, additional information about the type of fault will probably be included, categorised in one of two ways.

- loss of service
- poor performance.

A user will usually be able to tell you whether the fault is a complete loss of service, so the system is non-functioning or has some non-functioning aspects, or whether performance is merely poor. Poor performance is usually considered to be speed of response related, for example it takes a long time to:

- log on to the system or network
- open a file
- save a file
- edit an image
- load a web page
- download files from the internet.

In this instance, the system is still working, but might not be performing in a way that is expected when you consider its age or particular range of installed components.

It is also possible that a system that has now failed began as an issue of **poor performance**. For this reason, asking the user to go over any known history immediately prior to the fault occurring can be a very useful activity!

12.3.2 Sources of information

As the provision of technical support relies heavily on staff having access to a range of reliable information and data sources, this section is covered in both this unit and in Unit 4. As a significant amount of detail on this subject can be found in Unit 4, it will only briefly be covered here.

Make the Grade P4 M3

P4 is a practical task, requiring you to find the source of technical information you can use to provide advice and guidance – it has to be from a variety of sources (i.e. not just the internet!).

M3 asks you to make a judgement about different sources of support material. Which is best? Which is most reliable? Why?

Product specifications and manuals

Most products are sold with a product specification and a technical manual, although the actual medium used to provide this detail can vary. Some manufacturers choose to include a printed copy of a Quick Start guide and will provide a web link to the full manual, which provides more in-depth coverage. Other companies will simply provide a full manual as a printed publication. Alternatively, a CD or DVD could be provided, alongside a printed Quick Start guide.

The advantage of any information that is stored on a CD or DVD is that in addition to printed detail, in the form of a **PDF** (**P**ortable **D**ocument **F**ormat), for example, the disk could also contain a short Microsoft PowerPoint® presentation about the main features of the product or a video on troubleshooting. In addition, this format is cheaper and easier to transport.

Colleagues with specialist expertise

This is probably the best source of information, particularly for the novice technician, although some would argue that asking experienced colleagues is a time-consuming and wasteful activity! One of the main advantages of using this source of information is that you can ask **further questions** if you are unsure that you fully understand a process, an answer or an explanation. With many of the other sources of data, clarification may still need to be sought from a fellow human being with appropriate experience!

Knowledge bases

There are a range of knowledge bases available on the internet, although as suggested earlier in this chapter, the novice technician or inexperienced user must be very careful about relying on information that may not be valid or correct (i.e. people can post anything on a web page forum).

However, manufacturer's websites are generally thought to be **reliable** and **trustworthy**.

Fault records showing previously found solutions

As discussed further in Unit 13, once faults have been resolved, it is good practice to retain the fault record and file it for future use (e.g. in a solutions database) as it will contain a full life cycle of the problem (Figure 12.11).

What you may have noticed is that this life cycle is very similar to the life cycle models in a number of other units in this text – in each case, the diagram will have been modified into the context of the topic, but fundamentally it is still the same life cycle. A problem is defined, the fault or cause is diagnosed (investigated), the resolution to the problem must be found (designed) and the solution implemented.

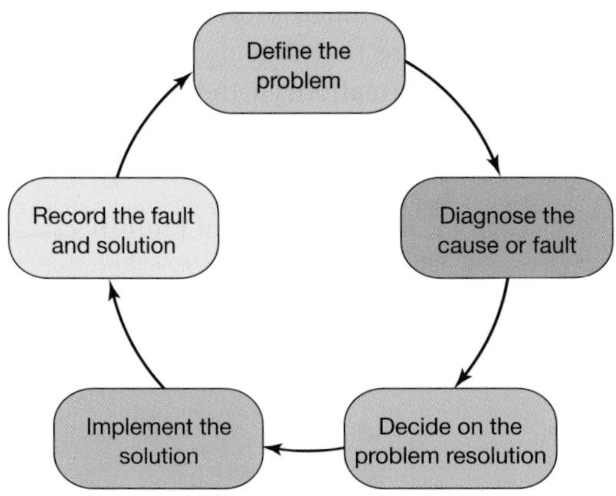

Figure 12.11 The fault resolution life cycle

Historical information about previous faults and remedies will be essential to the novice technician or engineer, who will effectively be able to learn from other people's experiences.

Internet sources

The internet is a very useful source of information that will help engineers resolve technical problems. Manufacturer's websites will usually contain **FAQ**s (**F**requently **A**sked **Q**uestions) about their products or services. This is where technical staff, employed by the manufacturer, will list information about problems and resolutions, answering questions posed by users of the product or service. These will tend to be reliable.

Equally, **technical forums** can be a useful route to finding answers to both simple and complex problems.

However, you should always bear in mind that some information might be invalid or even, at worst, intentionally misleading.

> **Unit link**
> For more on sources of technical information, see Unit 13 – IT systems troubleshooting and repair, section 13.3.1.

12.3.3 Validation of information

Cross-reference checks with user

There will be occasions when it will be possible to check that **other users** are experiencing the same problems on a particular system. If this system is a network, then it will help in the diagnosis of the fault to find out whether only one machine is experiencing problems or whether the fault is common to all machines attached to the network.

Confirmation from a number of users that a particular fault exists or that the fault is of a particular nature will give the technician confidence in how to approach formal diagnosis and remedy.

Problem reproduction

The best way for a technician to identify and diagnose a fault is if he or she can see the problem. However, if the fault is **intermittent**, it may prove difficult to **reproduce** the fault in the workshop. For this reason, it is essential that the user takes **screenshots** of any **error messages** he or she experiences, and prints these to be used as reference material as and when the system is being repaired.

If the cause is **environmental** – for example, interference from another system or device in the computer's usual location – it will be difficult for the technician to identify unless the technician carries out diagnosis in the machine's original location. In these situations, the technician has to go to the machine to experience the same effects.

Reliability of different types of information

One major consideration when trying to identify practical solutions to problems is deciding how valid the advice you have been given really is. Take the email shown in Figure 12.12 as an example.

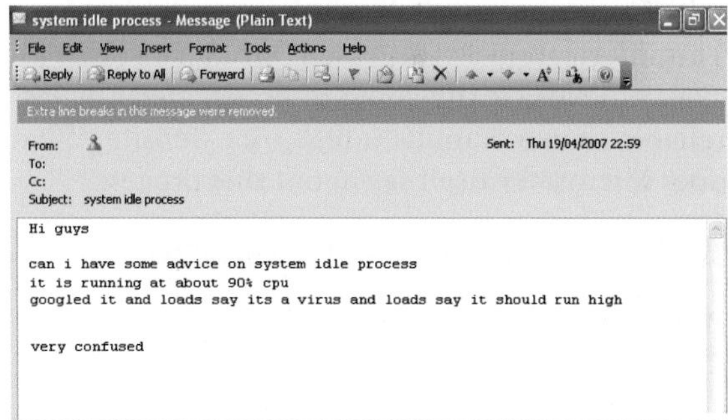

Figure 12.12 Query email

In this particular instance, the user has used the Microsoft Windows® Task Manager to establish what is running on his system and how much CPU is being used (see Figure 12.13).

Searching for advice on the internet produced two contradictory pieces of advice. On the one hand, individuals on forums were suggesting that this was probably a virus and should be eradicated,

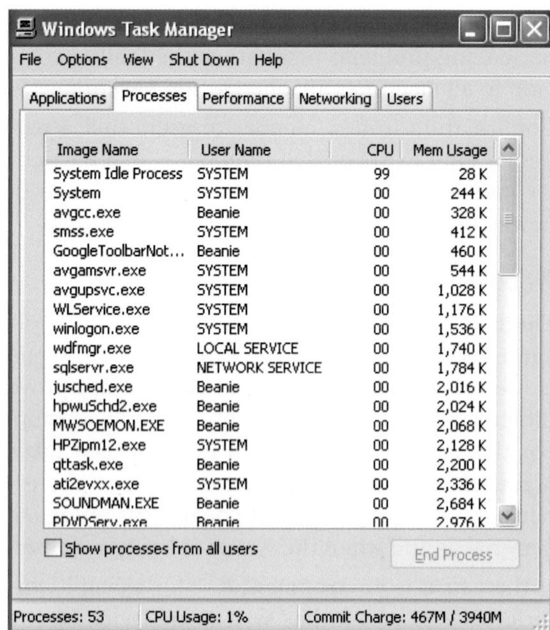

Figure 12.13 Windows® Task Manager

while conversely, others were saying that this was a normal part of a system and should be left alone.

So which answer was correct?

The latter! Task Manager was merely reporting that the computer was idle, so almost all CPU usage was being given over to doing nothing! In fact, this is correct – this value will be high if the system is idle. If the number had been low, then the CPU would have been busy undertaking other tasks.

This information was accessed through an open forum, which is clearly going to be significantly less reliable than a manufacturer's own website. What does Microsoft® itself say about this process?

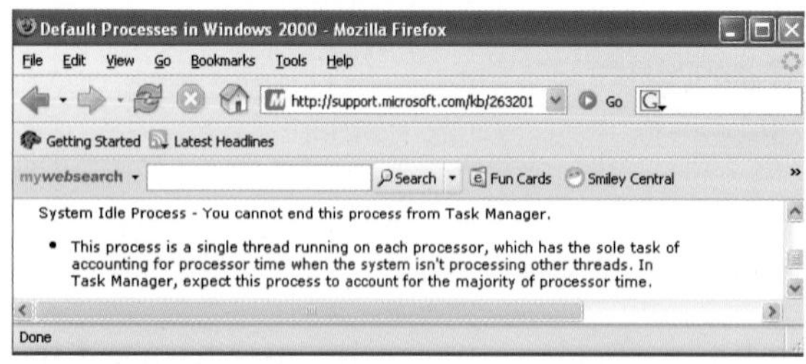

Figure 12.14 Microsoft® support information on system idle process

Had the enquirer gone directly to the manufacturer's website, he or she would have had the appropriate answer.

For this reason, individuals providing technical advice must make sure that they do so supported by accurate, valid information. Further sources of such information are discussed in the following section.

12.4 Be able to communicate advice and guidance

This section will cover the following grading criteria:

P5 P6 P7 M4 D2

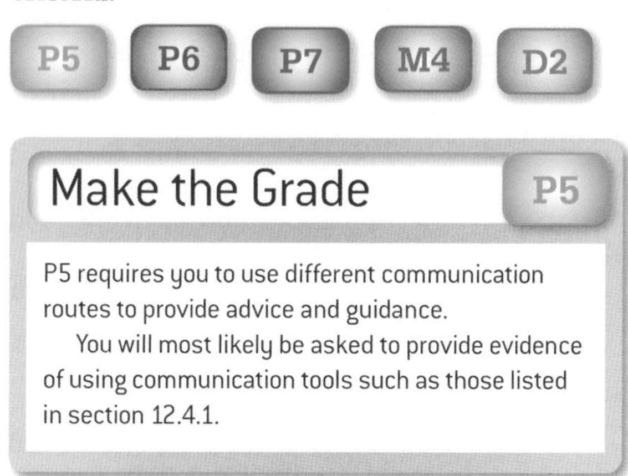

P5 requires you to use different communication routes to provide advice and guidance.

You will most likely be asked to provide evidence of using communication tools such as those listed in section 12.4.1.

12.4.1 Communication method

Unit 1 (Communications and employability skills for IT) covers the whole concept of communication in depth. For this reason, in this particular section only new detail will be added, so you may be asked to refer back to your previous learning in Unit 1.

Direct to user in response to a query

This is a fundamental part of technical support and doing this effectively will be an important aspect of your role.

As suggested, you can respond directly to queries in a number of ways:

- an email
- telling the user face to face
- via a telephone conversation.

Regardless of which medium is chosen, you will need to be able to use it successfully. For in-depth coverage of the use of email, face-to-face exchanges and telephone, see the unit link.

Additional support material

Alternatively, your communication with the user might be classed as secondary guidance because you were not the originator, but merely passed on infor-

Unit links

For more on interpersonal communication techniques see Unit 1 – Communication and employability skills for IT, section 1.2.3.
For more on written communication techniques see Unit 1 – Communication and employability skills for IT, section 1.2.4.
For more on successful communication see Unit 1 – Communication and employability skills for IT, section 1.3.1, and Unit 13 – IT troubleshooting and repair, section 13.2.5.

Make the Grade

To achieve M4 you must be able to provide additional support material for users. This might include: email, newsletters, access to FAQs and technical forums, help sheets or manufacturer's guides.

Evidence this by identifying what has been provided and how this will help the end user.

mation that was gained from other sources, or instructions on how to access this type of information.

Email

In this instance, the email may have been received from elsewhere (for example, in direct response to an email directed at a manufacturer – the received response could then be freely passed to relevant users).

Newsletters

You and your colleagues may receive regular technical updates from manufacturers when products have been registered, in the form of paper or electronic newsletters. In this instance, you may well choose to hold and file the newsletter until it is needed or you may choose to distribute it to users.

FAQs and technical forums

These will provide a wealth of information and it may well be a case of either directing users to the information, or copying and pasting it into a document that you may then pass to the user as appropriate. You must, however, remember to consider the issue of reliability of information, as suggested in section 12.1.2 earlier in this unit.

Unit link

For more on FAQs and technical forums see Unit 13 – IT systems troubleshooting and repair, section 13.3.1.

Help sheets

Many organisations, particularly those with a large number of users, create help sheets in response to faults that can then be given to users when problems occur. These may be stored electronically on the organisation's intranet, and users are instructed to look for guidance on the intranet prior to involving technical staff. Sometimes this can provide a quick resolution to the problem, particularly if the fault was simple to resolve and the user might have had to wait some time if he or she had involved a technician or engineer.

Manufacturer's installation instructions

These will also provide a useful source of information. In Figure 12.15, the instructions include both text and images, to help the user through the installation process.

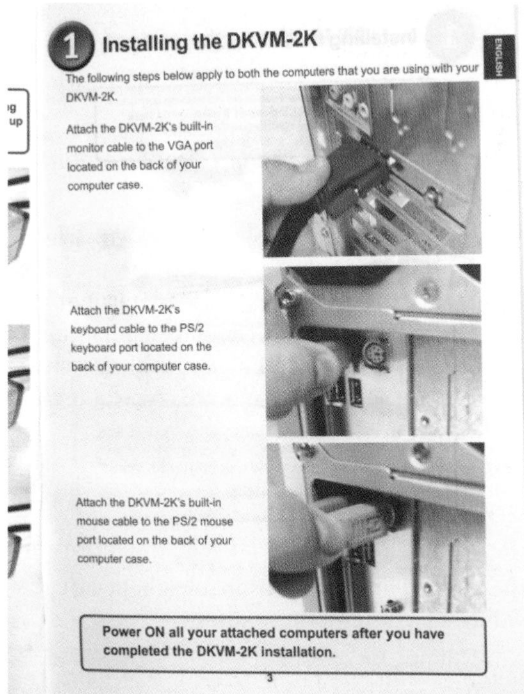

Figure 12.15 Installation instructions

Adding images will certainly help the novice user, who might be unfamiliar with terminology included in text.

Make the Grade **P6** **D2**

P6 requires you to **respond appropriately** to end users. This really involves the **type of advice** you give (section 12.4.2) and **how you conduct yourself** with the customer when giving the advice (section 12.4.3). Criterion D2 will check that your communication skills are effective when dealing with different types of end user.

This may be assessed practically based on role play of specific case studies, For example, what advice you give for specific faults and how you impart these with your tutor (who role plays the customer).

Activity 5

A user has discovered problems with their ATi Graphic card – they cannot understand how to use the Catalyst Control Centre.

Research and collect a list of support material they may want to read on the subject.

12.4.2 Types of advice

Recommendations for repair or replacement of components

In many situations, customers will look to a technical specialist to make recommendations about whether systems, peripherals or simply components should be repaired or replaced when faults occur. Thus, you may well find yourself in a situation where you will need to give this type of recommendation or advice.

Repair may well be the obvious solution if

A. cost is an issue

B. the repair is likely to be relatively straightforward

C. the repair will have a reasonable chance of providing a medium-term solution.

Repair will **not be** chosen if

D. it will be expensive

E. it will be complex and time-consuming to implement

F. it may not last very long.

If D, E or F are likely, then **replacement** of the system, peripheral or component may be the more logical solution to the problem. In most circumstances a customer will accept your recommendation, but you should anticipate that there will be times when a customer will insist that an item is repaired, even if you suggest that the repair may not last very long!

One of the key issues in this instance is that you make the right recommendation, for the right reasons: you should not, for example, recommend an expensive replacement if you know full well that the item can be repaired easily and cheaply and will still be usable for some time to come. This would clearly be dishonest. It will damage your reputation and that of your organisation if you engage knowingly in this kind of activity.

Provision of training or direct instruction

Another type of advice that you might be asked to give will be around the concept of training. Here there are two possibilities:

a) If the requirement is for an individual to receive a limited amount of training to resolve the situation, you may well find that you are asked to handle this yourself. If, on the other hand, a number of individuals might be able to come together as a group, you could be asked by your organisation to organise and deliver a direct training session to users.

b) As an alternative, you may well be asked to investigate and recommend training opportunities for individuals or groups of users to take place outside the organisation. In order to do this effectively, you will need to identify users' training needs and match them to the most relevant training opportunity.

Other advice

If the fault cannot be solved through one of the resolutions shown above, it may simply be a case of helping the user to work through the process.

Bug fixes and **patches** come under the heading of software maintenance tasks. From your perspective, when providing technical support you will probably need to have the relevant file that you can email to the user or you will need to have the URL to hand so that you can point the user in the right direction to download the file directly.

Once the user has the file, he or she may well ask what to do. In this instance you could either point the user at instructions on the internet, or you could provide a more personalised service by talking the user through the installation of the update or upgrade.

Unit link

For more on software maintenance tasks see Unit 2 – Computer systems, and Unit 13 – IT systems troubleshooting and repair, section 13.1.2.

Another alternative is to reset or reboot systems. In both of these cases, a novice user will probably be reticent about implementing instructions, purely because they will be unsure about what they are actually doing. In this situation you will need to give very clear and calm advice, reassuring them along the way.

12.4.3 Communication skills

Providing information to relevant people

There are different types of users, from the novice to the more experienced user, so part of a technical support role can be to decide how much information to give a user (why, for example, tell someone something he or she doesn't really need to know). This often applies to the level of detail you feel you need to provide. A novice user will often not wish to know the intricate details of why the system doesn't work; equally, an experienced user might wish to broaden his or her experience by fully understanding the reasons why something occurred, the range of resolutions that might have been possible, and why a particular solution was chosen.

Anger management skills (customer)

One thing is certain, when dealing with customers there will be times when you will find yourself faced with a customer's anger and aggression. This can be prompted by a whole range of different triggers, most of which will not have been caused by you – unless you have been rude to the customer or dismissive of their problem!

Most customers get frustrated when computers stop working properly – it's a common occurrence and you too have probably experienced it at some point when a program has crashed or a file won't load as expected!

Some technicians will have natural skills that will help them deal with aggressive and angry customers, others will have to learn particular skills or techniques to help them defuse situations they might have little experience of.

The most important and urgent action you must take if you are faced with a customer's anger is to assess whether you are in any **direct danger**. If you feel that you are, you must either immediately remove yourself from the situation by walking away, or you must call **someone else** to help you deal with the situation (preferably a manager).

You must then begin the process of finding a resolution to the problem. At this stage the key issue will be to **keep calm** and **objective**.

Keeping calm and objective (self)

This is not always easy, particularly when you feel personally threatened by the responses or reactions of someone else, but here are some simple tips:

- If you are in no danger, it may be appropriate and possible to allow the customer to get it out of his or her system. While this is happening, remain calm and try not to interject. If you are not answering back, then you are not giving the customer additional things to shout about. Ideally, you will have taken the customer into another room or place so as not to involve others in the process. **Be patient** and don't try to rush into resolving the situation – otherwise you might well make it much worse.
- Use time constructively! While you must show that you are listening to what the customer has to say, you can be using the time in deciding how to respond. Consider whether there are others you might be able to call on to help you deal with the situation. Think about what you **will** and **will not** be able to offer the customer.
- When the customer begins to calm down, you will find that they will be more responsive and likely to listen to what you have to say. This is because they will feel that they have at least been heard.
- Clearly you will need to come to some sort of resolution, even if this is ultimately a compromise. If you are not able to make concessions, you might need to involve someone who is.

- Try to discuss the situation rather than telling the customer – then the customer will feel that he or she had some input into the resolution. Throughout the process, take deep breaths yourself as it will help you to slow down your own heart rate and stay calm.

Ultimately, you must try to:

- stay in control
- be confident
- be calm.

If you do not feel confident about handling conflict situations like these, see whether you can find some appropriate training or ask your tutor whether your school or college offers any support.

Soft skills

As you mature, you will gain **soft skills** such as **empathy** and **patience**. You will be able to access direct training courses or may well find that these subjects are part of other courses you do. For example, if you are going into any type of customer service or customer support, it is likely that you will receive anger management, conflict, aggression and hostility training as part of your induction. If you are in a situation where you feel that this type of training would be useful, but it is not offered to you, don't be afraid to ask.

Key terms

Patience is the act of holding back and waiting for situations or circumstances to be right before beginning to act. It is extremely hard to do at times, but is very powerful as often the resolution will come more quickly and be more effective long-term.

Empathy is where you are able to understand someone's emotions and feelings because you can relate to them by being able to identify similar experiences yourself. If a customer believes that you really understand the way they are feeling, then they will be more open to discussing issues with you.

Escalating issues that are beyond the scope of an individual

If at any time you are, or you feel that you are, trying to deal with issues that are beyond your scope or experience, then you should **escalate** them to someone else who will be in a position to help.

Key terms

If you are unsure how to resolve a problem or issue, or if you do not have the relevant skills, the problem will be **escalated** (moved up or given) to a more experienced and skilled individual.

As discussed further in Unit 13, once a problem has been escalated it would be useful for a novice to take part in or observe the problem's resolution in order for him or her to learn.

Unit link

For more on escalation see Unit 13 – IT systems troubleshooting and repair, section 13.1.2.

Providing and communicating appropriate response times for resolution

Within an organisation, prioritisation and response times may well be defined as part of an IT support policy or procedure, however, when it comes to paying customers, it will clearly be in a technician's interest to try to resolve the problem as quickly as possible. In an attempt to do this, however, you should not be **unrealistic** in what you can achieve. There is no point, for example, promising a repair for a particular date if you need to get components from a third party and you cannot guarantee that they will arrive in time for you to repair and prepare the machine. Clearly, if you make unrealistic promises and then fail to deliver, it will not affect your supplier's reputation, it will affect yours.

In most cases, customers will be happy as long as you keep them informed about the progress of their problem – you must demonstrate that things are being done!

Estimating a realistic response time will become easier as you gain experience, and in some cases it can be predicted by analysing response times for identical or similar faults using historic data.

Unit link

For more on prioritisation of jobs see Unit 13 – IT systems troubleshooting and repair, section 13.1.1.

12.4.4 Checking solutions

Testing

After repair activities have been concluded and before returning the system or peripheral to the customer, you must ensure that adequate testing has taken place so that you can be sure that the system is fully functioning.

Successful testing should be planned as part of a **structured approach**. As part of the process, the following should be considered:

Test subject:	Description of what is being tested, e.g. hard drive, motherboard, system power-up.
Where and when:	Where the test will be carried out, e.g. in the workshop or at the customer's premises?
When will it happen?	This will be the actual date of the test.
Test procedure:	What aspect is being tested? How will it be tested? What is the expected outcome (what you expect to happen)? This will be repeated for each test.

The plan will then be recorded formally in a test plan (Figure 12.16).

TEST PLAN TEMPLATE

Test subject ....

Location of test ....

Date of test ....

Test #	What is being tested	Test Description	Actual results of test	Actions required

Figure 12.16 Test plan template

Once the tests have been planned and executed, the results of the tests will be recorded. Using a template like the one shown in Figure 12.16 will help you to test more effectively.

As with other technical support activity documentation, these records will be retained and will become a valuable source of information to the novice technician, as they will provide information about the sorts of tests that can be undertaken and how failed tests were resolved.

Make the Grade

P7 is a practical task asking you to check your solutions and record your actions. This is part of the review process discussed in 12.4.4.

A written report, blog or vblog may be appropriate ways of documenting this.

User review ensuring that advice was sufficient and correct or solution was successful

One of the best ways to ensure that you improve the advice and guidance you give will be if you ask the user to give you feedback on whether the advice was adequate, correct and whether the solution was successful.

Clearly, if the answer to any of the above is 'no' then you will need to investigate what went wrong and how you can improve next time.

Most IT support departments will also formalise this kind of feedback in an annual or bi-annual customer questionnaire.

Activity 6

It may be helpful to have an initial idea of how much time is needed to replace components in a system.

Assuming that the component was available, find out in each case how long it would take on average to replace the component. Assume that the computer case is closed and will need to be returned to the same state.

Activity	Time
Replace motherboard	
Replace processor	
Replace CD-ROM	
Replace memory	
Replace CPU	
Replace mouse	
Replace keyboard	
Replace video card	

12.4.5 End users

End users can often be difficult to categorise. This is because users are not always honest about their actual level of **technical knowledge** and **expertise**.

Key terms

Someone who is **experienced** will have built up an in-depth knowledge and understanding of something and will have developed skills through first-hand encounters with a particular problem, system or situation. An experienced user is likely to be able to help you in diagnosing the problem, and he or she may even be able to offer some sensible solutions. However, beware! As suggested previously, users might like you to think or believe that they are more experienced than they really are.

A **novice** user will be learning about a particular system and may be encountering problems or difficulties for the first time. Bearing in mind his or her lack of experience, some of the problems may have been caused by the user's own inappropriate actions (incorrect key presses for example), or other simple innocent errors. It is unlikely that the novice user will create problems or faults intentionally, and he or she is unlikely to be of much help in the diagnosis or resolution of the fault. However, all users (novice or otherwise) should be encouraged to take screenshots of error messages or write down what happened as this might assist in the diagnostic process.

A **technical** user will have more understanding of the system than an experienced user, as an experienced user may well only have a good understanding of their system, but not the wider technical issues of computing. For example, an experienced user will probably be able to tell you a great deal about his or her system. It is unlikely, however, that he or she will understand the network to which it is attached. A technical user will, however, have a greater understanding and will often be able to place a fault in the context of a wider system.

You need to be aware that in your role in technical support, you will encounter individuals who have the same level, a lower level or a higher level of technical knowledge and expertise than you.

Achieving success

This particular unit has 13 criteria to meet: 7 Pass, 4 Merit and 2 Distinction.

For a Pass: You must achieve all 7 Pass criteria.

For a Merit: You must achieve all 7 Pass and all 4 Merit criteria.

For a Distinction: You must achieve all 7 Pass, all 4 Merit and both Distinction criteria.

Unit link

Unit 12 is a **mandatory unit** for the Edexcel BTEC Level 3 National Diploma and Extended Diploma in IT (Networking and Systems Support pathway) and **optional** for all other qualifications and pathways of this Level 3 IT family.

Qualification (pathway)	Mandatory	Optional	Specialist optional
Edexcel BTEC Level 3 National Certificate in Information Technology		✓	
Edexcel BTEC Level 3 National Subsidiary Diploma in Information Technology		✓	
Edexcel BTEC Level 3 National Diploma in Information Technology		✓	
Edexcel BTEC Level 3 National Extended Diploma in Information Technology		✓	
Edexcel BTEC Level 3 National Diploma in IT (Business)		✓	
Edexcel BTEC Level 3 National Extended Diploma in IT (Business)		✓	
Edexcel BTEC Level 3 National Diploma in IT (Networking and System Support)	✓		
Edexcel BTEC Level 3 National Extended Diploma in IT (Networking and System Support)	✓		
Edexcel BTEC Level 3 National Diploma in IT (Software Development)		✓	
Edexcel BTEC Level 3 National Extended Diploma in IT (Software Development)		✓	

There are specific links to the following Units in the scheme:
Unit 13 – IT systems troubleshooting and repair
Unit 25 – Maintaining computer systems

Further reading

French, C. – *Computer Science, 5th Edition* (Thomson Learning, 1996) ISBN-10 0826454607, ISBN-13 978-0826454607

Knott, G. and Waites, N. – *BTEC Nationals for IT Practitioners* (Brancepeth Computer Publications, 2002) ISBN-10 0953884821, ISBN-13 978-0953884827

Websites

techrepublic.com

whatis.techtarget.com

www.pctechguide.com

Unit 13: IT systems troubleshooting and repair

By the end of this unit you should be able to:

1. Understand how organisational policies can affect IT troubleshooting and repair
2. Be able to use appropriate tools to troubleshoot IT problems
3. Be able to select and apply fault remedies to IT systems

Whether you are in school or college, passing this unit will involve being assessed. As with most BTEC schemes, the successful completion of various assessment criteria demonstrates your evidence of learning and the skills you have developed.

This unit has a mixture of pass, merit and distinction criteria. Generally you will find that merit and distinction criteria require a little more thought and evaluation before they can be completed.

The colour-coded grid below shows you the pass, merit and distinction criteria for this unit.

To achieve a pass grade you need to:	To achieve a merit grade you also need to:	To achieve a distinction grade you also need to:
P1 Explain the impact of organisational policies on the troubleshooting and repair process		**D1** Examine the potential impact of faults on an organisation
P2 Use hardware and software tools to troubleshoot simple IT problems	**M1** Communicate effectively with users during fault diagnosis activities	**D2** Compare a range of hardware and software troubleshooting tools
P3 Identify sources and select suitable fault remedies		
P4 Apply fault remedies safely to simple IT system problems	**M2** Justify an appropriate remedy for a complex hardware and a complex software fault	
P5 Demonstrate good working practices when applying fault remedies	**M3** Maintain data security and integrity when applying fault remedies	
P6 Keep accurate records of fault diagnosis and repair activities		

Introduction

Working with computer systems will require individuals who have the skills to both troubleshoot and repair, from both a hardware and a software perspective.

Technical staff must be able to diagnose problems and repair them efficiently so as not to have a detrimental effect on the organisation's ability to function. This unit also attempts to remind you of the professional approach needed when performing this type of IT technical support role.

This unit looks at this topic from both a theoretical and practical perspective and should ideally be studied after Unit 2 – Computer systems. It also has direct links with Unit 12 – IT technical support and Unit 25 – Maintaining computer systems.

How to read this chapter

This chapter is organised to match the content of the BTEC unit it represents. The following diagram shows the grading criteria that relate to each learning outcome.

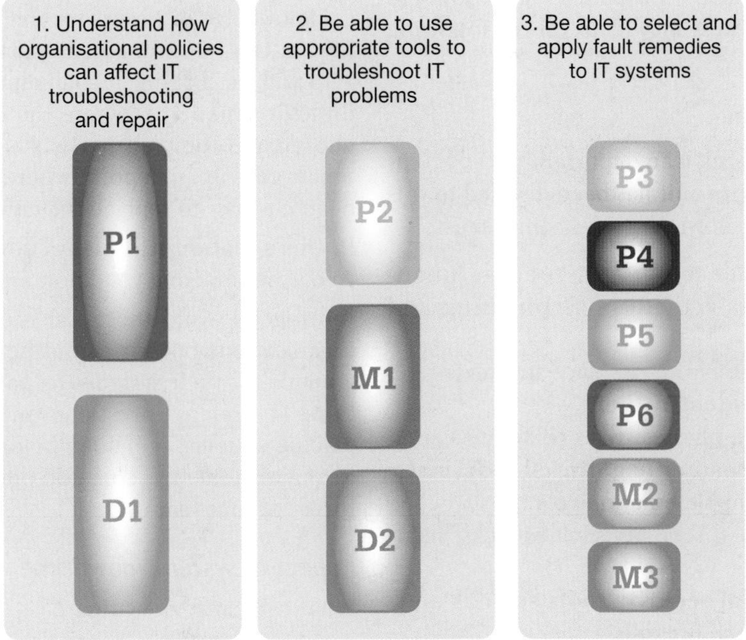

You'll find colour-matching notes in each chapter about completing each grading criterion.

Figure 13.00

13.1 Understand how organisational policies can affect IT troubleshooting and repair

This section will cover the following grading criteria:

13.1.1 Organisational policies

The process of IT troubleshooting and repair is typically controlled by the policies laid down in an organisation. These may focus on the following aspects.

Security

Systems security is such an important part of computing that an entire unit has been devoted to this subject (see link below). IT professionals must:

- Identify threats to systems such as unauthorised access activities like **phishing** and **hacking**.
- Ensure that systems are in place to prevent activities such as **identity theft**.
- Understand the physical risks to systems such as **natural disasters** (e.g. fire, flood), **malicious acts** or simple **human error**.
- Invest in **physical security** such as locks, security gates etc.
- Invest in **logical security tools** such as anti-virus, spyware and firewalls.
- Develop and implement procedures to define security activities.
- Be aware of legislation and ensure that it is complied with.

Make the Grade 

P1 requires you to be able to explain how the process of IT troubleshooting and repair is influenced by the policies in an organisation. In order to achieve this you will need to read carefully through sections 13.1.1 and 13.1.2. These will provide you with enough information to be able to tackle this task.

Costs

For any organisation, or individual for that matter, cost is a hugely important consideration and in most situations there will be a choice when it comes to resolving system problems: repair or replace.

Which option is ultimately taken is dependent on the fault, and likely cost, although you should not forget that not having access to the system because it is being repaired is also a cost (see Impact of systems downtime below). In addition, a replacement part may be difficult to obtain, especially if it is old or unusual.

Choosing whether to repair or replace parts in a system is a choice that users will generally find difficult to make because most will have little technical knowledge or expertise. You are therefore relying on the honesty and integrity of an engineer who will be making recommendations. The most difficult situation is where the option to repair is chosen and the fault persists – so the cost of the repair goes up, to a point where it might well have been cheaper to replace the component.

In this situation it is always advisable to take advice from someone you know and trust.

In order to avoid these kinds of decisions, many organisations opt for a routine replacement programme for their systems. As part of the organisation's IT strategy, investment in upgrading and replacing systems, hopefully before something goes wrong with them, is common practice, usually on a three- or four-year cycle.

Impact of systems downtime

What can cause downtime?

- Software failure or defect
- Hardware failure or defect
- Operator error
- Power failure (where systems will also then have to be fully rebooted)
- Disasters such as fire, flood, earthquake
- Routine maintenance

Because routine replacement of systems or systems components is usually planned into the activities of individuals or departments, it can be done at times that will cause minimum disruption:

- out of hours (so overnight or at weekends)
- during holiday periods (at Easter or Christmas, or in some cases in a summer shutdown)
- where alternative user activities have been planned (such as staff training).

It is not, however, possible to plan alternative activities for users when the other causes of downtime are experienced. For this reason, many organisations have a fall-back plan.

To deal with software or hardware failures many organisations carry stocks of units or components to speed up response time and thereby minimise the amount of downtime that will be experienced.

In an attempt to avoid operator error, most organisations will invest in regular training for users.

Some organisations invest in back-up generators that will automatically 'kick in' should a power failure be experienced.

Disasters such as fire, flood and earthquake are much more difficult to plan recovery strategies for, although most organisations do have a **disaster recovery plan**. In some cases this has been developed by one of the many companies that specialise in disaster recovery by helping organisations to recognise the actual risks they face and implement strategies to overcome them.

Unit link

For more on security and disaster recovery see Unit 7 – Organisational systems security, section 7.3.4.

Regardless of the causes of downtime, one issue is absolutely clear – an organisation *must* have backups of all its data, preferably held off-site, to give it a starting point when trying to re-establish its activities. If an organisation has multiple outlets or branches, it is common for each branch to act as a backup point for another branch (Figure 13.01).

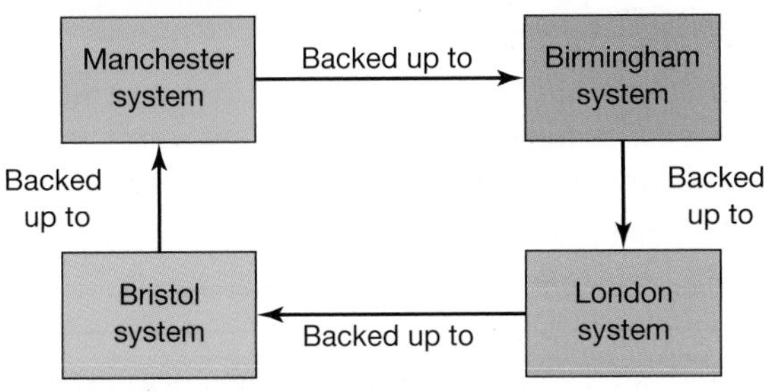

Figure 13.01 Backup strategy for organisation with multiple sites, outlets or branches

Make the Grade D1

A continuation of P1, D1 requires you to examine the potential impact of faults on an organisation. This is detailed throughout section 13.1.1, from the disruption of normal working to the costs involved in arranging preventative training and operating detailed disaster recovery plans.

This is useful for two reasons: firstly, it protects a recent copy of the data and in addition it keeps the data backup in-house and therefore under the control of the organisation. Clearly, an organisation that does not have these facilities will need to find a trustworthy external data storage facility.

Disruption of normal working

In some cases the consequence of a system disruption will be that users need to take written information that will subsequently be keyed into the system when it comes back online. If the disruption has been extensive, temporary input staff could be brought in to help resolve the backlog and this costs money.

In many cases, **minor disruptions** will have **minimal effect** and will merely **cause irritation**. However, if the company is trading online or is using sales staff to process orders by phone, the consequences of system downtime could be catastrophic. It could lead to **extensive loss of business** as customers place orders elsewhere. Similarly, if **distribution** and **delivery** are affected and customers cannot receive their orders, business will be lost.

For these reasons, companies **must** take steps to ensure that they understand the impact and implications of downtime and they must endeavour to put systems in place to minimise the effects.

Contractual requirements

There will inevitably be instances where the system problems will affect an organisation's ability to fulfil contracts and depending on the contract, this may have penalty implications and result in short-term financial issues and possibly a loss of goodwill. For this reason most companies will have procedures in place to help them to ensure that they will continue to meet their contractual requirements.

Trend analysis of faults reported

It is common for system faults to be analysed in order to identify any common themes or trends in the data so that steps can be taken to pre-empt some repetitive problems or faults, as shown in Table 13.01.

Table 13.01

Typical faults or problems	Possible remedy
Repetitive hardware failures	Change manufacturer used
Repetitive hardware failures	Plan regular maintenance
Recurring software failures	Change or upgrade software
Recurring software failures	Plan regular maintenance
Repeated user errors	Training and staff development programmes

Other issues could also exist and supervisors and managers should be aware of this. For example, in the case of persistent hardware failures, if changing the supplier or manufacturer of the hardware does not resolve the problem, and it clearly isn't a user error, the problem could lie with the engineer or technician who undertook the maintenance activity. In each case, however, as with any investigation, the most obvious possibilities would be looked into before the less likely ones!

Resource allocation and prioritisation of jobs

In most organisations this can be a political 'hot potato' as all departments or areas of the business will feel that they have a more pressing and justified need for particular resources, spending or priorities for getting jobs done than other areas. While handling this type of situation will become easier with experience, as a general rule most organisations would prioritise in the following order of function (Figure 13.02):

Management — Most important
Sales
Distribution
Payroll
Manufacturing
Accounts
Administration — Least important

Figure 13.02

Why? Without working systems:

- **Managers** will not be able to direct the activities of the organisation.
- The **sales team** will not be able to sell any products or services and thus will not be generating any income.
- The **distribution function** will not know who to deliver to and when, with the potential that customers and business could be lost if the service is then perceived as poor.
- **Payroll** must be a relatively high priority because without this system, the company could lose employees.
- The **manufacturing function** will not be able to make any new product to sell. While you might consider that the priority here should be higher (and it might be in some cases), most companies will be holding stocks of products and a delay in manufacturing could merely mean that stocks are not replaced as quickly as usual.
- The **accounting function** may not be able to send out invoices on time – while the knock-on effect of this could be that cashflow is affected, it is clearly a lower priority than losing customers!
- **Administration** is probably the lowest priority, particularly if the activity here is archiving and filing of historic transaction data or data that is not essential to the day-to-day operations of the organisation like personnel data.

This list is provided for guidance only as individual organisations may have different priorities – for example, a company that makes goods to order will clearly give its manufacturing department a higher priority than one where the department makes goods for stock!

Case Study

Kris Arts and Media have no current strategies for reducing the impact of system failure or downtime experienced as a result of faults.

Do not forget that KAM is a small business with only one office.

Activity 1

Using the above case study, prepare a list of recommendations that you would make to KAM and in each case justify your choices.

Discuss your recommendations with a tutor or other specialist.

An organisation may well have a series of policies on the circumstances in which items are repaired or replaced, or the time expected for faults to be resolved. If employed in an IT support capacity, you must ensure that you know the policies within your organisation and that you apply their rules.

13.1.2 Internal customer issues

In an organisation, one department can be considered to be the internal customer of another department. This is particularly true of an IT department that supports the business function of the entire organisation.

Communications

One of the key issues around providing a good service for your customers will be how you communicate. Although your customers will hope that faults can be found and resolved very quickly, this will often not be the case, and in this situation it is essential that you **keep your customer updated** with **progress reports**. You will need to be able to estimate **how long** a fault will take to resolve, and if the customer will be paying for the repair, how much this is likely to cost.

Your customer will need to feel that a resolution is being sought and even if your progress report does not always bear good news, the customer will feel that you are doing your best if you at least tell them what the current situation is. Some examples of work-in-progress reports are given in Figure 13.03.

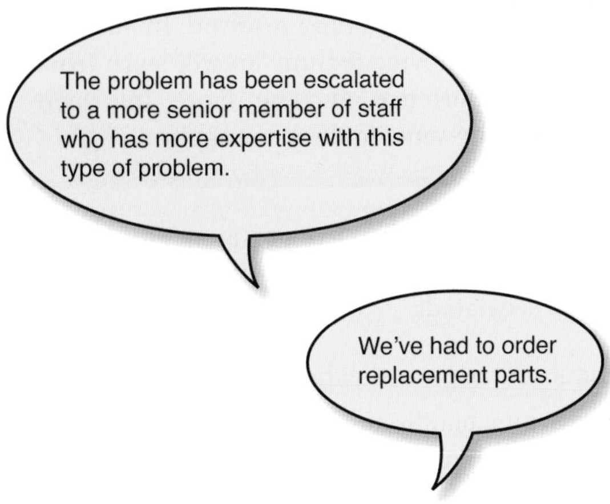

Figure 13.03

You will find that if you keep your customer informed about your progress, they will be happier!

Understanding impact

When it comes to computer systems, most users only have (or have access to) one! As a result, you must be sensitive to the user's concerns when the system is not working. From a user perspective, the following are examples of the impact that a non-working system will have on individuals.

In the business environment:

- **Cost** – most businesses will not worry particularly about the costs of repair, as long as the repair is financially viable and it wouldn't have been cheaper to purchase a new system.
- **Time** – this is the more important concern for businesses:
  - If they are IT dependant, the impact will be felt more drastically.
  - Employees will have to find other ways of doing their jobs – the usual solution is for the employee to write everything down with a view to updating the system once it is back online. This can, however, be stressful because of the duplication of effort.
- **Stress** – while it is likely that in a business environment another system may be found for the user to work with, this in itself can cause stresses, particularly if the machine is not set up in the way that is familiar to the user. In addition, it is likely to mean that the employee may need to work more slowly, or possibly might not be able to do aspects of his or her current role because the system is not set up appropriately.

Unresolved faults may result in individuals and organisations feeling a sense of frustration and irritation and it will depend on the situation as to whether or not the problem can be easily resolved. Organisations will probably have the capacity to replace items if the possible time for repair becomes unacceptable. For many individuals and home users, on the other hand, this may be difficult.

Customer handover and acceptance process following repair

It is standard practice that prior to handing items back to customers, an engineer will demonstrate that the item is now working and he or she will generally then ask the customer to sign an **acceptance document** that will be kept to say that the customer was happy with the repair work undertaken. Why is this done?

Firstly, so that if the system subsequently fails, it will be possible to establish whether the system was still faulty when it was returned to the customer or whether new faults have developed. Clearly for a paying customer, the distinction between the two is likely to be an important one.

Other considerations

Relevant legislation and legal issues

As with all aspects of computerised systems, legislation *must* be adhered to in the repair of IT systems. For example, an organisation's systems may well contain confidential data and data that will be subject to the Data Protection Act.

As such, it will be assumed that a responsible engineer or technician will observe the right of the individual or organisation to confidentiality in line with the legislation – for example, not disposing of hard disks which contain sensitive customer information in a careless manner!

In addition, some organisations make their technicians sign confidentiality agreements to prevent them from passing on any information they may have inadvertently had access to during repair activities.

Bearing in mind how heavily legislated the computer industry is, you should ensure that you are aware of all relevant legislation, particularly in relation to how it impacts on your role or job.

Unit link

For more on legislation see:

- Unit 3 – Information systems, section 3.2.1
- Unit 7 – Organisational systems security, section 7.3.3
- Unit 8 – e-Commerce, section 8.2.5

Level agreements

Key terms

A **service level agreement** (SLA) is a contractual agreement between a customer and a provider of a service (even in the same organisation), that sets out a range of behaviours that the customer will expect. These include:

- speed of response
- level of service offered
- maximum repair time (for different types of faults)
- costs (what is already included, what is not)
- penalties (in some cases customers can inflict penalties on service providers if they fail to provide the level of service described in the SLA)
- procedures for making a complaint about service received.

SLA performance is often measured through **metrics** such as:

- average time for helpdesk to respond to a call/email
- average open time for a logged fault
- number of faults resolved on first reporting.

Escalation procedures

Key terms

Escalation of a problem will occur in a number of situations:

- the problem is not being resolved in a reasonable timeframe
- the cause is difficult to diagnose.

Effectively, the problem will be escalated (moved up or given) to a more experienced and skilled technician or engineer if there are issues over it being resolved. In an ideal world, the novice technician will learn from their experience and be more informed should the same fault occur again.

Each organisation or IT department will have procedures and processes that define when problems will be escalated.

Documentation and reporting

Repair and maintenance activities should always be documented carefully and it will depend on the organisation as to how this is done, and in what level of detail.

For an individual customer's system, like a home user, an itemised invoice will usually be raised (Figure 13.04).

Milton House, Boxbush Parade, Waystone WA99 1AA (04156 987371)

INVOICE

Invoice Date: 14th January 2011

Customer Details

Mr John Jackson
Flat 17
Albermarle Mews
Waystone West
WA 98 1FM

Components Fitted:

A Provides a component list with relevant costs

Quantity	Description	Price (per unit)	Total
1	ASUS P5W DH Deluxe SKT 775 dual-core Core2Duo Motherboard	106.35	106.35
7	Case Screws	0.03	0.21
		Components total (ex-VAT)	106.56

Work Description:

B Describes what was actually done

Fault identified.
System dismantled.
Motherboard replaced.
System reassembled.
Missing case screws replaced.
System tested.

Invoice Summary:

Item	Total
Labour	30.00
Components	106.56
Total	136.56
VAT	23.90
Grand Total	164.46

VAT Registration Number: 99 9999 999

Figure 13.04 Repair invoice

It is standard practice to itemise both the work undertaken and the components fitted during the repair activity.

This document will serve as a record of the repair.

Clearly if the computers belong to an organisation, say an office of 12 machines or a classroom containing 25 machines, generating an invoice would not be an appropriate way of keeping a record of repair.

In an office situation it is likely that the fault would have been notified via email and once the work was finished, the user would have received a confirmation email identifying what the problem was and what was done to resolve it. In a classroom, however, where there would be lots of machines with transient users, it is more likely that the room would have a **fault log** that could be completed by students or teaching staff when faults occurred. Technicians would then regularly visit each room and check the fault log, carrying out repairs as necessary and logging activities in this centralised document.

A typical fault log will look like this (Figure 13.05).

Fault Log

Room: 12A

Machine Number	Date	Fault	Remedy	Rectified by	Date
6	4/12/06	Mouse not working	Replaced!	RW	5/12/06
8	16/12/06	KEYBOARD SPACE BAR FAULTY	Replaced!	RW	21/12/06
5	2/1/07	monitor icons too small	Resolution reset	[illegible]	2/1/07
17	5/1/2007	Loose cables			
12	6/1/07	CD jammed in drive			
1	8/1/07	WON'T BOOT UP!	Motherboard replaced	RW	9/1/07

Figure 13.05 Typical fault log

You should notice the following:

1. The repair of non-working systems will probably be a higher priority than issues like loose cables and CDs jammed in drives.
2. The repair date is also included so that managers or supervisors will be able to see how quickly faults are being resolved.
3. The signature of the technician or engineer is included so that supervisors can identify who was responsible for the repair activity.
4. Sometimes the users give too little information (e.g. loose cables – what loose cables?), so the technician won't necessarily know where to look first!
5. Writing can be difficult to read, as in the case of the CD jammed in the drive.

Once fault log sheets have been filled, they are usually kept in an archive file for reference purposes.

So, dependent on the situation, different reporting mechanisms will be used (although this is not exclusive):

Customer – Invoice

Office user – Email

Student – Fault log

13.2 Be able to use appropriate tools to troubleshoot IT problems

This section will cover the following grading criteria:

13.2.1 Hardware tools and techniques

Electrical/electronic test instruments

Figure 13.06 Cable tester (*Source*: http://www.warrenelectronics.com/Networking/Lantest.jpg)

A cable tester (Figure 13.06) is used to verify that a length of cable has no faults and that the connections have all been made and are functioning correctly.

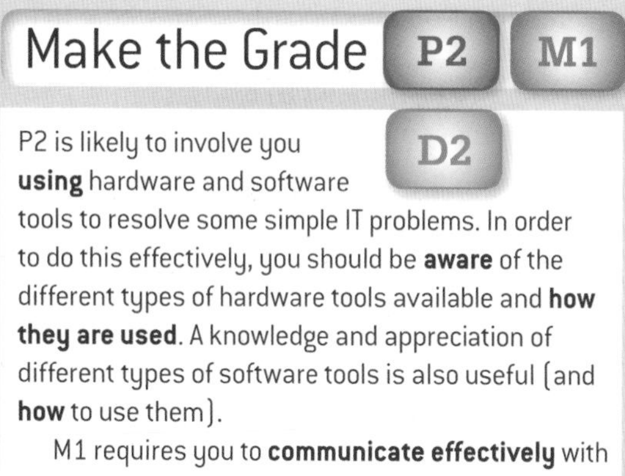

Make the Grade **P2** **M1** **D2**

P2 is likely to involve you **using** hardware and software tools to resolve some simple IT problems. In order to do this effectively, you should be **aware** of the different types of hardware tools available and **how they are used**. A knowledge and appreciation of different types of software tools is also useful (and **how** to use them).

M1 requires you to **communicate effectively** with users during your fault diagnosis activities – this will involve (a) keeping them informed of progress, (b) being sympathetic by using good interpersonal skills and (c) communicating your actions and their outcomes in a clear and appropriate manner. Think back to Unit 1 about how to do this.

D2 asks you to **compare** (check for similarities) between different hardware and software tools – typically this will be a case of **matching** the right tool for the right job!

Figure 13.07 Multi-meter (*Source*: http://ecx.images-amazon.com/images/I/41MNGSDM9NL._SS500_.jpg)

The multi-meter (Figure 13.07) is used to check electrical voltages and verify that there are no breaks in cables (continuity).

Other portable, specialist test instruments are also available, but the two items shown above are the devices most commonly used in hardware fault diagnosis.

Self-test routines

During the computer boot sequence, the system runs a series of self-tests. As a function of the BIOS and known as **POST** (**P**ower **O**n, **S**elf **T**est), the process checks the presence and function of peripherals such as the keyboard and mouse and components such as RAM, hard disks, CD or DVD drives.

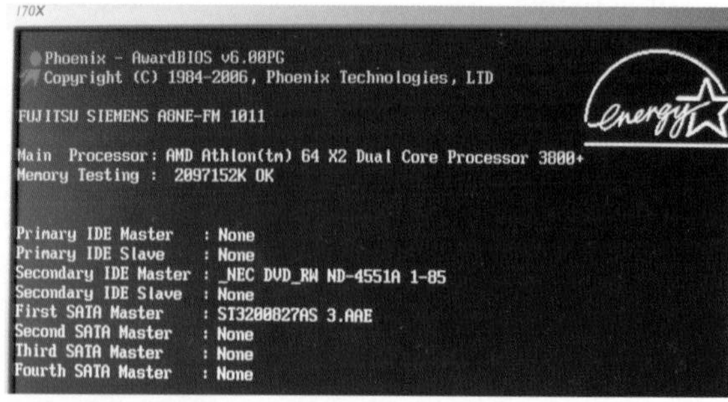

Figure 13.08 POST screen

Monitoring devices

The BIOS also provides some hardware monitoring functionality, such as CPU temperature and speed, so that in the case of the CPU becoming too hot, the system will shut down.

Unit link

For more on monitoring devices see Unit 2 – Computer systems, section 2.1.1.

Suitable tools (e.g. screwdrivers, pliers, torch)

You will need to ensure that you are familiar with different tools and their functions. Here are some examples (Figures 13.09–13.16):

Table 13.02

Item	Description
Mains testing screwdriver	This screwdriver has a small bulb in the handle that lights up if the screwdriver comes into direct contact with a live electrical supply. This is a useful tool as it will confirm that a device is safe to work on.
Pliers	Pliers are particularly useful for holding items that are being worked on and pinching connectors to grip wiring.
Torch	A torch is clearly going to be very useful in a situation where there is a low level of light. Some engineers prefer to use a headband torch, which is a torch that is secured on an elastic headband which goes over the engineer's head. The advantage of this is that the engineer will not need anyone to hold the torch while he or she is working.
Tweezers Alternative to tweezers	Tweezers are essential for holding and retrieving small items such as screws that may have fallen inside the machine. Often referred to as a three-pronged parts retriever, this is a useful alternative to tweezers for inserting screws into drive bay assemblies. It is often a personal preference which variation is used.
Anti-Static wrist strap	An anti-static wrist strap is an absolutely essential tool for anyone working with an electrical device. The strap, which is worn around the wrist and then attached to the metal case of the device being worked on, will minimise the possibility of an electrostatic discharge destroying components.
Screws, washers and jumpers	Anyone who works regularly with computer hardware will have containers, tubes or boxes of screws of various types and sizes, washers and jumpers. **Jumpers** are tiny connectors that make connections between pins on circuit boards to change how the board's connections are made and alter its functionality.
A standard toolkit	A relatively inexpensive but essential toolkit for anyone working with computer hardware and peripherals.

Figure 13.09 Alternative to tweezers

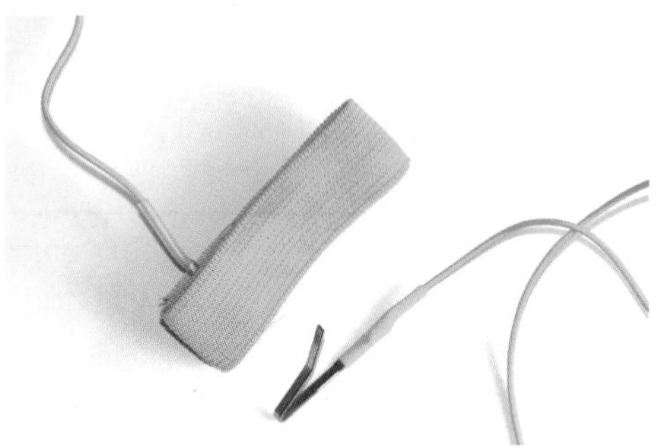

Figure 13.10 Anti-static wrist strap

13.2.2 Software tools and techniques

Diagnostics (e.g. virus software) and test utilities

There are a number of software products on the market today that can help an engineer to examine a system. One of the most obvious is anti virus software, such as Grisoft's AVG® software as shown in Figure 13.11.

Figure 13.11 AVG Technologies antivirus software

When run, this software will scan all or part of a system to detect and heal infected files (or destroy any viruses) it finds. This type of software must be updated regularly to ensure that it can continue to protect a system fully.

Although many other products exist, we should not forget the system tools or utilities that often come as part of the operating system. See Figures 13.12 and 13.13.

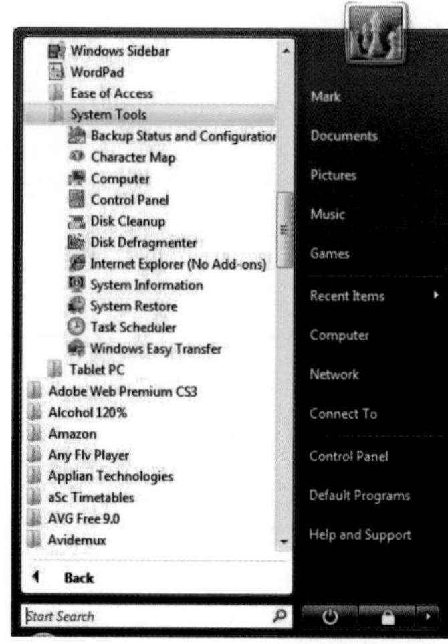

Figure 13.12 Microsoft Windows® System Tools

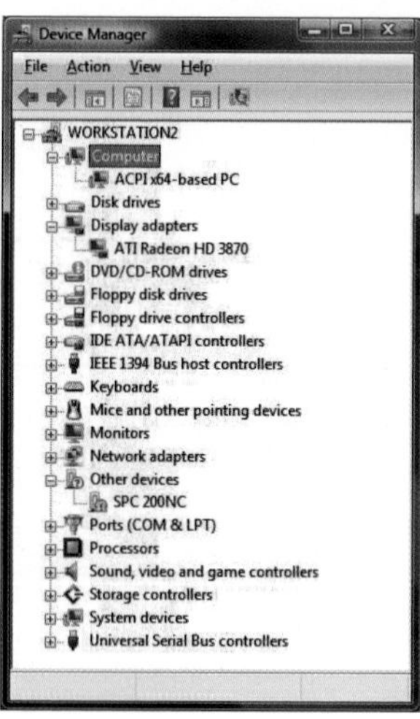

Figure 13.13 Microsoft Windows® Device Manager

Disk fragmentation and cleanup are system maintenance tools that can significantly improve the speed and performance of a system. There is also the **device manager** in operating systems such as Microsoft Windows®, which helps engineers instantly spot whether there is any conflict between devices. Many **third-party tools** (e.g. PC Tools Registry Mechanic™) are also available in abundance (Figure 13.14).

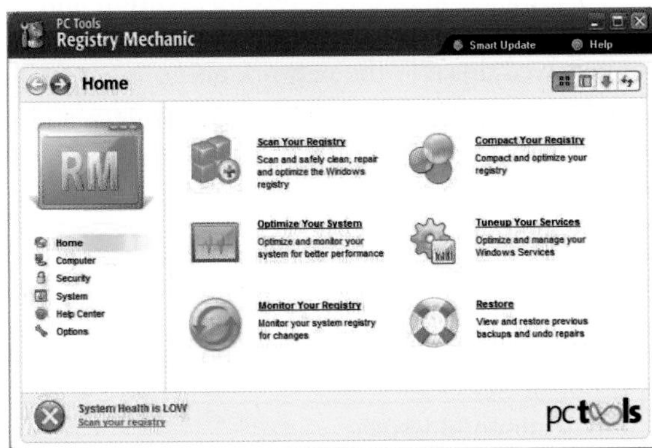

Figure 13.14 PC Tools Registry Mechanic™

Others (e.g. monitoring and error logging programs, system specific applications)

From Vista onwards, Microsoft Windows® has a Reliability and Performance tool (see Figure 13.15), which can track issues in system performance (in many different categories) over set periods of time. It can be accessed via the Control Panel's advanced tools and helps to identify repeating faults.

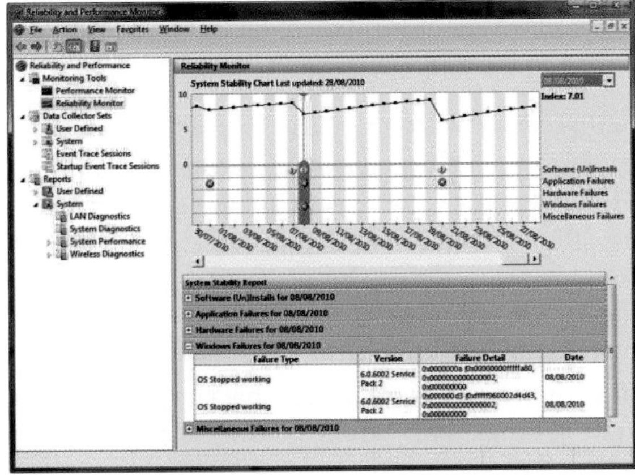

Figure 13.15 Microsoft Windows® Reliability and Performance Monitor

Some systems have additional software that performs specific tasks. For example **SpyTech SpyAgent 7.2®** (www.spytech-web.com/index.shtml) which:

- records all keystrokes typed, all website visits and all online searches performed
- logs programs and application use
- monitors social networking behaviours
- tracks all file usage and printing
- records online chat conversations
- logs windows opened
- shows every email sent and received
- logs internet traffic data and connections
- shows what users have uploaded and downloaded
- checks how active (or inactive) users are
- reveals user passwords.

This type of product, which can run stealthily on an employee's system, can produce a lot of helpful evidence in terms of IT troubleshooting as it reveals how the system has been used. However, from an **ethical standpoint**, many people feel that this type of software is intrusive and inappropriate because its use suggests that employers **do not trust** their employees. Others would say that when you are working and being paid for your labour, your organisation has the right to know what you are doing! It's an interesting dilemma.

13.2.3 Using troubleshooting techniques

When faced with a computer fault there are a number of techniques you can use to help you find the actual problem. There is no magic order in which these techniques should be used – in some cases you might need to apply a number of them while on other occasions your first option might well identify the fault.

As you become more experienced as a technician, you will begin to identify which of the techniques is more likely to help you to identify particular types of fault.

Substitution

Substitution is where a part that is suspected to be faulty is **simply replaced** with one that has already been tested and which is known to work. If this technique is successful, it can be a very swift and effective resolution to the problem! Substitution examples would include replacing a mouse, printer or keyboard. It can even extend to CD- or DVD drives.

Test

Sometimes what is required is a **structured approach** to testing a device or system and it will be the job of the engineer or technician to decide which tests would be most appropriate, and the order in which the tests will be undertaken.

Usually, at this stage, a **test log** is developed and all the possible tests will be listed and defined, with a column to record the **actual outcome** of running the test. The sample log in Table 13.03 might be used to identify why a machine has no power.

Table 13.03

Test	Description	Actual outcome
1	Check mains switch is on	
2	Check lead is plugged in correctly	
3	Check computer power master switch is on	
4	Check computer front power switch is on	
5	Replace main power lead between base unit and mains supply	

As each test is done, the **actual outcome** of the test is recorded. Notice that, in the first instance, the **obvious checks** are made, **before** any items are replaced.

Once the fault has been resolved, tests should be undertaken to check that the system is now working correctly. A modified test log would now be used as shown in Table 13.04.

After each test the actual outcome of the test will be recorded.

As suggested earlier in this unit, these sorts of completed logs will provide a mountain of information, ideas and strategies for a novice engineer!

Change

There are times when in order to diagnose a problem, the engineer might have to move the equipment to another location for testing. For example, to see whether a logging on problem is the fault of the machine or something to do with the network point. If the computer is moved to a second location and is then found to log on successfully, the problem can be narrowed down to the network point.

Consider also the increased use of wireless technologies. A home computer that is suffering from intermittent loss of internet access might have any one of the following problems:

- physical wireless device problems
- software problems
- reception problems due to interference from other devices
- environmental issues.

If the first three have been eliminated, moving the machine to other locations might identify environmental issues.

Upgrade

It has been known for the installation of new hardware components to trigger a need for a simultaneous software upgrade. Similarly, some software will only run on hardware with particular configurations or specifications – this could also apply in reverse.

For this reason, it is essential that engineers fully understand the **consequences** of upgrading any parts of a system, so that reductions in performance can be anticipated and eliminated.

Reinstall software

Reinstalling software is sometimes the only solution to a problem. In the case of an application, this is usually a straightforward process. However, if the software that needs to be reinstalled is the operating system, the engineer and user *must* take some pre-emptive action to ensure that data is not lost.

It is therefore essential that backups of all data and settings are taken *before* beginning the reinstallation.

Table 13.04

Test	Description	Purpose of test	Expected outcome	Actual outcome
1	Switch on system	To check that the system now has power	Power on and login screen accessed	
2	Log on to system	To check that power is maintained	Successful log on	
3	Activate an application and use for 10 minutes	To check that power is maintained	Successful use of system with no further power loss	

Elimination

This is the process of removing parts of the system to see what effect this has. Clearly there are some parts that cannot be removed because to do this would render the system unusable (e.g. CPU).

Applying bug fixes

One of the reasons why you need to register the purchase and installation of new software is that unless this has been done, the user will not be able to take advantage of any bug fixes that the manufacturer releases after the product has been purchased. Clearly, if your software is illegally copied, then you would not be able to download these patches (or mini programs) because doing so will identify that you are using someone else's registration code.

The downloaded fixes will usually be available for one of the following reasons:

- The software contains bugs that were not identified prior to release.
- New hardware or other new software products have minor conflicts with an application that can be resolved with the relevant patch.

As a technician or engineer, you will have to remember to apply the bug fixes to all machines that are affected. However, if users are sharing applications because they are being distributed through a server, then there may be fewer machines to worry about.

Generating error codes

In general, errors can be signposted in one of two ways:

1 using a user-friendly **dialogue box** (Figure 13.16).

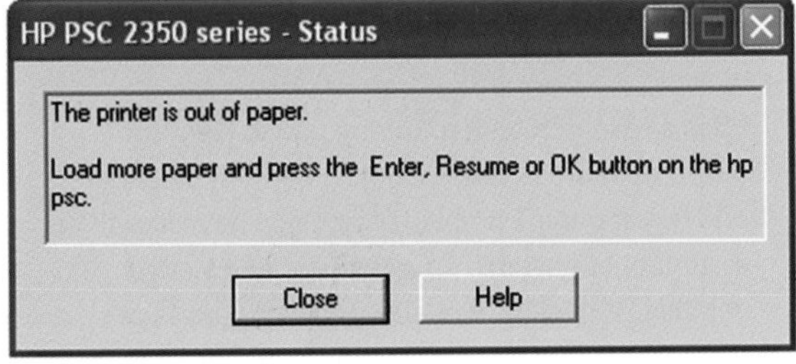

Figure 13.16 Error message

2 using a more specific **error code** (Figure 13.17).

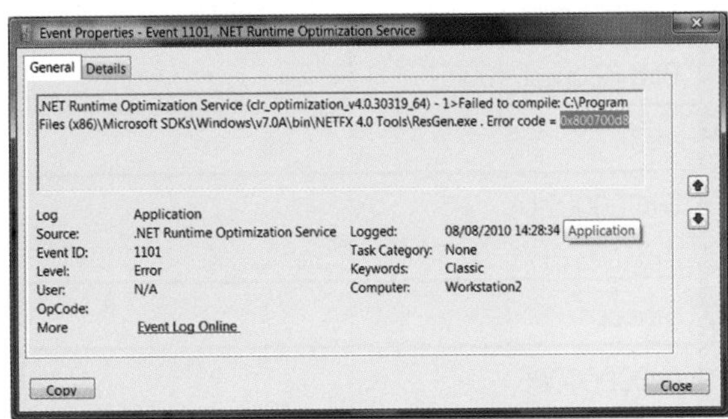

Figure 13.17 Error message with typical hexadecimal (base 16) error code

Each error code that is generated refers to one specific fault in a system. Keying this code into a search engine like Google may bring up a range of web pages that might help you resolve the problem.

When discussing errors with users, particularly where they subsequently try to describe what the error message said, encourage them to a) write down the message or b) write down the error code. It can be particularly helpful if you ask users to print a screen capture of any error messages or codes. They can even paste the image into an email to make life easier.

With some system errors, the system may not have booted sufficiently for the user to be able to see convenient error messages on screen. These errors are signposted by the **beeps** the computer makes. You will be asked to find out about some of these codes in the Activity below.

> **Activity 2**
>
> *Error codes!*
>
> Staff at Lee Office Supplies have been having a few headaches with error messages periodically popping up on their systems. They have given you a series of codes in a table. Complete the table by identifying the fault in each case! Be aware that while some of them are internet related, others are not! Use the internet to find the answer in each case.

Error code	Meaning
Bad Request 400	
488	
0xC000021A	
5 beeps	
0x000000BE	
Forbidden 403	
1 long 3 short beeps	
Gateway timeout 503	

13.2.4 Nature of reported faults

Trend analysis may show that faults can be categorised as being simple or complex in nature.

Simple faults:

- easy to identify
- can usually be remedied quickly
- caused by a common issue that is well known.

Complex faults:

- cause not easy to trace because there are multiple symptoms
- time consuming to resolve
- require a more complex solution that may require multiple steps
- may be easier to resolve through replacing rather than locating the problem.

13.2.5 Communication

Effective communication is essential when practising IT troubleshooting and repair. Communication should always be clear and in an appropriate format (i.e. verbal or written). The technician should have good communication and interpersonal skills and be able to check that the information they have provided has been understood clearly by its recipient: faults cannot be identified or remedied unless the information exchanged is accurate and agreed.

Unit link

A more detailed examination of communication and interpersonal skills can be found in Unit 1 – Communication and employability skills for IT.

13.3 Be able to select and apply fault remedies to IT systems

This section will cover the following grading criteria:

13.3.1 Identify remedies

Even the most experienced and knowledgeable IT technical staff cannot possibly know everything. In actual fact they are successful at what they do, not because of the knowledge they do have, but because they have the ability to find the answers if they do not know them already!

This section helps you to identify different ways of getting information to support IT systems.

Use knowledge databases

Key terms

A **knowledge database** is a special type of organised file containing a series of records that can be searched to provide answers to technical questions. Modern knowledge databases are often searched via a website interface.

Knowledge databases exist for more or less anything you can think of!

Where are knowledge databases found?

Make the Grade P3

P3 is a research task requiring you to identify different sources that may help you troubleshoot and repair your IT problem. Once you have identified a number of possible sources (e.g. knowledge databases, specific websites, newsgroups) you must select some suitable fault remedies from them.

- **Organisations** may have internal knowledge databases that are compiled by their IT staff, to record the answers to **FAQs** (Frequently Asked Questions). These would probably be found on the organisation's intranet.

- **Manufacturers' websites** often have knowledge databases about their products that can be accessed to answer common questions.
- **Usenet newsgroups** are discussion groups based around categories and topics. Accessed through an email client or using newsgroup clients, users can email queries and receive detailed responses and solutions.

Examples of newsgroups are:

- Comp.os.linux.networking
- Microsoft.public.windowsxp.hardware
- Comp.protocols.appletalk

When it comes to databases that need to be accessed through the internet, a search engine can be used to find the manufacturer's website, the relevant group or the topic of interest.

In addition, there are a series of technical support websites that offer free help to **diagnose** and **fix common problems**.

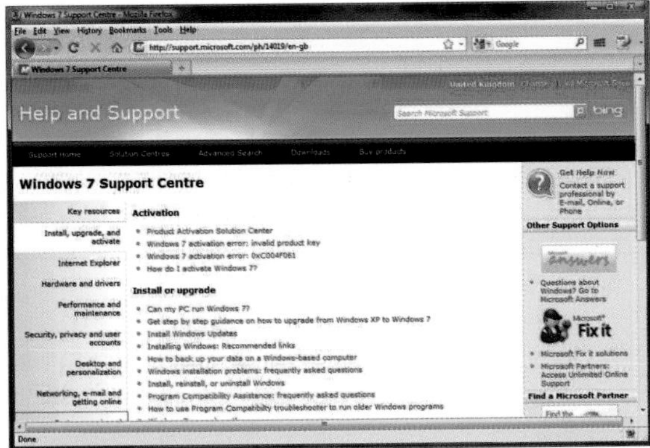

Figure 13.18 Accessing the Microsoft knowledge database for Windows 7®

The knowledge database in Figure 13.18 contains a series of key resources that have been categorised by the manufacturer. As you can see, this site contains 'How do I..?' articles on different aspects of Microsoft Windows 7®.

Similarly, enthusiasts will have contributed to knowledge databases that are devoted to particular software products. In Figure 13.19, the subject is The Sims!

This particular knowledge database may have been developed by the manufacturer of the software, with developers, testers and subsequently users contributing, or it might have come as the result of a group of enthusiasts who have decided to pool their knowledge to share with other enthusiasts.

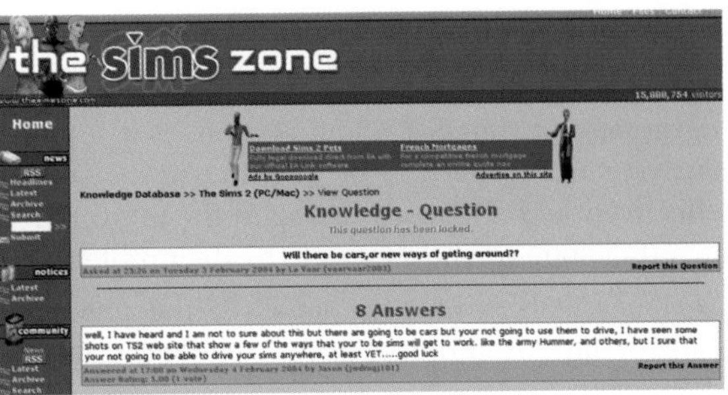

Figure 13.19 Knowledge database for a computer game

Use technical manuals

Most electrical and electronic products come with a technical manual. These documents are often referred to as **user guides** as they contain advice and guidance for the users, along with a list of FAQs and the technical specification of the components in the product.

In the case of computer components, some accessories and software packages, the minimum system requirements will also be specified because attempting to use some of these with equipment that is not of a suitable specification will result in poor (or no) performance.

In keeping with modern technology, some manufacturers choose to provide manuals on disk – usually on CD, although in some cases the manual may be on a DVD, particularly if the manufacturer has included a promotional video highlighting some of the product's main features.

Scorecard – On-disk manual

+	Content can be more in-depth and extensive as there are fewer limits on the size of the manual.
+	Material can be organised in several different ways on the same disk, for example, the whole manual in a single file or multiple files containing different sections.
+	Easier to carry around.
+	Cheaper to produce.
+	Environmentally friendly (less waste of paper).
–	More difficult to access as it requires a computer!

In addition to the help provided on disk and through printed manuals, many organisations also offer online help. The main advantage of online help is that it is the one medium that can be constantly updated as new issues arise. Clearly this would be difficult to achieve with a printed manual or one that has been supplied on disk!

Regardless of which medium is used, as a support analyst you will need to be able to use the source effectively and efficiently to obtain the information to either support the user or to fix the problem.

Most manuals have some or all of the following categorisations and listings for the content of the document.

Glossary

> **Key terms**
>
> A **glossary** is like a mini dictionary. It is a list of key terms, usually in alphabetical order, which explains the word at a level the user should be able to understand (Figure 13.20).

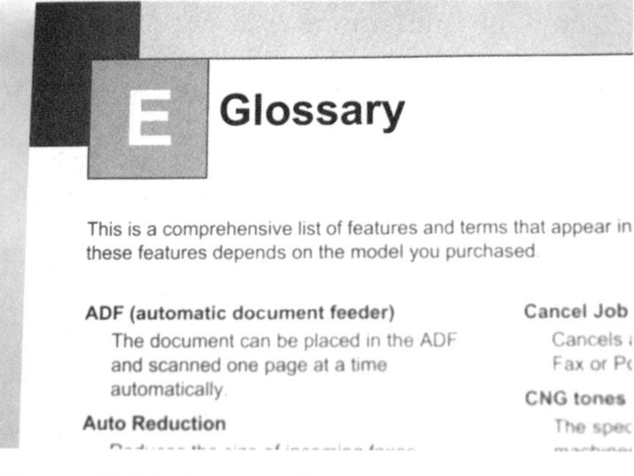

E Glossary

This is a comprehensive list of features and terms that appear in these features depends on the model you purchased.

ADF (automatic document feeder)
The document can be placed in the ADF and scanned one page at a time automatically.

Auto Reduction

Cancel Job

CNG tones

Figure 13.20 Brother MFC-660CN printer manual glossary

Index

Some books and manuals contain one or more **indexes**. Like a glossary, the index contains key words, but this time the word will be a signpost to where the information can be found in the book. For example: Visual Basic®...........page 123. There will be no written explanation included at this point, just a reference to where this particular subject is covered in the document (which may be more than once, in different parts of the book). To help the reader, books and manuals sometimes contain more than one index – an **alphabetical index** (which simply lists the words in order) and a **subject index**, where the relevant words are categorised and sub-categorised in topics or subject areas. For example, the following terms may be simply listed in an alphabetical index:

Content	Page
Accessories	47
Cables (network)	92
Network components	162
Network design	107
Network topologies	101
Software (network operating system)	166
Software (operating system)	75
Software (user applications)	254

A second index might now also be given, but this will then be organised differently to help the user to find the relevant content:

Content	Page
Computers	
Accessories	47
Operating system	75
User applications	254
Networks	
Cables	92
Components	162
Design	107
Operating system	166
Topologies	101
Software	
Network operating system	166
Operating system	75
User applications	254

What you will notice now is that some of the sub-categories have been listed more than once. 'Operating system' has been listed, for example, in all three main categories. This is because computers have operating systems, networks have operating systems and operating systems are pieces of software! The content has been listed from different perspectives.

Specifications

Particularly true of technical manuals that are provided with electronics or software, **specifications** provide a list of technical information about a product (Figure 13.21).

This could contain information about the electrical voltage the device needs to run, or in the case of software, include the **minimum hardware specifications** required to run the application. Technical specifications are often a good starting point when troubleshooting. For example, if you identify that an application requires a minimum of 512 Mb of RAM to run and you already know that the machine contains only 256 Mb, you may not need to look any further for an explanation about why the system is not working properly!

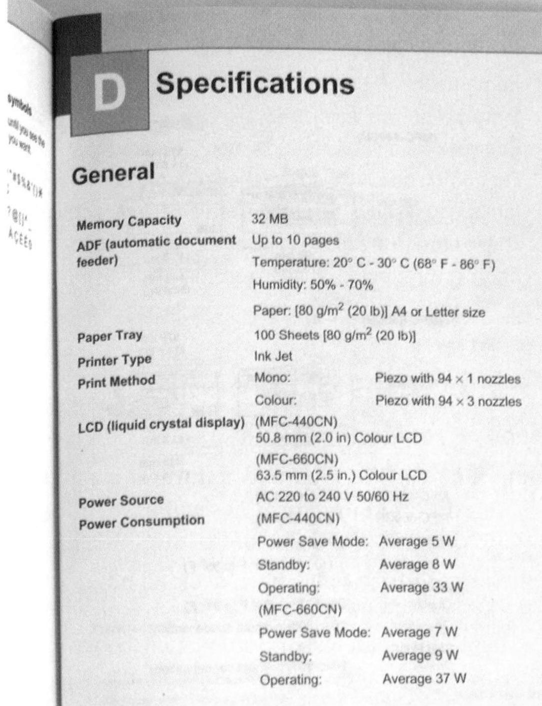

D Specifications

General

Memory Capacity	32 MB	
ADF (automatic document feeder)	Up to 10 pages	
	Temperature: 20° C - 30° C (68° F - 86° F)	
	Humidity: 50% - 70%	
	Paper: [80 g/m² (20 lb)] A4 or Letter size	
Paper Tray	100 Sheets [80 g/m² (20 lb)]	
Printer Type	Ink Jet	
Print Method	Mono:	Piezo with 94 × 1 nozzles
	Colour:	Piezo with 94 × 3 nozzles
LCD (liquid crystal display)	(MFC-440CN) 50.8 mm (2.0 in) Colour LCD	
	(MFC-660CN) 63.5 mm (2.5 in.) Colour LCD	
Power Source	AC 220 to 240 V 50/60 Hz	
Power Consumption	(MFC-440CN)	
	Power Save Mode:	Average 5 W
	Standby:	Average 8 W
	Operating:	Average 33 W
	(MFC-660CN)	
	Power Save Mode:	Average 7 W
	Standby:	Average 9 W
	Operating:	Average 37 W

Figure 13.21 Technical specifications for Brother MFC-660CN printer

FAQs

FAQ stands for **F**requently **A**sked **Q**uestions (Figure 13.22).

This is usually a list of questions that have been asked about a product, with answers or solutions then provided. For example:

Q. Why has my computer got no power?

A. Try checking the connections into the machine, and remember to check that the machine has been plugged into the socket and that the socket is switched on.

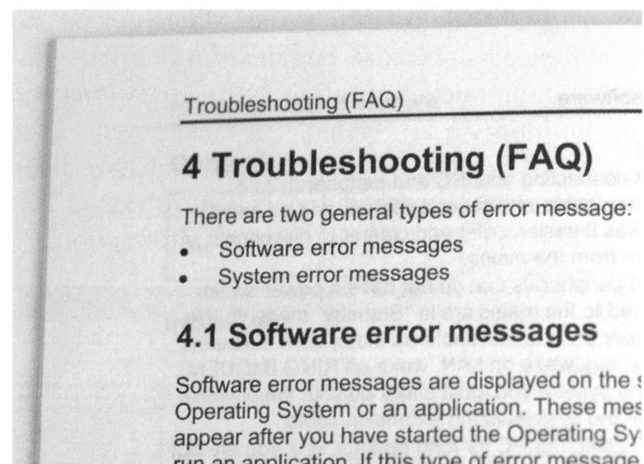

Troubleshooting (FAQ)

4 Troubleshooting (FAQ)

There are two general types of error message:

- Software error messages
- System error messages

4.1 Software error messages

Software error messages are displayed on the
Operating System or an application. These mes
appear after you have started the Operating Sy
run an application. If this type of error message

Figure 13.22 FAQs from a home PC user manual

Internet (e.g. discussion forums, manufacturers' websites)

While the internet will carry the same content as manuals to provide technical support, the main advantage of this medium is that it can be kept constantly up to date. For example, if a product develops a fault after it has been released, the manufacturer's website will be able to carry information about the fault and how to resolve it, that would not have been available when the manual was originally printed.

> **Activity 3**
>
> Understanding how to find remedies for common problems is a crucial skill for IT technicians performing troubleshooting and repair.
>
> Try to locate the following sources for these products:
>
> - a knowledge database for Microsoft Windows Vista®
> - an online discussion forum for Apple® iPad users
> - the manufacturer's website supporting HP printers
> - an online Usenet newsgroup (or Google Group) for Microsoft Visual C#®
> - a printed manual for a new motherboard
> - a CD or DVD with an electronic FAQ for a new hardware device.

Similarly, discussion forums exist where novice and experienced users and engineers will discuss aspects of products, including faults, irritations and resolutions! As an example, www.annoyances.org contains a collection of problems that have been identified and resolved by users (Figure 13.23). This sort of forum can be a goldmine of information.

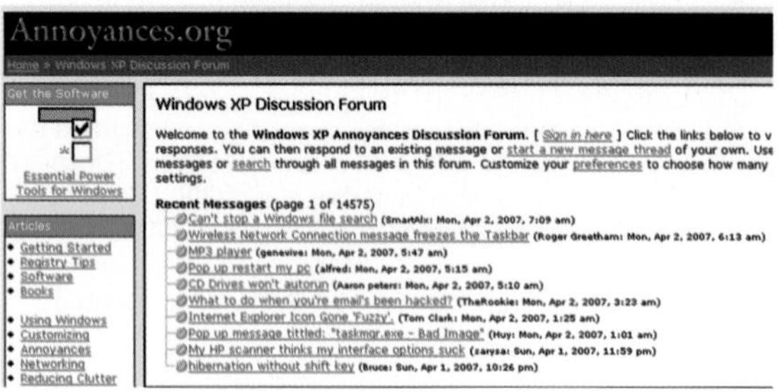

Figure 13.23 Windows XP® discussion forum from Annoyances.org

You should, however, bear in mind that sites such as Annoyances.org are not created by the manufacturers themselves, but by users and technicians working with the products.

Others (e.g. colleagues, training programmes undertaken, fault history)

Other useful sources of valuable information will be less obvious, but are still valid! For example:

Colleagues – other users, technicians or engineers. This is particularly useful inside an organisation as you will be able to gain a significant amount of in-depth knowledge that you know is directly relevant to the systems in use. This also links to the concept of escalation, which is covered later in this unit.

Training programmes – as part of your **CPD** (**C**ontinuous **P**rofessional **D**evelopment) you will at times be asked to attend training courses. These courses can be anything from a few hours to a number of days and may, on occasion, even be residential courses where you are required to stay away from home overnight. Some organisations invest more heavily in training courses for their employees than others, as these courses can be expensive. For this reason, it is not unusual for one employee to be sent on a course with the expectation that he or she will pass on (or cascade) their newly acquired knowledge to other staff.

Fault history – in most organisations, old fault logs containing information about the fault and how it was resolved will exist. These are often kept for reference and can be a valuable source of information, again specifically relevant to the organisation's systems.

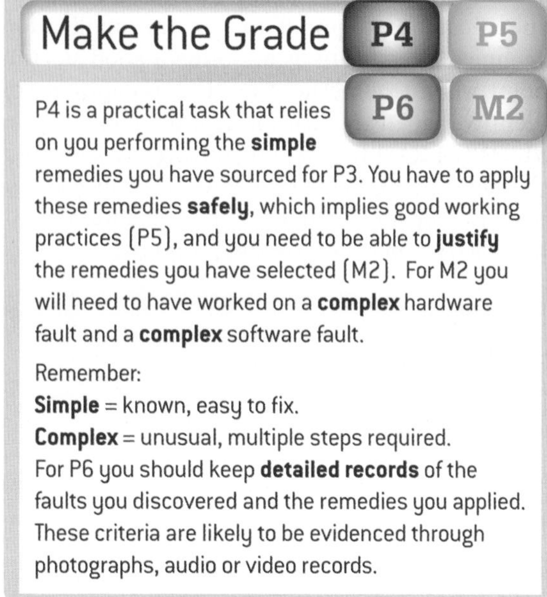

Make the Grade **P4** P5 **P6** M2

P4 is a practical task that relies on you performing the **simple** remedies you have sourced for P3. You have to apply these remedies **safely**, which implies good working practices (P5), and you need to be able to **justify** the remedies you have selected (M2). For M2 you will need to have worked on a **complex** hardware fault and a **complex** software fault.

Remember:
Simple = known, easy to fix.
Complex = unusual, multiple steps required.
For P6 you should keep **detailed records** of the faults you discovered and the remedies you applied. These criteria are likely to be evidenced through photographs, audio or video records.

13.3.2 Types of remedies

Repair or replace hardware

Depending on the type and nature of a particular fault, different organisations will have different policies on what should be done.

Some organisations may have decided never to repair any equipment if it goes wrong, but to replace the item immediately. For example, a CD drive will be instantly replaced if it develops a fault.

Other organisations, however, may well have a policy to always attempt to repair an item at least once, if at all feasible.

You must ensure that in an organisational setting you make yourself familiar with any relevant policies, so that you do not waste time trying to repair a device that the organisation will simply replace.

Why do some organisations repair and others replace?

This is usually a cost issue, although sometimes the reasons are less straightforward. It could, however, be down to the time it will take to carry out the repair, where the organisation cannot afford to have the system off-line.

Software remedy (e.g. reconfigure software, apply software patch)

Manufacturers' online help systems and the update links included on websites will give you lists of FAQs and offer advice on **reconfiguring** hardware and software when errors occur. In addition, instructions will be given on any **software patches** that have been developed to address particular faults in systems or software that may not have been known at the time of development.

Key terms

A **software patch** is a downloadable mini program containing code which, when run, will **modify** the existing software in some way. Patches are usually developed in response to problems experienced by users, for example, operating systems are patched routinely when **vulnerabilities** or **flaws** are discovered.

In addition, other software maintenance tasks can also be undertaken as part of troubleshooting and repair activities:

- upgrading software
- automation of scheduled tasks
- use of utility software such as defragmentation and disk clean-up tools
- compression utilities
- use of spyware and antivirus.

Further explanation can be found later in this unit and in the Unit link shown below.

Unit link

For more on software maintenance tasks see Unit 2 – Computer systems.

Other (e.g. instruct user in correct use of equipment, re-install software)

Part of the role of a technical support analyst is to help the user to use his or her system correctly. This can be by way of discussing problems and talking through solutions over the phone, demonstrating aspects of the system when necessary or through more formal situations such as user training.

Sometimes the support analyst has no other option other than to re-install the software. This is often done when an inexperienced user has changed so many settings that they have either compromised the system or made it unusable in some other way. In this instance, it may well be more logical to re-install the software than attempt to unpick all the changes. Some organisations have a system **image** – which contains all of the software the machine should have. In extreme circumstances, a technical support analyst may well be asked to **re-image** the machine's hard disk. This will effectively overwrite all the existing software and settings and return the machine to its base state. If you need to resort to this type of drastic action, ensure that your user has backed up any important files before you begin – otherwise data will be lost permanently and will not be recoverable.

13.3.3 Nature of reported faults – please see section 13.2.4

13.3.4 Working practices

Obtaining permissions before repairing

As cost can be a determining factor in decisions about repairing or replacing equipment or components, it is usually necessary to obtain permission to proceed before any repair activity takes place. Some organisations will have policies that specify different levels of permission that may be required, depending on the circumstances. Table 13.05 shows an example.

Table 13.05

Cost	Permission
Under £20	No permission needed
Between £20 and £100	Permission from budget holder required
Between £100 and £150	Permission from senior manager required
Over £150	Item will be written off automatically

Similarly, some individuals will give you a special instruction on when you may go ahead and when you should seek guidance, for example:

> 'If it is going to cost less than £50 then go ahead. If it is more then call me first.'

You should always ensure that you adhere to these types of request; otherwise you might find your customer refusing to pay the bill.

Preparing the worksite

Before any repair, installation or upgrade can take place, there will undoubtedly be a need to undertake some sort of preparation! In general, the following plan can be used as guidance:

1. Check that your workspace is safe and tidy.
2. Backup any data to ensure that there will be no data loss, even if you might not be working directly with hard disk devices (see the section on ESD on page 369).
3. Obtain the necessary hardware, software and so on. You should be aware that some aspects of this might need to be ordered in advance, so there may be a delay before you can begin.
4. Identify and lay out the relevant tools (you should never attempt to work on a system with the wrong tools)!
5. Ensure that you have sufficient rights to access the system, particularly if you will need to be able to do this to test it at the end of the activity.
6. Ensure that you know any configuration settings.
7. Check that any new equipment or components are undamaged. If working on an existing system, always ensure that anything you do will not invalidate any existing warranties.
8. Read the installation instructions that come with any component or equipment. These instructions may be paper-based, electronic, on a CD, or you may need to access the manufacturer's website (as suggested earlier in this unit).
9. Arrange for supervision (if appropriate).
10. Now you should be ready to begin!

This list is not exhaustive and might need to be modified based on your own experiences or situation, but it should provide a sound set of instructions for you to follow in preparing your working environment or, more specifically, in preparing you for an actual repair activity.

Recording information (e.g. product keys, license number, installation date)

Once the upgrade, installation or repair activity has been completed, you should ensure that all relevant documentation is completed. It is particularly important that product keys, license numbers and installation dates are recorded. This is often because registering products will activate the warranty period and activate accessibility to manufacturer support mechanisms.

For an individual, keeping purchase receipts in a safe place is essential (companies will put any receipts into their accounting processes, so they will be sure to have this information).

Key terms

Product keys– most software can only be installed by entering a valid product key or serial number as part of the installation process. Although some keys are unique, organisations may be allowed to use a number of them simultaneously. Some keys that are used illegally may be 'blacklisted' and refuse authentication when the user tries to register the product, access any support for the product or get free updates.

License numbers– some software is activated by a license number rather than a product key. In this instance, the same number is used for each installation of the software and once the number of purchased licenses is reached, no further licenses can be activated.

Make the Grade M3

M3 requires you to maintain data security and integrity when you are applying your chosen fault remedy.

This may include backing up important data, creating a restore point, updating virus protection or assigning correct access rights – the actual measures will depend greatly on the remedies being applied. Evidence this with screen captures or video for best effect.

13.3.5 Data security and integrity

It has been suggested a number of times in this unit that data should be backed up before work is undertaken on systems. How this is done and the range of media available to support this process forms part of the information systems coverage in Unit 3, with further discussion on security covered in Unit 7. Confidentiality of data is usually achieved through security measures and through the use of non-disclosure agreements that employees can be asked to sign when taking up employment.

Unit link

For more on data backup see Unit 3 – Information systems. For more on maintaining security see Unit 7 – Organisational system security.

13.3.6 Health and safety

All ICT users and practitioners have a responsibility to be aware of health and safety legislation as it affects them in their roles and they must ensure that they work safely while also considering those around them.

When working in a technical capacity, you will also need to ensure that you adopt safe working practises when using tools, devices and utilities.

Correct use of tools (e.g. screwdrivers, test meters, utility programs)

Clearly, the range of tools, devices and utilities that could be used in repair activities is vast. This section will merely provide an overview and some general guidance. This should never, however, be considered a substitute for reading any instructions that come with tools or other equipment.

As part of your technical role you may well need to use some of the following:

- **Screwdrivers** will be used to remove and replace screws in computer cases and where they are used to secure components. As a potentially **sharp** implement, the guidelines for the safe use of screwdrivers will be the same as for other items such as scissors (i.e. to avoid cuts and piercing).
- Using **test meters** involves **electrical contact** so you would follow the general safety guidelines for using any electrical devices.
- Implements such as **pliers** and **crimpers** have **squashing** or **squeezing potential** and should be used with care.
- IT personnel will often think nothing of holding screws, washers, nuts or jumpers between their teeth to leave hands free. Clearly this will present a **choking hazard** and the practice should be avoided!

Electro Static Discharge (ESD) and electrical safety

Advice and guidance on avoiding electrocuting yourself when working with direct current should be an essential part of your knowledge base. You might wonder why this is mentioned here as when working with a computer, you would make sure that it is isolated from any electrical supply. What you may not have considered is that there may be times when you are repairing systems that you need the systems to be 'live' for a number of reasons: one reason could be that you need to hear whether the device is making a particular noise. There are a number of websites that detail current guidelines, recommendations and legislation, and you should aim to become familiar with these, to ensure that your knowledge is up to date.

> **Key terms**
>
> The two types of electricity are defined as current and static.
>
> **Current** electricity comes directly from a battery or the mains whilst **static** electricity can build up on components or surfaces (including your body!).

Before you undertake any new activity with electrical devices, you should check the advice given by the manufacturer of the product or device (if this advice exists) or institutions like the Government's designated agencies like the Health and Safety Executive (Figure 13.24) or the Fire Service.

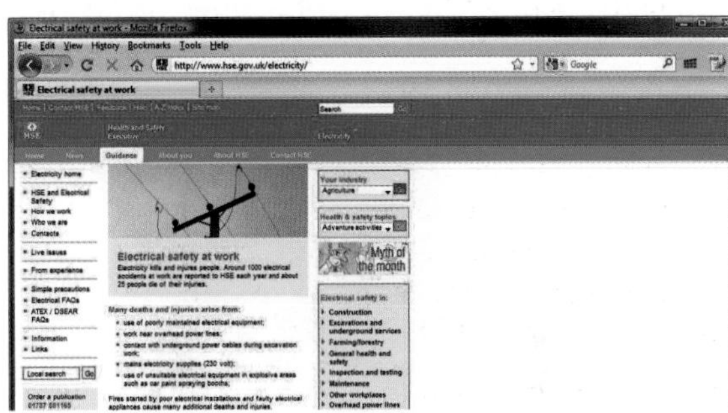

Fig 13.24 Electrical safety advice provided by the Health and Safety Executive

More general advice is also offered by a number of safety bodies such as the Electrical Safety Council (Figure 13.25), which offers tips on what to look out for when it comes to appliance or device general safety, and covers some of the legislation that applies to safe working practices. The most important advice that any of these websites will give you, however, is not to work with electricity unless you are absolutely sure that you know what you are doing and you are qualified to do so.

You are more likely to have to consider the ramifications of static electricity, which can build up slowly until there are sufficient volts on the component to cause damage or the need to be released. At this point the device will find the quickest route to

Figure 13.25 Electrical Safety Council

earth. This is called an **ESD** or **electrostatic discharge**. If the earthing route is through another device or component, the item may cease to work.

In an attempt to reduce the potential for static electricity build-up, some components are kept in anti-static bags or other packaging (Figure 13.26).

Figure 13.26 Anti-static bag

This packaging contains a special coating that reduces the opportunity for static build-up. It also protects the component while it is being moved from any static charge that may have built up on your body as you move around while carrying the item. The component should be kept inside the packaging until it is needed.

When working with computer base units, it is standard practice to isolate yourself from the device by using an anti-static wrist strap (Figure 13.27). This reduces the potential for static damage to circuit boards, memory and processor chips.

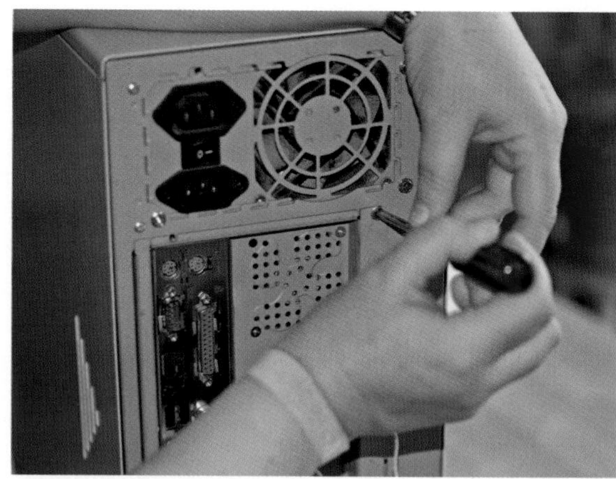

Figure 13.27 Anti-static wrist strap

The strap, which contains a wire, is worn around the wrist and connected with a crocodile clip or V-clip to the chassis of a computer (as long as it is connected to a mains socket, although this is clearly not recommended), a water pipe or other unpainted metal device that goes into the floor.

Further information on ESD protection can be found on the following website:

www.electronics-radio.com/articles/constructional_techniques/electro-static-discharge/esd-protection.php

Using correct manual handling procedures

Moving, lifting and occasionally positioning some IT equipment can be hazardous, particularly if the equipment is heavy or bulky. It can result in strains to virtually any part of the body, or more direct injuries, particularly to your back. Figure 13.28 shows the recommended weight-lifting tolerances for both men and women.

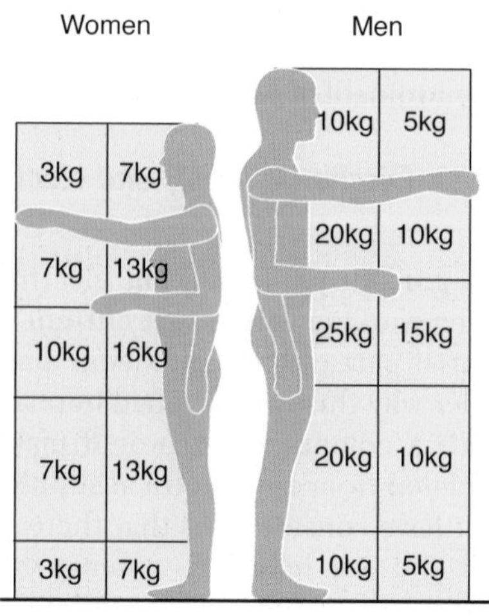

Figure 13.28 Recommended manual handling weights

The best advice is that if equipment appears to be heavy or bulky and needs to be moved, seek help. *Never* attempt to move anything like this on your own. It is far too easy to injure your back through careless lifting and while at a minimum you might experience back strain, at the other end of the spectrum you could cause permanent damage that might require surgery and leave you needing to manage a back condition for the rest of your life.

For more advice and guidance on safe manual handling practices see the following website: www.hse.gov.uk/pubns/manlinde.htm

Considering fire safety and the health and safety of other people

The potential for fires caused through the use of electrical equipment and through repair activities can be vastly reduced by following simple fire safety guidelines such as those published by the Government through the **Fire Kills** awareness programme and through websites belonging to regional fire brigades (Figure 13.29).

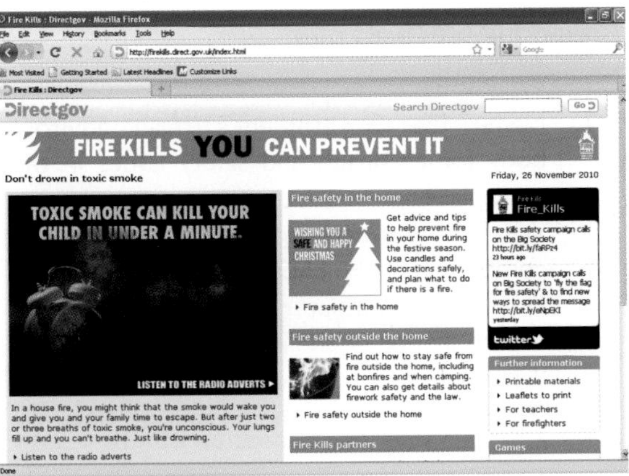

Figure 13.29 Fire Kills government website

In addition to this advice, IT personnel must ensure that they keep their workspace clean and tidy to avoid any hazards associated with fire safety such as the blockage of emergency exits with boxes or equipment, and also tripping and falling hazards that can be associated with trailing wires or broken components that have not been correctly disposed of.

As suggested in the Health and safety section in Unit 3, the responsibilities for workplace health and safety are shared by employers (or organisations) and employees alike, including employees taking care not to endanger the health and safety of others.

> **Unit link**
> For more on health and safety see Unit 3 – Information systems, section 3.2.3

Correct disposal of old parts and equipment

It is essential that organisations and individuals behave responsibly when disposing of both hardware and consumables, because this is an increasingly sensitive environmental issue.

As hardware costs fall and items such as printers, keyboards and mice become increasingly disposable, it is more common to buy replacement parts rather than attempt to repair them: it's simply the cheaper option! The consequence, however, is that we then end up with old components that we will need to dispose of safely. For example, some old motherboards can contain toxic materials which have to be disposed through a **waste broker**. This is a company that is licensed and trained to deal correctly with such materials.

Some consumable items, such as printer cartridges (both ink and toner varieties), can be reused (by being refilled) rather than being disposed of in household or business waste.

Complete systems can be recycled by being donated to charity (e.g. IT Schools Africa, Figure 13.30).

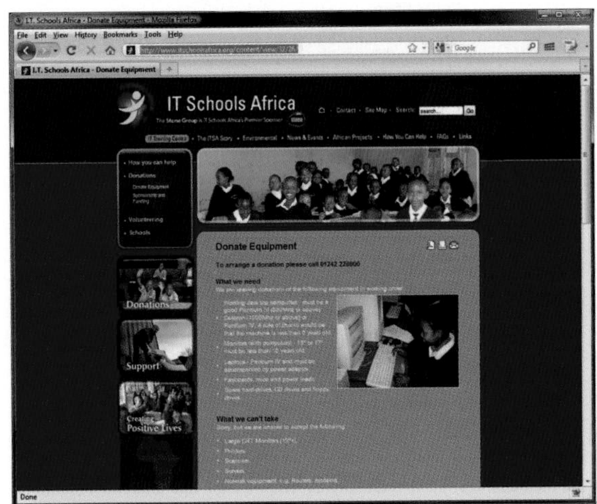

Figure 13.30 IT Schools Africa (*Source*: http://www.itschoolsafrica.org/content/view/32/26/)

Other organisations like **TECC** (**T**he **E**thical **C**omputer **C**entre) are community projects helping the unemployed and, as can be seen from their website on page 372, they also help developing countries. Figure 13.31 shows their approach to recycling and disposal.

Figure 13.31 TECC – The Ethical Computer Centre

You should ensure, however, that before you donate your old equipment any sensitive and confidential data has been removed from hard disks.

European legislation, primarily the **WEEE** (**W**aste **E**lectronic and **E**lectrical **E**quipment) directive sets out how unwanted IT equipment should be disposed of and imposes large fines for irresponsible disposal in the UK. This directive came into full effect in January 2007.

Availability of first aid and supervision

There is certainly UK legislation about employers making first aid provision for their staff as can be seen from the Health and Safety Executive's website in Figure 13.32.

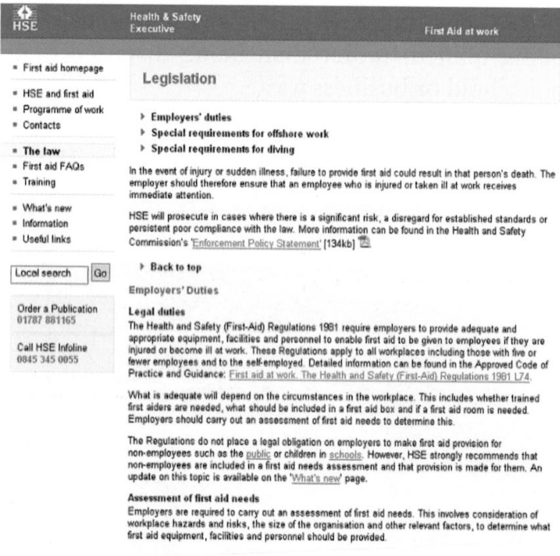

Figure 13.32 First aid legislation

However, as you can see, in order to establish the appropriate level of provision, the first aid needs of individual organisations need to be determined.

To facilitate this, each organisation will have to carry out an **audit** where it identifies hazards and risks, the size of the organisation and any other relevant factors so that the level of provision can be established.

When it comes to the issues of supervision, it would clearly be irresponsible if any organisation were to allow an inexperienced employee to do something that is known to be dangerous or hazardous. For this reason, organisations are supposed to carry Employers' Liability Insurance to comply with the Employers' Liability (Compulsory Insurance) Act 1969, although as with all legislation, there are organisations that will find that they are exempt from this.

For more on the Employers' Liability (Compulsory Insurance) Act 1969, see the following website, which contains an easy-to-read guide for employers: www.biba.org.uk/PDFfiles/Contents/766hse40.pdf

B Braincheck 2

Working practices quiz

1. What is ESD?
2. Name the Government's main advisory body for all health and safety issues in the workplace.
3. What do you need to use to protect your components from ESD?
4. How does a computer technician or engineer ensure that he or she is earthed?
5. What are the main danger signs that you should check for when considering electrical fire safety?
6. Name three workplace hazards.
7. List the correct options for disposing of old parts or equipment.
8. Name the legislation that sets out directives on how IT equipment should be disposed of.
9. Name the Act that sets out requirements for ensuring employee safety at work.
10. Name six of the possible steps in preparing the worksite.

Unit link

Unit 13 is a **mandatory unit** for the Edexcel BTEC Level 3 National Extended Diploma in IT (Networking and Systems Support pathway) and **optional** for all other qualifications and pathways of this Level 3 IT family.

Qualification (pathway)	Mandatory	Optional	Specialist optional
Edexcel BTEC Level 3 National Certificate in Information Technology		✓	
Edexcel BTEC Level 3 National Subsidiary Diploma in Information Technology		✓	
Edexcel BTEC Level 3 National Diploma in Information Technology		✓	
Edexcel BTEC Level 3 National Extended Diploma in Information Technology		✓	
Edexcel BTEC Level 3 National Diploma in IT (Business)		✓	
Edexcel BTEC Level 3 National Extended Diploma in IT (Business)		✓	
Edexcel BTEC Level 3 National Diploma in IT (Networking and System Support)		✓	
Edexcel BTEC Level 3 National Extended Diploma in IT (Networking and System Support)	✓		
Edexcel BTEC Level 3 National Diploma in IT (Software Development)		✓	
Edexcel BTEC Level 3 National Extended Diploma in IT (Software Development)		✓	

There are specific links to the following units in the scheme:

Unit 12 – IT technical support

Unit 25 – Maintaining computer systems

Achieving success

This particular unit has 11 criteria to meet: 6 Pass, 3 Merit and 2 Distinction.

For a Pass: You must achieve all 6 Pass criteria

For a Merit: You must achieve all 6 Pass and all 3 Merit criteria

For a Distinction: You must achieve all 6 Pass, all 3 Merit and both Distinction criteria.

Further reading

French, C. – *Computer Science, 5th Edition* (Thomson Learning, 1996) ISBN-10 0826454607, ISBN-13 978-0826454607

Websites

technet.microsoft.com

techrepublic.com

whatis.techtarget.com

www.pctechguide.com

Unit 42: Spreadsheet modelling

By the end of this unit you should be able to:

1. Understand how spreadsheets can be used to solve complex problems
2. Be able to develop complex spreadsheet models
3. Be able to automate and customise spreadsheet models
4. Be able to test and document spreadsheet models

Whether you are in school or college, passing this unit will involve being assessed. As with most BTEC schemes, the successful completion of various assessment criteria demonstrates your evidence of learning and the skills you have developed.

This unit has a mixture of pass, merit and distinction criteria. Generally you will find that merit and distinction criteria require a little more thought and evaluation before they can be completed.

The colour-coded grid below shows you the pass, merit and distinction criteria for this unit.

To achieve a pass grade you need to:	To achieve a merit grade you also need to:	To achieve a distinction grade you also need to:
P1 Explain how spreadsheets can be used to solve complex problems		**D1** Discuss how organisations can use interpretation methods to analyse data
P2 Develop a complex spreadsheet model to meet a particular need	**M1** Refine a complex spreadsheet model by changing rules and values	
P3 Use formulae, features and functions to process information		
P4 Use appropriate tools to present data	**M2** Analyse and interpret data from a spreadsheet model	
P5 Customise the spreadsheet model to a given requirement		
P6 Use automated features in the spreadsheet model to meet a given requirement	**M3** Compare different automation methods	

P7 Test a spreadsheet model to ensure that it is fit for purpose		D2 Evaluate a spreadsheet model incorporating feedback from others and make recommendations for improvements
P8 Export the contents of the spreadsheet model to an alternative format		
P9 Produce user documentation for a spreadsheet model	M4 Produce technical documentation for a spreadsheet model	

Introduction

Spreadsheet modelling is a 10-credit unit which builds on assumed basic spreadsheet skills to produce models to solve complex problems.

As a practical unit, there will be a significant emphasis on the hands-on use of spreadsheet software, with a consideration of spreadsheet technologies, such as the use of comma separated value (csv) formatting to enable import and export of data into other files or applications.

How to read this chapter

This chapter is organised to match the content of the BTEC unit it represents. The following diagram shows the grading criteria that relate to each learning outcome.

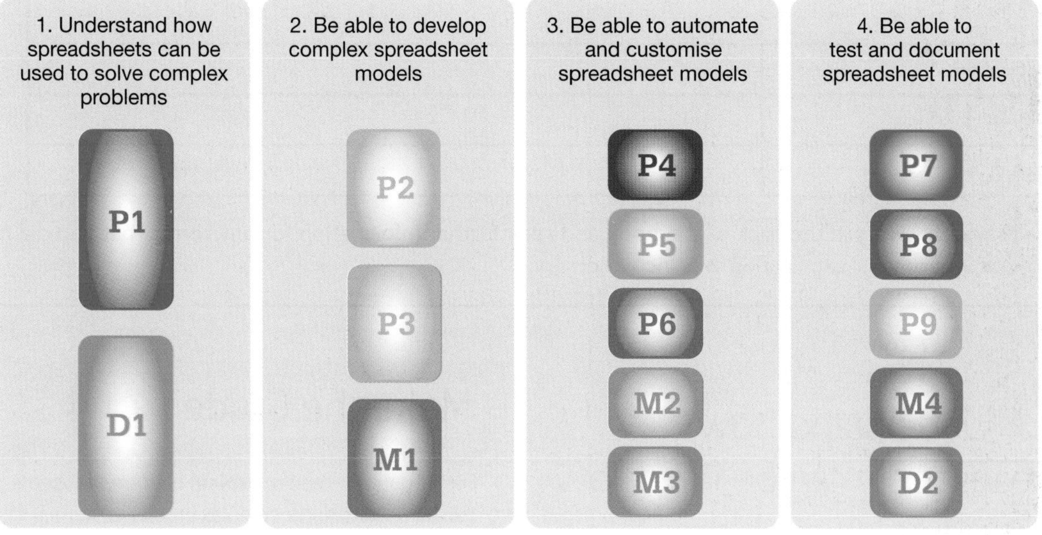

Figure 42.00

B Braincheck 1

What do you already know?

The title of this unit is Spreadsheet modelling and it builds on assumed spreadsheet skills. This means that basic concepts will not be covered and you will be expected to understand some of the terminology already. To demonstrate your understanding, complete the following grid:

Term	Explanation
Row	
Column	
Cell	
Operators	
Formulae	
Function	
Parenthesis	
BODMAS	
Condition	
Simple logical operators	
Format	
Alignment	
Merge	
Range	

Check your answers in the back of the book and seek further information for any terms that you did not know or where your explanation was incorrect.

42.1 Understand how spreadsheets can be used to solve complex problems

This section will cover the following grading criterion:

P1

Make the Grade P1

For P1 you will need to **explain** how spreadsheets can be used to solve complex problems. At this level, you will also need to **link** your explanations to **real examples**. You might find it helpful to link your examples to situations such as **decision-making**, **forecasting** and **budget control**.

A set of presentation slides with notes are a good way to evidence this criterion.

Although computers have been doing calculations since they first began, VisiCalc® was in fact the first commercial spreadsheet program. Released in 1979, the technology quickly grew with more versions of spreadsheet software becoming available containing increasingly complex functionality.

42.1.1 Uses of spreadsheets

So what are spreadsheets used for?

Manipulating complex data

Spreadsheets have changed the ways in which data can be manipulated and the speed in which calculations can be executed. Prior to the advent of spreadsheets, data users had to work physically with the numbers to calculate the answers and then they had to decide how they would present the information. This could mean typing out tables of information on a typewriter, with the possibility of numbers being transposed or simply being typed in incorrectly. There are a number of advantages to using spreadsheets:

- A simple change to a data item will mean that all numbers affected by the change will be updated automatically.
- Spreadsheets can be linked so that a change in one spreadsheet will update numbers in another automatically.

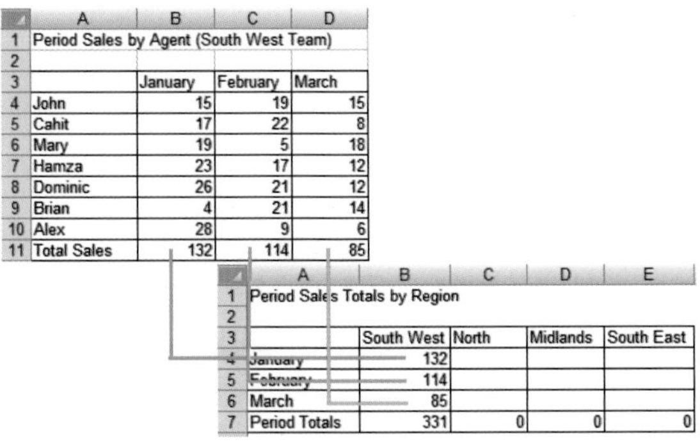

	A	B	C	D
1	Period Sales by Agent (South West Team)			
2				
3		January	February	March
4	John	15	19	15
5	Cahit	17	22	8
6	Mary	19	5	18
7	Hamza	23	17	12
8	Dominic	26	21	12
9	Brian	4	21	14
10	Alex	28	9	6
11	Total Sales	132	114	85

	A	B	C	D	E
1	Period Sales Totals by Region				
2					
3		South West	North	Midlands	South East
4	January	132			
5	February	114			
6	March	85			
7	Period Totals	331	0	0	0

Figure 42.01 Linked spreadsheet

Compare Figure 42.01 with the following spreadsheet (Figure 42.02) where the figures have been altered. Two numbers are now changed – Brian's figure of 4 in January has risen to 17. The change has been made in the spreadsheet entitled Period Sales by Agent (South West Team) and have automatically updated the Period Sales Totals by Region spreadsheet.

	A	B	C	D
1	Period Sales by Agent (South West Team)			
2				
3		January	February	March
4	John	15	19	15
5	Cahit	17	22	8
6	Mary	19	5	18
7	Hamza	23	17	12
8	Dominic	26	21	12
9	Brian	17	21	14
10	Alex	28	9	6
11	Total Sales	145	114	85

	A	B	C	D	E
1	Period Sales Totals by Region				
2					
3		South West	North	Midlands	South East
4	January	145			
5	February	114			
6	March	85			
7	Period Totals	344	0	0	0

Figure 42.02 Updated linked spreadsheet

In a real situation, similar spreadsheets or files would have been developed for the North, Midlands and South East data that would be linked similarly into the Period Sales Totals by Region file.

Although the range of functionality that can be applied to non-numeric data is more limited, as can be seen below, the agents in the first spreadsheets have been ordered alphabetically on the click of a button.

	A	B	C	D
1	Period Sales by Agent (South West Team)			
2				
3		January	February	March
4	Alex	28	9	6
5	Brian	17	21	14
6	Cahit	17	22	8
7	Dominic	26	21	12
8	Hamza	23	17	12
9	John	15	19	15
10	Mary	19	5	18
11	Total Sales	145	114	85

Figure 42.03 Alphabetical sort

Note: Care should be taken when sorting rows of figures to ensure that the corresponding data on the remaining part of the row is also included in the sort when executed, otherwise the data will no longer be attributed to the right agent (see highlighted area in Figure 42.04).

	A	B	C	D
1	Period Sales by Agent (South West Team)			
2				
3		January	February	March
4	Alex	28	9	6
5	Brian	17	21	14
6	Cahit	17	22	8
7	Dominic	26	21	12
8	Hamza	23	17	12
9	John	15	19	15
10	Mary	19	5	18
11	Total Sales	145	114	85

Figure 42.04 Selecting the data to sort

Presentation to requirements

When preparing data using spreadsheets, it is the responsibility of the person generating the spreadsheet to ensure that the information is presented in such a way that it will suit the requirements of the audience.

In simplest terms, this might be adjusting font sizes to ensure that all the information is legible for someone with a visual impairment. It could require that the data be presented as a comparative chart like the one shown in Figure 42.05.

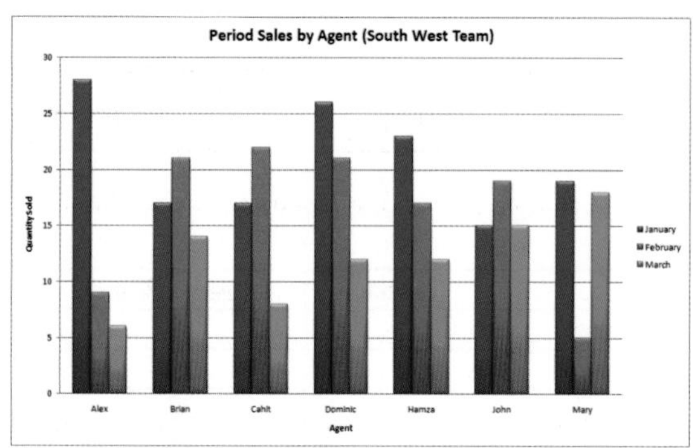

Figure 42.05 Comparison bar chart

Alternatively, the data users might wish to see a comparison of the total quantities sold between the various regions (see Figure 42.06).

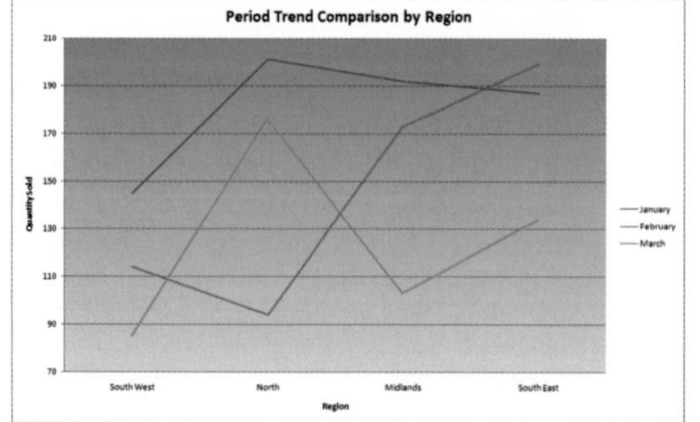

Figure 42.06 Trend comparison chart

Notice that the Y-axis scale (vertical) has been adjusted to have a maximum value of 210 and a minimum of 70. This is so that more efficient use is made of the visual display area. To effect this, simply click on the axis itself and select **Format Axis** from the menu. Change the values in the **Minimum** and **Maximum** boxes as required.

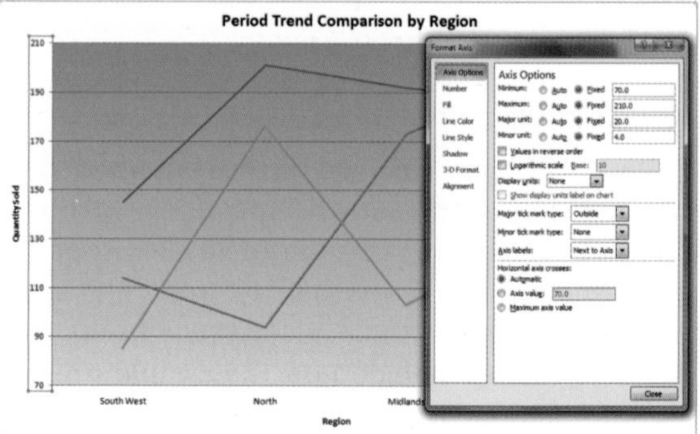

Figure 42.07 Format axis dialogue box

The Y-axis values on this occasion had been set to a maximum of 250 and a minimum of 0 by default. How the graph would have looked had the Y-axis scale not been changed can be seen in Figure 42.08.

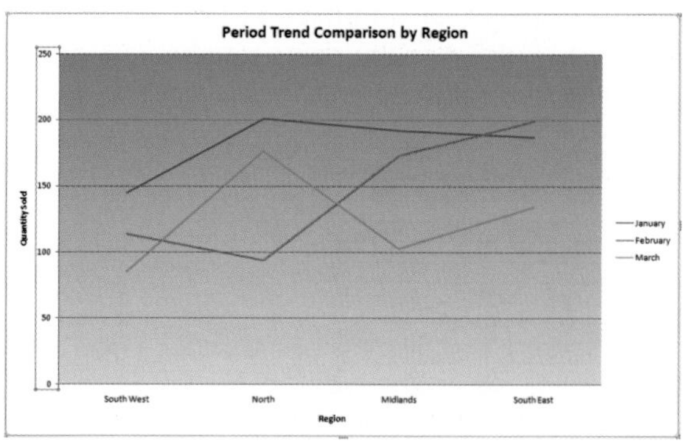

Figure 42.08 Period trend comparison graph before changing axis scale

Considering the needs of the audience is one of the most important skills that a spreadsheet developer needs to master. Reading more information about the principles of effective communication will help you to make important decisions about the presentation of spreadsheets.

Supporting decision-making

In order for managers to be effective in making decisions about the organisation, they must be able to access information about the organisation and how it has been operating. They might also need to have information about the activities of competitors or stakeholders.

The types of decisions that the information will need to support are operational issues such as monitoring and controlling the organisation's activities or helping the organisation analyse the past and plan for the future.

Whatever the intended use of the information, its preparation should have been **timely** (available for use at the right time) and **accurate** (correct and at an appropriate level of detail).

How can the use of a spreadsheet help in the process?

Analysis of data

Being able to compare data sets from different operational periods, the same periods from different years or comparing performance against that of a competitor is vital in ensuring that an organisation is able to stay ahead.

Viewing the data in different ways can highlight discrepancies in performance because unusual occurrences can be easier to spot in a graph or chart than if they are merely numbers represented in a table. Look again at the table of data in Figure 42.03. Is it easy to spot that Mary had the lowest monthly quantity overall and Alex had the highest? Look again at the chart of the same data in Figure 42.05. Is it easier to spot this detail in the chart?

Being able to manipulate tables of data, whether this is making charts and graphs, ordering, sorting, filtering or summarising the data (see later in this unit), makes data analysis a relatively simple process and enables users to understand their information in much more depth.

Goal seeking

This is part of the 'What-If' analysis functionality and is a term that is almost contradictory because what you are using the spreadsheet for is to find a value that contributes to the calculation rather than simply calculating an end result! When using the Goal Seek, you are able to find one value by making alterations to another value. What does this really mean? The best way to understand it is through the use of an example (see Case Study).

Case Study

Lee Office Supplies has decided to buy in some new spiral binders to sell on to customers. They already know that they can't charge more than £2.86 each for these items as their competitors are selling them for £2.90 and to gain the business, they must charge less.

They also know that they always make a 35 per cent profit on the goods they sell. They now need to calculate how much they can afford to pay for them to ensure they can still make 35 per cent profit when they sell them at the market price they have identified.

They have created a basic spreadsheet:

B3 | fx =(B1*B2)+B1

	A	B	C
1	Maximum cost price	£2.40	
2	Percentage Profit	35%	
3	Resale Price	£3.24	
4			

Figure 42.09 Lee Office Supplies spreadsheet

In Figure 42.09 you will notice that the spreadsheet contains three values:

- Maximum cost price – this is the value they are trying to calculate (the maximum they can afford to pay).
- Percentage profit – the percentage mark-up they always apply to goods they resell.
- Resale price – the price they will need to sell the item for if they want it to be competitive in the market.

The only formula in the spreadsheet is in cell B3, which is

(B1*B2)+B1

Or

(Maximum cost price * Percentage profit) plus Maximum cost price

So far they have guessed at a number of maximum cost price figures that they thought could give them the actual resale price of £2.86. However, they haven't found the right value as yet.

They now decide to use the Goal Seek function. To do this, click on Data then on What-If Analysis and then finally on Goal Seek. The following dialogue box appears:

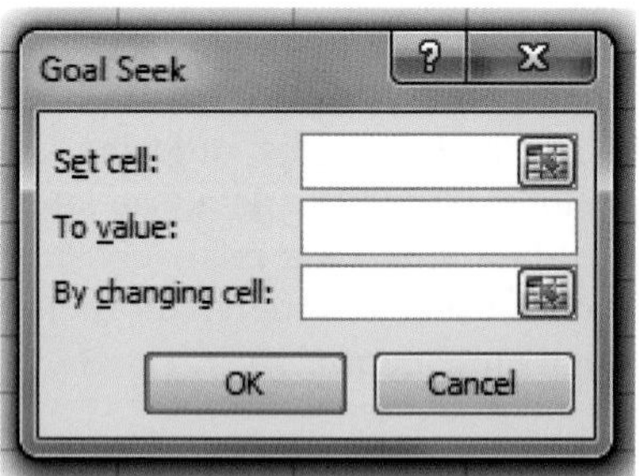

Figure 42.10 Goal Seek dialogue box

The figures and cell references now need to be completed. This is how to interpret the values to enter into the dialogue box:

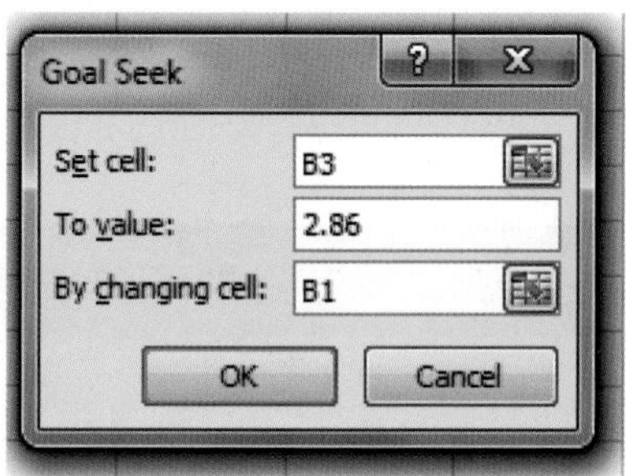

Figure 42.11 Inputting values into the dialogue box

Once these values have been input, click OK. The computer will now work incrementally through possible values until it finds a value for Maximum cost price that, when multiplied by the Percentage profit, will give the desired Resale Price.

Figure 42.12 The solution found by the Goal Seek function

Click OK to leave the Maximum cost price that has been calculated visible in cell B1.

While there are other ways to calculate the missing value without using Goal Seek, this is an easy-to-use, user-friendly interface that can resolve these kinds of queries quickly.

Lee Office Supplies has been advised by its landlords that the rent on the business premises is set to rise by 20 per cent as from 1 April.

The company's cash flow forecast spreadsheet, prior to the anticipated change, is shown in Figure 42.13.

As you can see, the previous projections show that the company will more or less break even if all goes as expected (without the increase in rent). Also, there is no evidence of a bank overdraft being required.

	A	B	C	D	E	F	G	H	I	J	K	L	M
1	Lee Office Supplies - Cashflow Forecast for January to December 2010												
2													
3		January	February	March	April	May	June	July	August	September	October	November	December
4													
5	Opening Balance	£12,500.00	£10,668.58	£8,944.29	£7,329.79	£5,827.85	£4,441.27	£3,229.69	£2,199.59	£1,357.69	£710.94	£266.57	£32.07
6													
7	Projected sales	£4,285.00	£4,392.13	£4,501.93	£4,614.48	£4,729.84	£4,904.84	£5,086.32	£5,274.52	£5,469.67	£5,672.05	£5,881.92	£6,099.55
8													
9	Expenditure												
10	Rent	£3,275.00	£3,275.00	£3,275.00	£3,275.00	£3,275.00	£3,275.00	£3,275.00	£3,275.00	£3,275.00	£3,275.00	£3,275.00	£3,275.00
11	Wages	£2,601.90	£2,601.90	£2,601.90	£2,601.90	£2,601.90	£2,601.90	£2,601.90	£2,601.90	£2,601.90	£2,601.90	£2,601.90	£2,601.90
12	Telephone	£56.40	£56.40	£56.40	£56.40	£56.40	£56.40	£56.40	£56.40	£56.40	£56.40	£56.40	£56.40
13	Energy	£78.56	£78.56	£78.56	£78.56	£78.56	£78.56	£78.56	£78.56	£78.56	£78.56	£78.56	£78.56
14	Vehicle Expenses	£104.56	£104.56	£104.56	£104.56	£104.56	£104.56	£104.56	£104.56	£104.56	£104.56	£104.56	£104.56
15													
16	Total Expenditure	£6,116.42	£6,116.42	£6,116.42	£6,116.42	£6,116.42	£6,116.42	£6,116.42	£6,116.42	£6,116.42	£6,116.42	£6,116.42	£6,116.42
17													
18	Closing balance	£10,668.58	£8,944.29	£7,329.79	£5,827.85	£4,441.27	£3,229.69	£2,199.59	£1,357.69	£710.94	£266.57	£32.07	£15.19

Figure 42.13 Lee Office Supplies' cash flow forecast

Case Study

Now we modify the spreadsheet to reflect the change in rent from April – with a 20% rise from £3,275 to £3,930.

The picture now is very different, with the company slipping into overdraft in July 2010. By the end of the financial year, the situation is far more serious, with a deficit of nearly £6,000. The organisation now has a number of choices:

- Sell more products
- Reduce expenditure (this could mean reducing staff for example)
- Refuse to accept the 20 per cent rise in rent
- Look for alternative accommodation

Scenario-based forecasting is one of the most powerful tools to help managers make decisions about future actions.

	A	B	C	D	E	F	G	H	I	J	K	L	M
1	Lee Office Supplies - Cashflow Forecast for January to December 2010												
2													
3		January	February	March	April	May	June	July	August	September	October	November	December
4													
5	Opening Balance	£12,500.00	£10,668.58	£8,944.29	£7,329.79	£5,172.85	£3,131.27	£1,264.69	-£420.41	-£1,917.31	-£3,219.06	-£4,318.43	-£5,207.93
6													
7	Projected sales	£4,285.00	£4,392.13	£4,501.93	£4,614.48	£4,729.84	£4,904.84	£5,086.32	£5,274.52	£5,469.67	£5,672.05	£5,881.92	£6,099.55
8													
9	Expenditure												
10	Rent	£3,275.00	£3,275.00	£3,275.00	£3,930.00	£3,930.00	£3,930.00	£3,930.00	£3,930.00	£3,930.00	£3,930.00	£3,930.00	£3,930.00
11	Wages	£2,601.90	£2,601.90	£2,601.90	£2,601.90	£2,601.90	£2,601.90	£2,601.90	£2,601.90	£2,601.90	£2,601.90	£2,601.90	£2,601.90
12	Telephone	£56.40	£56.40	£56.40	£56.40	£56.40	£56.40	£56.40	£56.40	£56.40	£56.40	£56.40	£56.40
13	Energy	£78.56	£78.56	£78.56	£78.56	£78.56	£78.56	£78.56	£78.56	£78.56	£78.56	£78.56	£78.56
14	Vehicle Expenses	£104.56	£104.56	£104.56	£104.56	£104.56	£104.56	£104.56	£104.56	£104.56	£104.56	£104.56	£104.56
15													
16	Total Expenditure	£6,116.42	£6,116.42	£6,116.42	£6,771.42	£6,771.42	£6,771.42	£6,771.42	£6,771.42	£6,771.42	£6,771.42	£6,771.42	£6,771.42
17													
18	Closing balance	£10,668.58	£8,944.29	£7,329.79	£5,172.85	£3,131.27	£1,264.69	-£420.41	-£1,917.31	-£3,219.06	-£4,318.43	-£5,207.93	-£5,879.81

Figure 42.14 Lee Office Supplies' revised cash flow forecast

Scenarios

What if scenarios can also be modelled using spreadsheet software. In this instance the values on the spreadsheet can be changed in order to forecast what will happen as a result of values changing.

Regression

Regression is a **statistical technique** for examining the **relationship** between **two or more variables.** Using the data in the spreadsheet, it will establish whether a variable **will change** as a **direct result** of a change in **another variable.** It is better explained as an example or a series of questions:

1. Do sales of DIY products go up if it is a wet summer?
2. If house prices go up, do the sales of holidays go down?
3. If the value of pound sterling falls in relation to other currencies, does that mean more people take holidays in the UK?

The regression analysis is done using historic data and the data is represented as a **scatter graph.** The **line of best fit** is added and the closeness of the scatter points is judged in relation to the line. The closer the scatter points fall to this line, the greater the relationship between the variables.

Data mining

Key terms

Data mining is a term applied to software applications that help users drill down into their data to find exceptional events.

The graph in Figure 42.15 was produced from organisational data.

At a glance, it is possible to see that something very unusual happened in August 2009 when production seemed to fall uncharacteristically low – not good for an ice cream manufacturer!

Using data mining software, users are not only able to identify unusual events, but they can drill down into the data on increasing levels to find out why the data appeared to be so different from the expected normal parameters.

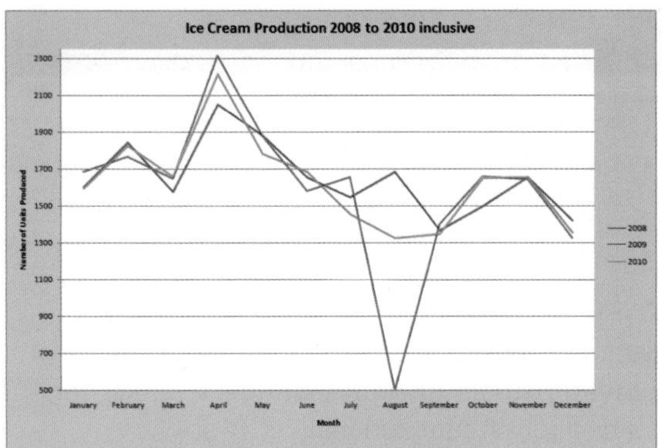

Figure 42.15 Trend analysis comparing ice cream production

It could be that the company unusually closed down for two weeks in August, or that there was a natural disaster, or they were unable to get the raw ingredients to support ice cream production. Through data mining, the anomaly is highlighted and then experienced analysts will investigate to establish the cause of the difference.

Typical data mining software has:

- number crunching and statistical functionality not usually found in software like Microsoft Access®
- the ability to analyse sub-levels in the data
- report-writing functionality
- the ability to be used with most database software.

42.1.2 Complex problems

With the advent of spreadsheets came the opportunity to set up templates to undertake a wide range of problem-solving tasks that would have been done previously by human beings using calculators, pens and paper. The following business problem-solving techniques are just some of the range of processes that can be automated using spreadsheet software.

Cash flow forecasting

As shown in Figures 42.13 and 42.14, cash flow forecasts are used to predict how certain events will impact on an organisation's financial situation. Simply by changing one or more of the variables, it is possible to see the effect that changes will have.

Cash flow forecasting often relies on best guesses, although with experience and historic information to support these hypotheses, some guesses are likely to be more accurate than others.

Cash flow forecasts are commonly produced for a quarter, half year, whole year or a number of years. You should remember that the further into the future you attempt to forecast, the less likelihood of accuracy! This is because the further from the present you get, the more uncertainty there is because less is known about the future events.

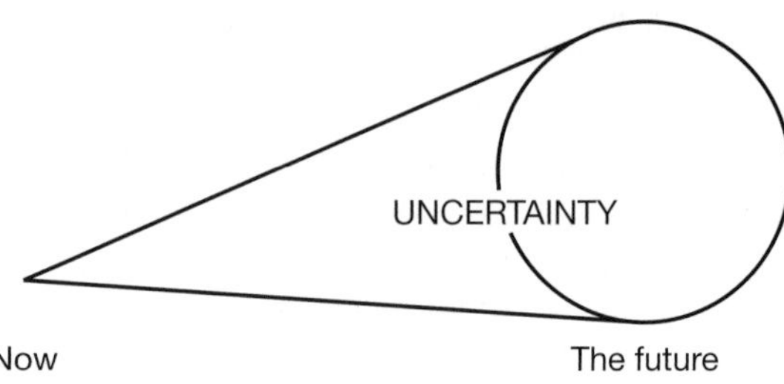

Figure 42.16 Predicting the future

Budget control

Another common use of spreadsheets is budget monitoring and control.

> **Key terms**
>
> A **budget** is an amount of money given to individuals or groups to be used for a particular purpose.
>
> Those given the budget usually have the responsibility to see that the budget is used appropriately, and that the best possible use is made of any money allocated.
>
> A budget is usually attached to a period – for example, money to support the manufacturing activities for a quarter (a period of three months) or a whole year (an annual budget).

Using a simple formula, the spreadsheet would be used to monitor the activity on the budget, recording the transactions and providing information about how much of the budget remains unspent. Figure 42.17 is an example of a **reducing balance** spreadsheet.

A little like a bank statement, the budget period will begin with an **opening value**, then each transaction or budget allocation will be itemised, reducing the **balance remaining** accordingly.

	A	B	C	D
1	Lee Office Supplies			
2				
3	1st January 2010 to 31st December 2010 - Temporary Staff Budget			
4				
5	Date	Nature of spend (and circumstances)	Cost	Balance
6				
7	**1st January 2010**	**Budget allocated**		**£5,000.00**
8	11th April 2010	3 days to cover staff absence for training (Mike Kidd)	£684.99	£4,315.01
9	9th July 2010	10 days to cover key staff holiday (Alicia Franks)	£1,766.40	£2,548.61
10	20th August 2010	5 days to cover key staff holiday (Jack Cahalit)	£837.45	£1,711.16
11	11th October 2010	2 days to cover staff sickness (Ruth Gibbons)	£456.11	£1,255.05
12				

Figure 42.17 Reducing balance budget control

The spreadsheet in Figure 42.17 shows the Temporary Staff Budget, controlled by the HR Manager at Lee Office Supplies. The year began with an opening budget allocation of £5,000 and a number of transactions have seen the balance fall to £1,255.05. This is the remaining amount available for the rest of the year. In the event that further temporary staff cover is needed, the HR Manager will have to make some decisions about whether to use all or some of the remaining budget, or try to make do without staff cover to retain the budget in the event that there is a more urgent need later in the year.

Figure 42.18 shows the formula view of the spreadsheet with the total for each line reduced by the cost on each subsequent line.

	A	B	C	D
1	Lee Office Supplies			
2				
3	1st January 2010 to 31st December 2010 - Temporary Staff Budget			
4				
5	Date	Nature of spend (and circumstances)	Cost	Balance
6				
7	**1st January 2010**	**Budget allocated**		**5000**
8	11th April 2010	3 days to cover staff absence for training (Mike Kidd)	684.99	=D7-C8
9	9th July 2010	10 days to cover key staff holiday (Alicia Franks)	1766.4	=D8-C9
10	20th August 2010	5 days to cover key staff holiday (Jack Cahalit)	837.45	=D9-C10
11	11th October 2010	2 days to cover staff sickness (Ruth Gibbons)	456.11	=D10-C11
12				=D11-C12

Figure 42.18 Reducing balance budget formula print

What if scenarios

While the budget control spreadsheet is an example of dealing with **actual events** (things that really have happened), the power of spreadsheets really is obvious when applying its techniques to **extrapolate** the results to the use of **what if scenarios.** Cash flow forecasting shown earlier in this unit is one example of using a spreadsheet to work out what will happen in the event that a certain criterion or set of criteria occurs.

But what if scenarios can be used in other ways that don't necessarily have anything directly to do with money! Here is an example:

> Question: If we adjust or change the formulation of our product (for whatever reason), how will our customers respond?
>
> Here, the quantities of different components that make up the product could be changed. The spreadsheet would be used to record how the formulation of the product is changed and then to analyse the results of the post-change customer testing questionnaire.

Within the functionality of Microsoft Excel® is a **scenario** function that allows you to change figures in designated cells and see the results of changing the numbers.

Case Study

Kris Arts and Media wishes to launch a new range of media products and services and has decided to put on a corporate event to introduce the developments, with an exhibition and a key note speaker.

They have asked five different venues to provide information that they will compare so they can decide which of the venues to use for the event.

The venues and offers are:

Hellaby Hall
Cost of venue £800
Number of delegates 250
Cost per delegate for catering (optional) £5.40

ARMCC Centre
Cost of venue £710
Number of delegates 205
Cost per delegate for catering (optional) £5.30

Mitton Villa Conference Rooms
Cost of venue £1050
Number of delegates 275
Cost per delegate for catering (optional) £6.15

Bentham Meeting Centre
Cost of venue £890
Number of delegates 195
Cost per delegate for catering (optional) £6.55

JPF Suite
Cost of venue £685
Number of delegates 245
Cost per delegate for catering (optional) £5.70

When making a simple visual comparison, it is difficult to decide which offer would be the most beneficial to Kris Arts and Media. Initially, the JPF Suite is interesting because it has the lowest venue cost. But it isn't the lowest when it comes to the costs of catering.

Using the spreadsheet scenario functionality will help to compare these offers. This is how it's done.

Activity 1

This activity will walk you through using the What If functionality.

1 Open a blank worksheet in Microsoft Excel®.

2 Now begin by entering the information for Hellaby Hall. See Figure 42.19.

3 In cell B8, calculate the Total Cost by taking B4 and adding the result of B5 multiplied by B6.

=B4+(B5*B6)

	A	B
1	**Venue**	
2	**Hellaby Hall**	
3		**Cost**
4	Cost of Venue	£800.00
5	Number of delegates	250
6	Cost per delegate for catering	£5.40

Figure 42.19 Details for Hellaby Hall

See Figure 42.20 showing the total cost for Hellaby Hall. Save the file.

	A	B
1	**Venue**	
2	**Hellaby Hall**	
3		**Cost**
4	Cost of Venue	£800.00
5	Number of delegates	250
6	Cost per delegate for catering	£5.40
7		
8	Total cost	£2,150.00

Figure 42.20 Total cost for Hellaby Hall

4 You are now going to use the scenarios functionality. With the spreadsheet still open, click on **Data** then on **What-If Analysis** and finally on **Scenarios** as shown in Figure 42.21.

5 This activates the **Scenario Manager** shown in Figure 42.22.

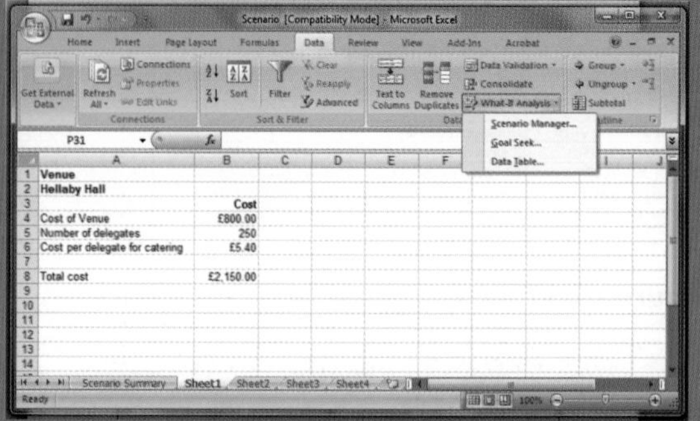

Figure 42.21 Finding the Scenarios function

At present there are no defined scenarios, so we need to use this interface to process the details for each of the five offers from venues.

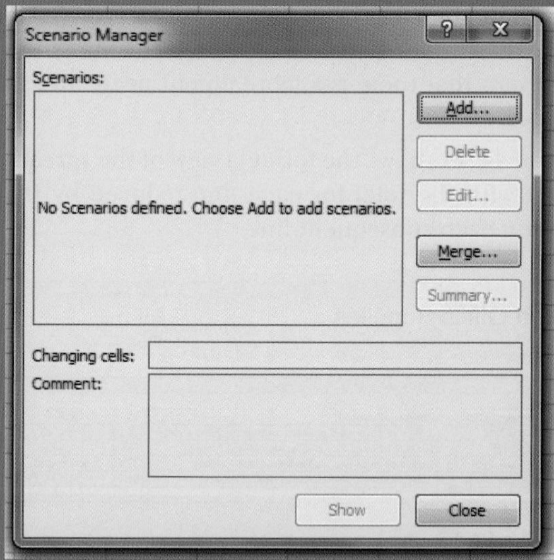

Figure 42.22 The Scenario Manager

6 You must now select **Add** so that you can begin to add each of the offers (including Hellaby Hall). The Add dialogue box is shown in Figure 42.23.

a) Give the Scenario a name (best practice would be to give it the venue name, e.g. Hellaby).

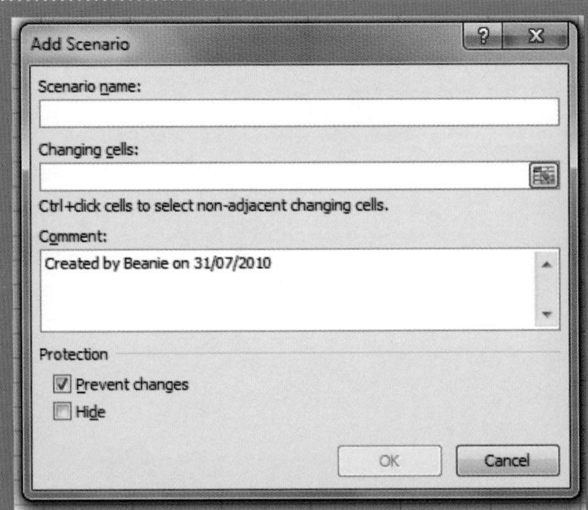

Figure 42.23 Add Scenario dialogue box

b) You now need to click in the Changing cells box and click one by one into each of the cells that will change, separating them with a comma (remember the name of the venue will also be one of the values that will need to change and the total cost), see Figure 42.24.

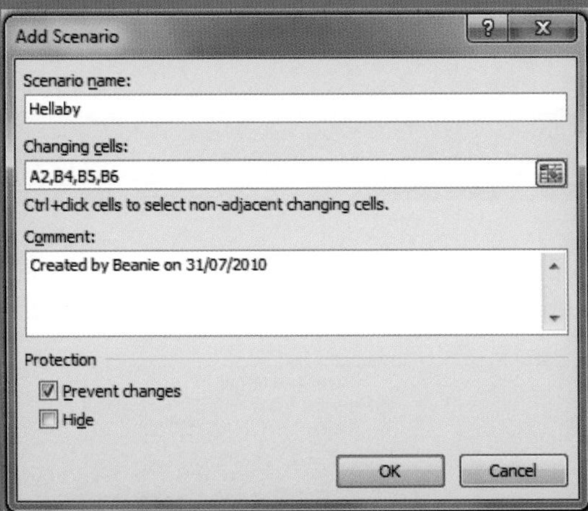

Figure 42.24 The first scenario is added (notice five cells will change)

7 Once you have done this, click on OK. The details for Hellaby Hall will appear. Click immediately on OK as you need to retain the details originally entered for this venue, see Figure 42.25.

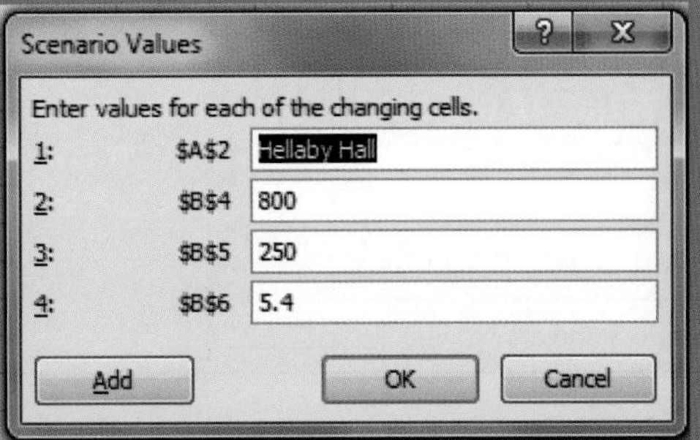

Figure 42.25 Figures entered for Hellaby Hall

Now click on **OK**.

8 The dialogue box will now change and will show the first of the scenarios you have added, as shown in Figure 42.26.

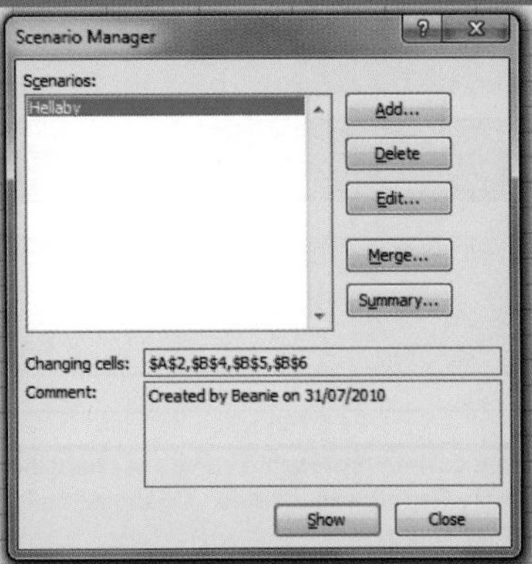

Figure 42.26 First scenario added

9 Repeat the process for the remaining four venues. The Scenario Manager will now look like the image in Figure 42.27.

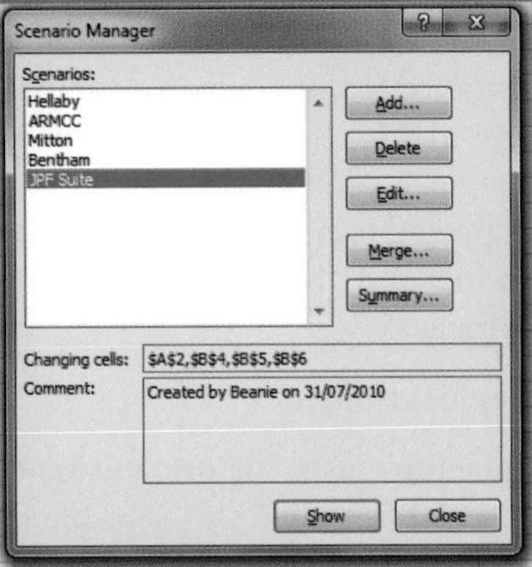

Figure 42.27 All scenarios added

10 Now to view all scenarios simultaneously, click on **Data**, then on **What-If Analysis**, **Scenarios** and finally on **Summary**. Make sure that the Scenario Summary report type is selected.

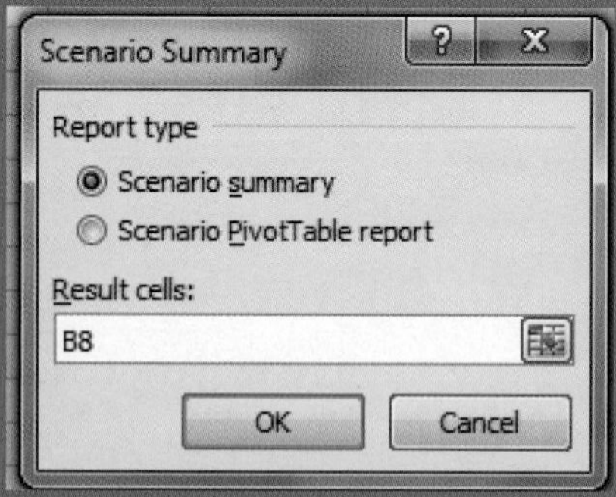

Scenario Summary

Report type

- Scenario summary
- Scenario PivotTable report

Result cells:

B8

OK Cancel

Figure 42.28 Set up the summary

Click on **OK**. You will now notice that the spreadsheet has gained an additional worksheet named **Scenario Summary**.

11 Open this spreadsheet and adjust the columns accordingly (hiding any data you do not wish to be seen on the print, adjusting column widths and alignment as required).

It is now easy to compare the venue offers and the anticipated costs. However, this does not take into account how many delegates Kris Arts and Media believe will attend their event!

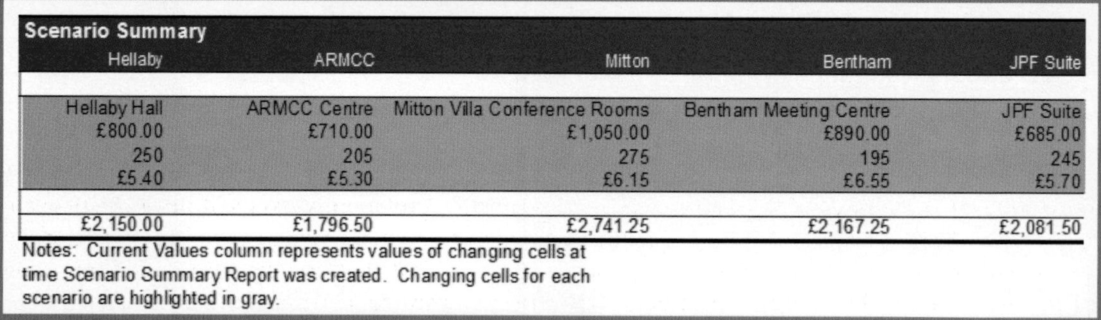

Scenario Summary

Hellaby	ARMCC	Mitton	Bentham	JPF Suite
Hellaby Hall	ARMCC Centre	Mitton Villa Conference Rooms	Bentham Meeting Centre	JPF Suite
£800.00	£710.00	£1,050.00	£890.00	£685.00
250	205	275	195	245
£5.40	£5.30	£6.15	£6.55	£5.70
£2,150.00	£1,796.50	£2,741.25	£2,167.25	£2,081.50

Notes: Current Values column represents values of changing cells at time Scenario Summary Report was created. Changing cells for each scenario are highlighted in gray.

Figure 42.29 Summary view

Sales forecasting

To forecast future sales it is usual to analyse historical data and use this to predict the future. The analysis could also incorporate the results of marketing activities or national statistics on anticipated growth. The potential for activity in the housing market, for example, is predicted based on how interest rates are expected to behave, which affects the cost of borrowing and thus the individual's ability to get a mortgage.

Let's consider a simpler example:

An ice cream manufacturer uses historic customer buying patterns to establish that the sale of ice cream is higher than the monthly average at Easter, again at Christmas, and is higher still in the summer months of June to August (inclusive). The graph in Figure 42.30 shows how this might have looked.

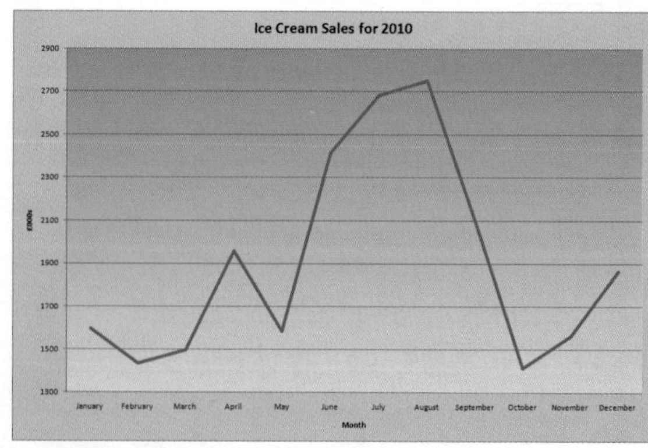

Figure 42.30 Ice cream sales analysis 2010

Based on this historic data, if the organisation now feels that through the introduction of new product lines it will be able to increase sales to in excess of £2,000,000 in January, applying the same expected buying patterns will place sales in the summer months to well over three million pounds at their peak.

Forecasting is one of the most useful tools an organisation has to support it in planning its future activities.

Payroll projections

Organisations generally pay staff in two ways:

Some staff work set hours each week or month and their pay does not change. In this instance, the organisation will always know in advance how much it will need to pay its employees and when.

However – this is not always the case.

In some organisations, some or all of the employees are paid a variable amount each week or month. This might be linked to production or sales performance, requirements for overtime to cover particular jobs or job roles, special projects and so on.

For most organisations, payroll will be a combination of both of the above. We should not forget, however, that there may be times when an organisation needs to buy in the services of temporary staff to enable a specific project or support increased activity for example.

In terms of projecting the payroll requirements for those staff that are variably paid, spreadsheets that calculate pay against expected sales or production, for example, will help organisations plan and ensure that there is sufficient money in the bank to pay employees when necessary.

Statistical analysis

While a range of statistical functions such as **STDEV** (Standard Deviation) are readily available in Excel® to help you carry out routine statistical analysis, there is also a series of Data Analysis tools that provide additional analytical functionality and that can be made available in Excel® through loading the Analysis Toolpak. This is not usually included with a standard installation, but can be added later.

Trend analysis

As with forecasting, **trend analysis** uses historical data to make decisions about past events and enable managers to apply lessons learned to future situations. Data mining, as suggested earlier, uses data to analyse trends and highlight unusual or exceptional events. Further analysis is then possible to establish the reasons behind particular situations.

42.1.3 Interpretation

This section will cover the following grading criterion:

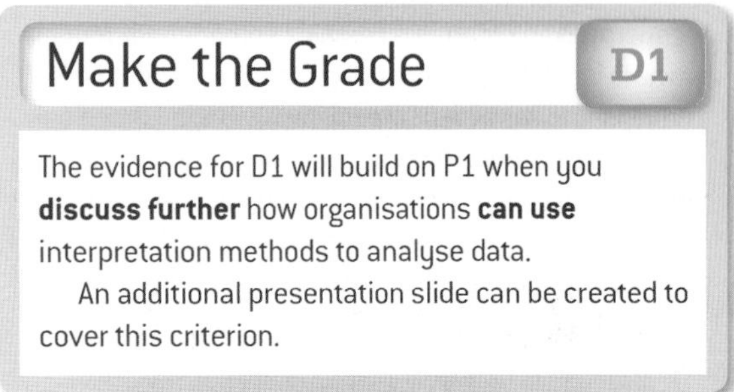

Interpretation methods

As an IT professional you will need to show that you can not only use the technology to manipulate the data, but that you can also confidently interpret or draw conclusions from the results.

Comparisons of totals

Using data replicated over weeks, months, periods, quarters, bi-annually (twice a year) or annually, will enable you to identify any unusual occurrences that can be further investigated through the use of the functions as described in earlier sections.

An additional functional aspect of a spreadsheet package is located on the Tools menu under the heading Compare and Merge Workbooks. Using this functionality will enable users to compare like files for different years where the files have essentially been used as templates.

Use of trend analysis to predict future events

Trend analysis is an exceptionally useful management tool to help predict what will occur in the future. The more data you have available when undertaking a trend analysis, particularly from other years and comparable operational periods, the more likely your predictions are to be accurate – although this is not always the case!

42.2 Be able to develop complex spreadsheet models

This section will cover the following grading criterion:

Make the Grade P2

As a highly practical unit, evidence for P2 will be generated by creating a complex spreadsheet model, where 'complex' requires that the spreadsheet contains some aspects of the following range (these aspects are covered in detail in subsequent sections, but you will need to consider using them in combination to provide a spreadsheet model/solution):

- multiple worksheets (with links)
- complex formulae, for example at least a two-step process
- large data sets
- linked cells
- data entry forms, for example menu systems
- list boxes, drop-down boxes, event controls, data validation and/or error trapping
- lookup tables and/or nested IF functions
- templates and activating cell protection.

42.2.1 Complexity

Multiple pages and cells linked between pages

Earlier in this unit we suggested that values in one spreadsheet could be linked dynamically to values in another spreadsheet in the same workbook or even with another workbook. In Figure 42.31 the formula for the North production totals is in fact a value that exists in a file named Linked Workbook 2.xls, on Sheet 1, in cell B15.

B2 = [Linked Workbook 2.xls]Sheet1'!B15

	A	B	C	D	E	F	G	H
1		Production						
2	North	43315						
3	South							
4	East							
5	West							
6	Midlands							
7								

Figure 42.31 Spreadsheet drawing a value from a linked workbook

Any values that are linked **within a workbook** will be **updated immediately** when the values they are linked to **change**.

Complex formulae

Over the years there has been significant disagreement about what constitutes a complex formula. In defining the word 'complex' you may find any of the following words used: complicated, multiple parts, related components.

In general, a simple formula can be considered to be one or maybe two parts. **A complex formula will have at least two parts.**

Example of a simple formula:

Invoice total = Quantity purchased * price
+ VAT

The following example is a complex formula because a number of steps must be carefully executed to get the final answer:

Invoice total = Quantity purchased * price – discount
(if more than 10 are purchased, discount is 10% otherwise discount is 0)
+ VAT

Large data sets

When you consider that a single worksheet contains 256 columns and 65,536 rows, this multiplies out to 16,777,216 cells in a single worksheet! It is, however, unlikely that all of these cells would contain values as some columns and rows are left blank to enhance the appearance of the spreadsheet.

Examples of large data sets could include the following:

- a sheet of wage calculations for 2,000 employees in a factory including gross figures, deductions, etc.
- a stock print-out for all items held in stock containing the current stock totals, cost price and overall stock values
- sales information from a supermarket checkout at the end of each day
- the results of marketing surveys.

The list is actually endless and in the real world you will find many more examples.

Cells linkage

Carefully linking cells **within** a spreadsheet and **between** spreadsheets will ensure that when a value changes, any other numbers to which the value has contributed will change accordingly.

This will enhance the **integrity of data** because changes are automatically updated.

Data entry forms

As with databases, modern spreadsheet software allows developers to create **data entry forms**.

An obvious example would be to use a worksheet as the basis for a menu, with command buttons to activate movement between worksheets.

Similarly, worksheets can be used to create mini applications. The example in Figure 42.32 uses list boxes, combo boxes and event controls to calculate the cost of a client project based on a number of variables.

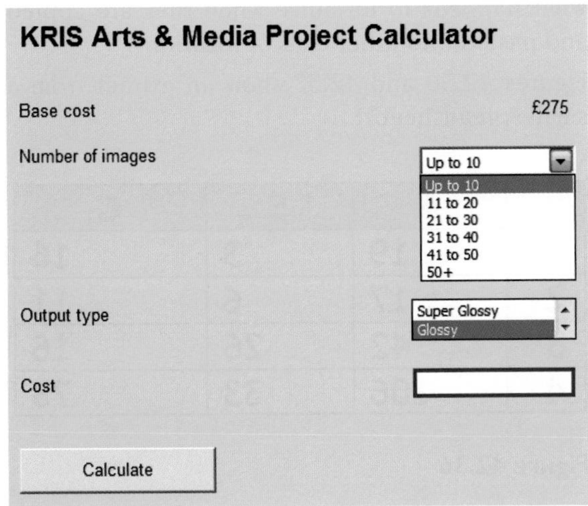

Figure 42.32 Form

Data validation and error trapping

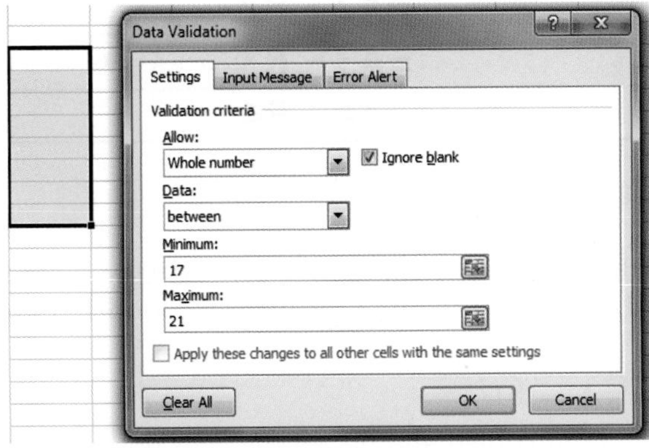

Figure 42.33 Implementing validation

Modern spreadsheet software includes **Data Validation** functionality on the **Data** menu, where for a cell or range of cells a developer can simply set up a **validation routine** to be applied for any data that is input. In the example shown in Figure 42.33, the developer has chosen that only a whole number between 17 and 21 can be input into the range of highlighted cells.

Using the **Input Message** tab, the developer can add a message to alert the user to the acceptable values or format, which is activated when the user accesses any of the validated cells.

Alternatively, the user can simply use the **Error Alert** to highlight the problem once the user has attempted to move out of the cell having input data (see Figure 42.34 below).

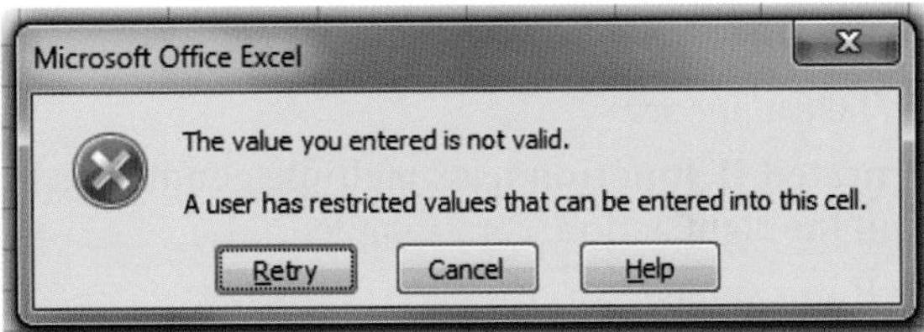

Figure 42.34 A customised error message alerting incorrect input!

Lookup tables

Lookup tables are really useful for accessing data stored in tables. Take the example in Figure 42.35. In the final system, the item information and prices would be hidden and the only part of the data that would be visible is highlighted.

B4 =VLOOKUP(B3,A9:B24,2)

	A	B	C	D
1	Frankoni T-shirts Price checker			
2				
3	Input item number (e.g. 12345)	12354		
4	Price	0.75		
5				

Figure 42.35 VLOOKUP

The user would simply key in the item number and the system, using the **VLOOKUP function**, would check the input value then search the table to find the relevant matching item number and its associated price.

The formula is shown at the top of the image. It means:

VLOOKUP (**Vertical Lookup**) – look down the vertical list in the first column, comparing each item in the list to the information in cell **B3**. Search the table which is defined as cells **A9** to **B24** inclusive, then give the value in the **second** column.

The table could just as easily have been stored the other way around, with the item numbers across the top and the prices below. In this instance, you would have used the **HLOOKUP function** (looking across a **horizontal list**).

Nested IF functions

The **IF function** is used to test a condition and carry out a particular action based on the result of the test. For example:

If it is sunny
　Then wear sunscreen
Otherwise
　Take a jumper

A **nested IF function** tests multiple conditions to find the right action. For example:

　If it is sunny
　　Then wear sunscreen
　Otherwise
　　If it is raining
　　　Take an umbrella
　　Otherwise
　　　Take a jumper

> **Unit link**
> **Unit 6** – Software design and development, section 6.1.4 'Features', provides further coverage of Nested Ifs.

Templates

Templates are **prepared worksheets** that have been developed to meet a **defined purpose**. Some organisations will have their own templates or **house styles** that dictate the way spreadsheets (and other organisational documents) are constructed and presented in order to achieve a **corporate 'feel'**.

Cell protection

Inexperienced spreadsheet users have been known to **accidentally delete data** or even functions and formulae in spreadsheets and if they are novice users they may well not be able to put the data or functionality back! **Protecting cells** ensures that accidental deletions cannot be made. This is covered in more detail later in the unit.

42.2.2 Formulae

This section will cover the following grading criterion:

Use relative and absolute cell references

When formulae are created, they are developed with either **relative** or **absolute cell referencing.** What does this actually mean?

In order to understand this we need to appreciate what happens to formulae when they are copied and pasted into other cells or locations.

Figures 42.36 and 42.37 show an extract from a small spreadsheet.

	A	B	C
1	19	3	16
2	17	6	11
3	42	26	16
4	106	33	73

Figure 42.36

Formulas in **column C**
=A1 - B1
=A2 - B2
=A3 - B3
=A4 - B4

Figure 42.37

What we actually did (having keyed data into cells A1 to B4), was to input the following formula into cell C1.

= A1 – B1

We then copied and pasted the cells down as far as cell C4.

As we did so, the formulae adjusted themselves dynamically and automatically to accommodate the changing row numbers (see Figure 42.38).

Formulas in column C
=A1 - B1
=A2 - B2
=A3 - B3
=A4 - B4

A1 to A2 to A3 to A4

Figure 42.38

This is known as relative referencing because as each cell is pasted into the next position, the software automatically changes all parts of the formula **relative** to the last cell position.

There are times, however, when we do not want the formula to change like this.

Look at the following example:

Here cell B1 contains a value that needs to be used (known as referencing) in every calculation. Without applying absolute cell referencing, as we copy and paste the cells down column C, B1 will become B2, then B3, then B4 (just as shown in the first example).

	A	B	C
1	7	6	42
2	22		132
3	5		30
4	18		108

Formual in Column C
= A1 * B1
= A2 * B1
= A3 * B1
= A4 * B1

Figure 42.39

Using the **$ (dollar) symbol** as part of the cell reference means that even when copied and pasted, that particular value **will not change**.

Why would we choose to use absolute cell referencing rather than merely keying the value 6 into the formula? Because if each copy of the formula had contained the number and the number had subsequently changed, we would have had to change four separate formulae, rather than just the contents of cell B1. This **saves a lot of time** and contributes to **easier spreadsheet maintenance**.

The types of data often declared as absolutes are things like interest rates, VAT rates or maybe a price. Choosing the absolute referencing option here will ensure that **only a single value needs to be changed** and thus all other formulae that rely on this particular data would be **automatically updated** through a single action.

Logical functions

Logical functions are different from mainstream formulae and functions because the latter are always executed whereas actions that result from logical functions may or may not be, depending on whether a criterion, or set of criteria, are met.

What now follows is a brief investigation into each of the following:

IF, OR, AND, NOT and SUMIF

IF

IF functions (commonly known as **IF statements**) are designed to allow the user to carry out different actions depending on whether or not a condition is fulfilled. These conditions can also be nested to test multiple conditions. In the following example, we are considering calculating whether an individual would qualify for a child, adult or concession ticket for entry into an art gallery:

IF (**the person's age is less than 18**)
  They will be classified as a child
Else
  Check again and IF (**the person's age is greater than or equal to 18 and is less than or equal to 60**)
    They will be classified as an adult
  Else
    They will be classified as a concession

This translates as

Check the person's age:
  Less than 18 is a child.
  Between 18 and 60 (inclusive) is an adult.
  If **neither** of the other two, they **must be a concession**.

All IF statements have the same structure:

IF (condition)
  Do **this** if **true**
Else
  Do **this** if **false**

Here is a spreadsheet example:

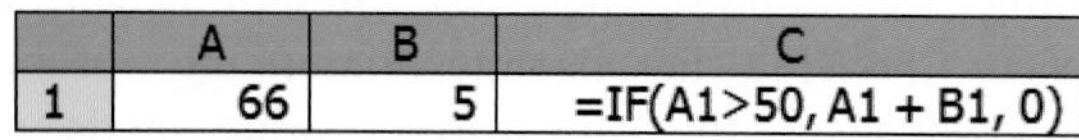

	A	B	C
1	66	5	=IF(A1>50, A1 + B1, 0)

Figure 42.40

which means in full:

IF (A1 > 50)

the cell containing this logic statement will take the result of adding A1 and B1

Else

the cell containing this logic statement will take the result of 0

Looking at the data, what will the above function return?

Is A1 greater than 50?

Yes – so add 66 and 5 together, which will give 71.

	A	B	C
1	**66**	**5**	=IF(A1>50, A1 + B1, 0)

Figure 42.41

OR

With the **OR** operator, the user can test multiple conditions but in a way that will allow the TRUE action to be undertaken in the event that any one of the conditions is evaluated to be true.

The structure is:

IF (condition A is True) **OR** (condition B is True)

Do this because **one of them** is True

Else

Do this because they are both False

Look at the example in Figure 42.42. What will the result be?

	A	B	C
1	**66**	**5**	=IF(OR(A1<50,B1>4,A1+B1,0)

Figure 42.42

Here A1 is false because the value in that cell is greater than 50. However, when the second part of the condition is tested you will find that B1 is indeed greater than 4 (so this will be true). The value 71 will be returned.

On the other hand, had the value of A1 been 66 and the value of B1 had been 2, both of the conditions would have been false and the value 0 would have been entered in C1.

AND

The **AND** operator again allows the user to check multiple cells, but unlike the **OR** operator where either part of the condition can be true for the condition to return the value of **True**, with the **AND** operator **both parts** of the condition **must be true** for the True part of the statement to be executed.

The structure is:

IF (condition A is True) AND (condition B is True)

Do this because **both of them** are True

Else

Do this because they are both False

Look at the example in Figure 42.44. What will the result be?

	A	B	C
1	**46**	**5**	=IF(AND(A1<50,B1>4,A1+B1,0)

Figure 42.43

Is A1 less than 50? **Yes**. Is B1 greater than 4? **Yes**. Therefore **both conditions are indeed met** and the result placed in C1 will be 51. If **either** of the conditions **had not been met**, the result would have been 0.

NOT

Trying to understand **NOT** can be quite challenging because you are effectively working with **reversed logic**!

Let's look at the following:

=NOT(3+3=6)

Will this evaluate to true or false?

It will evaluate to **false**! Why? Because 3 + 3 is 6, you would expect it to be true, but the NOT reverses the logic.

=**NOT**(3+3=8) would evaluate to true, because 3 + 3 is NOT 8!

SUMIF

The **SUMIF** function works slightly differently in that here all the values in a range are checked and any greater than or equal to the specified number (in this case 50) are added into the total and the others are ignored.

The total in Figure 42.44 would be **285**.

	A	B
1	January	75
2	February	41
3	March	52
4	April	16
5	May	24
6	June	67
7	July	91
8		=SUMIF(B1:B7,">=50")

Figure 42.44

To prove this is accurate, let's identify the relevant values and place them in column C before adding and check the result.

	A	B	C
1	January	75	75
2	February	41	
3	March	52	52
4	April	16	
5	May	24	
6	June	67	67
7	July	91	91
8		=SUMIF(B1:B7,">=50")	=SUM(C1:C7)

Figure 42.45

Totals would be **285** Check: **285**

As with other parts of a developed spreadsheet, the results of all **logical** functions must **be carefully tested** and **checked** as part of the spreadsheet testing strategy because it is very easy to make a mistake.

Finally, you should have a basic understanding of **relational operator** symbols:

- \> Greater than
- < Less than
- = Equal to
- \>= Greater than or equal to
- <= Less than or equal to

B Braincheck 2

Logical operators

Work out the answers to these complex expressions using the given values for A, B and C. In each case specify the outcome!

A = 100 B = 50 C = 12

1. =IF(A<75,A+B,A+C)
2. =IF(AND(A>75,B>30,C>9),A+B+C,0)
3. =IF(AND(A<50,B>30),A+B,0)
4. =IF(OR(A<50,B>30),A-B,0)
5. =SUMIF(A:C,"<=50")
6. =IF(A+B=150,"true","false")
7. =IF(OR(B=50,C<9),A,0)
8. =NOT(7+4=11)

42.2.3 Structure and fitness for purpose

While studying your BTEC, unless specified, the choice of spreadsheet structure is yours. However, be prepared to **justify** your choices!

Formatting

Whichever **format** you choose for numbers, dates and textual displays, you should ensure **consistency** in the use of the format. Table 42.01 briefly looks at some **format choices** that you could make.

Table 42.01

Format choice	Description
Integer	An **integer** is a **whole number with no decimal parts** – e.g. the numbers 7, 63 or 1507. Sometimes, particularly when you are displaying many numbers containing thousands, it might be helpful to include a comma after the leading number – so 1,507. If you do this, make sure you do this consistently for all affected numbers throughout the document.
Real	A **real** is a number **with a decimal part** – e.g. the numbers 2.5, 18.979 or 6,397.49795. You should make sure that you choose a display that is appropriate in terms of the level of detail you need to show.

Format choice	Description
Date	There are a number of date formats for you to use in the preparation of a spreadsheet. One aspect you should always remember, however, is that not all countries display day, month and year in the same order as in the UK. For example, in America and parts of Europe, the month precedes the day. 08/04/1960 08/04/60 1960-04-08 8-Apr-60 08 April 1960 There are many different formats for dates – here are some examples:
Currency	Currencies are usually preceded with a **symbol** that indicates what the currency actually is. For example a £ (pound sterling) sign precedes values to denote UK currency – £14.99. **Dollars** (American for example) will be preceded by **$**, although there are a number of other countries in the world that have adopted the dollar as their currency. The symbol for the **Euro €** is beginning to appear on many European keyboards, and can either be inserted through selecting a symbol in Excel® or through the Alt Gr + 4 key.
Text	Text can be manipulated in many ways, some of which follow in the next section, but the choice of the font is also an important decision. **Serif** fonts are described as **having embellishments** and flourishes. These can be additional lines or curves. **Sans serif** fonts are those **without embellishments**. Text set in **proportional fonts** allows each character to occupy a different amount of space, depending on which character it is. For example, in the word Bristol, the character 'i' uses less space than the remaining letters. W and M usually take up most space. Using **non-proportional fonts** (often also referred to as **fixed fonts)** will ensure that each character is allowed to occupy the same amount of space. Let's compare the two: Wiltshire `Wiltshire` The **former** is proportional, the **latter** non-proportional or fixed.

Styling e.g. bold, italics, borders, shading, column alignment, consistency

Additional formatting options are available to further enhance the presentation of a spreadsheet (see Table 42.02). These should be used carefully as the application of too many formats simultaneously can detract from the overall intention of the spreadsheet, which is to impart information.

Table 42.02

Format choice	Description
Bold	**This text has been emboldened. This means it has been thickened to make it stand out.**
Italics	*Italicised text usually leans to the right. This draws the reader's attention to particular words or phrases.*

Format choice	Description
Borders	Borders can be used around specific cells to make them stand out. Totals 6.45 425.10 87.00 167.61 12.26 **Figure 42.46** Borders
Shading	Shading can similarly make individual cells stand out – in this instance the shading has been applied to a cell containing a heading. Totals 6.45 425.10 87.00 167.61 12.26 **Figure 42.47** Shading
Column alignment	All data in a single column should be carefully **aligned** to make sure it is tidy. This text is left aligned This text is right aligned This text is centred The same options can be applied to tables of numbers, although traditionally these will be **right aligned** – in fact if you enter numbers into a cell in Microsoft Excel®, the system automatically aligns the numbers to the right by default.
Consistency	Whichever formats you choose to apply when developing your spreadsheet, you should ensure that they are applied consistently across the column, the row and ultimately the spreadsheet. Contrast Figures 42.48 and 42.49. Which looks better? Totals 6.4525 425.1 87 167.61 12.258 **Figure 42.48** Non-aligned Totals 6.45 425.10 87.00 167.61 12.26 **Figure 42.49** Aligned with fixed decimal places You will agree that Figure 42.49 is presented in a more appealing way.

To meet the needs of a particular context

As the range of possible contexts will be extensive, it is clearly difficult to define here! What would be most appropriate would be for you to look at examples of spreadsheets and decide how effective you think they are for the audience for which they are intended.

42.2.4 Features and functions

This section will also cover the following grading criterion:

> ## Make the Grade P3
>
> This criterion reflects the mechanics of your spreadsheet model and you will evidence this criterion by using formulae, features and functions to process information – this essentially means any topic covered in sections 42.2.2 and 42.2.4.
>
> This will probably be tested through a scenario supplied by your tutor and require you to carry out some sort of information processing such as a **cash flow forecast**, a **budgeting problem**, a **'what if' analysis, payroll projections** or another similar scenario.
>
> This should include **some aspects** from the following range: relative references, absolute references, logical functions (for example IF, AND, OR, NOT, SUMIF), using correct operators, implementing named ranges, file sharing, change tracking, consideration of security issues, configuration of the user interface, using add-ins and/or built-in functions, for example cell functions, lookup functions, text functions, statistical function and finding data.

Using named ranges to identify areas of a spreadsheet

As suggested earlier in this unit, most spreadsheet software also has limited database capabilities. This can be extremely useful if you need to insert values automatically based on other input values. Let's look at an example from Lee Office Supplies.

Firstly we need to imagine that they are using a standard Microsoft Access® database to record stock information and stock transactions. Some or all of the data could be exported into a spreadsheet to provide information that can then be searched and further information extracted. In the data sample shown in Figure 42.50, 12 records have been copied and pasted into the spreadsheet, with their Product Code, Description and Resale Price visible. The detail has been pasted into Sheet 2 of a workbook, starting at cell A2.

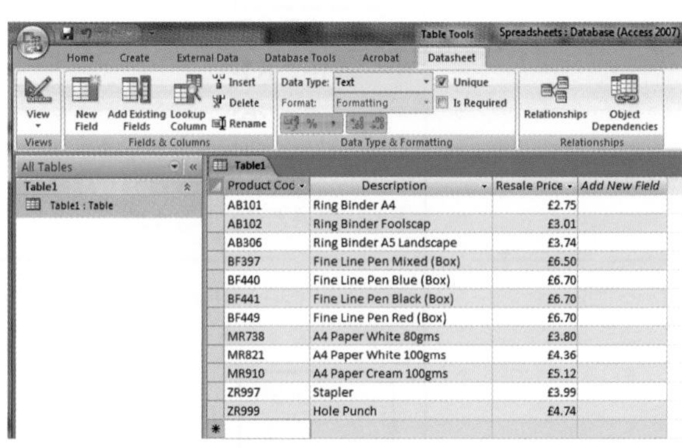

Product Code	Description	Resale Price	Add New Field
AB101	Ring Binder A4	£2.75	
AB102	Ring Binder Foolscap	£3.01	
AB306	Ring Binder A5 Landscape	£3.74	
BF397	Fine Line Pen Mixed (Box)	£6.50	
BF440	Fine Line Pen Blue (Box)	£6.70	
BF441	Fine Line Pen Black (Box)	£6.70	
BF449	Fine Line Pen Red (Box)	£6.70	
MR738	A4 Paper White 80gms	£3.80	
MR821	A4 Paper White 100gms	£4.36	
MR910	A4 Paper Cream 100gms	£5.12	
ZR997	Stapler	£3.99	
ZR999	Hole Punch	£4.74	

Figure 42.50 Data extract exported from Microsoft Access®

Once imported, the area of the spreadsheet that contains this data could be referred to in two ways (see Figure 42.52).

	A	B	C
1			
2	Product Code	Description	Resale Price
3	AB101	Ring Binder A4	£2.75
4	AB102	Ring Binder Foolscap	£3.01
5	AB306	Ring Binder A5 Landscape	£3.74
6	BF397	Fine Line Pen Mixed (Box)	£6.50
7	BF440	Fine Line Pen Blue (Box)	£6.70
8	BF441	Fine Line Pen Black (Box)	£6.70
9	BF449	Fine Line Pen Red (Box)	£6.70
10	MR738	A4 Paper White 80gms	£3.80
11	MR821	A4 Paper White 100gms	£4.36
12	MR910	A4 Paper Cream 100gms	£5.12
13	ZR997	Stapler	£3.99
14	ZR999	Hole Punch	£4.74

Figure 42.51

A2:C14 This would be the cell reference for the range.

StockInfo This would be a name that applies to the whole area.

What is the main advantage of naming the range? Simply that keying in row numbers and column identifiers each time you need a formula or function in the spreadsheet is more likely to generate **keying errors**. In the event that the **incorrect name** is keyed in, nothing will happen because the name, incorrectly spelt, would not exist in its own right!

So how do you name a range? Firstly, highlight the area that includes the cells you want as part of the range. You then right click and select **Name a Range** as shown in Figure 42.52.

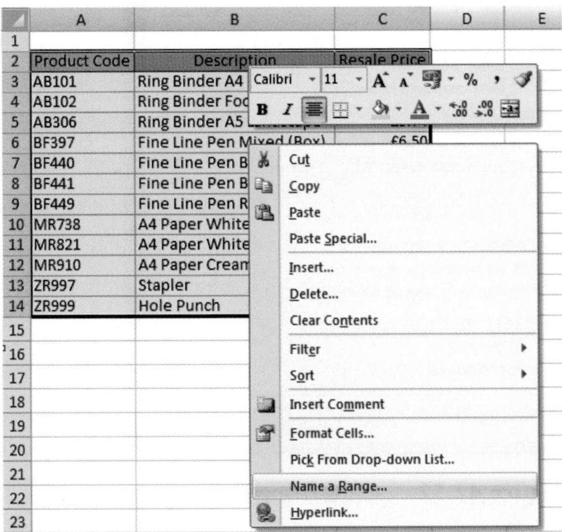

Figure 42.52 Naming the range

Now you need to create the name.

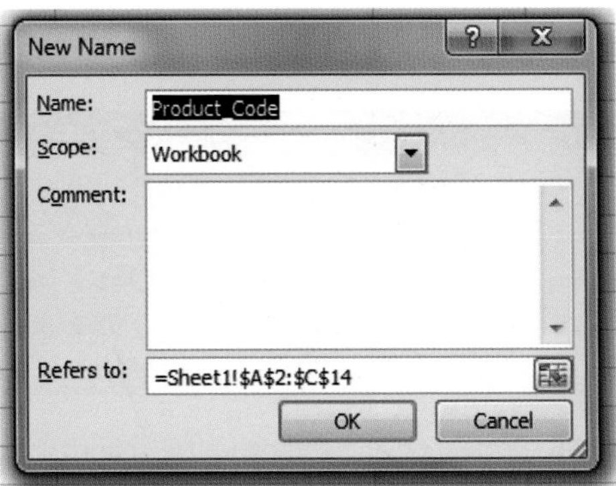

Figure 42.53 Naming the range

You will notice that the system has actually inserted a suggested name for the range – in this case **Product_Code** – which is taken from the content of the cell in the upper left corner of the range. You will also notice that the area you highlighted has been displayed in the bottom of the dialogue box.

To input your own name for the range, simply delete the words Product_Code and insert **StockInfo**. Click on OK. The area has now been named.

If you now move to other sheets, you will see the named range appear as one of the available options in the **Name Box** in any of the spreadsheets in the same workbook, although you should be aware that the option will not be available via this method in other workbooks. When this is visible, clicking on it will automatically take you to the range in the appropriate sheet.

StockInfo | fx Product Code

	A	B	C
1			
2	Product Code	Description	Resale Price
3	AB101	Ring Binder A4	£2.75
4	AB102	Ring Binder Foolscap	£3.01
5	AB306	Ring Binder A5 Landscape	£3.74

Figure 42.54 Name Box display containing the newly-created named range

Now, in Sheet 1, we will set up the items part of an invoice with a table containing the product code, description of the item, the quantity purchased, the price of the item and the total.

We now want the description of the item and the price to be automatically inserted based on the product code as input by the user.

To do this we use the VLOOKUP (vertical look up) function. It works like this:

VLOOKUP(cell, range, column)

This translates as 'look up the contents of the cell in the identified range and input the data for the column listed'.

To insert the description once the Product Code has been inserted would be achieved with the following:

= VLOOKUP(A2,StockInfo,3,0)

When executed, the system would perform a vertical lookup (looking down the first column of values in the named range), would compare the value on each line in the first column to the value in the designated cell, then extract the relevant value in column 3. In the event the value is not found, the 0 ensures that a default value is returned. See Figure 42.55.

When using this spreadsheet, the user will simply need to insert the Product Code into the cell beside Item and the remaining data appears.

Note: In order for the lookup function to work as intended, the data in the first column of the named range must be stored in **alphabetical** and/or **numeric order**. For this reason, numbering products sequentially without any gaps would be essential.

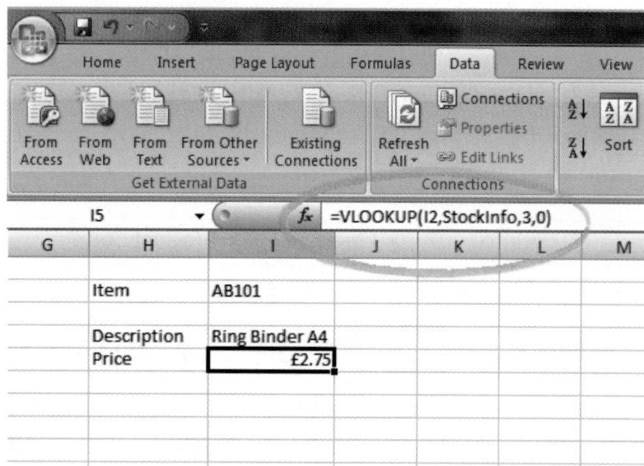

Figure 42.55 Automated lookup in a named range

Sharing files and data between users and tracking changes

If you need to share spreadsheet files and data with other users it is essential that changes are tracked.

In order to share a particular workbook you will need to **enable sharing activity** as this is usually locked by default. To enable sharing you need to have the spreadsheet file open, then click on the **Review** tab and then on **Share Workbook** (see Figure 42.56).

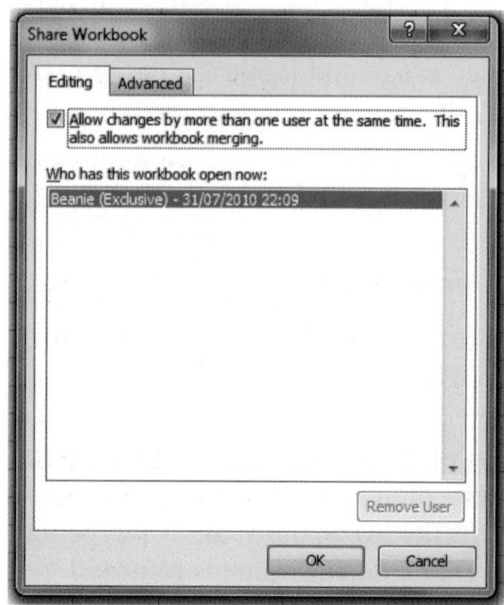

Figure 42.56 Enabling the Share Workbook facility

You will then need to check the **Allow changes by more than one user at the same time** option.

The second tab labelled **Advanced** on this dialogue box then allows you to select a range of tracking and updating options like whether changes are recorded for tracking purposes, for how many days these records should be retained and, importantly, whose changes should take priority in the event that there is a conflict between users (see Figure 42.57).

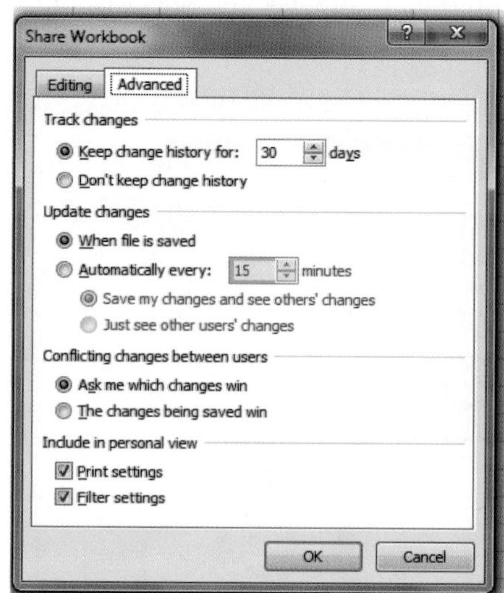

Figure 42.57 Tracking changes to the file

Security issues

Ensuring that the data in a spreadsheet is secure can be achieved two ways:

- Applying a password to a particular sheet or to the whole workbook, as shown in Figure 42.59.

Figure 42.58 Protecting and setting up file sharing

- Being **selective** about those to whom you **give access** and making sure that if they leave the organisation, their **permissions are revoked**.

Configuring the user interface

As with most software, the user interface can be configured to **personalise** the user's workspace.

For example, buttons or options can be added to toolbars (see Figure 42.59 on page 399).

Adding or removing options can be achieved by **clicking on the drop-down list** option in the toolbar and simply clicking on those options you want to include for quick access (or **unclicking them to remove**). See Figure 42.60.

Figure 42.59 The Quick Access toolbar

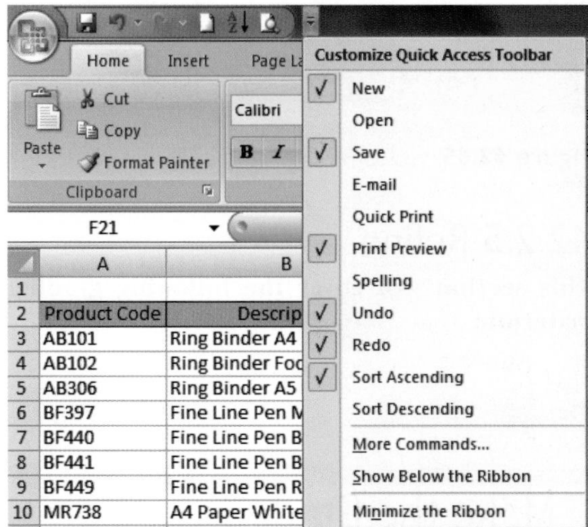

Figure 42.60 Choosing options

Using add-ins

A range of **add-ins** for less popular functionality is also available. Some generic features are installed during the standard installation (such as Publish to Website and Post to Blog). Additional features, however, may not be installed during a standard installation but can be added in at any time.

As with many of the old Options available on the Tools menu, these are now available through the Microsoft Office® button at the top left of each application (see Figure 42.61).

Figure 42.61 Microsoft Office® button

To view a list of add-ins, click on the **Microsoft Office® button**, then on **Excel Options** and finally on **Add-ins** (see Figure 42.62). The add-ins can then be added or removed to meet the user's needs.

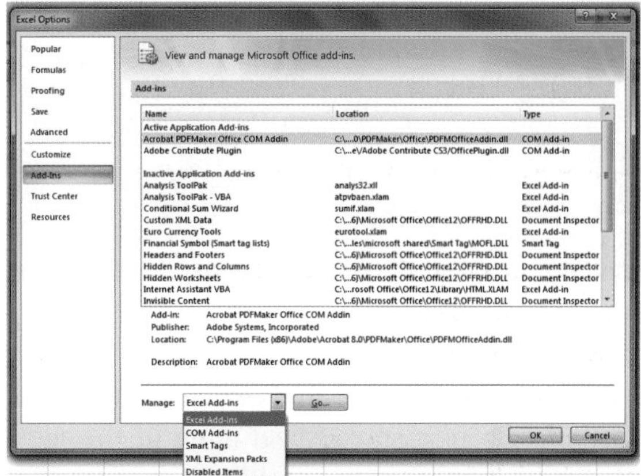

Figure 42.62 Managing Add-ins

Use a range of inbuilt functions

A range of inbuilt functions is provided in most spreadsheet software. This is accessible through the **Formulas tab** and then the **Function Library option** (Figure 42.63).

Figure 42.63 Functions Library

The formulae and functions are readily available and can be used at any time. Clicking on the function category will bring up a list of functions included. The list of functions, however, is very long, and to begin to explain the individual categories and the functions themselves would take up an entire book in its own right!

As a simple guide, if you need to use a function, first check whether it is already available within the software before you begin to develop your own formula!

> **Activity 2**
>
> *Functions*
>
> There is a wide range of pre-written functions that can be used within a spreadsheet and some of this functionality has already been considered.
>
> Create a table that names at least five text functions and five statistical functions, identifies their function type (e.g. text or statistical) and provides a brief description of what the function does.
>
> Keep an electronic copy for reference.

Finding data

There are a number of functions that help you to find data in a spreadsheet. One of the most commonly used ones is the **filter function** that extracts all instances of records that contain the chosen filtering term, numbers or range.

In this example, we want to extract all items that have a price in a given range.

We begin by **selecting** the **heading cells** of the data, clicking on **the Data tab**, then on the **Filter icon**. This will activate the **AutoFilter** (Figure 42.64).

We will then need to choose the values we want to display. To do this you would need to click on the **Filter icon** to the right of Resale Price. Clicking on **Number Filters** will then let you choose the criteria (such as a range with a maximum and minimum value), on which to filter (Figure 42.65).

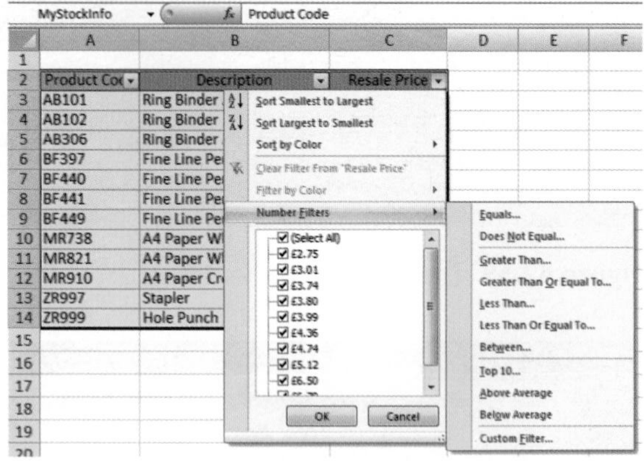

Figure 42.65 Custom Filter

42.2.5 Refine

This section will cover the following grading criterion:

> **Make the Grade** M1
>
> Showing that you can refine your spreadsheet is essential to achieve M1. You will need to demonstrate that you have improved the efficiency of your solution.
>
> This could be achieved by the addition of **shortcuts** or other methods to **aid navigation**, as well as improving the **presentation** of your solution by adopting **consistent** and **appropriate formatting** techniques and **styles**.
>
> Ultimately you must show that you have considered the development of your spreadsheet and that you can make it presentable and user friendly.

Figure 42.64 Filter

Refining a spreadsheet is essential to meet the Merit criteria in this unit. In order to do this you will have to show that you can improve the efficiency of your spreadsheet, format the data correctly and show that you can print selectively.

Improving efficiency

Shortcuts

Efficiencies can be made in a number of areas including adding **shortcuts** (e.g. a button with a macro to print three copies of a particular area of the spreadsheet, rather than have to highlight the area and select to print three copies through the usual dialogue boxes).

```
Sub Macro1()
Macro1 Macro
Macro recorded 20/07/2010 by Bernie
   Range("A1:A7,B3:B7").Select
'Choose these ranges
   Selection.PrintOut Copies:=3,
Collate:=True           'Print three
copies
End Sub
```

This macro could then be placed on a button so that as the figures are changed, the user would have the option to print the same area again and again.

Aiding navigation

There are also a range of options that can be used to aid navigation around the spreadsheet. For example, cells can be **locked** to restrict the cells that the user can actually access (so using the tab key between cells moves to the next unlocked cell) – this is covered in more detail later in the unit.

Period Sales by Agent (South West Team)			
	January	February	March
John			
Cahit			
Mary			
Hamza			
Dominic			
Brian			
Alex			
Total Sales			

Figure 42.66 Input screen

Developers should also consider the **input order for data** to ensure that it is reflective of wherever the data is coming from. For example, there is little point in ordering the spreadsheet input boxes as shown in Figure 42.66 in preparation for data input if the data, when received, is ordered as shown in Figure 42.67.

Period Sales by Agent (South West Team)			
	January	February	March
Mary	19	5	18
Alex	28	9	6
Brian	17	21	14
Hamza	23	17	12
Cahit	17	22	8
John	15	19	15
Dominic	26	21	12
Total Sales	145	114	85

Figure 42.67 Source data

Formatting

Professional spreadsheets reflect professionalism in their formatting and the way that they look to the reader. This is achieved through a range of formatting options, which are briefly explored here (although there are many others if you experiment).

Fonts

The key with fonts is not only the choice of font but also in being consistent with the use of the fonts (all headings in the same font, the main body of the text in the same font etc.).

Fonts come in two main types:

Serif Fonts with small embellishments

Sans serif Fonts without any embellishments

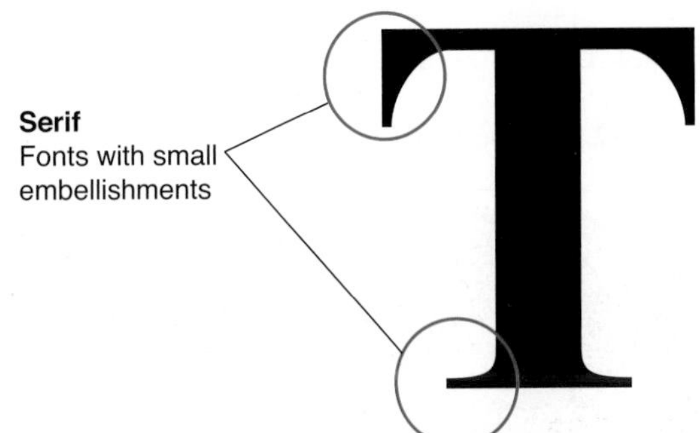

Figure 42.68 A font with serifs

'Sans', as you may be aware, is French for 'without', so sans serif literally means 'without serifs'. Some studies have indicated that text written in sans serif fonts is considered to be less formal and aids reading and recollection.

Figure 42.69 shows some examples. To be able to see the difference clearly, look at the capital T in each example.

Serif Fonts
The cat sat on the mat
The cat sat on the mat
The cat sat on the mat

Sans Serif
The cat sat on the mat
The cat sat on the mat
The cat sat on the mat

Figure 42.69 Fonts

In addition, fonts are classified as **proportional** or **non-proportional**.

A proportional font uses up a different amount of space for each character – for example, an 'I', which is tall and thin would take up much less space than an 'M' (see Figures 42.70 and 42.71 for comparison).

This font is Times New Roman **(14) and it is a** serif, proportional font **as it uses less space for an 'I' than it does for an 'M' and it has embellishments**.

Figure 42.70 Times New Roman

```
This font is Courier New (14) and it is a serif,
non-proportional font as it uses the same amount
of space for an 'I' as it does for an 'M'. This
```

Figure 42.71 Courier New

> Activity 3
>
> *Fonts*
>
> Investigate different font examples and identify five serif and five sans serif fonts.
>
> In each case state whether the font is proportional or non-proportional.
>
> Keep an electronic copy for reference.

Page orientation

Paper can be used in two different ways (this is called its **orientation**): landscape and portrait (Figure 42.72).

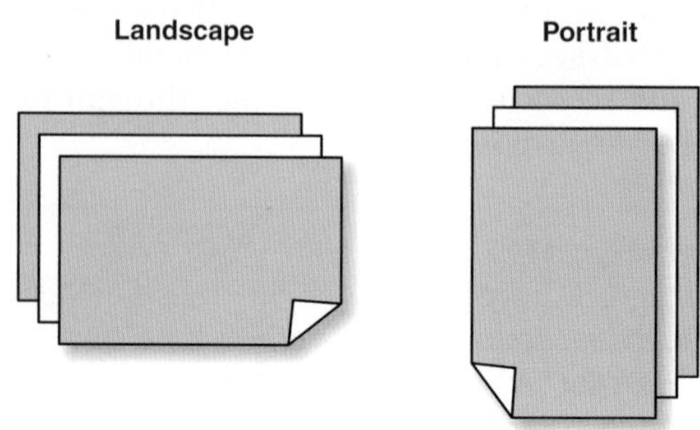

Figure 42.72

Charts and graphs are often created in landscape view, particularly bar charts and trend charts, to ensure that the image is as clear as it can be. Printing on paper in the same landscape orientation will ensure that the information is fully legible. Squashing it into a portrait view could make some or all of the information illegible.

Header and footer

Just as with Microsoft Word® documents, spreadsheets can be enhanced with headers or footers. A **header** appears in the white space at the top of a document or spreadsheet; a **footer** appears in the white space at the bottom. Inserting these is an option on the Insert tab, on the Text menu (see Figure 42.73).

Figure 42.73 Header and footer

Activating the Text menu brings up an additional tab (in this case the Design tab), which contains an extensive list of header and footer options. If you have chosen to insert a header, the Header box appears and the cursor flashes for text entry.

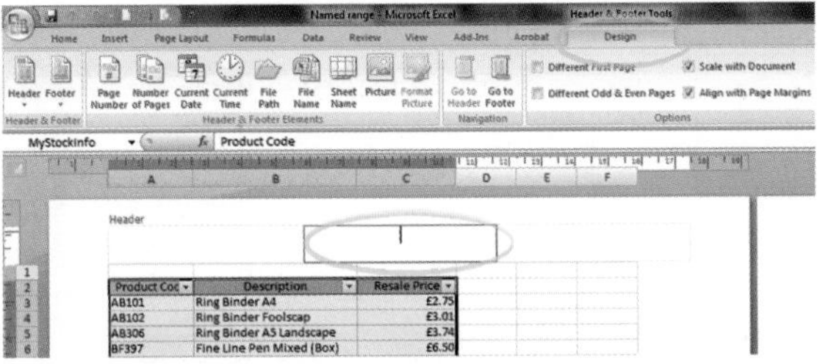

Figure 42.74 Header and Footer Tools

Print area

There will be instances where the user does not wish to print an entire spreadsheet, but instead decides to print a part of it. To do this, you need to highlight the area you want to print, then click on the **Page Layout tab** and the **Print Area** option. You can then set or clear a series of selected cells.

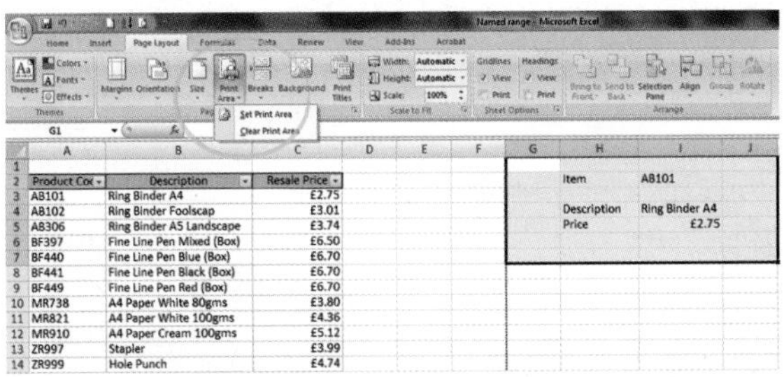

Figure 42.75 Setting the print area

Use of colour

Colours can also be used to improve the appearance of the spreadsheet. In the example in Figure 42.76, we have changed the colour of the row and column headings and have also used a different colour to highlight the highest sales value for each region over the period. You can clearly see that the Midlands, South West and North had their best month in January, while for the South East it was February.

Period Sales Totals by Region

	South West	North	Midlands	South East
January	145	201	192	187
February	114	94	173	199
March	85	176	103	134
Period Totals	344	471	468	520

Figure 42.76 Colours

42.3 Be able to automate and customise spreadsheet models

This section will cover the following grading criteria:

Make the Grade P4 M2

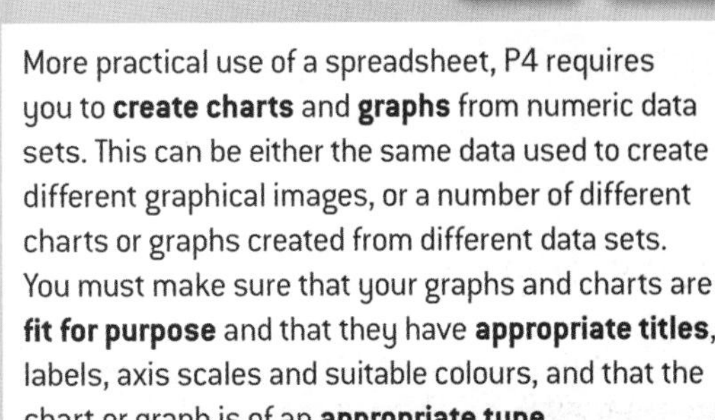

More practical use of a spreadsheet, P4 requires you to **create charts** and **graphs** from numeric data sets. This can be either the same data used to create different graphical images, or a number of different charts or graphs created from different data sets. You must make sure that your graphs and charts are **fit for purpose** and that they have **appropriate titles**, labels, axis scales and suitable colours, and that the chart or graph is of an **appropriate type**.

For M2 you will need to use the graphs or charts you have developed for P4 as a **method of analysing** and **interpreting data** from your spreadsheet model.

As an alternative you could be asked to use sub-totals or pivot tables, data sorting and data comparison (trends for example) techniques to analyse data.

Ultimately to achieve M2 you will need to **demonstrate** that you are using these techniques as **appropriate to the situation** to interpret the spreadsheet model.

42.3.1 Sorting and summarising data

Use of sub-totals and facilities

A **pivot table** is a tool that can be used to **summarise a data** set and allow the data users to see the data from **different perspectives**.

Using the data in Figure 42.77, we will use the pivot table facility to provide subtotals and different views of the data.

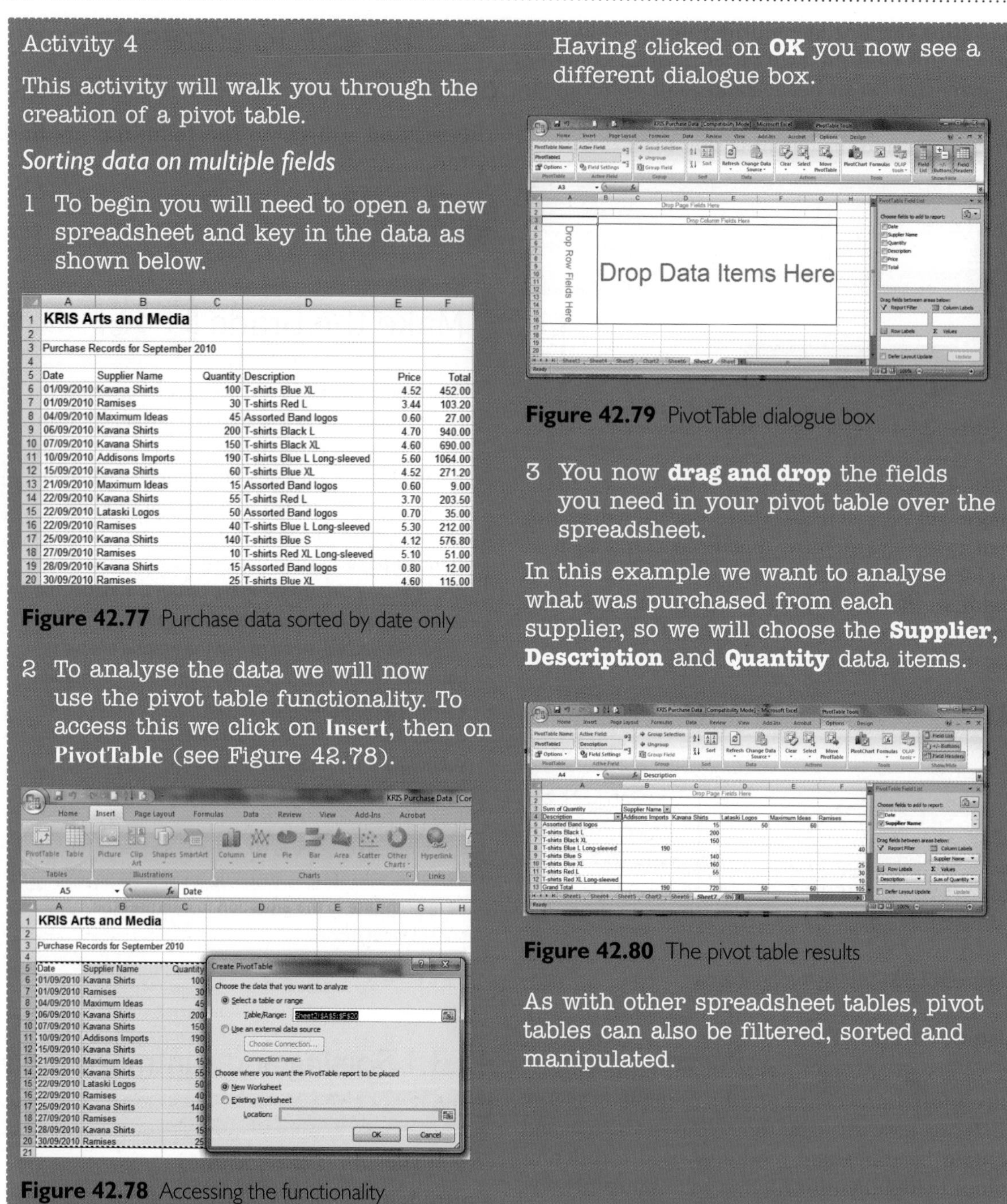

Activity 4

This activity will walk you through the creation of a pivot table.

Sorting data on multiple fields

1 To begin you will need to open a new spreadsheet and key in the data as shown below.

	A	B	C	D	E	F
1	**KRIS Arts and Media**					
2						
3	Purchase Records for September 2010					
4						
5	Date	Supplier Name	Quantity	Description	Price	Total
6	01/09/2010	Kavana Shirts	100	T-shirts Blue XL	4.52	452.00
7	01/09/2010	Ramises	30	T-shirts Red L	3.44	103.20
8	04/09/2010	Maximum Ideas	45	Assorted Band logos	0.60	27.00
9	06/09/2010	Kavana Shirts	200	T-shirts Black L	4.70	940.00
10	07/09/2010	Kavana Shirts	150	T-shirts Black XL	4.60	690.00
11	10/09/2010	Addisons Imports	190	T-shirts Blue L Long-sleeved	5.60	1064.00
12	15/09/2010	Kavana Shirts	60	T-shirts Blue XL	4.52	271.20
13	21/09/2010	Maximum Ideas	15	Assorted Band logos	0.60	9.00
14	22/09/2010	Kavana Shirts	55	T-shirts Red L	3.70	203.50
15	22/09/2010	Lataski Logos	50	Assorted Band logos	0.70	35.00
16	22/09/2010	Ramises	40	T-shirts Blue L Long-sleeved	5.30	212.00
17	25/09/2010	Kavana Shirts	140	T-shirts Blue S	4.12	576.80
18	27/09/2010	Ramises	10	T-shirts Red XL Long-sleeved	5.10	51.00
19	28/09/2010	Kavana Shirts	15	Assorted Band logos	0.80	12.00
20	30/09/2010	Ramises	25	T-shirts Blue XL	4.60	115.00

Figure 42.77 Purchase data sorted by date only

2 To analyse the data we will now use the pivot table functionality. To access this we click on **Insert**, then on **PivotTable** (see Figure 42.78).

Figure 42.78 Accessing the functionality

Having clicked on **OK** you now see a different dialogue box.

Figure 42.79 PivotTable dialogue box

3 You now **drag and drop** the fields you need in your pivot table over the spreadsheet.

In this example we want to analyse what was purchased from each supplier, so we will choose the **Supplier**, **Description** and **Quantity** data items.

Figure 42.80 The pivot table results

As with other spreadsheet tables, pivot tables can also be filtered, sorted and manipulated.

Sorting data on multiple fields

The key issue with sorting data is ensuring that you select all the data across the rows and columns to be included when the records are moved. Failure to do this could result in data becoming mixed up and effectively useless.

In Figure 42.80 (on the next page) the data had been sorted in date order. We will now use the same data and sort it on multiple fields. See Activity 5 for details.

Filtering data sets

With sorted or unsorted data there is also an **autofilter Function**. To activate the autofilter, highlight the headings at the top of the relevant data, click on **Data** and then on the **Filter icon.** The column headings will automatically become drop-down boxes. Selecting the drop-down menu beside Description, for example, will allow the user to choose which item to display and it will extract only those records from the list which match your

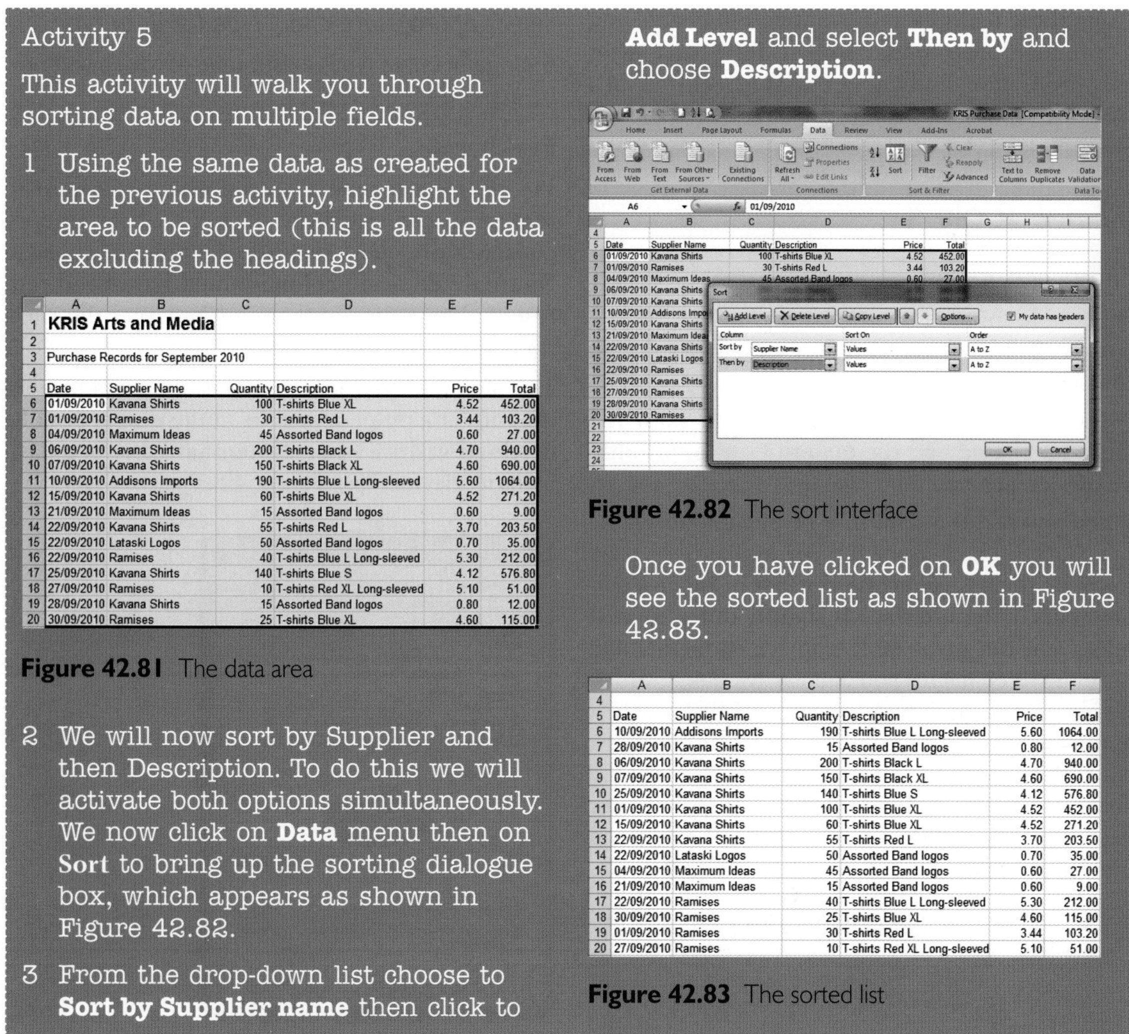

Activity 5

This activity will walk you through sorting data on multiple fields.

1 Using the same data as created for the previous activity, highlight the area to be sorted (this is all the data excluding the headings).

	A	B	C	D	E	F
1	**KRIS Arts and Media**					
2						
3	Purchase Records for September 2010					
4						
5	Date	Supplier Name	Quantity	Description	Price	Total
6	01/09/2010	Kavana Shirts	100	T-shirts Blue XL	4.52	452.00
7	01/09/2010	Ramises	30	T-shirts Red L	3.44	103.20
8	04/09/2010	Maximum Ideas	45	Assorted Band logos	0.60	27.00
9	06/09/2010	Kavana Shirts	200	T-shirts Black L	4.70	940.00
10	07/09/2010	Kavana Shirts	150	T-shirts Black XL	4.60	690.00
11	10/09/2010	Addisons Imports	190	T-shirts Blue L Long-sleeved	5.60	1064.00
12	15/09/2010	Kavana Shirts	60	T-shirts Blue XL	4.52	271.20
13	21/09/2010	Maximum Ideas	15	Assorted Band logos	0.60	9.00
14	22/09/2010	Kavana Shirts	55	T-shirts Red L	3.70	203.50
15	22/09/2010	Lataski Logos	50	Assorted Band logos	0.70	35.00
16	22/09/2010	Ramises	40	T-shirts Blue L Long-sleeved	5.30	212.00
17	25/09/2010	Kavana Shirts	140	T-shirts Blue S	4.12	576.80
18	27/09/2010	Ramises	10	T-shirts Red XL Long-sleeved	5.10	51.00
19	28/09/2010	Kavana Shirts	15	Assorted Band logos	0.80	12.00
20	30/09/2010	Ramises	25	T-shirts Blue XL	4.60	115.00

Figure 42.81 The data area

2 We will now sort by Supplier and then Description. To do this we will activate both options simultaneously. We now click on **Data** menu then on **Sort** to bring up the sorting dialogue box, which appears as shown in Figure 42.82.

3 From the drop-down list choose to **Sort by Supplier name** then click to **Add Level** and select **Then by** and choose **Description**.

Figure 42.82 The sort interface

Once you have clicked on **OK** you will see the sorted list as shown in Figure 42.83.

	A	B	C	D	E	F
4						
5	Date	Supplier Name	Quantity	Description	Price	Total
6	10/09/2010	Addisons Imports	190	T-shirts Blue L Long-sleeved	5.60	1064.00
7	28/09/2010	Kavana Shirts	15	Assorted Band logos	0.80	12.00
8	06/09/2010	Kavana Shirts	200	T-shirts Black L	4.70	940.00
9	07/09/2010	Kavana Shirts	150	T-shirts Black XL	4.60	690.00
10	25/09/2010	Kavana Shirts	140	T-shirts Blue S	4.12	576.80
11	01/09/2010	Kavana Shirts	100	T-shirts Blue XL	4.52	452.00
12	15/09/2010	Kavana Shirts	60	T-shirts Blue XL	4.52	271.20
13	22/09/2010	Kavana Shirts	55	T-shirts Red L	3.70	203.50
14	22/09/2010	Lataski Logos	50	Assorted Band logos	0.70	35.00
15	04/09/2010	Maximum Ideas	45	Assorted Band logos	0.60	27.00
16	21/09/2010	Maximum Ideas	15	Assorted Band logos	0.60	9.00
17	22/09/2010	Ramises	40	T-shirts Blue L Long-sleeved	5.30	212.00
18	30/09/2010	Ramises	25	T-shirts Blue XL	4.60	115.00
19	01/09/2010	Ramises	30	T-shirts Red L	3.44	103.20
20	27/09/2010	Ramises	10	T-shirts Red XL Long-sleeved	5.10	51.00

Figure 42.83 The sorted list

selection. To demonstrate this function, we click on Description, as suggested, and then deactivate the Select All option in the list and click only Assorted Band Logos (Figure 42.84).

	A	B	E	F
4				
5	Date	Supplier Name	Pri	To
6	10/09/2010	Addisons Imports	5.60	1064.00
7	28/09/2010	Kavana Shirts	0.80	12.00
8	06/09/2010	Kavana Shirts	4.70	940.00
9	07/09/2010	Kavana Shirts	4.60	690.00
10	25/09/2010	Kavana Shirts	4.12	576.80
11	01/09/2010	Kavana Shirts	4.52	452.00
12	15/09/2010	Kavana Shirts	4.52	271.20
13	22/09/2010	Kavana Shirts	3.70	203.50
14	22/09/2010	Lataski Logos	0.70	35.00
15	04/09/2010	Maximum Ideas	0.60	27.00
16	21/09/2010	Maximum Ideas	0.60	9.00
17	22/09/2010	Ramises	5.30	212.00
18	30/09/2010	Ramises	4.60	115.00
19	01/09/2010	Ramises	3.44	103.20
20	27/09/2010	Ramises	5.10	51.00

Sort A to Z
Sort Z to A
Sort by Color
Clear Filter From "Description"
Filter by Color
Text Filters
(Select All)
Assorted Band logos
T-shirts Black L
T-shirts Black XL
T-shirts Blue L Long-sleeved
T-shirts Blue S
T-shirts Blue XL
T-shirts Red L
T-shirts Red XL Long-sleeved
OK Cancel

Figure 42.84 Using the autofilter to filter data

The filtered list now shows **only** those suppliers from whom Kris Arts and Media have purchased that particular product. Notice that the drop-down icon on the Description column has now **changed** to a **Filter icon**. This is very useful to the user as he or she can immediately see **where a** filter has been applied (Figure 42.85).

C	D	E	F
Quant	Description	Pri	To
15	Assorted Band logos	0.80	12.00
50	Assorted Band logos	0.70	35.00
45	Assorted Band logos	0.60	27.00
15	Assorted Band logos	0.60	9.00

Figure 42.85 Autofilter results

Similarly, you could choose to filter for all the records for one particular supplier or for goods purchased on a single date. Usefully, the autofilter function can be switched **on** or **off** on demand.

Using these features and facilities will enable you to produce professional spreadsheets that meet user needs. If in doubt about what is required on a spreadsheet or how the audience requires the data presented – **ASK!**

42.3.2 Tools

Charts and graphs

Being able to create charts and graphs is an important skill for anyone working with data through spreadsheets.

Using another pivot table, prepared to show the items purchased and the quantities as totals only, we now create a column chart.

When you use the data in a pivot table to create the chart or graph, once the Wizard has been used to create the base chart (in the first instance a column chart), the interface is slightly different as it offers you the pivot table choices as menus and buttons which means you can easily change which pieces of data are used to make up the chart or graph (see Figure 42.86). The user can now draw conclusions based solely on the information in the chart – for example: long-sleeved T-shirts have not been purchased from Kavana Shirts (there is no pink or purple column against this supplier).

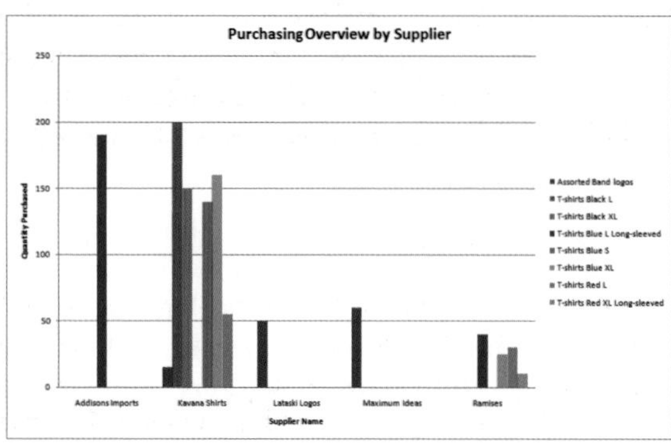

Figure 42.86 A chart made from a pivot table

As always, the title will need to be added, labels will need to be included or removed as required, the X-axis (across) will require a title (in this case **Supplier Name**) and the Y-axis (up and down) will require a title, which in this instance could be **Quantity Purchased**.

Similarly, as with all charts, an appropriate general title will be required.

In all charts created in Microsoft Excel® the **chart area** can be formatted and the background colours changed. Similarly, annotation can be added.

Select appropriate chart type for data type

A range of chart types exist, some of which will now be explored.

Pie charts

Pie charts are generally used where you want to represent data visually as part of a whole. Had we chosen a pie chart instead of a column chart in Figure 42.86, each column would have been represented by a slice of the pie. The larger the slice, the more it represents of the whole.

The pie chart you will see most often when working with computer systems is in the properties of a destination drive (such as your hard disk or a flash memory device) (see Figure 42.87).

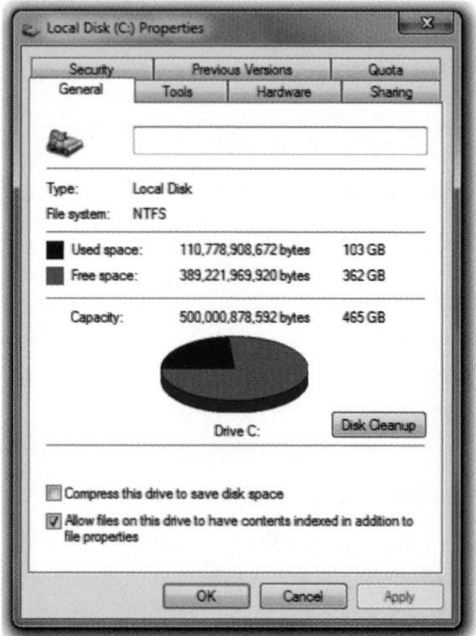

Figure 42.87 Pie chart used to display free and used disk space

Column charts

As shown in Figure 42.86, **column charts** contain vertical bars (upright). This is probably the most commonly used chart type and is usually offered as the default (or first choice) by the Wizard. Column charts are useful for allowing users to visually compare columns of data.

Bar charts

With horizontal bars (flat), **bar charts** are often used for comparing distances, for example. Many people, however, use the term "bar chart" regardless of whether the bars are vertical or horizontal.

Line graphs

Line graphs are good for comparing trends, as with the spreadsheet included at the beginning of this unit.

When using any chart or graph, users must make certain that the chart will actually mean something to the data user. Consider the pie chart in Figure 42.89. What is it telling you?

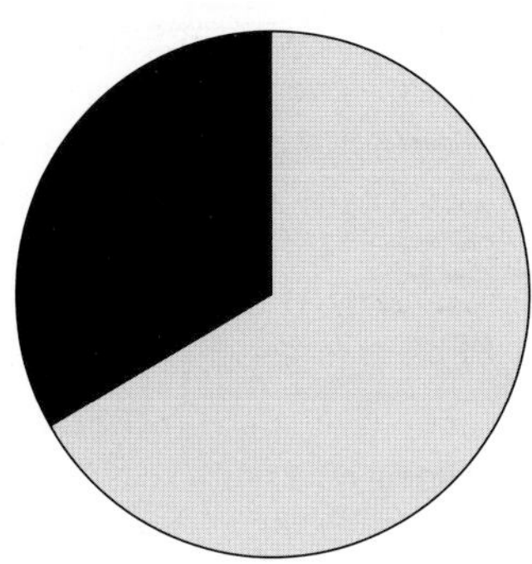

Figure 42.88 Pie chart without annotation

In fact, this pie chart is not very useful. As it has no title and no key or legend, the user is unlikely to understand what it is actually intended to present!

This is a very common error made by users in creating such charts.

Justify choices

When creating charts and graphs, be prepared to explain your choices to users or managers. To avoid errors in this respect, always make sure you fully understand what you are trying to achieve in using this medium to present information.

42.3.3 Presenting

Combining information

Professionally presented information is usually a combination of tables of data or information, charts or graphs and textual commentary that explains the images. In some cases, the images are used to provide a better understanding of the text.

Using combined information to support arguments will become easier with experience. As a general rule, always try to provide evidence to support both sides of an argument before drawing a conclusion.

Maintaining data

This topic has already been covered in section 42.1.1 earlier in this unit.

You should just remember that any links established between worksheets, workbooks or files are dynamic, and changing the source value will lead to all those values reliant on the source value automatically being updated. Remember that when re-opening a file that creates a dynamic link, you will be asked whether you wish to update the file when it is opened or not.

42.3.4 Analysing and interpreting data

One of the biggest advantages of using spreadsheet tools to help you to analyse data is that you can manipulate the data in many ways to give you different perspectives and help you to identify information that otherwise might be difficult to spot. The following section gives some examples.

Converting data

Creating charts in different formats from the same data can highlight unusual events.

Lists

These can be sorted – for example, sales values from particular representatives could be ordered highest to lowest at the touch of a button. This would show immediately the ranked order of successful sales for staff.

Similarly the data could be filtered, to exclude any records that have a particular value. One example would be to filter a stock table to show just those items that have a stock of fewer than 10 items (for reordering purposes).

Trends and patterns

Using charts, graphs, lists and so on, you should quickly be able to spot any trends or patterns in the data. Comparing year 1 sales with year 2 sales will show, for example, if a particular month shows high or low sales. In this instance, the data could then be interrogated to find out why that particular event occurred (was it the weather, was the product out of season, etc).

Data analysis and results

The data itself will be analysed in different ways, making use of different tools to produce the results of the analysis. At this stage no conclusion is drawn from this information – the data simply says that this is so and it is up to the data user (or spreadsheet user in some cases) to find the facts.

Conclusions

Conclusions are now drawn – the data is interpreted and meaning is found in the results. This gets easier with experience. Although novice data/spreadsheet users are unlikely to have to draw these conclusions, to learn how conclusions are drawn from information following a data analysis, ask the data user to share his or her conclusions with you.

42.3.5 Customisation

This section will cover the following grading criterion:

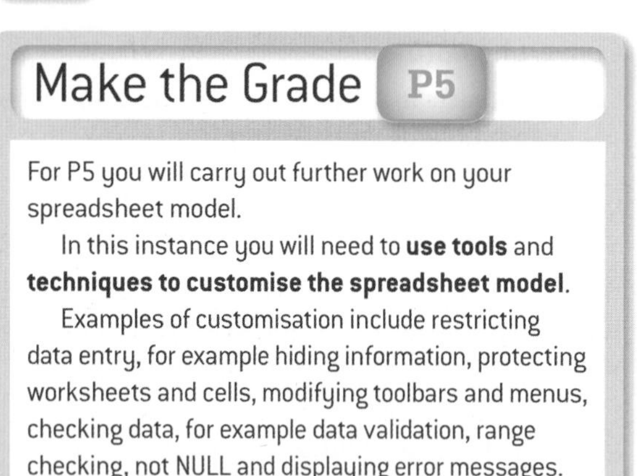

Make the Grade P5

For P5 you will carry out further work on your spreadsheet model.

In this instance you will need to **use tools** and **techniques to customise the spreadsheet model**.

Examples of customisation include restricting data entry, for example hiding information, protecting worksheets and cells, modifying toolbars and menus, checking data, for example data validation, range checking, not NULL and displaying error messages.

Restricting data entry

Hiding columns and rows of data in a spreadsheet to prevent access by particular users is a simple procedure.

Simply select the columns you wish to hide, then right click and choose **Hide** (this can be seen in Figure 42.89). The same technique is used for hiding rows.

This will not prevent the user accessing them if needed. To **Unhide**, the user simply highlights the columns to the left and right of where the column or columns are missing, and then right clicks and chooses **Unhide**.

Protecting the contents of rows or columns requires slightly reversed thinking! When protecting a whole sheet, the developer will simply click on the Home tab, then find the Cells submenu, and under the Protection options choose to **Protect Sheet** (see Figure 42.90).

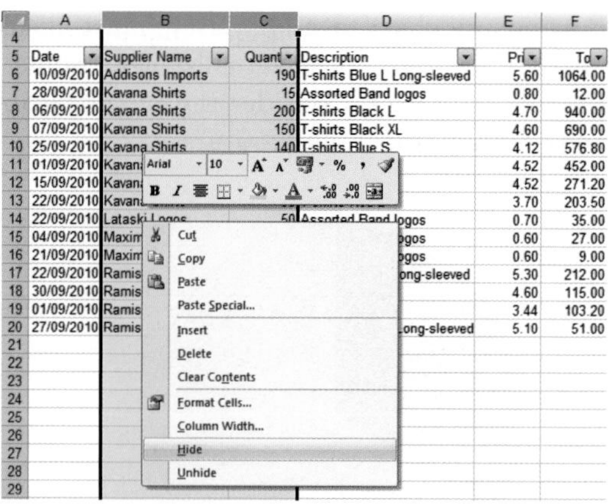

Figure 42.89 Hiding columns

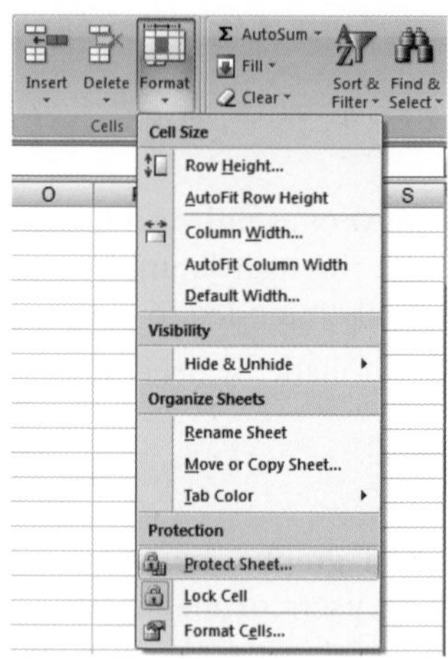

Figure 42.90 Protecting the worksheet

Sheet protection can be safeguarded using a password, effectively locking the whole worksheet and preventing users from being able to change any values.

On more modern versions of Microsoft Excel®, however, it is now also possible to give specific levels of worksheet access to users as can be seen in Figure 42.91.

Figure 42.91 Selecting protection

The developer might, on the other hand, wish to protect the important parts of the spreadsheet, such as headings and totals, and only enable (or leave accessible) those areas that are safe for a novice user to use.

To do this the developer will need to unlock (make accessible) those areas that the user is free to access, prior to protecting the worksheet.

In Figure 42.92, the area that the user will be able to key into has been identified.

	A	B	C	D	E	F
4						
5	Date	Supplier Name	Quant	Description	Pri	To
6	10/09/2010	Addisons Imports	190	T-shirts Blue L Long-sleeved	5.60	1064.00
7	28/09/2010	Kavana Shirts	15	Assorted Band logos	0.80	12.00
8	06/09/2010	Kavana Shirts	200	T-shirts Black L	4.70	940.00
9	07/09/2010	Kavana Shirts	150	T-shirts Black XL	4.60	690.00
10	25/09/2010	Kavana Shirts	140	T-shirts Blue S	4.12	576.80
11	01/09/2010	Kavana Shirts	100	T-shirts Blue XL	4.52	452.00
12	15/09/2010	Kavana Shirts	60	T-shirts Blue XL	4.52	271.20
13	22/09/2010	Kavana Shirts	55	T-shirts Red L	3.70	203.50
14	22/09/2010	Lataski Logos	50	Assorted Band logos	0.70	35.00
15	04/09/2010	Maximum Ideas	45	Assorted Band logos	0.60	27.00
16	21/09/2010	Maximum Ideas	15	Assorted Band logos	0.60	9.00
17	22/09/2010	Ramises	40	T-shirts Blue L Long-sleeved	5.30	212.00
18	30/09/2010	Ramises	25	T-shirts Blue XL	4.60	115.00
19	01/09/2010	Ramises	30	T-shirts Red L	3.44	103.20
20	27/09/2010	Ramises	10	T-shirts Red XL Long-sleeved	5.10	51.00

Figure 42.92 Identifying the user access area

If the user now right clicks on the identified cells, then clicks on Format Cells and finally on Protection, the dialogue box shown in Figure 42.93 will become visible. The user unchecks the Locked box in order to unlock those cells when the rest of the sheet becomes protected.

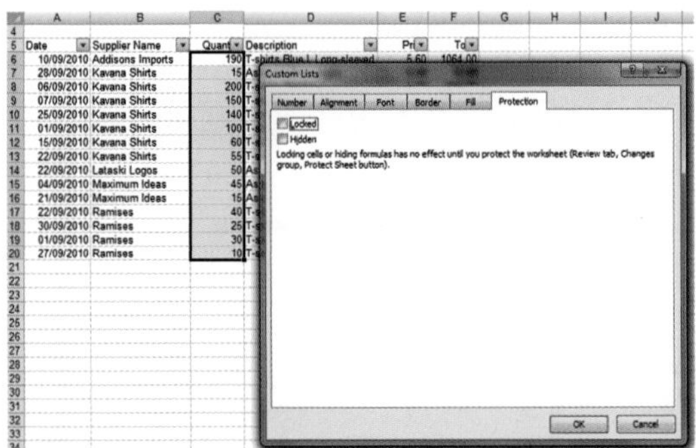

Figure 42.93 Unlocking cells

You will also notice that cells to be hidden can be identified in the same way.

Once the cells to be kept active have been unlocked, the sheet is protected in the usual way (see Figures 42.90 and 42.91).

Modifying toolbars and menus

Having already considered how data can be hidden or locked and how whole worksheets can be protected, you might also wish to **limit the functionality that** a user has access to by **removing buttons or menus**.

Data validation, range checking and error messages

Customising your spreadsheet to provide some data validation functionality is essential to maintain the integrity of your data and some suggestions for this activity have already been covered in section 42.2.1, including validation, range checking and the use of customised error messages.

42.3.6 Automation

This section will cover the following grading criteria:

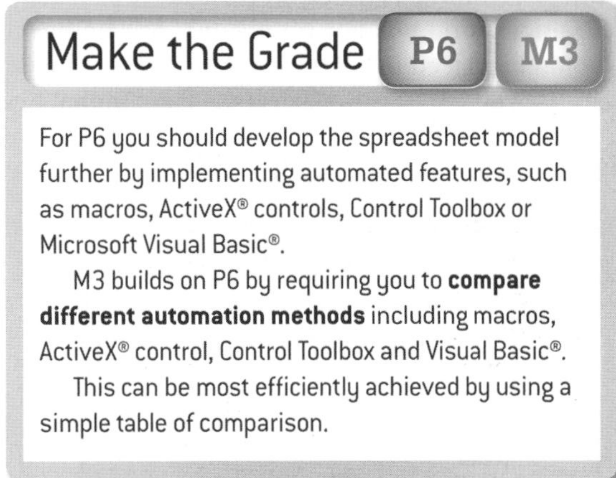

Make the Grade P6 M3

For P6 you should develop the spreadsheet model further by implementing automated features, such as macros, ActiveX® controls, Control Toolbox or Microsoft Visual Basic®.

M3 builds on P6 by requiring you to **compare different automation methods** including macros, ActiveX® control, Control Toolbox and Visual Basic®.

This can be most efficiently achieved by using a simple table of comparison.

Macros

Macros are mini programs that automate chosen functions in a spreadsheet. They can be stored within a particular workbook or stored globally so that they can be accessed by all workbooks.

Recording a macro is a very straightforward process. You can either select the **View tab** and then the **Macro submenu**, or you can use the **Developer tab** which contains many of the macro functions. This is not visible by default and may need to be added.

To add the Developer tab, click on the Microsoft Office® icon, Excel® Options and check the box as shown in Figure 42.94.

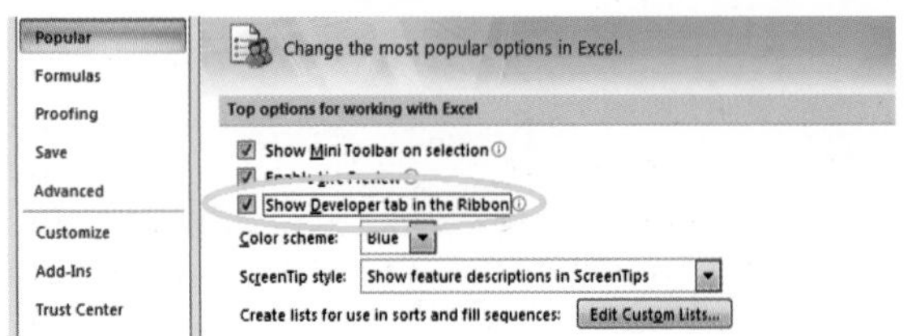

Figure 42.94 Adding the Developer tab

When you click on the Developer tab, you can then choose to Record a new macro (Figure 42.95).

Figure 42.95 Recording a macro

As soon as **Record New Macro** has been selected, the dialogue box shown in Figure 42.96 will appear. Here you will have to give the macro a name, and you will select whether the macro **will be visible** to the workbook open at the time it was created, a new workbook not yet created, or whether it should be placed in a **Personal Macro Workbook**. This is what effectively makes the macro global because the Personal Macro Workbook is visible to all spreadsheets. This is called '**scoping**'.

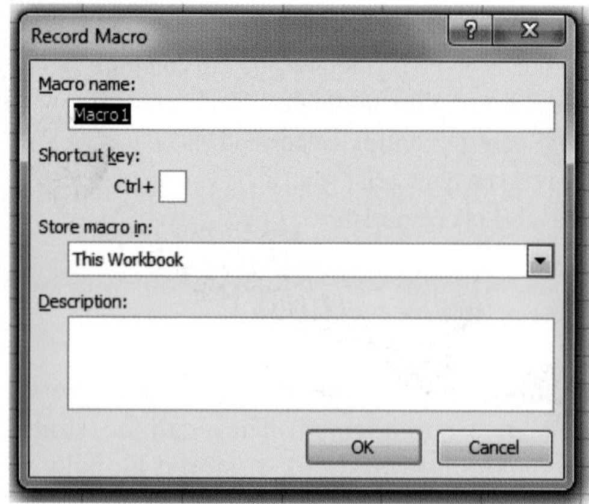

Figure 42.96 Scoping the macro

Once you click on OK, the macro will begin recording and every action you undertake will be logged, until you click on the Stop Recording button as shown in Figure 42.97.

Figure 42.97 Stop recording

Once the recording has been stopped, you can then add a button to the spreadsheet to activate the macro.

To do this you must select the **Developer tab**, click on the **Controls submenu**, click on **Insert** and then from the **Form Controls** click on the **button icon**.

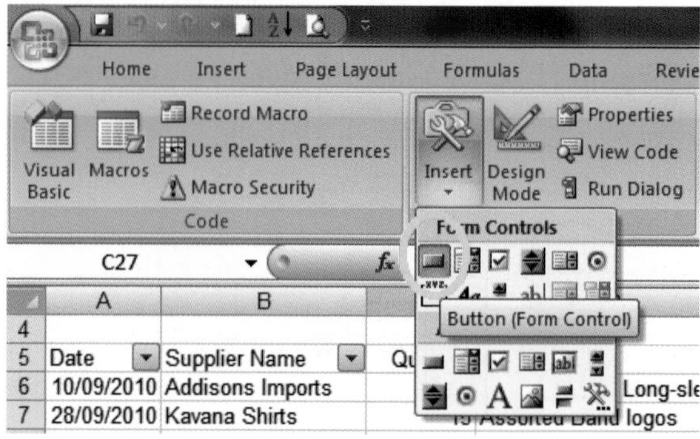

Figure 42.98 Adding a button

Draw a button on your spreadsheet and when you release the mouse the **Assign Macro** dialogue box will appear. **Choose** the macro you wish to assign.

You can also change the **caption** on the button to **describe** what the button does (e.g. Print).

Macros you might like to record to enhance your spreadsheet could include:

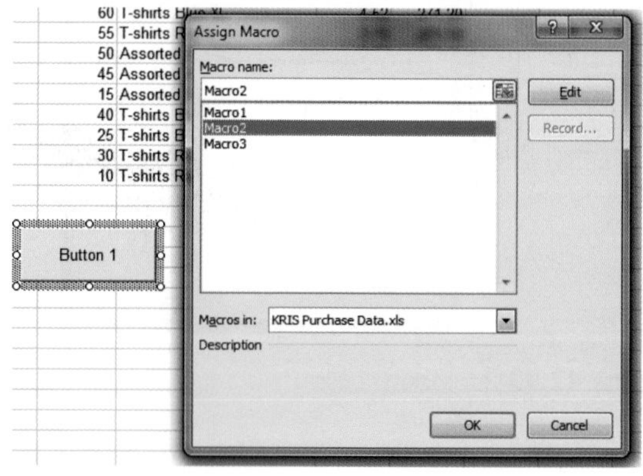

Figure 42.99 Assign a macro

- a print macro to always print a specific number of copies of a whole spreadsheet
- a macro to select a specific area in a spreadsheet for printing
- a macro that ensures that all columns are of the correct width to accommodate the data

- a macro that ensures that all numeric columns have two decimal places.

The list of possible options is **extensive** and would fill an entire book of its own! What you must ensure, however, is that you choose a macro that is going to be useful to the user, rather than just creating one to prove you can!

ActiveX® controls and Control Toolbox

These are objects that can be downloaded, written by the spreadsheet developer or imported from other software applications and which can be made available to different programs as well as different files in the system.

They can also be embedded into particular files to carry out pre-defined functions. These controls are reusable and can be accessed through the ActiveX® Controls, More Controls option as shown in Figure 42.100. Some examples are shown in Figure 42.101.

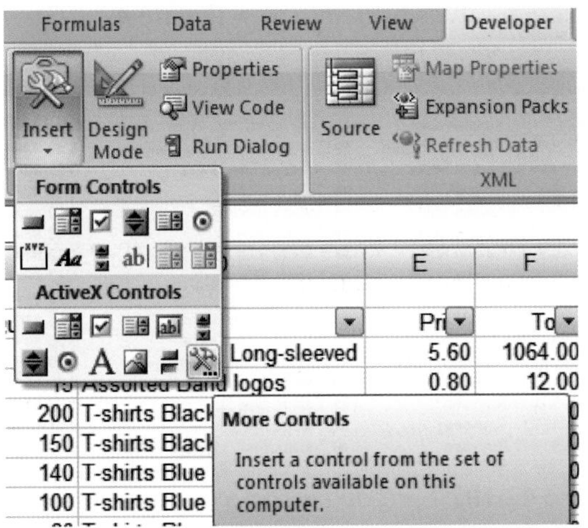

Figure 42.100 Controls

Figure 42.101 ActiveX® options

Visual Basic® for Applications (VBA)

Visual Basic® is the programming language used to support automated processes in most Microsoft® applications. Shown below is the macro that was introduced earlier in this unit:

```
Sub Macro1()
Macro1 Macro
Macro recorded 20/07/2010 by Bernie
   Range("A1:A7,B3:B7").Select
'Choose these ranges
   Selection.PrintOut Copies:=3,
Collate:=True          'Print three
copies
End Sub
```

Amending the print range or the number of prints is achieved by simply changing the relevant values in the code:

```
Sub Macro1()
Macro1 Macro
Macro recorded 20/07/2010 by Bernie
   Range("A1:A12,B3:B12").Select
'Choose a different range
   Selection.PrintOut Copies:=6,
Collate:=True          'Print six copies
End Sub
```

42.4 Be able to test and document spreadsheet models

This section will cover the following grading criteria:

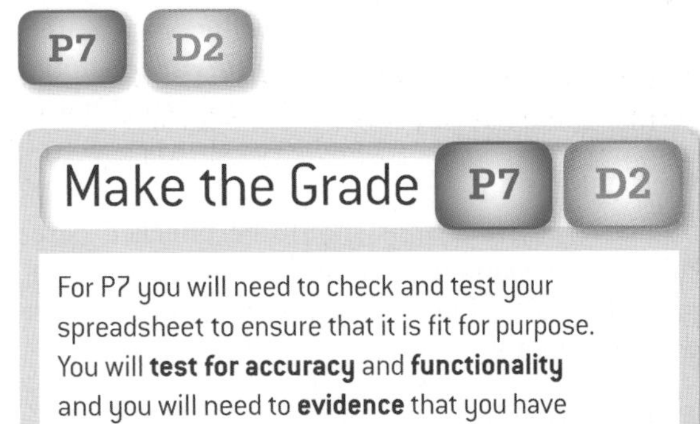

For P7 you will need to check and test your spreadsheet to ensure that it is fit for purpose. You will **test for accuracy** and **functionality** and you will need to **evidence** that you have **checked** the spreadsheet model in terms of the required **functionality**, **accuracy** of **calculations**, data **validation**, and ensured that the results of calculations and so on, are displayed with an

appropriate level of detail (columns for example to two decimal places). Evidence should be in the form of test plans and screen captures.

D2 builds on P7 by requiring you to **evaluate your spreadsheet model** incorporating **feedback** from **others**. You should be able to **reflect** on **your own performance** in building a spreadsheet model and consider what **hurdles you had to overcome** to achieve the desired result. Questions you should pose to focus the evaluation could include:

- Did the spreadsheet model meet the given requirements?
- What did other people think of the spreadsheet model?
- Was there any functionality that could be included or aspects that could be improved?

Reviewing the answers to these questions will also enable you to include some sensible recommendations for improvements.

42.4.1 Test

There are three main reasons for testing your spreadsheet. This would be to:

a. confirm the spreadsheet has the correct functionality
b. confirm the spreadsheet calculations and so on are correct
c. confirm the spreadsheet is simple to use (shortcuts, data forms etc.).

Formulae and functions

Those formulae and functions created by the spreadsheet developer need to be carefully checked.

Formulae, for example, should be checked to make sure that they include all the values in a range. The order of precedence in any formulae should also be checked (don't forget that incorrect use of BODMAS will still give an answer, it just won't be the right answer).

Similarly, any functions should be checked carefully, using manual methods to confirm the answers (the use of pen, paper and calculator is the most common)!

Data entry forms

The checks on data entry forms will largely consist of visual checks of the following:

- **completeness**
- **presence** of all the required functionality
- that the **tab order** of any inputs follows the natural progression of any input forms
- that any **user prompts are complete** and in place
- **spelling** of any labels.

Validation

Validation routines should be checked to ensure that **good values are accepted** and that **bad values are rejected**, with the **correct error message** displaying **as needed**.

Collecting or creating relevant test data is covered in the next section.

Layout

Firstly, columns should be made wide enough to accommodate all headings and the numbers themselves. If columns are not wide enough to accommodate the data within them, the numbers are shown as hashes. Widening the column will bring the actual values back into view (Figure 42.103).

	A	B	C	D	E	F
4						
5	Date	Supplier Name	t	Description	Pri	To
6	10/09/2010	Addisons Imports	##	T-shirts Blue L Long-sleeved	5.60	####
7	28/09/2010	Kavana Shirts	15	Assorted Band logos	0.80	####
8	06/09/2010	Kavana Shirts	##	T-shirts Black L	4.70	####
9	07/09/2010	Kavana Shirts	##	T-shirts Black XL	4.60	####
10	25/09/2010	Kavana Shirts	##	T-shirts Blue S	4.12	####
11	01/09/2010	Kavana Shirts	##	T-shirts Blue XL	4.52	####
12	15/09/2010	Kavana Shirts	60	T-shirts Blue XL	4.52	####
13	22/09/2010	Kavana Shirts	55	T-shirts Red L	3.70	####
14	22/09/2010	Lataski Logos	50	Assorted Band logos	0.70	####
15	04/09/2010	Maximum Ideas	45	Assorted Band logos	0.60	####
16	21/09/2010	Maximum Ideas	15	Assorted Band logos	0.60	9.00
17	22/09/2010	Ramises	40	T-shirts Blue L Long-sleeved	5.30	####
18	30/09/2010	Ramises	25	T-shirts Blue XL	4.60	####
19	01/09/2010	Ramises	30	T-shirts Red L	3.44	####
20	27/09/2010	Ramises	10	T-shirts Red XL Long-sleeved	5.10	####

Figure 42.102 Spreadsheet showing missing data hashes

Values

As part of the development of a spreadsheet, the results of calculations should also be carefully checked. Using **alternative means** of calculating the answers, such as a **pen and paper** or a **calculator**, is necessary to test the spreadsheet formally and thus ensure that formulae and functions are working as they should.

In addition, developers need to make decisions about the **level of detail** required in the numbers that are displayed.

With spreadsheets containing British currency, for example, there may be little point in displaying numbers to three decimal places – £15.947 – because no physical currency exists for 0.7 of a pence.

On the other hand, there will be instances where it is **appropriate** to display values to five or more decimal places (e.g. scientific measurements).

Suitability for client

Although your tutor may not be a paying customer, he or she is still the person for whom the spreadsheet is being created.

Clearly it is necessary to ask him or her for **feedback** on the **suitability** of the final solution. This process can be **formalised** (maybe with a feedback interview), but will more likely involve user testing (see below).

User testing

If the spreadsheet is going to be used by one or more users, you would ordinarily ask the users to test it. This can be very useful for checking the robustness of the spreadsheet. For example, if you have error trapping to trap incorrect numeric values, have you tested it by inputting a character or symbol? A real user could very easily make these kinds of mistakes!

Usually the user is given a form or some sort of feedback document to complete.

Test plans using normal, extreme and erroneous data

Data selected for testing purposes should cover the following range:

- **Normal data** – the program needs to be tested with data that is within a sensible range. This is the data that is expected to be input when the system is being used normally.
- **Extreme data** – the program should also be tested with data that, though still within a sensible range, is **less likely** to be input. For example, an age over 115 is not impossible, it's just unlikely!
- **Erroneous data** – this is data that is neither normal nor sensible! It is data that is blatantly incorrect. The data will contain values **outside valid ranges** and **incorrect types** of values (e.g. characters where numbers are expected and vice versa).

42.4.2 Feedback

Receiving feedback for any IT project is **essential** to ensure that a) the client or user is happy that he or she is getting the expected solution and b) there is confirmation that the system works as it should.

The methods used for obtaining feedback in this situation tend to be surveys, questionnaires and interviews. As these techniques support the investigation phase of the systems life cycle, they are explained in full in Unit 11 section 11.2.1.

Analyse results and make recommendations

Once received, feedback should be **carefully collated** and **analysed** and any errors or problems fixed in the short term. In the medium term, any additional functionality could also be added to improve the spreadsheet.

Activity 6

Complete the following test plan to reflect testing for normal, extreme and erroneous data. In each case, suggest at least two values!

Test	Normal data	Extreme Data	Erroneous data
Age is between 18 and 21			
Height is between 1.5 and 2.2 metres			
Quantity (must not be 0)			
Price (must be more than 0, but less than £20.00)			
Choice must be A, B, C, D or E			
Hours worked (must be greater than 0, but less than 50)			

42.4.3 Alternative formats

This section will cover the following grading criterion:

> In addition, you will have a **copy of the original file** and the **converted file** and to fully evidence the criterion, you could open the converted file and send it to print.

Make the Grade P8

A practical task, the P8 criterion requires you to **export** the contents of a spreadsheet model to an **alternative format**. This does not necessarily mean that you need to export the entire contents of a spreadsheet, but you will need to choose a **sensible section** of the spreadsheet and save it as a smaller file if you decide not to export the whole thing.

When the conversion is carried out, a **witness statement** could be used to record the activity.

For the occasions when you might want to export an entire spreadsheet file, Microsoft Excel® offers you the opportunity to save the files in different formats.

To save in a different format, you merely need to choose a different file type when going through the **Save As...** dialogue.

A range of common formats is explored in Table 42.03.

Remember that each of the formats will present the file in the file management system with a different icon.

What you should notice is that as the file extensions are different for each format, the file name can actually remain the same!

Table 42.03

<table>
<tr><th>Format choice</th><th>Description</th></tr>
<tr><td>xls</td><td>An eXceL Spreadsheet and the default format applied when you save a spreadsheet in Microsoft Excel 97~2003®.
This format is still supported in newer versions of Microsoft Excel®.</td></tr>
<tr><td>csv</td><td>This stands for comma separated value. If you save a spreadsheet in this format, the cells are separated by commas, and a new line denotes the beginning of a new line in the spreadsheet.
The spreadsheet in Figure 42.103 is saved in xls format.
<table>
<tr><th></th><th>A</th><th>B</th><th>C</th><th>D</th></tr>
<tr><td>1</td><td>Ice Cream Sales for 2010</td><td></td><td></td><td></td></tr>
<tr><td>2</td><td></td><td></td><td></td><td></td></tr>
<tr><td>3</td><td>Month</td><td>£000s</td><td></td><td>Percentage of total sales</td></tr>
<tr><td>4</td><td>January</td><td>1597</td><td></td><td>7</td></tr>
<tr><td>5</td><td>February</td><td>1438</td><td></td><td>6</td></tr>
<tr><td>6</td><td>March</td><td>1499</td><td></td><td>7</td></tr>
<tr><td>7</td><td>April</td><td>1957</td><td></td><td>9</td></tr>
<tr><td>8</td><td>May</td><td>1586</td><td></td><td>7</td></tr>
<tr><td>9</td><td>June</td><td>2417</td><td></td><td>11</td></tr>
<tr><td>10</td><td>July</td><td>2683</td><td></td><td>12</td></tr>
<tr><td>11</td><td>August</td><td>2751</td><td></td><td>12</td></tr>
<tr><td>12</td><td>September</td><td>2100</td><td></td><td>9</td></tr>
<tr><td>13</td><td>October</td><td>1414</td><td></td><td>6</td></tr>
<tr><td>14</td><td>November</td><td>1563</td><td></td><td>7</td></tr>
<tr><td>15</td><td>December</td><td>1866</td><td></td><td>8</td></tr>
<tr><td>16</td><td></td><td></td><td></td><td></td></tr>
<tr><td>17</td><td>Total</td><td>22871</td><td></td><td>100</td></tr>
</table>
Figure 42.103 .xlsx format</td></tr>
</table>

Format choice	Description

csv	If the file is now been saved as a .csv file and imported into Microsoft Word®, it will look like this:
	
	`Ice Cream Sales for 2010,,,`
	
	`Month,£000s,,Percentage of total sales`
	`January,1597,,7`
	`February,1438,,6`
	`March,1499,,7`
	`April,1957,,9`
	`May,1586,,7`
	`June,2417,,11`
	`July,2683,,12`
	`August,2751,,12`
	`September,2100,,9`
	`October,1414,,6`
	`November,1563,,7`
	`December,1866,,8`
	
	`Total,22871,,100`
	
	Figure 42.104 .csv format

txt	This format is a simple **text** file. The same ice cream sales data has now been saved in this format and the new file imported into Microsoft Word®. This is how the content of the file looks now:
	
	`Ice Cream Sales for 2010`
	
	`Month £000s       Percentage of total sales`
	`January    1597        7`
	`February   1438        6`
	`March 1499        7`
	`April 1957        9`
	`May   1586        7`
	`June  2417        11`
	`July  2683        12`
	`August     2751        12`
	`September  2100        9`
	`October    1414        6`
	`November   1563        7`
	`December   1866        8`
	
	`Total 22871       100`
	
	Figure 42.105 .txt format
	
	In this instance, the commas are missing and an attempt has been made by the software to align the information using **default tabs**. Text files are perhaps the **most flexible** and most basic format to save data because the majority of applications and operating systems will be able to read them.

pdf	This popular format will enable the user to export the spreadsheet as an Adobe Acrobat® **p**ortable **d**ocument **f**ormat file, to be read with the freely downloadable Adobe Acrobat Reader® application.
xlsx	An e**X**ce**L** **S**preadsheet XML workbook and the default format applied when you save a spreadsheet in Microsoft Excel 2007®.
html	The **h**yper**t**ext **m**arkup **l**anguage format option prepares the data to be used in the creation of web pages, exporting it in a web browser-friendly format.

42.4.4 Documentation

This section will cover the following grading criteria:

Make the Grade P9 M4

For P9 you will need to produce **user documentation** with instructions for users on **how to use** the spreadsheet model, especially when navigating the user interfaces. This can be achieved as a formal document or equally as a series of web pages.

M4 builds on P9 by requiring you to add **technical documentation**, which includes **the required hardware** and **software resources**, **instructions** and an **explanation of calculations** used in the spreadsheet model.

Again this could be a completely separate document or could be additional pages in a web-based help file. Screencast videos (see Unit 6, section 6.2.1 'Writing documentation') could also be used.

In order to make sure that any IT solution can be **properly maintained** (repaired if problems arise or enhanced if new functionality is needed) a range of documentation will need to be created that **explains the solution** from a number of perspectives. The same will be true for a spreadsheet solution. The documents created may be printed, could be held electronically in a .doc file, or as a series of web pages for users to access when needed (e.g. on an organisation's intranet).

User documentation

This documentation should be developed from a user perspective. It should contain:

- a **guide** on the overall purpose of the spreadsheet
- **instructions** on how to use the spreadsheet, in particular how to execute specific tasks
- **troubleshooting** information on what the user should do if the spreadsheet does not function correctly.

Technical documentation

The technical documentation may be a section in the user documentation or could be a completely separate document or series of web pages. This information will focus on:

- **Hardware resources** – this will usually specify any particular hardware requirements that are needed to run the spreadsheet successfully.
- **Software resources** – it is likely that the spreadsheet solution will have been created in a particular version of Microsoft Excel® and this should be recorded. This is because the spreadsheet might not be compatible with earlier versions of the software.

Instructions

Although modern software largely has electronic help files, many people still prefer books to support the general use of software. The following URL provides a link to a series of Microsoft Excel® books that can be purchased on www.amazon.co.uk:

http://www.amazon.co.uk/s/ref=nb_sb_noss?url=search-alias%3Dstripbooks&field-keywords=excel&x=14&y=17&fsc=-1

Calculations

All calculations and functions used or created should be recorded. With spreadsheet solutions it is useful if the holding cell (cell where the formula is written), the formula itself and a description of the formula or function is included (a print of the spreadsheet in formula view could also be included).

Formula

Cell A15	=A14*20%	This formula calculates VAT.

Functions used

Cell A14	=SUM(A1:A13)	This function adds together the values on the invoice to provide a pre-VAT subtotal.

To display the formula view of a spreadsheet, click on the Formula tab, then on the Formula Editing sub-menu choose Show Formulas (see Figure 42.106).

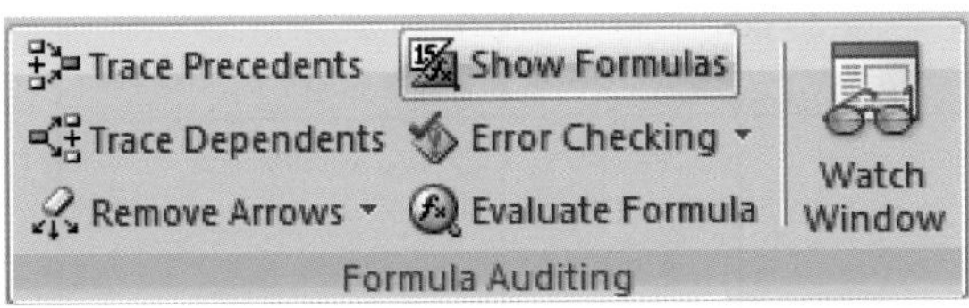

Figure 42.106 Show Formulas

On the view tab click the Formulas Checkbox in the Window options section. The screen will now appear as shown in Figure 42.107.

	A	B	C	D	E	F
4						
5	Date	Supplier Name	Quant	Description	Pri	To
6	40431	Addisons Imports	190	T-shirts Blue L Long-sleeved	5.6	=C6*E6
7	40449	Kavana Shirts	15	Assorted Band logos	0.8	=C7*E7
8	40427	Kavana Shirts	200	T-shirts Black L	4.7	=C8*E8
9	40428	Kavana Shirts	150	T-shirts Black XL	4.6	=C9*E9
10	40446	Kavana Shirts	140	T-shirts Blue S	4.12	=C10*E10
11	40422	Kavana Shirts	100	T-shirts Blue XL	4.52	=C11*E11
12	40436	Kavana Shirts	60	T-shirts Blue XL	4.52	=C12*E12
13	40443	Kavana Shirts	55	T-shirts Red L	3.7	=C13*E13
14	40443	Lataski Logos	50	Assorted Band logos	0.7	=C14*E14
15	40425	Maximum Ideas	45	Assorted Band logos	0.6	=C15*E15
16	40442	Maximum Ideas	15	Assorted Band logos	0.6	=C16*E16
17	40443	Ramises	40	T-shirts Blue L Long-sleeved	5.3	=C17*E17
18	40451	Ramises	25	T-shirts Blue XL	4.6	=C18*E18
19	40422	Ramises	30	T-shirts Red L	3.44	=C19*E19
20	40448	Ramises	10	T-shirts Red XL Long-sleeved	5.1	=C20*E20

Figure 42.107 Formula view

Validation procedures

All validation routines and procedures should be recorded, stating what the validation routine is set to check and annotating any error messages that will be displayed.

Macros and Visual Basic® code

All macros and Visual Basic® code should be described and annotated with simple comments that tell the reader what the line of code does (rather than describing the actual commands used).

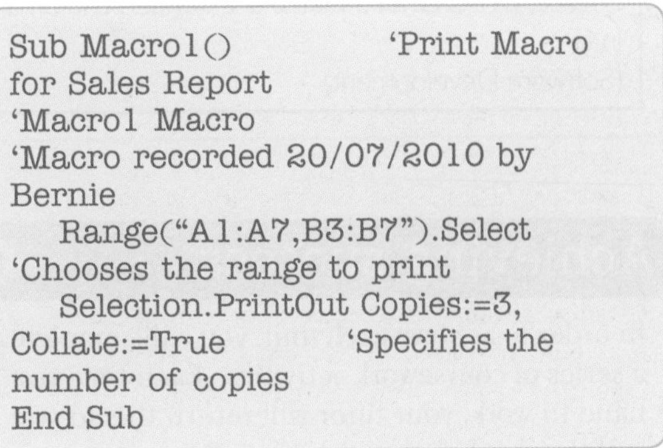

```
Sub Macro1()            'Print Macro
for Sales Report
'Macro1 Macro
'Macro recorded 20/07/2010 by
Bernie
    Range("A1:A7,B3:B7").Select
'Chooses the range to print
    Selection.PrintOut Copies:=3,
Collate:=True         'Specifies the
number of copies
End Sub
```

The key to working successfully with spreadsheets is to make any spreadsheet solution look professional, make sure it is as efficient as possible and check that any calculations, validation and macros work correctly.

Unit link

Unit 42 is a **specialist optional** unit for all qualifications and pathways of this Level 3 IT family.

Qualification (pathway)	Mandatory	Optional	Specialist optional
Edexcel BTEC Level 3 National Certificate in Information Technology			✓
Edexcel BTEC Level 3 National Subsidiary Diploma in Information Technology			✓
Edexcel BTEC Level 3 National Diploma in Information Technology			✓
Edexcel BTEC Level 3 National Extended Diploma in Information Technology			✓
Edexcel BTEC Level 3 National Diploma in IT (Business)			✓
Edexcel BTEC Level 3 National Extended Diploma in IT (Business)			✓
Edexcel BTEC Level 3 National Diploma in IT (Networking and System Support)			✓

Qualification (pathway)	Mandatory	Optional	Specialist optional
Edexcel BTEC Level 3 National Extended Diploma in IT (Networking and System Support)			✓
Edexcel BTEC Level 3 National Diploma in IT (Software Development)			✓
Edexcel BTEC Level 3 National Extended Diploma in IT (Software Development)			✓

Achieving success

In order to achieve each unit, you will complete a series of coursework activities. Each time you hand in work, your tutor will return this to you with a record of your achievement.

This particular unit has 15 criteria to meet: 9 Pass, 4 Merit and 2 Distinction.

For a Pass: You must achieve all 9 Pass criteria.

For a Merit: You must achieve all 9 Pass and all 4 Merit criteria.

For a Distinction: You must achieve all 9 Pass, all 4 Merit and both Distinction criteria.

Further reading

Day, A. – *Mastering Financial Mathematics with Excel* (Financial Times Prentice Hall, 2005) ISBN 0764597809

Hart-Davis, G. – *How to Do Everything with Microsoft Office Excel 2003* (McGraw-Hill Education, 2003) ISBN 0072230711

Heathcote, R. – *Further Excel 2000–2003* (Payne-Gallway Publishers, 2004) ISBN 1904467768

Koneman, P. – *Advanced Projects for Microsoft Excel 2000* (Prentice Hall, 2000) ISBN 0130885444

Simonn, J. – *Excel Data Analysis, 2nd Edition* (Hungry Minds Inc US, 2005) ISBN 0764597809

Zapawa, T. – *Excel Advanced Report Development* (Hungry Minds Inc US, 2005) ISBN 0764588117

Websites

www.office.microsoft.com/en-us/excel/default.aspx

www.support.openoffice.org/index.html

www.free-training-tutorial.com

Index